On the
ORIGINS
Of WAR
and the
PRESERVATION
Of PEACE

On the

ORIGINS
Of WAR
and the
PRESERVATION
Of PEACE

Donald Kagan

DOUBLEDAY

New York
London
Toronto
Sydney
Auckland

PUBLISHED BY DOUBLEDAY
a division of Bantam Doubleday Dell Publishing Group, Inc.
1540 Broadway, New York, New York 10036

Book design by Susan Yuran

Library of Congress Cataloging-in-Publication Data

Kagan, Donald.
    On the origins of war and the preservation of peace /
Donald Kagan.
       p.   cm.
    Includes bibliographical references and index.
    1. War—History. 2. Military history. I. Title.
  D25.5.K27 1995
  904′.7—dc20   94-12250
                                   CIP

*For Bob and Fred, who have taught me so much
and will teach many others*

CONTENTS

THE ROOTS OF this book may be found in a seminar I taught jointly with
Professor Walter A. Ralls of Hobart College in the summer of 1967 to a
group of very bright high school seniors at the Telluride House at Cornell
University. We studied some of the crises examined here, among others.
The experience stimulated me to invent a lecture course called "Historical
Studies in the Origins of War," which I first taught at Yale University in
the spring term of 1970 and have taught from time to time ever since. Over
the years students have told me that I had an obligation to put my thoughts
down on paper, and now, at last, I have done so. I have learned a great
deal from the professional literature over a quarter century and have
changed many of my views as a result. I have also been educated by the
questions and writings of generations of extraordinary students. I owe a
special debt to the outstanding graduate students who have served as teaching fellows in the course, many of them now distinguished historians in
their own right, but some of them doctors and lawyers. They are too
many to name, but I owe them much. I also want to thank Walter Ralls,
whose lively mind and masterful teaching set me a model and got me
started. I am grateful to Victor D. Hanson of Fresno State University,
my colleague Henry A. Turner, and Williamson Murray, whose careful
reading of several chapters saved me from errors. I absolve them from
responsibility for any that remain. I also received important help from
two budding historians, my sons Bob and Fred, to whom this book is
dedicated. Bob's advice, deriving from his experience as a practitioner in
the formation and execution of American foreign policy and his keen
understanding of international relations were invaluable. Fred's knowledge of Russian and Soviet history and his command of the Russian language were equally valuable. I am grateful to them and proud of their
achievements. Once again, I owe everything to my wife Myrna's patience
and support.

In 1987 I tried out some of my ideas in an article called "World War I,
World War II, World War III," in *Commentary* magazine. I am grateful to
the publishers of the magazine for permitting me to adapt parts of the
article for use in several places here.

It remains to give thanks for more tangible support to Yale University, which gave me a year's leave to work on this project, to the Center for

Advanced Study in the Behavioral Sciences at Stanford University, which provided me with a fellowship during that year, and to the Hoover Institution, which graciously extended its hospitality to me during my stay in Palo Alto.

HAMDEN, CONNECTICUT

HE COLLAPSE OF the Soviet Union put an end to the dangerous rivalry between the great powers that threatened the peace and safety of the world for almost half a century. For many, the victory of the West over the East, of the free market over command economies, of democracy over Communist dictatorship, promises a new era of security, prosperity, and peace. Some place their hopes for lasting peace on the victory of a free market economy and its spread throughout the world and on the communications revolution, believing that increased travel and mutually valuable commercial relations will make war unlikely if not impossible. Others hope that the extension of democracy will make for a more peaceful world, since in modern times democratic states have not fought one another. Some find reason for confidence in the new balance of power, so favorable to the forces satisfied with their place in the world and, therefore, eager for peace. Others find comfort in the thought that nuclear weapons will prevent major wars involving the great powers. It has even been suggested that the triumph of the Western ideas of economic and political liberalism over communism has brought history to an end, and with it, the danger of major wars between the great, modern states.[1]

At such a time it may seem perverse to undertake a study of the origins and causes of wars. Even a casual look at history suggests otherwise, however. This is not the first time that new conditions and ideas have led many to believe that a unique prospect of lasting peace was at hand, and yet over the past two centuries the only thing more common than predictions about the end of war has been war itself. Past theories of war's obsolescence were much the same as today's. In 1792 the English scientist Joseph Priestley believed "the present commercial treaties between England and France, and between other nations formerly hostile to each other, seem to show that mankind begin to be sensible of the folly of war, and promise a new and important era in the state of the world in general, at least in Europe."[2] Thomas Paine expressed a similar belief in his pamphlet *The Rights of Man,* which appeared in the same year: "If commerce were permitted to act to the universal extent it is capable, it would extirpate the system of war."[3] Paine also believed, following Montesquieu and Kant, that the substitution of republics for monarchies would guarantee lasting peace. Paine applied this theory to the new republic established by the French Revolution:

"The instant the form of government was changed in France the republican principles of peace and domestic prosperity and economy arose with the new government; and the same consequences would follow in the case of other nations."[4]

A generation after the Congress of Vienna introduced an unusually peaceful century for the nations of Europe, many Europeans, especially the subjects of Queen Victoria, had fond expectations of a new millennium. In 1848 John Stuart Mill sang the praises of commerce, which was "rapidly rendering war obsolete, by strengthening and multiplying the personal interests which act in natural opposition to it. . . . [T]he great extent and rapid increase of international trade . . . [is] the principal guarantee of the peace of the world."[5] Contemporary liberal free traders such as Richard Cobden combined a high romantic idealism with evangelical moralism to portray free trade as the antidote to war:

> If I were not convinced that the question [of Free Trade] comprises a great moral principle and involves the greatest moral world's revolution that was ever accomplished for mankind, I should not take the part I do in this agitation. Free Trade! What is it? Why, breaking down the barriers that separate nations; those barriers behind which nestle the feelings of pride, revenge, hatred and jealousy, which every now and then burst their bonds and deluge whole countries with blood.[6]

Such men as he and John Bright combined this confidence in the pacific power of commerce with the conviction that the growth of democracy would also help put an end to war. The people, they believed, wanted peace; it was only the upper classes who sought war and gained from it. When the people ruled so would peace.[7]

The advance of technology convinced many that future wars would be too awful for any rational leader or people to embark upon. At the end of the century Ivan Bloch, a Polish entrepreneur who had organized the railway supply for the Russian Army in the war against the Turks in 1877–78, published a monumental study describing what might be expected from a future war fought in the new conditions. Encompassing political considerations and analysis of the latest military technology, as well as new economic developments, Bloch's *La guerre future; aux points de vue technique, économique et politique* concluded that modern war would be not only futile but also suicidal. The last volume, translated into English, was called *Is War Now Impossible?,* and the answer was plainly yes, at least in regard to major states: "The dimensions of modern armaments and the organisation of society have rendered its execution an economic impossibility." The range, speed of fire, and accuracy of modern weapons would prevent decisive battles. The deadlock on the battlefield would produce "increased slaughter on so terrible a scale as to render it impossible to push the battle to a decisive issue." Then there would be "a long period of continually increasing strain on the resources of the combatants, [an] entire dislocation of all industry and severing of all the sources of supply by which alone the community is enabled to bear the crushing burden. . . . That is the future of war—not fighting, but famine, not the slaying of men but the bankruptcy of nations and the break-up of the whole social organization."[8]

Opinions similar to Mill's, Bright's, Cobden's, and Bloch's were expressed frequently in the years prior to the outbreak of World War I. In the first decade of this century Norman Angell argued that the development of new conditions had made war useless. It only remained to educate everyone in the new realities to make it impossible. Angell took it for granted that nations go to war chiefly for economic gain, but the capitalist knows, he said, "that arms and conquests and juggling with frontiers serve no ends of his and may very well defeat them." Economically, there was no longer anything to be gained from war and conquest. "If credit and commercial contract are to be tampered with in an attempt at confiscation the credit-dependent wealth is undermined, and its collapse involves that of the conqueror; so that if conquest is not to be self-injurious it must respect the enemy's property, in which case it becomes economically futile."[9]

It is a special characteristic of the modern Western world, as opposed to other civilizations and the premodern Western world, to believe that human beings can change and control the physical and social environment and even human nature to improve the condition of life. The revolution in science and technology since the sixteenth century has encouraged the belief that nature can be mastered for that purpose, and the intellectual revolution it produced in the eighteenth century encouraged the idea that human society and the behavior of individual human beings similarly can be manipulated to produce progress, peace, and prosperity. Like the elements of nature, people and their institutions have been seen as infinitely malleable, requiring only intelligence, good will, and determination to improve and perfect them. So it is not surprising to come upon these hopeful expectations by men of the Enlightenment and their intellectual heirs.

Yet in the same year that Paine assured himself that republican principles would bring peace and prosperity, the new French republic was at war with its neighbors, and France, Britain, and Europe had entered more than two decades of devastating general war. The Congress of Vienna established a remarkable and durable peace, but the hopes of Mill, Bright, and Cobden were disappointed by the middle of the century. Democracy and war proved compatible when the British people enthusiastically supported their country's participation in the Crimean War. When the First World War broke out in 1914, it, too, was greeted with great popular enthusiasm, in democratic countries no less than elsewhere.

The First World War was even more horrible and destructive than Bloch and his contemporaries imagined. Yet that frightful experience did not prevent the outbreak of an even more disastrous war only two decades later. Hopeful descendants of the nineteenth-century free traders and democrats put their faith in the League of Nations, the apparent fulfillment of the dreams of world government that dated back to Kant in the eighteenth century. The new organization, however, did not bring peace, either through greater international understanding or through collective security. Fearful successors to Angell and Bloch beheld the new dangers posed by aerial bombardment, believed that it would mean the extinction of civilization in the event of another war, and expected that the threat would prevent its outbreak. But the resulting terror was not shared by all nations and their leaders and was not enough to deter the Second World War.

Over the past two centuries the optimists and pessimists, each predicting the end of war for different reasons, have been proven wrong. Believing in and hoping for progress, they forgot that war has been a persistent part of human experience since before the birth of civilization.[10] In 1968 Will and Ariel Durant calculated that there had been only 268 years free of war in the previous 3,421.[11] From the Stone Age, at least as far back as ten thousand years ago, organized armies in formation fought one another and built fortifications to protect themselves and their people from attacks by other armies.[12] The earliest civilizations of Egypt and Mesopotamia added powerful new elements to the character of warfare and were from the first occupied with war, as were later Bronze and Iron Age cultures all over the world. The earliest literary work in the Western tradition, Homer's *Iliad,* tells of a long, bitter war and the men who fought it.

The Rigvedic hymns of the ancient culture of India tell of the warrior god, Indra, who smashes the fortifications of his enemies. The earliest civilizations of China were established by armies equipped with spears, composite bows, and war chariots. In the sixth century B.C. the Greek philosopher Heracleitus observed that *polemos pater panton,* "war is the father of all things." Ancient philosophers like Plato and Aristotle took an enduring human nature and the persistence of war for granted. They believed that men were naturally acquisitive and aggressive and that governments and laws existed to curb those tendencies. Since they did not imagine any government broader than that of individual city-states, they assumed that war was inevitable for mankind.

The ancient Greeks, wracked as they were by perpetual war, were eager to investigate its causes. The "Father of History" began his account as follows: "What Herodotus of Halicarnassus has discovered by inquiry is published here, so that the great and marvelous deeds done by both Greeks and barbarians should not be erased from human memory by time, and *especially the reasons why they fought against one another* [emphasis added]."[13] Thucydides, writing soon after Herodotus about a different war, sought its causes for more pragmatic purposes. He expected his history to be useful "to those who wish to have a clear understanding both of events in the past and of those in the future which will, in all human likelihood, happen again in the same or a similar way." That is why he set forth with great care the quarrels between the Athenians and the Peloponnesians and the reasons they broke their treaty: "*so that no one may ever have to seek the cause that led to the outbreak of so great a war among the Greeks* [emphasis added]."[14]

The careful study of the origins of war declined for many centuries to follow, perhaps because it was such a common occurrence, both seeming inevitable and even, to many, desirable. In our own time the shock and destructive consequences of the First World War led to a new interest in the subject, and by far the fullest and most intense study of the causes and origins of war have come since that war. Of course, in this modern era scholars and laymen have sought to understand the causes of war not merely out of Herodotean curiosity. They are right to believe that the catastrophe threatened by modern war makes a better understanding of its origins an inescapable assignment, so that informed policies may be pursued in the attempt to prevent it.

How well has the modern world fared in understanding the causes of war? The answer, I believe, is that we have not done as well as the ancient Greeks. It has been characteristic of our time to seek the causes and origins of war in impersonal forces: monarchy and aristocracy and the military ethos of an earlier age that surrounds them; atavistic reversions in the modern age to these outmoded ways; the class struggle; imperialism; arms races; alliance systems, etc. Yet the fall of monarchy and aristocracy in the modern era has not brought an end to war. Struggles between classes are at least as old as the ancient city-state; on a few occasions they have been involved in the origins of wars, but usually not. Imperialism is at least as old as ancient Egypt, Mesopotamia, China, and India, and Persia, Greece, and Rome, but there have been empires without wars and wars without empires. Alliance systems are common in history; arms races less so. Sometimes they contribute to the outbreak of a war, even more significantly to its intensity and duration, but at least as often they contribute to its prevention. Typically they are not causes but symptoms, reflections, or effects of more basic elements.

The wisest modern students of war have concluded that something more fundamental produces wars: the competition for power. Such is the view of a distinguished historian of modern warfare: "in 1914 many of the German people, and in 1939 nearly all of the British, felt justified in going to war, not over any specific issue that could have been settled by negotiation, but to maintain their power, before they found themselves so isolated, so impotent, that they had no power left to maintain and had to accept a subordinate position within an international system dominated by their adversaries."[15] To many in the modern world the word *power* has an unpleasant ring. It seems to imply the ability to impose one's will upon another, usually by the use of force. Power is felt inherently to be bad. That, however, is an unduly restricted understanding. In itself power is neutral. It is the capacity to bring about desired ends, and these may be good or bad. It is also the capacity to resist the demands and compulsions of others. In this latter sense power is essential for the achievement and preservation of freedom. In the Kingdom of Heaven, we are led to believe, human beings will not require power, but in the world in which we all live, it is essential, and the struggle for it inevitable. That point of view is basic to two schools of thought among modern political scientists who study international relations, the "realists" and the "neorealists." "Realists" believe that all states and nations seek as much power as they can get, as something desired not only for what it can do but for itself. The desire for it is almost like original sin, unattractive, deplorable, and regrettable, but inescapable. "Neorealists" understand the behavior of states in their international relations in a tamer and less reprehensible form, as the search, not for power itself, not for domination, but for security that, in turn, requires power. The realist view is a gloomy one, for it envisages no way to stop the unlimited search for power and the conflict it must engender except the conquest of all by one power, or the maintenance of an uneasy peace by reciprocal fear. The neorealist vision seems less frightening because it leaves hope that systems can be devised and people educated in such a way as to arrange and control power to provide security for all without an unending struggle for power, although it cannot be said that any system has yet fulfilled such hopes.

The realists say little about the uses to which the states wish to put the power they acquire. The neorealists imply that states seek power chiefly to retain the good things they already have in peace and safety. Most modern students of the question assume that states want power to achieve tangible and practical goals such as wealth, prosperity, security, and freedom from external interference. But the range of goals that move people to fight wars is broader and not always so practical. All war aims, says another student of the causes of war,

> are only varieties of power. The vanity of nationalism, the will to spread an ideology, the protection of kinsmen in an adjacent land, the desire for more territory or commerce, the avenging of a defeat or insult, the craving for greater national strength or independence, the wish to impress or cement alliances—all these represent power in different wrappings. The conflicting aims of rival nations are always conflicts of power.[16]

The list, however, is not of varieties of power alone but also includes purposes for which power is sought.

In the fifth century B.C., I believe, Thucydides provided a clearer, more profound, more elegant, and comprehensive explanation of why people organized in states are moved to fight wars. He, too, understood war as the armed competition for power. He certainly anticipated the modern realists in the famous Melian Dialogue, where he presents the Athenian spokesman trying to persuade the besieged Melians to yield to the might of Athens without moralistic debate, on the grounds that both in heaven and on earth the unlimited seeking of power is natural: "by a necessity of their nature [human beings] rule as far as their power permits,"[17] and he also explained why they sought it. In the struggle for power, whether for a rational sufficiency or in the insatiable drive for all the power there is, Thucydides found that people go to war out of "honor, fear, and interest."[18]

I have found that trio of motives most illuminating in understanding the origins of wars throughout history and will refer to them frequently in this work. That fear and interest moves states to war will not surprise the modern reader, but that concern for honor should do so may seem strange. If we take honor to mean fame, glory, renown, or splendor, it may appear applicable only to an earlier time. If, however, we understand its significance as deference, esteem, just due, regard, respect, or prestige we will find it an important motive of nations in the modern world as well. Honor, in these senses, is desirable in itself, but it also has practical importance in the competition for power. When it is on the wane, so, too, is the power of the state losing it, and the reverse is also true. Power and honor have a reciprocal relationship. It is obvious that when a state's power grows, the deference and respect in which it is held are likely to grow as well. But the opposite is also true: even when its material power appears to remain the same, it really declines if in some manner these attitudes toward it change. This happens most frequently when a state is seen to lack the will to use its material power. The reader may be surprised by how small a role in the instances studied here, and, I believe, in many other cases, considerations of practical utility and material gain, and even ambition for power itself, play in bringing on wars and how often some aspect of honor is decisive.

What, then, is the best method for gaining an understanding of how and why states and nations go to war? Since honor, fear, and interest are at issue, a grasp of the particular ways in which these were appreciated and related to one another in the outbreak of each war is essential, for these may differ in different societies and at different times. The well-known lines of the ancient Greek poet Archilochus present the two fundamental choices: "The fox knows many tricks, the hedgehog only one;/one big one." Philosophers and most social scientists are the hedgehogs; they seek to explain a vast range of particular phenomena by the simplest possible generalization. But in the world of human affairs, wildly complicated by the presence of individual wills, and of particular ideas of what produces or deprives people of honor, in what does interest consist, and even of what is there to fear, extremely general explanations are neither useful nor possible. Historians should, in the first instance, be foxes, using as many tricks as they can to explain as many particular things as accurately and convincingly as possible. Then, they should try to find revealing examples from the wide variety of human experiences to support generalizations of varying breadth. They should not expect to find the one big trick that will explain everything, but the lesser generalizations, to be tested by other understandings of the evidence and by new human experiences as they arise, which can still be interesting and useful. It is this mixed path taken by the historian, chiefly of the fox but with a necessary element of the hedgehog, that I believe promises the best results.

Many historians have examined the origins of particular wars, some with great success, without trying to make general observations based on the study of several different wars. A few writers, on the other hand, have used historical examples as the main source for their understanding of the origins of war in general, but none, so far as I know, has examined carefully the origins of a number of wars in some detail to illuminate the general question. That is what will be attempted here. The method might be called comparative narrative history. This is a study of the origins of the Peloponnesian War (431–404 B.C.), World War I (1914–18), the Second Punic War (218–202 B.C.), and World War II (1939–45). The last study is of the Cuban missile crisis of 1962, an unusual event when it was believed widely that a serious war threatened, but the crisis passed without fighting. It is included because it appears to have been the closest the world has come to a war between major powers since the coming of the nuclear age. It has often been asserted that analogies drawn from international conflicts that took place before the invention of nuclear weapons have no bearing on the nuclear era, that the very existence of nuclear weapons with their unprecedented capacity for destruction creates a "minimal deterrence" that is adequate to prevent a major war. The study of the Cuban missile crisis, therefore, is essential to test such assertions as best we can. The recent publication for the first time of documents vital to its understanding, moreover, reveal important aspects of the situation that shed important light on the general question of the causes and origins of wars. The new material has changed my own understanding and interpretation of the crisis and has reinforced my conviction that sound analyses of international relations and the origins of wars in earlier times remain relevant to our own world.

In each study at least the following questions are considered: What were the character and goals of the opponents? How did each state make decisions in foreign policy? What was the character of the international system? What was the nature of the peace that was broken? What started the states on the road to war? How and why did each make the decision to fight? What choices were available, and more importantly what choices did they believe were available? I try to answer these questions in each case by means of an analytic narrative that is meant to provide an interesting and instructive story.

It remains to explain my choice of subjects among the myriad of wars in human history. They are all part of the experience of the Western world, in part because that is the world I know best and where I can read many of the sources and studies in the original languages. In part, however, it is because I am interested in the outbreak of wars between states in an international system, such as we find in the world today. The Greeks and the Romans of the republican era lived in that kind of a world, and so has the West since the time of the Renaissance. Most other peoples have lived either in a world without states, or in great empires where the only armed conflicts were civil wars or attempts to defend the realm against bands of invaders. Within the Western experience I have tried to select examples from different historical periods involving a variety of types of states living in different kinds of international systems. Each case has been chosen also because a lively and instructive debate has sprung up among the scholars studying each of them. Because there is so little evidence for the ancient period compared with the modern the accounts of the ancient wars necessarily will be shorter, less rich and detailed, yet I think there is enough information to permit useful discussions. It would be possible, of course, to make a different selection, but I believe the choices made here permit an instructive and interesting inquiry.

As this page is written a civil war rages in the former state of Yugoslavia that has already involved the armed forces of NATO, an intervention publicly opposed by Russia. The Russians themselves are engaged in border conflicts with peoples formerly part of the Soviet Union. Poland, Czechoslovakia, and Hungary feel sufficiently threatened by the possible revival of Russian power to seek membership in NATO urgently, a course strongly opposed by the Russians. North Korea, probably in possession of nuclear weapons or, at least, the capacity to build them, has great armed forces massed on the South Korean border, threatening war if the United States persists in demanding inspection of nuclear sites and forbidding nuclear weapons. Not every serious crisis, fortunately, leads to war. All these problems may have been resolved peacefully by the time this work is in print, but if so they will surely be replaced by others no less serious and challenging. It should be plain that threats to peace similar to those in the past persist to this very day and will continue in the future. The need to cope with them wisely, in an age of nuclear weapons, is greater than ever.

The secret of the success of our species has been its ability to learn from experience and to adapt its behavior accordingly. The aim of this book is to provide some useful studies that may help in that effort. The Chinese sage Sun Tzu said: "The art of war is of vital importance to the state, It is a matter of life and death, a road either to safety or ruin. Hence it is a subject of inquiry which can on no account be neglected."[19] No less vital is the art of avoiding war, and no more may the attempt to understand its origins and causes safely be neglected.

1. Francis Fukuyama, "The End of History?" *The National Interest* 16(1989) p.18.

2. Cited by E. L. Jones, *The European Miracle,* Cambridge, 1981, pp. 125–26.

3. Thomas Paine, *Collected Writings,* vol. 1, London, 1894, p. 456.

4. Paine, p. 453. Relevant passages in Montesquieu and Kant are cited by Michael Howard, *War and the Liberal Conscience* (London, 1978). My debt to that excellent work will be evident throughout this section.

5. J. S. Mill, *Principles of Political Economy,* London, 1848, p. 582.

6. From a speech in a Covent Garden demonstration on September 28, 1843, cited by Correlli Barnett, *The Collapse of British Power* (New York, 1972), p. 49.

7. Concern for the balance of power, said Bright, is only "a gigantic system of outdoor relief for the aristocracy of Great Britain" (G. M. Trevelyan, *John Bright,* London, 1913, p. 274).

8. Michael Howard, "Men Against Fire: The Doctrine of the Offensive in 1914," in Michael Howard, ed., *The Lessons of History,* New Haven, 1991, pp. 97–99.

9. Howard, "Men Against Fire," pp. 70–71.

10. Arther Ferrill, *The Origins of War* (London, 1985, p. 13), says that "organized warfare appeared at least by the end of the Palaeolithic Age." Others would place it after the beginning of civilization. My reading of the evidence agrees with Ferrill's, but no one doubts that war is at least as old as civilization.

11. *The Lessons of History,* New York, 1968, p. 81.

12. Such is the evidence produced by Arther Ferrill, *The Origins of War* (pp. 18–31).

13. Herodotus, 1.1. (References to the ancient writers are to the divisions into books, chapters, and sections that are now conventional.)

14. Thucydides, 1.23.

15. Howard, "The Causes of Wars," in *The Causes of Wars,* edited by Michael Howard, Cambridge, Mass., 1983, p. 16.

16. Geoffrey Blainey, *The Causes of War,* London, 1973, pp. 149–50.

17. 5.15.2.

18. 1.76.2. The Greek words are *timé, deos,* and *ophelia.*

19. Sun Tzu Wu. *The Art of War,* translated by Lionel Giles, Harrisburg, 1944, p. 40.

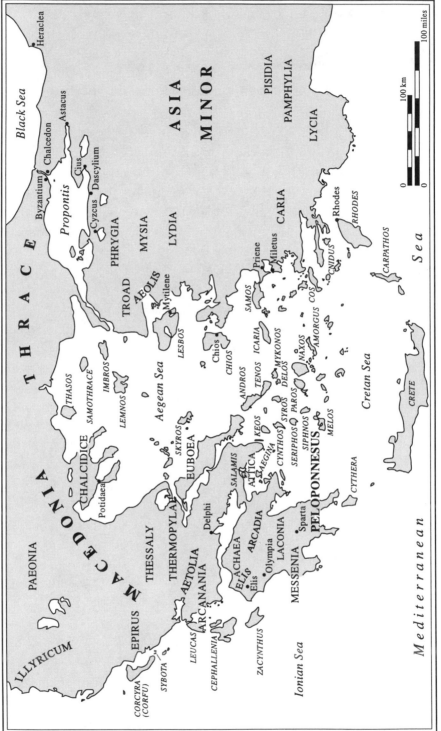

Classical Greece

1

THE
PELOPONNESIAN
WAR

431-404 B.C.

OR ALMOST THREE decades at the end of the fifth century B.C. the Athenians and their allies fought the Spartans and theirs in a terrible war that changed the Greek world and its civilization forever. A half-century before its outbreak the Greeks had fought off an assault by the mighty Persian Empire, preserving their independence and liberty by driving its armies and navies out of Europe and recovering the Greek cities on the coasts of Asia Minor from its grasp. It opened a proud era of growth and achievement. The Athenians especially flourished, growing in population and establishing an empire that brought them wealth and glory. Their young democracy came to maturity and spread to bring political rights, opportunity, and power to even the lowest class of citizens, and their novel constitution spread, taking root in other Greek cities as well. It was a time of extraordinary cultural achievement, probably unmatched in its originality and fecundity in all of human history. Dramatic poets like Aeschylus, Sophocles, Euripides, and Aristophanes raised tragedy and comedy to a level never surpassed. Architects and sculptors created the buildings on the Acropolis in Athens, at Olympia, and all over the Greek world that influenced the course of Western art so powerfully and still do so today. The natural philosophers, like Anaxagoras and Democritus used unaided human reason to seek an understanding of the physical world, and such pioneers of moral and political philosophy as Protagoras and Socrates did the same in the realm of human affairs. It was a time of great progress, prosperity, and confidence.

To all this the great conflict put an end. Thucydides tells us that he undertook his history as the war began,

> in the belief that it would be great and noteworthy above all the wars that had gone before, inferring this from the fact that both powers were then at their best in preparedness for war in every way, and seeing the rest of the Hellenic people taking sides with one side or the other, some at once, others planning to do so. For this was

the greatest upheaval that had ever shaken the Hellenes, extending also to some part of the barbarians, one might say even to a very large part of mankind. (1.1.2)[1]

The war was a terrible watershed in Greek history, causing enormous destruction of life and property, intensifying factional and class hostility, dividing the Greek states internally and destabilizing their relationship to one another, ultimately weakening the Greek capacity to resist conquest from outside. Sparta's victory also reversed the tendency toward the growth of democracy. When Athens was powerful and successful, its democratic constitution had a magnetic effect on other states, but its defeat was the turning point in the political development of Greece that sent it in the direction of oligarchy instead of democracy.

The war was a tragic event, a great turning point in history, the end of a period of confidence and hope, and the beginning of a darker time. It was a war of unprecedented brutality, violating even the rugged code that previously had governed Greek fighting and breaking through the thin veneer that separates civilization from savagery. Anger, frustration, and the desire for vengeance increased as the fighting dragged on, producing a progression of atrocities that included maiming and killing captured opponents, throwing them into pits to die of thirst, starvation, and exposure, and hurling them into the sea to drown. Bands of marauders murdered innocent schoolchildren. Entire cities were destroyed, the men killed, the women and children sold as slaves. On the island now called Corfu the victorious faction in a civil war brought on by the larger struggle

went to the sanctuary of Hera and persuaded about fifty men to take their trial, and condemned them all to death. The mass of the suppliants who had refused to do so, on seeing what was taking place, slew each other there on the consecrated ground; some hanged themselves upon the trees, and others destroyed themselves as they were severally able. During seven days . . . they were engaged in butchering those of their fellow-citizens whom they regarded as their enemies. . . . Death thus raged in every shape; and as usually happens at such times, there was no length to which violence did not go; sons were killed by their father, and suppliants dragged from the altar or slain upon it. (3.81.2–5)

Soon the violence spread, and with it came a collapse in the habits, institutions, beliefs, and restraints that make civilized life possible:

> Later on, one may say, the whole Hellenic world was convulsed, struggles being everywhere made by the popular chiefs to bring in the Athenians, and by the oligarchs to introduce the Spartans. . . . Words had to change their ordinary meanings and to take those which were now given to them. Reckless audacity came to be considered the courage of a loyal ally; prudent hesitation, specious cowardice; moderation was held to be a cloak for unmanliness. . . . Frantic violence became the attribute of manliness; cautious plotting, a justified means of self-defence. The advocate of extreme measures was always trustworthy; his opponent, a man to be suspected. . . .
>
> Religion was in honour with neither party; but the use of fair phrases to arrive at guilty ends was in high reputation. . . .
>
> Thus every form of iniquity took root in the Hellenic countries by reason of the troubles. The ancient simplicity into which honour so largely entered was laughed down and disappeared; and society became divided into camps in which no man trusted his fellow. (3.82.1, 8; 3.83.1)

Such was the conflict that inspired Thucydides's mordant observations on the character of war as "a savage schoolmaster that brings the characters of most people down to the level of their current circumstances." (3.82.2) What brought on this terrible war?

"Epidamnus is a city on your right as you sail into the Ionian Gulf. The Taulantians, a barbarian people of the Illyrian race live near by." (1.24.1) That is how Thucydides begins his narrative of the events that led to the war. He needed to do so, because few of his fellow Greeks would have known where the city was or anything else about it, as few Europeans knew anything about Sarajevo when the heir to the Austro-Hungarian Empire was assassinated there in June of 1914. It was one of those remote places, unimportant in themselves, where occasionally an event occurs, unleashing a chain of sequential events that lead to catastrophe.

The city, called Dyrrachium by the Romans and Durazzo by the modern Italians, is now the site of Durrës in Albania. It was well to the north of the normal sailing route from Greece to Italy, not remarkably rich

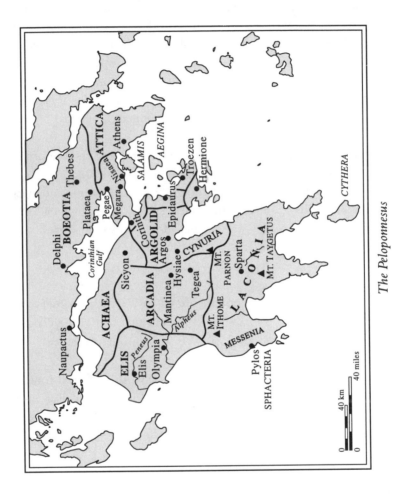

The Peloponnesus

or strategically situated, nor was it part of the alliance system that divided Greece when its troubles began to roil the waters in the mid 430s.[2] No one could have predicted that an internal quarrel in this remote city on the fringes of the Hellenic world would lead to the terrible and devastating Peloponnesian War[3] that deserves, from the perspective of fifth-century Greeks, to be thought of as a world war no less than the great war of 1914–18 seemed to the Europeans of the time.

THE HEGEMONIC POWERS AND THEIR ALLIANCES

Sparta and the Peloponnesian League

On the eve of the Peloponnesian War Greece was divided into two great alliances that had regarded one another with suspicion for almost half a century, sometimes coming to blows. The older organization was led by Sparta, a state like no other. Centuries earlier, the Spartans had conquered their neighbors, reducing some, called *perioikoi,* to subordination and others, the helots, to a condition of state slavery or serfdom. The helots farmed the land and provided the Spartans with food, while the *perioikoi* manufactured what was needed and engaged in the little commerce the Spartans required and permitted. This liberated them from the toil men normally undertook, leaving them free to devote themselves to military training.

The helots were guarded closely and treated severely. They outnumbered their Spartan masters by some ten to one and, as an Athenian who knew Sparta well put it, "They would gladly eat the Spartans raw." (Xenophon, *Hellenica,* 3.3.4–11) From time to time they broke out in rebellions that endangered the existence of the Spartans and their state. To meet this challenge, as well as to enhance their military prowess, the Spartans subordinated individual and family to the needs of the state. Only physically perfect infants were permitted to live; boys were taken from home at age seven to be trained and toughened in military school until they were twenty. From twenty to thirty they lived in barracks, helping to train the young. They could marry but visit their wives only by stealth. At thirty the Spartan male became a full citizen an "equal" *(homoios).* He took his meals at a public mess with fourteen comrades. He dined simply, often on a black soup that appalled the other Greeks. Military service was required until age sixty. The entire system was designed to produce soldiers whose physical powers, training, and discipline made them the best in the world.[4]

In the sixth century the Spartans developed a system of perpetual alliances to safeguard their peculiar community from internal and external dangers. The allies were required to send contingents of soldiers at the request of the Spartans and to serve under Spartan command. The alliance made Sparta the first great power in classical Greek history. Modern scholars call the Spartan Alliance the Peloponnesian League, and the term has become so common that it is hard to avoid, but it was less a league than a loose organization consisting of Sparta, on the one hand, and a group of allies connected to her by separate treaties on the other.[5] Each state swore to have the same friends and enemies in return for Spartan protection and recognition of its integrity and autonomy. The language of the treaties was ambiguous about such important questions as whether the allies or the Spartans would determine what friends and enemies they held in common and whether the allies were bound to aid the Spartans in offensive as well as defensive wars. Reality, not theory, provided the interpretive principle.

When Sparta was strong and secure it could call the tune. The Spartans helped their allies when it was to their advantage or unavoidable, compelling others to join in when it was necessary and possible. The entire alliance met only when the Spartans chose, and we hear of few meetings. The rules that chiefly counted were imposed by military, political, or geographical reality, and they reveal three discernible, if informal, categories of allies. One consisted of states that were small enough and close enough to Sparta as to be easily controlled. A second category, including Megara, Elis, and Mantinea, were stronger, more remote, or both, but so powerful and distant as to escape ultimate punishment. Thebes and Corinth were the only states in the third group, states so remote and powerful that their independence rarely was tampered with and their conduct of foreign policy rarely subordinated to Spartan interests.[6]

Once they had established their leadership of the Peloponnesus, the power and prestige provided by their alliance did not make the Spartans bold and aggressive. In spite of the great military superiority given them by their unmatched training and discipline and the forces provided them by their alliance, they were usually reluctant to go to war; the further the objective the greater the reluctance. The chief source of their restraint was fear that the helots would take advantage of any long absence of the Spartan Army to rebel. Thucydides pointed out that "most institutions among the Spartans have always been established with regard to security against the helots" (4.80.3) and Aristotle said that the helots "are like someone sitting in wait for disasters to strike the Spartans." *(Politics* 1269a)

Argos presented another problem to the Spartans. A large, populous, and potentially powerful state to the northeast of Sparta, it was not a member of the Spartan Alliance. The two states, in fact, had a long history of enmity and war. The Spartans always were worried about the union of a rejuvenated Argos with other enemies, and especially of Argive assistance to a helot rebellion.

Security against helot rebellions and Argive ambitions depended heavily on the reliability of the Spartan Alliance. Anything that threatened the integrity of the Peloponnesian League or the loyalty of any of its members was a potentially deadly menace to the Spartans. When the Persians invaded Greece in 480, however, the alliance was solidly under Spartan hegemony, and the Spartans were the obvious choice to lead all the Greek states who defied and defeated "the barbarian."

Sparta's political constitution was also unlike that of any other Greek state. Theorists regarded it as a "mixed constitution," containing monarchic, oligarchic, and democratic elements. The assembly, consisting of all Spartan men over thirty, was the democratic element. The Gerousia, a council of twenty-eight men over the age of sixty elected from a small number of privileged families,[7] represented the oligarchic principle. The royal element appeared in the form not of one but of two kings. The five ephors represented a fourth, anomalous element.

The two kings served for life, led Sparta's armies, and performed important religious and judicial functions. Unless they were unusually incompetent they enjoyed great prestige and influence. Their views on matters of war and peace carried great weight, but it sometimes happened that the two kings disagreed, and factions formed on different sides of an issue. The Gerousia sat with the kings as the highest court in the land and were the court to which the kings themselves were brought to trial. They appear to have had no formal role in the formation of foreign policy, but the prestige they held because of family connections, age, and experience in a society that venerated such things, and the honor of their election, must have given them great unofficial influence.

The ephorate was invented in the sixth century, chiefly to serve as a check on the kings. By the fifth century, however, the role of the ephors was more complex, and it was important, especially in foreign affairs. They alone summoned the assembly and presided over it. They sat with the

Gerousia, were its executive officers, and had the right to bring charges of treason against the kings. They received foreign envoys, negotiated treaties, and ordered expeditions once war had been declared. They have been called the foreign ministry of Sparta.[8]

Formal decisions on treaties, foreign relations, war, and peace belonged to the assembly, but its real powers were limited. Meetings occurred only when called by officials. There was usually little or no debate; such as took place was usually limited to kings, members of the Gerousia, or ephors. The ordinary Spartan appears never to have spoken. Voting was usually by acclamation, the equivalent of a voice vote; division and the counting of votes was rare. On most occasions decisions on matters presented to the assembly must have been a forgone conclusion, but when the leadership was divided the real decision might be left to the assembly, "the organ of the collective warriors and ex-warriors."[9]

For three centuries from its establishment this remained Sparta's constitution, undisturbed by lawful change, coup d'état, or revolution. Such stability might seem to promise a consistent foreign policy, especially compared with the instability made possible by the democratic constitution of Athens. In theory, and sometimes in practice, the Athenians could adopt a policy one day and reverse it the next or accept the plan of one leader and put its execution into the hands of another. The realities behind Sparta's formal constitution, however, reveal the possibility of similar instability. Conflicts between the kings, between ephors and kings, among the ephors themselves, and by the annual rotation of boards of ephors, in fact, could weaken Sparta's control of its alliance. An ally could pursue its own interests and policy by exploiting Sparta's internal divisions and the paradox inherent in its situation. Sparta's mighty army and its command of the alliance gave the Spartans enormous power, but if they used it against a strong enemy outside the Peloponnesus, they ran the risk of a helot rebellion or an Argive attack. If they did not use it when called upon by their more important allies, they risked their defection and the dissolution of the alliance on which their security rested. In the crisis leading to the war Spartan decision making would be affected by both these difficulties.

Athens and Its Empire

In the Persian Wars the Athenians played a part not less crucial than that of the Spartans and, before long, they found themselves at the head of

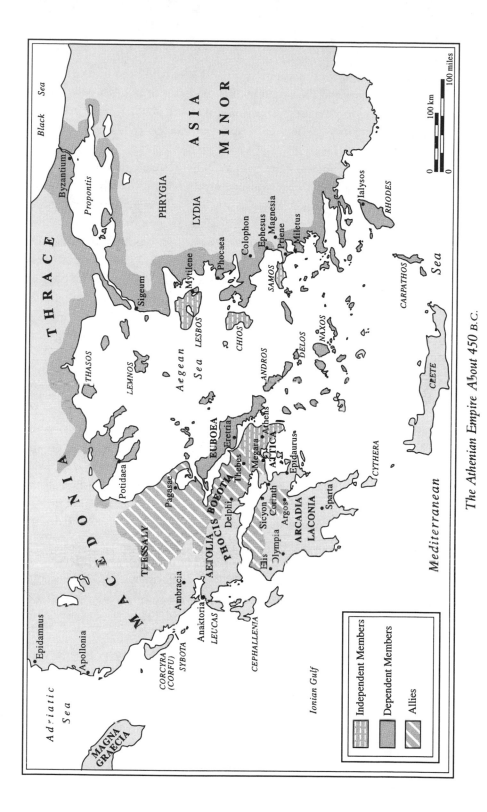

The Athenian Empire About 450 B.C.

Independent Members

Dependent Members

Allies

an alliance of Greek states separate from and later at odds with the Spartan Alliance. To understand the situation and character of the Athenian state as it entered the Peloponnesian War it is useful to think of it as the "Athenian Imperial Democracy," with significance connected to each part of the designation.

Athens had a unique history that helped shape its character long before it became a democracy and acquired an empire. It was the chief town of the region known as Attica, a small triangular peninsula extending southeastward from central Greece. Attica has an area of about one thousand square miles, but much of it is mountainous and rocky and unavailable for cultivation. Little of the rest is first-rate farming land, so that early Attica was relatively poor, even by Greek standards. This proved a blessing when invaders from the north swept down and occupied the more attractive lands of the Peloponnesus, regarding Attica as not worth the trouble of conquest. Unlike the Spartans, the Athenians claimed to have sprung from their own soil and to have lived in the same place since before the birth of the moon. They were, therefore, free to go their way without the burden of oppressing a discontented underclass.

Another secret of Athens's ultimate success was that it had quite early unified the entire region under its control. The Athenians, therefore, unlike the Thebans, who constantly fought for control of Boeotia on the northern frontier of Attica, were not distracted by quarrels and wars with neighboring towns. Attica was fully and successfully unified, so that all the communities of Attica were part of the Athenian city-state, and all their free, native-born inhabitants were Athenian citizens on an equal basis.

The absence of intense pressures, internal and external, may help explain Athens's relatively easygoing, nonviolent early history and its emergence in the fifth century as the first democracy in the history of the world. By mid century the democratic constitution basically had reached the completion of its development toward the full and direct participation of all adult male citizens in their own government.

The power and prosperity of the Athenian democracy depended on its command of its great maritime empire, which was centered on the Aegean Sea, of the islands in it, and of the cities along its coast. It began as "the Athenians and their allies" (modern scholars call it the Delian League), a voluntary alliance of Greek states who invited Athens to take the lead in continuing the war of liberation and vengeance against Persia. It gradually became an empire under Athenian command functioning chiefly for the advantage of Athens. Over the years almost all the members gave up their own fleets and chose to make a money payment into the common treasury instead of contributing their own ships and men. The Athenians used the money to increase the number of their own ships and to pay the rowers to stay at their oars for eight months each year, so that the Athenian Navy became by far the biggest and best fleet ever known. On the eve of the war only two islands, Lesbos and Chios, of some 150 members of the league, had their own fleets and enjoyed relative autonomy. Even they were unlikely to defy Athenian orders. During the era of the Cold War it was common to compare the conflict between the Spartans and their allies and the Athenians and theirs with the rivalry between the Soviet Union and the United States, often in a misleading manner.[10]

Athens's imperial revenue was large enough to provide a considerable surplus beyond the needs of the Navy, and the Athenians used it for their own purposes, including the great building program that beautified and glorified their city and gave work to its people and the accumulation of a large reserve fund. The Navy protected the ships of their merchants in their prosperous trade all around the Mediterranean and beyond. It also gave the Athenians access to the wheat fields of Ukraine and the fish of the Black Sea with which they could supplement their inadequate home food supply and even replace it totally, with the use of imperial money, if forced to abandon their own fields by war. Once they completed the walls surrounding their city and connecting it by long walls to its fortified port at Piraeus, as they did in mid century, the Athenians could be invulnerable.

The sovereign in Athens, which made all decisions on policy, foreign and domestic, military and civil, was the assembly. All male citizens were eligible to attend, vote, make proposals, and debate. The assembly met no fewer than forty times a year in the open air, overlooking the marketplace and beside the Acropolis. At the start of the war about forty thousand Athenians were eligible, but attendance rarely exceeded six thousand. This was the body that had to approve treaties of peace and declarations of war. Whatever strategic decisions were taken had to be proposed, discussed, and debated in the open before thousands of people, a majority of whom must approve every detail of every action. For any expedition the assembly voted on its target and purpose, the number and specific nature of ships and men, the funds to be spent, the commanders to lead the forces, and the specific instructions to those commanders. The Council of Five Hundred, chosen by lot from the Athenian citizenry, prepared bills for the assembly's consideration but was totally subordinate to the larger body.

The most important offices in the Athenian state, among the few filled by election rather than by lottery, were those of the ten generals. Because they commanded divisions of the Athenian Army and fleets of ships in battle they had to be military men; because they needed to be elected for a one-year term, and could be reelected without limit, they had to be politicians. In the fifth century most generals had skills in both directions, although some were stronger in one respect than the other. These men could and did impose military discipline on campaign, but they were not very potent in the city. At least ten times a year there were formal opportunities for them to face complaints against their conduct in office, and at the end of their terms they had to make full accountings of their behaviors in office, military and financial. On each occasion they were subject to trial if accused and serious punishment if convicted.

The ten generals together did not make up a cabinet or a government; the assembly was the government. Sometimes, however, a general would gain so much political support and influence as to become the leader of the Athenians in fact, if not in law. Such was Cimon for the seventeen years between 479 and 462, when he appears to have been elected general each year, to have led every important expedition, and to have persuaded the Athenian assembly to support his policies at home and abroad. After the departure of Cimon, Pericles achieved similar success over an even longer period.

Pericles was one of those rare people who place their own stamp on their time. An Athenian aristocrat, he first became a democratic political reformer, and then the leader of the Athenian democracy. He personally commanded armies and navies, negotiated treaties, selected the sculptors and architects who beautified the Acropolis, and counted among his friends and associates the leading artists, poets, philosophers, and historians of his age. It is hard to think of any political leader who ever had so direct and versatile a role in guiding the life of his people. For three decades before the war he seems to have been general each year, to have assisted the election of some of his associates, to have conducted those campaigns he thought necessary, and to have gained the support of the Athenians for his domestic and foreign policies. It is important to note, however, that he never had any greater formal powers than the other generals and never tried to alter the democratic constitution. He was still subject to the scrutiny provided for in the constitution and required a vote in the open and uncontrolled assembly to take any action. He did not always get what he wanted and, on some occasions, his enemies persuaded the assembly to act against his wishes, but an accurate description of the Athenian government on the eve of the war was that it was a democracy led by its first citizen. Pericles was influential not because of any hidden power or the control of armed force, for he had none. The Athenians followed his lead because of his reputation for intelligence, wisdom, ability, honesty, and patriotism, because of his remarkable talents as a public speaker, and because of the success and popularity of his policies and leadership. Thucydides introduces him into his history as "Pericles son of Xanthippus, the leading man in Athens at that time and the ablest in speech and in action." (1.139.4) It would be wrong to go as far as Thucydides does in saying that Athens in Pericles's time, though a democracy in name, was becoming the rule of the first citizen, in fact (2.65.7), for it always remained a thoroughgoing democracy in every respect, but in the crisis leading to war, in the adoption of a strategy to fight it, and into the second year of its conduct, the Athenians invariably followed the advice of their great leader. Under Pericles's leadership the Athenian democracy had the capacity for deciding upon policies for itself and its allies without outside influence and holding to them with firm consistency.

THE ORIGIN OF THE RIVALRY

The rivalry between Sparta and Athens developed in the decades after the Persian Wars as the Delian League grew in success, wealth, and power and was transformed gradually into the Athenian Empire. From the first, there was a faction in Sparta suspicious and resentful at the growth in Athenian power. The Spartans opposed the Athenians' desire to rebuild their walls after the Persians had fled. When the Athenians rejected their views in no uncertain terms, the Spartans made no formal complaint, "but they were secretly embittered." (1.92.1) By 475 resentment had grown to the point that a proposal emerged in the Gerousia to go to war against the Athenians in order to destroy their new alliance and gain control of the sea.[11] After some debate the plan was rejected, but the event reveals that an anti-Athenian faction continued to exist in Sparta. In later years some of the Spartans' allies would blame them for their sluggishness and isolationism for not nipping the growth of Athenian power in the bud, for not performing their function as preservers of the peace and the prewar balance of power, but that critique was unjustified. In the early years of Athenian power the memory of their recent collaboration in the great war of Greek independence against Persia argued against a conflict. The Athenians appeared to be continuing the good fight against the Persians and for the liberty of the Greeks. The Spartans, moreover, would soon be distracted by troubles closer to home in the form of wars within the Peloponnesus. By the time the danger from Athens could no longer be ignored its power was daunting, and the Spartans' capacity to overcome it was open to question.

There was no trouble for two decades, but in 465 the Athenians besieged the island of Thasos and met fierce resistance. The Thasians sent word to the Spartans, urging them to come to their aid by invading Attica. In a secret decision, unknown to the Athenians, they made the promise and, Thucydides tells us, "they meant to keep it." (1.101.1–2)[12] They were, however, prevented from doing so by a terrible earthquake in the Peloponnesus that led to a major revolution of the helots. Unable to drive the rebels from their mountain stronghold, the Spartans called on their allies for help. Among those who came were the Athenians, still formally tied to the Spartans under the terms of the Greek alliance against Persia sworn in 481 and uniquely qualified to help by their skill at siege warfare. Before they had a chance to demonstrate their talent, the Athenians were asked to leave, alone among Sparta's allies, on the specious grounds that they were no longer needed. Thucydides reports the true motive: "the Spartans were afraid of the boldness and the revolutionary spirit of the Athenians, thinking that . . . if they [the Athenians] remained they might be persuaded . . . to change sides. . . . It was because of this expedition that the Spartans and Athenians first came to an open quarrel." (1.102.1–3)

The incident, clear evidence of the suspicion and hostility felt by many Spartans, brought about a political revolution in Athens and then a diplomatic revolution in Greece. The Spartans' insulting dismissal of the Athenian Army brought down Cimon's pro-Spartan regime, which had maintained friendly relations between the two powers since the Persian Wars. The anti-Spartan group, which had opposed sending help to the Peloponnese, drove Cimon from Athens, withdrew from the old alliance with Sparta, and made a new alliance with Sparta's old and bitter enemy, Argos. (1.102.4; Plutarch, *Cimon* 17.2)[13]

Relations between Sparta and Athens soon deteriorated further. When the besieged helots could hold out no longer, the Spartans allowed them to leave the Peloponnesus under a truce, provided they never return.

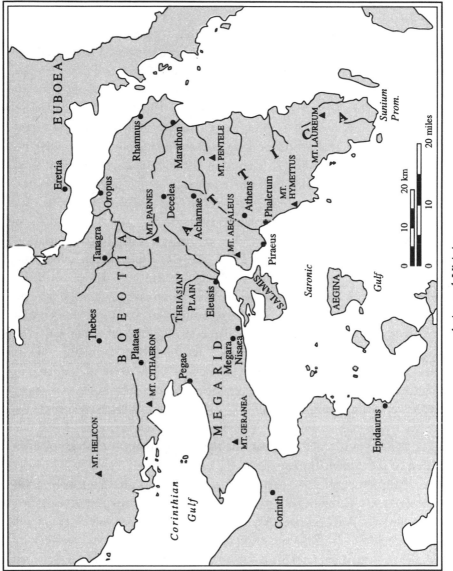

Attica and Vicinity

The Spartans must have thought they would scatter harmlessly, but the Athenians settled them as a group at a strategic site on the north shore of the Corinthian Gulf, in the city of Naupactus that Athens had recently acquired, "because of the hatred they already felt toward the Spartans." (1.103.3)

Next, the Athenians took an action that annoyed the Spartans even more. Two allies of Sparta, Corinth and Megara, were at war over the boundary between them. Megara was losing. The Spartans did not choose to be involved, so the Megarians proposed to secede from the Spartan Alliance and join with Athens in exchange for help against Corinth. The incident reveals how the breach between Athens and Sparta created a new instability in the Greek world. So long as the two hegemonal states were on good terms, each was free to deal with its allies as it chose; dissatisfied members of either alliance had nowhere to go. Now, however, dissident states could seek support from their leader's rival. To some degree, the existence of the rivalry encouraged dissent.

Megara, on Athens's western border, had great strategic importance. Its western port, Pegae, gave access to the Corinthian Gulf, which the Athenians could otherwise reach only by a long and dangerous route around the entire Peloponnesus. Nisaea, its eastern port, lay on the Saronic Gulf, where an enemy could use it to launch an attack on the port of Athens. Even more important, Athenian control of the mountain passes in Megarian territory, possible only with a friendly Megara, would make it difficult if not impossible for a Peloponnesian Army to invade Attica. An alliance with Megara would, therefore, bring Athens enormous advantages, but it would also bring war against Corinth and probably with Sparta and the Peloponnesian League. The Athenians accepted Megara into their alliance, "and it was chiefly because of this action that Corinth's powerful hatred of the Athenians first arose." (1.103.4)

This, although the Spartans did not become directly involved for several years, was the beginning of what modern historians call the "First Peloponnesian War." It lasted for more than fifteen years, including periods of truce and lapses of action, and, at one time or another, involved the Athenians from Egypt to Sicily. It ended when the Megarians defected from the Athenian alliance and returned to the Peloponnesian League, opening the way for the Spartan king Pleistoanax to lead a Peloponnesian Army into Attica. The Athenian Army marched out to defend their land, and a decisive battle seemed certain, but at the last moment the Spartans returned home without a fight. Ancient writers explain this behavior by claiming that Pericles had bribed the king and his adviser to abort the battle, and at first the Spartans were angry with the commanders, punishing both severely. (Plutarch, *Pericles,* 22–23)[14] A more likely explanation is that Pericles met with them and offered them acceptable peace terms, making a fight unnecessary. A short while later, in any case, the Spartans and Athenians concluded a peace treaty.

THE PEACE

The Thirty Years' Peace was ratified in the winter of 446–45. We do not have its text or a single full account of all its provisions, but its essential elements are clear in Thucydides' account. In the only territorial clause the Athenians agreed to give up the Peloponnesian lands they had acquired during the war. In return, the Spartans granted what amounted to official recognition of the Athenian Empire, for Sparta and Athens each swore the ratifying oaths on behalf of their allies. The Greek world was formally divided in two by a provision forbidding the members of each alliance to change sides, an obvious attempt to prevent a repetition of the last war, which began when Megara did precisely that. A clause that looked to the future permitted neutrals to join either side, an apparently innocent and sensible item that would cause a surprising amount of trouble. The most novel and interesting provision required both sides to submit future grievances to binding arbitration. This seems to be the first attempt in history to maintain perpetual peace through such a device.

Peace treaties are not all the same. Some come at the end of a war in which one side is destroyed or thoroughly defeated, such as the last war between Rome and Carthage (149–46). Others impose harsh terms on an enemy who has been defeated but not destroyed. Such was the peace that Prussia imposed on France in 1871, or, as the common view has it, the victors imposed on Germany at Versailles in 1919. This kind of treaty often plants the roots of another war, because it humiliates and angers the loser without destroying the capacity for revenge. A third sort of treaty ends a conflict, usually a long one, in which both have become aware of the costs and dangers of war and the virtues of peace, whether or not there has been a winner on the battlefield. The Peace of Westphalia in 1648 ending the Thirty Years' War and the settlement with which the Congress of Vienna concluded the Napoleonic Wars in 1815 are good examples of this. Such a treaty does not aim at destruction or punishment but seeks a guarantee of stability against the renewal of war. Success for this kind of peace requires that it accurately reflect the military and political situation and that it rest on a sincere desire to make it work.

The Thirty Years' Peace of 446–45 belongs in this last category. In a long war both sides had suffered losses and experienced dangers. Neither could win a decisive victory; the sea power had been unable to sustain its victories on land, and the land power had been unable to win at sea. Neither had been able to win the war in its favored element and impose its will on the enemy. The peace, therefore, was a compromise that contained the essential elements of success. It accurately reflected the balance of power between the two rivals and their alliances. It committed both sides to maintain the status quo in regard to each other and their allies. By recognizing Sparta's hegemony on the mainland and Athens's in the Aegean it accepted the dualism into which the Greek world was divided and so provided hope for a lasting peace.

Like any peace treaty, this one also had elements of possible instability. In each state minority factions were dissatisfied. Some Athenians favored expansion of the empire, and some Spartans resented sharing hegemony with Athens. Others, including some of the allies, feared Athenian ambition, believing the very existence of a powerful Athenian naval empire threatened the independence of the other Greeks. Athenians knew of these suspicions and feared that the Spartans and their allies were not truly committed to peace but only waiting for a favorable opportunity to renew the war. Some Spartans were frustrated with the way the war ended, thinking that total victory was at hand when King Pleistoanax withdrew their army from Attica without a fight. The Corinthians were still angry at Athens for its interference against the Megarians; Megara, itself, was now ruled by oligarchs who had massacred an Athenian garrison in gaining control of their city, and they were bitterly hostile to Athens, as the Athenians were to them. Boeotia, and especially its chief city Thebes, also was under the control of oligarchs who resented the Athenians' emplacement of democratic regimes in their land during the First Peloponnesian War.

Any or all these things might one day threaten the peace, but the men who agreed to it, made weary and cautious by the war, intended to preserve it. The arbitration clause was not a conventional boilerplate, but a fresh new idea. Its acceptance suggests that both sides truly wanted peace and were ready to seek unusual means to avoid wars in the future. To do so

Sicily and Southern Italy

each side needed to allay suspicion and build confidence; in each state the friends of peace had to maintain power instead of their warlike opponents; each state needed to control any tendency its allies might have to create instability. When the peace was ratified there was reason to believe that all this was possible.

TESTING THE PEACE

Within five years the peace was tested twice, the second time most severely. In 444–43 Sparta and Athens received a request from some former citizens of the recently reestablished colony of Sybaris in southern Italy, some of them Athenians who had joined as individuals. Decimated by quarrels and civil wars, the Sybarites sent to mainland Greece for help in founding a new colony at a place called Thurii, near by. Sparta had no spare population to provide colonists and had earlier indicated a lack of interest. (Diodorus 12.10.3–4) The Athenians agreed to help, but in an unusual manner. They sent messengers all over Greece to advertise for settlers for a new colony. It was not, however, to be Athenian, but to be a panhellenic colony. This was a thoroughly new idea, without precedent. Why did Pericles and the Athenians conceive it?

Some scholars believe that the Athenians were expansionists without limit and see the foundation of Thurii as part of an uninterrupted Athenian imperial growth, in the west as well as the east. But, apart from Thurii, the Athenians sought neither territory nor allies in the years between the Thirty Years' Peace and the crisis that brought on the Peloponnesian War, so the test of the theory must be Thurii itself. In that colony Athenians made up only one of the ten tribes in the city, and the largest single group were the Peloponnesians, so Athens could not have hoped to control the place and use it for Athenian purposes. The city's early history, moreover, shows that Athens never intended to control it. No sooner was Thurii founded than it fought a war against one of Sparta's few colonies, Taras. Thurii lost and the winners set up a trophy of victory and an inscription at Olympia for all the assembled Greeks to see: "The Tarantines offered a tenth of the spoils they took from the Thurians to Olympian Zeus."[15] If the Athenians meant Thurii to be the center of an Athenian Empire in the west they should have taken some action, but they did nothing, allowing the Spartan colony to flaunt its victory in the most public gathering place in Greece.

A decade later, in the midst of the crisis that led to war, a dispute arose in Thurii as to whose colony it was. The matter was settled at Delphi, where the priests declared that Apollo was the founder of the colony. The panhellenic character of Thurii thereby was reaffirmed, the connection with Athens denied, and again Athens did nothing, even though Delphic Apollo was friendly to Sparta, and the colony could be useful to the Spartans in case of war. The Athenians clearly regarded Thurii as a panhellenic colony and consistently treated it that way.

How can the Athenian actions be explained? If they had no designs on the west and wished to avoid provoking such Peloponnesian states as Corinth, who had colonies and interests in that direction, they simply could have refused to take part in the establishment of Thurii. Such inaction would have attracted little notice, but by inventing the idea of a panhellenic colony and planting it in an area outside Athens's sphere of influence, Pericles and the Athenians may have been sending a diplomatic signal. Thurii would stand as tangible evidence that Athens, rejecting the opportunity to establish its own colony, had no imperial ambitions in the west and would pursue a policy of peaceful panhellenism. The reception and persuasiveness of that message would soon be tested.[16]

In the summer of 440 a war broke out between Samos and Miletus over control of Priene, a town lying between them. The island of Samos was autonomous, a charter member of the Delian League, and the most powerful of the only three allies that paid no tribute and possessed its own navy. Miletus also had been a member of the league from the first, but it had twice revolted and been punished accordingly. It had been subjugated, deprived of its fleet, forced to pay tribute and to accept a democratic constitution. When the Milesians asked for help the Athenians could not refuse, for the leader of the alliance could not stand by and allow a powerful member to impose its will on a helpless Athenian ally. The Athenians asked the Samians to submit the quarrel to arbitration, but they refused. Athens could not ignore this defiance of its leadership and authority. Pericles himself led a fleet against Samos, replaced the ruling oligarchy with a democratic government, imposed a large indemnity, took hostages as a guarantee of good behavior, and left an Athenian garrison to guard the island.[17]

The speed of the Athenian reaction had taken the Samian leaders by surprise, but they were unwilling to accept their defeat. They now turned from defiance to revolution. Some of them persuaded Pissuthnes, the Persian satrap in Asia Minor, to help them against Athens. He allowed them to hire a mercenary army in his territory and stole the hostages from the island where the Athenians were holding them, thereby freeing the rebels to go forward. With their mercenary army, the rebels surprised and defeated the democratic government and the Athenian garrison on Samos. As a supreme act of defiance they sent the captured garrison and other Athenian officials to the Persian satrap.

News of these events sparked more trouble in the empire. Byzantium, an important city located at a choke point on the Athenian grain route to the Black Sea, also revolted. Mytilene, the chief city of the island of Lesbos and another autonomous ally possessing a navy, awaited only Spartan support before joining the rebellion.[18] The danger to Athens was acute. Two elements of the coalition that would later cause the defeat of Athens in the great Peloponnesian War were in place: revolt in the empire and support from Persia. Everything depended on Sparta, for without its commitment the rebellions would be defeated and the Persian would draw back. Sparta's decision, in turn, was sure to be influenced by Corinth for, in case of a war against Athens, the Corinthians would be the most important ally expected to produce a fleet.

The test of the peace and of Athenian policy since its conclusion was at hand. If that policy, especially in the west, seemed to Sparta and Corinth to be aggressive and ambitious, this was the time to seize this "incomparable opportunity . . . to make a sudden attack on Athens while her sea power was seriously engaged."[19] The Spartans called a meeting of the Peloponnesian League, proving that they took the matter seriously. According to the Corinthians it was they who intervened to decide the question, saying: "We did not vote against you when the other Peloponnesians were divided in their voting as to whether they should aid the Samians." The decision went against attacking Athens, which was then free to crush the Samian rebellion and to avoid a general uprising aided by Persia and a war that might have destroyed the Athenian Empire.[20]

Why did the Corinthians, whose hatred of Athens went back for two decades and who would be the major agitator for war in the final crisis, intervene to save the peace? The most plausible explanation is that they had received and understood the signal sent by the Athenian action at Thurii. Certainly, they would have been inflamed had they believed it was meant to be part of a new Athenian expansion in the western regions so important to Corinth. They must have been reassured sufficiently by its establishment as a panhellenic colony to speak in favor of peace in 440. The Samian crisis produced a dangerous threat of war, but its outcome strengthened the prospects of peace. Since the agreement of 446–45 both sides had shown restraint and a refusal to seek advantages that might endanger the peace. Prospects for the future were hopeful, when a quarrel in a remote city created new and unexpected problems.

The Crisis

Epidamnus, where the trouble began, was governed by an aristocracy, but internal struggles against the democratic faction and war against neighboring non-Hellenic Illyrian tribes had weakened the city and the aristocrats' hold on it. When the democrats gained the upper hand and drove their enemies from the city, the defeated aristocrats joined forces with the Illyrians and attacked their native city. Since Epidamnus had been founded by Corcyra (modern Corfu) about two centuries earlier, the democrats within the city sent to the mother country, asking for help in ending the fighting. The Corcyraeans, who had done well with their policy of isolation from the brotherhood of Corinthian colonists as well as from another alliance, refused. The desperate and beleaguered Epidamnians then turned to Corinth, offering to become a Corinthian colony in return for assistance. This was not surprising, for Corinth had founded Corcyra and, as was the custom, had provided the founder for the city founded by its own daughter city. It was, however, a dangerous action, for unlike Corinth's warm ties with her other colonies, relations between Corinth and Corcyra were bad. For centuries the two cities had quarreled and fought wars, often over control of some colony that both claimed as their own.

The Corinthians, nonetheless, accepted with enthusiasm, knowing full well that they would thus annoy the Corcyraeans, probably to the point of war. They sent a considerable garrison to reinforce the faction in the city and brought along many whom they invited to be permanent settlers of the reestablished colony, but they sent it by the more difficult land route "out of fear that the Corcyraeans might prevent them if they went by sea." (1.26.2) Scholars have sought in vain to find a tangible, practical, material reason for the decision,[21] but Thucydides provides an explanation on other grounds. In part, the Corinthians accepted the dangerous offer because they chose to contest Corcyra's claim to be the mother city of Epidamnus, but at the same time also out of hatred for the Corcyraeans, for they paid no attention to the Corinthians even though they were their colonists. In the common festivals they did not give them the customary privileges, nor did they begin by having a Corinthian commence the initial sacrifices, as the other colonies did, but treated them contemptuously. (1.25.3–4)

The Corinthian decision, no doubt, was part of the continuing contest over disputed colonies, a form of imperial competition familiar among European states late in the nineteenth century. It has long been clear that many of the European empires were unprofitable from a material point of view, and that the practical reasons given for acquiring them were excuses rather than true justifications. The real motives were often psychological and irrational rather than economic and practical, that is, they derived from questions of honor.[22] States seeking to assert or reclaim their status among the great powers of their time sometimes resort to imperial rivalry and the conflict it often engenders.

So it was with the Corinthians. Corinth had been a rich and powerful state when Athens and Sparta were of much less consequence. In the sixth century Sparta grew to be the dominant power in the Peloponnese, the head of a powerful league of allies, and had been given the honor of leading the Greek resistance to the Persian invasion in 480–79. Since the Persian Wars Athens had become the leader of her own alliance and an equal to Sparta. The Corinthians had seen her prestige shrink in comparison with the two superpowers, but they were determined to build a sphere of influence in the Greek northwest to compensate for their diminished prestige elsewhere. This brought them into conflict with Corcyra, whose power and influence had grown while Corinth's declined. Corcyra remained aloof from the foreign and domestic wars that troubled Greece in the fifth century and did well by it. The Corcyraeans had acquired a fleet of 120 warships, second in size only to Athens. For years they had challenged Corinthian hegemony in the northwest.[23] To these injuries they added the insult of public disdain for Corinth at the public festivals common to them and Corinth's other colonies. These public insults must have been at least the last straw for the Corinthians. Spoiling for a fight they seized the excuse offered them by the Epidamnian invitation. It was a matter of respect and prestige, that is, honor.

Nothing compelled the Corinthians to intervene in Epidamnus when they knew their involvement could mean war with Corcyra. Since the Corcyraeans had remained aloof, no interest of theirs was threatened, nor any diminution of their power or prestige. They seized the opportunity to annoy and humiliate their insolent colony. If that meant war, so much the better, for that could provide an opportunity to crush Corcyra forever. In the Thucydidean triad of motives the Corinthians acted to increase their honor, taking the initiative because the opportunity beckoned.

The Corcyraeans already had shown their lack of interest in who would win the civil war at Epidamnus, but Corinth's intervention changed their minds. They sent a fleet to Epidamnus and presented their demands: the faction holding Epidamnus must send away the garrison and colonists sent by Corinth and take back the exiled aristocrats. This was not a proposal for negotiation; it was an ultimatum, delivered in insolent language, whose terms were unacceptable. Corinth could not agree to accept them without disgrace, and the faction holding Epidamnus could not accept them in safety.

Corcyra's confident arrogance rested on its current naval superiority. Apart from Athens, Corcyra was the only state to maintain a fleet in peacetime, and a powerful one. Although Corinth was a great commercial state, it had no warships to speak of. The Corcyraeans, therefore, did not hesitate to deliver their ultimatum nor, when it was refused, to take action. They, too, since they had shown their lack of interest in Epidamnus, acted in defense of their honor. They sent forty ships to besiege the city, while the Epidamnian exiles and their Illyrian allies enclosed it by land. In relying on the correlation of forces at the beginning of the quarrel the Corcyraeans made a great mistake. Corinth was rich, adaptable, angry, and determined. It was allied to Sparta and a member of the Peloponnesian League. In the past the Corinthians had more than once been able to use those alliances to their own advantage, and they expected to do so again against Corcyra.[24] The Corcyraeans should have been able to foresee the danger, but they, too, were angry.

Corinth responded with vigor, announcing the foundation of a completely new colony at Epidamnus and inviting settlers from all over Greece to join it. Many responded and were sent to Epidamnus, accompanied by thirty Corinthian warships and three thousand soldiers. Additional help came from several cities asked by Corinth to supply ships and money. Several of them, including the major states of Megara and Thebes, were members of the Spartan Alliance, but the Spartans themselves gave no help.

Even a token force from the Spartans might have intimidated the Corcyraeans, but we have no evidence that they were asked. Perhaps they already
had expressed disapproval of the Corinthian expedition.

The force of Corinth's action and the character of the support it had
collected shook the Corcyraeans' confidence, so they turned to diplomacy
as a way out of their trouble. They sent negotiators to Corinth "with
Spartan and Sicyonian ambassadors, whom they had invited along."
(1.28.1) The Corcyraeans first repeated their demands that the Corinthians
withdraw from Epidamnus. Failing that, Corcyra was willing to submit the
dispute to arbitration by any mutually acceptable Peloponnesian state or, if
the Corinthians preferred, to the oracle at Delphi. After this offer of a
peaceful solution to the quarrel came a threat. If the Corinthians refused
and insisted on war, Corcyra would be forced to seek friends elsewhere.
The reference was unmistakable: if necessary, the Corcyraeans would seek
an alliance with Athens.

There is no reason to doubt the sincerity of the Corcyraeans in
seeking a negotiated or arbitrated settlement. They had underestimated
Corinth's latent power and did not want to suffer for that mistake. At the
same time, they had little to fear from arbitration. Any Peloponnesian state
they would accept as arbitrator would be under the influence of Sparta and
unlikely to side totally with Corinth. The oracle at Delphi was also very
much under Spartan influence. (1.112.5; 1.118.3) Such an arbitrator might
recommend the restoration of the status quo ante, with instructions for
some reconciliation between the warring factions and the withdrawal of
the Illyrians. That would leave Epidamnus in native hands and compel the
Corinthians, their colonists, and their allies to withdraw and would delight
the Corcyraeans. But any judgment that compelled the Corinthians to
withdraw—and any possible arbitrator would be likely to insist on that—
would be satisfactory. The Corcyraeans, however, would not accept the
humiliation of surrendering to the Corinthians. Rather than that they
would seek an alliance with the Athenians and fight.

A minor incident in a remote corner of the Greek world had produced a crisis that now began to threaten a major war. So long as the affair
involved only Epidamnus and Corcyra the problem was purely local, for
neither belonged to either of the international alliances that dominated
Greece. When Corinth took a hand, however, and began to embroil members of the Spartan Alliance, prompting Corcyra to seek the help of Athens,
a major war became conceivable.

The Spartans had foreseen the danger; that is why they agreed to join the Corcyraean negotiators and lend support to a peaceful settlement of the quarrel. The Corinthians would not yield. A flat refusal under the eyes of the Spartans would have been embarrassing, but they made a counteroffer that was not serious: if the Corcyraeans withdrew their ships and the Illyrians, the Corinthians *would think about* Corcyra's proposal. That would have left the Corinthian forces in Epidamnus where they could gain a strategic advantage by strengthening their hold on the city, taking in supplies, and bolstering its defenses against a siege. Although the Corinthian proposal was plainly not sincere, the Corcyraeans did not break off negotiations even then. They offered a mutual withdrawal of forces or a truce while the two sides negotiated in place. The Corinthians refused, declaring war and sending a fleet of seventy-five ships along with two thousand infantrymen to Epidamnus. On the way they were intercepted by a Corcyraean force of eighty ships and thoroughly defeated at the battle of Leucimne. On the same day Epidamnus was forced to surrender to the Corcyraean besiegers. Corcyra ruled the sea and the disputed city. To add to the Corinthians' humiliation, they could not prevent the Corcyraean fleet from ravaging and burning the territory of their allies in the west. (1.29–30)

THE CRISIS WIDENS

The Corinthians' first miscalculation, of their own strength against Corcyra's, had led to defeat on land and sea, as well as humiliation. Their second, of the diplomatic situation in the larger world of Hellas, would have broader and deadlier consequences. The Corcyraeans had warned that if pressed hard they would seek new allies, and it was clear that they meant the Athenians. The Spartans were alarmed sufficiently by the prospect to support Corcyra's offer of a negotiated settlement, but the Corinthians were undeterred. Their answer to defeat was to spend the next two years preparing for revenge. They built their largest fleet ever and hired experienced rowers from everywhere, including cities in the Athenian Empire. The Athenians did not object, which may have strengthened the Corinthians' opinion that Corcyraean talk of getting help from Athens was unrealistic.

The Corcyraeans were frightened thoroughly by Corinth's determination and of its preparations. Apart from its own wealth and power,

Corinth could expect to gain the support of at least some of its fellow members of the Spartan Alliance, perhaps ultimately of Sparta itself, while Corcyra was neutral, without allies. The Corinthians had raised the bet and called Corcyra's bluff. Corcyra, therefore, sent an embassy to Athens to seek an alliance and assistance against Corinth. When the Corinthians heard about it, they, too, sent ambassadors to Athens "to prevent the addition of the Athenian fleet to the Corcyraeans' since that would impede their victory." (1.31) The crisis, heretofore confined to a conflict between Corcyra and Corinth, was on the verge of reaching a higher and more dangerous level, involving at least one of the great powers and alliances of the Greek world.

It is hard for a modern reader to imagine the scene on the Pnyx in the summer of 433 when the Athenian assembly met to hear the Corcyraean ambassadors. The very men who would need to fight in any war that might result heard every word spoken by the foreign ambassadors, debated the issues themselves, and determined the course to take by their own votes. It is hard to imagine any convenant arrived at more openly, in Woodrow Wilson's phrase. The Corcyraeans faced a difficult task in trying to per-suade the Athenians to join them in their conflict against Corinth. There was no previous friendship between them, and Athens owed them nothing. No Athenian interests were involved in the quarrel. Since 445, moreover, the Athenians had been committed to a policy of peace and conciliation with Sparta and her allies. Why should they consider an alliance that would involve them in hostilities against Corinth, at least, and possibly the Pelo-ponnesian League?

The Corcyraeans argued for the moral rightness of their cause and for the legality of the alliance they proposed, since the Thirty Years' Peace expressly permitted alliance with a neutral.[25] Like most people, however, the Athenians were more concerned with questions of security and inter-est, and the Corcyraeans were prepared to satisfy them: "We have a navy that is the greatest except for your own," a force that would be added to Athenian power. "In the entire course of time few have received more advantages all at once, and few when they come to ask for an alliance offer to those whom they ask as much security and honor as they expect to receive." (1.33.1–2)

The most powerful appeal, however, was to fear. The Athenians needed the alliance as much as those proposing it, and they needed it at once, for the Corcyraeans argued that a war between Athens and the

Spartan Alliance was inevitable and on its way. "If any of you thinks it will not happen his judgment is in error, and he does not see that the Spartans are eager for war out of fear of you, and that the Corinthians have great influence with them and are your enemies." (1.33.3) Since war could not be avoided, Athens must accept the Corcyraean alliance.

> There are three fleets worthy of mention in Greece, yours, ours, and the Corinthians'; if the Corinthians get control of us first, you will see two of them become one, and you will have to fight against the Corcyraean and Peloponnesian fleets at once; if you accept us you will fight against them with our ships in addition to your own. (1.36.3)

The task of the Corinthian spokesman was no easier. Corinth was the first to intervene at Epidamnus and had rejected every offer for a peaceful solution, even against the advice of its allies. All the Corinthians could do was remind the Athenians of past favors and assault the character of the Corcyraeans. They had a stronger argument about the legality of an Athenian treaty with Corcyra. Technically, the Thirty Years' Peace permitted an alliance since Corcyra belonged to neither bloc, but it certainly violated the spirit of the treaty and common sense: "although it says in the treaty that any of the unenrolled cities may join whichever side it likes, the clause is not meant for those who join one side with the intention of injuring the other." (1.40.2) No one who negotiated or swore to the treaty could have imagined approving an alliance by one side with a neutral at war with the other. The Corinthians, at any rate, made their attitude clear: "if you join with them, it will be necessary for us to include you in our revenge against them." (1.40.2–3)

There remained Corcyra's most weighty argument, that war was in any case inevitable, so that the Athenians could not afford to let Corcyra's fleet fall into Corinthian hands. The Corinthians responded by denying that war *was* inevitable. They reminded the Athenians of past favors they had received from Corinth, especially their service during the Samian uprising when they helped to dissuade Sparta and the Peloponnesian League from attacking Athens at a moment of great danger. They believed they had confirmed on that ocasion the key principle governing the relations between the two alliances, the one vital to the maintenance of peace: noninterference by each side in the other's sphere of influence.

Circumstances have brought us under the principle that we our-selves expressed at Sparta, that each side should punish its own allies. Now we come to you demanding the same thing: that you should not injure us with your vote, since we helped you with ours. Pay us back in equal measure, knowing that this is the crucial moment when assistance is the greatest friendship and hostility the greatest enmity. Do not accept the Corcyraeans as allies against our wishes, nor help them to do wrong. In doing what we ask you will be behaving properly and serving your own interests in the best way. (1.43)

The Corinthian argument was not entirely sound. Corcyra was not a Corinthian ally, as Samos had been allied to Athens, and even the broadest interpretation of the treaty did not prevent the Athenians from assisting a neutral attacked by Corinth. Athens would be on solid legal ground in accepting Corcyra's proposal. But the Corinthians were right in a deeper sense: there could be no lasting peace if either side chose to help unaligned states at war with the other.

The behavior of the Athenians since 445 and right on through the crisis makes it clear that they wanted to avoid war. It is hard to imagine their joining any other neutral at odds with an ally of Sparta's, but Corcyra was unique. Its defeat and the transfer of its navy would have created a Peloponnesian fleet powerful enough to challenge Athenian naval suprem-acy, on which the power, prosperity, indeed the very survival of Athens and its empire depended. The Athenians' situation resembles that faced by Great Britain in the early years of the twentieth century. When Germany, as we shall see (see pp. 132–44), began to build a navy of a size and quality to challenge British supremacy at sea, the British, who preferred to live in "splendid isolation" from the Continent, reversed a century-old policy and aligned themselves with their traditional enemies France and Russia. Like most states whose security depends on control of the sea, Britain was ready to fight a great and dangerous war to defend its naval supremacy.

The Athenians' problem was even more difficult, for they were threatened with a deadly change in the balance of power at one stroke, almost overnight. The Corinthians did not grasp the point, although their Spartan allies seem to have done so. They appear to have been confident that Athens would refuse the alliance, possibly even to join the Corinthians against Corcyra, as they had the audacity to suggest. (1.40.4) Why did they miscalculate so badly? For them, Corcyra was merely a local affair. They were persuaded that the Athenians wanted peace and had no ambitions in the region, and believed that Athens would respond in kind to their friendly behavior in the Samian affair. In the pursuit of their narrow interests, intensified by a long-standing exasperation and anger at their humiliation by a lesser state outside the world of the great powers, they ignored or underestimated the significance of their action to the balance of power in the international system. They did not make sure that the Athenians would stand aside before making war on Corcyra. Instead, they ignored the danger and plunged ahead, hoping and assuming that all would be well. Corinth would not be the last state in history to let passion overcome prudence.

The Athenians faced the most difficult of choices. If they accepted the Corcyraean alliance, it would surely mean war against Corinth and, sooner or later, probably against the Spartans and their allies. If they refused, they ran the risk of a Corinthian victory and capture of the Corcyraean fleet and the resulting major change in the correlation of forces at sea. In case of a future war against the Peloponnesians, and continued peace was far from certain, that would seriously threaten Athenian security. Almost all debates in the Athenian assembly ended in a single day, but the argument over the Corcyraean alliance required a second meeting. On the first day opinion inclined toward rejection. We may assume feverish discussion overnight, and on the second day a new plan emerged. Instead of the full offensive and defensive commitment that was usual in a Greek alliance *(symmachia)* the proposal was to make an alliance that was defensive only *(epimachia)*, the first we hear of in Greek history. The chances are great that the innovative Pericles was its author. Throughout the crisis he was able to shape Athenian policy, and Plutarch tells us that it was Pericles who "persuaded the people to send help to the Corcyraeans who were fighting the Corinthians and to attach themselves to a vigorous island with naval power." *(Pericles, 29.1)*

Thucydides says that the Athenians voted for the treaty because they believed that war with the Peloponnesians was inevitable, and they wanted to gain a strategic advantage before it came. That is a major element in his interpretation, but it is by no means certain that he is right.[26] Certainly, the many Athenians who opposed the treaty could not have agreed. It is possible that the defensive alliance was invented as the best that could be gotten, for the Athenians were plainly reluctant to act in such a way as to bring on a war with the Peloponnesians. The danger to Athens was remote and problematical. Why, many must have asked, should Athens risk war on behalf of Corcyra? But the Athenians' action is also consistent with the choice of a policy aimed not at preparing for war but at deterring it, a middle way between the unpleasant choices of refusing the Corcyraeans, thereby risking the loss of their fleet to the Peloponnesians, and accepting an offensive alliance likely to bring on an unwelcome war. Their subsequent behavior indicates that they chose this middle policy of moderation and deterrence and held to it as long as possible.

The defensive alliance was a precisely crafted diplomatic device meant to bring the Corinthians to their senses without war. To meet their new commitment the Athenians sent a fleet to Corcyra, but of the hundreds of warships in their navy they sent only ten. If the intention was to fight and defeat the Corinthians, Athens could have sent two hundred warships. Together with the Corcyraeans, a force of that size would either have forced the Corinthians to reconsider or have guaranteed a smashing victory and probably the destruction of the enemy fleet. The small force actually sent could not have had any great effect once the fighting began; it was clearly of more symbolic than military significance, meant to show that Athens meant business and to deter the Corinthians. The choice of Lacedaemonius, the son of Cimon, as one of the commanders is also significant. He was an experienced cavalryman, but we know nothing of his naval experience. His very name, which can be translated as "Spartan," is evidence of his father's close ties with the leaders of the Peloponnesian League. The choice was no coincidence; it was meant to disarm Spartan suspicion of his mission.

Even more striking were the orders received by the Athenian commanders. They were not to engage unless the Corinthian fleet sailed against Corcyra itself or one of its possessions with the intention of making a landing. "These orders were given in order not to break the treaty." (1.45.3) Such orders are a nightmare for any naval commander. In the melee of a naval battle, how can anyone be certain of the intentions of the enemy? Caution and patience might prevent a timely intervention; swift reaction to what might be a feint or a misunderstood maneuver could lead to engagement against orders. In the latter case it might be helpful if the crucial decision was taken by Lacedaemonius, the son of Cimon.

The policy, with all its difficulties, was an effort at what is called in current jargon "minimal deterrence." By their actions the Athenians indicated that if Corinth would refrain from attacking Corcyra and seizing her fleet there need be no war. The presence of an Athenian force demonstrated Athenian determination to prevent a shift in the balance of naval power; its small size showed that the Athenians did not intend to diminish or destroy Corinthian power. If the plan worked the Corinthians would sail home without a fight, and the crisis would pass. Even if the Corinthians chose to fight, the Athenians might still hope to stay out of the battle. Perhaps the Corcyraeans might win without Athenian aid, as they did at Leucimne. Perhaps some Athenians hoped "to wear the two sides out as much as possible against each other so that they might find Corinth and the other naval powers weaker in case it should be necessary to go to war with them." (1.44.2) Either way, the Athenians could stay out of the fight.

The Corinthian and Corcyraean fleets met at the battle of Sybota in September of 433. The small Athenian squadron did not deter the Corinthians, as a larger fleet might have done. There is a considerable difference between the thought that one's actions may have unpleasant consequences at some time in the future and the fact of overwhelming forces before one's eyes that will bring immediate destruction. Eight allied cities had given help to Corinth in the previous battle at Leucimne. Only two, Elis and Megara, were at Sybota. The others may have been deterred by Corinth's earlier defeat or by the new Corcyraean alliance with Athens. It is also possible that Sparta worked to persuade its allies to stay out of the conflict. With 150 ships, 90 of their own and 60 more provided by colonies and allies, the Corinthians attacked 110 Corcyraean warships while the Athenians remained apart.

Soon, however, the Corinthians gained the upper hand, and the Athenians could no longer stand aloof.

> When the Athenians saw the Corcyraeans pressed, they began to help them without reservation. At first they held back from making an actual attack on the enemy ship, but when it became plain that a rout was taking place and that the Athenians were in hot pursuit, then at last each man took part in the work, and fine distinctions were no longer made. The situation had developed to the point where the Corinthians and Athenians necessarily had to fight one another. (1.49.7)

As the Corcyraean and Athenian fleets prepared to defend the island, the Corinthians, who had launched their attack already, backed off. They saw what turned out to be a force of twenty Athenian warships, sent to reinforce the original contingent. After the original ten had sailed, a debate broke out in Athens as to their sufficiency. Pericles's opponents criticized his plan as being excessively subtle and falling between two stools: "he had provided little help for the Corcyraeans by sending ten ships, but a great pretext for complaint by their enemies." (Plutarch, *Pericles*, 29.3) They insisted on sending reinforcements, but the relatively small contingent suggests that the result was a compromise.

In the heat of battle the Corinthians could not be sure how large the new Athenian squadron was. Even if they could count the ships, they could not be sure that they were not the earliest of many more still to arrive. Night fell without further fighting. The next day, bolstered by thirty undamaged Athenian ships, the Corcyraeans offered battle, but the Corinthians refused. They were afraid that the Athenians might regard the first day's skirmish as the beginning of a war against Corinth and seize the chance to destroy the Corinthian fleet, but the Athenians allowed them to sail away. Each side was meticulous in disclaiming responsibility for a breach of the treaty. Corinth could not win a war against Athens without enlisting the support of Sparta and its allies. But the Spartans had tried to restrain Corinth; if the Corinthians could be blamed for breaking the treaty they could not expect to gain their support. The Athenians, on the other hand, were careful not to give Sparta a reason to enter the quarrel.

Corcyra and its fleet had been saved only by the arrival of additional forces. The Athenians had not prevented the battle nor destroyed the Corinthians' capacity to fight. "Minimal deterrence" had failed. The Corinthians sailed off, most of their fleet intact. On their way home they seized Anactorium, a colony disputed with Corcyra, regardless of what Athens might think or do. Frustrated and angry, they were determined to bring in the Spartans and their allies to achieve their own goals and to gain vengeance against their enemies.

It was now clear to the Athenians that they must prepare for war, at least against Corinth, even as they tried to avoid involving the Spartans and their other allies. Even before the battle of Sybota the Athenians had interrupted their grand building program to preserve the money that would be needed in case of war. After the battle they undertook a series of diplomatic missions and military expeditions to shore up their position in northwest Greece, Italy, and Sicily.[27] The most clear-cut instance of Athenian preparation for war against Corinth was the ultimatum they delivered in the winter following Sybota to Potidaea, a city in the northern Aegean. The Potidaeans were members of the Athenian alliance and at the same time colonists of Corinth, unusually close to the mother city. Knowing that the Corinthians were planning revenge, the Athenians feared they might join with the hostile king of neighboring Macedon to spark a rebellion in Potidaea. From there it might spread to other states and cause serious problems in the empire.

Perhaps in the month of January 432, without any specific provocation, the Athenians ordered the Potidaeans to pull down the walls that protected them on the seaward side, to send away the magistrates they annually received from Corinth, and to give hostages. This action would separate the city from Corinthian influence and put it at the mercy of Athens. The aim of the ultimatum was to deter a rebellion and prevent Corinth from gaining new allies and extending the area of conflict. Once again, the Athenian action should be understood as a diplomatic response to a looming problem, a moderate choice between unwelcome extremes. Taking no action might invite rebellion; sending a military force to gain physical control of Potidaea would make the city safe for Athens, but it could be provocative. Issuing the ultimatum was a matter of imperial regulation, clearly permitted by the Thirty Years' Peace.

The Potidaeans sent an embassy to Athens to object to the ultimatum, and discussions went on all winter. At last, the Athenians became suspicious and ordered the commander of an expedition they had sent to Macedonia previously "to take hostages from the Potidaeans, pull down their walls, and keep watch on the cities near by so that they would not rebel." (1.57.6) The Athenian suspicions were justified; at the same time the Potidaeans had sent envoys to Athens they secretly dispatched another embassy to Sparta. Supported by the Corinthians, they asked for help in their rebellion. Spartan magistrates, probably the ephors, promised to invade Attica if Potidaea launched a rebellion. What caused such a remarkable reversal of policy at Sparta?

During the same winter (in close proximity to the Potidaean ultimatum, but whether before or after it is unclear) the Athenians took still another action. They passed a decree barring the Megarians from the harbors of the Athenian Empire and from the Athenian agora, its marketplace and civic center. Economic embargoes are sometimes used in the modern world as diplomatic weapons, as means of coercion short of war. In the ancient world we know of no previous embargo employed in peace-time.[28]

This was certainly another of Pericles's innovations, for contemporaries blamed the war on the decree and him for the decree, and he defended it stubbornly to the end, even when it appeared to become the sole issue on which war or peace depended. Why did the Athenian leader introduce the decree and he and the majority of Athens's citizens approve and hold fast to it? Scholars have seen it variously as an act of economic imperialism, a device intended deliberately to bring on the war, an act of defiance to the Peloponnesian League, an attempt to enrage the Spartans into violating the treaty, and even the first act of war itself.[29] The official version was that the decree was provoked by the Megarians' cultivation of sacred land claimed by the Athenians, their illegal encroachment upon borderlands, and their harboring of fugitive slaves. (1.139.2) The modern theories do not bear close scrutiny,[30] and the ancient complaints are a mere pretext. The purpose of the Megarian Decree should be understood to have been a moderate intensification of diplomatic pressure to help prevent the spread of the war to Corinth's allies. The Corinthians could succeed only if the other Peloponnesians, especially Sparta, could be made to join the fight. Corinth had defied Spartan wishes by rejecting a negotiated peace. Megara had done the same by sending help to Corinth at Leucimne and also at Sybota, even when most of the other Peloponnesian states had held back, and had suffered no punishment. In time, other states might join the Corinthians in another encounter with Athens; if enough of their allies took that step, the Spartans could stay aloof only at the risk of their leadership of the alliance and their own security. Pericles and the Athenians decided to punish the Megarians in order to deter further help to Corinth.

Once again, the Athenian action should be seen as a middle path. To do nothing might encourage further assistance to Corinth by Megara itself and might make it easier for other states to join them. To attack the city by any military means would have been a breach of the treaty and would bring Sparta into the war against Athens. The embargo would not bring Megara to its knees or do unbearable damage. It would cause general discomfort to most Megarians and do significant harm to the men who prospered from trade with Athens and her empire, some of them, no doubt, members of the oligarchic council that governed the city. The punishment might persuade Megara to stay out of future trouble and warn other trading states that they were not immune from Athenian retaliation, even in a period of formal peace.

For all its intended moderation, the Megarian Decree was not without risks. The Megarians were sure to complain to the Spartans, who might feel compelled to come to their aid, but there was reason to doubt that they would respond. Once again, the measure had been crafted not to violate the terms of the treaty, which said nothing about trade or economic relations. Besides, Pericles was a personal friend of Archidamus (2.12.4), the only king in Sparta at that time (Pleistoanax had been sent into exile in 445). He knew that Archidamus favored peace and could expect that his royal friend would understand his own peaceful intentions and the limited purposes of the decree and help the other Spartans to understand. He was right about Archidamus, but he underestimated the passions aroused in some Spartans by the combination of events that had taken place since the alliance with Corcyra.

THE DECISION FOR WAR: SPARTA

Among those angered and alarmed were at least three of the five ephors, the majority needed to make the promise to invade Attica that was given to the Potidaean envoys. It was a secret promise, not endorsed by the Spartan assembly, and it was not kept in the spring of 432. Neither their king nor a majority of the Spartans were prepared to go to war yet, but an influential faction was eager to change their minds.

Encouraged by the ephors' promise, the Potidaeans launched their rebellion, and the Athenian force sent to prevent an uprising was too little and arrived too late. The Corinthians wasted no time in exploiting the new opportunity. They did not dare send an official expedition, which would have been a formal violation of the treaty. Instead, they organized a corps of "volunteers" commanded by a Corinthian general, who led a force of Corinthians and Peloponnesian mercenaries to help the Potidaeans. The Athenians responded by making peace with Macedon to free the force fighting there for use against Potidaea and sending reinforcements from Athens. By the summer of 432 a large force of men and ships surrounded the city, beginning a siege that lasted more than two years and cost a vast sum of money.

The Athenians were besieging a city defended by Corinthians and other Peloponnesians, whatever their informal status, and the Megarians were injured and insulted by the Athenian embargo, so the Corinthians now had grievances other than their own with which to inflame the Spartans against Athens.[31] They encouraged all the states that had grievances against Athens to put pressure on the Spartans. But in spite of the ephors' promise, they had not been able to get a vote for war against Athens in the assembly. At last, in July 432, the ephors called a meeting of the Spartan assembly to which they invited any allied state with a complaint against Athens to come to Sparta and speak out. This is the only known occasion when allies were invited to speak, not at a meeting of the Spartan Alliance, but in the Spartan assembly. The most plausible explanation for this unique event is that the bellicose ephors did not believe they could bring the majority of the Spartans around to their view unaided, so they invited the angry foreigners to help make the case.

Several spoke, the most vehement being the Megarians, but the Corinthians were the most effective. Faced by the fact that the Athenians had been careful to abide by the letter of the treaty, aware that their engagement at Epidamnus had created the crisis and that their subsequent behavior, against the wishes of the Spartans, had fanned the flames of war, they said as little as possible about particulars. Their strategy was to persuade Sparta that its traditional policy of caution and reluctance to fight was disastrous in the face of the dynamic power of Athens, and their tactic was to draw a sharp distinction between the characters of the two peoples.

> You have never considered what sort of men you are going to fight and how totally different they are from you. They are revolutionary and quick to formulate plans and put them into action, while you preserve what you have, invent nothing new, and when you act do not even complete what is necessary. Again, they are daring beyond their power, run risk beyond wisdom, and are hopeful amidst dangers, while it is your way to do less than your power permits, to distrust your surest judgments, and to think you will be destroyed by any dangers.
>
> Besides, they are unhesitating while you delay, they are always abroad while you stay at home, for they think that by their absence from home they may gain something while you are afraid you will lose what you already have. When they have conquered their enemies they pursue them as far as possible, and if beaten yield as little ground as they can. In addition to that they use their bodies in the

service of the city as though they belonged to someone else, at the same time as they keep their judgment their own so as to use it for the city. And when they have thought of a plan and failed to carry it through to full success, they think they have been deprived of their own property; when they have acquired what they aimed at, they think it only a small thing compared to what they will acquire in the future.

If it happens that an attempt fails, they form a new hope to compensate for the loss. For with them alone it is the same thing to hope and to have, when once they have invented a scheme, because of the swiftness with which they carry out what they have planned. And in this way they wear out their entire lives with danger, and they enjoy what they have the least of all men because they are always engaged in acquisition and because they think their only holiday is to do what is their duty and also because they consider tranquil peace a greater disaster than painful activity. As a result one would be correct in saying that it is their nature neither to enjoy peace themselves nor to allow it to other men. (1.70)

Both halves of the comparison were exaggerated. The Spartans could not have become leaders of the great alliance that led the Greeks to victory over the Persians if they were as sluggish as they were painted. Whatever one might think about the Corinthians' picture of the Athenian character, it did not fit the behavior of the Athenians since the Thirty Years' Peace began. Athens had acted in full accord with its letter and spirit, as the Corinthians themselves acknowledged when they restrained their allies at the time of the Samian rebellion. Athens's troubling behavior in the last year plainly had been a reaction to actions initiated by Corinth. The Corinthian tactic was to say as little as possible about recent, concrete events. Instead they described the Athenian character, arising inescapably from its institutions, as one that made peaceful coexistence impossible, regardless of the resolution of any specific crisis. Prejudice, suspicion, and fear were employed to obscure the facts of recent history and to drive the Spartans toward war.

The Corinthians concluded with a threat: the Spartans must come to the aid of Potidaea and their other allies and invade Attica, "lest you betray your friends and kinsmen to their worst enemies and turn the rest of us to some other alliance." (1.71.4) The threat was empty; there was no other alliance to which they could turn, but it still had an effect. Sparta's security and its way of life rested, to some considerable degree, on the integrity of its alliance, so even the suggestion of defections that might lead to dissolution was alarming.

The next speaker was a member of an Athenian embassy that, Thucydides says, "happened to be present beforehand on other business." (1.72.1) We are not told what that "business" might be, and it seems clear that it was merely a pretext to allow the Athenians to present their views. For Pericles and the Athenians it was important not to send an official spokesman to a Spartan assembly to answer complaints, for that would concede Sparta's right to judge Athenian behavior rather than to submit disagreements to arbitration, as the treaty required. At the same time, they wanted to affect the debate. They intervened to prevent Sparta from making a serious mistake by yielding to the arguments of their allies; to show that Athens had gained her power justly, and that Athenian power was formidable. They ascribed the growth of their empire not to ambition but explained it as a response to a series of necessities imposed by the demands of fear, honor, and a reasonable self-interest—matters that the Spartans, who exercised a similar power, should understand. Their tone was not conciliatory, but businesslike, and their conclusion insisted on the precise letter of the treaty: the submission of all disputes to arbitration. Should the Spartans refuse, however, "we shall try to take vengeance on those who have started the war when you have led the way." (1.78.5)

Some scholars have understood the speech as deliberately provocative, meant to move the Spartans to violate their oaths and start the war. Such a view, not uncommon in our time, assumes that attempts to appease anger, to explain differences charitably, to make concessions, are the only ways to seek peace. Sometimes, however, the best way to prevent war is through deterrence, by conveying a message of strength, confidence, and determination. This policy can be especially effective when it leaves the other side an honorable way out, as the arbitration clause provided for the Spartans. The best contemporary witness, at any rate, tells us that war was not the Athenians' goal: "they wanted to make clear the power of their city, to offer a reminder to the older men of what they already knew and to the younger men of the things of which they were ignorant, thinking that because of their arguments the Spartans would incline to peace instead of war." (1.72.1)

So the Athenians placed their hopes for peace in a combination of deterrence and the honorable alternative to war—arbitration. That hope must have seemed reasonable, since Sparta's kings traditionally were influential in decisions of war and peace and in 432 the only king in Sparta was Archidamus, a personal friend of Pericles's, "a man with a reputation for wisdom and prudence" (1.79.2) who would soon demonstrate his opposition to the war. After the foreigners had spoken they all withdrew. The aggrieved allies had been successful in stirring strong feeling against Athens, and the Athenian response did not allay it. In the face of a Spartan assembly in a hostile mood and confident that Athens could be beaten easily in a brief war, the king endorsed the Athenians' assessment of their strength. Athens's power was greater than Sparta was accustomed to facing and of a different kind. A walled city, with lots of money, a naval empire, and command of the sea could wage a war such as the Spartans had never fought. He feared, rather, "that we shall pass this war on to our children." (1.81.6)

The mood of the assembly was so angry that Archidamus could not simply decide in favor of the Athenian offer, so he proposed a moderate alternative. The Spartans should send an embassy to Athens to make an official complaint, without yet committing themselves to any course of action. At the same time, they should prepare for the kind of war they would really face if discussion failed. They should seek ships from the barbarians (primarily the Persians) and from the Greeks. If the Athenians gave satisfaction there need be no war. If not, there would be plenty of time to fight when the Spartans were better prepared, *in two or three years.*

These suggestions would have suited the Athenians well. Whatever the result of discussions, so long a delay would certainly cool Spartan ardor and allow the crisis to pass. For that reason they were unwelcome to the Corinthians, the other complaining parties, and those in Sparta who wanted war. Any chance at saving Potidaea required swift action. No form of arbitration or negotiation would satisfy the Corinthians. They did not want a settlement of grievances, they wanted a free hand to crush Corcyra once and for all, and they wanted revenge against the Athenians, indeed, the destruction of the Athenian Empire. The advocates of war in Sparta had come to the same conclusion; most Spartans agreed with them. Individually, the affairs of Corcyra, Potidaea, and Megara were not decisive but, taken all together with a selective choice of the history of the last fifty years, they seemed to confirm the Corinthian picture of the arrogance of the Athenians and the danger presented by their growing power.

The response to Archidamus and the Athenians by the bellicose ephor Sthenelaidas, therefore, could be short and blunt:

> I don't understand the lengthy arguments of the Athenians. They praise themselves highly, but they don't deny that they are doing wrong to our allies and to the Peloponnesus. . . . If we are wise we will not look on while they wrong our allies. . . . Others may have much money, ships, and horses, but we have good allies whom we must not betray to the Athenians. Nor should we submit to judgments by courts or words, for we have not been injured by words. Instead, we must take swift vengeance with all our forces. And let no one tell us that we must take time to consider when we have been wronged; rather let those who contemplate doing a wrong reflect for a long time. So vote for war, Spartans, in a manner worthy of Sparta. Do not allow the Athenians to grow stronger and do not betray your allies, but let us, with the help of the gods, march out against those who are doing wrong. (1.86)

Then the ephor called for a vote on the question of whether the Athenians had violated the peace treaty. Claiming he could not tell which side made the louder clamor, but "wanting to make them more eager for war by an open demonstration of their opinion" (1.87.2) he called for a division. A large majority voted that the Athenians had broken the peace; it was a vote for war.

Why did the Spartans decide to fight what might be a long and difficult war against a uniquely powerful opponent, facing no immediate threat, for no tangible benefit, provoked by no direct harm to themselves? What had dissolved the normally conservative Spartan majority favoring peace, led by the prudent and respected King Archidamus? Thucydides explained that the Spartans voted for war, not because they were persuaded by the arguments of their allies, "but because they were afraid that the Athenians might become too powerful, seeing that the greater part of Greece was already in their hands." (1.88) His general explanation for the origin of the war was this: "I think that the truest cause, but the least spoken of, was the growth of Athenian power, which presented an object of fear to the Spartans and forced them to go to war." (1.23.6) That is, they launched a preventive war to forestall events that they believed posed threats for the future.

But the power of Athens was not growing in the dozen years between the peace and the battle of Sybota, nor was Athenian policy aggressive, as even the Corinthians had recognized in 440. The only growth in Athenian power was the alliance with Corcyra in 433, made in response to a Corinthian initiative taken against Spartan advice, and the evidence was clear that the Athenians had acted reluctantly and defensively, seeking only to prevent the Corinthians from causing a major shift in the balance of power. They represented no immediate threat to Sparta. But, as one perceptive student of the history of war has put it, wars have normally arisen "from almost a superabundance of analytic rationality. Sophisticated communities . . . do not react simply to immediate threats. Their intelligence . . . enables them to assess the implications that any event taking place anywhere in the world, however remote, may have for their own capacity, immediately to exert influence, ultimately, perhaps to survive." All kinds of events may "precipitate or strengthen a trend, set in motion a tide whose melancholy withdrawing roar will strip us of our friends and influence and leave us isolated in a world dominated by adversaries deeply hostile to us and all we stand for."[32]

So it was with the Spartans, who took fright when it seemed to them that "the power of the Athenians began to manifest itself and to lay hold on their allies. Then the situation became unendurable, and the Spartans decided they must try with all their resolution to destroy that power if they could and to launch this war." (1.118.2) All three components of Thucydides's explanation justify the Athenians' analysis of the motives at work in the relations between states (1.75.3): fear, honor, and interest. The deepest self-interest of the Spartans required them to maintain the integrity of the Peloponnesian League and their own leadership of it. Their honor, their conception of themselves, depended on the recognition of that leadership and on maintaining their peculiar polity, whose security, in turn, depended on the same things. In the view of those who voted for war, all this was put at risk by the recent behavior of the Athenians. They feared that its growing power would allow Athens to annoy Sparta's allies still further to the point where the allies would pursue their own interests without regard to Sparta, thereby dissolving the league and Sparta's security with it. The Spartans felt the need to expose themselves to the great dangers of a preventive war to preserve an alliance they had created precisely to save them from danger. They had formed it to serve their own interests but found that to preserve it they had to serve the interests of their allies, even if those threatened their own safety. It was not the last time that the leader of an alliance would find itself led by lesser allies to pursue policies it would not have chosen for itself.

The threat of the Corinthians to secede in 432 and to take other aggrieved states with them may or may not have convinced the Spartans but, together with the complaints by the allies against Athens's recent actions and the terrifying picture the Corinthians painted of the Athenians' fundamental character, it revived old suspicions and raised fears for a future when Athenian power and intentions might challenge Sparta's survival, so the Spartans voted that the Athenians had broken the peace.

In spite of that, the Spartans took no military action. Instead, the ephors called for a meeting of the Spartan Alliance to take a formal vote on the decision for war, but the allies did not gather until August. Not all the allies came to the meeting; presumably those who stayed home disapproved of its purpose. The Corinthians lobbied furiously, and the other aggrieved allies repeated their complaints. Of those who were there, a majority (not a large majority, such as Thucydides reports in the purely Spartan vote) voted for war. Among the allies, therefore, we may deduce that not everyone thought the war was inevitable; not everyone thought it was just; not everyone thought it would be easy and successful; not everyone thought it was necessary.

The vote for war opened the way for an invasion of Attica that would have redeemed the promise to the Potidaeans only months late. The simple preparations for the invasion needed no more than a few weeks, and September and October would provide good weather either for a battle or for doing harm to property if the Athenians should refuse to fight. Although the Athenian grain crop had been harvested long since, there was still time to do significant harm to grapevines and olive trees and to the farmhouses outside the walls. If the Athenians were going to come out and fight, as the Spartans expected, a September invasion would give them plenty of reason to do so.

All this argued for an immediate advance into Attica, but the Spartans and their allies took no military action for almost a year. Even then, it was the Thebans, attacking Athens's allies the Plataeans without consulting Sparta, who began hostilities in March 431. In the interim, moreover, the Spartans sent no fewer than three missions to Athens, of which at least one seems to have been sincere. (1.126–139)[33] The long delay and the attempt at negotiation suggest that after the emotion of the debate had passed the cautious and sober arguments of Archidamus took effect and restored the mood in Sparta to its usual conservatism. Perhaps war might yet be averted.

THE DECISION FOR WAR: ATHENS

The first Spartan mission demanded that the Athenians "drive out the curse of the goddess" (1.126.2–3), referring to an act of sacrilege committed two centuries earlier by a member of Pericles's mother's family with which Pericles was widely associated. The Spartans thought it would be easier to win concessions from the Athenians if Pericles were banished, but they had no real hope of bringing about his exile. They hoped, instead, that he would be blamed for Athens's troubles and discredited, because, "as the most powerful man of his time and the leader of his state, he opposed the Spartans in everything and did not allow the Athenians to yield but kept driving them toward war." (1.126.3) Pericles always had opposed concessions without arbitration; after the Spartans and their allies had voted for war, he thought that further negotiations were merely tactical maneuvers meant to undermine Athenian resolve.

The Spartans' effort at psychological and political warfare, however, suggests that they believed there was enough opposition in Athens to Pericles and his policy to make it worthwhile. Pericles, however, was experienced and skilled in the art of political propaganda. He crafted an Athenian response that demanded in return that the Spartans expiate not one but two old religious violations by expelling the appropriate people. The first sacrilege involved the killing of helots who had taken sanctuary in a temple, and called attention to the fact that the Spartans, who would wage the war under the slogan "freedom for the Greeks," ruled despotically over a vast number of Greeks in their own land. The second recalled the deeds of a Spartan king who had tyrannized his fellow Greeks before treasonously going over to the Persians.

Undaunted by this rebuff, the Spartans sent envoys making various demands, but finally settling on one: "they proclaimed publicly and in the clearest language that there would be no war if the Athenians withdrew the Megarian Decree." (1.139.1) This demand clearly reflects a compromise and indicates a change in Sparta's political climate since the vote for war. Plutarch says that Archidamus "tried to settle the complaints of the allies peacefully to soften their anger" (*Pericles,* 29.5), but neither he nor his opponents was firmly in command. If Archidamus were in control he could have submitted the complaints to arbitration; if the advocates of war had had the upper hand they could have ended negotiations after the first embassy. Archidamus, apparently, was strong enough to force a continuation of negotiations, but his opponents could demand concessions without arbitration. The compromise still rejected arbitration but reduced the demands to one.

This was no light concession by the Spartans, for it amounted to a betrayal of Corinthian interests. On the other hand, by supporting and protecting the Megarians without submitting to arbitration, the Spartans demonstrated their power and reliability as leaders of the alliance, thereby isolating Corinth. If the Corinthians threatened secession in those circumstances, Archidamus and the majority of Spartans were ready to let them try. Perhaps the time had come to show Corinth who was leader of the alliance. The Spartans had made a serious effort, at some risk, to avoid war. The decision now lay in Athens.

In spite of the softened Spartan position Pericles remained obdurate. He insisted on nothing less than arbitration, as required by the treaty, but the Spartans' offer of compromise persuaded many Athenians. By dropping all their other demands the Spartans made it seem that Athens would go to war simply over the Megarian Decree, originally a mere tactical maneuver and certainly not in itself worth fighting over. Pericles could not ignore the pressure for a response. The official charges that ostensibly had provoked the embargo were now embodied in a formal decree and sent to Megara and Sparta as a defense of the Athenian action. "This decree was proposed by Pericles and contained a reasonable and humane justification of this policy," says Plutarch. (Pericles, 30.3) In answer to repeated Spartan requests, Pericles explained his refusal to rescind the embargo by pointing to some obscure Athenian law that forbade him from taking down the tablet on which the decree was inscribed. The Spartans answered: "Then don't take it down, turn the tablet around, for there is no law against that." (Pericles, 30.1) True or not, the story reflects what must have been great pressure to yield, rescind the decree, and avoid war, but Pericles held fast and kept the majority with him.

At last, the Spartans sent a final embassy with an ultimatum: "the Spartans want peace, and there will be peace if you give the Greeks their autonomy." (1.139.3) This amounted to a demand for the dissolution of the Athenian Empire, and Pericles would have liked the debate in the Athenian assembly to focus on that obviously unacceptable requirement, but his opponents were able to set the terms of the debate. The Athenians "resolved to give an answer after having considered everything once and for all." (1.139.3) Many spoke, some arguing that the war was necessary, others that "the decree should not be a hindrance to peace but should be withdrawn."

Pericles's defense of his policy rested on what might seem a legal technicality. The Spartans consistently had refused to submit to arbitration, as the treaty required. Instead, they sought to win their point by threats or force. "They want to resolve their complaints by war instead of discussion, and now they are here, no longer requesting but already demanding. . . . Only a flat and clear refusal of these demands will make it plain to them that they must treat you as equals." (1.140.2,5) Pericles was willing to yield on any specific point. If the Spartans had submitted to arbitration, Pericles would have been compelled to accept the decision and ready to do so. What he could not accept was direct Spartan interference in the Athenian Empire at Potidaea and Aegina or with Athenian commercial and imperial policy as represented by the Megarian Decree. That would concede that Athenian hegemony in the Aegean and control of her own empire depended on the sufferance of the Spartans. If the Athenians gave way when threatened now, they would abandon their claim to equality and open themselves to future blackmail. Pericles carefully spelled this out in his speech to the assembly:

> Let none of you think that you are going to war over a trifle if we do not rescind the Megarian Decree, whose withdrawal they hold out especially as a way of avoiding war, and do not reproach yourselves with second thoughts that you have gone to war for a small thing. For this "trifle" contains the affirmation and the test of your resolution. If you yield to them you will immediately be required to make another concession which will be greater, since you will have made the first concession out of fear. (1.140.5)

For many Spartans and for some Athenians, as well, it must have been as difficult to understand why the Athenians were ready to fight for this trifle of a decree as it would later be for Germans and Britons to understand why Great Britain was willing to fight in 1914 for the "scrap of paper" that guaranteed Belgian neutrality. But in both cases the apparently trivial source of contention masked the important political and strategic considerations. Pericles's statement is a classic rejection of appeasement under pressure, remarkably similar to the arguments made by Churchill and others in the 1930s. Was it justified?

The grievances at hand were important only as part of the quarrel between the two sides. Sparta's single nonnegotiable demand contained nothing of material or strategic importance. If the Athenians had withdrawn the Megarian Decree, the crisis would probably have blown over. That danger averted, several circumstances might have encouraged a continuation of the peace. Sparta's betrayal of Corinth surely would have led to a coolness between the two states, possibly a rift that would distract the Spartans from conflict with Athens. Other distractions might arise in the Peloponnesus, as they had in the past. The longer the peace, the greater the chance that all would be reconciled to the status quo. While this is only speculation, it suggests that a war between Athens and Sparta was not inevitable if the current crisis could be overcome.

On the other hand, there was a faction in Sparta, dating back at least half a century, that was jealous and suspicious of the Athenians and implacably hostile to Athens. An Athenian concession might have calmed the fears of a majority of the Spartans for a time, but the enemies of Athens were always there. Yielding in 431 might lead to a harder line in future crises. Concession, in fact, might encourage greater Spartan intransigence and make war in the future more likely.

Such considerations were foremost in Pericles's mind, but his decision rested also on the strategy he had formulated for fighting the war. Strategy is not merely a matter of military plans, as tactics may be. As Clausewitz pointed out, it is the continuation of politics by other means and has a political purpose. Peoples and leaders turn to war to achieve their goals when other means have failed, and they select a strategy that they believe will attain them through force of arms. Before the outbreak of war, however, different strategies can have different effects on the very decisions that bring on the war or avoid it. In the crisis of 432–1 both Sparta and Athens chose strategies that inadvertently helped bring on the war.

The usual pattern of warfare between Greek states was for one phalanx to march into the territory of the enemy and there be met by the enemy's phalanx. The two armies would clash and, on a single day, the issue would be decided.[34] That was the style of fighting for which the Spartans had organized their state and their way of life, and it had brought them security, power, and the admiration of the other Greeks. In spite of the warnings of King Archidamus, that is what the majority of the Spartans and their allies expected would be the nature of a war against the Athenians. Since their forces would greatly outnumber the Athenians they had every reason for confidence if the Athenians responded in the usual way, and most Spartans had no doubt that they would. If not, the Spartans were certain that a year, or two, or three, of ravaging Athenian territory would bring either the decisive battle they sought or an Athenian surrender. So thought the Spartans at the beginning of the war, and so thought the rest of the Greeks. (7.28.3)[35] Confidence in that strategy helped the Spartans decide for war. It was an offensive strategy that promised swift and sure victory, just the plan for a state dissatisfied with the state of affairs and eager to force a change. Had they believed that would need to fight a long, difficult, costly war of uncertain outcome, as the Athenians and Archidamus tried to persuade them it would be, they might have decided differently.

What of the strategy that Pericles persuaded the Athenians to adopt? He understood the likely outcome of a traditional war in the same way as did the Spartans, so he devised a novel strategy made possible by the unique character and extent of Athens's power. It was a naval power that permitted the Athenians to rule over an empire that provided them money with which they could sustain their naval supremacy and to obtain what they needed by trade or purchase. Its lands and crops were open to attack, but Pericles had all but turned Athens into an island by constructing long walls that connected the city with its port and naval base at Piraeus. In the current state of Greek siege warfare these walls were invulnerable when defended, so that the Athenians could safely move within them and allow their fields to be ravaged, using the income from the empire to provide them with necessities and to maintain the fleet. If the Athenians were willing to withdraw within the walls the Spartans could neither get at them nor defeat them.

The strategy Pericles had in mind, which the Athenians employed so long as he was alive, was fundamentally defensive, although it contained some limited offensive elements. Pericles said that "if the Athenians would remain quiet, take care of their fleet, refrain from trying to extend their empire in wartime and thus putting their city in danger, they would prevail." (2.65.7) In detail this meant that the Athenians were to reject battle on land, abandon the countryside, and retreat behind their walls while the Spartans ravaged their fields to no avail. Meanwhile the Athenian Navy would launch a series of commando raids on the coast of the Peloponnesus, not meant to do serious harm but to annoy and harass the enemy and to give them a taste of how much damage the Athenians could do if they chose. The strategy was intended to demonstrate that the Spartans and their allies had no way to defeat Athens and to exhaust them psychologically, not physically or materially. The natural divisions within the loose organization of the Spartan Alliance, such as the one between the more vulnerable coastal states and the safer ones in the interior, would assert themselves in costly quarrels. Soon it would be obvious that the Peloponnesians could not win, and a peace would be negotiated. Thoroughly discredited, the Spartan war faction would lose power to the reasonable men who had kept the peace since 446–45. Athens could then look forward to an era of peace founded more firmly on the enemy's awareness of his inability to defeat Athens.

It was a strategy with much to recommend it, certainly compared to the traditional one of confrontation between phalanxes of infantry, but it had serious flaws, and reliance on it helped cause the failure of Pericles's diplomatic strategy of deterrence. Its first weakness was its lack of credibility. Events would show that Pericles was able to persuade the Athenians to adopt his strategy and hold to it so long as he was their leader, but few Spartans, indeed few Greeks, would believe that until they saw it happen. The Athenians would need to tolerate the insults and accusations of cowardice the enemy would hurl at them from beneath their walls. That would violate the entire Greek cultural experience, the heroic tradition that placed bravery in warfare at the peak of Greek virtues. Most of the Athenians, moreover, lived in the country, and they would have to stand by passively while their crops were destroyed, their trees and vines damaged, their homes looted and burned. No Greeks who had any chance of resisting had ever been willing to do that, and the Athenians had come out to fight rather than allow the devastation little more than a decade earlier. In spite of the sober warnings of Archidamus, the Spartans and Peloponnesians, understandably, did not believe that the Athenians would adopt the unorthodox strategy they did. They counted, instead, on a standard kind of war that they would win quickly and easily. Athenian power and warnings, therefore, did not deter them.

A second weakness in the Periclean strategy is related to the reason it lacked credibility. Since it went strongly against the grain of Greek habit and culture, it was very difficult to execute. It would be hard to persuade the Athenians to go to war with such a strategy and harder still to hold them to it once the war began. On the eve of the war Pericles told the Athenians, "If I thought I could persuade you I would tell you to go out yourselves and lay [your fields and houses] waste and show the Spartans that you will not give way to them for the sake of these things." (1.143.5) But, of course, he could not persuade them. When the Spartans invaded, the Athenians were "dejected and angered at having to abandon their homes and the temples that had always been theirs, ancestral relics of the ancient polity, at facing a change in their way of life, at nothing less than each man having to abandon his own *polis*." (2.16.2) When the invaders came closer the Athenians became even angrier, and many, especially the younger men, insisted on going out to fight. They turned with fury against Pericles "because he did not lead them out to battle, and they held him responsible for all their suffering." (2.21.3) Finally, he was forced to use his extraordinary influence to prevent meetings of the assembly, "fearing that if the people came together they would make a mistake by acting out of anger instead of using their judgment." (2.22.1)

The difficulty of Pericles's task was recognized by a distinguished military historian who placed the Athenian leader "among the greatest generals in world history" for his ability to impose upon a free people the difficult, unpopular, but necessary strategy of exhaustion.[36] No one but Pericles could have done it, but he was in his mid-sixties. If the crisis passed without a fundamental resolution and the conflict flared up again when Pericles was gone, the strategy would no longer be possible, and the alternative was almost certain defeat. Such thoughts may well have made Pericles's diplomacy more intransigent.

Seen from the proper perspective, in which a military strategy is judged as part of a continuum of devices whereby a state seeks to achieve its goals, the Athenian strategy had still another flaw. At first glance it might seem to have been especially appropriate: Athens had defensive aims, and it also had a defensive strategy. But since the most desirable goal was to avoid war by means of deterrence, the defensive strategy was not appropriate. The goal of deterrence is to arouse such fear in the enemy as to make him to decide against fighting, but Pericles's strategy presented the Spartans, even if they believed the Athenians might carry it out, with little to fear. Suppose the Athenians refused to fight. The only cost to the Spartans would be the effort it took to march into Attica for a month or so and do what damage they could. Suppose the Athenians landed forces on the

Peloponnesus: unless they built forts they could do little harm. If they built
forts away from the coast they could be surrounded and starved out. If they
built them on the coast, they could be cut off and prevented from doing
any damage. None of this would be painful or costly to the Spartans.

More perceptive individuals might see that over time the Athenians'
ability to damage at least the coastal states by raids and by interfering with
their trade, while Sparta could do nothing to protect them, might erode
the Spartan leadership of the alliance and produce dangerous defections,
which is just what happened in 421. But few could have had the imagination to see that prospect in the dim future. Fewer still, if any, could have
foreseen the strategy adopted by the Athenians after the death of Pericles:
the establishment of an impregnable walled fort at Pylos on the coast of
Messenia, the homeland of the helots, and the seizure of the island of
Cythera, at the other end of the Peloponnesian coast.

The first action provided a place to which the helots could escape and
terrified the Spartans into a reckless response that led to a defeat and the
capture of many Spartan prisoners that shook their resolve. The helots,
using Pylos as a base, launched raids that were especially effective and
frightening because they knew the territory and spoke the local dialect.
The Spartans

> had never before been exposed to this kind of predatory warfare
> and, when the helots began to desert, they feared that the revolu-
> tionary movement would grow among the people of the territory
> and took it badly. Although they did not want to show their alarm
> to the Athenians, they kept sending embassies to them in the at-
> tempt to recover Pylos and the prisoners. (1.42.3)

The capture of Cythera produced even greater panic:

> [E]xpecting descents of the same kind on their coasts, the Spartans
> nowhere opposed them in force, but sent garrisons here and there
> through the country, consisting of as many heavy infantry as the
> points menaced seemed to require, and generally stood very much
> upon the defensive. After the . . . occupation of Pylos and Cy-
> thera, and the apparition on every side of a war whose rapidity
> defied precaution, they lived in constant fear of internal revolution.
> . . . Besides this, their many recent reverses of fortune, coming

close one upon another against all calculation, had thoroughly unnerved them, and they were always afraid of another disaster . . . and scarcely dared to take the field, but thought that they could not stir without a blunder, for being new to the experience of adversity they had lost all confidence in themselves. (4.55)[37]

Had the Spartans imagined such a strategy and such results they might have thought more carefully before committing themselves to war, but that was no part of Pericles's plan or its transmission through the warning given by Archidamus. Without an obvious, credible, frightening offensive threat Pericles's diplomatic strategy of deterrence was crippled and doomed to failure.

Had he believed that, Pericles might have pursued a more conciliatory policy, might not have imposed the Megarian Decree, or might have withdrawn it as the Spartans asked, accepting the risks of future trouble. But Pericles was confident that his own defensive strategy would succeed, so he remained firm. He persuaded the Athenians to adopt his very language in their answer to the Spartans: "They would do nothing under dictation, but they were prepared to resolve the complaints by arbitration according to the treaty on the basis of reciprocal equality." (1.145.1)

THE OUTBREAK OF WAR

The Spartans sent no more embassies, but even then, they did not move. In March 431 the Thebans attacked Plataea, a city friendly to Athens, either as a preemptive strike on the assumption that war was imminent or as a stroke meant to prevent the Spartans from backing out. The Spartans could no longer hold back and launched their invasion in May. Even at the last moment Archidamus, in command of the invading army, sent an envoy to Athens in the hope that the Athenians might yield when they saw the army on the march. But the Athenians barred the envoy from their city:

They sent him away without listening to him and ordered him to be outside their boundaries on the same day. In the future the Spartans must withdraw to their own territory if they wanted to send an embassy. . . . When he arrived at the frontier and was about to depart, he went off speaking these words: "This day will be the beginning of great evils for the Greeks." (2.12.1–4)

The Spartans then marched into Athenian territory, beginning the war that, as Archidamus had predicted, they would leave to their sons.

THE CAUSES OF THE WAR

Thucydides believed that the war was the inevitable result of the growth of the Athenian Empire, its insatiable demand for expansion, and the fear it must inspire in Sparta, and his interpretation has dominated modern scholarship.[38] In his own day, however, his was a new explanation meant to overcome a different view that had considerable currency. Many Athenians thought that war could have been avoided if only the Athenians had not invoked the Megarian Decree or withdrawn it at the Spartans' request. Since Pericles was behind the decree and was the man who most powerfully opposed its withdrawal "they held him alone responsible for the war." The comic poet Aristophanes explained Pericles's actions in two different ways, perhaps reflecting two kinds of scurrilous attacks launched by his opponents, perhaps inventing them for comic purposes. In either case, these explanations were taken seriously by ancient writers and became part of the tradition. According to one story, told in *Acharnians,* performed in 425, some Athenians stole a Megarian whore, and the Megarians responded by stealing three from the house of Aspasia, Pericles's common-law wife. Pericles's response was to enact a law "that the Megarians must leave our land, our market, our sea and our continent. Then, when the Megarians were slowly starving, they begged the Spartans to get the law of the three harlots withdrawn. We refused, though they asked us often. And from that came the clash of shields."[39] Aspasia did not keep a bawdy house, and the story of the rape and counterrapes reads like a parody of the story of the origins of the Trojan War as told by Homer and of the Persian War as told by the Phoenicians and Persians in Herodotus.

It is hard to believe that this explanation had much currency, but the second, the one Plutarch called "the worst charge of all," was more plausible. In the years before the war Pericles's political opponents, frustrated by their inability to defeat him in elections or in debates in the assembly, brought a series of charges in the courts, first against his close associates, then against him. His friend, the philosopher Anaxagoras, and his common-law wife, Aspasia, were charged with religious violations. He and his friend Phidias, the great sculptor who planned the temples on the Acropolis and created the great gold and ivory cult statue of Athena in the Parthenon, were charged with stealing public funds. The attacks failed of their purpose and Pericles maintained his position of preeminence. When the war broke out not many years later, Pericles's enemies connected these events and offered the explanation that he had started the war in order to divert attention from his internal political troubles. Here is the story as told by Diodorus of Sicily, a compiler of history from the first century B.C.:

> But Pericles, knowing that during the operations of war the popu-
> lace has respect for noble men because of their urgent need of
> them, whereas in times of peace they keep bringing false accusa-
> tions against the very same men because they have nothing to do
> and are envious, came to the conclusion that it would be to his
> own advantage to embroil the state in a great war, in order that the
> city, in its need of the ability and skill in generalship of Pericles,
> should pay no attention to the accusations against him and would
> have neither leisure nor time to scrutinize carefully the accounting
> he would render of his funds.[40]

Here we have an early, perhaps the first, assertion of what German scholars investigating the causes of the First World War would call the *Primat der Innenpolitik,* the formation and execution of foreign policy to deal with domestic problems. In Pericles's case, at least, it is patently absurd, although it was taken seriously in antiquity and by at least one modern scholar.[41] One reason Thucydides wrote his history was to dispel such simple-minded explanations, and most historians since have accepted his explanation.[42]

The argument here, however, is that Athenian power did not grow between 445 and 435; that the imperial appetite of the Athenians was not insatiable but, under the leadership of Pericles, was satisfied fully; that the Spartans as a state were not so afraid of Athens as to seek war, at least until the crisis had developed very far. There was good reason to believe that the two great hegemonal states and their alliances had come to terms and could live side by side in peace indefinitely, so that it was not the underlying causes but the immediate crisis that produced the war.

It is true that the war would not have taken place without certain preexisting conditions. If there had been no history of Athenian expansion and no sentiment in Sparta hostile to Athens, Corinth could not have driven the two powers into conflict. But tensions and suspicions exist in many international relationships; it remains to be proven that they must bring on war. Perhaps the First Peloponnesian War was made inevitable by the growth of Athenian power, but that long, costly, and indecisive struggle had taught restraint to both sides, and the treaty concluding it reflected reality and the will for peace. The situation between 445 and 435 was not inherently unstable.

The war broke out in a particular international structure that political scientists call "bipolar," and theorists believe that structures help explain the coming of wars. The trouble is that they disagree about their significance, some thinking that bipolar systems are more dangerous than multipolar ones, others less.[43] At best, general theories explain "war's dismal recurrence through the millennia,"[44] they do not explain why particular wars come about. That is not very satisfying. We may believe that either bipolarity or multipolarity is more conducive to war, but we observe that each system sometimes leads to war and sometimes not. What we want to know is why particular wars happen when they do and, if possible, what of general value we can learn from their experience.

To learn what we can we must attempt a historical analysis of the events leading to war. At each step it is clear that the decisions were not preordained, although the options narrowed as each decision precluded others. Any assertion that war was inevitable after the Thirty Years' Peace of 446–45 does not arise from the evidence but must be imposed a priori. The peace was working until the civil war in Epidamnus. That affair had no necessary relation to the outside world and need not have affected the international situation. The Corinthians' decision to intervene was neither predetermined nor necessary for the Corinthians' well-being, security, or even prestige. Had they remained aloof, there would have been no crisis and no war, but they seized the opportunity to humiliate and avenge themselves on the hated Corcyraeans. That decision may be judged irrational or merely a miscalculation of likely consequences, but it is like many similar ones throughout history in which passion inspired by old hatreds and wounded honor are the cause of dangerous actions. The Corinthians understood that their action might well mean war against Corcyra, but they did not shrink from it. They were influenced by their understanding of the structure of international relations. Their optimistic understanding was that the Thirty Years' Peace had divided the Greek world into two discreet spheres of influence and the Athenians would not challenge the Peloponnesians in western waters. The Corcyraeans, neutral and isolated, might be deterred from challenging Corinth by the knowledge of their association with the Spartan Alliance. If not, Corinth, with the help of its allies, could defeat Corcyra. They did not fear Athenian intervention. They were confident that a war against Corcyra would be localized and victorious. Their driving motive was neither interest nor fear but honor, a determination to avenge the slights they had suffered from the Corcyraeans and to elevate their prestige among the Greek states.

Had they planned a war against any other neutral, their calculations would have been correct, but Corcyra was unique. The size of its navy made it a formidable opponent and forced any threat to its independence upon the attention of Athens. Corinth's allies, Sparta and Sicyon, perceived the danger and tried to dissuade the Corinthians. But they clung to their willful misunderstanding of the true situation in spite of the warnings of their friends, and the crisis became more intense. Corinth launched a vast program of naval construction. Like others in later history, it was an arms race in which only one side raced, for the Corinthians were determined to change the correlation of forces in their favor in order to defeat Corcyra.

The choice facing the Athenians in 433 was grim. They had no interest in Corcyra and no desire to fight Corinth, but they knew that a decisive Corinthian victory over Corcyra might deliver the Corcyraean fleet to the enemy to create a naval force capable of changing the Athenians' supremacy at sea and, therefore, their security. A war against Corinth would be unwelcome but tolerable, yet it might lead to a general war between the alliances, which the Athenians wanted to avoid. It is hard to see how the Athenians could simply have rejected Corcyra's request. They chose, instead, an inventive policy aimed at steering a middle course that would frustrate Corinth's aims without bringing on a general war. The Athenian response came out of fear, a common reaction among status quo powers to sudden unfavorable changes in the balance of power, actual or potential.

The result was a standoff at the battle of Sybota. The Corinthians were not conciliated, defeated, nor deterred. Instead, they undertook a policy meant to annoy and weaken Athens and also to bring on a general war. The Athenians continued their moderate policy aimed at deterrence: the response to Corinthian machinations within the Athenian Empire was the ultimatum to Potidaea; the response to Megara's continuing support of Corinth was the Megarian Decree. That policy was either too weak or too strong. It did not prevent the Potidaeans from rebelling or from trying to involve Sparta in the quarrel, nor did it compel the Megarians to stop their anti-Athenian activities. On the other hand, it did not persuade the Spartans of Athens's peaceful intentions, providing instead fuel for Corinthian propaganda and Spartan fear. At the meeting of the Spartan assembly in the summer of 432 the Athenian spokesman continued the same middle policy, warning of Athens's power and determination and offering to arbitrate all grievances as the treaty required. Such subtle policies are always difficult and dubious ways to achieve deterrence.

The Spartans faced an equally difficult problem. Before the Athenian actions over the winter of 432–33 the majority of Spartans did not want war; from the beginning of the crisis Sparta had tried to restrain the Corinthians and to keep their allies from getting involved. Even after Athens had promulgated the Potidaean ultimatum and the Megarian Decree the bellicose majority on the board of ephors was unable to get the Spartans to keep their promise to invade Attica in support of the rebellion at Potidaea. The influential King Archidamus argued vigorously and skillfully for peace, but the angry and crafty Corinthians, determined to avenge themselves on the Corcyraeans and Athenians, were too much for him. They gathered all the aggrieved parties and brought them to the assembly to help convince the Spartans of the unremitting danger posed by Athens and its empire.

Corinth's quarrel with Corcyra was none of Sparta's affair. The rebellion Corinth had stirred up at Potidaea had no importance for Sparta, and the terms of the treaty clearly permitted the Athenians to do as they wished in their own empire. Corinth's threat to withdraw from the Spartan Alliance ought to have been understood as a bluff safe to call. The Megarian Decree, however, was more difficult. As a measure regulating trade in the Athenian Empire, like the alliance with the neutral state of Corcyra, it was allowed by the treaty, but like that alliance, it had an unanticipated aspect that caused trouble. The Corcyraean alliance was with a state already at war with a Spartan ally, and the Megarian Decree was a means of bringing heavy pressure on another Spartan ally. Could the Spartans assert and maintain the leadership of their alliance—the guarantee of their security— if they did not defend their allies from the novel weapons employed by the ever inventive Athenians? The Spartans might have accepted the use of arbitration as the device for protecting their allies, running the risk of disaffection. Instead, the frightening picture painted by the Corinthians persuaded them to vote for war. They, too, were moved by fear of future threats to their security.

So difficult was their decision that disagreement continued for some time, and the Spartans offered peace if only Athens would withdraw the Megarian Decree. Many Athenians would have liked to accept, but Pericles had made up his mind and could persuade the majority of Athenians to support him. For him the Spartan vote had made war inevitable. Anything short of an agreement to arbitrate would undo the essence of the peace treaty: equality between the great powers. The insistence that Athens must back down, even on the one point, under threat of war, was unacceptable. All that remained was to hold fast to the chief principle, bolster Athenian morale, and wait for his novel strategy to compel the Spartans to reason and a more lasting peace. The Athenians rejected the Spartan proposal and ended further discussions.

If the Corinthians were led astray by the passion for vengeance and the Spartans by jealousy and fear, the Athenians may have suffered from an excess of reasoned calculation. Pericles's diplomacy counted on the Spartans to see Athenian actions as what he intended—moderate responses to provocations—responses meant not to bring on war or challenge Spartan leadership, but to deter war and preserve the status quo. He counted on equally cool calculation, first on the part of the Corinthians, then of the Spartans, but passion proved stronger. Their decisions should not be seen as miscalculations, for that implies a simple error of judgment. In both cases passion, for honor in the form of revenge for the Corinthians, for the Spartans in the shape of defense of their allies, and for the Spartans also the passion of fear, were stronger than interest, reasonably understood. It would not be the last time that states would be driven to war by the dominance of such passions.

Peace does not keep itself. After the First Peloponnesian War responsibility for its maintenance fell upon the leaders of the two great Greek coalitions, Sparta and Athens. The Athenians' deliberate public policy of restraint was rewarded when the Corinthians helped dissuade the Spartans from war during the Samian rebellion, and again when the Spartans tried to cool off the conflict between Corinth and Corcyra. When Sparta's efforts failed the burden fell more heavily on the Athenians.

The problem facing the Athenians was very difficult and the resources available to them limited. They needed to deter the Corinthians from creating a dangerous crisis in such a way as to avoid frightening and angering the Spartans, because they lacked the military power to deter Sparta effectively. In the end, they failed to deter the Corinthians, and yet they frightened and angered the Spartans. One Athenians error lay in making inadequate allowance for the role of such passions as fear and anger in important decisions. A policy of deterrence can work even where passions reign, but to be effective it must counterbalance passion with passion, fear with fear. Athens's best chance of deterring Corinth would have been to make a clearer and larger commitment. Perhaps a full offensive and defensive alliance such as the Corcyraeans proposed would have convinced the Corinthians that Athens was serious. It is far from clear that it would have brought Sparta into the war more quickly. If the Athenians had sent an armada to Sybota instead of ten ships, that would surely have prevented the battle and might have compelled the Corinthians to put off their hopes for revenge against Corcyra entirely. If that had led to a battle the result would have been the destruction of Corinth's fleet and the end of its challenge to Corcyra. Such an outcome need not have brought Spartan involvement in the conflict; it might well have discouraged it. In any case, the outcome could not have been worse than what happened. Later on, if the Athenians had sent a powerful force to Potidaea at once they could have prevented the rebellion and presented their enemies with a discouraging fait accompli instead of a live and promising rebellion, with the besieged rebels calling for war.

When Pericles's moderate policy failed to deter Corinth, however, deterrence of Sparta was no longer possible. The Athenians simply did not have enough manpower to offer a credible offensive threat. Talk of seaborne raids and fortified bases on the Peloponnesus would not work. Most Spartans did not have the imagination to understand the threat the skillful use of such devices could pose to them and their alliances. Only the challenge of a superior army could have held them back, and the Athenians had no way to produce that. Their policy, therefore, was not consistent with their strategic capacity. Had they understood that better they might have refrained from the Megarian Decree and taken a more conciliatory approach, since their capacity for deterrence was inadequate and since no strategy was available to them that guaranteed victory in war. Pericles and the majority of Athenians, however, had great confidence in the promise of the new, untried, strategy that their navy, walls, and empire allowed them alone to pursue. They counted on it to deter their enemies from fighting and, when that failed, to bring victory. So the war came.

ENDNOTES

1. Adapted from the translation of Richard Crawley. In this chapter references are to Thucydides's history of the Peloponnesian War unless otherwise indicated. The numbers refer to the traditional divisions by book, chapter, and section.

2. All dates in this chapter are B.C. unless otherwise designated.

3. It is the "Peloponnesian War," of course, from the point of view of the Athenians; the Spartans, no doubt, thought about it as the "Athenian War," but as so much of Greek history, we see it from the Athenian perspective. Most of what we know about it comes from the history written by Thucydides, the son of Olorus, an Athenian contemporary who served as a general in 424 and was condemned and sent into exile for the rest of the war when a city for which he had partial responsibility fell to the enemy. His personal calamity was fortunate for posterity, for his exile enabled him to travel about the Greek world and to talk with participants on both sides. The result is an account of unusual evenhandedness and great profundity. It is necessary, however, to fill out and test his account with the evidence from contemporary inscriptions and from the versions of other ancient writers.

E. Badian ("Thucydides and the Outbreak of the Peloponnesian War," in June Allison, ed., *Conflict, Antithesis, and the Ancient Historian,* Columbus, 1990, pp. 46–91) rejects Thucydides's claim to the pursuit of objectivity and regards his methods as "much more like that of the journalist than like that of the historian." (p. 48). He argues that "it is Thucydides' main aim, in his account of the origin and outbreak of the War, to show that it was started by Sparta in a spirit of ruthless *Realpolitik,* and that this was the culmination of a long series of attempts, unscrupulous and at times treacherous, to repress Athenian power" (p. 50). If that was Thucydides's aim, he failed badly, because almost all writers on the subject through the centuries either have accepted Thucydides's overt explanation, that the war was the inevitable outcome of the growth of Athenian power and the fear it inspired among the Spartans, or have placed the blame chiefly on Athens.

4. For useful accounts of Spartan history and institutions see W. G. Forrest, *A History of Sparta 950–192 B.C.* (New York, 1968), and Paul Cartledge, *Sparta and Lakonia* (London, 1979).

5. For a different point of view, containing a critique of the one presented here see G. E. M. de Ste. Croix, *The Origins of the Peloponnesian War* (London and Ithaca, 1972), pp. 9–30. The differences between the two positions, in fact, are less great than they may seem. In general, I would accept Ste. Croix's formulation: "there were a few basic 'constitutional' rules governing the behavior of members of the Peloponnesian League, and . . . we can identify some of them, even if on occasion they were ignored or overriden either by Sparta or herself or by allies whose position was strong enough to make it unwise for Sparta to attempt to coerce them" (pp. 122–23). I would emphasize, however, that the rules were few and the occasions when they were ignored or overridden many.

6. For a fuller discussion of the Spartan Alliance see Kagan, *Outbreak,* pp. 9–26.

7. Ste. Croix, *Origins,* pp. 353–54.

8. A. H. J. Greenidge, *A Handbook of Greek Constitutional History,* London, 1902, pp. 102–6. See also Georg Busolt and Heinrich Swoboda, *Griechische Staatskunde,* 2 vols. (Munich, 1920–26), pp. 683–91. Ste. Croix has many valuable discussions of the Spartan constitution scattered throughout his *Origins* and an excellent index that allows the reader to piece them together. For a different view see A. Andrewes, "The Government of Classical Sparta," in *Ancient Society and Institutions. Studies presented to Victor Ehrenberg on his 75th Birthday,* edited by E. Badian (Oxford, 1966).

9. Ste. Croix, *Origins,* p. 127.

10. When making this comparison it is important to remember that if the American constitution and way of life are closer to those of the Athenians and the Soviet Union's internal arrangements were closer to those of Sparta, the workings of NATO are more similar to those of the Spartan Alliance and those of the Warsaw Pact more like the Athenian Empire.

11. Diodorus Siculus, 11.50.

12. For a defense of Thucydides's credibility on this point see Kagan, *Outbreak,* p. 61, note 15.

13. At the same time the Athenians made an alliance with Thessaly, in northern Greece. The sources give no reason, but the Thessalians were famous cavalrymen, and it is possible that the new Athenian leaders already were anticipating their value in a war against Sparta.

14. See Kagan, *Outbreak,* p. 124, note 13 for discussion.

15. W. Dittenberger, *Sylloge Inscriptionum Graecarum,* vol. 1, no. 6, 4th ed., Leipzig, 1915; reprinted Hildesheim, 1960.

16. For a discussion of Athens's policy in the west and the significance of Thurii see Kagan, *Outbreak,* pp. 154–69.

17. For a discussion of the Samian rebellion see Kagan, *Outbreak,* pp. 170–78.

18. Kagan, *Outbreak,* p. 172, note 2.

19. E. Meyer, *Geschichte des Altertums,* 4.1, p. 713.

20. A Corinthian speech in the Athenian assembly in 433 is our source for the meeting. (1.40.5–6;41.1–3;43.1) Ste. Croix *(Origins,* pp. 201–3) takes the Spartans' decision to call a meeting to mean that they had already determined to attack Athens. R. Meiggs *(Athenian Empire,* pp. 190, 461–62) argues that such an interpretation is not necessary, that the Spartans might have called the meeting to help them make the decision. I agree with Meiggs, but the Spartans would not have called their allies together unless they were at least taking the possibility seriously.

21. Kagan, *Outbreak,* pp. 206–19.

22. W. L. Langer, "A Critique of Imperialism," *Foreign Affairs,* 14(1935–36): 102–19.

23. Kagan, *Outbreak,* pp. 213–18.

24. Kagan, *Outbreak,* pp. 22–26.

25. There has been massive debate about the reliability of the speeches reported by Thucydides. I believe that, among other things, they are attempts to give an accurate account of the arguments made in speeches really given. All of those elements have been questioned. I have tried to justify my practice in "The Speeches in Thucydides and the Mytilene Debate." *Yale Classical Studies* 24(1975): 71–94, and in appropriate places in the volumes of my history of the Peloponnesian War.

26. Kagan, *Outbreak,* is devoted to arguing against that interpretation. See especially pp. 357–74.

27. Kagan, *Outbreak,* pp. 251–54.

28. An attempt to deny that the Megarian Decree was intended as an economic embargo is the central thesis of a thick and detailed volume by G. E. M. de Ste. Croix, *The Origins of the Peloponnesian War* (Ithaca, 1972). As far as I know, the theory has won no other adherents.

29. Kagan, *Outbreak,* pp. 261–64.

30. Ste. Croix *(Origins,* pp. 381–83) presents a rogue's gallery of more than forty modern opinions he judges mistaken, including the one presented here.

31. The island of Aegina, forced into the Athenian alliance during the First Peloponnesian War, secretly joined the Corinthians in complaining about mistreatment at the hands of Athens and stirring up the resentment of the other Peloponnesians (1.67.2), but the precise basis of their complaint is unclear.

32. Michael Howard, *The Causes of Wars and Other Essays,* Cambridge, Mass., 1983, pp. 14–15.

33. Kagan, *Outbreak,* pp. 317–42.

34. For an excellent description of Greek warfare see Victor D. Hanson, *The Western Way of War* (New York, 1989).

35. For a discussion of Sparta's strategy and expectations see Kagan, *The Archidamian War* (pp. 18–24).

36. Hans Delbrück, *Geschichte der Kriegskunst I, Das Altertum,* Berlin, 1910, reprinted 1964, pp. 124–33.

37. The translation is adapted from the eloquent version of Richard Crawley.

38. Few have doubted that Thucydides holds to this theory of inevitability. For a discussion and criticism of that view see Kagan, *Outbreak,* pp. 345–56, 357–74, especially p. 345, n. 1, and p. 365, n. 34.

39. Aristophanes, *Acharnians,* lines 532–39.

40. Diodorus of Sicily, *The Library of History,* vol. 4, 12.39.3, translated by C. H. Oldfather, Cambridge, Mass., and London, p. 455.

41. See Karl Julius Beloch, *Die Attische Politik seit Perikles* (Leipzig, 1884, pp. 19–22) and *Griechische Geschichte,* 2nd ed. (Strassburg, Berlin, and Leipzig, 1912–27, pp. 294–98).

42. Among the exceptions are E. Badian (see note 3), who appears to place the blame for the war chiefly on Athens, and Ste. Croix (see note 5), who blames Sparta exclusively. To accept the first view it is necessary to believe that Thucydides is engaged in extensive and deliberate deception, which does not seem justified. To accept the second it is necessary to believe that the Megarian Decree had no political or economic purpose, which no one, to my knowledge, is willing to do. It also requires the reader to ignore entirely Sparta's attempt to mediate a peaceful solution alongside the Sicyonians and Corcyraeans, as well as the sincerity of at least one of their attempts to achieve a peaceful settlement with Athens just before the war, and to discount completely the Spartans' long delay in beginning the fighting, to the point where it took the Thebans to strike the first blow.

43. For discussions of these issues specifically in the context of the Peloponnesian War see *Hegemonic Rivalry from Thucydides to the Nuclear Age,* Richard N.

Lebow and Barry S. Strauss, eds. (Boulder, 1991). See also essays by Robert Gilpin, Kenneth N. Waltz, and Bruce Bueno de Mesquita in *The Origin and Prevention of Major Wars,* R. I. Rotberg and T. K. Rabb, eds. (Cambridge, England, 1989).

44. Kenneth N. Waltz, "The Origins of War in Neorealist Theory," in Rotberg and Rabb, *Origin and Prevention,* p. 44.

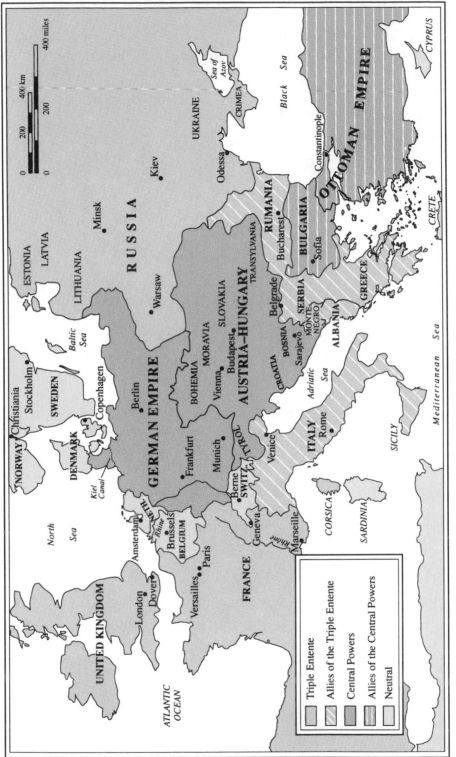

Europe in 1914

Triple Entente
Allies of the Triple Entente
Central Powers
Allies of the Central Powers
Neutral

2

THE
FIRST
WORLD
WAR
1914-1918

HE FIRST WORLD WAR, like the Peloponnesian War, brought a
terrible end to an extraordinary period in the history of a great
civilization. In the century after the Congress of Vienna ended
the Napoleonic Wars in 1815 Europeans experienced an amazing growth in personal and material well-being; in the richness and greatness of their cultural achievements; in the understanding, control, and
exploitation of the resources of nature; in their power to influence and
control people and nations in the rest of the world; and in the prestige that
such things bring with them.

Although there were critics and dissenters, the dominant mood of
Europeans in the late nineteenth century was confident and hopeful:

> They thought that mankind had progressed in enlightenment, in
> humanity, in reason, to a point where the old might be peacefully
> and usefully absorbed into the new. They understood that the
> means to untold affluence were at hand. They believed that with it
> the planet might ultimately produce a civilization of perpetual
> peace and progress, guided by the light of exact knowledge that
> was rapidly being revealed to mankind. . . . By the sun of what
> was vaguely called "science" all things were to be illuminated: the
> secrets of the universe made known, superstition dispelled, the
> nature of human existence revealed, the means to a richer and
> wiser world fashioned. . . .
>
> There was no doubt about it: a new world was being made.
> . . . Modern ideas were triumphing everywhere. Europe would
> soon be organized on a rational basis, its political and social sym-
> metries would reflect the symmetry of nature and the universe.[1]

The Great War, as its contemporaries called it, shattered that mood
and the world that had given rise to it. It destroyed four empires, leaving a

collection of insecure and mutually suspicious petty states in place of the Habsburgs' Austria-Hungary, a Turkey limited to Asia Minor and a toehold in Europe in place of the Ottoman Empire, a Germany reduced in size to the always troubled Weimar Republic, and the Soviet Union in place of the dynasty of the Romanovs. While ending the era of European monarchy and aristocracy, it also reversed the trend toward constitutional, limited government and democracy, producing a Communist tyranny in Russia and providing the conditions for the rise of autocratic and totalitarian regimes in Italy, Germany, Spain, and several other European states.

The war greatly hastened the decline of Europe's power compared to the rest of the world, badly damaged its relative economic position, began the process that would put an end to its colonization of foreign lands, and assisted the rises of Russia and the United States, the huge, flanking super-powers of the future that would come to control its fate. It raised the human costs of war to new levels of frightfulness and introduced horrors unknown in previous conflicts. It killed about twice as many people as had died in all the wars of the previous two centuries, which included the wars of the French Revolution and Napoleon and the American Civil War. Winston Churchill described its character in almost Thucydidean language:

> The Great War through which we have passed differed from all ancient wars in the immense power of the combatants and their fearful agencies of destruction, and from all modern wars in the utter ruthlessness with which it was fought. All the horrors of all the ages were brought together, and not only armies but whole populations were thrust into the midst of them. The mighty edu-cated States involved conceived with reason that their very exis-tence was at stake. Germany having let Hell loose kept well in the van of terror; but she was followed step by step by the desperate and ultimately avenging nations she had assailed. Every outrage against humanity or international law was repaid by reprisals often on a greater scale and of longer duration. No truce or parley mitigated the strife of the armies. The wounded died between the lines: the dead mouldered into the soil. Merchant ships and hospital ships were sunk on the seas and all on board left to their fate, or killed as they swam. Every effort was made to starve whole nations into submission without regard to age or sex. Cities and monuments

were smashed by artillery. Bombs from the air were cast down indiscriminately. Poison gas in many forms stifled or seared the soldiers. Liquid fire was projected upon their bodies. Men fell from the air in flames, or were smothered, often slowly, in the dark recesses of the sea. The fighting strength of armies was limited only by the manhood of their countries. Europe and large parts of Asia and Africa became one vast battlefield on which after years of struggle not armies but nations broke and ran. When all was over, Torture and Cannibalism were the only two expedients that the civilized, scientific, Christian States had been able to deny themselves: and these were of doubtful utility.[2]

Once again we are moved to ask, how did such a war come about?

THE EMERGENCE OF GERMANY AND THE CHALLENGE TO THE OLD ORDER

On June 28, 1914, Archduke Franz Ferdinand, heir to the throne of the Austro-Hungarian Empire, was assassinated in the Bosnian capital of Sarajevo, not very far from the ancient town of Epidamnus, where the crisis that had provoked the Peloponnesian War began. The assassination also led to a crisis that produced the First World War within less than six weeks. Like the ancient war, however, its roots went back half a century to the emergence of a new power, whose strength and dynamism had threatened the old order, challenging it to find a new equilibrium. The old European order, resting on a balance among the five great powers of Austria, France, Great Britain, Prussia, and Russia, had been established at Vienna in 1815 as a way of preventing the domination of a single state over all of Europe, such as had almost been achieved by Napoleon Bonaparte. The great powers agreed to confer and to work together as the Concert of Europe to defend the new balance. The system was designed to maintain the independence of the leading states more than to preserve the peace, but the one purpose was generally supportive of the other, and between 1815 and 1914 Europe was far more peaceful than it had been for centuries.

The main threat to the new order was the powerful force of nationalism unleashed during the French Revolution. Successful rebellions brought independence to Greece and Belgium without shaking the foundations of the system, while others in Poland, Italy, Germany, and Hungary were put down in the first half of the century. Even the Crimean War (1853–56), the first among European great powers since 1815, appeared to leave the system intact. The unification of Italy (1859–61), however, introduced a new nation ambitious to join the circle of great powers, and the unification of Germany, concluded in 1871, created an entirely new international situation.

Germany's unification was carried out by Prussia under the leadership of Otto von Bismarck, and it was accomplished by force. In a series of lightning campaigns the Prussians defeated Denmark (1864), Austria (1866), and France (1870–71). On the eighteenth of January 1871, in the Hall of Mirrors in the Palace at Versailles built by Louis XIV, King William of Prussia was crowned Emperor of Germany, the Second Reich, the first being the Holy Roman Empire founded by Charlemagne. Suddenly the center of Europe was occupied by a new nation that had in swift succession decisively beaten two of the other four charter members of the Concert of Europe. Its population was greater than all but Russia's; its people were well educated and hardworking; its resources, especially the iron and coal needed to produce steel, had been increased greatly by the acquisition of Alsace-Lorraine from France; and its splendid educational system and scientific and technological excellence gave it a great advantage in the new and burgeoning chemical and electronic industries. Finally, the Germans had just demonstrated that they had the most powerful army in Europe.

To be sure, the new German Empire was not without disadvantages. From the beginning it faced the hostility of a France that was still wealthy and strong but bitterly resentful at its defeat, and where many Frenchmen burned for vengeance, eager to recover their lost provinces. The annexation of Alsace-Lorraine also added to the considerable number of non-German subjects who were imperfectly and, to some degree, unwillingly incorporated in the empire. Germany's greatest disadvantage came from its geography. Unprotected by the seas, like the islands of Great Britain, or by vast spaces, like Russia, Germany sat in the center of Europe surrounded by potential enemies, especially between a hostile France and a powerful Russia, with no defensible borders to the east and none to protect its new conquests in the west.

These difficulties by no means outweighed Germany's assets. As far back as 1816 Adolf Ludwig Heeren had foreseen the power available to a united Germany and the problem this would create for Europe:

If this state were a great monarchy with strong political unity, furnished with all the material strength that Germany possesses— how could any safe existence be left for Germany's neighbours? Would such a state for any length of time resist the temptation to make a bid for hegemony over Europe, in keeping with its position and power? The rise of a single and unrestricted monarchy in Germany would before long be the grave of freedom in Europe.[3]

If, however, the fears inspired by the powerful new arrival could be assuaged and a stable new balance of power established, Germany's inherent advantages were sure to establish it as the dominant power in Europe. The emergence of the new empire had shattered the old international system. Germany's, and Europe's, challenge was to create a new one into which it would fit comfortably.

THE EUROPEAN POWERS

Germany

The constitution of the German Empire has been described as

a clumsy and illogical document. It created an imperial government without sufficient administrative agencies to give it much meaning, a federal state that was prevented from being truly federal by the special position of one of its members, and a parliamentary system based on universal suffrage that was rendered ineffective by limitations placed on its responsibility.[4]

Theoretically, the governing body was the Bundesrat, the upper legislative chamber, whose delegations were appointed and controlled by the rulers of the twenty-five states that constituted the empire. The size of each delegation was determined by the size and power of each state. Prussia dominated the Bundesrat by its prestige and power and also by special privileges that were written into the constitution. No changes in the military sphere could be made without Prussian approval, and Prussia had an effective veto over other changes. The King of Prussia was the German Emperor and the Minister President of Prussia was usually also the German Chancellor. The

King, through his control of Prussian foreign affairs, ultimately controlled the seventeen Prussian votes in the Bundesrat.

The Reichstag, the lower house of the imperial parliament, elected by universal vote of men over twenty-five and representative of the people rather than of the states, had far less power than the upper house. For the most part it dealt only with matters put before it by the Bundesrat or the government. The Kaiser appointed the Chancellor, who served at his pleasure. The Reichstag might criticize or express no confidence in him, but only the Kaiser could dismiss him, and only the Chancellor could dismiss his state secretaries.

The Reichstag's most important power was in its control of the budget, but even here its strength was limited. The military budget was voted for a period of seven (later five) years, depriving the lower house of regular, close control of the most significant item. Still, its power over the purse gave the Reichstag the capacity to obstruct the government and to try to extend its own powers. Sometimes this worried the government enough to contemplate a coup d'état to reduce or destroy its powers, but they never chose to take so drastic an action. Neither the Bundesrat nor the Reichstag, in any case, had much influence on the shaping of foreign policy or its military and diplomatic tools.

The constitution placed these responsibilities directly in the hands of a single man, the Kaiser. He was the supreme commander of the armed forces; he alone had the privilege of making foreign policy and of making war and peace. To be sure, no man could carry out those responsibilities alone, nor was the Kaiser free from pressures that influenced his decisions, yet it would be a mistake to ignore the degree to which the Kaiser and his appointed officials were free to make the most fateful decisions for his nation and people. One scholar rightly calls the German Empire, "an autocratic monarchy with a few parliamentary trimmings. . . . [I]t is not an exaggeration to say that [in foreign affairs] the Reich Constitution endowed the House of Hohenzollern with an almost absolutist position."[5]

France

By 1875 a series of fundamental laws had established a republican regime in France that lasted until the defeat of France by Germany in 1940. The Third Republic, as it was called, had probably the most democratic constitution of any European state. The legislature, called the National

Assembly on those few occasions when it sat as a unit, consisted of two houses, the Chamber of Deputies, whose members were elected by universal male suffrage for a four-year term, and the Senate, whose three hundred members were elected indirectly for terms of nine years. The two houses were ostensibly equal, but in fact the directly elected, more democratic, Chamber of Deputies was the more powerful. Ministries and governments needed a majority in the Chamber to win appointment, and a vote of no confidence there brought them down. The two houses met jointly as the National Assembly to elect the President of the Republic who served a seven-year term. In practice he was usually only the titular head of state, a ceremonial figurehead. After 1877 no president ever dissolved the Chamber and when, in 1924, a president went beyond the precedents limiting his involvement in partisan politics, the Chamber compelled him to resign.

The true executive power rested with the Cabinet of Ministers. The real decisions were made in negotiations among the leaders of the parties, and the ministers were responsible to the Chamber. The French political system consisted of a multitude of parties ranging from Anarchists and Marxists to Monarchists of various allegiances. All governments, therefore, were composed of coalitions and could be dissolved by disagreements on a wide range of questions. Between 1890 and 1914 France had forty-three governments and twenty-six prime ministers. In this apparent chaos, however, there was a surprising degree of stability. There never was a question of a ministry's choosing to dissolve the Chamber and hold new elections rather than resign. The Chamber ruled.

Most governments were formed from the center of the political spectrum, and it was not unusual for politicians to move from one party to another. The fall of one government and its replacement by another usually meant a reshuffling of Cabinet offices, with the same people undertaking different assignments, or ministers in previous governments returning to office after a brief stay outside. One consequence of the frequent coming and going of ministers was the increased power and importance of the permanent civil servants. In foreign and military policy this provided a significant element of stability, yet the fluidity of the political system sometimes made it difficult to sustain policies over a period of time. The Third Republic was a bourgeois democracy whose government and foreign policy were more open to the influence of partisan politics, the press, and public opinion in general than were those of other countries. Such a regime is cautious in launching initiatives in foreign affairs, more likely to react than to act.

While segments of French opinion continued to crave the return of Alsace-Lorraine, most Frenchmen lost interest as the prospect seemed dimmer and less practical with the passage of time. In the years between 1871 and 1914 the chief concern of French foreign policy was security from attack by Germany, the new empire to the east whose advantage in population and industrial production continued to grow. France had a low birth rate, so its population remained stable, while Germany's advanced rapidly during this period. By 1914 Germans in the empire numbered well over sixty million compared to only forty million Frenchmen. While German industry was growing by leaps and bounds, overtaking and, in some areas, even surpassing Great Britain, the home of the Industrial Revolution, France remained primarily an agricultural country. As late as 1914 more than half the population still lived in rural areas, and its industrial production lagged far behind the Germans'. One reason for this was that a large portion of France's considerable wealth was invested abroad, while most of Germany's capital investment was in its own industries. Perhaps a third to a half of French savings were available for investments outside the country, which sometimes proved useful in foreign policy even as it reduced France's potential industrial strength.

The French had a keen sense of their history and the power and greatness they had enjoyed in the centuries between the reign of Louis XIV and the Napoleonic Empire. In spite of their defeat by the Germans, they used the succeeding decades to expand their overseas empire. From Algeria, which they had taken in the 1830s, they moved eastward into Tunisia. They expanded their domain in western and equatorial Africa and later moved eastward toward Egypt; they acquired the island of Madagascar off East Africa and established a new empire in Indo-China in Asia. Whatever tangible gains this brought France and whatever flattery to its sense of grandeur, it also brought friction with the Italians, who had their own ambitions in Africa, and it exacerbated the age old rivalry with the British. When Germany became interested in colonial acquisitions the French Empire in Africa became an important bone of contention.

Great Britain

Great Britain, the island kingdom that included England, Ireland, Scotland, and Wales, was formally a constitutional monarchy but in fact an increasingly democratic parliamentary government. Queen Victoria, Edward VII, and George V were little more than figureheads who reigned but did not rule. The true executive element in the constitution was the Cabinet, theoretically chosen by the monarch but really by the party holding a majority in the House of Commons. Led by a prime minister of the party's choosing, the Cabinet appointed officials, supervised the administration, and introduced legislation in Parliament. In turn, it was responsible to the Parliament. It could be expelled from office by a vote of no confidence or by failing to pass an important piece of legislation. For the most part the Parliament was divided between the major parties, Conservatives and Liberals. When the ruling party failed on a key vote it could resign and allow the other party to try to form a Cabinet or it could dissolve the Parliament and force new elections to determine which party could form the new government.

Britain's true sovereign was Parliament, divided into two houses, Lords and Commons. Throughout this period Commons was the dominant member, but until 1909 the House of Lords had the right to delay or even to block legislation passed by the Commons. In that year the Lords were deprived of that power, and the Commons ruled without hindrance. The House of Commons was elected by popular vote for a term of six years, which might be shortened if the Cabinet dissolved it to hold new elections. The reform bills of the nineteenth century had broadened the franchise considerably, but it left as many as one third of the men of Britain without the vote. Both major parties were led by the upper and wealthier classes: aristocrats, industrialists, financiers, most of whom had been educated at the elite public schools and then at Oxford or Cambridge. A surprising number of ministers were men of intellectual interests and accomplishments as writers, historians, and philosophers. Their training inculcated the idea that the advantages enjoyed by the elite imposed an obligation for public service.

British Foreign Ministers had an extraordinary degree of autonomy.[6] The appointees were always men of considerable standing in their own right, wealthy, experienced, and respected. They usually stayed in office for a long time and, after their party had been defeated and then reelected, they often returned to the same post. The Prime Minister, of course, needed to be informed and to support his Foreign Minister, and so, sometimes, did a few selected Cabinet ministers, but the Cabinet as a whole was not an effective instrument of control. Parliament, of course, had even less influence and control over foreign policy. Even during parliamentary debates and in question periods the Foreign Minister was able to keep from the Parliament what he did not wish it to know. The Parliament needed to approve only those treaties that involved financial commitments or the cession of territory in peacetime, and many were not even debated.

> It may appear somewhat paradoxical that, in a country where parliamentary government and cabinet responsibility were so deeply rooted [Sir Edward] Grey [foreign secretary 1906–16] enjoyed more freedom than his German counterpart. While in Berlin the Kaiser and Chancellor, the heads of the army and navy, politicians, industrialists and agriculturalists all brought their influence to bear, in Britain these pressures were channelled along customary paths which left Grey surprisingly free.[7]

In the two decades surrounding 1870 Britain led the world by far in economic and industrial power. Its pioneering role in the Industrial Revolution vaulted it to an astonishing preeminence.[8] By 1860 it was producing 53 percent of the world's iron and half of its coal and lignite. It produced and consumed many times more energy than any other country. With only 2 percent of the world's population its trade represented a fifth of the world's commerce and two-fifths of the trade in manufactured products. A third of the ships that carried all these goods around the world, moreover, were British. In addition to being the world's leading manufacturer and merchant Britain was also its leading financier and insurer. Between 1870 and 1875 British investments overseas reached the astonishing figure of 75 million pounds annually, producing a vast income that was regularly reinvested. Alongside the vast income earned by the visible items of trade in raw materials and manufactured goods, the British also enjoyed the lion's share of the so-called invisible profits earned from shipping, insurance, and banking. As Britain became less agricultural and more industrial it came to depend on imports not only for the cotton and other raw materials needed for its factories but even for the food needed for its survival. For the insular British, this meant the need to keep the seas free for trade and the world free of major war, which might interfere with their food supply and the income they received from trade and its ancillary activities.

The same needs arose from Britain's position as the ruler of the largest and most populous empire in the history of the world. It included colonies of one sort or another on all the inhabited continents; the sun, as the saying went, never set on the British Empire. The argument still continues as to whether European colonialism was profitable for the imperial powers, but there can be no doubt that Great Britain benefited more than the others. Unlike most colonial powers, the British imported great quantities of natural resources and carried on a high percentage of their trade with their colonies. Even more singular, the British Empire included such self-governing areas as Canada, Australia, New Zealand, and South Africa, ruled by emigrants from Britain who retained such loyalty to the mother country as to be willing to assist her on land and sea in wartime. The jewel in Britain's imperial crown, as another saying went, was the vast Asian subcontinent of India. With a population of some three hundred million it contained perhaps 80 percent of the empire's subjects and provided a considerable portion of the imperial profit.

All the advantages that came from intercourse with other countries and the benefits that came from the empire depended on free access to natural resources and markets and these, in turn, on freedom of the seas and the absence of major wars. At the height of her power in the middle decades of the nineteenth century it is remarkable how little money and effort Britain needed to spend in order to maintain these desired conditions. The cost of its armed services during these years was only about 2 to 3 percent of the gross national product, a very low figure compared with other nations, not to speak of the world's greatest empire. The British Army was the smallest among the European powers: by 1880 it numbered less than a quarter of a million men, less than half the size of France's and not much more than a quarter of Russia's.[9] It was not an army meant to fight a war against European armies or to defend the home islands from invasion but an imperial police force—and a very small force even for that purpose.

Great Britain could escape heavier burdens for defense in part because the balance of power that obtained in Europe before the Franco-Prussian War prevented any serious challenge to British interests arising from the

Continent. The British also relied for the security of their islands and empire on the great superiority of their navy. Even here the unthreatening condition of Europe allowed the British to reduce its size and still be guaranteed of superiority over any plausible combination of the fleets of other nations.

This happy situation permitted the British to continue their traditional hostility to standing armies that went back at least to the seventeenth century and allowed them to avoid the burden of military conscription required by the Continental powers. The Liberal ideas that prevailed regarded war as the result of folly and unlikely to occur in a world increasingly shaped by free trade, prosperity, and British ways of thinking, and they considered the expenditure of any public money beyond the minimum as unproductive and wasteful. "However preeminent the British economy in the mid–Victorian period . . . it was probably less 'mobilized' for conflict than at any time since the early Stuarts."[10]

In retrospect it is clear that Britain's economic position, while still the strongest in the world absolutely, had begun to decline relative to other nations in the world. Between 1885 and 1913 Britain's industrial production increased by 2.11 percent, but Germany's increased by 4.5 percent and the United States's by 5.2. By 1906 the Americans had passed Britain in the production of coal and iron and both Germany and the United States led Britain in steel production.[11] By the turn of the century Britain's share of the world's industrial production had decreased and been surpassed by the United States. Austria's and Russia's were growing, and Germany's had multiplied almost two and one-half times since 1860 and was closing in on the British lead.

Even during the middle of the century, and in spite of the low level of imperialist rhetoric, the British Empire had grown considerably, according to one estimate at the rate of about 100,000 square miles a year between 1815 and 1865.[12] The defense of all this new territory, which spanned the globe from Hong Kong and Singapore to Aden to the Falkland Islands, put an additional burden on British resources. The latter part of the century, however, saw what has been called the "New Imperialism" in which the European nations sought to establish colonies wherever it was still possible and competed with one another aggressively for the privilege. Britain's concern for the security of India led, on the one hand, to increased conflict with Russia, which was expanding southward toward the Indian borders, leading to conflict in Persia, Afghanistan, and Tibet. When the Suez Canal was built the British felt the need to acquire control of it and to secure the rest of the water route to India through Gibraltar and the Mediterranean. This produced tension with the Mediterranean nations, especially France, and again with Russia, whose fleet the British were eager to lock up in the Black Sea.

British interests in China produced tensions, once again with Russia, but also with Japan, France, Germany, and the United States. Britain had investments and colonies in the West Indies and South America, which caused friction with the United States. The race to divide Africa caused more trouble when the British desire to connect their Egyptian protectorate with their colony in South Africa by means of a "Cape to Cairo" railroad from North to South conflicted with the French wish to expand their Equatorial African Empire from west to east. It also led to conflict with Germany when the Germans experienced a burst of colonial activity in the 1880s.

These new dangers and burdens imposed themselves soon after the unification of Italy and the emergence of the powerful new German Empire disrupted the old, secure European balance of power. The British would have preferred to cling to their favored policy of what was called "splendid isolation," but over time the new circumstances made it seem ever less splendid. Economic competition created ill will; intensified colonial rivalries carried over into European relations. The appearance, once again, of a new state that might have the power to impose control over the Continent should it choose to do so made it impossible any longer to ignore the vital questions of the balance of power that had forced the British to fight wars in Europe from the reign of Louis XIV to the defeat of Napoleon.

Russia

In 1871 the Russian Empire was the last of Europe's absolute monarchies untouched by the wave of constitutionalism that had altered, to one degree or another, even such conservative regimes as Prussia's and the Habsburgs'. The Tsar was Autocrat of all the Russias, who ruled by divine right, unchecked by legislature or human law and responsible only to God. Defeat in the Russo-Japanese War and the revolution that ensued in 1905 forced Tsar Nicholas II, last of the Romanov dynasty, to accept a constitution and the establishment of a popularly elected national legislature called the Duma. As the revolution waned the Duma's powers and prospects were swiftly curtailed. It has been said that the Duma was little more than a debating society, but as a place for the expression of public opinion that could be spread and amplified by the press, it was not without influence on the Tsar's ministers and even on the Tsar.

The introduction of the constitution and the Duma, nonetheless, did not significantly alter Russia's autocratic rule. As the Tsar told a German envoy to the Rusian court in 1908: " 'I am the master here.' The Duma, said Nicholas, might be a useful safety valve 'where everyone could air their views and where one might gather advice and even approval' but as regards important policies, 'I myself decide.' "[13]

The Russian Empire stretched along the Eurasian land mass from the borders of Germany and Austria on the west to the northern Pacific Ocean that touched the eastern shore of Siberia. By the end of the nineteenth century it was the largest among European powers in both area and population, and as a world empire it was second only to the British. The technical and industrial developments of the nineteenth century, however, left Russia far behind. At mid century less than 8 percent of the population lived in towns or cities and all of Russia contained only 660 miles of railroad. Illiteracy was widespread, and the prospects for educational improvement dimmed by the dominance of the obscurantist Russian Orthodox Church and the reactionary government.

Shocked by defeat in the Crimean War of 1853–56 and by the emergence of a powerful new German Empire on the western frontier, the Tsars and their governments undertook significant reforms that led to real progress. Conditions of travel and transportation, however, were still primitive in most of Russia, the railroad system well behind that of the other great powers and inadequate for Russia's commercial and industrial development and military needs, and Russia's industrial production lagged far behind Britain's or Germany's. In spite of the great strides made in education, moreover, the ratio of schoolteachers to the population as a whole was the lowest of any major state, including Italy and Japan, and the rate of literacy was only 30 percent.[14]

The Russians also faced special internal problems that caused them concern. Ethnic minorities formed part of the populations of all the European powers, but in 1897 only 45 percent of the subjects of the Tsar were Great Russians. Attempts to "Russify" some of these minorities caused such anger that "by 1914 Petersburg had good reason to fear trouble in

Finland and Poland in the event of war."[15] Ukrainian nationalism was strong enough to gain encouragement and support from the Austrians, an intervention that frightened and annoyed the Russian rulers. They also feared the possible development of a Panislamic movement along the vast southern border from the Caucasus to China. Although such concern probably was exaggerated, it was one of the reasons the Russians maintained large military forces along the Central Asian border, at considerable cost to an already strained budget. Quite apart from their problems with ethnic minorities, the Russians were threatened by the hostility of many of their own people, especially the intelligentsia and the increasingly militant urban industrial workers, and by a relatively dangerous and revolutionary socialist movement.

None of this prevented the Russians from continuing to pursue, with varying degrees of vigor, an expansive foreign and imperial policy along the borders of their vast empire. Pressure on Manchuria, Korea, and China brought them into conflict chiefly with Japan and Britain. Advances in Tibet, Persia, and Afghanistan led to serious differences with Britain. Russia's traditional efforts to gain control of the sea route between the Black Sea and the Mediterranean, "the Straits," as the Bosphorus, Sea of Marmora, and Dardanelles were called, brought conflict not only with the faltering Ottoman Empire, but also with Britain, France, and Austria. Efforts, as the most powerful Slavic nation and as "the Third Rome," successor to Byzantium as the home and paladin of Orthodox Christianity, to help liberate the Christian Slavs of the Balkans and to assert its leadership there brought conflict with the Turks and Austrians and even the Italians, who had Balkan ambitions of their own. The rise of a powerful German state, finally, had posed a new challenge whose character was yet to be determined.

Austria-Hungary

In the Middle Ages the German family the Habsburgs began forging a great empire in central Europe from the borders of Russia and Rumania on the east to the Alps and the Adriatic in the west. Early in the twentieth century it was the third largest state in Europe, behind Russia and Germany. It was unique among the great powers in being a polyglot empire in which the ruling nationality was a small minority of the population. Of the Habsburg emperor's more than fifty million subjects in 1910 only about

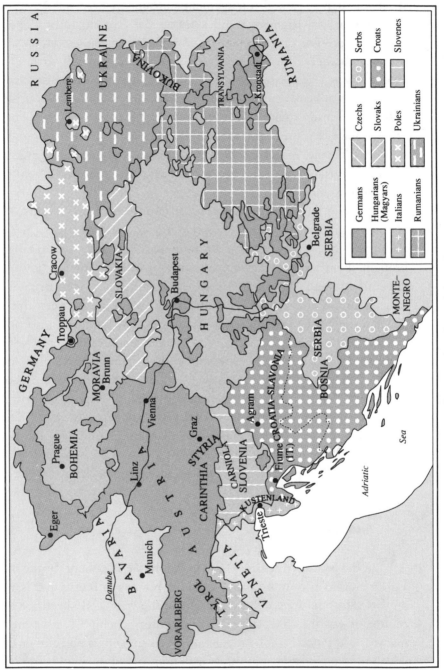

Nationalities Within the Habsburg Empire

twelve million were Germans; ten million were Magyars, the ruling people of Hungary. The rest were Czechs, Slovaks, Poles, Ukrainians, Rumanians, Serbs, Croats, Slovenes, Italians, Slavic Muslims, and a scattering of others.

In 1867 the Habsburg realm was divided into two separate states called the Empire of Austria and the Kingdom of Hungary, united under a single flag and under the sovereignty of a single monarch, called Emperor of Austria in one land and King of Hungary in the other. Each state had its own language, its own constitution, officials, and Parliament. In practice the Parliaments were powerless and ineffective. "While Austria in the years preceding the war of 1914 nominally had a constitutional parliamentary government, in actual fact she had a government which was a bureaucratic absolutism functioning under a 'constitutional cloak.' "[16]

Questions of finance, foreign policy, and war were dealt with jointly. For these purposes the Emperor appointed joint ministers. Neither the separate national ministers nor the joint ones were responsible to any Parliament but only to the Emperor. To coordinate the regular joint business of the Dual Monarchy, the Common Ministerial Council met frequently, dealing chiefly with foreign policy and the military and naval budgets. It consisted of the Prime Ministers of the two states and the three common ministers, usually under the chairmanship of the Foreign Minister.[17]

Like the emperors of Germany and Russia, Franz Josef (1848–1916) retained control of foreign policy, command of the armed forces, and decisions on war and peace. Regardless of the constitution that theoretically gave him his authority, he always believed that he ruled by divine right, that duty required him to exercise his powers in the interests of his dynasty and his people according to his own best judgment. In the years before the outbreak of war he was the most experienced statesman in Europe, loved by his people and respected by the other monarchs and statesmen of Europe. Even so, especially as the Emperor grew older, the regular conduct of affairs, the response to new problems, and the planning of initiatives inevitably fell to his ministers, most importantly to the Foreign Minister. Both Franz Josef and his Foreign Minister, moreover, had to face the fact that they governed a double monarchy. Technically, neither half could veto an important decision, like a declaration of war, but since success depended on gaining the full material and moral support of both states, it would be disastrous folly to proceed without the approval of both prime ministers. Since the two states had different approaches to very important questions, this sometimes led to damaging disagreement, delay, and even, on occasion, to paralysis.

Austria's defeat by Prussia in 1866 drove it from its traditional place as the most powerful of the Germanic states, out of Germany entirely, and left it isolated in a political arrangement in which the Germans were a distinct minority whose privileged position was immediately and constantly under challenge. For most of his long reign Franz Josef conducted a cautious, conservative policy emphasizing compromise and the avoidance of war. That program was made more difficult by the decline and then the disintegration of the Ottoman Empire in Europe. The emergence of Serbia and Montenegro, formerly under Ottoman rule, as independent Slavic states in the Balkans encouraged a Yugoslav (south Slav) movement that threatened to separate the Croats, Serbs, and other south Slavs from the Habsburg monarchy and join them with Serbia and Montenegro to form a great Yugoslav state. The kingdom of Rumania served as a magnet for the Rumanians in the empire, mostly in Transylvania, where they lived unhappily under Magyar rule.

The newly unified Italy had a similar appeal to the Italians who lived in the Habsburg-ruled Tyrol, Trieste, Istria, and Dalmatia. These issues created conflicts with the states who had significant numbers of their ethnic group within the Dual Monarchy, with the Ottoman Empire, and with Russia. The Russians' eagerness to profit from Turkey's weakness to gain control of the Straits and their assumption of the role of liberator and protector of the Slavs often put them at odds with Austria-Hungary, posing the greatest threat.

As ethnic quarrels intensified within the Dual Monarchy, and foreign dangers grew and multiplied, it seemed to many that after the imminent death of the Ottoman Empire, Austria-Hungary would succeed it as the "sick man of Europe" whose illness might lead to a similar fate. In spite of these problems it would be a mistake to look upon Austria-Hungary as doomed. Its importance and value for the stability of Europe had long been appreciated. In 1848 the Czech statesman Frantisek Palacky insisted on the importance "for the whole of Europe, indeed for mankind and civilization itself" of preserving the Habsburg Empire: "Truly, if the Austrian empire had not existed for ages, it would be necessary, in the interest of Europe, in the interest of mankind itself, to create it with all speed."[18] With remarkable prescience he forecast the consequences of a Europe without the empire: "Imagine if you will Austria divided into a number of republics and miniature republics. What a welcome basis for a Russian universal monarchy!"[19]

Granted the desirability of the empire's survival, was it possible? For all its problems the Habsburg Empire retained considerable vitality. To Edvard Beneš, another Czech writing sixty years after Palacky and just a few years before the outbreak of war, at any rate, the end of the empire seemed inconceivable: "People often have spoken of the dissolution of Austria. I do not believe in it at all. The historic and economic ties which bind the Austrian nation to one another are too strong to let such a thing happen."[20] There was wisdom as well as wit in the typically cynical Viennese observation that the empire's situation was "hopeless but not serious." No solution for the monarchy's problems likely to produce unanimous satisfaction was available, but there is no reason to be confident that without the extraordinary pressure of the Great War it could not have continued.

Italy

Italy emerged as a unified country in the modern world only in 1861 and did not acquire the city of Rome, its ancient and modern capital until 1870. The new nation was a constitutional monarchy with a bicameral legislature.

Normally, the formation and conduct of foreign policy lay in the hands of the Foreign Minister and the professional bureaucracy. Individual deputies could have an effect through their personal influence or connections, but "debate in the Chamber never openly decided foreign policy on the basis of party division."[21] The system gave very much power to the Prime Minister, so it is not surprising that in times of crisis he often took control of foreign affairs himself.

Italy was a great power only to the degree that it claimed to be one and by courtesy of the real powers. In spite of its formal unification it was still a country deeply divided by geography, history, and tradition. As one distinguished Italian leader said soon after the unification, "We have made Italy; we must now make Italians."[22] In 1870 its population was only about 26 million. By 1910 it had grown to some 35 million, still fewer than France's 40 million and well short of Austria-Hungary's 50 million and Germany's 65 million. Even this number was smaller than Italy's economy could sustain, and each year millions of Italians left the country to find temporary work abroad or to emigrate permanently, chiefly to the Americas.

In spite of these problems Italy from the first tried to act as though it were a great power. The fact that some Italians still lived under the rule of the Austrians in the Trentino and Trieste and elsewhere gave its leaders an immediate goal: the restoration of *Italia irredenta,* unredeemed Italy. But beyond that, memories of the greatness of ancient Rome and the myths of repressed glory pressed every Italian government to pursue an active foreign policy among the European powers and then to seek colonial empires overseas. The first goal led to friction with Austria, the others to quarrels with France over competing imperial designs in Africa, and all of them to an involvement in the terrible war that had so little to do with Italy's fundamental needs and problems:

> In the final analysis, Italy entered the First World War quite deliberately because not to do so would have been to admit that her pretensions of being a Great Power were false, and therefore, by implication, that her pretensions to liberalism, parliamentarianism and a constitutional centralised monarchy were equally false.[23]

BISMARCK'S ERA

Bismarck's unification of Germany under the leadership of Prussia was an astonishing achievement. His ability to solidify the place of the new and threatening entity in a European system shattered by its emergence and to create a new international order in which Germany could live in peace and prosper may have been even more remarkable. For the two decades after 1871 that he remained in power there were no wars among the great powers. Even after he was dismissed in 1890 by the new German emperor, William II, it took his successors another quarter of a century to undo and reverse his policies and so distort the system he created as to produce a major war.

Bismarck's second great achievement rested, in part, on Germany's strong military and industrial power, which gave his policies weight and respect. But history has many examples of a state achieving a powerful position by means of might in arms and then only by its menacing demeanor and behavior frightening the others into hostile coalitions that resort to war to restore a more satisfactory balance. The exceptions are few. Pericles, as we have seen, concluded that the Athenian Empire was large enough and that its interests would best be served by consolidation and peace. Augustus, the first Roman emperor, came to a similar conclusion, putting an end to centuries of Roman expansion. Bismarck belongs in their company as one of the rare leaders of mighty states who chose to limit his ambitions. His decision may have been even more remarkable, for Pericles and Augustus accepted these limits only after being sobered by military defeats, while Bismarck's Germany was undefeated and uniquely formidable when he chose to pursue peace in place of expansion.

Central to his goal was the need to convince the other powers that Germany was what he repeatedly asserted: a "saturated" power that needed to turn inward to consolidate in peace what had been gained in three swift wars.[24] What he feared most was a French war of revenge in which the other powers would join rather than see the power of Germany grow further. One aspect of his response was to treat France in such a way as to salve the wounds of its defeat and help the French forget. "I wish," he told the French ambassador in 1884, "to reach a point where you would forgive Sedan [the decisive battle of the Franco-Prussian War] as you have forgiven Waterloo."[25] That was the period, too, when Bismarck encouraged the French focus on expanding their colonial empire overseas as a way of turning their thoughts and energies elsewhere.

In the 1870s, however, the war was too recent and the bitter memories it produced too powerful to be overcome by cajolery. For a time, at least, Germany must count on its own strength, and to increase that strength while isolating France Bismarck turned to the great Eastern conservative powers, Austria and Russia. Prussia had ties of friendship with Russia that went back to their comradeship in the victory over Napoleon. The new Germany and Russia shared a common interest in resisting Poland's independence, since both had gained from its partition, and both were conservative monarchies who wished to resist the forces of republicanism, democracy, and socialism. Bismarck was especially eager to draw close to Russia, since an alliance between Russia and France was the most dangerous possible Continental coalition Germany might face.

Even so, Bismarck did not want to rely on Russia alone, where Pan-Slavic and anti-German sentiment was growing, so he wanted to draw closer to Austria, as well. As a German diplomat put it, "Only when mounted were we as tall as the Russian giant. Austria was intended to be our mount."[26] Bismarck had been careful to seek good relations with Austria ever since Germany's victory in 1866. He imposed generous terms, taking no territory and imposing no indemnity. Austria, nonetheless, was alienated by its defeat in the war, but Prussia's victory over France in 1871 made Austria's situation between its vast rival to the east and the new giant of central Europe too dangerous to sustain. The Magyars who ruled Hungary hated and feared the Russians and were worried about being engulfed in a sea of Slavs. They looked to Germany for protection, and the Germans of Austria, reconciling themselves to the new circumstances, were also ready to draw nearer to the German Empire.

With careful maneuvering, therefore, the League of the Three Emperors came into being in 1873. A vague agreement without teeth, it nevertheless committed William I of Germany, Alexander II of Russia, and Franz Josef of Austria-Hungary to consult with one another so that "the maintenance of the peace of Europe [might] be secured, and if necessary be enforced, against attack from any quarter."[27] Bismarck liked to say that in a world of five powers "try to be a *trois*,"[28] and in spite of its nonbinding character the new league brought the three conservative empires together and seemed to leave France friendless. Its great and obvious flaw was that Russia and Austria continued to have serious disagreements that might well lead to conflict, and the league did nothing to solve them.

Bismarck had imposed a heavy war indemnity on the French in order to cripple the French economy for a long time and to keep the French in line by means of the occupying army until they paid.[29] By September 1873, however, they had paid the sum in full, and the German Army was forced to withdraw. France's return to independence was soon followed by the emergence of a ministry that seemed, to alarmed Germans, to seek the restoration of the monarchy, French military power, the lost provinces, and France's lost glory. When the new regime enacted a law increasing the size of the French Army, the German General Staff became alarmed and began to talk of preventive war. Bismarck had no desire for war, but he probably wanted to frighten the French into reducing their armaments. It is even possible that he hoped to force France into friendship, perhaps even an alliance, by impressing them with Germany's power. Counting on the support of Russia and Austria, perhaps even of Britain,[30] he approved a press campaign in 1875, including an article called IS WAR IN SIGHT? suggesting that highly placed Germans thought it was. This rather obvious attempt at bullying played into the hands of the French Foreign Minister, who used it to suggest that Bismarck was planning war against France and to seek the support of Britain and Russia. These two states, by no means friendly toward one another, concerted their efforts and delivered diplomatic warnings to Berlin.

Bismarck had suffered a diplomatic defeat that he never forgot, but he learned from the experience. Decades later his successors would seek to get their way, even to win allies, with the threat of force. Bismarck learned that the new Germany could not use such tactics. Its power was too great for the other states to permit it to grow further. They would not allow the destruction or greater weakening of France without resistance. Even traditional enemies would come together for that purpose. He also learned that the League of the Three Emperors was a weak reed on which to build German security.

The Eastern Crisis that roiled the waters in the years 1875 to 1878 emphasized that weakness. In the summer of 1875 rebellions broke out in Herzegovina and Bosnia that soon spread to Bulgaria. They were assisted by Serbia, which aspired to be the Balkan Sardinia, the spearhead of a new Yugoslav nation, and also by Montenegro. It is quite true that "once the Balkan Slavs were astir, the Russian government dared not let them fail; Austria-Hungary dared not let them succeed."[31]

Russia's continuing expansion had brought it to the Black Sea in the eighteenth century; thereafter it sought to get hold of the Straits and control of access to and from the Mediterranean. The treaties governing the Straits in 1875 forbade Russia to send her warships into the Mediterranean but allowed the Turkish Sultan to permit foreign navies to sail into the Black Sea, the worst possible arrangement for Russia.[32] The hope of gaining control of the Straits, therefore, was one reason for Russian involvement in the Balkans.

Since the fall of Constantinople in 1453, moreover, Moscow had claimed to be the "Third Rome" and the Russian Tsars the leaders and protectors of Orthodox Christianity. In eight wars against Turkey they had gained much territory and the grateful devotion of Slavic Christians in the Balkans who looked to them for liberation. "Even older than the desire to secure control of the Straits was the more sentimental aspiration . . . to regain control of Constantinople and place the Christian cross on the church of St. Sophia, as well as to aid the oppressed Christians of the Balkans in their fight for liberty." In the two decades before these rebellions the thin sliver of the upper crust of Russian society that constituted significant public opinion had been strongly influenced by the movement called Pan-Slavism. A mixture of mysticism and nationalism, in various schemes it called for the liberation of all the Slavs and Balkan peoples and their organization into a grand confederation under Russian leadership. The great barrier to achieving the goal was not so much the crumbling Turkey as "Germanism," represented chiefly by Austria. Pan-Slavism, therefore, was a challenge not only to the survival of the Ottoman Empire but also to the Austro-Hungarian Empire. In 1875 Austria-Hungary's Foreign Minister told a Crown Council that "Turkey maintains the status quo of the small Balkan states and impedes their aspirations. . . . If Bosnia-Herzegovina should go to Serbia or Montenegro, or if a new state should be formed there . . . then we should be ruined and should ourselves assume the role of the 'Sick Man.' "[33]

The British, too, were alarmed at the prospect of the disintegration of the Ottoman Empire and an increase in Russian power that would also allow them to control the Straits. If matters were allowed to run their course the three interested powers might be drawn into war, taking the rest of Europe with them.

For all their ambitions and concerns both Russia and Austria feared the consequences of a quarrel, so the two rivals sought to cooperate. The Emperors of Russia and Austria met privately at Reichstadt, where they agreed not to intervene in the fighting and made vague plans for the division of European Turkey should the Turks be defeated. But the Turks stubbornly refused to collapse, and in April 1877 Russia, soon joined by Rumania, declared war on Turkey. After a slow start the Russian Army defeated the Turks and was on the point of taking Constantinople. Clear warnings from Austria and Britain persuaded the Russians to stop short and make peace with the Turks.

The resulting Treaty of San Stefano shocked the European powers. Turkey was all but driven from Europe. Serbia, Montenegro, and Rumania each gained recognition of their full independence, as well as some additional territory. Russia gained the Dobrudja, which it then exchanged with Rumania for Bessarabia, which had been lost in the Crimean War, and lands in the Caucasus region east of the Black Sea. The most troubling item of all was the creation of a very large Bulgaria running from the Black Sea almost to the Adriatic and from the Danube to the Aegean. Not unreasonably, the powers, especially Austria, feared that the new state, created by Russian arms and scheduled for occupation by Russian troops for two years, would become a Russian satellite, as would the other newly independent Balkan states. The Austrians were also angry at what they believed they had been promised at Reichstadt, the acquisition of Bosnia and Herzegovina, which the treaty left to Turkey, and because their hopes of running a railroad from Vienna to Saloniki on the Aegean would be thwarted by the creation of so large a Bulgaria.

The British expressed concern that the new arrangements threatened their control of the eastern Mediterranean, which seemed more important than ever since the opening of the Suez Canal had created a shorter route to India. They joined with the Austrians in rejecting the Treaty of San Stefano and demanded an international conference to consider its terms. The Russians opposed such a plan, but their army had been worn down by the stiff Turkish resistance, and they feared another coalition such as had humiliated them in the Crimean War. British Prime Minister Disraeli sent a fleet to the Dardanelles, and the threat of a war against Britain and Austria compelled the Tsar to yield.

All this time, Bismarck and Germany had remained aloof in spite of pressure from the Russians. They had asked the Germans to support them by holding back Austria while they thrashed the Turks, in gratitude for Russia's friendly neutrality during Prussia's wars with Austria and France in 1866 and 1870. Bismarck refused. Germany had no interest in gaining advantages in the Balkans for itself. In a speech to the Reichstag on December 7, 1876, he made his famous remark: "The whole of the Balkans is not worth the healthy bones of a Pomeranian musketeer," and his actions showed that he meant what he said. He was, in fact, willing for Russia to gain its ends in the Near East but only with the agreement of Austria and without war. He especially rejected a war that would destroy Austria as a great power and with it the balance of power.[34]

To avert a war Bismarck offered to serve as a mediator, the term he used was "honest broker," and invited the powers to settle matters at a general conference. The British insisted on concessions by the Russians before they would take part in a conference. The Russians were reluctant to have the gains won by blood and force of arms judged and diminished by a conference of other powers. To his ambassador in London Gorchakov, the Foreign Minister, made it clear that Russian honor was at issue: "It is no longer a question of interests being at stake here, but rather amour-propre and prestige. . . . After a bloody and victorious war, we cannot conceive of abasing the dignity of Russia before the prestige of England, even as a matter of form."[35] Finally, however, resistance ceased. In June of 1878, under Bismarck's presidency, Europe's leading diplomats gathered at the Congress of Berlin, "easily the most distinguished diplomatic gathering between the Vienna Congress of 1814–15 and the Paris Peace Conference of 1919."[36]

The Russians were forced to accept major revisions of the treaty of San Stefano. The British acquired Cyprus from the Turks, a key to the security of Suez and the right to bring their navy through the Straits into the Black Sea. Disraeli returned in glory, asserting that he had brought "peace with honour."[37] Austria gained the right to occupy and administer Bosnia and Herzegovina, and the unspoken but general understanding that it could annex them at will, and to garrison the sanjak of Novibazar, the area that separated Serbia from Montenegro. The large Bulgaria was divided into three sections; only the northernmost part became Bulgaria, an autonomous principality paying an annual tribute to the Turkish sultan.

The Russians were permitted to keep their conquests in the Caucasus and Bessarabia. They could claim the honor of bringing full independence to Montenegro, Rumania, and Serbia and of forcing the Turks to improve their treatment of Christians and to pay a war indemnity. Objectively, that was quite an achievement and amounted to more than Russia had sought at the beginning of the war: "Russia had gone to war for reasons of national pride and of Pan-Slav sentiment, not to achieve any practical aim; and the congress was a blow to her prestige rather than a setback to her policy."[38] For this they did not blame the limitations of their own army but focused their resentment upon Bismarck; the Tsar called the Congress of Berlin "a European coalition against Russia under the leadership of Prince Bismarck."[39]

Such a description was entirely unfair. Bismarck truly had served as an "honest broker," and his efforts brought Russia a better outcome than it could have achieved whether by separate negotiations with Austria and Britain or by fighting a war against them, which was, in any case, out of the question. The Congress of Berlin was a great moment for the new Germany. In 1856 Prussia barely had been permitted to attend the Peace of Paris that concluded the Crimean War. In 1878 it was the center of diplomacy, an essential element in settling disputes among the great powers and preserving the peace of Europe. Purely for German interests Bismarck wanted to keep the peace, to avoid a re-creation of the Crimean coalition that would bring France into alliance with Austria and Britain, to avoid even a war that might bring victory to Germany. He knew that another war between Russia and Britain or Austria would draw in Germany, and he feared that France would take advantage of the chance to undo the Franco-Prussian War. "The treaty of Frankfurt made a reconciliation between France and Germany impossible; therefore a war in the Near East would become general."[40] Because Bismarck, like Pericles before him, was willing to limit Germany's ambitions and to conserve what had been achieved rather than to endanger it by running new risks, his policy fostered the cause of European peace. "The congress of Berlin demonstrated that a new Balance of Power, centred on Germany, had come into existence. None of the statesmen at Berlin expected the settlement to last long, and they would have been astonished to learn that the congress would be followed by thirty-six years of European peace."[41]

But Europe had not yet devised a system that would consistently permit the peaceful resolution of disputes. It might appear that the success at Berlin heralded a return to the Concert of Europe in a form adjusted to the new realities, but the tensions that emerged from the congress were too great to permit that. The Russians were outraged and deeply resentful of Germany, and Bismarck would have liked to revive the League of the Three Emperors but saw that it was impossible. He therefore undertook a new path, leading ultimately to the construction of a new system that would attempt to maintain the peace through a set of alliances.

In October 1879 he negotiated the Dual Alliance with Austria that was to last into the First World War. To persuade his emperor, the strongly pro-Russian William I, of the need of such an alliance Bismarck claimed to fear Russian hostility toward Germany, but what he really feared was the realization of his nightmare of a Franco-Russian alliance with Germany in the middle. It is also possible that from the outset he meant the Dual Alliance to be only the first step in the formation of a new Three Emperors' League to reassure Austria and prevent its association again with France and Britain as in the Crimean War: "I wanted to dig a ditch between her and the Western powers."[42] The treaty called for mutual assistance in case either state were attacked by Russia and for friendly neutrality if either suffered attack from any other power.

This alliance was the keystone of the Bismarckian system of preserving the German Empire by keeping peace in Europe. Previous treaties among the powers had been for specific purposes and for a limited duration, usually for a particular war, not in peacetime with the purpose of preserving peace. The Dual Alliance was renewed consistently until November 1918, when both empires were destroyed: "the first permanent arrangement in peace-time between two Great Powers since the end of the *ancien régime.*"[43]

The alliance was praised by contemporaries,[44] but after the First World War it was criticized for fostering the alienation between Austria and Russia and encouraging the Russo-French alliance that helped bring on that war. Bismarck, however, used it as a device for *preventing* conflict between Austria and Russia. On several occasions he reminded Austria of its defensive character and refused to support the Austrians in their Balkan ambitions or in quarrels with the Russians. It is wrong to hold Bismarck responsible for the reversal of his policies by the ministers who succeeded him and the new emperor who dismissed him.[45]

Bismarck probably counted on the powerful ideological conflict between Russia and France to help keep the two nations apart. Russia was the chief example and supporter of absolutism in Europe, and France was the mother of republicanism. Whether or not he expected or planned it, the Dual Alliance produced results most satisfactory to Bismarck. Worried about being isolated by Bismarck's diplomacy and fearing a British attack through the Straits, the Russians sought an accommodation with the new coalition instead of trying to befriend France. They approached Bismarck for a rapprochement with Germany alone, but he insisted on a renewal of the Three Emperors' League, including Austria. The treaty was signed in June of 1881 for a period of three years. The Austrians refused a longer duration, as Bismarck preferred, but he did not insist, on the grounds that "when Austria has worn that flannel next to her skin for three years she will no longer be able to discard it without running the risk of catching cold."[46]

Like the Dual Alliance's, the terms were secret. The chief clause provided that each state would maintain a benevolent neutrality if one of the others were at war with a fourth power, protecting each from the danger of a hostile alliance. A second provision pleased the Austrians by recognizing their right to annex Bosnia and Herzegovina when they thought it appropriate. They would have liked to retain their unique connection with Germany, but "it was unreasonable to suppose that Bismarck would ever tie himself to the chariot wheels of Austrian policy."[47] The treaty pleased the Russians by safeguarding them against a naval attack in the Black Sea and by agreeing to prevent Turkey from recovering its power in the Balkans. Bismarck had not instigated these alliances, but he soon came to see their value and worked hard to conclude them, for he thoroughly understood their advantages to Germany. One should not lose sight, he said, of

> the importance of being one of three on the European chess-board. That is the invariable objective of all cabinets and of mine above all others. Nobody wishes to be in a minority. All politics reduce themselves to this formula: to try to be one of three, so long as the world is governed by an unstable equilibrium of five Great Powers.[48]

The new alliance brought the advantages of uniting the three conservative monarchies, preserving the peace between Russia and Austria, sparing Germany the danger of being involved, and, most attractive of all, it prevented an alliance between France and Russia. The weakness in the new Three Emperors' League was the continuing rivalry between Austria and Russia in the Balkans but, as a keen student of this period observed, "the treaty helped to take the edge off this antagonism. Thereby it served not only the interests of the three parties, but the cause of general peace."[49]

In 1882 the Italians also came to Bismarck early to seek an alliance. In the previous year the French had seized Tunis, making the Italians fear that they would be excluded entirely from North African colonies. Aware of the potential trouble between Austria and Italy Bismarck told the Italian ambassador that "the door that leads to us must be sought in Vienna."[50] Although that meant the Italians must put aside hopes of regaining *Italia irredenta* in the Austrian Empire, they joined with Germany and Austria in May 1882 to form the Triple Alliance. This, too, was a secret treaty for three years and was meant to be defensive. It promised aid if Italy or Germany were attacked by France or if Austria or Germany were attacked by two powers. Here, too, the initiative did not come from Bismarck, and he insisted that the proposed alliance should not be bilateral but should bring together into a triad two states with significant disagreements. In later years Italy and Austria would try to use the Triple Alliance for aggressive purposes, but for Bismarck it was always defensive, "our League of Peace,"[51] and he often stood in the way of the ambitions of his allies.

In October 1883 Rumania joined the system by signing agreements of mutual assistance with Austria and Germany providing that if either Rumania or Austria were attacked the other two states would come to its assistance. The treaties were secret and for a duration of five years, but they were renewed down to the outbreak of the war. To please the German Emperor, Russia's name was not used, but the treaties clearly were aimed at Russia. In asking the Austrians to enter these agreements Bismarck laid out his fundamental understanding: "Except for Russia and France, there is no state in Europe today which is not interested in the maintenance of peace. The firm pivot for the crystallization of any such scheme [the spread of what Bismarck called the League of Peace to Rumania, and then, perhaps, Serbia and Turkey] would always be our own permanent Dual Alliance."[52]

These diplomatic arrangements left France isolated, and her own decision to pursue colonial expansion soon intensified that condition. The Tunisian adventure had alienated Italy. Then, in 1882, a quarrel over control of Egypt damaged French relations with Britain for the next two decades. Bismarck did not use the Egyptian dispute as a way to split France off from Britain, which was not his goal. When the split came of its own accord, however, he gave the British moral and political support that was significant: "Bismarck may be said to have kept the ring for the English and to have made the occupation of Egypt possible."[53] Such policies established good relations with the British and help explain why the British Foreign Minister, Lord Salisbury, regarded Bismarck's dismissal from office in 1890 as "an enormous calamity of which the effects will be felt in every part of Europe."[54] The outcome, in any case, left France more isolated than ever and Germany allied to or on good terms with every other European power.

Bismarck could play so helpful a part because, unlike many statesmen of the time, he placed little value in colonial expansion. He had compared German colonies to sable coats on the backs of Polish noblemen who had no shirts underneath[55] and firmly resisted pressures to acquire any throughout the 1870s. A key element in his policy of helping the French forget their defeat in 1870–71 and the loss of Alsace-Lorraine was to encourage them to acquire new colonies in Africa and Asia. He told the French ambassador at the Congress of Berlin that "the Tunisian pear is ripe and it is time for you to pick it." In 1881 he instructed the German ambassador to France that "France can be certain that we shall never oppose her justifiable policy of expansion in the Mediterranean."[56] There is no reason to doubt his sincerity when he told someone pressing him to acquire colonies for Germany: "Your map of Africa is very fine, but my map of Africa is here in

Europe. Here is Russia and here is France and here we are in the middle. That is my map of Africa."[57]

In spite of that attitude Bismarck undertook a series of actions in 1884–85 that brought Germany colonies in Togo, Cameroon, Southwest and East Africa, and on several islands in the Pacific Ocean. Scholars continue to disagree on the purpose and significance of this change in policy,[58] but it seems clear that Bismarck's venture into colonialism was a brief aberration from his continuing relegation of it to unimportance. Whether he spoke the truth to a member of the Prussian Ministry of State in saying, "All this colonial business is a sham, but we need it for the election,"[59] or had other and more complicated reasons, he turned his back on further colonial ventures. In October of 1889 he made it clear to the German Consul General in Zanzibar that he had "had enough of colonies,"[60] and, at some political cost, he resisted further pressure from the colonial lobby. Attempts, in any case, to link Bismarck to Germany's future course of aggressive colonial ambition are ill-founded. When he told the colonialist enthusiast that Germany's position in Europe was his map of Africa, "this sentence defined the greatest difference between him and his successors in the reign of William II. He thought solely in continental terms; they imagined that Germany could go over to 'world-policy' before she had secured the mastery of Europe. . . . Bismarck was never distracted by colonial issues."[61]

In 1885 a crisis once again arose in the Balkans that severely tested Bismarck's new alliance system. The Russians had been the sponsors of Bulgarian independence and expected to have great influence in the new nation, especially when the Bulgarians chose Alexander of Battenberg, the Tsarina's nephew, as their ruler. Prince Alexander proved to be too independent for Russian tastes, however, and his independence made him more popular with the Bulgarian people. In 1885 a revolution in Eastern Rumelia enabled Alexander to unite it with Bulgaria, restoring two-thirds of the "Big Bulgaria" dismantled by the Congress of Berlin. Then he defeated a Serbian army that attacked in search of compensation. The Russians, fearing the loss of all influence in Bulgaria, then sponsored a conspiracy that attempted to replace him with a monarch who would be subservient to Russia. The Bulgarians resisted and chose as their ruler Ferdinand of Saxe-Coburg, a German prince who was friendly not to Russia but to Austria.

By 1886 the Russians, Austrians, and Bulgarians were preparing for war, the new Three Emperors' League was threatened with destruction, and Bismarck faced a most difficult problem. In his view, "Germany was standing between Austria and Russia like a man between two vicious dogs who would fly at each other as soon as they were unleashed."[62] He could not allow Austria to be defeated, but if he openly took Austria's side and thereby prevented war, he ran the risk of driving Russia into the arms of a France currently under the influence of General Boulanger, a fervent nationalist who spoken openly and heatedly about the need to regain Alsace and Lorraine. Germany was faced with the possibility of an alliance between a disgruntled and resentful Russia and a revanchist France.

To deal with the French Bismarck demanded from the Reichstag an increase in the size of the German army. The higher number of troops was less important than the rhetoric Bismarck used in the heated electoral campaign his request produced. While disclaiming any idea of attacking France he warned against the dangers inherent in the approach and ambitions of Boulanger and the French nationalists. At the same time, he concluded a renewal of the Triple Alliance increasing French concern about Italian involvement in a German war against France. This exercise in deterrence by military, political, and diplomatic means was effective. The French soon lost interest in *boulangisme* and in a Russian alliance.

In the East Bismarck needed to support the Russians' claims without allowing them so much success as to drive Austria to war. He took a strong line with Austria, urging the view that Bulgaria was a Russian sphere of influence while the western Balkans were Austria's and making it clear that Germany would not fight Russia to achieve Austrian goals in the Balkans. Since the Magyars were the most aggressive advocates of war against Russia, Bismarck said: "We have no intention of allowing ourselves to be bound by the alliance to the tail of the Hungarian comet, but to establish a regular order of calculable dimensions."[63]

To protect Bulgaria, and thereby satisfy Austria, he undertook some complicated maneuvers. Taking advantage of Italian proposals, Bismarck renewed and strengthened the Triple Alliance, providing for the defense of the status quo in the Balkans. The Italians, however, were a weak reed on which to rest the deterrence of Russian ambitions, so he also urged them to seek the support of Austria and Britain. Bismarck, eager for Britain to check the Russians and protect the Austrians, worked hard and effectively behind the scenes. The result was the Mediterranean Agreement completed in March of 1887 whereby the three powers agreed to maintain the status quo in the Mediterranean, Adriatic, Aegean, and Black seas. Italy promised Britain support in Egypt in exchange for British support for Italian aims in Libya. The latter provisions were aimed at France, but for Bismarck the most important achievement was that Britain would now serve to protect Austria against Russian ambitions in a way that Germany could not. "By making England an associate of the Triple Alliance, [the Mediterranean Agreement] promised to be a deterrent to both French and Russian adventurism."[64]

Bismarck then undertook to repair relations with the Russians, concluding in June 1887 the three-year secret agreement that is called the Reinsurance Treaty. Each side promised to remain neutral in a war fought by the other, except if Germany attacked France or Russia attacked Austria. Germany recognized Russia's "preponderant and decisive influence" in Bulgaria and both sides agreed not to permit territorial changes in the Balkans without their prior agreement. In a "very secret supplementary protocol" Germany promised that if Russia were forced to take control of the Straits and Constantinople in order to defend the entrance to the Black Sea "to accord her benevolent neutrality and her moral and diplomatic support to the measures which His Majesty may deem it necessary to take to control the key to his empire."[65]

Here, as before, the Russians were more frightened by the danger of isolation from Bismarck's system than angry at his inadequate support of their goals. The new treaty freed Germany from the threat of a Franco-Russian alliance and the immediate danger of a war between Russia and Austria. The Reinsurance Treaty, more than any other part of Bismarck's system, has been the subject of dispute and the object of criticism. The main charge was that it was inconsistent with the Dual Alliance and thereby deceived Austria. But Bismarck had many times made it plain to the Austrians that he regarded Bulgaria and the eastern Balkans as a Russian sphere of influence and that he would not fight for Austria's goals there.

A more justified complaint is that Bismarck was misleading Russia and England. In sponsoring the Mediterranean Agreement he worked to check Russian goals in the East. Only months later he concluded an agreement encouraging Russia to pursue those very goals. Months later than that, when the Russians' dissatisfaction with Bulgaria's new ruler threatened anew to provoke a war in the Balkans, Bismarck again encouraged an agreement among Austria, Britain, and Italy to check them. The Second Mediterranean Agreement[66] repeated their support of the status quo and specifically mentioned Bulgaria and the Straits, and that warning led Russia to abandon its Bulgarian activities, "probably not without some bitter reflections about the disadvantages of having an ally who took away with his left hand what he had given with his right."[67] A leading student of these negotiations makes the point in defense of Bismarck that these arrangements were made not to protect German special interests but to help others protect their own. Nor did the treaty do more than give the Russians a free hand to seek their goals without direct German opposition; they could not have expected the treaty to bring an end to Austrian and British resistance.[68] Even so, the Russians had no reason to expect that the Germans would work behind the scenes to help frustrate their wishes. If there is a defense of his duplicity, perhaps it is this: "What Bismarck had really done was to establish a sort of balance of power, a system under which Russia would be held in check by the Mediterranean coalition, and the peace of Europe preserved."[69]

The Russians were not the only ones frustrated. Within Germany there were those who sought not peace but a confrontation with Russia. Within the Foreign Office Friedrich von Holstein urged the Austrians to take a tough line with Russia over Bulgaria, and he was supported by General Alfred von Waldersee of the army's General Staff. Waldersee argued for a preventive war against Russia and tried to get General Helmut von Moltke to go behind Bismarck's back and use his influence with the Emperor in support of that policy. Bismarck confronted the generals directly and forced Moltke and the others to back down and deny any intention of meddling in foreign policy. He also indirectly lectured the Emperor on the purely defensive character of the Dual Alliance. To his ambassador in Vienna he wrote: "I cannot avoid the impression that it is the aim of certain military circles in Vienna to distort our alliance. . . . We must both take care that the privilege of giving political advice to our monarchs does not in fact slip out of our hands and pass over to the General Staffs."[70] This was one of several models that Bismarck's successors proved unwilling or unable to emulate.

The Character of the Peace

The conclusion of the Reinsurance Treaty and the Second Mediterranean Agreement produced the final form of Bismarck's continuing efforts to preserve German security by maintaining peace among the great powers. This peace is the base from which began the path to war in 1914. How

sound was it? A. J. P. Taylor, by no means an uncritical admirer, character-
izes the completion of Bismarck's system by comparing the world he
shaped with that of his successors:

> The days of European upheaval were over; they would not come
> again until one of the Powers felt itself strong enough to challenge
> the balance which had been established at the Congress of Berlin.
> That Power could only be Germany. Ever since 1871 Bismarck
> had followed a policy of restraint. His motive was always fear, not
> conquest. The new Germany was conscious only of its strength; it
> saw no dangers, recognized no obstacles. German explorers, scien-
> tists, and capitalists spread over the world. Germans were every-
> where—in the Balkans, in Morocco, in central Africa, in China;
> and where they were not, they wished to be. So long as William I
> lived, Bismarck could keep a hold on the reins. His system was
> doomed, once an emperor representative of the new Germany was
> on the throne. Bismarck in office had been to the great powers a
> guarantee of peace, even though a peace organized by Germany.
> Now the Powers had to seek other guarantees, and ultimately
> guarantees against Germany herself.[71]

Bismarck's diplomacy and policy was the target of criticism in his
own time, and especially after Kaiser William II dismissed him and reversed
his policies. As we have seen, there were powerful forces pressing for
change, for more ambitious and, in Bismarck's view, more dangerous policies ranging from vigorous colonial expansion to preventive war against
Russia. "All the world is really pro-war here," said the critical Holstein in
1888. "With the almost exclusive exception of His Excellency, who exerts
himself to the utmost for the maintenance of peace."[72] The restraint, the
satisfaction with the status quo, the determination to continue balancing
one power against another without achieving a permanent and satisfactory
settlement that would increase German power and glory, even at the cost of
war, seemed stodgy and old-fashioned.

> The thought of war as a possibility in international politics entered
> the consciousness of the generation succeeding Bismarck with
> gathering force. A new emotion was raging, an emotion which

perceived the status quo as inadequate and sought by means of final solutions what was adjudged inevitable. . . .

Bismarck's pragmatic peace policy was anything but popular in contemporary Germany. By contrast, Wilhelm II's soon proclaimed *Weltpolitik* . . . met with the enthusiastic approval of rulers and ruled alike.[73]

The generation shaped by memories of the wars of the French Revolution and Napoleon and that treasured the blessings of peace was gone, to be replaced by a new one convinced that change and progress were the same thing. It is not necessary to admire Bismarck's personality, his reactionary political opinions, or the constitutional system he established in order to appreciate his remarkable achievement in conducting Germany's foreign affairs in the years 1871–90.

Bismarck stood out against the new spirit with a stubbornness that ultimately helped bring him down. For him Germany's interests and security demanded peace. He understood, as he wrote to the Prussian Minister of War in 1886, that "one campaign taking an unfortunate course could possibly even lead to the collapse of the Reich,"[74] just as Pericles knew that one defeat in a land battle could bring down the Athenian Empire. Like Pericles in the 430s B.C. Bismarck tried to restrain new forces to preserve what had already been achieved. "So long as he was at the head of state in peacetime he pursued a moderate policy and preserved it in safety, and it was under his leadership that the state reached its fullest greatness."[75] Such was Thucydides's judgment of Pericles's leadership and policy, and it seems to fit Bismarck's conduct of foreign affairs equally well. Both states, however, contrary to the aims of these leaders, entered wars that destroyed what they had created. Was such an outcome inevitable for Bismarck's Germany? Was his system doomed to fail?

Such, certainly, was the view of his successors who rejected it, so they claimed, because it was overly complicated and self-contradictory. But, as we have seen, the complications were manageable. There was only one contradiction, and that one was made necessary by the central task of keeping the peace between two states divided by serious conflicts. It was not the system that was at fault in this regard but the underlying realities which the system was meant to control. What was essential was not the maintenance of any particular arrangement of states into alliances but the combination of German power, disinterest, and commitment to peace. So long as these were in place Germany's interests were consistent with Britain's. Together they could keep the peace of Europe with or without an alliance. It did not require Bismarck's genius to maintain his system, once it was in place, only an adherence to his goals and general policies.

Some modern claims that the system could not last focus on social and economic forces that they believe were bound to undermine it. The depression that started in 1873 and lasted into the 1890s put an end to free trade on the Continent and led to tariff wars, embittering international relations, especially between Germany and Russia. These concerns were troubling but transient and in no way central to the collapse of the system. The same forces also, the argument runs, caused pressure for expansion in Europe, the drive for overseas colonies, the building of a fleet, all of which were bound to undermine Bismarck's arrangements. It is, of course, the duty of a statesman to resist such pressures when they promote unwise or dangerous policies. Pericles's ability to do that won Thucydides's admiration: he "restrained the multitude and . . . led them rather than being led by them."[76] Bismarck did the same with a high degree of success. There is no factual basis for asserting that his successors could not have held to his line for, as we shall see, they never tried. Instead, they took the lead in reversing his policies and sought diametrically opposite goals, just as Pericles's successors did in his day.

A recent critique rejects the idea of a "system" entirely, suggesting that Bismarck's work was no more than a brittle and precarious "system of stopgaps," a set of responses to crises, providing no long-term solution, without perspective and without a future.[77] It is certainly right to correct an older view that gave Bismarck undue credit for long vision and the conscious creation of a system planned in advance and consistently followed. His work *was* a system of stopgaps, as what conduct of foreign policy over a comparable period is not? What were the available alternatives? To contemporaries the favorite choices were territorial expansion, overseas colonization, or preventive wars that do not, in retrospect, appear attractive. Modern critics suggest the dismantling of Germany's social, economic, and political system to produce greater equality and democracy. Leaving aside the question of its practicability, at least one scholar doubts that it would have helped:

> [A]n internal parliamentarisation, corresponding in some respect to
> the current of the age, would in all probability have encouraged the

tendency to external expansion rather than controlled it. . . . As is indicated by the strengths and weaknesses, opportunities and limitations, stabilities and susceptibilities of German foreign policy in the age of Bismarck, in some respects there was no alternative to the "system of stopgaps."[78]

In the Melian Dialogue Thucydides reports the following statement by an Athenian spokesman in 416, more than a decade after Pericles's death: "In the realm of the gods we believe and of human beings we clearly know that by a necessity of their nature they rule as far as their power permits."[79] That was the voice of the new generation Pericles had tried to restrain who wanted to seek new glories and expand the empire. Its most potent spokesman was Alcibiades, the ward of Pericles who designed and advocated the great Sicilian expedition of 415–13, a major contributor to Athens's disastrous defeat. In his view a great dynamic state like Athens could not stand still:

"You must understand . . . that by sinking into inaction, the state, like everything else, will wear itself out, and its skill in everything decay, while each fresh struggle will give it a fresh experience, and make it more used to defending itself in word and deed. . . . A city not inactive by nature could not choose a quicker way to ruin itself than by suddenly adopting such a policy."[80] These are views strikingly similar to many expressed in Germany in the two decades before the Great War, of inevitable and salutary conflict, of ambitions impossible to limit, of *Weltmacht oder Niedergang* (world power or decline).[81]

Is it true that there can be no limit to the ambitions of power, or that at least some kinds of states that grow to great power status through aggressive, dynamic policies cannot in their maturity restrain and control the forces they have unleashed and put limits to their growth and desires? If so, Pericles and Bismarck may be seen as old men fruitlessly trying to consolidate the gains of their youth by trying to hold back a whirlwind.

In the case of Bismarck, at least, we must remember that the peace he worked for lasted for a quarter of a century after his dismissal from office, not a short time as such matters go. As we shall see, moreover, it took extraordinary efforts and a willful and complete rejection of his goals to bring on a war even then. It therefore seems questionable to call his system a failure and to blame it for the war that came after his death. It is well to remember that not long before his dismissal, Bismarck could take satisfaction in the fact that his network of alliances was still in good repair and, indeed, had been strengthened by Great Britain's association with the junior members of the Triple Alliance. There was no immediate prospect of new troubles in Europe. The warmongers in France and the Pan-Slavs in Russia were in eclipse, and the attention of all Powers was becoming increasingly absorbed by problems of territorial expansion and colonial exploitation in areas far from the European centre.[82]

Testing the Peace

Germany's "New Course"

Eighteen eighty-eight was the year of the three emperors in Germany. In March the ancient William died. His son Frederick III died after only ninety-nine days on the throne, and on June 15 Frederick's son William II became Kaiser. Unlike his grandfather, who relied heavily on Bismarck to manage the state and its affairs and rarely interfered, the young Kaiser was determined to rule his empire himself. Even after rebuffs and failures had made him more diffident he continued to play an important and often decisive role in political, diplomatic, and military decisions. It is not possible, therefore, to understand Germany's behavior in the years from 1888 to 1914 without taking account of the ideas and personality of William II.

Even late in the nineteenth century, when constitutional monarchy had become the normal form of kingship in Europe, the young Kaiser asserted an absolutist theory: "I regard my whole position and my task as having been imposed on me from heaven, and that I am called to the service of a Higher Being, to Whom I shall have to give a reckoning later."[83] He was also a dedicated militarist, delighting in uniforms, surrounding himself with a military entourage, and sharing in the ethic of the Prussian soldier. His military and naval officials had easier access to him than his chancellor. When he was thwarted or when things were going badly, these ideas often led him to think and talk of launching a military coup to abolish the constitution and restore absolute rule, although he never undertook such an action.

Another important part of his character involved his attitude toward

Great Britain. His mother was the daughter of Queen Victoria. William came to detest her domination of his father, her preference for English over German ways, her Liberal politics. By the time he came to the throne the relations between them were very bad, and they never improved. On the other hand, the Kaiser was very proud of his English lineage. He was much taken with the code of the English gentleman, although he never got it quite right, frequently behaving in such a way as to create amusement and embarrassment, to which he reacted with fury. England exerted a powerful but ambiguous attraction upon him. He wanted to win the liking, respect, and acceptance of the royal family and the aristocracy, but he was jealous of England's power, represented most strikingly by its empire and the fleet that preserved it. He always suspected that the British did not take him or his country quite seriously and that they accorded neither due respect, and these prejudices had important consequences. As a biographer has put it:

> The last Kaiser's most pronounced—and most fatal—characteristic was his habitual inclination to act almost entirely on the basis of his personal feelings. The most momentous decisions in his early life— his renunciation of his English mother and her country, his embracing the life and ethos of a Prussian lieutenant, his implementation in the mid-1890s of a reactionary domestic regime, and the campaign a few years later to construct a gigantic navy—can be traced to vanity or to pique. This ineffable tendency to personalize everything stands revealed in the Kaiser's correspondence . . . or his marginal comments . . . on countless documents, which display passion but rarely judgment.[84]

The young Kaiser, determined to rule and not merely to reign while his Chancellor made the important decisions, soon came into conflict with Bismarck. The two had significant disagreements about both domestic and foreign policy, as well as fundamental differences that reflected the generational distance between them. The Kaiser's memoirs reveal his strong commitment to the colonial and naval policies he would one day pursue and the old Chancellor's very different perspective. The young William told Bismarck of the popular enthusiasm for Germany's first colonial acquisitions in Africa; "The Prince remarked that the matter hardly deserved this." Bismarck always had the intention only "to utilize the colonies as commercial objects, or objects for swapping purposes, [rather] than to make them useful for the fatherland or utilize them as sources of raw materials." William "pointed out that steps must be taken for *getting a fleet constructed* [emphasis in the original] in time; . . . that since the Prince had unfurled the German flag in foreign parts . . . there must also be a navy behind it." The idea that an English fleet could land in Germany unopposed was "unbearable for Germany." To make that impossible, he argued, "we . . . needed a sufficiently strong navy." Bismarck's sardonic answer was "If the English should land on our soil I should have them arrested."

Bismarck's attitude toward England was particularly annoying:

> England, to be sure, was one of the five balls in his diplomatic statesmanly game, but she was merely one of the five, and he did not grant her the special importance which was her due.
>
> For this reason it was that the Foreign Office likewise was involved entirely in the continental interplay of politics, had not the requisite interest in colonies, navy, or England, and possessed no experience in world politics. The English psychology and mentality, as shown in the pursuit—constant, though concealed by all sorts of little cloaks—of world hegemony, was to the German Foreign Office a book sealed with seven seals.[85]

But the most fundamental reason for the rift was a contest of wills. As the Kaiser put it, "it was merely a question of who was to be the 'top dog.' "[86] In such a contest the Kaiser was bound to win, and in March 1890 he compelled the "Iron Chancellor" to resign.

The new chancellor was General Leo von Caprivi, a respected military man with no previous experience either in domestic affairs or diplomacy who had once asked, "What kind of a jackass will dare to be Bismarck's successor?"[87] Almost immediately Germany broke with the most fundamental policy of Bismarck's system: the need to maintain a connection with the Russians in order to keep them isolated from France. It has been suggested that this "first foreign political action in . . . the Wilhelmine New Course was the most crucial of all those made between 1890 and the outbreak of the First World War and that it set in train the whole chain of calamity that led toward that catastrophe."[88]

In the confused and busy week of Bismarck's firing the Kaiser met with the Russian ambassador without consulting Caprivi and told him

Germany was ready to renew the Reinsurance Treaty. He then asked Caprivi to set the process in motion. Caprivi fell under the influence of the experienced, mysterious, but influential Foreign Office official, Friedrich von Holstein. Holstein was uncomfortable with Bismarck's system and hostile to Russia, and he soon convinced Caprivi that renewal of the treaty would be a mistake. Caprivi, supported by the leading officials of the Foreign Office and key ambassadors, then told the Kaiser that the secret treaty with Russia was incompatible with Germany's other obligations to Austria, Rumania, and Italy, that it exposed Germany to Russian blackmail, and that it was not an effective check on the French. It would be better to let the Russian treaty lapse and pursue a simpler, more straightforward policy. Confronted by this unanimous advice, the Kaiser agreed to the lapse of the treaty.

The news came as a devastating blow to the Russians, who came back in May and offered concessions, to abandon the supplementary protocol that seemed most in conflict with the Austrian alliance, even to substitute an exchange of notes for a formal treaty. Hans Lothar von Schweinitz, the German ambassador to Russia, who had opposed the renewal of the treaty, now changed his mind and supported the Russian proposal. "I do not consider it advisable to reject the hand which the Tsar is once again offering us," he told Caprivi. "In fact I think it is perfectly possible, in view of the reduced Russian demands, to conclude something in writing which, even if it should become known, could not be used against us and would still assure us of Russian neutrality, at least during the first weeks of a French war of aggression."[89] But the others stood fast, inventing all sorts of reasons for refusing. On June 18, 1890, the Reinsurance Treaty lapsed.

The arguments used by the opponents of the treaty seemed to them to make sense. The Russians were unalterably hostile to Germany, they claimed, and nothing had changed that in the past or could do so in the future. With or without a treaty they would attack Germany if the French did. On the other hand, a German treaty with Russia always endangered its alliances with Austria, Italy, and Rumania and would make it impossible to achieve an alliance with England. In fact, this reasoning is remarkable in its failure to distinguish reality from prejudice and what was central from what was peripheral:

> There is something ludicrous about an argument that considers relations with Rumania or even with Italy on the same terms as

relations with Russia. The argument also totally failed to appreciate the enormous difference between a Russia tied to Germany, no matter how loosely or unreliably, and a Russia firmly allied with France. As soon as Russian statesmen realised they could expect no more from Germany they were forced to seek the support of France and to co-operate with France on the big questions of international diplomacy. For France, the certainty of Russian support as compared to the hopeful expectation of such support enormously increased French authority and self-respect in international affairs. France and Russia together were to form a power bloc which fully balanced the Triple Alliance. For Germany the actuality of a Franco-Russian alliance increased the danger of a future French war of revenge.[90]

Why did the Germans take this remarkable action? When the arguments they presented are so easily refuted it is reasonable to seek other explanations. The new policy reflected the views of the professionals in the foreign office, especially Holstein's. "Instead of Bismarck's complicated system of checks and balances, the Caprivi administration intended to build up a great alliance of states with interests similar to Germany's, an alliance in which Britain would take the place of Russia. In such an alliance Russia played no part and could only disrupt German plans."[91] For some years Holstein and others had been angered by Russia's behavior in the Balkans and, behind Bismarck's back, had been pressing the Austrians to take a hard line against Russia. The "New Course" sought an alliance with Britain, and one of Holstein's chief reasons for rejecting the Reinsurance Treaty was that its revelation would offend England, especially the supplementary protocol closing the Straits. But Holstein persisted in his opposition even after the Russians were prepared to abandon the protocol. His hostility to Russia was visceral and went beyond rational diplomacy. Apart from that, he had personal motives. Bismarck and he had become enemies, and Holstein was convinced that a renewal of the treaty would bring Bismarck back to office, and that would mean the end to his own career. In the spring of 1890, however, he was the only man of experience and weight in the diplomatic corps, "he was the one-eyed man in the country of the blind,"[92] and his influence on his colleagues was decisive.

When the Kaiser heard of the diplomats' opposition to the treaty he said, "Well, then, it can't be done whether I like it or not,"[93] and it is true that his role in the affair was passive. Throughout his career, however, he repeatedly rejected advice, from whatever source, when he disagreed with it strongly. In this instance there is good reason to believe that his first instinct, to renew the treaty, was automatic rather than the product of careful thought and that the decision to let it lapse represented his true preference. From the mid 1880s he had been increasingly displeased with the Russians. By 1887, persuaded that France and Russia were plotting a war against Austria and Germany, he wrote Bismarck in support of Waldersee's idea of a preventive war. The Chancellor wrote a friend, "that young man wants war with Russia and would like to draw his sword straight away if he could. I shall not be a party to it."[94] In 1889, after he had come to the throne, he held the same views. He promised the Austrian emperor Franz Josef, in direct opposition to Bismarck's policy of restraint, that he would support Austria in a war against Russia, whether Bismarck liked it or not, and he told friends that if Bismarck did not support a war against the Russians the Chancellor would have to go.[95] In the same year the Kaiser put an end to negotiations by Bismarck and his personal banker for a large loan to the Russians.[96] The decision "to cut the wire to St. Petersburg," therefore, did not represent a reversal of William's previous views.

There appears to have been yet another reason for the reversal in policy, intangible and difficult to document, but no less real. William II represented the arrival in power of a new generation after a long reign by the previous one. William I had reigned into his nineties, and Bismarck had managed affairs for almost three decades. By any objective evaluation they had achieved remarkable success: the unification of Germany under Prussian leadership, its rise to primacy in Europe, enormous economic progress, and the maintenance of peace for twenty years. Yet there was discontent as the old achievements were taken for granted and new problems came to the fore. People were tired of the rule of those old men, especially the irascible and domineering Chancellor. There was considerable pressure, especially among the younger elite surrounding the young Kaiser, for change, almost any change. From the Kaiser's point of view, how could he rid himself of the dead hand of the past and establish his own place as leader of his people if he merely walked the paths paved by his predecessors? What was the point of dismissing Bismarck only to be ruled by his system and his policies?

But change is not always for the better and movement not always progress. A keen critique of the new policy points up its shortcomings:

What Bismarck's successors neglected to consider was the effect their Russian policy might have on their allies or on powers they hoped to secure as allies. These countries had interests of their own which were not necessarily connected with those of Germany. By casting Russia adrift, the Germans considerably lowered their bargaining power with Austria and Italy, and they lost perhaps their most effective lever for prying the British out of their isolationism. Once Russia had made an alliance with France, which she was virtually compelled to do as a result of German policy, the Austrians and Italians recognized that by threatening to defect to the rival power bloc they could make Germany pay an increasingly high price for their friendship, and the friendship of both was made less reliable. As for the British, they saw that Germany was now compelled to support Austria and Italy or risk the disintegration of the Triple Alliance, and in consequence they felt much less reason than in Bismarck's day to make binding commitments to these powers in order to balance the power of Russia in Eastern Europe and France in the Mediterranean. They could only regard with satisfaction the German break with Russia and the reestablishment of the balance of power on the continent which allowed them to play the profitable role of balance wheel. They certainly had no intention of supporting a German bid for the diplomatic domination of the continent, though for many years the Germans convinced themselves that some day the British would provide that support.[97]

The folly of the new policy soon became apparent. The Germans successfully negotiated a treaty with the British, acquiring the little island of Heligoland in exchange for recognizing the British protectorate over Zanzibar and other significant colonial concessions in Africa. Heligoland had no importance to the Germans, who "welcomed it solely as a display of national prestige,"[98] and many Germans rightly thought the British had gotten by far the best of the bargain. But Holstein and Caprivi, caring little for colonies, thought they were well on the way to an alliance with Britain. Attempts to draw the British closer to the Triple Alliance, however, failed. When Italy tried to use Germany's increased dependence on the Triple Alliance to gain support for its interests against France, Holstein tried to get the British to promise Italy protection from a French attack. Salisbury would not agree. He knew that "as long as France was afraid of Germany she could do nothing to injure us."[99] When Gladstone and the Liberals came to power in July 1892, moreover, German plans for an English alliance to replace the Russian came crashing to the ground. Gladstone favored the French, but even more he favored the old policy of isolation.

The Russians, however, were shaken badly by Germany's turn away from them and toward the British, and they continued to hope and work for a return to closer relations with Germany. When the French urged them in May of 1890 to join them in a military agreement against Germany the Russians refused. Undeterred, the French tried again, this time using their great financial power as a diplomatic weapon. At a moment when the Russians were in serious need of money, the French got the House of Rothschild to cancel a large loan, and the Russians received the message. In July 1891 a naval squadron from France, the mother of European revolution, arrived in Kronstadt, the Baltic port of Tsarist Russia, the bulwark of reactionary autocracy, and was greeted with tumultuous cheers. In August the two nations concluded a secret diplomatic agreement. A year later French and Russian generals negotiated a military convention, subject to final approval, that committed the Russians to attack Germany in case the Germans attacked France and vice versa. In October 1893 the Russian fleet reciprocated the Kronstadt visit with a voyage to the French naval base at Toulon where they also received an enthusiastic reception, and in January 1894 the French government formally endorsed the alliance, approved by the Tsar a week earlier. Bismarck's worst nightmare had become reality. "The system by which Germany directed the affairs of Europe" had come to an end.[100]

At first the Germans were not greatly alarmed by the growing rapprochement between France and Russia. But as the British remained cool and the Franco-Russian romance grew warmer Germany was forced to face the prospect of a two-front war.[101] The elder Moltke's plan for such a contingency had been to divide his armies roughly equally between east and west, "ready to take the offensive in both the East and West—but only as a means of defence."[102] The more powerful attack was to go against Russia, then thought to be the weaker opponent, first, while holding the French at bay in the west. Since the Russians were likely to retreat and make good military use of the great size of their country, as they had against Napoleon, the plan did not place a great premium on swiftness of attack. If the Germans were compelled to fight Russia, they hoped to

Area of the Schlieffen Plan

restrain or contain the French by increasing their forces but staying on the defensive on the western front.

In February 1892 Count Alfred von Schlieffen became Chief of the General Staff, a change as significant as the installation of the new Emperor and his new Chancellor.

> Thanks to Bismarck's masterly diplomatic preparations and to the vast technical and material superiority of the Prussia-German army, Moltke had been able to start all his wars with a high expectation of success (one might almost say 80 per cent). Now, from decade to decade, this expectation had diminished. Only by studying Moltke's deployment plans after 1871 can one understand why Bismarck felt so oppressed by the *cauchemar des coalitions,* and why he employed such elaborate, and finally such daring, tricks to avoid a conflict with Russia. The new generation of diplomats, standing on the firm political foundations which Bismarck had created, were much more confident. They simplified their work by finally dropping the "reinsurance" with Russia and steered full ahead for the high seas of a "world policy" which was soon to antagonise England as well. The same confident attitude was reflected, after Moltke, among the younger generation of German chiefs-of-staff.[103]

Schlieffen devised a new plan which, in spite of several significant changes, remained the basic strategy with which the Germans entered the war in 1914. France, though seen to be the more formidable opponent, could be defeated swiftly if the attacking force were strong enough. Schlieffen's plan, therefore, in all its forms, called for an immediate attack in the west to knock out the French before the Russians could bring their power to bear in the east. Even a war beginning in the Balkans, therefore, required a German attack on France: "though the prospect of war on two fronts produced Schlieffen's plan of campaign, this plan first made war on two fronts inevitable."[104]

A. J. P. Taylor ridicules the notion that the system of alliances that existed in 1914 caused the war, pointing out that "with or without alliances an Austro-Russian war had to involve the west, once Schlieffen's plan was adopted."[105] The target is a broad one and deserves to be hit, for blaming the alliance system as the cause of the war began at once and continues to this day. On August 1, 1914, Alfred Zimmermann, undersecretary of the German Foreign Office, told the British ambassador in Berlin: "It all came from this damned system of alliances, which was the curse of modern times,"[106] and the most influential of the revisionist historians went so far as to say that "the greatest single underlying cause of the War was the system of secret alliances which developed after the Franco-Prussian War."[107] The purpose of both statements was to clear the Germans of blame for the war begun by its invasion of neutral Belgium. As we have seen, however, the alliance system that emerged after 1871 kept the peace for two decades, and the very different one that arose after 1890 survived for another quarter century before collapsing into a general war. Both systems were not causes of war but the results of more basic goals and policies pursued by European powers, so that exposing the vacuousness of such claims is a useful activity.

Even so, Taylor's argument misses the point at issue in 1892. The Schlieffen plan was adopted in response to the emerging alliance between Russia and France, an alliance Bismarck had worked long, hard, and successfully to avoid and one virtually forced on the Russians by the new diplomatic course stubbornly pursued by the Germans after 1890. It was immediately clear that the new strategy required a larger army, and the Reichstag was compelled to vote funds for a large increase. Bismarck and other critics were quick to point out the failure of the new policy that had brought France and Russia together "while following the will-o'-the-wisp of an alliance with Britain, a notoriously unreliable Power that was now clearly intent upon using the Triple Alliance for its own purposes while giving nothing in return."[108]

The Kaiser angrily abandoned Britain and tried to mend fences with the Russians. He expended considerable effort and badly annoyed the agrarian conservatives who were the monarchy's strongest supporters by backing Caprivi's trade agreement of 1893 that was very favorable to the Russians. This sharp reversal gained the support even of Holstein, who was now "willing to give up Rumania, Bulgaria, Turkey and the Straits, and to conclude an alliance with Russia with or without the sanction of Austria."[109] Whatever the merits of this *volte-face,* it was no longer possible. Russia was committed to the new French alliance and suspicious of the Germans, even bearing gifts of low tariffs.

Paul Hatzfeld, Germany's ambassador in London, acutely assessed the lack of constancy and steadiness in his country's foreign policy in 1894. If only, he said, the Germans would learn "to sit quietly and wait, broiled turtle-doves would fly into their mouths; as it was, however, they defeated their own interests by 'incessant hysterical vacillations.' "[110] The government turned next to the pursuit of popularity and prestige by involving Germany in colonial disputes. The Kaiser liked the idea because colonies were becoming popular with elements of the German people. It also attracted him because the policy was certain to produce conflict with Britain, the greatest of the colonial powers, and thereby counteract the new regime's reputation for being too accommodating to the British. Holstein liked the plan because he saw in it a chance of annoying the British and thereby showing them that they would do better to join Germany and the Triple Alliance. In spite of his own appreciation of the dangers of Germany's hyperactivity, Hatzfeld participated in this policy, pointing out different ways that colonies could be used to put pressure on the British: "By its treaty with the Congo State, the English Cabinet has given us a new weapon for demonstrating the disadvantages of our hostility. . . . This is therefore . . . the way we can exercise pressure and perhaps make the English more amenable." The Kaiser was delighted with the advice, commenting, "Splendid! Corresponds entirely with my views and our policy is to be conducted as recommended here."[111] This curious idea of winning friends and allies by bullying continued to appeal to Holstein and to his protégé Bernhard von Bülow, later Foreign Minister and Chancellor. Their misreading of the British character would cause much trouble.

In 1894 the Germans challenged or quarreled with Great Britain about Samoa, the Congo, the Sudan, Morocco, Turkey, and Portugal's African colonies. The dismissal of Caprivi as Chancellor and his replacement by Prince Chlodwig zu Hohenlohe-Schillingsfürst did not interrupt the pattern. In 1895, though they had no Far Eastern interests, they intervened in the settlement of Japan's war against China, because of the groundless fear that Britain would otherwise make new gains in the region.[112] The Germans were not always wrong in these disagreements, but their unpleasant tactics and apparent lack of motive confused and annoyed the British without achieving anything of consequence for Germany. In June of 1894 the British Foreign Secretary wrote his ambassador in Berlin: "if this is to continue it may have far-reaching consequences and it is difficult to understand what advantage they expect to gain by such a policy."[113] But the Germans were unaware that their policy and manner were causing increasing ill will in England, "nor did they seem to realise that this policy had seriously undercut the possibility of an eventual agreement between Britain and the Triple Alliance, an agreement which had previously been the major goal of German diplomacy." Instead, Holstein chided Hatzfeld for being too soft on the British, and the German ambassador responded indignantly, "You are wrong if you believe that I am in any way reluctant to make myself disagreeable here."[114]

On December 29, 1895, Dr. Leander Starr Jameson, the Administrator of Rhodesia for the British South Africa Company, led an armed raid into the independent Boer state of the Transvaal aimed at causing a revolt among British and other settlers against Boer rule. The British disavowed Dr. Jameson, and within a few days he was defeated and captured; the affair seemed to be over.

The Jameson raid, however, infuriated the Kaiser. He talked of war against Britain and of making the Transvaal a German protectorate. It was to ward off these reckless ideas that Marschall persuaded him instead to send the following telegram of congratulation to President Paul Kruger of the Transvaal:

> I congratulate you most sincerely on having succeeded, with your people, without calling on the help of foreign powers, by opposing your own force to an armed band which has broken into your country to disturb the peace, in restoring quiet and in maintaining the independence of your country against external attack.[115]

When Holstein objected to the telegram Marschall urged him not to interfere: "you've no idea of the suggestions made in there. Everything else is even worse."[116]

But the telegram, which "probably . . . did more to inflame British and German public opinion against each other" than any single act before 1914,[117] was bad enough. Its message angered the British because they regarded the message as an improper intervention into the internal affairs of the British Empire. They were angered further by the implicit suggestion that Germany was one of the unnamed "foreign powers" who might have been willing to help the Boers had it been necessary. Beyond that, South Africa was very important to the British. Their Foreign Secretary had lately told the Germans that it was "perhaps the most vital interest of Great Britain because by the possession of it communication with India was assured . . . [it was] of even greater importance to England than Malta or

Gibraltar."[118] The result was a great outcry in the press and the first public demonstrations of anti-German feeling among ordinary people, who smashed the windows of German shops and wrote insulting and threatening letters to the German ambassador, who reported "an entirely changed situation . . . a deep-seated feeling of bitterness among the public, which has shown itself in every way . . . if the Government had lost its head or had wished for war for any reason, it would have had the whole of public opinion behind it."[119] In 1896 German relations with Britain had sunk to their lowest level. The new course, which aimed at a rapprochement with Britain, had produced the opposite result and, at the same time, had created a Franco-Russian alliance. By any reasonable reckoning the Kaiser's policies were a disastrous failure.

In Germany, however, the Kaiser's telegram provoked a great wave of popular enthusiasm for a bold approach to foreign and colonial policy and the humiliation of England. Those in the government, on the other hand, who understood its ramifications were worried and appalled. Holstein called the telegram "a match to set fire to an accumulation of inflammable material," and the German military attaché in St. Petersburg declared that "the Kaiser must be *mad, mad, mad!*"[120] No doubt, the Kaiser truly was angered, but if he was mad there was method in it. In 1895 the Kaiser was pressing hard for a major increase in the German Navy, for which there was little support in the Reichstag or the country at large. As one scholar puts it, "behind the Kaiser's emotional outbursts there sometimes lay a certain cunning calculation." Some months before the Jameson raid the Kaiser anticipated an international crisis arising over British relations with the Boers, saying "we must make all the capital we can out of the business, also for ev[entua]l naval appropriations to protect our growing commerce."[121] To the conference he called to consider a response to the raid he brought three admirals, and "the Kaiser, [Admiral] Knorr and [Admiral] Senden certainly wanted to exploit the 'wonderful' wave of anglophobia produced by the crisis to demand huge sums from the Reichstag to enlarge the Navy."

Naturally, shipbuilders, iron and steel manufacturers, suppliers of a navy's needs, financiers, and other businessmen and industrialists who would profit directly gladly supported the Kaiser's plans. Nationalistic, superpatriotic organizations like the Colonial Union and the Pan-German League were vigorously in favor of colonies and hostile to the British. In 1895–96 they were readily brought round to the idea of a navy, as were the many nationalistic intellectuals, popular writers, and university professors. Often they made arguments apparently based on alleged practical needs and advantages, typically economic. Thus Admiral Georg von Müller, a man who sought to pursue *Weltpolitik* and its benefits not at the expense of but in alliance with England, asserted that "central Europe *(Mitteleuropa)* is getting too small and that the free expansion of the peoples who live here is restricted as a result of the present distribution of the inhabitable parts of the earth and above all the world domination of England."[122] But the economic advantages of colonial imperialism usually were assumed and proclaimed rather than demonstrated. Time and subsequent study have shown that there was rarely any profit to be gained from the acquisition of such colonies as were still available or could be acquired. "Germany's colonial policy had a very narrow economic base. Its advocates were professors, school-teachers and clergymen rather than businessmen."[123] Major colonial and imperial projects, such as the Berlin-Baghdad railroad, generally were started by politicians who could get financiers to invest only by offering government guarantees.[124]

Nor is it clear that contemporaries really were convinced or moved to action by economic motives. Germany's swift rise to power and influence in the quarter century since its creation had filled the heads of the new generation, especially of intellectuals, professionals, and businessmen with national pride and ambition. In a famous lecture in 1895 Max Weber argued that Germany needed to pursue world power:

> We must understand that the unification of Germany was a youthful folly, which the nation committed in its declining days and which would have been better dispensed with because of its expense, if it should be the conclusion and not the starting point for a German Weltmachtpolitik [policy of world power]."[125]

Such ideas fit into the framework of the Social Darwinism that was influential in Germany and elsewhere around the turn of the century. It transferred the concept of a struggle for survival and the survival of the fittest from the experience of species in nature to the sphere of nations in the world.

The remarks of Hunold von Ahlefeld, Director of the imperial Shipyards at Kiel, were typical: "The 'struggle for survival' is raging between individuals, provinces, parties, states. The latter are engaged in it either with the force of arms or with economic means; there is nothing we can do about this, except to join in. He who doesn't will perish."[126]

Only months before the war Chancellor Theobald von Bethmann Hollweg complained that "every day Germany sees its population growing by leaps and bounds; its navy, its trade and industry are making unparalleled developments . . . it is forced to expand somehow or other; it has not yet found that 'place in the sun' which is its due."[127]

Over and over again in the two decades before the war the British tried to find a way to accommodate German interests but were hard pressed to understand them. As one perceptive scholar has put it, the Germans "wanted *Geltung* [respect], *Anerkennung* [recognition], *Gleichberechtigung* [equal authority], a whole host of emotionally loaded and psychologically revealing objectives."[128] It is hard to escape the sense that Germany's demand for colonies and world empire were based far less on a concern for "interest," in Thucydides's language, than in the search for "honor."

Among European countries at the turn of the century the definition of excellence and greatness was shaped by Great Britain, whose power had to be confronted if Germany was to achieve her destiny. Even the moderate historian and influential essayist Hans Delbrück,

> one of the few German "critic[s] of the Wilhelmine era," focussed on the centrality of England:
> We want to be a world power and pursue colonial policy in the grand manner. That is certain. Here there can be no step backward. The entire future of our people among the great nations depends upon it. We can pursue this policy with England or without England. With England means in peace; against England means— through war.[129]

Britain's greatness was thought to rest on her empire which, in turn, depended on the command of the seas exercised by the British Navy. To be a great power one needed a colonial empire and a fleet. These ideas were given a powerful boost by the publication in 1890 of the American Alfred T. Mahan's book *The Influence of Sea Power Upon History 1660–1783*. Choosing appropriate historical examples Mahan observed that the hierarchy of nations was always in flux and that constant international competition led to the rise of some states and the decline of others. He argued that naval power always had been the decisive factor. Although it is far from clear that its argument is correct,[130] the book had a tremendous impact on the Kaiser. From his childhood he had had a passionate interest in sailing, the sea, and navies. One of his first acts as Emperor was to reorganize the structure of naval administration and another was the novelty of appointing a naval officer as one of his adjutants. Delighted when Queen Victoria raised him to the rank of a British admiral, he bombarded her and British naval officials with criticism and advice that was not much appreciated. He read Mahan's book in 1894, committed it to memory, and ordered all German naval officers to master it.[131] But, as one biographer has put it, "at bottom his attitude to the fleet was part of his love-hate relationship with his mother's country. He wanted a navy because the English had one, because it was a sign of being a world Power, because it was a means of forcing the English to pay him attention.[132] Another offers a similar explanation:

> [T]he German fleet was to him not so much a calculated ingredient of domestic or foreign policy but a romantic emblem of Hohenzollern glory. . . . A navy was to him a gorgeous apparition through which to humble Germany's enemies and create respect and riches both for ruler and people. . . . Without a navy the Kaiser knew that he could take no effective action in either the Atlantic or the Pacific and that this impotence would lead ineluctably to a humiliating decline in Germany's prestige as well as his own. He therefore must have a fleet.[133]

The Kaiser's commitment to the Navy "was the only constant in a life that was otherwise notable for its vacillation . . . the one subject on which the Kaiser was inflexible in his opinions,"[134] and this was of the greatest importance, because Germany in the 1890s was far from willing to embark on a major program of naval construction. As late as January 1896 Admiral Senden complained that "the King and Kaiser has no majority in the Government, nor in the Bundesrat, nor in the Reichstag. . . . The entire country is ignorant about the purpose and function of the Navy. We must rouse support in the Reichstag and country as a whole."[135] The years during which the policy of building a great battleship fleet to challenge

British supremacy at sea took shape, 1897–1900, were also the years of William II's greatest political power. "From 1897 until Bülow's assumption of the Chancellorship in October 1900, Kaiser Wilhelm II was 'his own Chancellor. . . . For these three years. . . . [he] held a position akin to that of a modern prime minister or president."[136] Without his strong determination, his discovery and constant support of Alfred von Tirpitz, the genius of propaganda and politics who was able to win over the nation and its politicians, there is little reason to believe that Germany would have launched its great naval program.

In the excitement after the Jameson raid the Kaiser pressed Admiral Friedrich von Hollmann, the State Secretary of the Reich Navy Office, and Chancellor Hohenlohe to put a Navy bill before the Reichstag at once, arguing that "we shall never again have such a favourable opportunity of proving to the country that the Navy cannot continue in its present state,"[137] but they found that the support was not available and that the bill must be postponed until the next session. The Kaiser was furious and Hollmann told Hohenlohe that "the Kaiser hopes to find a Reich Chancellor who will pose large naval demands, dissolve the Reichstag if necessary, and execute a *coup d'état.*"[138] What Hollmann did not know was that the Kaiser would replace him soon as well, for William II was determined to build a great German fleet able to challenge the British for command of the sea.

In June 1897 Alfred Tirpitz was appointed State Secretary of the Imperial Navy, an extraordinary honor for the son of a middle-class family. He was convinced that Germany's future would be determined at sea, that Great Britain was Germany's chief enemy, the barrier to its achievement of world power, and that the battleship was the only instrument for combating British power. His abilities and vitality had gained the admiration of his superiors; when Senden contemplated the massive task of gaining public and political support for a naval program he concluded that "an energetic man with a broad view as State Secretary must bring about a change, perhaps Tirpitz."[139] At once Tirpitz turned the Navy Office into a great center of propaganda. "Using the techniques of modern advertising, Tirpitz carried [his] message to all classes and all ages—through the printed word, through lectures, through visits by junior officers to schools and by officers of higher rank to politicians, and through invitations to the public to board and inspect naval vessels."[140] He used public funds and persuaded interested businessmen to contribute private funds to found and support the Naval League, which itself became a powerful and effective propaganda weapon, and he gained the support of other nationalistic organizations. With remarkable and unprecedented skill in winning the favor of politicians and parliamentary committees, in April 1898 Tirpitz was able to bring about the passage of a law that granted four hundred million marks for new naval construction meant to bring Germany's Navy up to a strength of nineteen battleships with proportionate numbers of cruisers, torpedo boats, and other vessels. Two years later he carried a Supplementary Bill that planned for twice as many battleships over a period of years. The battleships and heavy cruisers were to be replaced automatically every twenty-five years, the light cruisers, every fifteen.

Here was the beginning of Germany's great naval program that soon provoked fear and suspicion in Great Britain, a naval race of unprecedented size and cost, a diplomatic revolution that saw the emergence of two antagonistic power blocs and, almost every scholar would agree, played a vital part in bringing on the war. For what purposes was it undertaken? For a quarter century scholars have debated the assertion that the chief goals of *Weltpolitik,* colonial imperialism, and especially the building of a great navy were not driven chiefly by considerations of foreign policy, *Aussenpolitik,* but by internal social, economic and political motives, *Innenpolitik.*[141] The following is a statement of that thesis:

> Tirpitz's naval policy was nothing less than an ambitious plan to stabilise the Prusso-German political system and to paralyse the pressure for change. The Navy was to act as a focus for divergent social forces which the government hoped to bribe into a conservative *Sammlung* [collection, or rallying] against the "Revolution." Promises of a great political economic future were made with the aim of maintaining big landowners, the military and the bureaucracy in their key positions within the power structure. . . .
>
> The idea of a big navy . . . had the power "to revive the patriotism of the classes and to fill them again with loyalty to, and love for, the Emperor and the Reich." . . . The danger of a genuine parliamentary system or even a collapse of the monarchy under the impact of a revolutionary upheaval would disappear once and for all. . . .
>
> The decision to build a large battle-fleet represented an "inner-

political crisis strategy" designed to contribute to the survival of the Prusso-German political system: with the help of the Navy, the monarchy wanted to overthrow the *status quo* internationally in order to preserve it at home.[142]

The resulting policy is referred to as "social imperialism."

In a more serious and scholarly way this theory resembles the ancient writers' version of the *Primat der Innenpolitik* in the fifth century B.C., i.e., that Pericles started the war to solve domestic troubles in Athens,[143] but the evidence supports it no better. Critics have shown that the author of *Sammlungspolitik* regarded the building of the fleet as a menace to the success of his plan to bring together the nonsocialist parties, and that Tirpitz's goals had little to do with internal political considerations.[144] But the most impressive refutation lies in the course of events from 1898 to 1914. "Instead of acting as an integrating focus, the Navy would turn into a divisive force."[145] The enormous cost of the Navy, which continued to grow year after year, created intense domestic problems that would not have arisen otherwise. It required the levying of new taxes, which created strife between the major groups supporting the monarchy and the internal status quo and made it hard, and sometimes impossible, to govern. By 1905 "the idea of a monarchy, based on the prestige of a popular Kaiser and a powerful fleet, had failed to capture the imagination of a majority of Germans. Under the glimmering surface of Wilhelmine optimism and rising prosperity, there emerged anew the old fear of 'Revolution.' " As early as 1903 the Kaiser spoke of " 'the coming revolution and its defeat' by the Army."[146] In 1905 Tirpitz himself was afraid to try to increase the size of the Navy. He knew that no majority could be found in the Reichstag to support it and that a dissolution and new elections would be dangerous. "The deficit in the budget and the need for tax increases, 'the general inflation of prices (shortage of meat and the effect of the commercial treaties [i.e., of the higher agricultural tariffs],' Tirpitz warned, would quite possibly turn the elections into a fiasco and weaken the internal and external prestige of the monarchy."[147] By 1908 there was no avoiding divisive new taxes.

> The Anglo-German naval rivalry . . . had . . . become a German domestic problem of the first order. The more the arms spiral was set in motion, the more powerful grew the chorus of those

who argued that a continuation of the arms race was financially intolerable. . . . Tirpitz's naval programme . . . polarised public opinion at home by unlocking the dynamic contained in the peculiar financial constitution. More and more people came to suspect that the Navy was doing the opposite of what it was expected to do: rather than integrating German society on the basis of the *status quo* it was a divisive force upsetting that *status quo*.[148]

In July 1909 Chancellor Bülow was replaced by Bethmann Hollweg. "The internal situation was . . . a complete shambles, and just as German naval armaments policy was responsible for the country's isolation, it was also due to the ambitious naval programme of the turn of the century that confusion reigned at home."[149] If the goals of *Weltpolitik* and the construction of a great navy were internal, why didn't the Kaiser and his advisers turn back from them when the plan was not working? In fact, they never considered retreat, regardless of the cost and the trouble caused by the Navy, pushing forward relentlessly.

The new Chancellor wanted to stop the naval race, but the Kaiser angrily supported Tirpitz. The increase of taxes on the common man, who bore the brunt of the cost of the Navy, was a great help to the growth of the Social Democrats. By 1912 the Socialists had won a smashing electoral victory that made them the largest party in the Reichstag, and the government could not count on a reliable conservative coalition. Evidence of this domestic political trouble came early and often. It was serious enough to make the Kaiser contemplate a coup d'état on more than one occasion. The only plausible explanation for these actions is that the naval policy was driven not by domestic considerations but by the pursuit of power and glory, by *Aussenpolitik,* at any cost, at the risk of disruption at home and world war abroad.

It is only with such goals in mind that one can understand the Kaiser's and Tirpitz's plans for the German Navy. In its final stated form the plan envisioned a navy of sixty battleships to be replaced automatically every twenty years without new approval by the Reichstag. As early as 1897 Tirpitz laid out his basic approach. "For Germany, the most dangerous enemy at the present time is England. It is also the enemy against which we must urgently require a certain measure of naval force as a political power factor." There was no point in trying to attack British commerce on the high seas. "Our fleet must be constructed so that it can unfold its greatest military potential between Heligoland and the Thames. . . . The military situation against England demands battleships in as great a number as possible."[150] The fleet was to be used against the Royal Navy and the decisive battle was to be fought in the North Sea. As one scholar has put it, "Tirpitz saw his battlefleet in the form of a sharp knife, held gleaming and ready only a few inches away from the jugular vein of Germany's most likely enemy."[151]

In less dramatic language the German battle fleet was meant to serve as a deterrent. The threat of this weapon would make England conciliatory, prevent her from interfering with German interests, force her to get out of the way of Germany's new *Weltpolitik*. "Tirpitz's battle fleet was to be used as a lever whereby the overseas gains and successes necessary to allow the continuous growth of Germany into the outside world and to satisfy the Kaiser and the German public were to be prised from those 'dying' empires which the British would probably seek to protect from German occupation. . . . [It] was a shortcut to *Weltpolitik*."[152]

The British fleet, of course, was larger even than the one publicly planned by Tirpitz. How could the Germans hope to frighten the British with an inferior fleet? The answer was the "risk theory" that assumed that the British could not afford or be able to man a fleet larger than ninety battleships. Since the common belief was that an attacking fleet needed at least a three-to-two advantage to win, Tirpitz calculated that the Germans would have a good chance to win, especially since he believed Germany to have better ships, better training, and a better command structure. But the British fleet, with its need to protect the Mediterranean and its imperial responsibilities all over the globe in any event would not be able to concentrate its forces against Germany. Even a British victory in such a decisive battle, however, would be very costly, leaving the British vulnerable to their other naval enemies, France and Russia. In the face of such a prospect they were bound to seek an accommodation with Germany or at least stand out of the way of its *Weltpolitik*.

If this really was Tirpitz's plan it was full of assumptions whose falseness would become obvious soon. In case of war a British fleet need not take the offensive; Britain's geographical position allowed it to blockade Germany at a distance and keep the German fleet bottled up without risking an attack. For the Germans to get any use out of their fleet it was they who must attack and who would, therefore, need a numerically superior force. Britain, moreover, was richer than Germany and better able to sustain an arms race at sea, especially since, as islanders, they managed with only a tiny army while Germany's much larger one competed for limited resources. The plan also assumed stability in the international situation, but why should Britain use its ships to defend far-off colonies instead of bringing them home when threatened by a dagger aimed at her vitals? And why should Britain not abandon some of her enmities and make new alliances when confronting such a danger?

Tirpitz himself saw one possible flaw that worried him greatly. In the years when the fleet was under construction but not yet strong enough to withstand an attack, wouldn't the British be tempted to launch a preventive attack and destroy it in port? That fear focused on a historical precedent. In 1807, in time of peace during a lull in the Napoleonic wars, a British admiral seized the neutral Danish fleet in Copenhagen harbor to prevent its falling into French hands when the war resumed. Tirpitz and many Germans lived in constant terror of such an attack during the "period of greatest danger," before the German fleet was complete. In 1904, in fact, Sir John Fisher, Britain's First Sea Lord, suggested to King Edward VII that they "Copenhagen" the German fleet before it got too strong. "My God, Fisher," the King responded, "you must be mad!" and there never was a plan to take such action, yet "the belief that 'Fisher was coming' actually caused a panic at Kiel in 1907, and cautious parents kept their children home from school for two days."[153]

Most of the other flaws in the risk theory and in Tirpitz's stated plans seem obvious enough as to raise the question of whether he failed to see them. If not, he and those who supported his plan must seem not only dangerously fanatical but also foolish. The alternative is to believe that his true intention was different, and there is persuasive, though not conclusive evidence to support the view that Tirpitz planned ultimately to build a fleet large enough to defeat the Royal Navy in a decisive battle in the North Sea. Both the Kaiser's mother and Holstein reported that it was William II's lifetime determination to have a navy larger and stronger than the British, and others heard Tirpitz proclaim the same goal. "When it reached the size which Tirpitz and the Kaiser *ideally* desired for it, this fleet would be used to sweep British naval control from the seas."[154]

Britain's Reaction

The beginnings of the new naval policy did not attract much notice in Britain, even though they occurred in a period of considerable ill will. The wounds inflicted by the Kruger telegram were still sore. On a visit to the Kaiser, Cecil Rhodes explained the outcome of the Jameson raid and the Kruger telegram:

> "You see," said Rhodes, "I was a naughty boy, and you tried to whip me for being a naughty boy, but directly *you* did it, they said, 'No, if this is anybody's business, it is *ours.*' The result was that Your Majesty got yourself very much disliked by the English people, and I never got whipped at all."[155]

The outbreak of the Boer War (1899–1901) rubbed these feelings raw. Although the Kaiser behaved correctly and with caution, the German press and public opinion openly favored the Boers and was very hostile to Britain. There was also considerable British resentment against the growing competition offered to British manufacturers by the burgeoning German industries, trade and shipping. Britain remained first in the world in these activities, but its relative position was declining.[156] The press made much of this trade rivalry and public feeling was further exercised by politicians such as Joseph Chamberlain who wanted to replace Britain's traditional policy of free trade with one of tariffs and imperial preference. In time, this feeling faded; by 1909 the German ambassador could tell his Chancellor that "Germany's trade and industry no longer stand in the foreground of British fears."[157] At the turn of the century, however, it still had force.

Even before the Boer War, however, the situation facing Britain around the world seemed menacing. In 1898 Germany and Russia were challenging the territorial integrity of China and threatening British interests there, and France was pushing eastward into the Sudan, seeming to seek control of the Upper Nile, the Russians were applying pressure in Central Asia, and there was conflict with several nations over the status of Turkey. The pressure of worldwide responsibilities was proving too great. Salisbury decided that the British Navy could no longer protect the Straits and shifted the focus in the eastern Mediterranean to the Nile. It was also seen as hopeless to exercise power in the Western Hemisphere in the face of the rising power of the United States. The British were forced to abandon their old naval standard, which committed them to maintaining a fleet at least as great as the next two most powerful navies, and limit its application to the combined fleets of France and Russia. At the Colonial Conference in 1902 Joseph Chamberlain described his country as "the weary Titan staggering under the too-vast orb of its fate."[158] Britain's isolation no longer appeared so splendid. Retrenchment must be assisted by diplomacy if Britain was to meet its remaining commitments.

An attempt to come to an agreement with Russia failed, and so the British turned to Germany. They made concessions in Africa and Samoa to establish a friendly climate. What they wanted chiefly was German help in resisting Russian expansion in the Far East. Between 1898 and 1901 they made several overtures for cooperation, but the Germans were cool. They felt that Britain was weak and declining and was bound to come back with a sweeter offer if the Germans only waited. Suggestions that the British might seek allies elsewhere, with the French or the Russians, were brushed aside as fantastic. "In my opinion," Chancellor Bülow told his ambassador in London, "we need not worry about such remote possibilities."[159] At bottom the basis for alliance did not exist. German policy, so recently adopted, aimed at competition with and challenge to Britain, not cooperation, and public opinion in both countries was hostile. "A German alliance was never within the realm of practical politics. British and German interests did not mesh; no true *quid pro quo* existed."[160]

The failed attempt was not without cost. The Kaiser and his government were annoyed with the British, and the press treatment of the discussions and negotiations fanned anti-British feeling in Germany. The British were no less annoyed. The Prime Minister, Lord Salisbury, said of the Kaiser that "there are dangers of his going off his head." Opinion in the Foreign Office grew that the Germans were ill disposed, fishing in troubled waters, and trying to squeeze something out of Britain at every opportunity. Thomas Sanderson, permanent undersecretary in the Foreign Office and sympathetic to Germany, complained of the growing hostility to Germany among his colleagues. Whenever they were mentioned he was forced "to labour to show that the conduct of the German government has in some material aspect been friendly. There is a settled dislike of them, and an impression that they are ready to play us any shabby trick they can."[161]

The failure of negotiations with Germany led the British to conclude a treaty with Japan in January 1902 in which each promised to assist the other if attacked in the Far East by two other powers. For the British it "prevented any Japanese alliance with Russia and added a barrier against any further Russian advance." Its immediate effect was to confirm Britain's isolation from the European continent by ending the necessity of seeking German support in defense of its interests in China. Its value as a way of limiting imperial responsibilities and freeing resources for European concerns only became apparent later. Still, the menace of the German Navy was becoming more obvious. The First Lord of the Admiralty, Lord Selborne, wrote: "I am convinced that the great new German navy is being carefully built up from the point of view of war with us. Sir F. Lascelles [ambassador to Germany] is equally convinced that in deciding on a naval policy we cannot safely ignore the malignant hatred of the German people or the manifest design of the German Navy."[162] The two-power standard limited to France and Russia, therefore, was no longer adequate, but cost put the notion of building to a three-power standard out of the question. As a result, "members of the Foreign Office and the public were beginning to argue that the only alternative left was a rapproachement with France, perhaps even with Russia also."[163]

When Bülow dismissed the idea of a British alliance with France or Russia he had history on his side. Throughout the second half of the nineteenth century the British had been in conflict with the Russians from the Balkans to the Far East, and at the turn of the century their rivalry was as hot as ever. France, of course, was Britain's traditional enemy. From the Hundred Years' War to the competition between Francis I and Henry VIII, to the contest with Louis XIV and his successors, to the long struggle against the Revolution and Napoleon, the British had fought the French. At the turn of the century they remained colonial rivals from Africa to the Far East. As Lord Palmerston frequently said, however, "England had no eternal friendships and no eternal enmities, but only 'eternal interests.'" Of these continuing interests the most basic were three: control of the seas, especially those around the British Isles; control of the Low Countries and their ports on the English Channel; and the prevention of control of Europe by a single power. At the turn of the century there was no chance that France or Russia would threaten any of these interests. No one yet foresaw any threat to the latter two, but Germany was emerging as a menace to the most basic interest of all: control of the seas.

THE ROAD TO WAR

This was the context in which Britain ended its estrangement from France, although the primary motive for the Entente Cordiale of 1904 was not the situation in Europe. In 1898 a force under Colonel Jean-Baptiste Marchand marching from the Congo to establish French claims in the Sudan on the upper Nile was met by a superior British force under General Horatio Kitchener at Fashoda. An armed clash and the possibility of a war between Britain and France was avoided when the new French Foreign Minister, Théophile Delcassé, repudiated Marchand and ordered him to withdraw. Delcassé, who would serve until 1905, the longest term for a foreign minister in the history of the Third Republic, had come to office with the intention of mending fences with the British.[164] The French colonialists, Delcassé among them, were eager to gain control of Morocco. He gained Italian approval for those ambitions in exchange for a free hand in Libya, and sought to get British approval, as well. The accession of the pro-French King Edward VII helped smooth the way, and the outbreak of the Russo-Japanese War in February 1904 lent urgency to the discussions, for neither party wanted to be dragged into a war by its ally. In April 1904 the old rivals signed a series of colonial agreements called the Entente Cordiale. Britain gave France some territory in Africa to end a dispute about fishing rights off Newfoundland, and the two states compromised disagreements in Siam and the New Hebrides. Most important of all, each side gave the other a free hand in Morocco and Egypt, respectively. The agreement was in no way an alliance and dealt only with colonial questions. Each state was free to conduct an independent policy, "but what was most important was the spirit of the Entente Cordiale. As it replaced the main source of friction between the two powers with a new cordiality it presaged an even closer union."[165]

The First Moroccan Crisis

Delcassé was eager to press forward with his plan to complete French control of Morocco. In January 1905 a French delegation went to Fez to propose a series of reforms that would have the effect of turning Morocco into a French protectorate. The Madrid Convention of 1880 supported the independence of Morocco and the principle of the "open door" to all nations who wished to do business there. Germany, as one of its signatories and guarantors, had a right to be consulted, but Delcassé had ignored the Germans, probably fearing they would object to his plans. No doubt, he thought that if he presented the Germans with a fait accompli they would have to accept it in the face of the acquiescence of the other powers.

This turned out to be a mistake. The Germans were annoyed and determined to exploit the situation. Since they had not been consulted about French plans for Morocco, they acted as though nothing had happened, treating Morocco as an independent country and waiting for the French to make them an offer regarding the protection of their commercial interests there and compensation for the advantages France had gained. When time passed and no offer came forth, Bülow persuaded the Kaiser, much against his will, to stop at Tangier during his cruise of the Mediterranean at the end of March 1905. There the Kaiser asserted Germany's equal rights in Morocco, its defense of free trade, and its support of Moroccan independence "and pointedly told the French consul that he knew how to defend German interests in Morocco and would expect the French to recognize that fact."[166] He had launched an international crisis.

It is far from clear what the Germans intended to achieve. Some have thought that Holstein, one of the shapers of Germany's Moroccan policy, aimed at war against France.[167] In this view, Holstein agreed with Schlieffen, who was worried that the plan of pursuing a world policy before Germany's control of the Continent was assured was a dangerous error. Schlieffen already had raised the spectre of a Germany encircled by enemies that haunted its leaders increasingly, until 1914, and he thought of preventive war:

> We are surrounded by an enormous coalition, we are in the same position as Frederick the Great before the Seven Years' War. Now we can escape from the noose. . . . [N]ow we can settle the account with our bitterest and most dangerous enemy, France, and would be fully justified in doing so.[168]

If such a plan really were contemplated the time could hardly have been better chosen. Russia experienced both military defeat and domestic revolution in 1905 and was in no condition to fight. The French Army and Navy were also not ready, and Great Britain was not yet committed to the defense of France in any way. Neither Bülow nor the Kaiser, however, wanted war. They may have sought to disrupt the new Anglo-French entente by diplomatic pressure, to gain prestige by the display of their power, to obtain territorial compensation, or merely to fish in troubled waters to see what they could catch.

Delcassé tried to conciliate the Germans by offering to maintain the open door policy as a protection to German commerce in Morocco. But the Germans insisted on calling an international conference to deal with the Moroccan question. Holstein and Bülow were confident that the display of German will and power would shatter the Entente, and according to the curious logic of German diplomacy in this period, even force the French to move closer to Germany. "The French," said Holstein, "will only consider approaching us when they see that English friendship is not enough to obtain Germany's consent to the French seizure of Morocco."[169] He and Bülow also were confident that a conference would turn out to Germany's liking. "It is out of the question," wrote the Chancellor, "that the conference should result in a majority handing over Morocco to France."[170]

The demand for a conference backfired. Delcassé had prepared the ground well, and the powers refused to accept a conference without French approval. The Germans then turned to intimidation. Although they made no military preparations, they talked of war and insisted on Delcassé's resignation. France's Prime Minister, Maurice Rouvier, feared an attack by Germany and believed that the dismissal of Delcassé would clear the way for better relations with Germany, which he favored. On June 6, 1905, Delcassé was forced to resign. On the same day, to reward the diplomatic triumph, the Kaiser raised Bülow to the rank of Prince.

The Germans, however, still would not recognize French control of Morocco and continued to insist on a conference that, in July, Rouvier was no longer able to resist. The conference on Morocco, the first such international conference for two decades, met at Algeciras in Spain from January to April 1906. To the surprise and dismay of the Germans only two of the thirteen attending nations, Austria–Hungary and Morocco, supported their position. The conference reaffirmed the independence and integrity of Morocco, but undermined that verbal assertion by its more practical actions. It gave control of the police to France and Spain and gave France the dominant position in the national bank, which amounted to the economic control of the country.

Germany's Moroccan adventure had ended in humiliating defeat. The French had gotten most of what they had wanted, and the Germans received nothing in return. In pressing their demands they frightened, angered, and alienated the French, saw Italy's unreliability as an ally publicly revealed, and instead of splitting the Entente, had made it stronger. Lord Lansdowne regarded it as a strictly colonial agreement; when the French pressed for British support in May 1905 he offered only that the two countries

> should continue to treat one another with the most absolute confidence, should keep one another fully informed of everything which came to their knowledge, and should, as far as possible, discuss in advance any contingency by which they might in the course of events find themselves confronted.[171]

He saw the fall of Delcassé as evidence of France's weakness and worried about its usefulness as an associate, but he continued to offer the French moral support.

When the Liberals gained control of the government in December 1905 Sir Edward Grey, the new Foreign Minister, felt the need to do more. Grey was an English gentleman from the north country who loved walks in the country and bird-watching. To many he seemed "a simple fisherman happier with his ducks than with the dispatch boxes."[172] But he was also a man of high principle and determined commitment to his rather traditional beliefs. He was devoted to the idea of the "concert of Europe" and, for all his gentle and tolerant demeanor, not a man to be bullied. The Liberals were Britain's "peace party" as compared with the Conservatives, and some members of the Cabinet were avowed pacifists. Grey, on the other hand, was a "Liberal Imperialist" who had supported the Conservative government's policy in the Boer War while the radical Liberals were opposing it. He promised to continue the general line taken by Lansdowne, but unlike him, he regarded Germany as Britain's most serious problem. As early as 1903 he said that Germany was "our worst enemy and greatest danger. I do not doubt that there are many Germans well disposed to us, but they are a minority; and the majority dislike us so intensely that the friendship of their Emperor, or their Government cannot be really useful to us."[173] During the crisis, moreover, he agreed that France could not be abandoned safely lest the European balance of power be upset, permitting Germany to gain effective domination of the continent.

At the same time, he knew that the pacific radicals, who were very powerful in the party, the Parliament, and the Cabinet, were opposed to any action that committed Britain in advance to military action. In part, his response was to consult little with the Cabinet and to say nothing to the Parliament or the public. For the rest, he followed a very tortuous policy that often seemed to offer a commitment with one hand and take it back with the other. Thus, he told the German ambassador in January 1906 that "the British people would not tolerate France's being involved in a war with Germany because of the Anglo-French agreement and in that case any English government, whether Conservative or Liberal, would be forced to help France."[174] Yet at the end of that same month he told the French ambassador not to expect the English people to risk a war to give France control of Morocco. If it seemed that Germany was forcing a war on France to break up the Entente, he said, public opinion would surely favor the French, but he could not be sure if that feeling would be enough to overcome the "great reluctance which exists amongst us now to find ourselves involved in a war."[175] To the French this must have seemed exasperatingly equivocal, but similar equivocations characterized Grey's statements and policies up to the war. They did not contribute to firm, well-coordinated measures that may reassure friends or to clear warnings that may deter enemies.

Even if the French believed in the reliability of a British commitment, the question remained, what could Britain do to help the French if they were attacked by Germany? The British Navy would be of little use in the kind of swift war, on the model of Prussia's victories, that was generally expected. As Rouvier pointed out during the crisis, "it could not run on wheels."[176] At the beginning of 1905 the British relied on their Navy alone to protect their native islands, and their Army, laughably small by Continental standards, was chiefly an imperial police force and garrison, most of it stationed to defend India. Not since the "war-in-sight" crisis of 1875 had the British any reason even to think of using their Army on the Continent, but the Moroccan crisis was the first step away from the unquestioned domination of the "blue water" school that relied entirely on the Navy for the defense of Britain and toward the Continental commitment that would place a British expeditionary force in defense of Belgium and France on the European Continent.

In the course of the crisis the General Staff considered the possibility of a German attack through Belgium and an appropriate British response:

> An efficient army of 120,000 troops might just have the effect of preventing important German successes on the Franco-German frontier and of leading up to the situation that Germany, crushed at sea, also felt itself impotent on land. That would almost certainly bring about a speedy and, from the British and French point of view, satisfactory peace.

This approach "was to shape British military planning until the outbreak of war."[177] In January 1906 Grey gave permission for talks between the British and French general staffs. After consulting with the King and the Prime Minister, he kept them secret from the rest of the Cabinet (they would not learn of them until 1911) on the debatable grounds that they represented no questions of policy since he insisted that they be "solely provisional and non-committal," but really because he feared the reaction of the radical majority. Grey insisted that the decision gave him greater freedom of action, "to be free to go to the help of France as well as free to stand aside." He compared the conversations to talks "between the London Fire Department and the Metropolitan Water Works,"[178] as the American President Franklin D. Roosevelt on the eve of the Second World War would explain the Lend-Lease Program of aid to Britain as the lending of a garden hose to a neighbor whose house was on fire. Both were homey similies meant to soften or conceal the dangers of commitments taken without formal consultation and approval.

In both cases, as also in Pericles's policy before the Peloponnesian War (see pp. 45ff.), it was an attempt to find a middle way meant to protect Britain's interests and security without making a firm alliance or commitment to fight. Critics would later blame Grey either for being too bold or too timid, but what is clear is that his decision committed Britain to a new policy and a new strategy that basically would guide British actions until the war. The British had concluded that their own safety was tied up with the fate of France, that "a second overthrow of France by Germany . . . would end in aggrandisement of Germany to an extent which would be prejudicial to the whole of Europe, and it might therefore be necessary for Great Britain in her own interests to lend France her active support should war of this nature break out."[179] A historian of European diplomacy has characterized the change and its significance well:

> Though the French accepted Grey's statement that "no British government will ever commit itself on a hypothesis," the talks were the substitute for an alliance—and in some ways a more decisive one. Once the British envisaged entering a continental war . . . they were bound to treat the independence of France . . . as the determining factor. The European Balance of power, which had been ignored for forty years, again dominated British foreign policy. . . . A vital change of emphasis followed. . . . In Salisbury's time, Great Britain made arrangements with European powers in order to defend her empire; now she made concessions outside of Europe in order to strengthen the Balance of Power. . . . The conflict over Morocco . . . was a true crisis, a turning point in European history. It shattered the long Bismarckian peace.[180]

The Triple Entente

Grey's private secretary wrote that "we must go to Algeciras, determined to back up the French and see them through," and that is exactly what Grey did, firmly supporting France all the way.[181] An agreement with France's ally, Russia, was a natural complement to such a policy, and Grey soon moved to achieve it. For a decade the British had been thinking about coming to some settlement with the Russians as a way of easing the pressure of their imperial responsibilities. Even after their defeat by Japan they remained Britain's major rival in Central Asia and a possible threat to India. Russia's continued expansion southward toward the Indian frontier led the government in India to demand great increases in military manpower and weapons that would be difficult to supply. The alternative was to ease the pressure by diplomatic means.

From the Russian perspective, defeat at the hands of the Japanese and the domestic revolution that had accompanied it produced a frightening sense of weakness. The cornerstone of the Russians' policy was the alliance with France, which protected them from the dangers of a German attack and, through loans floated by French bankers, provided them with vitally needed funds for military recovery and economic development. As the

French drew closer to England they tried to bring their Russian allies along with them, but establishing friendship between Russia and Britain was not easy. Apart from their traditional rivalry, the mutual distrust between the mother of parliamentary government—the homeland of liberalism—and the most reactionary of autocracies, as well as Britain's alliance with Japan, there was the fresh memory of the Dogger Bank incident. In 1904 the Russian fleet sailing for the Far East, mistaking some British fishing boats off Dogger Bank for Japanese warships, fired on them, almost bringing on a war. Seeking to take advantage of the resulting ill will, the Germans tried to make an alliance with Russia, first in 1904 and again in the summer of 1905. Their hope was to bring France into the agreement, too, to have a Continental alliance aligned against an isolated England. The second attempt, conducted by the Kaiser alone, without the knowledge of his Chancellor or Foreign Office experts, produced the Treaty of Björkö, signed by Tsar Nicholas II, likewise without the knowledge of his experts. The latter soon persuaded the Tsar that it was inconsistent with the French alliance and with Russian interests in general and persuaded him to back away from it. When compelled to make a choice, the Russian government "would opt for Paris rather than Berlin."[182]

After more than a year of difficult and complicated discussions the Russians and the British signed a convention on August 31, 1907, in which they agreed to settlements in Persia, Afghanistan, and Tibet meant to put an end to all colonial frictions. In this they were not entirely successful, for disagreements and quarrels resumed and continued right up to the war, but the shaky entente held, for the European situation required it. Since the Russians found it imperative to cling to France, they must face the prospect of German enmity, in which case they could not afford hostility from England. For the British, on the other hand, the entente with Russia, apart from relieving pressure on the Indian frontier, provided a check on Germany that promised to preserve the balance of power in Europe. For a long time Grey had hoped for a good relationship with Russia. In the midst of the Moroccan crisis he said, "An entente between Russia, France, and ourselves, would be absolutely secure. If it is necessary to check Germany it could then be done."[183] The British knew that their association with Russia would further alienate Germany, but their estimate of Germany's strength and purposes made them willing to take the risk. The view of British military leaders was that "Germany's avowed aims and ambitions are such that they seem bound, if persisted in, to bring her into armed collision with us sooner or later, and therefore a little more or less enmity on her part is not a matter of great importance."[184] Grey himself did not think an armed clash was inevitable, nor did he abandon the idea of conciliation. The heart of his policy, however, although the term was not yet current, was deterrence, and the new "Triple Entente" was central to that policy.

The Anglo-Russian entente was the final nail in the coffin of the new course undertaken for the Kaiser by Holstein and Bülow. Instead of intimidating Britain into complaisance with Germany's global aims the construction of a menacing battle fleet had produced a diplomatic revolution and a new alignment the Germans had thought inconceivable. Instead of opening the way to the high seas and *Weltpolitik* the new policy left the Germans with only one ally, the troubled Austro-Hungarian Empire. Increasingly, they spoke of being victims of *Einkreisung,* encirclement by their enemies. The problem, however, was of Germany's own making. What the Germans saw as their encirclement "is more aptly described as a reactive policy of containment; in effect Germany had 'circled herself out' of the great power concert."[185] By their own misguided efforts the Germans had turned against themselves Bismarck's formula of always being one of three states in a system of five.

The Naval Race

Since Germany's new policy was proving disastrous both in its foreign and domestic goals, it might seem reasonable to change, or even reverse it. A naval agreement with Britain, for instance, would have gone a long way toward easing the tension, but the Kaiser would not consider it. In the next few years the naval race intensified greatly and played a central role in alienating Britain and solidifying the Triple Entente. In the early years of the German naval build up few in Britain paid much attention, but soon alarmed concern reached the popular level. Beginning in 1871 a series of thrillers depicting imaginary wars in which the French invaded England gained wide popularity. In 1903 for the first time a very successful one made the Germans the invaders, and a series of novels and plays continued the theme for years. In 1906 William Le Queux's *The Invasion of 1910* began to appear in serial form in the *Daily Mail.* It depicted an invasion in which a ferociously brutal German army sweeps easily to victory. It sold a million copies and made a deep impression. Nor did it escape the attention of the

Foreign Office, where Sir Francis Bertie asserted that "the Germans' aim is to push us into the water and steal our clothes."[186]

By 1904 the Conservatives began responding to the German program by proposing the construction of four large armored ships annually. In October of the same year the promotion of Admiral Sir John Fisher to the position of First Sea Lord gave a great boost to the growth and improvement of the British fleet. Dispositions of the fleet were changed to concentrate them in European waters, training in gunnery and other battle tactics was vastly improved, outmoded ships were removed from service, recruiting techniques were revolutionized, and Fisher's formidable skills in politics and publicity, which, in some minds, made him the British Tirpitz, were set to work gaining support for building a great fleet.

Fisher's best known innovation was the introduction of a new type of warship, HMS *Dreadnought,* and his decision to base Britain's naval power and security on a fleet composed of these big, fast battleships armed with big guns, all of the same calibre. After the war Tirpitz claimed that Fisher's introduction of the *Dreadnought* was a mistake, because it wiped out Britain's numerical lead and gave its competitors the opportunity to begin anew only slightly behind the British. But Fisher had little choice. The Japanese had destroyed the Russian fleet at Tsushima with ships that were faster and had larger guns than their opponents', and they, the Russians, and the Americans were known to be planning or building bigger and faster ships on the new model. General advances in naval technology, quite apart from thoughts about the German rivalry, required the change.

The introduction of the *Dreadnought,* however, was a terrible blow to Tirpitz's plans; to the quantitative arms race Fisher had added a very costly qualitative element: "The news of this new ship not only rendered obsolete all of his recently-built battleships, but it upset all his design and construction calculations for a certain while. And, when he decided to follow up with German dreadnoughts, the cost was appalling."[187]

Here was one of those critical moments when the Germans had to decide whether to continue the race after most of the assumptions underlying the Tirpitz plan had been undermined by events, when the cost of naval construction was putting a severe strain on the internal stability of the political system and the crown itself, or of curtailing the naval program and trying to reach an accord with England. The decision was to go foward. In 1906 Tirpitz presented a supplementary naval bill that included building six new cruisers, changing to dreadnought battleships, and the prolongation of the annual three-battleship tempo for an additional seven years, among other costly additions.[188]

In Britain the Liberal party was committed to cuts in defense spending as part of their plan for increasing expenditure for social services. They were pleased with Fisher, whose elimination of outmoded ships and concentration of naval forces at first saved money. The Liberals' reaction to the increase in German naval construction was to seek an arms limitation agreement and unilaterally to scale back Britain's own program to only three battleships for 1907–8 instead of the four originally scheduled. Then the radicals in the Cabinet persuaded the government to delay starting even one of those "as a gesture to the forthcoming Hague Peace Conference."[189] The Germans rejected the idea of disarmament talks; instead, in November 1907 they announced a new supplement to the Naval Law providing for four dreadnoughts annually instead of three for the years 1908–9 through 1911–12 and reduced the time of replacement from twenty-five to twenty years. As U. S. Secretary of Defense Harold Brown would later say of the missile race with the Soviet Union, "We have found that when we build weapons, they build. When we stop, they nevertheless continue to build."[190] In 1908 the Kaiser's comment on an ambassador's report demonstrated his determination to continue his naval policy at any cost:

> I have no desire for a good relationship with England at the price of the development of Germany's Navy. If England will hold out her hand in friendship only on condition that we limit our Navy, it is a boundless impertinence and a gross insult to the German people and their Emperor. . . . The [Navy] Law will be carried out to the last detail; whether the British like it or not does not matter! If they want war, they can begin it, we do not fear it![191]

Between 1908 and 1912 the naval rivalry dominated the relationship between the two countries and also played an important role in domestic political arguments in England. The dispute over the meaning of Germany's swiftly growing navy and the correct response to it divided the British public, the two major parties, and the ruling Liberal party itself. Some minimized the importance of the German Navy and saw no need for a British response. In 1910, for instance, *The Economist* asserted that "the German fleet which has struck such panic is largely imaginary, and the supposed danger is entirely due to the fact that the Admiralty invented the Dreadnought and fostered the impression that this type of ship had super-seded all others."[192] Eyre Crowe of the Foreign Office, on the other hand, thought such talk contributed to Britain's problem: "The more we talk of the necessity of economising on our armaments, the more firmly will Germans believe that we are tiring of the struggle, and that they will win by going on."[193]

The years 1908 and 1909 saw a naval scare in Britain. There were frequent warnings in the press of a "bolt from the blue" in the form of a German surprise attack on the fleet and an invasion. The Kaiser made matters worse in an interview with an unnamed Englishman that was published in the *Daily Telegraph* in October 1908. "You English," he said, "are mad, mad as March hares" for thinking that the German Navy was directed against Britain. The Kaiser was England's friend and wanted to restrain the majority of Germans who were hostile, but English suspicions made his task difficult, he said, among several other indiscreet and irritating remarks. "Never," said Grey, "since I have been in office has opinion here been so thoroughly wide awake with regard to Germany, and on its guard as it is now."[194]

The extreme navalists insisted on laying down eight new dread-noughts in the 1909 budget—"We want eight, and we won't wait!" was their slogan. The First Lord of the Admiralty proposed six, splitting the Liberal Cabinet. The "economists," led by David Lloyd George and Win-ston Churchill, argued that four would be enough. Grey threatened to resign unless the six were approved. Herbert Asquith, the new Prime Minister, found an acceptable compromise: four ships would be begun at once and the other four later in the year, if German behavior justified it. The debate in Parliament caused great alarm in the country, and rumors circulated that the Germans were secretly increasing their capacity to build warships and using it to accelerate the growth of their fleet. Finally, in July 1909, news that the Austrians and Italians were building dreadnoughts led to the decision to build the remaining four. In Churchill's words: "The Admiralty had demanded six ships: the economists offered four: and we finally compromised on eight."[195] Years later Churchill rightly insisted that his opponents' arguments had been overstated and their fears excessive, "but, although the Chancellor of the Exchequer and I were right in the narrow sense we were absolutely wrong in relation to the deep tides of destiny. The greatest credit is due to the First Lord of the Admiralty, Mr.

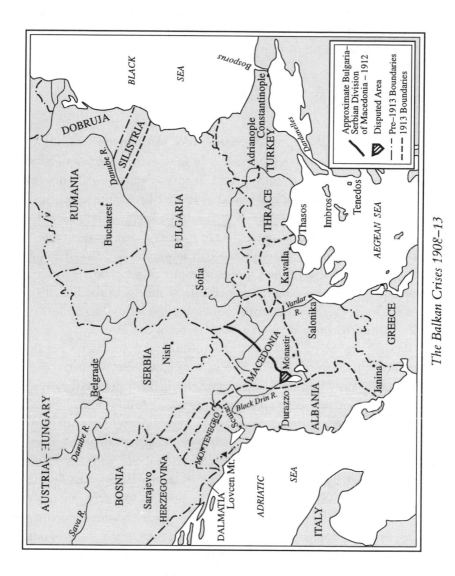

The Balkan Crises 1908–13

Legend:
- Approximate Bulgaria–Serbian Division of Macedonia – 1912
- Disputed Area
- Pre-1913 Boundaries
- 1913 Boundaries

McKenna, for the resolute and courageous manner in which he fought the case and withstood his Party on this occasion."[196] That view is endorsed by the leading naval historian of the period: "Had the four contingent ships not been approved in 1909, in January 1915 the Grand Fleet would have had only twenty-one capital ships available . . . to fight Germany's twenty. In a word, it was the contingent four capital ships of 1909 that gave the Navy its rather bare margin of security in the critical early months of the war."[197]

The Bosnian Crisis

The great naval debate in Britain took place in the context of a serious international crisis in the Balkans. In spite of their mutual suspicions and conflicting ambitions Russia and Austria-Hungary had not only avoided military conflict but had joined in alliance from time to time in the 1870s and 1880s as part of Bismarck's system for keeping the peace. Even after Bismarck's dismissal, as late as 1897, they had joined in an entente that lasted down to 1908. It was motivated by the mutual fear that the apparently imminent collapse of the Ottoman Empire might produce incalculable consequences threatening to each empire's interests in the Balkans and Near East. Each preferred to work to preserve the status quo and its own position rather than to risk all in a new throw of the dice.

Russia's defeat by Japan and the revolution it produced began to change the situation in 1905–6. The defeat caused the Russians to turn their attention away from Asia and toward the Balkans, where they sought to pursue their interest more vigorously and regain lost prestige. The Russians tried to bring the British into Balkan questions to help restrain Austria.[198] The situation was changed further by the advent of a new Foreign Minister in each country in 1906, Baron Alois Lexa von Aerenthal in Austria and Alexander Izvolsky in Russia. Aerenthal planned to deal with the south Slav agitation that came from Serbia and Montenegro and disturbed the provinces of Bosnia and Herzegovina by bolder action in the Balkans. His idea was to annex Bosnia and Herzegovina formally, nominally under Turkish suzerainty but occupied by Austria-Hungary since the Treaty of Berlin in 1878. He thought that with the provinces formally part of Austria, the Serbs would give up hope of gaining them in the event of the collapse of Turkey and with it their schemes for a "greater Serbia" or a Serbian-based Yugoslavia. Over the years Austria had gained theoretical approval for annexing the provinces from Germany, Italy, and Russia. Aerenthal was eager to demonstrate Austria's independence and vitality, although he hoped not to disrupt the entente with Russia and counted on its current weakness to gain its approval.

Izvolsky was eager to mend fences in all directions to give a badly weakened Russia time to recover from its recent reverses. He negotiated the entente with England in 1907 but also an agreement with Germany to keep peace in the Baltics, and he was careful to assure the Austrians of his continued cooperation. Russia "was not in a position to challenge anybody, and [Prime Minister] Stolypin's demand for twenty years of peace to crush the revolution at home had the force of law in the Foreign Office."[199] At the same time, Izvolsky was alert for any opportunity through diplomacy to gain an advantage and restore Russia's prestige.

The trigger for action was the rebellion of the Young Turks who took power in Constantinople in July 1908. The Young Turk movement was liberal, forcing a constitution on the Sultan and talking of democracy, but even more, it was nationalistic. Its leaders hoped to reinvigorate Turkey and regain control of places like Bulgaria, Crete, Macedonia, Bosnia, and Herzegovina. By August rumor was rife that the Turks were planning action to regain Bosnia and Herzegovina. In reaction, the Catholic population of those provinces clamored for the granting of a constitution and annexation to Austria. On August 19 the Austrian government decided to announce the annexation of the two provinces at the first convenient moment. They also agreed to withdraw from the sanjak of Novibazar, a corridor running southeast from Bosnia, separating Serbia from Montenegro deemed militarily indefensible, which could be presented as a concession to Turkey.[200] Aerenthal intended to act without consulting the other powers, merely informing them of his action a few days before taking it.

Russia, however, required different treatment, not merely because of its special interest in the Balkans, but because Izvolsky himself had raised the question of annexation in an earlier note. Izvolsky saw that circumstances might impel the Austrians to annex the provinces. He knew that Russia was in no condition to prevent it and hoped, instead, to gain compensation in the form of a change in the status of the Straits. Instead of being prevented from sending Russian warships into the Aegean, as they currently were, he wanted free access for the Russians while barring it to all but the nations bordering the Straits and the Black Sea. The Russo-Japanese War had illustrated the great disadvantage of having a fleet locked up in the Black Sea in wartime, and a recent closure of the passage for a few months by Turkey had done terrible harm to the Russian economy, for many of Russia's exports, especially grain from the Ukraine, used that route. It was entirely understandable, therefore that the Russians should be eager to revise the rules governing passage of the Straits, and it was one of Nicholas II's most deeply desired goals. The recent entente with Britain, moreover, promised to remove a major barrier to achieving that goal. Izvolsky, therefore, obtained the Tsar's permission to suggest the quid pro quo.

In mid-September 1908 Aerenthal and Izvolsky met at Buchlau, the Bohemian estate of Count Leopold Berchtold, Austria's ambassador to Russia.[201] Although there was some heated argument, there appears to have been agreement on several points: Austria would annex the provinces and withdraw from the sanjak; Bulgaria would receive complete and formal independence from Turkey; and the Austrians would support Russia's claims at the Straits and help persuade Germany to accept them, as well. Although Izvolsky, aware of the strong Pan-Slav sentiments in the Duma, the press, and other powerful circles in Russia, had proposed concessions and compensations to Serbia and Montenegro as well, these were not agreed to. Questions of timing would later take on great importance, but there seems to have been no clear statement about it. There was no doubt, however, that the announcement of the annexation would be made before the meeting of the Austro-Hungarian Delegations early in October. Izvolsky continued on his tour of Western capitals seeking support for his plan for the Straits, expecting, no doubt, that Aerenthal would warn him before announcing the annexation.

Even before the announcement, however, things began to go wrong. On October 2 the details of the Buchlau agreement were revealed to the Russian Council of Ministers for the first time. The Russian constitution left foreign affairs entirely in the hands of the Tsar and his Foreign Minister. Besides, Izvolsky knew that Stolypin and other influential ministers liked the idea of cooperation with Austria, so he expected no trouble. He was badly mistaken, for Stolypin and the others were appalled by what they took to be a betrayal of the Slav cause and uninterested in the question of the Straits. Under their onslaught the Tsar falsely disclaimed any knowledge of Izvolsky's doings, and his opponents sent a message to the Foreign Minister denouncing his arrangement and ordering him to reverse his policy. He was to reject the annexation as a violation of the Treaty of Berlin and to demand an international conference to review it. Izvolsky sent a defiant telegram in return pointing out that nothing could stop the annexation, since even his critics were not prepared to fight: an empty denunciation was worth nothing. It would be better to acquiesce and seek a valuable compensation. The Russian press, however, assaulted him and the agreement, and the Tsar deserted him, even while allowing him to continue to seek support for the opening of the Straits.

Other surprises were the announcement by Bulgaria of its independence from Turkey on October 5 and the announcement of the annexation of Bosnia-Herzegovina on the next day, without any warning. Aerenthal had encouraged the Bulgarians, in the hope of diverting attention from the annexation, but he had denied any knowledge of their intentions when questioned by the British. When the two actions occurred almost simultaneously everyone thought they were parts of an Austrian plot to dismember what remained of the Ottoman Empire. The British, particularly, were annoyed, for they placed great hopes in the Young Turks both for their reputed liberalism and because their pro British feelings promised to give Great Britain primacy in Turkey at the expense of Germany. For the remainder of the growing crisis they would be suspicious and hostile to Aerenthal and fiercely supportive of Turkish interests.

Izvolsky received word of the annexation in Paris and was outraged. His policy had been disavowed by his government and by Russian public opinion, and he felt betrayed by Aerenthal's action without warning, before Izvolsky could achieve his part of their deal, and he was afraid that Aerenthal would reveal the details of their bargain showing his complicity in the annexation and his willingness to surrender Serbian and Montenegrin interests to achieve his purpose. For the rest of the crisis he would work to salvage what he could by denouncing Austria's action and demanding an international conference and by seeking revision of the Straits agreement and compensation for Serbia and Montenegro. The Austro-Russian entente was dead, replaced by a bitter hostility that would last until the outbreak of war.

Izvolsky was able to get Britain and France to join him in a call for a conference, but he was badly disappointed by the behavior of these entente partners. The French wanted Austrian help in a dispute they were having with the Germans in Morocco and made it clear the Russians could expect little support from them. Various British leaders, including Lord Grey, had said on several occasions that they would not stand in the way of Russia's desire to gain access to the Straits, but in response to Izvolsky's request, Grey refused. He was unwilling to humiliate the Turks further and insisted that the Russians wait until some unspecified later occasion before raising the question again. He stood in Izvolsky's path in yet another way, as well. Izvolsky must have expected that compensation for Serbia and Montenegro, needed to quiet the uproar in Russia, could be extorted from Turkey, but once again Grey would not have it. Even as the crisis deepened and the threat of war seemed real he insisted both that the Serbs should be compensated and that the compensation should come at the expense of Austria, not Turkey. It is possible that the crisis could have come to a much earlier end at a lesser cost in mutual suspicion and hostility had Grey not chosen to play so important a role in events so far from home, had he agreed to allow the Russians to put forward their claim to the Straits and to permit compensation for the Serbs at Turkish expense. He was, however, furious with Aerenthal, whom he thought a cheat and a liar, eager to support the Russians in the matter of Serbian compensation to demonstrate the solidarity of the entente, yet determined to pursue the Turkish opportunity by championing the interests of the Young Turks. As it happened, his hopes in the Young Turks were misplaced, as he ruefully admitted years later: "Those who knew Turkey well warned us that the 'young' Turks . . . were much like the 'old' Turks, but it was so pleasant to indulge the larger hope that I would not heed these warnings. The sequel destroyed the hopes and underlined the warnings."[202] One can sympathize with Grey's feelings and concerns and yet find fault with his policy. However unpleasant the deal between Russia and Austria, the tearing up of international agreements, riding roughshod over the claims of Turkey, Serbia, and Montenegro, Britain's interests, and Europe's too, lay in peace in the Balkans, and that would best be served by a continuance of the entente between Russia and Austria. Grey should have understood that and acquiesced in the changes that by common understanding and by his own admission were, in any case, inevitable. Instead, with no direct interest in the issues, as he admitted, and with no intention of committing British forces or resources to their resolution, he helped prevent a peaceful outcome. It was not the last time that the ambiguity of his policies would cause trouble.

The Germans were also taken by surprise by the annexation, and the Kaiser's first response was indignation at not being told in advance and at the threat it posed to their interests in Turkey. But Bülow argued that Germany could not afford to abandon Austria:

Our position would indeed be dangerous if Austria lost confidence and turned away. So long as we stand together, we form a bloc that no one will lightly attack. In eastern questions above all, we cannot place ourselves in opposition to Austria who has nearer and greater interests in the Balkan peninsula than ourselves. A refusal or a grudging attitude in the question of annexation of Bosnia and Hercegovina would not be forgiven.[203]

Austria's Chief of Staff, Franz Conrad von Hötzendorf, long an advocate of preventive war against Italy and Serbia to establish and safeguard Austria's predominance in the region, seized the opportunity to begin military conversations with his opposite number in Germany, Helmut von Moltke (the younger). In January 1909 he asked what the German Army would do if Austria invaded Serbia and the Russians then attacked Austria. Moltke replied: "that would be the *casus foederis* for Germany. . . . As soon as Russia mobilizes Germany will mobilize, too, and with its whole army."[204] Within a week the Kaiser had assured Emperor Franz Josef that "Austria-Hungary's interests are most closely tied to ours and her enemies are our enemies."[205]

Moltke also pointed out the strategic implications of German support. A war resulting from the Austro-Russian conflict in the Balkans would not be confined to that region. The Schlieffen plan required that if Germany came to Austria's aid against Russia, it would assume that the French would mobilize in support of their Russian allies, and the Germans would attack in the west. A Balkan war, therefore, because of Germany's strategic decision, would inevitably mean a war on the entire continent, and the violation of Belgium required by the plan would probably also bring Britain in as well. The Kaiser and the Chancellor were fully informed of Moltke's communications with Conrad and made no objection. The Bosnian crisis revealed how thoroughly the new regime had rejected Bismarck's policies. He had insisted on alliances with both Russia and Austria in order to keep control of the two states most likely to produce a European war, but the new course broke with Russia. Bismarck had insisted on the unimportance to Germany of Balkan and Near Eastern questions; he checked Austrian adventures, and made it clear that Germany was bound to defend Austria only if it was attacked. The new course made Austria's Balkan quarrels Germany's own, made no objections to an Austrian attack on Serbia, and promised military support if the Austrians did so. "In effect,

Moltke had changed the treaty of 1879 from a defensive to an offensive treaty and placed his country at the mercy of the adventurers in Vienna."[206]

The crisis dragged on until the end of March 1909. In spite of pressure, chiefly from Britain, Aerenthal, firmly backed by Germany and confident that Russia would not fight because it could not, refused to make concessions. He would not agree to an international conference unless his actions were approved in advance, nor would he grant any compensation either to Turkey or to Serbia. In January, at last, Austria agreed to make a money payment to the Turks, and that part of the crisis subsided. The Serbian problem was more difficult. Immediately after the annexation the Serbian press launched bitter attacks against Austria, the government supported the formation of a nationalistic, anti-Austrian organization called *Narodna Odbrana* (National Defense) and mobilized the Serbian Army. Conrad was given permission to mobilize additional forces and to bring the army of the Dual Monarchy to a heightened state of readiness. At once and throughout the crisis he pressed for a military attack on Serbia that would wipe it from the map and end the South Slav threat to the empire. Given the incapacity and unwillingness of the Triple Entente powers to fight and Austria's overwhelming military superiority over Serbia and Montenegro, there was little question of the outcome.[207] Franz Josef and Aerenthal, however, were opposed both to the expense and the risks of war. Aerenthal meant to achieve the suppression of the Serbian menace by humiliating Serbia and then bringing it under Austrian power by economic means. At the end of February he insisted that Serbia accept the annexation, put an end to anti-Austrian agitation, and promise to live at peace with Austria in return for some economic concessions. On March 15 the Serbs refused "in a note that was considered insolent and unacceptable even in London and St. Petersburg."[208]

At this point even Aerenthal was ready to go to war. The British ambassador to Vienna tried to find a way out of the impasse, but Grey adamantly rejected the result of his efforts. Finally, the Russians collapsed. Terrified at the prospect of an Austrian attack that would humiliate and possibly eliminate Serbia while the Russians looked on helplessly, Izvolsky asked for German mediation to provide him with a dignified way out. Instead, the Germans responded "with a brutality that the situation did not require."[209] Their ambassador was told to demand the immediate acceptance of Austria's claims and to tell Izvolsky "that we expect an answer—

yes or no; we must regard any evasive, conditional, or unclear answer as a refusal. We would then draw back and let things take their course. The responsibility for further events would then fall exclusively on M. Izvolsky."[210] In the face of this ultimatum the Russians capitulated, and the British were reluctantly compelled to abandon their objections. Serbia was forced to capitulate totally, recognizing that none of its rights had been injured, to accept the annexation, to reduce her army to its precrisis level, to disarm and dismiss volunteers, and "to live henceforth on a good-neighborly footing."[211]

The crisis was over. Bülow claimed that it had "torn the encirclement net to pieces."[212] The Kaiser boasted that Germany had stood by its ally "in shining armor," and the Germans and Austrians congratulated themselves on their success, but they had gained a Pyrrhic victory. If Aerenthal wanted to demonstrate Austria's strength and independence, Germany's decisive intervention demonstrated the opposite. If the chief goal of the annexation was to put an end to trouble from Serbia as a hostile center of Yugoslav agitation, it was a failure. The Serbs resolved their quarrels with Montenegro, and the two states strengthened their military and political ties to Russia. They were bitterly eager for revenge, so in spite of their promises, they intensified anti-Austrian propaganda, permitted and supported the work of *Narodna Odbrana* and more extreme organizations, which carried on terrorist activities within the empire. "From here the road led straight to Sarajevo."[213]

The most important consequence of the crisis was its effect on the Russians, who were determined never to be humiliated in the same way again. Even during the crisis Izvolsky had responded to Aerenthal's threat to use force with the warning that "the Eastern Question cannot be resolved except by a conflict. . . . Perhaps this conflict will not break out for five or ten years, but it is inevitable."[214] In April 1909 the German ambassador in St. Petersburg, Russia, reported that

> our Russian and non-Russian enemies here have coined the slogan: Germany has used Russia's present weakness and the general European wish for peace to humiliate Russia and force her capitulation to Baron Aerenthal by the clumsy threat that otherwise she will impose her will by force of arms. . . . This talk, for the moment, does not fail to have effect. The legend that Germany threatened her with the "mailed fist" finds credence in wide circles

and has for the moment made feeling run high against us, even in circles usually well-disposed to us.[215]

Conrad, still eager to fight a preventive war against Serbia, warned his emperor that "Russia cannot and will not accept this diplomatic failure— but instead will bring its armed forces back to their full level if only for reasons of prestige,"[216] and he was right. To avoid another such humiliation the Russians set out to bolster the Triple Entente, but even more to strengthen their military forces. The Duma voted a large increase in funds for the army in 1908, raised the amount still higher in 1909, maintained that high level for two more years, and raised it further in 1912 and 1913. The Russian Army was galvanized into action, reorganizing its mobilization plans, improving its deployment and supply and training of troops, and modernizing its weapons and equipment. By 1910 a Prussian General Staff report said, "The reorganization has brought the Russian army a more unified structure and a better provision of curved-trajectory artillery and technical troops; and hence altogether a significant increase in preparedness," and Austrian intelligence called the changes "such a vast and radical enactment of army reforms as would scarcely have been possible anywhere else."[217] In the final crisis that resulted in the First World War German civilian and military officials would think and talk often about their fear of Russia's growing military might, which led some of them to seek preventive war before it was too late for Germany to have a chance and others to accept the war with resignation on the same grounds. They had themselves chiefly to blame for "ignoring the good diplomatic rule that defeated enemies should be given a golden bridge across which to retire with honour"[218] during the Bosnian crisis.

By insisting on gaining his ends by the open threat of force, yet without the cost and risk of war, Aerenthal committed an error all too common in history. As the Athenians' intervention against Corinth and their embargo against Megara infuriated their objects without rendering them impotent, leaving them angry and potentially dangerous, so the Austro-German treatment of Serbia and Russia had the same effect. A soft answer to Izvolsky's appeal for a dignified retreat might have had a conciliatory effect, but even an effective attack on Serbia, with all its costs and dangers, might have been better than the terrible middle path taken, which left the Russians angry and increasingly able to seek vengeance. Both sides appear to have learned lessons from the crisis, but they were dangerously at odds. The Austrians and Germans knew that by standing together and threatening the use of force they had achieved their goals and forced the Serbs and Russians to back down. In the final crisis of 1914 some of their leaders expected the same result. The Russians looked at the same experience but drew different conclusions:

> In 1914 Austria again threatened unilateral action against Serbia and on 29 July Germany again intervened in Petersburg to demand that the Russians cease their military preparations and thus capitulate to Austrian pressure. Sazonov's furious refusal of Pourtalès' [the German ambassador at St. Petersburg] demand both reflected the extent to which Russian ruling circles had felt their previous humiliation in March 1909 and showed their determination not to knuckle under to Germany a second time.[219]

The Bosnian crisis was a crucial step on the road to war. By putting an end to the Austro-Russian entente, the substitute the two empires had evolved in place of Bismarck's system for keeping the peace, it produced a situation in which future Balkan troubles would always find them at odds. By its staunch and brutal support of its ally and by adopting the strategy of the Schlieffen Plan, Germany encouraged the newly emerged system of competing associations and guaranteed that a war between any two states would embroil them all. Scholars still ask: how did it happen that a Balkan dispute led to a world war? The outcome of the Bosnian crisis is an important part of the answer.

Agadir: The Second Moroccan Crisis

The Bosnian crisis raised European rivalries to a new level of intensity. It is hard to disagree with the view that "the Bosnian crisis first showed Europe the shadow of a general war,"[220] for between 1909 and 1911 the powers certainly drew back as if they had been frightened by such a shadow. The Germans backed away from their promise of unconditional support to Austria, and Bethmann Hollweg, the new Chancellor who succeeded Bülow in July 1909, tried to arrive at a détente with the British. The Austrians abandoned their aggressive ways and resorted again to diplomacy, and each member of the Triple Entente tried to mend fences with the Germans. They made an agreement with the Germans about Russian railroads in northern Persia and the German Baghdad railroad, which worried Great Britain. The British tried to reach a naval and political accommodation with Germany. The French had deserted their Russian ally during the Bosnian crisis, and an important faction in France sought an accommodation with Germany. The Triple Entente seemed to be falling apart, but it was brought back to life by Germany's reaction to France's Moroccan ambitions.

In April 1911 France sent an army to Fez, under siege from insurgent tribesmen. The condition of Morocco really was approaching anarchy, but the French acted without consulting Germany and Spain, and their continued occupation of Fez also went beyond what was permitted by the Act of Algeciras and the Franco-German agreement of 1909. It was clear that the French intended to use the incident as a pretext for making Morocco their protectorate, presenting the matter as a fait accompli. It was a reckless and risky action by the colonialist element in the French government and quickly sparked a crisis. Alfred von Kiderlen-Wächter, German State Secretary in the Foreign Office since 1910, had a plan for using the French coup in Morocco to gain territorial concessions elsewhere in Africa, perhaps in the Congo. He warned the French that a lengthy occupation of Fez would violate the Algeciras agreement, but then said nothing more for over a month. Sir Arthur Nicolson, the new permanent undersecretary in the Foreign Office, rightly divined his purpose: "I expect that Germany calculates that in that time France will have plunged herself up to her neck in Moorish affairs and that the moment will have arrived for Germany to step in and demand her price."[221]

Kiderlen was seeking a success both for the conduct of his foreign policy and for domestic purposes, in light of the disarray of the Triple Entente, which appeared to leave the French isolated, especially in a colonial dispute in which they were plainly in the wrong. Part of his plan appears to have been to impress the French with Germany's strength and determination as a preliminary step to an accord. "He had only to take a firm line and France would pay; when opinion in both countries would be satisfied, and a lasting reconciliation would follow."[222] The other part was to reverse the diplomatic defeat of Algeciras and raise German prestige. Accordingly, he made it clear that Germany expected compensation: "bring us something back from Paris," he told the French ambassador on June 21. To his own people he explained, "It is necessary to thump the table. However, the only object of this is to make the French negotiate."[223]

The domestic goal was to stem the tide that was running strongly against the government and the political groups supporting it. In 1909 the demands of the naval program had driven Bülow to attempt a tax reform thoroughly unpopular with the agrarian Conservatives. The result was the destruction of the "Bülow bloc," the latest version of the *Sammlung* of "respectable" parties against the Socialists. The failure guaranteed Bülow's dismissal from office, alienated the commercial and industrial groups, and left the political scene splintered into three groups: Conservatives, middle parties, and Social Democrats. Adolph Wermuth, State Secretary of the Reich Treasury, wrote to Tirpitz "that the internal structure of the Reich, its defence capabilities and its internal prestige demand not merely a standstill, but an energetic reduction of [our] expenditure. . . . [Otherwise] the development will end inescapably in the complete collapse of our finances and all national activities stemming from them."[224] *Weltpolitik* and the naval program had not brought about a safe and sound union of non-Socialist parties that could protect the monarchy and the old order. Instead it had produced economic crisis and political disaster in the form of a shattering of friendly political forces and the rapid growth of the Social Democrats. Had these policies been undertaken to achieve domestic ends their proponents ought to have abandoned them when it became obvious, as it was at least as early as 1909, that they were having the opposite effect.

The new Chancellor, Bethmann, understood the situation and sought to reach an agreement with England that included limitations on the German Navy, but Tirpitz opposed him and could count ultimately on the Kaiser's support. In 1911 Tirpitz introduced another very expensive supplementary naval bill that heightened the arms race and the domestic crisis. In July 1910 Albert Ballin, managing director of the Hamburg-American shipping lines and a friend of the Kaiser, wrote: "we are in the midst of a revolution today, for the fact that all by-elections to the Reichstag return Social Democrats supports the conclusion that a great change is in the making."[225] He and others looked to some foreign policy success to help turn the tide and, to some extent, this was also a motive for Kiderlen.

On July 1, 1911, the German gunboat *Panther* anchored off Agadir, a Moroccan port on the Atlantic Ocean. France's response was fuzzy, because of divisions within the government. The Foreign Office was dominated by aggressive young men ready to challenge Germany. The Prime Minister, Joseph Caillaux, on the other hand, was deeply committed to a rapprochement with Germany, although determined to make Morocco thoroughly French. He also had no confidence that Russia and Britain would provide military support against Germany. His idea was to conduct secret negotiations with the Germans, make concessions outside of Morocco, and come to a peaceful general agreement. Since this was very much in the direction pursued by Kiderlen there is reason to believe that a less bellicose approach might have achieved acceptable compensation for Germany without a crisis. What Kiderlen wanted, however, was a visible success, a demonstration of German power, a gesture of respect and a gain in prestige, and that called for open intimidation.

On learning of "the Panther's leap" the anti-German French Foreign Minister, Justin de Selves, undeterred by Caillaux's disapproval, asked the British to respond by sending a warship to Mogador, a port near Agadir. Britain's reaction was complicated. The Foreign Office, deeply suspicious of Germany, saw the German action as a threat to the Entente meant to force France to Germany's side, destroying the balance of power in Europe. Eyre Crowe, the office's German expert and its most anti-German member, stated their view forcefully:

> Germany is playing for the highest stakes. If her demands are acceded to either in the Congo or in Morocco or—what she will, I believe, try for—in both regions, it will mean definitely the subjection of France. The conditions demanded are not such as a country having an independent foreign policy can possibly accept. The details of the terms are not so very important now. It is a trial of strength, if anything. Concession means not loss of interest or loss of prestige. It means defeat with all its inevitable consequences.

Nicolson spelled out what those consequences would be: the collapse of "our policy since 1904 of preserving the equilibrium and consequently the peace in Europe."[226] They wanted Grey to send a gunboat to Morocco.

At the other end of the spectrum was the Cabinet led by the radical Liberals, especially Lords Loreburn and Morley. Inclined toward isolationism and disarmament, they tended to sympathize with Germany and to resist strong support of France and Russia, especially in colonial matters. Unlike the Foreign Office officials and Grey, they were suspicious of and little concerned with questions of the balance of power, counting on reasonableness and restraint to keep the peace. In this crisis, unlike the first Moroccan crisis, the Cabinet played an important part. They met on July 4 and instructed Grey as to Britain's policy: they would meet the obligations of the 1904 agreement with France by lending diplomatic support only; they strongly hinted that the French should offer something to the Germans; they were prepared even to concede the Germans an unfortified commercial port on the Atlantic coast of Morocco.[227]

Grey stood between the extremes. He was staunch for support of the French and aware of the balance of power issue, but he was quite willing to have the French make colonial concessions. The question was, as so often, what did the Germans want? The answer came on July 15: they demanded almost the entire French Congo in exchange for recognizing the French protectorate in Morocco. This seemed so excessive that the French thought the demand was meant to break up negotiations. The radical-dominated British Cabinet continued to hold Grey to the policy of pressing the French to make some concession pleasing to Germany. The alarmed Foreign Office pressed him to stand firmly by the French. Nicolson argued that the British had "to decide whether they will remain true to their engagement to France . . . or whether they will leave Germany to settle with France."[228]

Trying to make his way between Scylla and Charybdis, Grey suggested that Britain propose an international conference should the Franco-German talks collapse, as they seemed likely to do. To force a return to negotiations he wanted to add the threat that if Germany refused to attend, "we should take steps to assert and protect British interests."[229] That was far too strong for the radicals, who feared that Britain might be drifting into war. They insisted that Grey tell the French to submit counterproposals and that Britain would not regard a German insistence on a share of Morocco as grounds for war.

The softness of this position was too much for Grey, who feared that British inaction might end the Entente and drive France into the hands of Germany. He was also becoming increasingly annoyed at what he judged to be the Cabinet's excessive involvement in the management of foreign affairs. He sounded out Prime Minister Asquith about warning the Germans that an end to negotiations with France would bring British intervention in Morocco; now he even considered sending a British warship. As one scholar has put it: "These demands marked a turning point in Grey's approach to the Moroccan crisis. His policy of restraint upon France was henceforth joined by one of rigid sternness toward Germany."[230] On the one hand, the British delivered the Cabinet's message on July 20. The

French were shocked and alarmed by what seemed to them desertion by the British, a blow to the Entente whose "consequences might be very serious." The next day, on the other hand, Grey persuaded the Cabinet to let him take a harder line with the Germans, making clear that if Franco-German negotiations failed Britain would insist on taking part in any decision about Morocco.

That same night, July 21, 1911, Lloyd George, a leading radical member of the Cabinet, one of the "economists" in the naval debate of 1908–9, with a pro-German reputation, delivered a speech at the Mansion House in London which ended as follows:

> I believe it is essential in the highest interests, not merely of this country, but of the world, that Britain should at all hazards maintain her prestige among the Great Powers of the world. . . . I would make great sacrifices to preserve peace. I conceive that nothing would justify a disturbance of international good-will except questions of the greatest national moment. But if a situation were to be forced upon us in which peace could only be preserved by the surrender of the great and beneficent position Britain has won by centuries of heroism and achievement, by allowing Britain to be treated, where her interests were vitally affected, as if she were of no account in the Cabinet of nations, then I say emphatically that peace at that price would be a humiliation intolerable for a great country like ours to endure.[231]

To this day it is not clear whose idea the speech was and what Lloyd George's purpose was. There seems little doubt, however, that it had the support of Grey, Asquith, and Churchill, the last of whom was a fellow radical who was ready for a harder line, and that selected newspapers were alerted which would give it an anti-German slant.[232] The speech achieved all of Grey's goals; it "effectively muted the Cabinet's direction of foreign policy, alarmed the Germans, and assured the French."[233]

The *Panther*'s leap to Agadir had been greeted with enthusiasm in Germany. "Hurrah! A deed," said one newspaper, and there was widespread enthusiasm for the project, led by the nationalist, navalist, and colonialist groups sponsored by the government. Their excitement turned into an embarrassment for the government when British support of France and resistance to German claims proved to be greater than anticipated. As the crisis dragged on voices were heard calling for war if Germany did not get what she deserved. "By the middle of August, Kiderlen had to admit that he could no longer control the spirits he had raised. The Agadir venture began to backfire on the Reich government as the First Moroccan Crisis had done."[234] By September the German press was full of talk of war with Britain.

The prospect of war, even a victorious one, frightened Kiderlen. "After the victory of 1870 we had to pay with universal suffrage. Another victory will bring us a parliamentary regime."[235] The Kaiser and the Chancellor were likewise against it, and so was Tirpitz. He knew that the German Navy was no match for the British and would be humiliatingly kept in harbor or be destroyed in case of war. "He preferred a continuation of the Cold War against Britain which would help him with his projected naval bill." In his view, "the Agadir enterprise, whatever its outcome, will be very useful naval propaganda."[236] An embarrassment, in fact, would be better than a success.

Although agitation continued and the war scare reached its height in September, Grey's policy of restraint on France and firmness toward Germany helped push the negotiation to a peaceful conclusion. In November France and Germany agreed on the cession of a small and worthless piece of the Congo to Germany in return for its abandonment of Morocco.

In Germany the response to the outcome of Agadir was very hostile. There were many angry references to Britain's role, especially to the Mansion House speech, and there was considerable talk in military and colonialist circles of the need for war, which was often spoken of as inevitable. Bethmann Hollweg and the Kaiser were subjected to virulent attacks in the Reichstag and in the press. One newspaper referred to the Kaiser as *"Guillaume le timide,* the brave coward." The Moroccan settlement repeatedly was called a second Olmütz, a reference to Prussia's backing down from a confrontation with Austria in 1850, which was widely regarded as a terrible humiliation. A Liberal newspaper described the reaction in the Reichstag to the Chancellor's speech in defense of the settlement:

> Perhaps people turned to the past for an instance in which a German Chancellor during a debate on foreign affairs encountered a mood among the people's representatives similar to that which Herr von Bethmann Hollweg met today; they turned, but in vain. The only precedent is found in Prussia; when Manteuffel . . .

[explained his policy of surrender] after his return from
Olmütz. . . .[237]

The experience would make it harder for either Chancellor or Kaiser to
counsel moderation or back away from a fight in the future.

On the side of the Triple Entente the outcome of the crisis was
ambiguous. On the one hand, the entente between Britain and France had
held together and thwarted Germany's attempt to split it and to bully
France into major concessions. British and French military conversations,
begun in the first Moroccan crisis, were intensified during the second.
Under the determined leadership of the new, very pro-French, director of
military operations, General Henry Wilson, plans were made to send a
British expeditionary force to the Continent soon after an attack on France
and, to a limited extent, coordinated with the French. In a speech defending his policy after the crisis was over, Grey made Britain's commitment to
the entente clear, denouncing the advocates of "splendid isolation" and
taking pride in his stand alongside France:

> I trust that the fact that we have with France during the last seven
> months gone hand-in-hand through a great deal of rough diplo-
> matic weather, without for a moment losing touch with each
> other, will have its influence in perpetuating in France and here
> confidence in our mutual good faith and goodwill, our intention
> to keep in touch.[238]

On the other hand, the exact nature of Britain's commitment was far
from clear. The Navy had no plan for landing the Army on the Continent
and was bitterly hostile to the idea. The appointment of Churchill as First
Lord of the Admiralty began to change that situation, but it did not stop the
dispute between those for and against a Continental commitment. Grey
and Asquith were forced to repeat over and over again that they had made
no binding commitment to fight alongside France in case it was attacked,
that Britain was left with an entirely free hand. Nonetheless, opposition to
Grey and his policy from radicals within the British Cabinet and outside
was strong during the crisis and increased after it was over. The radicals in
the Cabinet were appalled to learn that military talks with the French had
been going on since 1906, and they insisted on limitations on them and
greater Cabinet control. A movement even was started to give greater

control over foreign policy to the House of Commons, and a campaign asserting that "Grey Must Go" had to be taken seriously.

Repeatedly during the crisis the French had asked Grey what Britain would do in case a war broke out over Morocco. The Foreign Secretary always evaded a direct answer and pressed the French to continue conversations and make concessions. During the crisis Grey said that his policy was "to give France such support as would prevent her falling under the virtual control of Germany and estrangement from us,"[239] but he was completely unclear as to what kind of support he was ready to give, how much of it, or under what circumstances he would give it. Some French leaders doubted not only Britain's commitment but its capacity to make a significant contribution in light of the the tiny size of its army. In 1909 General Wilson had asked Marshall Ferdinand Foch what was the smallest British military force that would be of practical value to a France attacked by Germany. "One single private soldier," Foch replied, "and we would take good care that he was killed."[240] In 1911 some French leaders doubted that the forces Britain might send to avenge that mythical soldier would be enough. None had reason to be fully confident that even he would be sent.

The Haldane Mission

The war scare during the Agadir crisis sharply increased criticism, especially from the radicals, of Grey's foreign policy. They were opposed to any commitment that might bind Britain even to "support French diplomacy in any future controversy, by the weight of the armed forces of this country, or by any such diplomatic action as might imply such assistance in the last resort."[241] People holding these views "wanted nothing less than the abandonment, or at least the erosion, of the Triple Entente,"[242] and they also wanted an accommodation with Germany. Grey, too, wanted better relations with Germany, but he insisted on preserving Britain's supremacy at sea and a free hand to support France against a German attack that would lead to German domination of the Continent, so he was not entirely optimistic about the prospects for an agreement. Political considerations, to be sure, pressed him to resume conversations with the Germans, but he was quite happy to do so.

The criticism of Grey and his policy by the radicals and some Conservatives also encouraged Bethmann Hollweg, who took comfort from these "pro-German statements," to try once again to pursue his main goal, the loosening of the Entente"[243] by coming to an agreement with Britain. He sought three goals: to reach a political agreement with the British that would at least keep them neutral in case of war with Russia and France; to reduce expenditure in such a way as to avoid raising taxes and thereby further to disturb the domestic political scene; and to rein in the naval arms race, which was the major barrier to achieving the first two goals. The first step was to try to stop Tirpitz's plan for a new and very expensive supplementary naval bill meant to take effect in 1912, when the current law would allow the pace of building to drop from four to two dreadnoughts annually. The new bill would maintain the four-ship pace; it would also make it impossible to come to terms with Britain or balance the budget without new taxes.

During the Morocco crisis Bethmann argued strongly against the new bill, and succeeded in postponing a decision, to the great annoyance of the Kaiser, who privately raged: "If the Chancellor is not willing he must go, I must be my own Bismarck."[244] Playing a crafty game, Bethmann encouraged the Army to present a request for military increases as a way of undercutting the Navy. The Army was receptive, as it had not been in the past, when it had resisted Army expansion in order to defend the aristocracy's domination of the officer corps. Bethmann's support and the Agadir crisis helped change their thinking. Those Germans who saw the agreement as a capitulation blamed it in part on alleged military weakness. The generals themselves began to believe in the reality of the prospect of a war against an increasingly formidable Triple Entente and the need for a larger army if they were to win such a war. In the end, Bethmann's plan backfired; the Kaiser's support of Tirpitz and the naval policy was too strong, and both an Army bill and a reduced Navy bill were passed in May 1912.

At the beginning of that year, however, Bethmann still hoped to stop the Navy bill and to make an agreement with Britain. First Churchill, then Grey were invited, but the Cabinet decided to send Lord Haldane, Secretary of State for War, a Liberal imperialist close to both Grey and Asquith and known to be friendly toward Germany. Tirpitz, supported by the Kaiser, destroyed all chances of success beforehand. Bethmann was forced to set the condition that Tirpitz's new naval increase, not yet made public, be included as part of the existing German Navy in the naval discussions. As if that were not enough, Tirpitz publicly announced the new supplementary bill the very day Haldane arrived in Berlin. Even the leading radical in the Cabinet, Lord Morley, said that the British government would be thought of as "idiots" if they made concessions in such an environment.[245] Apart from the naval problems, there was no chance of an accommodation, for the Germans insisted on British "benevolent" neutrality as the minimum for any agreement. They were not prepared to abandon their naval aspirations but wanted the British to get out of their way on the Continent. The Germans "wanted to eliminate Great Britain from the balance of Power." Tirpitz said that Britain ought to "give up her existing ententes and we should take the place of France," but he still would not have reduced his naval program, for he counted on the German fleet to force Britain onto the German side and keep it there.[246] This was very much the Kaiser's view. After the failure of the Haldane mission he clung to the approach that had characterized his policy from the beginning: "I have shown the English that, when they touch our armaments, they bite on granite. Perhaps by this I have increased their hatred but won their respect, which will induce them in due course to resume negotiations, it is to be hoped in a more modest tone and with a more fortunate result."[247]

Although the British rejected the German demands, the conversations themselves worried the "hawks" in the Foreign Office and the French. Characteristically, Grey shied away from giving firm guarantees. It was always his policy to defend the balance of power in Europe, but he refused to accept the proposal of the French Prime Minister, Poincaré, to declare that England and France would "co-operate, if necessary, to maintain the European balance." The most he would say to an anxious Nicolson was: "although we cannot bind ourselves under all circumstances to go to war with France against Germany, we shall also not bind ourselves to Germany not to assist France."[248]

In fact, the revelation of Germany's plans and attitude forced Britain both to continue the naval race and to move closer to France. In March 1912 Churchill, now first Lord of the Admiralty, announced an increase in naval construction and, even more important, the withdrawal of most of the Mediterranean fleet from Malta to the British Isles, and the rest to Gibraltar. The French took the hint; in September they moved their fleet from Brest to Toulon. Without any formal agreement Britain now relied on France to defend the Mediterranean and France on Britain for the defense of its northern coasts. In light of these events the French tried again to get more positive assurances from Britain, asking for an agreement that in case of the threat of aggression the two countries "would discuss the situation and seek means to assure in concert the maintenance of peace and to remove any attempt at aggression." Even then the British Cabinet watered down the language and added a preamble declaring that "consultation between experts is not and ought not to be regarded as an engagement that commits either Government to action in a contingency that has not arisen and may never arise." The French had to be satisfied with this slim formality, but what they had gotten was "a formal assertion that an alliance did not exist."[249] The practical arrangements, however, could not be ignored. "No objective observer could deny that Britain's obligation to defend France from attack was now stronger than it had been and that Germany was responsible for this."[250]

The Balkan Wars

The Second Moroccan Crisis had one consequence that none of the major participants had imagined. The Italians took advantage of French distraction to declare war on Turkey and invade Libya. Within a year they had forced the Turks to cede to them Libya and the Dodecanese Islands. This renewed evidence of Turkish weakness emboldened the Balkan states and frightened the Russians. During the war against Italy the Turks had closed the Straits for a period, fearing an Italian attack. The importance of gaining control of them suddenly loomed larger than ever. The Russians focused on the turbulent Balkan states, fearful of an Austrian attack on them and ambitious to take advantage of Turkey's collapse. Through their ambassadors at Belgrade and Sofia they managed the difficult task of bringing Serbia and Bulgaria together into an alliance. The Russians thought of this as a defensive union against Austrian or German ambitions, but the new allies had other ideas. The Bulgarians were eager to attack Turkey and drive it out of Europe entirely, annexing whatever they gained along the Aegean coast and inland, all the way to Constantinople. The Serbs were willing to help in the expectation that Bulgaria would then join them in an attack on Austria, which would give them the rest of the Turkish Balkans, much of which was inhabited by Albanians. Greece soon joined the alliance, eager not to miss a chance at dismembering Turkey. Along with Montenegro, which also hoped to despoil Turkey-in-Europe, this constituted the Balkan League.

In spite of their differences, neither Austria nor Russia wanted to be dragged into a Balkan war at that time, and the other powers likewise sought to preserve the peace, but on October 8, 1912, Montenegro declared war on Turkey; within ten days its allies had done the same. The action of the Balkan League marked a new phase in European history. As a French diplomat put it: "For the first time in the history of the Eastern question the small states have acquired a position of such independence of the Great Powers that they feel able to act completely without them and even to take them in tow."[251]

To the general surprise, and to the great consternation of the Austrians, the armies of the league quickly defeated the Turks wherever they offered battle. The Austrian Foreign Minister, Count Leopold von Berchtold, adopted a cautious attitude to the formation of the Balkan League. On only two points was he prepared to stand firm: the independence of Albania and the barring of Serbia from access to the Adriatic. The official policy was that Serbia must be contained: "A Serbia denied free access to the sea would still be a dependent Serbia; Albanian independence would help assure Vienna's policy."[252] It is far from clear, however, that cutting Serbia off from the Adriatic would have made it dependent. It seems more likely that Berchtold, appalled at the Serbian victories but unwilling to go to war, needed to "reassert the monarchy's 'prestige,' "[253] and selected this way for doing so. The league's swift victories, however, shattered Turkish resistance and imperiled the strategy of containment as the Montenegrins took the Albanian city of Scutari and the Serbian Army reached the Albanian city of Durazzo (Durrës) on the Adriatic. The Russians supported Serbia's position and increased their forces in Galicia on the Austrian border. The Austrians increased their forces in Galicia and Bosnia-Herzegovina, and war seemed possible.

In November, however, the Turks defeated the Bulgarians in a significant battle, and peace talks began in London in December. The Russians' main interest was that Bulgaria should not take Constantinople; Serbia's ambitions were secondary, at best. The Russians retreated from an intransigent support of Serbia's claims, and tension eased for the moment. Austrian military leaders, supported by the heir apparent, Franz Ferdinand, pressed for military action to end the menace from Serbia and Montenegro once and for all. They were convinced that Russia would not fight to gain Serbia a port on the Adriatic, which was exactly what the Russian diplomat Sergey Sazonov had told the Serbs.[254] Berchtold continued to oppose war, in considerable measure because of the attitude of Germany. When consulted, the Germans assured the Austrians of their full support, but in various ways they sent the message that they opposed war and sought a diplomatic solution at a conference of the great powers. Bethmann Hollweg made a nuanced speech in the Reichstag whose passages promising support for Austria won ringing cheers, but Berchtold understood the underlying message: "Upon closer inspection there is comminatory diplomatic pressure on St. Petersburg and a fatherly warning to Vienna kindly to keep still."[255] Emperor Franz Josef came down on the side of peace, and his was the decisive word.

In spite of continued stress, the conference made progress. Austria made some concessions to Serbia, but Britain and Russia accepted the Austrian position on Scutari and Durazzo. Britain and Germany worked to produce a peaceful settlement, each restraining its partner. The British were eager for better relations with Germany and Austria. Bethmann wanted to use the opportunity to win England away from the Entente, telling Berchtold: "we may look for a new orientation of British policy if we can get through the present crisis without any quarrels."[256] In March the Russians and Austrians released many of their troops, and the crisis seemed to be over. Regardless of the great powers, however, Serbia and Montenegro held to their demands. Pressed by the Russians, the Serbs withdrew, but King Nikita of Montenegro stood firm and finally took Scutari. This, at last, was too much for the Austrians, for whom acquiescence would mean a terrible and damaging loss of prestige. Even István Tisza, the Hungarian Prime Minister usually opposed to military intervention, told Berchtold that the issue was "whether Austria-Hungary was a 'viable power' or had fallen into a 'laughable decadence.' "[257] Berchtold and everyone else decided to call up the remaining reserves and deliver an ultimatum to Montenegro. Nikita agreed to abandon Scutari and the Serbs Durazzo. The First Balkan War was over. Once again, a conference, even with unanimous support of the powers, had humiliated Austria, but the threat of military action had brought success.

After their great victory over Turkey the allies fell out. The Serbs seized all of Macedonia, refusing to give Bulgaria its promised share. In June 1913 the Bulgarians thereupon attacked both Serbia and Greece, thinking they could impose their will on both their erstwhile allies. They were mistaken. They were getting worse than they gave when the Rumanians took advantage of the moment to gain control of Dobrudja and attacked Bulgaria from the north. At the Peace of Bucharest concluded in August, Bulgaria was stripped of almost all its gains from the first war.

Turkey gained Adrianople, an important city north of the Aegean Sea, and some self-respect. Rumania gained Dobrudja. Greece and Serbia were the big winners, and they refused to submit the settlement to the examination of the great powers.

The outcome was a disaster for Austria. Serbia had acquired a great deal of territory, a million and a half new subjects, and a new confidence and independence. Turkey and Bulgaria, whom the Austrians relied upon as a counterweight to Serbian ambitions, were defeated and of little use for that purpose. Serbia had shown itself capable of acting with an independent, aggressive determination that disregarded the great powers and was hard even for the Russians to control. The Serbs had been humiliated by the Austrian ultimatum and bitterly eager for revenge. The ranks of the Black Hand, a secret society committed to south Slav unification, were increased by angry military men, and Serbia's hostility and ambition were obvious. Serbia and Montenegro now all but surrounded the Austrian provinces of Bosnia and Herzegovina, and there was talk of their union into a single country. After that, many Slavs hoped that the next step would be the separation of Bosnia Herzegovina, Dalmatia, and other south Slavic territories from Austria-Hungary and the formation of a Yugoslav state. At Bucharest in 1913 Serbia's Prime Minister, Nicola Pashitch, told his Greek ally, "The first round is won; now we must prepare the second against Austria."[258] The Austrians increasingly saw the Serbs as a menace to the existence of the empire.

Relations between Austria and Germany had been difficult during the crisis. In spite of their reassuring words the Germans had not backed the Austrians firmly, but held them back, leading Berchtold to complain that they might as well belong to the Entente for all the good the German alliance had done them. The taming of Serbia was critical for Austria, but the Germans refused to understand that. The lessons Berchtold and his colleagues learned from the Balkan wars was that diplomacy would not work against Serbia, only the threat of force or its use; that even as the Germans restrained the Austrians, they doubted their resolve and competence. The Austrians relied on German support to keep the Russians out of a clash with Serbia or to fight them in case of a general war. On the one hand, they were nervous about getting the support they needed; on the other, they felt the need to act strongly and decisively to guarantee that support.

Berchtold and his colleagues have been criticized for their conduct in these years: "By converting issues into prestige matters on which compromise was impossible, the minister necessarily had to escalate his pressures if the other party balked. Prestige politics, that most dangerous and self-fulfilling of all diplomatic pursuits, had replaced interest politics."[259] The fact is that much of what had been happening in Europe since Germany embarked on its "new course" was prestige politics. *Weltpolitik* and the naval program, far from being to Germany's practical advantage economically or politically, domestically or abroad, were either of little or no value or, more frequently, seriously detrimental.

But the Kaiser and Tirpitz and the nationalistic forces they called forth and encouraged wanted power and the prestige it would bring; the arguments for practical advantage were chiefly rationalizations. The German battleship Navy was, after all, what Churchill called it, a "luxury fleet." Though it played a major part in causing the war, it took no significant part in the fighting and never did Germany any practical good. The colonies acquired were of little or no intrinsic value. The pursuit of recognition, respect, and association through bullying produced only fear and resistance. Both Moroccan crises were provoked in search of prestige, as was the excessively harsh and unnecessary ultimatum in the Bosnian crisis. The Germans clung to their policies even after these methods had clearly failed and instead produced serious dangers at home and abroad. These were the policies that created the prewar alliance system and the arms race on land and sea. They had separated Austria from Russia, setting the two nations on a collision course in the Balkans. It was the union of these elements that turned the collapse of the Ottoman Empire and the decay of the Habsburg Empire from local or regional problems, to which Europe could have adjusted without a major war, into the trigger for a world war. It is, therefore, hard to blame Berchtold and his colleagues "for believing that, at some point, prestige was worth fighting for—one great commonplace of his or any age."[260]

In the nineteenth century the British had helped support Austria by restraining Russia, and a well-known article has critized them for abandoning that useful activity. "Britain undermined Austria's position before the war . . . and assisted in her destruction during it, in a fit of absence of mind. . . . The basic point is that everyone saw the central threat to the European system in the decline of Austria, and no one would do anything about it."[261] It is quite true that Britain, for the most part, did not support the Austrians. Grey refused to do so even when urged to use British support as a lever to pry them away from the German alliance. He refused because he believed that the Germans had worked themselves into such a panic of self-created isolation that the defection of their only reliable ally might drive them to war. The fact is that the British regarded *not* the decline of Austria, but the menace of Germany to be the greatest threat, a very reasonable conclusion. Under the Kaiser the German Navy was a dagger at Britain's throat and its army a deadly menace to the states of Europe on whose independence Britain relied; together they posed the most serious danger to British security since Napoleon. In these circumstances it is unreasonable to expect the British to have worked to strengthen Germany's only true ally. It is, indeed, more surprising that they did not try to turn the Entente into a true alliance, to contain the threat more effectively and deter challenges to the status quo and to British security.

The outcome of the Balkan wars presented Austria with a problem to which it had no satisfactory solution. Berchtold and the others had no choice but to pursue a policy of prestige; they were too weak to do otherwise. The sense of the Austrians' weakness had encouraged the Serbs and Montenegrins to challenge their policies in the Balkans. Failure to change that perception could well lead to the disintegration of the empire. Fear of such a development, to use the Thucydidean triad once again, turned a policy of prestige (honor) into one of interest, as it has done so often throughout history. From the point of view of Austrian survival, Conrad might have been right to urge a decisive military attack against Serbia in 1908–9, when the Russians were too weak to fight and Serbia could have been crushed. After that, such a policy was no longer safe. As that fact became clear, provocation by the Serbs became more tempting and a moderate response by Austria more difficult. The next Balkan crisis would not end peacefully.

THE FINAL CRISIS

The months following the Balkan Wars contained troubles and tensions, but few, if any, felt apprehensions of a major war. The Austrians, for all their troubles and fears, were working on diplomatic schemes to solve their problems. The Russians, too, continued their diplomatic maneuvers in the Balkans and sought to move closer to their Entente partners. The British worked further to improve relations with the Germans, negotiating amicable agreements with them about the Baghdad railway and the future of Portugal's African colonies. The Russian Foreign Minister, Sazonov, might think that "the peace of the world will be secure only when the Triple Entente . . . is transferred into a defensive alliance without secret clauses. Then the danger of a German hegemony will be finally ended, and each of us can finally devote himself to his own affairs: the English can seek a solution of their social problems, the French can get rich, protected from any external threat, and we can consolidate ourselves and work on our economic reorganization,"[262] but Grey was of a different opinion. In 1914 Britain had more serious disagreements with Russia, chiefly about Persia, than with Germany. In 1913 Churchill had proposed a naval holiday, which the Germans refused, but Bethmann and the needs of the German Army had curbed the growth of the Navy anyway. The British had won the naval race, and there were no more negotiations to roil the waters. Grey wanted to continue his policy of friendship with Russia, and he was prepared to defend France if it were attacked by Germany, but he rejected the idea of alliances: "He could not understand an alliance as a security for peace; like most Englishmen, he regarded all alliances as a commitment to war."[263] To please France and secure Russian good will he got Cabinet permission for naval talks with Russia, which never came to any result. Grey clung to what he thought was a policy of maintaining a free hand.

The French, although nervous about Britain's relations with Germany, were gratified by Britain's efforts toward Russia. In any case, the French themselves were not thinking about war. In the summer of 1913 they had passed the Three Years' Law that raised military service from two to three years in order to increase the size of the French Army to meet the recent German increases. Elections in the spring of 1914, however, produced a legislature whose majority opposed it. The left-wing victory compelled Poincaré, now President of the Republic, to appoint René Viviani, a leftist, as Prime Minister. The Socialists, who had done very well in the election, always opposed close relations with autocratic Russia and sought to move closer to Germany. As a student of France in these years puts it: "during 1913 and 1914 France was more concerned with Syria than Bosnia, and more preoccupied with reaching an agreement with Germany over the future of the Ottoman Empire than with supporting her ally, Russia, in the Near East."[264]

The situation in Germany was complex and has been the subject of much controversy. In December 1912, in the midst of the Balkan crisis, the British had shattered German dreams when Lord Haldane told Prince Karl

Lichnowsky, the German ambassador in London, "that England, if we attacked France, would unconditionally spring to France's aid, for England could not allow the balance of power in Europe to be disturbed."[265] In a fury, the Kaiser called a meeting on December 8 to which he invited his chief military officials, but not the Chancellor or the Foreign Secretary.[266] He denounced the British and also Bethmann's policy of seeking to get close to them and insisted on an immediate war against France and Russia. "Austria," he said, "must deal energetically with the foreign Slavs [the Serbs], otherwise she will lose control of the Slavs in the Austro-Hungarian Monarchy." Moltke, the Chief of Staff of the Army, said: "I believe a war to be unavoidable and the sooner the better." The Kaiser and others favored a press campaign to prepare the nation for war. Tirpitz opposed the idea of war on the grounds that the fleet would not be ready for another eighteen months, but Moltke retorted that "the navy would not be ready even then and the army would get into an increasingly unfavorable position, for the enemies are arming more strongly than we, as our money is very tied up."[267] Such sentiments dominated the meeting and some scholars believe that this was the beginning of the plan for the war that broke out in 1914.[268] There is little support for such a view. A meeting that excluded the Foreign Secretary and Chancellor was neither official nor authoritative. Nor was there any follow-up to the suggestions put forward. There was no press campaign; Germany restrained the Austrians and worked with the British for a peaceful solution to the Balkan crisis. There was no declaration of war against France or Russia. Admiral von Müller, whose diary is our source for the meeting, points out the failure to take action and says that "the result was pretty well zero."

It is argued that this was only "War Postponed,"[269] that a compromise was reached in which the plan was made to prepare for war in 1914. The events of those intervening months and Germany's behavior in the final crisis, in which the vast documentation available has no reference to such a preconceived plan of war, do not support that interpretation either. Bethmann and Germany continued to try to work with Britain to preserve the peace. As late as June 1914 the Chancellor wrote to Lichnowsky, his ambassador in London: "If we both act together as guarantors of European peace, which as long as we follow this goal according to a common plan neither Entente nor Triple Alliance obligations shall prevent, war will be avoided."[270] There is no reason to doubt his sincerity.

Which is not to say that the forces moving Germany toward war were not powerful. The Kaiser was emotional and impulsive, and we must never forget that he had the constitutional authority to make foreign policy and declare war. Moltke and many others in the military were truly in favor of what they saw as a preventive war. They saw the power of Russia as a terrible menace as it recovered from its earlier weakness. They believed that by 1917 Russian military power would be capable, with the aid of France, to defeat the Central Powers and feared that the Russians would use that power against Germany. Their views could not be ignored lightly, and they played an important role in the final crisis. Nor was Germany's drive for increased power, influence, and prestige forgotten. To be sure, the failure of Tirpitz's policy had weakened support for a naval program and *Weltpolitik,* but for many Germans these were replaced by the goal of extending Germany's political and economic power and interest to the southeast, through the Balkans and into the Ottoman Empire. In the years 1912–14 the idea of *Mitteleuropa* gained considerable support. At the least it meant a German-dominated customs union; in the minds of the more extreme imperialists it meant a German Empire from the North Sea to the Persian Gulf; for some, even that was only a beginning in which the base of German power was to be established on the Continent as a first step to *Weltpolitik.* A peaceful policy of living within Germany's current boundaries and refusing to use force to extend its power and influence would have to tame these forces that the new course had done so much to encourage, but it is not clear that it could not have been done.

The difficulty was that the idea of imposing restraint had come late in the day. By 1912 German policy had created the Entente, which pursued a policy that we might call containment and the Germans called *Einkreisung,* encirclement. They found themselves associated with a weak and unreliable Italy and a decrepit Austria-Hungary. If they did not support the Dual Monarchy in its Balkan struggles, which always risked war against Russia, it might turn to the Entente or, more likely, collapse, in either case leaving Germany alone and surrounded by increasingly powerful enemies. The problem worried the Germans, who often longed to be rid of their Austrian burden, but to do so would mean giving up hope of expansion to the southeast, as the Austrian ambassador to Constantinople was quick to point out, presenting the alternatives: "Either the abandonment of the Bosphorus and of Germany's position in the Near East or marching on the side of Austria through thick and thin."[271] Even those uninterested in expansion might have been concerned that the collapse of the Dual Monarchy would result in Russian control of the Balkans and bring Russian power to Germany's southern as well as eastern frontier. For most German leaders then, the support of Austria in some form, which meant risking war with Russia, which, in turn, meant risk of a general war, was unavoidable. For some, such as Moltke, this meant preventive war. For others, such as Bethmann, remembering one of Bismarck's famous remarks, preventive war was "like committing suicide for fear of death." His approach was to work with England. The best outcome would be to break Britain free from the Entente, which would permit the preservation of peace without prejudice to Germany's interests. Failing that, he might win the promise of British neutrality; in that case he was confident of Germany's victory against its Continental opponents. Those who believe that he was complicit in a plan for war, preventive or aggressive, and that his talk of peace and his attempts to work with Britain were either false or instrumental, meant to guarantee victory, not to preserve peace, must ignore much of the evidence. Bethmann regarded the possibility of a general European war not as an opportunity but as a calamity in which the monarchy and the conservative institutions he cherished would be swept away. He specifically rejected the idea of preventive war. For him the decision for war, when it came, was "a calculated risk," a "leap in the dark" that he took reluctantly and fearfully. The trouble was that the situation that had evolved since 1890 left only dangerous choices.

Even so, war was not inevitable in the spring of 1914. None of the major powers wanted war. Germany's Chancellor was working to avoid it. So independent an observer as the Russian ambassador was certain that "the Berlin cabinet does not share the views of the belligerent circles of Germany, who, as I am told, desire to bring about an immediate warlike confrontation with Russia, and that it would prefer to try all peaceful means to reconcile our interests before taking a decisive step." Although these "belligerent circles" complained of Bethmann's policies, the ambassador did not doubt that "the German government is strong enough to be able to curb the warlike tendencies of the German chauvinists."[272]

On June 28, 1914, Archduke Franz Ferdinand and his wife were assassinated at Sarajevo, the chief city of Bosnia. The assassins, young Bosnians, were arrested quickly; it was thought more than probable that they were working for nationalist groups with connections to Serbia. In Vienna important civilian and military officials called for an attack on Serbia, but Berchtold was cautious. He knew that Emperor Franz Josef was not eager for war and that Hungarian Prime Minister Tisza would be against it; beyond that, he was far from sure what Germany's attitude would be.

The police were able to identify all the conspirators and to establish connections between some of them and Serbian officials. Subsequent evidence shows that the plot was organized and assisted by members of the Black Hand and *Narodna Odbrana,* including the head and at least one other member of Serbian military intelligence. Before the assassination the Serbian government learned of the transportation of the armed assassins from Serbia into Bosnia but never warned the Austrian government. Although the Serbian state did not concoct the plot, some of its officials did.[273] The evidence available at the time was not conclusive, but the Austrians did not doubt Serbian complicity and acted accordingly.

On the day after the assassination Berchtold met Conrad's demand for mobilization against Serbia by conceding that it was time "to solve the Serbian situation" but suggested instead making a series of demands that Conrad dismissed as being too acceptable without having any useful result.[274] Whatever Berchtold's personal inclinations may have been, he knew that a decision to make war on Serbia required German support. Even Conrad, the most aggressive of Austrian hawks, insisted on getting Germany's support before taking action.[275] On July 4, therefore, Berchtold sent his young *chef du cabinet,* Count Alexander Hoyos, to Berlin carrying two documents to be passed on to the German government. The first was the memorandum already prepared, outlining Austria's diplomatic plans for the Balkans, reworked for the occasion, and the second was a private letter from Franz Josef to William II. The memorandum asked for German assistance in winning Rumania back to a reliable relationship with the Dual Alliance and in trying to bring Bulgaria into the Triple Alliance, thereby isolating Serbia. The original memorandum was now strengthened by new references to the aggressiveness of Russia and France and by a forceful paragraph at the end. Franz Josef's letter blamed Russian and Serbian Pan-Slavism for the assassination. He wrote that "the band of criminal agitators in Belgrade" must be punished, but neither the Emperor's letter nor the memorandum ever used the word "war." Together, argues one scholar, the two documents "could have left little doubt in Berlin that this time Vienna would act."[276] But act how? was a reasonable question. Provocations in the recent past had not produced military action, and even under the immediate impact of the assassination the Austrians had not mentioned war plainly in seeking the support of their allies. Some scholars believe that Berchtold and the Austrian regime in general had already decided upon war with Serbia and were asking for German approval. But the evidence seems to give more support to the view that the Austrians were telling the Germans of their determination to take action, but awaiting German reaction before deciding on its character.

The Germans' first reactions, before the Hoyos mission, were in accord with the policy of restraint they had pursued during the Balkan wars. Alfred Zimmerman, undersecretary of state, who was in charge of the Foreign Office at the moment, "displayed no belligerence and exercised a pacifying influence on all quarters."[277] On June 30 the German ambassador to Vienna, Count Heinrich von Tschirschky, reported that he took every opportunity "to advise quietly but very impressively and seriously against too hasty steps. First of all, they must make sure what they want to do, for so far I have heard only indefinite expressions of opinion."[278] What Tschirschky did not yet know was that the Kaiser was in a very different mood. In the margin of the ambassador's report he wrote some comments. Next to Berchtold's wish to have a final reckoning with the Serbs he wrote, *Now or never. As to Tschirschky's efforts at restraint the Kaiser wrote: Who authorized him to act that way? That is very stupid! It is none of his business, as it is solely the affair of Austria what she plans to do in this case. Later, if plans go wrong, it will be said that Germany did not want it! Let Tschirschky be good enough to drop this nonsense! The Serbs must be disposed of and that right soon!*

On July 5 the Austrian ambassador to Berlin, Count Ladislaus Szögyény-Marich, had lunch with the Kaiser at his palace in Potsdam. The Kaiser read the documents and responded cautiously that he could not respond without consulting the Chancellor, but after lunch he changed his tune. He now said he "did not doubt that Herr von Bethmann Hollweg would agree with him" that Austria "might in this case, as in all others, rely upon Germany's full support." In case that led to a war between the Dual Monarchy and Russia, Szögyény reported in his telegram to Berchtold, "we might be convinced that Germany, our old faithful ally, would stand by our side." But the Kaiser emphasized the need for quick action: "this action must not be delayed. . . . [I]f we had really recognized the necessity of warlike action against Serbia, he [Kaiser Wilhelm] would regret it if we did not make use of the present moment, which is all in our favour."[279]

That same afternoon the Kaiser met with Bethmann, Zimmermann, the Kaiser's adjutant, Hans von Plessen, and two military officials, Moritz von Lyncker and Erich von Falkenhayn. The Kaiser swiftly read the Austrian documents aloud and reported on his conversation. The next day Bethmann and Zimmermann met with Szögyény and Hoyos and gave formal and constitutional ratification of the Kaiser's commitment. Why did the Kaiser act with such speed and force? He was, of course, an impetuous man who often spoke without deliberation, later regretting what he had said and reversing himself. During the Balkan crisis he made some very similar statements that came to nothing. Conrad reports a conversation in which the Kaiser assured him of support in a war against the Serbs in 1913, concluding that, "finally a situation arises in which a Great Power . . . must draw the sword." On a report about the same time of Berchtold's wish that the Serbs might give in before war was necessary the Kaiser commented: "This would be very regrettable! Now or never! For once things down there have to be put right and calm restored!"[280] But that was only loose talk. At Potsdam in 1914 William established formal policy that was constitutionally ratified.[281] In part, his behavior was a reaction to the assassination of a royal personage, something he found truly shocking. The Archduke and the Kaiser, moreover, had enjoyed unusually cordial relations. Beyond that, the Kaiser was keenly aware of his reputation for backing away from a fight. We may conjecture that the recent accusations that he was *Guillaume le Timide* made him more bellicose and eager to demonstrate his courage. On July 6 he talked to the industrialist Alfred Krupp: " 'This time,' he assured Krupp repeatedly. . . . 'I shall not chicken out.' It was almost pathetic, Krupp thought, to see how William tried to prove he was not a coward."[282] On a more practical plane, it seems clear that he believed that a strong German stance would deter Russian intervention, allowing the affair to be localized and the Austrians to defeat Serbia without interference. He thought the Russian Army was still unready for war and that Nicholas II, on whom he always imagined he could exert personal influence, would be reluctant to fight on behalf of regicides. In that case he could show his toughness to his critics and his loyalty to his ally without great risk.

But why did Bethmann change his course so sharply from the restraint he had employed in 1913 to the approval for war in 1914? The simplest answer is that he had little choice. Although he had held views different from his master before and argued them vigorously and sometimes successfully, there was no precedent for the situation in which he found himself at Potsdam. The Kaiser had essentially committed himself and his Chancellor to a foreign ambassador. Bethmann could hardly embarrass the

Kaiser by refusing to endorse his commitment.[283] Beyond that we can only speculate, with some help from the diary entries of Kurt Riezler, his young aide and adviser.[284] These reveal a man weighed down with sorrow and fear for the future. His fear of Russia was central: "the future belongs to Russia, which grows and weighs upon us as an increasingly terrifying nightmare." At the same time, the decay of Austria had grown too serious in his eyes to withstand another display of weakness. A failure to act could lead to the defection of Austria from the German alliance or its collapse. Yet "an action against Serbia can lead to world war." About such a war he was pessimistic. Win or lose, however, "the chancellor expects from a war, however it ends, a revolution of all existing order."

In spite of that, he thought action less dangerous than inaction. He still hoped that war could be avoided. Perhaps Russia or France might balk, as they had in the past. In that case Austria could strengthen itself in the Balkans and the Entente might even be split. In case it came to Continental war he thought Germany could win, put an end to the danger from Russia, and break through the ring of encirclement that limited German economic expansion and threatened its world policy. If Britain fought alongside France and Russia, however, he thought Germany would lose. A critical element in his policy during the crisis, therefore, would be to keep Britain neutral, but he recognized the danger. Riezler wrote that "the chancellor thinks I am too young not to succumb to the fascination of the unknown, the lure of the new, the great movement. For him the action is a leap in the dark and, as such, the most serious duty."[285]

Perhaps, in the end, he was encouraged by his recent success with the British, which may have led him to count on them to restrain the Russians and permit the Austrians to punish Serbia. In the days after the assassination feeling in every European capital was certainly hostile to the Serbs. Most of the British newspapers, in fact, blamed the deed on "the impossible Serbians."[286] In any case, he took his calculated risk and gave his formal approval.

The German response to the Austrian inquiry has gone down in history as the "blank check," which implies that it was left up to Austria to fill in the amount, i.e., to decide what to do and how to do it. That is how official German documents treat it, but there is reason to believe that this underestimates the amount of direction given by the Germans. Those involved seem to have had serious doubts about what the Austrians intended and how capable they were of carrying out a strong action. In his report to Moltke written right after the July 5 meeting with the Kaiser and Bethmann, General Falkenhayn seemed to think Austria would take no military action. The Austrian documents did not convince him that "the Vienna Government had taken any firm resolution. . . . [N]either [document] speaks of the need for war, rather both expound 'energetic' political action such as the conclusion of a treaty with Bulgaria, for which they would like to be certain of the support of the German Reich." Falkenhayn thought that Bethmann "appears to have as little faith as I do that the Austrian government is really in earnest." He told Moltke that he should not cut short his vacation: "Certainly in no circumstances will the coming weeks bring any decision. It will be a long time before the treaty with Bulgaria is concluded."[287]

The Chancellor, therefore, and the Foreign Office pressed the Austrians to move quickly, in part, no doubt, to take advantage of the general outrage felt in the capitals of Europe, but also to be sure that the notoriously bumbling Austrians would act. By July 4 Tschirschky obviously had learned of the Kaiser's opinions, perhaps even of his marginal notes. Through a German newspaperman he had sent a message to the Austrian Foreign Office assuring them of full German support, adding that "the sooner Austria-Hungary went into action the better. Yesterday would have been better than today, and today would be better than tomorrow."[288] On July 8 Tschirschky passed on to Berchtold his instructions from Berlin: "to emphasize here that Berlin expects the Monarchy to take action against Serbia and that Germany would not understand our letting the opportunity slip without striking a blow. . . . From other utterances of the Ambassador I could see that Germany would interpret any compromise on our part with Serbia as a confession of weakness, which would not remain without repercussions on our position in the Triple Alliance and the future policy of Germany."[289] This was more than a blank check. As one of the most important historians of the origins of the war says, the Germans gave Austria "incitement and encouragement to take action against Serbia."

Would the Austrians have taken action without German pressure? Even a scholar who emphasizes Austria's independent action and believes Berchtold wanted to attack Serbia answers, "probably not."[290] The reason is that István Tisza, the Hungarian Prime Minister, stood as a formidable barrier to war. Without his approval nothing could happen, and he was firmly against war. Without German pressure he could not have been moved. At the Ministerial Council of July 7 everyone opposed him, but he stood fast, threatening to veto steps toward war. For a week Austria could do nothing while the Hungarian Prime Minister held fast. Finally, concern that a failure to act against Serbia might encourage the Rumanians to make trouble among the Rumanians in Hungary, added to the German pressure, convinced the reluctant Tisza.[291]

After Tisza finally had given way a second Ministerial Council was held on July 19 to carry out the policy agreed to by the majority at the earlier meeting and to make further plans. Austria-Hungary would send an ultimatum blaming Serbia for the assassination, demanding a joint Serbian-Austrian committee to investigate it, public admission of Serbian responsibility, and a pledge of future good behavior. The Serbs would be given forty-eight hours to reply, and they were expected to reject the demands. War would follow. The ultimatum was to be delivered only on the afternoon of July 23, after the impending visit of Poincaré and Viviani to Russia was over, so that the allies might not be able to plan a response together. Meanwhile German and Austrian officials went on vacation, and everyone acted as though nothing serious or dangerous was being contemplated

It is important to recognize that this plan was a compromise. Conrad and others had argued for an immediate war. Had that been possible Austria could have taken advantage of the general disapproval of Serbia; if an attack could bring quick victory Europe might be presented with a fait accompli that the Entente would dislike but might not choose to fight over. It is usually easier to persuade a country to go to war to prevent an unwelcome development than to undo one. Some such outcome is what the Germans hoped to achieve when they pressed the Austrians to act. Tisza preferred no war but diplomatic efforts. This had its disadvantages, but it would avoid war. The advocates of the position actually adopted assumed that a swift attack would be too provocative and hoped that a more deliberate approach, including the pretense of diplomacy, might persuade the Entente to accept the punishment of Serbia. The trouble with this middle road was that the delay gave the shock of the assassination time to fade and replaced it with the shock of the Austrian ultimatum, turning the anger against Austria and shifting sympathy toward Serbia, without removing Serbia from the picture.

The Germans' official position was that they knew nothing of Austria's plans of action or of the ultimatum and its contents, and revisionist historians accepted that view for years, although a report of Hans von Schoen, the Bavarian chargé d'affaires at Berlin, published very soon after the war, proves otherwise.[292] The Germans were fully informed of what was happening, including the terms of the ultimatum and, of course, they made no protest. Their main concern was that Vienna would not act swiftly enough or at all. Writing to his prime minister in Munich the Bavarian chargé reported that the German government wanted Austria to move against Serbia even at the risk of war with Russia, "but whether they will actually rise to the occasion in Vienna still seems doubtful to Mr. von Jagow and Mr. Zimmermann." Zimmermann went so far as to refer to Austria as "the Sick Man of Europe." He thought that Germany's unconditional support was unexpected, "that it is almost embarrassing to the always timid and undecided authorities at Vienna not to be admonished by Germany to caution and self-restraint." Schoen also reported that Berlin would have liked the Austrians to move much faster so as not to give the Serbians time to make a counteroffer, initiating diplomatic discussions and permitting the intervention of outside nations, thereby removing the opportunity to launch a war.

The ultimatum was delivered in Belgrade at 6 P.M. on July 23 and at 9 A.M. the next day to the other European capitals. Grey called it "the most formidable document I had ever seen addressed by one state to another that was independent," and Sazonov exclaimed, *"C'est la guerre européenne."*[293] We are not well informed about the discussion in Serbia. The Serbian response accepted nine of the ten demands and tempered even the rejection of the remaining one, which required Austrian participation in the investigation inside Serbia. It was a diplomatic triumph that won widespread approval and swung opinion against the Austrians, as even the Kaiser's marginalia reveal: "A brilliant performance for a time-limit of only 48 hours. This is more than one could have expected! A great moral success for Vienna; but with it every reason for war drops away."[294] But the Kaiser's remarks, written on July 28, were far behind developments and out of tune with Austrian and German policy.

Upon hearing of the Serbian rejection of the ultimatum Franz Josef had ordered partial mobilization of the army against Serbia to take effect on the twenty-eighth. The Austrians did not plan to declare war until August 12, the first time their troops would be in position to fight, but on the twenty-fifth the Germans pressed them to begin some kind of military operation immediately, since "any delay in the beginning of war operations is regarded as signifying the danger that foreign powers might interfere. We are urgently advised to proceed without delay and to place the world before a *fait accompli.*"[295] The fiery Conrad did not see the point of declaring war two weeks before his army was ready to fight, but the Germans were eager to use the "window of opportunity" to launch the local war before offers of mediation became embarrassing and irresistible. As Berchtold said, "the diplomatic situation will not last as long as that."[296] On July 28 Austria-Hungary declared war on Serbia, and on the next day its ships on the Danube fired on Belgrade. Technically, the local war had begun.

European attention to the crisis had revived sharply on the twenty-fourth on the arrival of news of the ultimatum. Britain, France, and Russia tried to extend the time limit, and suggested mediation between Vienna and Belgrade or Vienna and St. Petersburg, but the Austrians and Germans rejected or ignored them. The news hit Sazonov like a bombshell, and he accused the Austrians of starting a general war: "You are setting fire to Europe," he said.[297] From the Bosnian crisis on the Russians had avoided mobilizing their forces, even at the cost of embarrassing retreats. In 1909 they had accepted the German ultimatum; during the Balkan wars they had refused to back Serbia or Montenegro in the face of Austrian threats. Even when German General Otto Liman von Sanders had been put in charge of the Turkish Army in Constantinople, a serious threat to their interests in the Straits, the Russian government allowed the problem to end in a compromise, to heavy criticism in the press. On hearing of the ultimatum, however, Sazonov at once thought that Austria and Germany intended to attack Serbia, and that Russia could not stand aside. In July 1914 Russia was not ready for war. Its industry was devastated by a wave of strikes, which raised fears of revolution. If domestic considerations influenced foreign policy they should have argued firmly against risking a war. Russia's military and naval preparations were far from complete. Its finances were less prepared to support a war than they had been ten years earlier. Sazonov, besides, had serious doubts about Britain's reliability if war should break out.[298]

At the Council of Ministers that met on July 24 Sazonov nevertheless argued that accepting the ultimatum would make Serbia a protectorate of the Central Powers. To accept that would mean to abandon Russia's " 'historic mission [to gain the independence of the Slavic peoples], she would be considered a decadent state and would henceforth have to take second place among the powers,' losing 'all her authority' and allowing 'Russian prestige in the Balkans' to 'collapse utterly.' " Besides, concessions would not save the peace, since previous conciliation had failed. "Germany had looked upon our concessions as so many proofs of our weakness and far from having prevented our neighbours from using aggressive measures, we had encouraged them."[299] The other ministers agreed, and the council decided to ask the Austrians to extend the time limit of their ultimatum; to ask Serbia, "to show a desire for conciliation and to fulfil the Austrian Government's requirements in so far as they did not jeopardize the independence of the Serbian state"; and to ask the Tsar to permit a partial mobilization of the armed forces against Austria, should that be needed. The next day Nicholas II sat with the Council and confirmed its decisions.[300]

In this ministerial council, where no one had reason to suppress other considerations, it is striking to observe the dominant role of prestige. Russia's material interests in Serbia and the other Balkan states were nugatory, but the Balkans were the place where its power and reputation were most on display and at risk. The state of its prestige made it more or less able to defend its clients and press its claims about such fundamental matters as access to the Straits, and more or less attractive as an alliance partner to those states on whom it depended for security. In that sense defense of its prestige *was* the defense of a most important interest, and fear of its loss the most powerful motive for risking war. Here, again, Thucydides's triad of interconnected motives help us understand the behavior of states and their international relations.

The Russians' policy in 1914 is also strikingly analogous to that of Athens in 433–31. The Athenians, too, thought it necessary to take a stand lest a failure to do so lead to a weakening of their power to act in the future, and they, too, sought a middle road between passivity and provocation. At the Council of July 24 the influential Minister of Agriculture, A. V. Krivoshein "outlined Russia's dilemma: if they acted too strongly they might bring about a war; if they acted too weakly, as experience showed in the past, they would suffer diplomatic defeat and encourage further demands and 'the public would not understand it.' "[301] So they hit upon the idea of partial mobilization, a device for which there was no plan, which would be a severe hindrance to a general mobilization, should that be needed, and which would not be effective even for war against Austria alone, since it did not include the Warsaw district for fear of alarming Germany. In case of war, that would have left Poland open to an unopposed Austrian attack, but that did not matter, because the Council knew that "partial mobilization against Austria alone could only be a means of supporting diplomacy."[302] It was like the Athenians' sending ten ships to Corcyra where they could not be of any military significance; they were meant as a diplomatic signal to deter Corinthian aggression. Like the Athenians, the Russians were seeking to avoid war through firmness, not to bring it on, but the Russian signal was no more successful than the Athenian.

On July 26 the period preparatory to war began and the measures it required proceeded. For a couple of days conversations with the German and Austrian ambassadors made Sazonov hope for a peaceful solution, but Austria's rejection of the Serbian response, declaration of war, and bombardment of Belgrade convinced him that the Central Powers meant to invade and destroy Serbia. On July 28 news of the Austrian declaration of war against Serbia convinced the Tsar to agree to partial mobilization against Austria. The next day the Germans warned that if Russia did not stop its mobilization German mobilization and war would follow. The bombardment of Belgrade convinced Sazonov that war was inevitable and that Russia could not safely wait any longer for full mobilization. After considerable uncertainty and hesitation, the Tsar finally approved general mobilization on the thirtieth, and the Germans immediately responded in kind. For the Germans, unlike the Russians, mobilization meant war.

The Germans, as we shall see, made much of the priority of Russian mobilization, using it to blame the Russians for bringing on the war. That charge is without merit. The real decision was taken when the Russians decided not to permit the attack on Serbia. "Given Austrian determination to crush Serbia and German willingness to back Vienna even if war with Russia and France should ensue, Petersburg's stand made a European conflict probable."[303] It has often been said that in 1914 "mobilization meant war," but that was true only for Germany. The Russians could stay mobilized behind their own frontiers for a very long time, permitting negotiations for peace, as could France. As Bethmann Hollweg himself told his colleagues in the Prussian State Ministry, "although Russian mobilization has been declared its measures for mobilization can not be compared with those of the states of Western Europe. The Russian troops could stay in their mobilized positions for weeks. Russia does not intend any war but has been compelled to take its measures only because of Austria."[304] It was only Germany, whose need to fight on two fronts and commitment to the Schlieffen plan for whom mobilization had to mean war.

The proper question is, was Russia right to resist? It is hard to disagree with the estimates of the situation given by two Russian diplomats, "both moderate men without Panslav leanings." One said that if Russia yielded, "our prestige in the Slav world and in the Balkans would perish never to return," and the other wrote that giving way to German power would bring Turkey and the Balkan states under the control of the Central Powers and would "result in the total destruction of our prestige and of our power in the Near East."[305] To expect a Great Power to accept such a defeat without a fight was completely unreasonable, yet that was the gamble the Central Powers had decided to take.

France's response to the crisis was distorted by the fact that President Poincaré and Prime Minister Viviani were at sea and largely out of touch with events fron July 23 to 29.[306] Revisionist historians have made much of alleged French instigation of Russian intransigence in the hope of bringing on a war that would bring back Alsace-Lorraine, but modern scholarship rightly has rejected it. The skimpy evidence about the discussions between Poincaré, Viviani, and the Russians between July 20 and 23 suggests that the French leaders did not attempt to inflame the situation. They repeated French support for Russia and its defense of Serbian independence, in part to soothe the Tsar's fears about French reliability caused by the recent electoral victory of the left, in part because they were fearful that the Germans might succeed in their aim of splitting the Entente.[307] Maurice Paléologue, French ambassador to Russia, deliberately delayed reporting the news of Russian mobilization for fear that Viviani, and possibly Poincaré, would react badly, but there is no reason to think earlier information would have made a difference. Most Frenchmen had long given up hopes for *revanche* and a restoration of the lost provinces, if they had ever held any, and a careful study of French opinion from 1905 to 1914 shows that there was no widespread surge of nationalistic, patriotic, *revanchiste* opinion.[308]

Throughout the crisis France's action was reactive and defensive, moved not by ambition but by fear. "France more than any other power in July 1914 was following events rather than leading them."[309] As the crisis drew nearer to its climax, the French looked increasingly and with considerable trepidation to Great Britain.

As early as July 6 Prince Lichnowsky, the German ambassador, warned Grey that the crisis would be serious since the Austrians, with German support, were planning to take strong action against Serbia. Grey looked back fondly on the success of his previous collaboration with the Germans and believed they could be persuaded to restrain the Austrians again if the Russians could be kept under control. He assured Lichnowsky that Britain had no secret agreements with France and Russia and that Britain wanted to maintain an "absolutely free hand, in order to be able to act according to her own judgment in the event of continental complications," and the ambassador passed his words on to Bethmann.[310] "I would continue the same policy," Grey said, "as I had pursued through the Balkan crisis. . . . The greater the risk of war the more closely would I adhere to this policy."[311] He asked the French and Russians to soothe the Germans, but as time passed, alarming news came in from Berlin and Vienna. On July 16 Grey told the Russian ambassador that "we can no longer count on the Germans being peacemakers under all circumstances."[312]

Grey then suggested that Russia and Austria try to settle the Austrian problem between them, but Poincaré and Sazonov wanted to have the Entente issue a warning to Vienna. Grey preferred to have Britain keep its distance and did not want to alienate Germany. Even on July 22 he told Lichnowsky of his willingness to press Serbia to accept Austrian demands if they were moderate. News of the Austrian ultimatum intensified the sense of crisis. Eyre Crowe represented the sense of the Foreign Office when he wrote that the struggle was not about Serbia "but one between Germany aiming at a political dictatorship in Europe and the Powers who desire to retain individual freedom."[313] Grey, however, continued to count on people like Bethmann and Jagow, whom he thought of as wanting peace, to restrain the Austrians. He asked the Germans to join him in urging an extension of the time limit, and he proposed mediation by Britain, Germany, France, and Italy, the four powers not involved directly.

Whatever may have been his previous misgivings, Bethmann worked assiduously to carry out the policy Germany determined at Potsdam. He rejected an extension of the deadline and mediation between Austria and Russia as well as the four-power mediation. But he still believed that Britain could be kept out of the Continental war that was plainly becoming likely. The Germans, therefore, undertook merely to pass on Britain's four-power mediation proposal to Vienna, not recommending it, "because the conflict with Serbia was a question of *prestige* for the Austro-Hungarian monarchy . . . ," but claimed to support mediation in principle. In passing on the proposal, however, Jagow told the Austrians that Germany "assures in the most decided way that it does not identify itself with these propositions."[314]

Austria's declaration of war and the bombardment of Belgrade put an end to the first phase of the crisis. Grey's approach had not prevented the small war, and he now moved in the direction desired by the Foreign Office. On July 29 he called in Lichnowsky and warned him that Britain would not stand aside if France came into the war. "Grey's statement came as a shattering blow, and in the small hours of 30 July Bethmann Hollweg tried to reverse the wheels of German policy."[315] Scholars have argued that a clear statement of Britain's intention to support France, as early as possible but even as late as July 26, might have had the same effect in time to prevent Germany from pressing Austria to declare war, thereby preventing Russian mobilization and possibly providing time for a negotiated settlement. Against that view it is asserted that Grey was not authorized to make such a declaration and, indeed, the Cabinet refused to make such a commitment up to the last moment. But, it has been pointed out, Grey had no more authorization on the twenty-ninth than he would have had on the twenty-sixth; he could just as well have spoken on the earlier date, before the outbreak of war. There can be no certainty, of course, that an earlier statement would have deterred the Germans, but in view of the Kaiser's conversion to a peaceful solution and Bethmann's sharp reversal on the thirtieth, the idea is more than plausible. It took the outbreak of war, however, to shake Grey from his illusions that the Germans were interested in avoiding a war.

After reading the Serbian reply on the twenty-eighth the Kaiser produced his "halt in Belgrade" scheme for preserving peace. He proposed that the Austrian Army march into Belgrade and hold it as security for Serbia's carrying out its promises. Meanwhile, Germany would join the mediation process.[316] Since Austria already had decided not to annex Serbian territory and Grey was friendly to the idea of a halt in Belgrade, there seemed to be a prospect for a peaceful solution. Bethmann Hollweg sent the proposal along as part of instructions to the German ambassador in Vienna. Bethmann has been accused of deliberately delaying the message until the Austrians had declared war, of altering the message so as to play down its more peaceful aspects.[317] That judgment seems unduly harsh. The time between the Kaiser's note, which was sent not to Bethmann but to Jagow, and its dispatch to Vienna by Bethmann was less than half a day. Bethmann's telegram talked about the need to make concessions to opinion, both of other nations and of the German people, lest the Central Powers incur the responsibility for bringing on war, and it does try to avoid the impression that Germany was holding Austria back. Such a tone might merely have been prudent, given the mood in Vienna, and Bethmann certainly included the Kaiser's plan as part of his advice. Still, he seems to have been more interested in acting in such a way as to put the blame for war on Russia, thereby gaining support for his policy in Germany and the neutrality of Britain than in pressing as hard as possible for a reversal in policy. We cannot know with how much enthusiasm he acted, but it is too much to suggest that he sabotaged the plan.

By the time the message arrived Austria had declared war, and it would have been difficult to reverse that action. Besides, even as Berchtold was studying it Conrad heard from Moltke that any more delay in mobilizing the Austrian Army would lead to disaster. When Conrad reported this Berchtold threw up his hands and asked, "Who actually rules in Berlin, Bethmann or Moltke?"[318] which suggests that he, at least, thought Bethmann really was proposing a delay. After some further delay he gave an evasive answer, and the crisis continued.

Hereafter the pressure on policy by the German military became more intense as the needs of the Schlieffen plan made themselves felt. Moltke and his colleagues wanted the swiftest possible mobilization so that an attack on Belgium and France would bring quick success before the vast forces of Russia could come into play. Bethmann, on the other hand, never gave up hope fully of keeping the British neutral. He was also very concerned to prevent socialist opposition within Germany in case of war. Both of these goals required that the Russians be made to seem the aggressors, so he tried desperately to delay the German decision to mobilize until after the Russians had made theirs. Under great pressure, he was forced to agree to German mobilization by noon on July 31, still hoping that the Russians would announce their general mobilization first. Bethmann's tactics were rewarded: at 11:55 the anxious, assembled German political and military leaders received a telegraph from St. Petersburg announcing Russian mobilization. They were free now to blame the Russians for forcing them to mobilize immediately and, thereby, for starting the war. His plan worked both in the short and the longer run: when war came the Social Democrats rallied to the national cause, comfortable in the thought that it was an imperialist war forced on Germany by an autocratic Tsarist Russia that had been the first to violate the peace, and as we have seen, after the war, Russian mobilization became a major part of the revisionist case that sought to lighten Germany's share of the blame.

The Germans formally demanded that the Russians immediately stop all their preparations for war, and when that was refused they declared war on August 1. They also asked the French to promise neutrality in a war between Germany and Russia that, among other things, would have required a violation of France's treaty with Russia. Had they agreed, the French also would have been required to turn over to Germany their major fortresses on the German border. Prime Minister Viviani refused, answering: "France will act in accordance with her interests."[319] The French were desperately worried that Britain might stand aloof. To make it inescapably clear that when war came France could not be accused of aggression, they ordered their troops to withdraw to at least ten kilometers from the German border. Finally, the Germans invented some stories of French violations of German territory and declared war on August 3.

Britain's decision had not been made yet. As late as August 1 Grey was still talking to the German ambassador about ways in which Britain might remain neutral. On the same day the French Minister of War hopefully told the British attaché, "We rely on ourselves first and on you,"[320] but the French probably felt more anxiety than hope. Churchill believed that the Cabinet was overwhelmingly pacific: "At least three-quarters of its members were determined not to be drawn into a European quarrel unless Great Britain was herself attacked, which was unlikely."[321] Within the Cabinet there was a bloc of at least four men whose views were close to those of John Burns: "Splendid Isolation. No Balance of Power. No incorporation in a continental system."[322] On hearing of the Austrian ultimatum to Serbia on July 24 Prime Minister Asquith wrote a friend that he expected a Continental war involving France and Germany, as well as Austria and Russia, "a real Armageddon," but he took comfort in the thought that "Happily there seems . . . no reason why we should be more than spectators." On August 2, only ten days later, he wrote again, telling her of the six principles that shaped his thinking:

1   We have no obligations of any kind either to France or Russia to give them military or naval help.

2   The despatch of the Expeditionary Forces to help France at this moment is out of the question and wd. serve no object.

3   We mustn't forget the ties created by our long-standing and intimate friendship with France.

4   It is against British interests that France should be wiped out as a Great Power.

5   We cannot allow Germany to use the Channel as a hostile base.

6   We have obligations to Belgium to prevent her being utilized and absorbed by Germany.[323]

He did not make clear how he weighed these contradictory principles, but he must have had them in mind when he made his cheery observation on July 24. Asquith was not a pacifist but a Liberal imperialist close to Grey and Haldane. That he should have held such views helps explain the nervousness of the French and also Bethmann's persistence in working to achieve British neutrality.

Only with the greatest difficulty did the Cabinet decide to become involved. On July 31 they were ready to abandon France and stay out entirely.[324] After a Cabinet meeting the next day Grey told Paul Cambon, the French ambassador, that even if Britain entered the war it would not send an expeditionary force to France, as had been agreed on in military talks in 1912 and thereafter, nor would it commit its Navy to defend France's northern coast, abandoned by the French fleet that was now entirely in the Mediterranean. In despair, Cambon asked if the word "honor" had been erased from the British dictionary and told Nicolson *"Il vont nous lâcher* [They are going to drop us]."[325]

German actions, however, soon began to change British attitudes. On August 2 the Germans invaded neutral Luxembourg, leading the Cabinet to promise to defend the French coast. During Cabinet discussions some members did not believe Britain was bound to fight, and four resigned rather than permit a single step toward war, two of them later withdrawing their resignations. The government was threatened by a serious division, even a collapse, but the defection of the pacific faction was checked by a letter sent to Asquith by the Conservatives. Their leader, Bonar Law, wrote: "it would be fatal to the honour and security of the United Kingdom to hesitate in supporting France and Russia at the present juncture; and we offer our unhesitating support to the Government in any measures they may consider necessary for that object."[326] That made it clear that if the Liberals split a government more solidly for war would replace them.

On the same evening the Germans presented an ultimatum to Belgium due to expire in a matter of hours on the next morning. The news reached Asquith on the morning of August 3 and was soon followed by an appeal for help from the King of Belgium. Britain was one of five guarantors of Belgian neutrality by a treaty signed in 1839, which had been reaffirmed in 1870 by France, Prussia, and Britain. Even then some Cabinet members still hesitated, but the Cabinet and country were swept toward war. Even without the invasion of Belgium it is hard to believe that Britain would have stood by and permitted a German defeat of France, but the invasion permitted the Liberals to remain in power and it unified British opinion. Those who would not fight for the balance of power and British security could console themselves that they were fighting for international law, the sanctity of treaties, and the protection of helpless neutrals. On the afternoon of August 3 Grey sent an ultimatum to the Germans demanding German respect for Belgian neutrality. It expired on midnight of the fourth, and Britain declared war. Even then there was hesitation and delay, and the decision to send a British expeditionary force to France came only on August 6. All the major powers were now engaged, and the First World War had begun.

On August 3 Grey went to Parliament and delivered a speech setting forth the situation and how it had developed. He said that Britain could keep out of the war by issuing a proclamation of unconditional neutrality, but he rejected that course:

> If we did take that line by saying: "We will have nothing whatever to do with this matter" under no conditions—the Belgian Treaty obligations, the possible position in the Mediterranean, with damage to British interests, and what may happen to France from our failure to support France—if we were to say that all those things mattered nothing, were as nothing, and to say we would stand aside, we should, I believe, sacrifice our respect and good name and reputation before the world, and should not escape the most serious and grave economic consequences.[327]

Years later he wrote that "the real reason for going into the war was that, if we did not stand by France and stand up for Belgium against this aggression, we should be isolated, discredited, and hated; and there would be nothing for us but a miserable and ignoble future."[328] Grey and the British, to be sure, were moved by fear of the danger Germany presented to their most vital interests, but they could be made to understand them and face their consequences only when they understood the danger to their honor.

THE CAUSES OF THE WAR

No war has produced so long and heated a debate about its causes as the First World War. The chief cause for that, no doubt, is the famous "War Guilt Clause," number 231, of the Versailles Treaty at the end of the war. That clause assigned full blame to the Central Powers and served as the moral basis for what many saw as the punitive character of the peace, especially the reparation assessments. Naturally, the Germans set out at once to demonstrate that responsibility for the war rested chiefly, or at least equally, with others, and the war of documents and monographs was on. Claims by U.S. President Woodrow Wilson and others that the war had been fought for noble motives that excluded self-interest and concern for security, such as self-determination and democracy; that it was to be ended by a just peace without victors, that it was not against the people but only against their leaders—all gone by 1919—produced angry disillusionment and a wave of revisionist histories, chiefly in the United States and Great Britain. Remarkably, these came to dominate informed opinion in those countries and to a considerable extent in Europe as well, until the work of Fritz Fischer and his followers beginning in the 1960s. Today there are few reputable scholars who would deny that Germany and Austria, but primarily Germany, bear the chief responsibility for the war.

In the 1980s, however, a new wave of revisionists emerged. They generally ignored the new scholarship and seemed to be moved by contemporary Cold War issues to suggest that greater understanding and flexibility by Great Britain might have avoided the war.[329] The central assumptions of what we might call the neorevisionists, though they rarely state them directly, are that Wilhelmine Germany was not really dangerous and that its actions in the two decades before 1914 did not require the strong reaction they received from Britain: Germany's intentions were not unappeasably aggressive, and the Germans had no clear goals incompatible with Britain's security. One formulation of the view goes even farther, finding fault not with German aggressiveness but with the reaction to it:

> Geography and history conspired to make Germany's rise late,
> rapid, vulnerable, and aggressive. The rest of the world reacted by

crushing the upstart. If, in the process, the German state lost its bearings and was possessed by an evil demon, perhaps the proper conclusion is not so much that civilization was uniquely weak in Germany, but that it is so fragile everywhere. And *perhaps the proper lesson is not so much the need for vigilance against aggressors, but the ruinous consequences of refusing reasonable accommodation to upstarts.*[330] [emphasis added]

The question is, what "accommodation" could the European states have made to the German "upstart" that would have brought satisfaction to Germany and stability to Europe? What, in fact, did Germany want? At the turn of the century Germany was the strongest military power in the world. It also had the strongest and most dynamic economy on the Continent. In 1897, without any previous naval tradition, without any new challenge from the sea to require an expensive change in policy, the Germans undertook the construction of a major battle fleet concentrated in the North Sea where it threatened British naval superiority and the only security available to Britain. The British gradually became alarmed as they came to recognize the threat Germany posed.

In the Foreign Office, Eyre Crowe, the resident expert on Germany, suggested in 1907 that the Germans might be "aiming at a general political hegemony and maritime ascendancy, threatening the independence of her neighbors and ultimately the existence of England." Concern over German intentions already had caused Britain to abandon its policy of isolation and enter into a series of understandings and alliances with other countries. Repeated statements by the German Emperor and many other leaders in and outside the government asserted that Germany was aiming at "world power," that it demanded "a place in the sun," that "no question of world politics must be settled without the consent of the German emperor."

In the two Moroccan crises the Germans tried to bully France and break the link between Britain and France. They continued to build big battleships in numbers that would destroy the security of Britain unless the British were willing to divert large sums of money from domestic purposes to hold up their side in a naval race. All this gradually converted the Foreign Minister, Sir Edward Grey, and the Liberal British government, which came into office committed to arms reduction and was full of isolationists and quasi pacifists, to Crowe's dark view of German intentions.

To be sure, Grey's policy met criticism from the isolationists and pacifists inside and outside the government and the party. Some claimed that Germany represented no threat at all: fear of war was being stirred up by militarists and the arms manufacturers, the "merchants of death" who were their associates. Others believed that the British fleet was strong enough and did not need to grow. Many opposed new naval construction because it would interfere with the domestic welfare program to which the Liberals were committed. Those influenced by Norman Angell's book *The Great Illusion* thought war impossible and so considered participation in an arms race irrational and unnecessary. In spite of such opposition the British competed in and won the naval race; they also maintained and strengthened their ties with France and maintained them with Russia because they feared the growth of the German Navy and the uses to which it might be put.

Even on the evidence available to Crowe, Grey, and their colleagues their fears were well-founded. However often the Kaiser might proclaim his friendly feelings for England and Tirpitz declare that the fleet had no offensive purposes, the continued construction of big battleships concentrated in the North Sea and the acceleration of that construction justified British suspicion and fear, even without inside information about German intentions. Scholarship, of course, has now made clear that Britain really was the target of the new German Navy and that the likeliest explanation of Tirpitz's otherwise irrational naval program is that it aimed at least at equality with the British fleet; when combined with Germany's military power it would give the Germans the ability to change the status quo in its favor and to the great and dangerous disadvantage of other powers, especially Britain. It would be some years before the Germans could hope for parity at sea, but the British expected that even before the Germans were prepared for a confrontation at sea, they would try to use their "risk" fleet to force concessions.

What concessions would they demand? Were they reasonable enough for Britain to make without endangering its security? Would an attempt to understand the feelings and needs of the new empire and to meet them have averted the conflict? What, in fact, were Germany's goals? Fritz Fischer, now followed by many other historians, believes that the Germans wanted to conquer and dominate the European Continent from the English Channel to the Ukraine, to exploit its economic resources and use it as a base for a world empire.[331] His main evidence is the program of war aims they drew up soon after the war broke out in 1914, the "September Program," which spells out the European part of such a plan.

We need not accept Fischer's thesis that Germany planned and unleashed the war precisely to achieve that program to believe that at least something of what the Germans hoped for before the war is reflected in the plans approved by Bethmann Hollweg only a month after it began. The central principle of those plans was "the safeguarding of the German empire for the foreseeable future in the East and West. Hence France must be so weakened that it cannot rise again as a great power. Russia must be pushed back from the German frontier as far as possible, and its rule over the non-Russian peoples must be broken."

Since victory in the West seemed imminent, while the situation in the East still was unclear, the bulk of the September Program dealt with the West. The military would decide whether the French should cede Belfort, the western slopes of the Vosges, the coast from Dunkirk to Boulogne, and destroy their forts on the German frontier; the military at once decided that they should. Germany would acquire the iron mines of Briey. A preferential trade treaty would make France "our export land," and the French would be required to pay an indemnity that would make it impossible for them to manufacture armaments for at least twenty years. Belgium would lose Liège, Verviers, and probably Antwerp, and would become a vassal state, accepting German garrisons in its ports. To this Belgian subsidiary of Germany would be attached French Flanders and the Channel ports of Dunkirk, Calais, and Boulogne. Holland would be ostensibly independent, "but essentially subject to us." Luxembourg would be incorporated directly into the German empire. Apart from these territorial provisions, but by no means less important, was the plan for establishing "an economic organization of *Mitteleuropa* through mutual customs agreements . . . including France, Belgium, Holland, Denmark, Austria, Poland, and perhaps Italy, Sweden, and Norway" that would guarantee German economic domination of Europe.

Plans for the East were not formulated yet so early, but what we know of ideas that were entertained shows that they led naturally to the settlement imposed on the new Bolshevik government of Russia by the Treaty of Brest-Litovsk in 1918. It deprived Russia of Poland, Finland, the Baltic states, Ukraine, and parts of the Caucasus. Although the treaty contained language about self-determination, there can be no doubt that all these lands would be under German control, one way or another.

We should remember that Bethmann Hollweg was a moderate in the context of Wilhelmine Germany and that his program fell short of the wishes not only of right-wing extremists, both civilian and military, but also of most intellectuals and political moderates. A "Petition of Intellectuals" published in July 1915 was signed by a great number of theologians, teachers, artists, writers, and some 352 university professors; it demanded a program of annexations that went far beyond the September Program. At the same time Bethmann was producing his own scheme, the leader of the Catholic Center party, Matthias Erzberger, was demanding the annexation of Belgium, parts of France, and the entire Congo, the conversion of the Baltic states and Ukraine into German dependencies, and the imposition of a reparation bill that would more than pay off the entire German national debt.[332]

The course of the war shows that the Chancellor would have had to yield to more extreme opinions or make way for more extreme leaders. The chances are that a victorious Germany would have claimed more than what was set down at Brest-Litovsk. In any event, Britain would have been faced with the domination of Europe by a single power far stronger and more dangerous than the Spain of Philip II or the France of Louis XIV, or even of Napoleon. It would have the greatest army the world had ever seen, unprecedented economic resources with which to make its already formidable navy, now able to operate from a series of Channel ports, stronger than the British fleet, and reserves of manpower the British could not hope to match. The new Germany would have the power to exclude British trade from the Continent, doing fearful damage to the British economy. If necessary, it could even be capable of invading and subjugating the British Isles.

Wilhelmine Germany was not just another European nation seeking to maintain its national interest or even to advance it by means tolerable to its neighbors. From the 1890s imperial Germany was a fundamentally dissatisfied power, eager to disrupt the status quo and to achieve its expansive goals, by bullying if possible, by war if necessary.

It might be argued that these grandiose aims, clear evidence for which only appears after the outbreak of war, grew and developed only after a long period of frustration and Cold War, as a result of British intransigence. If the British had been more forthcoming, some might say, a settlement might have been reached on more acceptable terms. The historical record will not support any such claim. As one keen student of the subject has put it:

The historian aware of the pressures for expansion in imperial Germany is bound to wonder whether a change of tone on Britain's part, a greater generosity over this or that colonial boundary, would really have had a significant difference. They might have papered over the cracks in the Anglo-German relationship for a few more years, but it is difficult to see how such gestures would have altered the elemental German push to change the existing distribution of power—which, unless the British were willing to accept a substantial diminution in national influence and safety, was bound to provoke a reaction on their part.[333]

If the British could not have avoided the war by greater flexibility, was there no other way? No sooner had the war broken out than the charge was leveled at the British government, especially at Lord Grey, that the British might have deterred the Germans from launching the war if they had made formal and open military alliances with France and Russia and if Grey had made Britain's support of those countries clearer during the crisis and the years before it. One possible response is that the charge is unfair. Britain and Grey, it has been argued, made their position clear enough for anyone who did not avert his eyes. Haldane had made it plain that Britain would stand by France in case of attack by Germany as early as 1912, and the news had sent the Kaiser into a tantrum. The mutually dependent dispositions of the British and French fleets made it even more obvious that Britain could not abandon France. The German ambassador in London repeatedly and correctly informed Berlin of Grey's intentions. Finally, Britain's guarantee to Belgium, going back to 1839 and reaffirmed in 1870, should have told the Germans that the British would not stand aside when they invaded Belgium, as the Schlieffen plan required them to do.

Yet that argument has significant flaws. Grey, still less the British Cabinet, never fully accepted the implications of their own policy. Having abandoned "splendid isolation," they clung, nevertheless, to the notion of the "free hand." To the end they firmly denied that they had a binding obligation to France and saw themselves as free to act or not, and so they told the French and also the Germans. Almost to the last, Grey refused to abandon the hope that he could work with Germany to defuse whatever crisis might arise, to the great alarm of his French and Russian associates. Up to the last prewar days Grey was discussing with the Germans what it would take to keep Britain neutral; the majority of the Cabinet regarded it as possible not to come to the aid of the French; many thought that Britain need not go to war if Belgium was invaded; and even after the idea of war was accepted, many thought Britain should not send an army to the Continent. Not only could Britain's friends and enemies not be sure what the British would do until the last minute, *the British themselves did not know.* In those circumstances it may not be surprising that even so cautious and conservative a man as Bethmann was willing to take the great risk that brought on the war. "Grey had followed the wrong course during July. He had hoped until the very end that by not coming down on either side he would delay the adoption of extreme measures. . . . Grey exaggerated his ability to play a 'floating role.' Though he never intended to abandon his friends, by attempting to mediate between the groups of powers, he may have encouraged Bethmann to gamble on his ultimate neutrality."[334]

There is not, however, reason to be confident that the clearest statement of British intentions clung to steadily over a period of time would have succeeded in deterring the Germans, for the British failed to take the actions needed to make deterrence effective. Strengthening the fleet and making new friends were not enough to stop the Germans from trying to change the world balance in their favor, even if it meant war, because neither action nor both together guaranteed the defeat of Germany's plan for a quick victory in a land war in the West followed by another swift victory on land against Russia. The British fleet could do nothing to prevent such victories, and any blockade it might impose would have little effect on a Germany that controlled the resources of all Europe. The only sure deterrent of any German leader who was not insane was the certainty of the presence on the Western front, soon after the outbreak of war, of an army large enough to make a quick victory impossible, an army of such a size as the British ultimately put into the field too late to deter war but just in time to avoid defeat.

The British, of course, had long opposed maintaining a large army in peacetime and refused to recruit their small regular armed forces by conscription, as the Continental powers did. After the Franco-Prussian War no less convinced a liberal than John Stuart Mill favored military conscription, but his appears to have been a solitary voice. After the Boer War one Minister for War raised the question of conscription, but he was attacked from all sides. At the turn of the century such an idea was one of those "unthinkable thoughts" that form no part of serious discussions of policy. Only after the outbreak of war and the deaths of hundreds of thousands of

British soldiers did the idea of compulsory military service seem both possible and necessary, and it was put into effect, too late to serve as a deterrent.

The Germans had long known the significance of Britain's military impotence. They knew that the British Army was a small volunteer force meant to serve as a colonial constabulary and not intended for Continental service. The fact that the British had no conscription also meant that they had no trained reserve that could be brought to bear quickly on the Western front. Schlieffen himself assumed that the British would intervene in a Continental war, but he was not troubled by the prospect. In an appendix to his plan prepared in 1906 he discussed the possibility of a British expeditionary force of 100,000 men, which he thought would probably land at Antwerp. There, he said, "They will be shut up, . . . together with the Belgians."[335] Schlieffen, therefore, thought it safe to ignore Britain's army in his strategic calculations, and his successors did the same. That is what explains Germany's willingness to go forward even after it was clear that Britain would fight.

No peace keeps itself. After the Franco-Prussian War Bismarck judged it to be in the interests of Germany to exercise restraint and maintain the peace of Europe. For twenty years under his guidance Germany accepted the major burden of keeping the peace by maintaining a powerful military force and using it to help avoid war. When William II and his ministers abandoned that role and became the chief menace to the status quo and the peace of Europe, the only power capable of taking its place and checking the movement toward war was Great Britain. Reluctantly, slowly, and ultimately inadequately, the British assumed some part of that burden. They undertook just enough responsibility to avoid defeat narrowly but not enough to deter war.

General Henry Wilson called Lord Grey "an ignorant, vain, weak man, quite unfit to be the Foreign Minister of any country larger than Portugal. A man who knew nothing of policy and strategy going hand in hand."[336] The first charge is entirely unfair. Grey was able to maintain and strengthen the system of ententes that was essential to Britain's safety and to win the naval race without which Britain would have been conquered. He was able to do so in spite of a Cabinet and a party that often opposed and tried to undercut his major policies. He was not weak, as the Germans learned repeatedly to their dismay.

The second charge, however, is more defensible. His determination to pursue a middle course, the policy of the "free hand," was increasingly unwise and dangerous, as Germany's policies made war more likely and effective deterrence more necessary. The entente with France, strengthened by the Moroccan crises, military talks, and naval arrangements meant that England would need to go to war if France were attacked by Germany and that Britain would need to send an army to the Continent, but Grey and the British never faced fully what that meant. The thought was too unpleasant, the price of facing it too high. Logic might lead to the conclusion that British commitments and safety required a large conscripted army, but their ability to appreciate that was undermined by the fact that Britain had none and was not willing to acquire any. In the decade before the war many Englishmen proposed it, but neither party would support it. In the liberal world of Edwardian England, even across party lines, armies were connected with aggression, oppression, and evil, and compulsory service was viewed as an intolerable violation of individual liberty. One radical went so far as to call the advocates of conscription part of "a covert conspiracy to militarise the country and to undermine civil liberties."[337] Naval power, on the other hand, was seen as defensive and in the service of peace. Grey and Britain, therefore, clung to Mahan's theory of sea power and refused to think seriously about the Continental commitment. "Neither Grey nor his advisers understood the dangers of a European role backed by a powerful navy but a small army." There are many explanations for this blindness; the moral one should not be overlooked. "If the Foreign Office continued to accept the doctrines of Captain Mahan uncritically it was because naval power was dressed in the clothes of righteousness."[338] Like Pericles and the Athenians, therefore, Grey and the British pursued policies that overemphasized the importance of the Navy and undervalued the significance of the Army.

Suppose, however, that the British had looked at their predicament clearly, honestly, and courageously in the years between 1898 and 1914. Suppose they had faced the fact that only the assurance of a large, well-trained British army that could quickly come to France's aid in case of attack could make a German victory in the West impossible and obviously so. Suppose they had swallowed the bitter pill of introducing conscription, and in a time of peace, at that. It would have meant going against an honored and comfortable tradition; it would have been costly and would have strained the British economy at a time when there was great pressure for domestic spending; it would have been at odds with the great libertarian ethic central to the British character—but the result would have been the presence of a standing army and a large trained reserve in 1914. That would have made the Schlieffen plan or any conceivable German plan of war obviously absurd and certain to fail. Whatever Germany's ambitions and frustrations, such a course of action could have forced Germany to abandon its reckless and unnecessary challenge to the stability of Europe with untold benefit to itself and the world. However painful such sacrifices might be, they could have spared Britain and Europe more than four terrible years of war, horrendous casualties, and the rapid loss of their place in the world.

Unlike the Athenians, the British had the capacity to take all the measures needed to keep the peace through deterrence, though at great cost in money and to their traditional way of life. To achieve that purpose, however, required an action they were unwilling to take, even to contemplate and confront. Their refusal to adjust their strategic capacity to their policy undermined their ability to conduct that policy. The unacknowledged, perhaps unconscious, understanding of the gap between their goals and their capacity to achieve them led Grey and the British to pursue an indecisive middle course that made it even harder to keep the peace.

1. Laurence Lafore, *The Long Fuse,* New York, 1971, pp. 25–26, 28.

2. Winston S. Churchill, *The World Crisis 1911–1918,* London, 1938, pp. 2–3.

3. Quoted by Michael Stürmer, "A Nation State Against History and Geography: The German Dilemma," in *Escape Into War?,* Schöllgen, p. 71.

4. Craig, *Europe Since 1815,* p. 339.

5. V. R. Berghahn, *Germany and the Approach of War in 1914,* New York, 1973, pp. 9–10.

6. For an excellent account of the workings of British foreign policy in this period see Zara S. Steiner, *The Foreign Office and Foreign Policy* (New York, 1969), and *Britain and the Origins of the First World War* (New York, 1977).

7. Steiner, *ibid.*

8. The following discussion is based chiefly on Kennedy, *The Rise and Fall of the Great Powers,* pp. 151–58.

9. See the table in Kennedy, *Rise and Fall,* p. 154.

10. *Ibid.,* pp. 152–53.

11. Felix Gilbert, *The End of the European Era 1890 to the Present,* New York, 1970, pp. 28–29.

12. A. G. L. Shaw, ed. *Great Britain and the Colonies 1815–1865,* London, 1970, cited in Kennedy, *Rise and Fall,* p. 155.

13. *Ibid.,* p. 56.

14. *Ibid.,* pp. 8–9.

15. *Ibid.,* p. 11.

16. F. Lee Benns, *European History Since 1870,* 3rd ed., New York, 1950, p. 267.

17. S. R. Williamson, Jr., *Austria-Hungary and the Origins of the First World War,* New York, 1991, pp. 13–14.

18. Quoted by Joachim Remak, "The Healthy Invalid: How Doomed the Habsburg Empire?" *Journal of Modern History* 41(1969): p. 132.

19. *Ibid.,* p. 131.

20. Remak, "The Healthy Invalid," p. 141.

21. *Ibid.*, p. 26.

22. Quoted by Benns, *European History*, p. 128.

23. Bosworth, *Italy*, p. 34.

24. W. L. Langer, *European Alliances and Alignments 1871–1890*, 2nd ed., New York, 1966, p. 16.

25. Quoted by S. B. Fay, *The Origins of the World War*, vol. 1, 2nd ed. (New York, 1966), p. 53, n. 2 (my translation).

26. General Hans von Schweinitz, quoted by Langer, *European Alliances*, p. 20.

27. Gordon A. Craig, *Germany 1866–1945*, New York, 1978, p. 104.

28. Hajo Holborn, *A History of Modern Germany*, vol. 3, 1840–1945, New York, 1969, p. 236.

29. A. J. P. Taylor, *The Struggle for Mastery in Europe 1848–1918*, Oxford, 1957, p. 216.

30. Such is the suggestion of Craig, *Germany*, p. 108.

31. Taylor, *Struggle*, p. 229.

32. Fay, *Origins*, vol. 1, pp. 72–73.

33. Quoted by G. H. Rupp, *A Wavering Friendship: Russia and Austria 1876–1878*, Cambridge, Mass., 1941, p. 39.

34. "We could endure that our friends should lose or win battles against each other, but not that one of the two should be so severely wounded and injured that its position as an independent Great Power, taking its part in the councils of Europe, would be endangered." (Prince Otto von Bismarck, *Reflections and Reminiscences*, vol. 2, translated by A. J. Butler, New York, 1899, p. 234). For a very similar statement, which makes Bismarck's concern for the future of Austria clear, see Taylor, *Struggle*, p. 239, n. 2.

35. Quoted by Craig, *Germany*, p. 111.

36. Craig, *Europe Since 1815*, p. 255.

37. Langer, *European Alliances*, p. 171.

38. Taylor, *Struggle*, p. 252.

39. Quoted by Craig, *Germany*, p. 113.

40. *Ibid.*, p. 254.

41. *Ibid.*

42. Bismarck to William I, August 31, 1879, *Grosse Politik* iii, no. 455, cited by Taylor, *Struggle,* p. 263.

43. Taylor, *Struggle,* p. 264.

44. Fay, *Origins,* I, p. 70.

45. *Ibid.,* p. 71.

46. Quoted by Langer, *European Alliances,* p. 210.

47. *Ibid.,* p. 212.

48. Quoted by Craig, *Europe,* p. 257.

49. Langer, *European Alliances,* p. 212.

50. *Grosse Politik,* iii, no. 208.

51. Fay, *Origins,* I, p. 86.

52. *Ibid.,* p. 88.

53. Langer, *European Alliances,* p. 278.

54. Quoted by Paul M. Kennedy, *The Rise of the Anglo-German Antagonism 1860–1914* (London, 1980), p. 204. Kennedy believes that underlying the surface of good relations between Britain and Germany in these years lay a more fundamental discomfort resting on "ideological and domestic-political aspects." (p. 161). For a critique of that view see Klaus Hildebrand, *German Foreign Policy From Bismarck to Adenauer, The Limits of Statecraft,* translated by Louise Willmot (London, 1989), pp. 64–83.

55. Langer, *European Alliances,* p. 283.

56. Fay, *Origins,* I, p. 99.

57. Craig, *Germany,* pp. 116–17.

58. Some emphasize economic problems such as the depression that hit Germany in the 1870s that led some to look to colonies for new markets, others on domestic politics, still others on considerations of European foreign policy. Good examples include: Henry A. Turner, Jr., "Bismarck's Imperial Venture: Anti-British in Origin?" in *Britain and Germany in Africa: Imperial Rivalry and Colonial Rule,* P. Gifford and W. R. Lewis, eds. (New Haven, 1967), pp. 47ff.; H.-U. Wehler, *Bismarck und der Imperialismus* (Cologne and Berlin, 1969), which is discussed critically by P. M. Kennedy, "German Colonial Expansion: Has the

'Manipulated Social Imperialism' Been Ante-Dated?" *Past and Present* 54(1972): 134–41. Three valuable contributions appear in S. Foerster, W. J. Mommsen, and R. Robinson, eds., *Bismarck, Europe, and Africa* (London, 1988); H. Pogge von Strandmann, "Consequences of the Foundation of the German Empire: Colonial Expansion and the Process of Political-Economic Rationalization," pp. 105–20; K. J. Bade, Imperial Germany and West Africa: Colonial Movement, Business Interests, and Bismarck's 'Colonial Policies,' " pp. 121–47; W. J. Mommsen, "Bismarck, the Concert of Europe, and the Future of West Africa, 1883–1885," pp. 151–70.

59. N. Rich and M. H. Fisher, eds., *The Holstein Papers,* Cambridge, England, 1957, p. 161.

60. Bade, *Bismarck, Europe, and Africa,* p. 147.

61. A. J. P. Taylor, *Struggle,* p. 294.

62. Langer, *European Alliances,* p. 370.

63. *Ibid.*

64. Craig, *Germany,* p. 131.

65. Langer, *European Alliances,* pp. 422–23.

66. Langer *(Ibid.* p. 440) prefers to call it the *Near Eastern Understanding* or *Entente.*

67. Craig, *Germany,* p. 132.

68. Langer, *European Alliances,* pp. 423–24.

69. *Ibid.,* p. 424.

70. Craig, *Germany,* p. 134.

71. *Struggle,* p. 324.

72. Klaus Hildebrand, "Opportunities and Limits of German Foreign Policy in the Bismarckian Era, 1871–1890: 'A System of Stopgaps?' " in Gregor Schöllgen ed., *Escape into War? The Foreign Policy of Imperial Germany,* New York, 1990, p. 88.

73. *Ibid.*

74. *Ibid.,* p. 85.

75. Thucydides, 2.65.5.

76. *Ibid.,* 2.65.8.

77.   Lothar Gall, *Bismarck, Der weisse revolutionaer,* Frankfurt, 1980, pp. 634–36.

78.   Hildebrand, "Opportunities and Limits," p. 90. In light of the growing power of the Social Democrats, Hildebrand's dark predictions about the consequences of greater democracy in Germany may be too pessimistic.

79.   Thucydides, 5.15.2.

80.   Thucydides, 6.18.6–7. Adapted from the Crawley translation.

81.   See pp. 132–34.

82.   Craig, *Germany,* p. 134.

83.   Craig, *Germany,* p. 227.

84.   Lamar Cecil, *Wilhelm II Prince and Emperor 1859–1900,* Chapel Hill and London, 1989, p. xii.

85.   *William II, Emperor of Germany, The Kaiser's Memoirs, 1888–1918,* translated by Thomas R. Ybarra. New York, 1922, pp. 6–9.

86.   *Ibid.,* p. 170.

87.   J. A. Nichols, *Germany After Bismarck, The Caprivi Era 1890–1894,* Cambridge, Mass., 1958, p. 32.

88.   Craig, *Germany,* p. 230.

89.   Norman Rich, *Friedrich von Holstein, Politics and Diplomacy in the Era of Bismarck and Wilhelm II,* vol. 1, Cambridge, England, 1965, p. 320.

90   *Ibid.,* p. 323.

91.   *Ibid.*

92.   Taylor, *Struggle,* p. 328.

93.   Nichols, *Germany After Bismarck,* p. 56.

94.   Cecil, *Wilhelm II,* p. 116–17.

95.   *Ibid.,* p. 131.

96.   *Ibid.,* p. 142.

97.   Rich, *Holstein,* p. 323.

98.   Taylor, *Struggle,* p. 228, n. 3.

99.   *Ibid.,* p. 333.

100. Ibid.

101. The following discussion of the military consequences of the Franco-Russian alliance starts from the views of Taylor, *Struggle,* pp. 338, 340.

102. Gerhard A. Ritter, *The Schlieffen Plan: Critique of a Myth,* London, 1958, p. 18.

103. Ibid., p. 21.

104. Taylor, *Struggle,* p. 340.

105. Ibid., n. 2.

106. G. P. Gooch and Harold Temperley, eds., *British Documents on the Origins of the War, 1898–1914,* vol. 11. London, 1930, no. 101.

107. Fay, *Origins,* vol. 1, p. 34.

108. Craig, *Germany,* p. 237.

109. Rich, *Holstein,* vol. 1, p. 358.

110. Craig, *Germany,* pp. 239–40.

111. Hatzfeld's letter and the Kaiser's comments can be found in *Grosse Politik,* vol. VIII, pp. 435–39.

112. Erich Brandenburg, *From Bismarck to the World War,* Oxford, 1933, pp. 53ff.

113. Rich, *Holstein,* vol. 1, pp. 373–74.

114. Ibid., p. 374.

115. *Grosse Politik,* vol. XI, no. 2610, pp. 31–32.

116. *Holstein Papers,* vol. 1, p. 162.

117. Rich, *Holstein,* vol. 2, p. 469.

118. Paul M. Kennedy, *The Rise of Anglo-German Antagonism 1860–1914,* London, 1980, p. 220.

119. Ibid.

120. *Holstein Papers,* vol. 3, p. 585; Cecil, *Wilhelm II,* pp. 288–89.

121. Rich, *Holstein,* vol. 2, pp. 468–69.

122. Quoted in J. C. G. Röhl, *Germany Without Bismarck: The Crisis of Government in the Second Reich, 1800–1900,* London, 1967, p. 162.

123. Wolfram Fischer, *Germany and the World Economy during the Nineteenth Century,* London, 1984, p. 26.

124. Gregor Schöllgen, ed. *Escape Into War? The Foreign Policy of Imperial Germany,* Oxford, New York, Munich, 1990; "Introduction," p. 10.

125. Immanuel Geis, ed. *July 1914, The Outbreak of the First World War, Selected Documents,* New York, 1974, p. 21.

126. V. R. Berghahn, *Germany and the Approach of War in 1914,* New York, 1973, p. 35.

127. Fritz Fischer, "The Foreign Policy of Imperial Germany and the Outbreak of the First World War." In *Escape,* Schöllgen, p. 26.

128. Steinberg, "The Copenhagen Complex," p. 42.

129. Jonathan Steinberg, "The Copenhagen Complex," *Journal of Contemporary History,* vol. 1, 3(1966): 25.

130. See Paul M. Kennedy, "Mahan *versus* Mackinder: Two Interpretations of British Sea Power," *Strategy and Diplomacy* (London, 1984), pp. 43–85.

131. Cecil, *Wilhelm II,* p. 299.

132. Michael Balfour, *The Kaiser and His Times,* New York, 1972, p. 197.

133. Cecil, *Wilhelm II,* p. 300.

134. *Ibid.,* p. 293.

135. Röhl, *Germany,* p. 169.

136. *Ibid.,* pp. 278–79.

137. *Ibid.,* p. 167.

138. *Ibid.,* p. 168.

139. *Ibid.*

140. Craig, *Germany,* p. 307.

141. The pioneering work arguing for the primacy of internal politics *(Primat der Innenpolitik)* was done by Eckart Kehr, *Schlachtflottenbau und Parteipolitik 1894–1901,* Berlin. A collection of his essays has been published by Hans-Ulrich Wehler as *Der Primat der Innenpolitik,* Berlin, 1965. Other works following his lead include Wehler's own *Bismarck und der Imperialismus,* Berlin, 1969, and *The German Empire, 1871–1918,* translated by Kim Traynor, New York and Oxford, 1985; Fritz Fischer,

War of Illusions, translated by Marian Jackson, New York, 1975; Volker Berghahn, *Der Tirpitz-Plan,* Düsseldorf, 1971; and *Germany and the Approach of War in 1914,* New York, 1973, among others.

142. Berghahn, *Germany,* pp. 29, 31, 40.

143. See pp. 68–69.

144. See Geoff Eley, *"Sammlungspolitik,* Social Imperialism and the Navy Law of 1898," pp. 29–63. See also W. J. Mommsen, "Domestic Factors in German Foreign Policy before 1914," *Central European History* (1973): 3–43.

145. Berghahn, *Germany,* p. 43.

146. *Ibid.,* pp. 54–55.

147. *Ibid.,* p. 59.

148. *Ibid.,* p. 77.

149. *Ibid.,* p. 72.

150. Steinberg, *Yesterday's Deterrent,* pp. 126–27.

151. Paul M. Kennedy, "Tirpitz, England and the Second Naval Law of 1900: A Strategical Critique." *Militärgeschichtliche Mitteilungen* 2(1970): 38.

152. *Ibid.,* pp. 39–40.

153. A. J. Marder, *From Dreadnought to Scapa Flow,* vol. 1, Oxford, 1961, pp. 113–14.

154. Kennedy, "Tirpitz," p. 53.

155. Balfour, *The Kaiser,* p. 196.

156. Paul M. Kennedy, *The Rise of the Anglo-German Antagonism 1860–1914,* London, 1980, p. 229.

157. *Grosse Politik,* vol. 28, no. 47.

158. Paul M. Kennedy, *The Rise and Fall of British Naval Mastery,* London, 1983, p. 220.

159. Craig, *Germany,* p. 312.

160. Steiner, *Britain,* p. 27.

161. *Ibid.*

162. George Monger, *The End of Isolation, British Foreign Policy 1900–1907*, London, 1963, p. 82.

163. Kennedy, *Rise and Fall of British Naval Mastery*, p. 215.

164. Christopher M. Andrew, *Théophile Delcassé and the Making of the Entente Cordiale*, London, 1968, p. 91.

165. John F. V. Keiger, *France and the Origins of the First World War*, New York, 1983, p. 20.

166. Craig, *Germany*, p. 318.

167. Such an argument is made by Craig in *Germany*, pp. 318–20.

168. Fischer, *War of Illusions*, p. 55.

169. Andrew, *Delcassé*, p. 269.

170. Taylor, *Struggle*, p. 429.

171. *British Documents*, vol. 3, no. 94.

172. Steiner, *Britain*, p. 37.

173. *Ibid.*, p. 40.

174. *Grosse Politik*, vol. 21, 1, no. 6923.

175. *British Documents*, vol. 3, no. 219.

176. Taylor, *Struggle*, p. 437.

177. Michael Howard, *The Continental Commitment*, London, 1989, p. 42.

178. Steiner, *Britain*, p. 43; Taylor, *Struggle*, p. 437.

179 Kennedy quotes the views of the Admiralty and War Office in 1905 in *Rise*, p. 280.

180. Taylor, *Struggle*, pp. 439–41.

181. Kennedy, *Rise*, p. 283.

182. Lieven, *Russia and the Origins of the First World War*, p. 28.

183. *British Documents*, vol. 3, no. 299.

184. Monger, *End of Isolation*, p. 282.

185. Berghahn, *Germany*, p. 47.

186. *Ibid.,* p. 48.

187. Kennedy, "Tirpitz," pp. 51–52.

188. Kennedy, *Rise,* p. 286.

189. Steiner, *Britain,* p. 49.

190. P. Glynn, *Closing Pandora's Box,* New York, p. 304.

191. Marder, *From the Dreadnought to Scapa Flow,* vol. 1, p. 143.

192. E. L. Woodward, *Great Britain and the German Navy,* Oxford, 1935, p. 503.

193. Steiner, *Britain,* p. 53.

194. Marder, *From the Dreadnought to Scapa Flow,* vol. 1, pp. 144–45.

195. W. S. Churchill, *The World Crisis,* p. 24.

196. *Ibid.*

197. Marder, *From the Dreadnought to Scapa Flow,* pp. 178–79.

198. F. R. Bridge, "Izvolsky, Aerenthal, and the End of the Austro-Russian Entente, 1906–8," *Mitteilungen des Österreichischen Staatsarchivs* 29(2976): 322.

199. *Ibid.,* p. 324.

200. *Ibid.,* p. 331.

201. Subsequent accounts of the meeting by each man disagree and, of course, the versions of each man differs from those of the other, yet publication of contemporary documents describing the conversations make it possible to attempt a reasonable reconstruction of what took place. See I. V. Bestuzhev, *Borba v Rossii po voprosam vneshnei politiki 1906–1910* (Moscow, 1961). A valuable translation of selected documents is provided by Bridge, "Izvolsky" (pp. 343–62).

202. Viscount Grey of Fallodon, *Twenty-Five Years 1892–1916,* vol. 1, New York, 1925, p. 168.

203. Craig, *Germany,* p. 322.

204. Franz Conrad von Hötzendorff, *Aus meiner Dienstzeit,* vol. 1, pp. 380–81.

205. *Grosse Politik,* vol. 36, 2, no. 9193.

206. Craig, *Germany,* p. 323.

207. For an excellent account of the military situation see David G. Herrmann, *Armies and the Balance of Military Power in Europe, 1904–1914* (Yale University Dissertation, 1992), pp. 261–62.

208. F. R. Bridge, *From Sadowa to Sarajevo: The Foreign Policy of Austria-Hungary, 1866–1914,* London and Boston, 1972, p. 317.

209. Craig, *Germany,* p. 322.

210. *Grosse Politik,* vol. 26, 1, no. 195.

211. Bridge, *From Sadowa,* p. 438.

212. Albertini, *Origins,* vol. 1, p. 293.

213. *Ibid.,* p. 321.

214. *Grosse Politik,* vol. 26, 2, no. 9191.

215. Albertini, *Origins,* vol. 1, p. 293.

216. Herrmann, *Armies,* p. 268.

217. Herrmann, *Armies,* p. 283.

218. Lieven, *Russia,* p. 36.

219. *Ibid.,* p. 37.

220. Taylor, *Struggle,* p. 457.

221. S. R. Williamson, Jr., *The Politics of Grand Strategy, Britain and France Prepare for War, 1904–1914,* Cambridge, Mass., 1969, p. 142.

222. Taylor, *Struggle.,* p. 466.

223. *Ibid.,* pp. 466–67.

224. Berghahn, *Germany,* p. 84.

225. *Ibid.,* p. 93.

226. *Ibid.,* pp. 95–96.

227. Williamson, *Politics,* p. 146.

228. *British Documents,* vol. 7, no. 386.

229. Steiner, *Britain,* p. 72.

230. Williamson, *Politics,* p. 151.

231. Grey, *Twenty-Five Years,* vol. I, p. 216.

232. Williamson, *Politics,* p. 153–54.

233. *Ibid.,* p. 154. Recollecting Lloyd George's speech in tranquillity after the war, Grey was still very appreciative: "when he spoke out the Germans knew that the whole of the Government and the House of Commons had to be reckoned with. It was my opinion then, and it is still, that the speech had much to do with preserving the peace in 1911. It created a great explosion of words in Germany, but it made Chauvinists there doubt whether it would be wise to fire guns." *Twenty-Five Years,* p. 217.

234. Berghahn, *Germany,* p. 96.

235. *Ibid.,* p. 97.

236. *Ibid.,* pp. 98, 100.

237. Fischer, *War of Illusions,* p. 89.

238. Williamson, *Politics,* pp. 166–67.

239. Keith M. Wilson, *The Policy of the Entente,* Cambridge, England, 1985, p. 89.

240. Williamson, *Politics,* p. 226.

241. This is from a resolution by the Manchester Liberal Federation in January 1912. Cited by Williamson, *Politics,* p. 250.

242. *Ibid.,* p. 251.

243. Konrad Jarausch, *The Enigmatic Chancellor,* New Haven, 1973, p. 126. The reference to "pro-German statements" is in note 29, pp. 459–60. He expressed his optimism to his friend Karl von Eisendecher as follows: "The British *parties* favor an understanding with us and I hope to be able to overcome the resistance of Sir Edward Grey and especially his aides in the Foreign Office *in time*—if here everything were not dictated by the mood of the moment and by the political sophistication of a kindergarten." (p. 126).

244. Jarausch, *Enigmatic Chancellor,* p. 93.

245. Taylor, *Struggle,* p. 477.

246. *Ibid.,* p. 478.

247. Craig, *Germany,* p. 331.

248. Taylor, *Struggle,* pp. 478–79.

249. Ibid., pp. 480–81.

250. Craig, *Germany*, p. 331.

251. Fischer, *War of Illusions*, p. 150.

252. Samuel R. Williamson, Jr., *Austria-Hungary and the Origins of the First World War*, New York, 1991, p. 125.

253. Taylor, *Struggle*, p. 491. For a critique of the Austrians' rationale for the policy see note 2 on the same page.

254. Ibid., p. 492.

255. Fischer, *War of Illusions*, p. 159.

256. Taylor, *Struggle*, p. 495.

257. Williamson, *Austria-Hungary*, p. 152.

258. Fay, *Origins*, vol. 1, pp. 445–46.

259. Williamson, *Austria-Hungary*, p. 155

260. R. J. W. Evans, "The Habsburg Monarchy and the Coming of the War." In *The Coming of the World War*, Oxford, 1988, p. 36.

261. Paul W. Schroeder, "World War I as Galloping Gertie: A Reply to Joachim Remak." *Journal of Modern History* 44(1972): 319–45.

262. Taylor, *Struggle*, p. 511.

263. Ibid., pp. 511–12.

264. Keiger, *France*, p. 144.

265. John Röhl, "Admiral von Müller and the Approach of War, 1911–1914," *Historical Journal* 4(1969): 661. See also *Grosse Politik*, vol. 39, no. 15612.

266. For accounts and discussions of this "War Council" see Röhl, loc. cit., pp. 651ff. and Fischer, *War of Illusions* (pp. 160–69).

267. Fischer, *Ibid.*, p. 162.

268. For a concise and unequivocal statement of this view see Immanuel Geiss, *German Foreign Policy, 1871–1914* (London, 1976), pp. 142–45.

269. That is the title of Fischer's chapter. For the arguments see the previous note.

270. Jarausch, *Enigmatic Chancellor*, p. 143.

271.   Taylor, *Struggle,* p. 514.

272.   Jarausch, *Enigmatic Chancellor,* p. 146.

273.   The most thorough account, though too easy on Serbian responsibility, is by Vladimir Dedijer, *The Road to Sarajevo* (New York, 1966).

274.   Immanuel Geiss, *July 1914,* New York, 1967, pp. 63–64.

275.   Albertini, *Origins,* vol. 2, pp. 124–25.

276.   Williamson, *Austria,* p. 194.

277.   Geiss, *July 1914,* p. 61.

278.   *Ibid.,* p. 65.

279.   *Ibid.,* pp. 76–77.

280.   *Ibid.,* p. 45.

281.   Here the absence of a Cabinet in the German constitutional system, where such an important decision would have had to be reviewed and discussed at length, may have had important consequences.

282.   Berghahn, *Germany,* p. 193.

283.   As Williamson, *Austria,* p. 196, points out, "the emperor's decided opinion would be difficult to overturn." Berghahn, *Germany* (p. 193), says "there can be little doubt that this mental state of the Kaiser [i.e., to avoid the appearance of cowardice] also pushed his Chancellor into accepting the highest risks."

284.   Although the authenticity of the published portion of Riezler's diary for July 1914 has been challenged (see B. Sösemann, "Die Tagebücher Kurt Riezlers. Untersuchungen zur ihrer Echtheit und Edition," *Historische Zeitschrift,* 236(1983): 328–69), most scholars regard it as authentic. For a challenge to Sösemann see K. Erdmann, "Zur Echtheit der Tagebücher Kurt Riezlers. Ein Antikritik," *Historische Zeitschrift* 236(1983): 371–402.

285.   Jarausch, *Enigmatic Chancellor,* pp. 157–59.

286.   Steiner, *Britain,* p. 220.

287.   Geiss, *July 1914,* p. 78.

288.   Albertini, *Origins,* vol. 2, p. 150.

289.   *Ibid.*

290.   Williamson, *Austria,* p. 197.

291. Ibid., p. 200.

292. Max Montgelas and Walter Schücking, eds., *Outbreak of the World War: German Documents Collected by Karl Kautsky,* Supplement IV. Translated by the Carnegie Endowment for International Peace. 2(1924): 616–18.

293. James Joll, *The Origins of the First World War,* London and New York, 1984, p. 12.

294. Fay, *Origins,* vol. 2, p. 348.

295. Geiss, *July 1914,* p. 201.

296. Taylor, *Struggle,* p. 523.

297. Joll, *Origins,* p. 14.

298. D. W. Spring, "Russia and the Coming of War." In *Coming,* Evans and Pogge von Strandmann, pp. 63–65.

299. Lieven, *Origins,* pp. 141–42.

300. Ibid., pp. 143–44.

301. D. W. Spring, "Russia and the Coming of War." In *Coming,* Evans and Pogge von Strandmann, p. 77.

302. Ibid., p. 73.

303. Lieven, *Russia,* p. 147.

304. Immanuel Geiss, *Julikrise und Kriegsausbruch 1914,* vol. 2, Hanover, 1964, pp. 372–73.

305. Ibid.

306. For good newer discussions of the French role in the crisis see Keiger, *France,* 145–64, and Gerd Grumeich, *Armaments and Politics in France on the Eve of the First World War,* translated by Stephen Conn (Leamington Spa, 1984), pp. 215–30.

307. Krumeich, *Armaments,* pp. 218–19.

308. See Jean-Jacques Becker, *1914: Comment les français sont entrés dans la guerre* (Paris, 1977).

309. Keiger, *France,* p. 167.

310. Geiss, *1914,* p. 104.

311. Steiner, *Britain,* p. 221.

312. Michael G. Ekstein and Zara Steiner, "The Sarajevo Crisis." In *British Foreign Policy Under Sir Edward Grey,* edited by F. H. Hinsley, Cambridge, England, 1977, p. 400.

313. Steiner, *Britain,* p. 222.

314. Geiss, *July 1914,* p. 236–37.

315. Ekstein and Steiner, "The Sarajevo Crisis," p. 402.

316. Geiss, *July 1914,* pp. 256–57.

317. *Ibid.,* p. 223.

318. Joll, *Origins,* p. 18.

319. Taylor, *Struggle,* p. 524.

320. Joll, *Origins,* p. 23.

321. Steiner, *Britain,* p. 233.

322. *Ibid.,* p. 234.

323. Michael Brock, "Britain Enters the War." In *Coming,* Evans and Pogge von Strandmann, pp. 145–46.

324. Nicolson to Hardinge in Steiner, *Britain,* p. 228.

325. Joll, *Origins,* p. 26.

326. Brock, "Britain," p. 156.

327. Sir Edward Grey, *Speeches on Foreign Affairs 1904–1914,* London, 1931, p. 313.

328. *Twenty-Five Years,* pp. 15–16.

329. See, for example, Miles Kahler, "Rumors of War: The 1914 Analogy," *Foreign Affairs* 2(1979–80): 374–96; the issue of the *Journal International Security* devoted to deriving contemporary lessons from the war of 1914, published separately as *Military Strategy and the Origins of the First World War,* Steven E. Miller, ed. (Princeton, 1985); Geoffrey Barraclough, *From Agadir to Armageddon,* London, 1982.

330. David Calleo, *The German Problem Reconsidered,* Cambridge, Mass., 1978, p. 6.

331. See his *Germany's Aims in the First World War,* New York, 1967, and *War of Illusions.*

332. Gordon A. Craig, *Germany 1866–1945,* Oxford and New York, 1978, pp. 359–60.

333. Kennedy, *Rise,* p. 469.

334. Steiner, *Britain,* p. 227.

335. L. C. F. Turner, "The Significance of the Schlieffen Plan." In *The War Plans of the Great Powers 1880–1914,* Paul M. Kennedy, ed., Boston, 1985, p. 204.

336. *Ibid.,* p. 200.

337. Brock, *Britain,* p. 167, n. 88.

338. Steiner, *Britain,* p. 166.

3
HANNIBAL'S WAR: THE SECOND PUNIC WAR
218-201 B.C.

N THE SPRING of 218[1] the Carthaginian general Hannibal, son of Hamilcar Barca, twenty-six years old, led an army out of Spain consisting of about 50,000 infantry, 9,000 cavalry, and 37 war elephants.[2] His daring plan was to march as swiftly as possible through Gaul, over the Alps, and into northern Italy. There he would gain allies from the Celtic Gauls, who were hostile to Rome. He also would proclaim a policy of liberating the Italian peoples from their Roman masters, thereby breaking up the Roman confederacy and winning allies for himself. That would permit him to defeat Rome, vastly increase the power of Carthage, and avenge the defeat and disgrace suffered by the Carthaginians a quarter of a century earlier.

By November Hannibal had arrived in northern Italy with a force reduced to 20,000 infantry and 6,000 cavalry, a pitiful number with which to challenge the vast armies available to Rome.[3] Within two years he had crushed Roman armies in three major battles, the last at Cannae, where almost 70,000 Romans were killed and almost 20,000 taken prisoner.[4] The defeat led to the defection of most of southern Italy and such panic among the Romans that they resorted to human sacrifice, a practice the Roman historian Livy deplored as "wholly alien to the Roman spirit."[5] For years Hannibal's army roamed freely, ravaging much of Italy while no Roman army dared confront him. From antiquity to modern times some have thought that he could have won the war had he marched on Rome immediately after Cannae. However that might be, the Romans were forced to fight for sixteen years, in Italy, Spain, Greece, and Africa, suffering fearful casualties and terrible economic damage before they were able to prevail. Hannibal's War was the greatest and most dangerous one they were compelled to fight on their way to the conquest of the Mediterranean and the

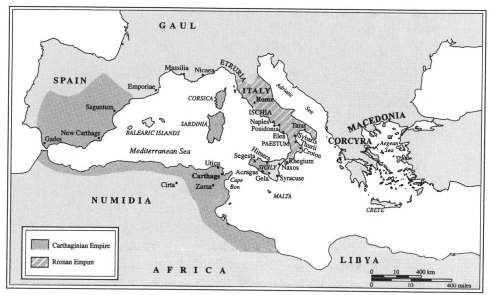

The Western Mediterranean Area During the Rise of Rome

establishment of an empire that would last another seven hundred years, and it almost derailed that journey before it was fairly started. For the Carthaginians it meant the end of their power and the possibility that an empire based in Africa, instead of one based in Europe, would rule the entire Mediterranean. A little more than half a century after the war it also meant the physical destruction of Carthage and the abandonment of its site. As the Greek historian of the Punic Wars who wrote less than a half-century after Hannibal's War put it, "Can anyone be so indifferent or idle as not to care to know by what means, and under what kind of polity, almost the whole inhabited world was conquered and brought under the dominion of the single city of Rome, and that, too, within a period of not quite fifty-three years?"[6] The story of the origins of the war that began that process well deserves our study.

THE NATURE OF THE OPPONENTS

Rome

Rome began as a small city-state on the Tiber River in central Italy. It had few natural advantages, being without natural defenses, rich soil, valuable or useful metals, or an excellent port. Its rise to power rested on its people, sturdy farmers and tough, determined infantrymen, and on its social institutions and republican constitution. Many of the elements that made for Roman success were shaped before the Roman Republic was founded, when the Romans were ruled by kings. The Romans were a very conservative people, and they attributed their success to their holding fast to the *mos maiorum,* the customs of their ancestors, going all the way back to the royal period.

Tradition places the foundation of Rome in the mid-eighth century B.C. By the sixth century Rome had come under the control of the Etruscans, a more civilized and sophisticated people to the north. Led by their Etruscan kings, the Roman Army, equipped and organized like the Greek phalanx, gained control of most of the territory of Latium in which Rome was situated. They achieved this success under an effective political and social order that gave extraordinary power to the ruling figures in both public and private life.

To their kings, the Romans gave the awesome power of *imperium,* the right to issue commands and to enforce them by fines, arrests, and corporal or even capital punishment. But the elected kings needed the approval of the Senate, and *imperium* had to be granted formally by a vote of the people in assembly. The basic character of Roman government was already clear: great power was granted to executive officers, but it had to be approved by the Senate and was derived ultimately from the people. Ostensibly the Senate had neither executive nor legislative power; it met only when summoned by the king and then only to advise him. In reality, its authority was great, for the senators, like the king, served for life. The Senate, therefore, had continuity and experience, and as it was composed of the most powerful men in the state, it could not be ignored lightly.

In early Rome, citizenship required descent from Roman parents on both sides. All citizens were organized into the third branch of government, an Assembly made up of thirty groups. It met only when summoned by the king; he determined the agenda, made proposals, and recognized other speakers, if any. For the most part, the Assembly was called to listen and approve. Voting was not by head but by group; a majority within each group determined its vote, and the decisions were made by majority vote of the groups. Group voting was typical of all Roman Assemblies in the future.

The center of Roman life was the family. At its head stood the father, whose power and authority within the family resembled those of the king within the state. Over his children, he held broad powers analogous to *imperium* in the state, for he had the right to sell his children into slavery, and he even had the power of life and death over them. As the king's power was more limited in practice than in theory, so it was with the father. His power to dispose of his children was limited by consultation with the family, by public opinion, and most of all, by tradition. His wife could not be divorced except for stated serious offenses, and even then she had to be convicted by a court made up of her male blood relatives. The Roman woman had a respected position and the main responsibility for managing the household. The father was the chief priest of the family. He led it in daily prayers to the dead that reflected the ancestor worship central to the Roman family and state.

Clientage was one of Rome's most important institutions. The client was "an inferior entrusted, by custom or by himself, to the protection of a stranger more powerful than he, and rendering certain services and observances in return for this protection."[7] The Romans spoke of a client as being in the *fides,* or trust, of his patron, so that the relationship always had moral implications. The patron provided his client with protection, both physical and legal; he gave him economic assistance in the form of a land grant, the opportunity to work as a tenant farmer or a laborer on the patron's land, or simply handouts. In return, the client would fight for his patron, work his land, and support him politically. These mutual obligations were enforced by public opinion and tradition. When early custom was codified in the mid-fifth century B.C., one of the twelve tablets of laws announced: "Let the patron who has defrauded his client be accursed." In the early history of Rome, patrons were rich and powerful whereas clients were poor and weak. But as time passed, it was not uncommon for rich and powerful members of the upper classes to become clients of even more powerful men, chiefly for political purposes. Because the client-patron relationship was hereditary and sanctioned by religion and custom, it was to play a very important part in the life of the Roman Republic. It also powerfully shaped the Roman conception of honor, both in domestic and foreign relations.

Roman society was divided in two by a class distinction based on birth. The upper class was composed of the patricians, the wealthy men who held a monopoly of power and influence. They alone could conduct the religious ceremonies in the state, sit in the Senate, or hold office, and they formed a closed caste by forbidding marriage outside their own group. The plebeians must originally have been the poor and dependent men who were small farmers, laborers, and artisans, the clients of the nobility.

As Rome and its population grew in various ways, families who were rich but outside the charmed circle gained citizenship. From very early times, therefore, there were rich plebeians, and incompetence and bad luck must have produced some poor patricians. The line between the classes and the monopoly of privileges remained firm, nevertheless, and the struggle of the plebeians to gain equality occupied more than two centuries of republican history.

Roman tradition tells us that the Republic replaced the monarchy at Rome suddenly in 509 B.C. as the result of a revolution sparked by the outrageous behavior of the last kings and led by the noble families. The republican constitution was an unwritten accumulation of laws and customs that had won respect and the force of law over time. The Romans' conservativism prevented them, even after the expulsion of the kings, from depriving their chief magistrates of the great powers exercised by the monarchs. They elected two patricians to the office of Consul and endowed them with *imperium*. As the kings, the Consuls led the Army, had religious duties, and served as judges—but their power was limited legally and institutionally as well as by custom. The vast power of the consulship was granted not for life but for a year only. Each Consul could prevent any action by his colleague by simply saying no to his proposal, and the religious powers of the Consuls were shared with others. Even *imperium* was limited, for though the Consuls had full powers of life and death while leading an army, within the sacred boundary of the city of Rome the citizens had the right to appeal to the popular Assembly all cases involving capital punishment. Besides, after their one year in office, the Consuls would spend the rest of their lives as members of the Senate. It would be a most reckless Consul who failed to ask the advice of the Senate or who failed to follow it when there was general agreement.

The many checks on consular action tended to prevent initiative, swift action, and change, but this was just what a conservative, traditional, aristocratic Republic wanted. Only in the military sphere did divided counsel and a short term of office create important problems. The Romans tried to get around the difficulties by sending only one Consul into the field or, when this was impossible, allowing the Consuls sole command on alternate days. In serious crises, the Consuls, with the advice of the Senate, could appoint a single man, the dictator, to the command and could retire in his favor. The dictator's term of office was limited to six months, but his own *imperium* was valid both inside and outside the city without appeal. These devices worked well enough in the early years of the Republic, when Rome's battles were near home, but longer wars and more sophisticated opponents revealed the system's weaknesses and required significant changes. Such long campaigns prompted the invention of the proconsulship in 325 B.C., whereby the term of a Consul serving in the field was extended. The introduction of the office of praetor also helped provide commanders for Rome's many campaigns. Their basic function was judicial, but they also had *imperium* and served as generals. By the end of the Republic, there were eight praetors, whose annual terms, as the Consuls', could be extended for military commands when necessary. At first, the Consuls classified the citizens according to age and property, the bases of citizenship and assignment in the Army, but after the middle of the fifth century two censors were elected to perform this duty.

The Senate was the single continuous deliberative body in the Roman Republic. Its members were leading patricians, often heads of clans and patrons of many clients. The Senate soon gained control of finances and of foreign policy. Its formal advice was not ignored lightly either by magistrates or by popular Assemblies. The centuriate Assembly was the most important legislative and elective body in the early Republic. In a sense, it was the Roman Army acting in a political capacity, and its basic unit was the century, theoretically one hundred fighting men classified according to their weapons, armor, and equipment. Because each man equipped himself, the organization was by classes according to wealth. The rules of the game gave very great advantages to the older and wealthier citizens, and the votes of younger and poorer Romans counted only when a vote was very close.

The laws and constitution of the early Republic clearly reflected the class structure of the Roman state, for they gave to the patricians almost a monopoly of power and privilege. The plebeians undertook a campaign to achieve political, legal, and social equality, and this attempt, which succeeded after two centuries of intermittent effort, is called the "Struggle of the Orders." The most important source of plebeian success was the need for their military service. Rome was at war almost constantly, and the patricians were forced to call on the plebeians to defend the state. According to tradition, the plebeians, angered by patrician resistance to their demands, withdrew from the city and camped on the Sacred Mount. There they formed a plebeian tribal Assembly and elected plebeian tribunes to protect them from the arbitrary power of the magistrates. They declared the tribune inviolate and sacrosanct, and anyone laying violent hands on him was accursed and liable to death without trial. By extension of his right to protect the plebeians, the tribune gained the power to veto any action of a magistrate or any bill in a Roman Assembly or the Senate. The plebeian Assembly voted by tribe, and a vote of the Assembly was binding on plebeians. They tried to make their decisions binding on all Romans but could not do so until 287 B.C.

The next step was for the plebeians to obtain access to the laws, and by 450 B.C., the Twelve Tables codified early Roman custom in all its harshness and simplicity. In 445 B.C. plebeians gained the right to marry patricians. The main prize was consulship. The patricians did not yield easily, but at last, in 367 B.C., new laws provided that at least one Consul could be a plebeian. Before long plebeians held other offices, even the dictatorship and the censorship. In 300 B.C. they were admitted to the most important priesthoods, the last religious barrier to equality. In 287 B.C. the plebeians completed their triumph by securing the passage of a law whereby decisions of the plebeian Assembly bound all Romans and did not require the approval of the Senate.

It might seem that the Roman aristocracy had given way under the pressure of the lower class, but the victory of the plebeians did not bring democracy. An aristocracy based strictly on birth had given way to an aristocracy more subtle but no less restricted, based on a combination of wealth and birth. The significant distinction was no longer between patrician and plebeian but between the *nobiles*—a relatively small group of wealthy and powerful families, both patrician and plebeian, whose members attained the highest offices in the state—and everyone else. These same families dominated the Senate, whose power became ever greater. It remained the only continuous deliberative body in the state, and the pressure of warfare gave it experience in handling public business. Rome's success brought the Senate prestige and increased its control of policy and its confidence in its capacity to rule. The end of the struggle of the orders brought domestic peace under a republican constitution dominated by a capable, if narrow, senatorial aristocracy. The government was managed by the Senate; the *comitia centuriata* voted on questions of war and peace, but the sources report no case in which the people rejected a senatorial decision for war.[8] This outcome satisfied most Romans outside the ruling group because Rome conquered Italy and brought many benefits to its citizens.

By about 350 B.C. the Romans had established their leadership of central Italy, and their success in turning back powerful attacks by Gallic tribes added still more to their power and prestige. As the Romans tightened their grip on Latium, the Latins became resentful. In 340 B.C. they demanded independence from Rome or full equality, and when the Romans refused, they launched a war of independence that lasted until 338. The victorious Romans dissolved the Latin League, and their treatment of the defeated opponents provided a model for the settlement of Italy. They did not destroy any of the Latin cities or their people, nor did they treat them all alike. Some in the vicinity of Rome received full Roman citizenship; others farther away gained municipal status, which gave them the private rights of intermarriage and commerce with Romans but not the public rights of voting and holding office in Rome. They retained the rights of local self-government and could obtain full Roman citizenship if they moved to Rome. They followed Rome in foreign policy and provided soldiers to serve in the Roman legions.

Still other states became allies of Rome on the basis of treaties, which differed from city to city. Some were given the private rights of intermarriage and commerce with Romans and some were not; the allied states were always forbidden to exercise these rights with one another. Some, but not all, were allowed local autonomy. Land was taken from some but not from others, nor was the percentage always the same. All the allies supplied troops to the Army, in which they fought in auxiliary battalions under Roman officers, but they did not pay taxes to Rome.

On some of the conquered land, the Romans placed colonies, permanent settlements of veteran soldiers in the territory of recently defeated enemies. The colonists retained their Roman citizenship and enjoyed home rule, and in return for the land they had been given, they served as a kind of permanent garrison to deter or suppress rebellion. These colonies usually were connected to Rome by a network of military roads built as straight as possible and so durable that some are used even today. They guaranteed that a Roman army could reinforce an embattled colony swiftly or put down an uprising in any weather.

The Roman settlement of Latium reveals even more clearly than before the principles by which Rome was able to conquer and dominate Italy for many centuries. The excellent army and the diplomatic skill that allowed Rome to separate its enemies help explain its conquests. The reputation for harsh punishment of rebels and the sure promise that such punishment would be delivered, made unmistakably clear by the presence of colonies and military roads, help account for the slowness to revolt. But the positive side, represented by Rome's organization of the defeated states, is at least as important. The Romans did not regard the status given each newly conquered city as permanent. They held out to loyal allies the prospect of improving their status, even of achieving the ultimate prize, full Roman citizenship. In so doing, the Romans gave their allies a stake in Rome's future and success and a sense of being colleagues, though subordinate ones, rather than subjects. The result, in general, was that most of Rome's allies remained loyal even when put to the severest test.

The next great challenge to Roman arms came in a series of wars with a tough mountain people of the southern Apennines, the Samnites. Some of Rome's allies rebelled, and soon the Etruscans and Gauls joined in the war against Rome, but most of the allies remained loyal. In 295 B.C., at Sentinum, the Romans defeated an Italian coalition, and by 280 they were masters of central Italy. Their power extended from the Po Valley south to the Greek cities of southern Italy, which they soon conquered. By 265 B.C., Rome ruled all Italy as far north as the Po River, an area of 47,200 square miles.

The Romans gained their control of Italy through military victories, and there can be no doubt that they were a warlike people. A Roman male owed the state sixteen years of military service between the ages of seventeen and forty-six, although legislation could extend that period to twenty, and no Roman could hold public office until he had completed ten years of service.[9] To a remarkable degree, moreover, the Romans were almost always at war. In more than six decades before the First Punic War in 264 only four or five years were without war.[10] Most modern historians, nonetheless, have not portrayed the Romans as aggressive or eager for war. The most common view has been that most of their wars, especially before the end of the Second Punic War, were defensive, fought to protect their own land and safety and those of their allies and friends, and to ward off dangerous peoples on their frontiers.[11] These views find support among some of the Romans themselves. A speaker in one of Cicero's dialogues says, "our people has now gained power over the whole world by defending its allies," and that Rome had always undertaken its wars either in defense of its safety or its *fides*.[12] As we shall see, moreover, Polybius, though he believed Rome came to seek domination of the inhabited world, explained their entry into the First Punic War in just such terms. They saw that Carthage was aggressive not only in Africa but also in Spain, that it had acquired the islands in the seas west of Rome: "they were beginning, therefore, to be exceedingly anxious lest, if the Carthaginians became masters of Sicily also, they should find them very dangerous and formidable neighbors."[13]

Another support for this view has been drawn from the very solemn religious ceremony the Romans employed before going to war, at least in the early centuries. If the Senate received any complaints about the actions of another state they send a board of priests, the *fetiales,* to investigate the matter. If there was reason they then sent one or more of the priests to the offending people with a *rerum repetitio,* a statement of grievance and a demand for satisfaction, reciting the formula, "If I unjustly or impiously demand that the aforesaid offenders be surrendered, then permit me not to return to my country." If, after thirty days, redress was not forthcoming, the priests returned and called upon the gods to note that their cause was just. When the Senate and the people had then voted for war one of the *fetiales* would return and hurl a charred spear into the enemy's territory as a declaration of a just war. The formal and religious nature of this process has convinced some scholars that the Romans were barred from aggressive or other unjust wars.

These defensive concerns they also extended to cover the safety of their allies and friends, applying the deeply rooted internal principle of clientage based on *fides* to the arena of relations between peoples and states. A people defeated by the Romans was required to make an unconditional surrender. Then the Romans granted them a relationship, usually as an ally on one basis or another, but the defeated power was in the position of seeking a favor from Rome from a position of inferiority, as in private life an individual might have the status of a client seeking to be accepted into the *fides* of a patron. When the Romans accepted a state into its alliance and *fides,* they expected the performance of specified duties, and they expected allegiance and loyalty. In return they undertook a moral obligation to provide protection. The Romans sometimes established a relationship that was not as formal as an alliance *(societas),* but was merely a "friendship" *(amicitia).* Even so, they came to regard these as involving their *fides* and felt entitled, and sometimes obliged, to come to the aid of their "friends" if these were threatened or attacked.

A good example of the process came in the year 298. When the Lucanians, a people in southern Italy, were attacked by another Italian people, "they asked the Fathers [the Roman Senate] to accept the Lucanians into their *fides* and protect them against violence and injury at the hands of the Samnites,"[14] and the Romans agreed. Similar cases extended Roman protection to all of Italy. One scholar's examination of the process leads him to this conclusion: "Rome claims . . . the right to extend her alliance to any free state and to protect it against its enemies, even if the attack actually preceded the alliance. Thus the principle of the fetial law which prohibited aggressive wars was overcome and the legal form was developed which later permitted the conquest of the Mediterranean without clear infringement of this principle."[15]

Rome's relations with other states, however, often seem less the extension of protection than the imposition of a protection racket, and there is considerable reason to believe that the Romans' remarkable expansion did not occur in a fit of absentmindedness or exclusively in defense of honor and friendship. Although Cicero emphasizes the defense of allies and honor as the causes of Rome's many wars and the roots of its power, he tells us that its "wars were fought on behalf of allies or for empire *(de imperio)*" and that "our ancestors took up arms not only to be free but also to rule."[16] The full story of Roman expansion, moreover, does not suggest that concern for their *fides* did very much to restrain the Romans from going to war. On the contrary, it often was the reason given for entering into a war that ended with the growth of Rome's territory and power; sometimes, perhaps it was just a pretext. Nor did the solemn legalities of the fetial law have a restraining effect. The Romans' demand for satisfaction of their grievances generally was framed in such a way as to guarantee a negative answer. We know of only one case in which the demand was complied with: it was an offer meant to be refused and to provide a morally and psychologically acceptable reason for going to war when the decision had already been made in the minds of the Romans.[17] Considerations of justice, *fides,* and especially self-defense played an important role in Roman decisions to go to war, sometimes a decisive one, but there were others, as well.

It is natural in our time to think of economic motives when we seek to explain expansion and imperialism, and there should be no doubt that in the long story of Rome's emergence as the ruler of the Mediterranean world thoughts of acquiring land, booty, and other forms of wealth helped persuade the Roman people and their leaders to fight wars. What may seem surprising is that these motives did not play a very significant role until after the Punic Wars. To be sure, the Romans enjoyed the benefits of conquered land and booty from an early time, but the evidence for these as motives for war before the Punic Wars is circumstantial and slight. A seeker after such motives whose eye is sharp and unclouded by sentiment, can make no stronger claim than this: "Apparently the aristocrat whose views are best known to us in this period [Fabius Pictor] . . . did at least recognize that economic ambitions of a certain kind had been part of Roman motivation."[18]

The "certain kind" of motive to which economic gain contributed was the one chiefly at play, the search for *laus* and *gloria,* (praise and glory), the "honor," in Thucydidean terms, we have seen at work elsewhere. The nobles who served as magistrates and senators placed this kind of public recognition at the center of their system of values. The highest goals, the chief magistracies, were themselves largely military in character. Military success was the quickest and best way to reach them, and the military successes a man could achieve in them were the basis of the high reputation every Roman sought to win and pass on to his progeny. A magistrate serving as general could hope to win a battle or campaign in such a way as to win the Senate's award to him of a triumph, and Polybius illustrates the great importance of the Senate by saying, "even to the successes of the generals the Senate has the power to add distinction and glory, and on the other hand to obscure their merits and lower their credit. For these high achievements are brought in tangible form before the eyes of the citizens by what are called 'triumphs,' " which must be approved by the Senate.[19] Here is an account of the triumph celebrated by Lucius Aemilius Paullus in 168:

The people erected scaffolds in the forum, in the circuses, as they call their buildings for horse races, and in all other parts of the city where they could best behold the show. The spectators were clad in white garments; all the temples were open, and full of garlands and perfumes; the ways were cleared and kept open by numerous officers, who drove back all who crowded into or ran across the main avenue. This triumph lasted three days. On the first, which was scarcely long enough for the sight, were to be seen the statues, pictures, and colossal images which were taken from the enemy, drawn upon two hundred and fifty chariots. On the second was carried in a great many wagons the finest and richest armour of the Macedonians, both of brass and steel, all newly polished and glittering; the pieces of which were piled up and arranged purposely with the greatest art, so as to seem to be tumbled in heaps carelessly and by chance. . . . On the third day, early in the morning, first came the trumpeters, who did not sound as they were wont in a procession or solemn entry, but such a charge as the Romans use when they encourage the soldiers to fight. Next followed young men wearing frocks with ornamented borders, who led to the sacrifice a hundred and twenty stalled oxen, with their horns gilded, and their heads adorned with ribbons and garlands; and with these were boys that carried basins for libation, of silver and gold.

After his children and their attendants came Perseus himself [the captured King of Macedon], clad all in black, and wearing the boots of his country, and looking like one altogether stunned and deprived of reason, through the greatness of his misfortunes. Next followed a great company of his friends and familiars, whose countenances were disfigured with grief, and who let the spectators see, by their tears and their continual looking upon Perseus, that it was his fortune they so much lamented, and that they were regardless of their own.

After these were carried four hundred crowns, all made of gold, sent from the cities by their respective deputations to Aemilius, in honour of his victory. Then he himself came, seated on a chariot magnificently adorned (a man well worthy to be looked at, even without these ensigns of power), dressed in a robe of purple, interwoven with gold, and holding a laurel branch in his right hand. All the army, in like manner, with boughs of laurel in their hands, divided into their bands and companies, followed the chariot of their commander; some singing verses, according to the usual custom, mingled with raillery; others, songs of triumph and the praise of Aemilius's deeds; who, indeed, was admired and accounted happy by all men, and unenvied by every one that was good.[20]

Even after death bravery in war received public celebration and was used to encourage that quality in the future. At the funerals of men who had held the highest offices their bodies were carried into the forum and their deeds of bravery praised in public speeches. Lifelike wax masks of similarly illustrious ancestors were worn by men resembling the originals in appearance, wearing uniforms of the appropriate rank. "By this means," says Polybius, "the glorious memory of brave men is continually renewed; the fame of those who have performed any noble deed is never allowed to die; and the renown of those who have done good service to their country becomes a matter of common knowledge to the multitude, and part of the heritage of posterity."[21] With such incentives to drive them, the leaders of the Roman Republic had powerful reasons not to shrink from the opportunities provided by war, even if the justice of the cause was somewhat doubtful.

At the same time, it would be wrong to conclude that the Romans were always eager to fight and aggressive. Sometimes the state was worn out by lengthy and hard fighting and ready for a breathing space. Prudential strategic considerations could argue against a war against one potential enemy at a time when a serious threat loomed elsewhere. Finally, ambition for honor was coupled with fear of dishonor. Magistrates and senators, especially, might shrink from a war for which they judged Rome unprepared and that threatened defeat or hard fighting without success. Each Roman decision for war, therefore, requires independent analysis without preconceptions.

Carthage

Rome's acquisition of coastal territory and its expansion to the toe of the Italian boot brought it face-to-face with the great naval power of the western Mediterranean, Carthage. Late in the ninth century, the Phoenician city of Tyre had planted a colony on the coast of northern Africa near modern Tunis, calling it the New City, or Carthage. The Romans called

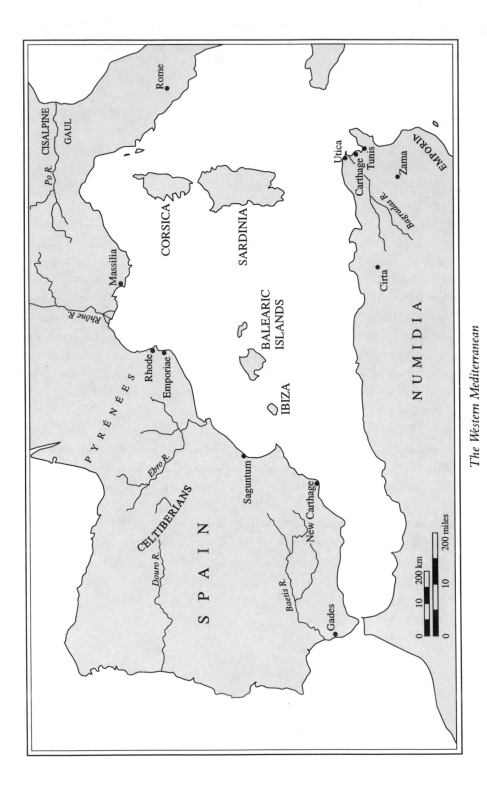

The Western Mediterranean

the Carthaginians Poeni or Puni, hence the Punic Wars. In the sixth century, the conquest of Phoenicia by the Assyrians and the Persians made Carthage independent and free to exploit its very advantageous situation.[22]

The city was located on a defensible site and commanded an excellent harbor that encouraged commerce. The coastal plain grew abundant grain, fruits, and vegetables. An inland plain allowed sheep herding. The Phoenician settlers conquered the native North African inhabitants and used them to work the land. In the sixth century, the Carthaginians began expanding their domain to include the coast of northern Africa west beyond the Straits of Gibraltar and eastward into Libya. Overseas, they came to control the southern part of Spain, Sardinia, Corsica, Malta, the Balearic Islands, and western Sicily. The peoples of these territories, though originally allies, all were reduced to subjection as the natives of the Carthaginian home territory had been. They all served in the Carthaginian Army or Navy and paid tribute. Carthage also profited greatly from the mines of Spain and from the absolute monopoly of trade Carthage imposed on the western Mediterranean.

Carthage, too, was an aristocratic republic headed by two magistrates serving one-year terms called Suffetes (cognate to the Hebrew word that means judges). The Senate of Three Hundred Men and the Council of Thirty, a subcommittee of the Senate that included the Suffetes, were the effective government of the state. When there was disagreement within these groups, and on some unusual occasions, matters were brought to the Assembly. Judicial authority rested with the Council of One Hundred and Four, chosen from the Senate. The popular Assembly of citizens enjoyed freedom of speech, and the people elected the Suffetes as well as both councils. As in Rome, the leaders appear to have come from a small number of families.

Unlike Roman nobles of the third century, who derived their wealth almost entirely from agriculture, the Carthaginian governing class was active in commerce and industry, as well as in large-scale farming, using slave labor and more advanced methods. At first, the Carthaginians fought their own wars, but by the third century they no longer fought in the ranks but served only as officers, except when the fighting was in Africa and threatened their city. The ranks were filled by African subjects and allies and by mercenaries from the rest of the Empire. Carthage, unlike Rome, also maintained a large and excellent navy, a match in size and skill for any in the Mediterranean, with which they were able to keep the western Mediterranean a closed sea. For these purposes the Carthaginians needed a great deal of money to build and maintain their ships and to pay their soldiers and sailors, money they obtained as tribute from their subjects and in the form of customs duties from their extensive trade. Their motives for fighting wars were much more clearly economic and commercial than was common in the ancient world, yet their ruling class and generals were moved by considerations of pride and honor no less than were the Romans, as the careers of the family of Hamilcar Barca, especially his son Hannibal, will show.

THE ORIGINS OF THE FIRST PUNIC WAR

The first record of contact between Rome and Carthage is a treaty between the two states agreed to in 509, the year the Romans drove out their Etruscan kings and established the Republic. At that time Roman power was confined to the region of Latium in central Italy, while Carthage was already an important commercial power with holdings and interests all over the western Mediterranean. The treaty forbade the Romans from sailing south or west of the Gulf of Tunis or to execute any contracts in Libya or Sardinia except under the eye of a Carthaginian official. They were permitted to trade in the Carthaginian portion of Sicily. In return, Carthage promised to keep out of Latium. It appears to have been part of the Carthaginians' policy to keep Rome from trading in their sphere of influence, as it probably had been doing as an Etruscan city. The new Roman Republic had little interest in commerce.

The treaty was renewed in 348, when the terms were made even more favorable to Carthage. Now the Romans were excluded entirely from Libya and Sardinia and from the Mediterranean west of the Gulf of Tunis on the African side and Cartagena on the European. In the Carthaginian sphere they were allowed to trade only in Carthage itself and in Carthaginian Sicily. Occupied in wars against their Italian neighbors and still uninvolved in commerce, Rome was willing to make this agreement in return for a guarantee that powerful Carthage would stay out of Latium.[23]

Since the sixth century Carthage had contested the control of Sicily with the Greek cities there, especially Syracuse, the most important among them. The death of Syracuse's powerful tyrant, Agathocles, in 289 produced anarchy in the Greek portion of Sicily. A collection of the late tyrants' Italian mercenaries took advantage of the confusion to seize the city of Messana (modern Messina) just across the strait from Italy. They called themselves Mamertines after the Sabellian war god Mamers (the equivalent of the Roman Mars) and set about ravaging and stealing from neighboring peoples. During the same period the Carthaginians seized the opportunity to expand their power in Sicily at the expense of the Greeks.

Meanwhile, the Romans were pushing south in Italy toward the region so populated by Greek cities that they called it Magna Graecia. In 285 a number of Greek cities began asking for Roman help against attackers from Italy and warlords from abroad such as Alexander of Epirus across the Adriatic. In 282 they agreed to help Thurii against the menace of Tarentum, the leading Greek city of southern Italy. When a Roman fleet appeared in their harbor the Tarentines attacked and sank several of them before marching an army to Thurii, driving out the garrison Rome had placed there and sacking the place. To meet Rome's inevitable response the Tarentines sent for Pyrrhus of Epirus. One of the leading *condottieri* of the Hellenistic world, he brought an army of twenty-five thousand crack professional soldiers and a horrifying new kind of weapon into Italy never seen before by the Romans: twenty war elephants. He defeated the Roman legions in battle, but he took heavy losses that he could ill afford, and was unable to shatter the Roman confederation. He began to look for what he hoped would be easier pickings and thought he would find them in Sicily, where Syracuse, hard-pressed by the Carthaginians, were asking for his help.

Eager to keep Pyrrhus out of Sicily, the Carthaginians sent a fleet to Italy in 279 to offer help to the Romans, who declined. They did, however, make another agreement to meet the new challenge in which each side agreed that either should be free to assist the other in case it was attacked by Pyrrhus, and the Carthaginians were to provide naval assistance if needed. Pyrrhus, nonetheless, soon arrived in Sicily, where he helped prevent a complete Carthaginian victory. In 275 he returned to Italy, where he was checked by the Roman Army before deciding to withdraw to Greece. Carthage had not asked for Roman help against Pyrrhus in Sicily nor had the Romans sought Punic aid against him in Italy, for neither side wanted the other in its domain.

On leaving Sicily Pyrrhus is reported to have said, "What a cockpit we are now leaving for the Carthaginian and Roman to fight in,"[24] and events proved him correct. Since the death of Agathocles the Syracusans gradually had been pushed back into eastern Sicily, where they found themselves harassed by the Mamertines. Under their new king, Hiero, they fought back and drove them back to Messana and laid siege to the city. One faction of Mamertines called upon the Carthaginians for help; they responded by sending a garrison to protect the city, and Hiero was forced to withdraw. Another faction, however, had sent to Rome for help, offering to place their city in the *fides* of the Romans. The request forced the Romans to face a major decision, for it was obvious that a positive answer probably would bring war with Carthage, a state of a different kind and with greater power than the Romans had ever faced.

Polybius tells us that the Roman Senate found itself in a quandary. Some years earlier the people of Rhegium, a Greek city just across the strait from Messana, had been threatened by Pyrrhus and worried about the Carthaginian fleet, so they had asked Rome for help. The Romans sent in a garrison of four thousand Italians from Campania to safeguard Rhegium, but soon the garrison imitated the Mamertines, seizing the city and driving out its inhabitants. As soon as they were able the Romans recovered Rhegium and returned it to the remainder of its citizens. Those Campanian rebels who survived the assault were taken back to Rome, where they were publicly scourged and beheaded, for the Romans wished, "as far as they could, to vindicate their good faith in the eyes of the allies."[25] How could they take into their custody a band of brigands who had done the same things for which the Romans had executed the Campanian renegades who had seized Rhegium? That would be "a breach of equity hard to justify."[26]

Concern for their honor, however, was not the only thing that made the Senate hesitate. Some senators might have preferred to push farther into the territory of the Gauls in northern Italy before crossing into Sicily. Others might have realized how potent an enemy Carthage would be and how different from any they had faced. Perhaps they knew how important navies would be in any such war and how inferior the Romans were at sea.[27] For many senators, however, the very greatness of Punic power argued for accepting the request of the Mamertines. Polybius says they saw that the Punic Empire extended beyond Africa to Spain and the islands surrounding Italy, and they worried that "if the Carthaginians became masters of Sicily also, they should find them very dangerous and formidable neighbors, surrounding them as they would on every side, and occupying a position which commanded all the coasts of Italy." They believed that unless they helped the Mamertines, Carthage would, in fact, gain control of all Sicily and concluded that "it was absolutely necessary not to let Messana slip, or allow the Carthaginians to secure what would be a bridge to enable them to cross into Italy."[28]

In a rare case of such division and hesitation the Senate was unable to arrive at a decision, so the momentous choice was passed on to the people in their Assembly. In their public addresses before the Assembly gathered to vote the Consuls plainly argued in favor of accepting the Mamertines's request, for they "suggested that individually [the people] would get manifest and important benefits from it."[29] The Consuls, no doubt, saw an opportunity for winning glory for themselves, and it is unlikely that the people understood their promises as anything but "booty, pure and simple."[30] Although these private motives must have played a part, it seems likely that the motive proposed by Polybius, even though it is the most respectable and the one favored by Roman propagandists, was the most basic and the one that united many who held different views. The Romans did not enter the war with the intention of conquering the Carthaginian Empire, or even all of Sicily. As the harshest interpreter of Rome's motives for expansion concedes, "we should probably accept Polybius' account of the growth of Roman ambitions *after* the fall of Agrigentum [in 262, emphasis added]," when he says they first decided to drive the Carthaginians out of Sicily.[31] The Carthaginians truly were a powerful, bold, and dangerous neighbor. They possessed a fleet that dominated the western Mediterranean. With a base at Messana it readily could raid the coast and threaten the cities of Magna Graecia. Carthage could present a choice to the newly incorporated Greek states of Italy, threatening to unravel the Roman confederation. If the Romans refused the Mamertines it might seem to others, and perhaps to themselves, that they had recoiled out of fear. They had not become masters of Italy by prudently avoiding risky entanglements, and their image of themselves, their concept of honor, did not permit such an evasion easily. Faced with the challenge of the Carthaginians in command of all Sicily, entrenched across the narrow strait from Italy, the Romans were not likely to back away.

The First Punic War was long and hard, lasting until 241. To win it the Romans were forced to become a great naval power, to expend unprecedented sums of money and to suffer horrendous numbers of casualties. It ended with Carthage's brilliant General Hamilcar Barca locked up in his stronghold in western Sicily, the only place still held by Carthage. The sinking of yet another Carthaginian fleet forced him to surrender, although he remained unbeaten in any land battle, still in possession of the fortress at Lilybaeum. So came to an end what Polybius called "the longest, the most continuous, and most severely contested war known to us in history." The Romans lost seven hundred *quinqueremes,* the new, larger model ship of the line that had replaced the *triremes* of classical Greece used in the Persian and Peloponnesian wars, and the Carthaginians five hundred. Taking into account the increase in ship size he concludes that "never in the whole history of the world have such enormous forces contended for mastery of the sea."[32]

THE PEACE

Such great exertions and losses had exhausted the Romans, too, and the Carthaginians, though defeated, were not helpless. As a result, the Roman Consul G. Lutatius Catulus, offered Hamilcar a generous peace. The Carthaginians were required to leave Sicily and to promise not to make war on Hiero of Syracuse, who had joined the Romans early in the war, or his allies; to return Roman prisoners; and to pay an indemnity of 2,200 silver talents over twenty years, a sum Carthage could afford to pay.[33] Hamilcar agreed, but the treaty had to be ratified by the Roman people, and they refused to accept it. Instead they sent a commission of ten men to make revisions, and they added a thousand talents to the indemnity—to be paid immediately—cut the time available to pay the rest to ten years, and required Carthage to evacuate not only Sicily but also the Lipari and Aegates islands that lie between Italy and Sicily. Perhaps they were stirred to this action by the jealous rivals of the Consul, eager to discredit his achievement, but the Roman people clearly thought that victory in so long and difficult a war deserved a greater reward.

Even so, the revised treaty, however annoying, was one the Carthaginians could accept, especially in light of the great troubles that threatened the safety of their own city in Africa. Withdrawn from Sicily, twenty thousand mercenaries gathered in one place and demanded arrears in their wages be paid in full at once. When the Carthaginians would not comply, the mercenaries launched a rebellion and marched against the city of Tunis. Soon the Libyan subjects of Carthage on the east and the Numidians on the west joined in the general revolt, called "the truceless war" because of the merciless ferocity with which it was waged. The Carthaginians themselves were forced to fight in defense of their own city.

After three years of hard warfare they were able to subdue the rebels but were worn down by the effort.

At first the Romans did not use these distractions to trouble Carthage further, in spite of some provocation and opportunity. When some Italian merchants were caught selling provisions to the mutineers in Africa, the Carthaginians captured and imprisoned as many as five hundred of them. The Romans were annoyed but recovered them through diplomacy, and even restored the Carthaginians captured in the war in Sicily. Thereafter they forbade trade with the rebels and permitted commerce with Carthage. While Carthage was fighting for its life in Africa its mercenaries on Sardinia also launched a rebellion and seized most of the island. When they appealed to Rome for help the Romans refused, as they also did when mercenaries who had seized the city of Utica, near Carthage, made a similar request.[34] The Romans, no doubt, were enjoying the respite from fighting after the long and costly war against Carthage, yet events would soon show how easy it would be to despoil or harm the Carthaginians if they chose. The sources do not say why they held back, but as late as 239 Rome clearly was not aggressive.

It is all the more puzzling, therefore, that the Romans reversed their course in the following year. When the mercenaries on Sardinia again asked for help against the natives of the island, probably in expectation of a Carthaginian expedition to recover the island, the Romans agreed. This was a clear violation of the treaty of 241 and without any respectable pretext. When the Carthaginians objected, the Romans demanded that they give up Sardinia and pay an additional 1,200 talents or else face war. The Carthaginians had no choice but to accept. The Romans claimed that the Carthaginians had been making military preparations not for the recovery of Sardinia from the mercenaries but against Rome. Polybius, normally sympathetic to the Roman point of view, rightly dismisses this as a false pretext. "The Carthaginians," he tells us, were beyond question compelled by the necessities of their position, *contrary to all justice,* to evacuate Sardinia and pay this enormous sum of money."[35] (emphasis added)

As Talleyrand said of Napoleon's murder of the Duc d'Enghien, however, "it was worse than a crime, it was a blunder," and Polybius calls the Roman humiliation of Carthage over Sardinia "the most important cause of the subsequent war."[36] Defeat in the First Punic War must itself have caused hard feelings among some Carthaginians, none more than their general, Hamilcar Barca. Polybius tells us:

> The result of the war in Sicily had not broken the spirit of that commander. He regarded himself as unconquered; for the troops at Eryx which he commanded were still sound and undismayed: and though he yielded so far as to make a treaty, it was a concession to the exigencies of the times brought on by the defeat of the Carthaginians at sea. But he never relaxed in his determined purpose of revenge; and, had it not been for the mutiny of the mercenaries at Carthage, he would at once have sought and made another occasion for bringing about a war, as far as he was able to do so.[37]

Polybius regards the exasperated anger of Hamilcar as one of the causes of the Second Punic War and supports it with a story Hamilcar's son Hannibal told King Antiochus of Syria many years later in 195. When the boy was nine years old his father "took me by the right hand and led me up to the altar, and bade me lay my hand upon the victim and swear that I would never be friends with Rome. So long, then Antiochus, as your policy is one of hostility to Rome, you may feel quite secure of having in me a most thoroughgoing supporter."[38]

The "Wrath of the Barcids" and the "Oath of Hannibal" came to be the heart and soul of the Roman tradition, explaining the origins of the Hannibalic War.[39] They served Roman interests in escaping blame for bringing on the war, but that does not make them false. Regarding any war, each side produces claims of its own innocence and the enemy's culpability; some of these claims are justified nonetheless. We need not believe the details of these stories, though they are in no way incredible,[40] to accept their general sense: that Carthage's leading general felt frustrated, angry, and possibly betrayed when he was forced to surrender an army unbeaten in the field; that he would very much have enjoyed gaining revenge in a renewed war; and that he passed that anger and those ambitions on to his devoted, talented, and ambitious son. It has been suggested that "one Carthaginian general in particular [Hamilcar Barca] may have been left with feelings akin to those of many German soldiers in 1918,"[41] and he and his son could not have been alone in such feelings.

Still, there is no reason to believe that most Carthaginians held similar feelings when Lutatius offered them a reasonable peace in 241. Rome's stiffened terms, however, must have embittered more of them, and its brutal behavior in the Sardinian affair, which Polybius regarded as a second cause of the Hannibalic War, could hardly have left many Carthaginians feeling anything but anger and loathing for their conquerors. When Hannibal launched his daring and dangerous assault on the Romans two decades later, therefore, his people supported him with zeal.

The peace that ended the First Punic War was very different from those broken by the great Peloponnesian War or the First World War. Each of those reflected the true power relationship among the major states with considerable accuracy. In each case the major powers were satisfied sufficiently with the situation as to want to maintain the resulting status quo. After the peace of 445 the chief burden for keeping the peace fell on Athens, and Pericles and the Athenians were prepared to accept it. After the Franco-Prussian war that responsibility fell on Germany, which, under the leadership of Bismarck, did the same. It took unexpected and unusual circumstances to bring on a new war in each instance.

The peace that concluded the First Punic War, however, differed from these in every crucial respect. It reflected the relationship of power between Rome and Carthage at a moment when Carthage was unnaturally weak. Unless the Romans took steps to destroy its enemy or cripple it permanently, Carthage had the capacity to recover its strength and to become formidable again. The peace imposed in 241 and 238, therefore, failed in this most basic way. It was faulty, also, because the Carthaginians were deeply dissatisfied with it, and many of them were determined to undo it whenever the opportunity arose. As late as 221, Polybius tells us, "the Carthaginians were meditating revenge for their defeats in Sicily."[42] In these circumstances it fell to the Romans to preserve the peace. As we shall see, however, they were distracted by other interests, and they were arrogant in their confidence that Carthage no longer posed a threat. When, at last, they recognized the danger it was not only too late to avoid a war but almost too late to avoid defeat and disaster. The peace they finally imposed on Carthage in 238 was of the least stable kind: it embittered the losers without depriving them of the capacity for seeking revenge and without establishing a system able to restrain them—and then taking the trouble to make it work.

So strong is our modern desire for peace that we tend to regard it as an unalloyed good, but the arrangement imposed by the Romans raises serious questions. Their behavior and the peace they forced on Carthage were, by the admission of one of their own defenders, entirely unjust. To keep the peace in those circumstances, to insist that its victims abide in it rather than resort to war, is to perpetuate an injustice. We must recognize that much of the time whatever international arrangement is in place has produced an injustice somewhere, and a sense of injustice, warranted or not, among many people. The result among people of conscience may be a serious conflict of basic values between a desire for peace and a desire for justice. It is hard to see how such conflicts can be avoided. Our study, however, deals with the more limited question of how wars come about and how peace is maintained, even if that peace be unjust.

TESTING THE PEACE

After putting down the rebellions in Africa the Carthaginians turned to Spain as the place best suited to restore their wealth and strength. It had rich silver mines, plenty of men to serve in the Punic armies, and was not as yet of any interest to the Romans. Even if the Carthaginians had no thought of a war of revenge against Rome there were good reasons for them to seek to regain and expand their Empire in Spain. Polybius, however, tells us that Hamilcar "set about securing the Carthaginian power in Iberia with the intention of using it as a base of operations against Rome." He calls Carthage's success in Spain the third cause of the Hannibalic War, "for it was confidence inspired by their forces there which encouraged them to embark upon it."[43]

Such an explanation accords with the Roman tradition of a war of revenge deliberately planned by the Barcid family from the first, and on those grounds is suspect, but once again, it is psychologically plausible and impossible to reject with confidence. If Hamilcar and other Carthaginians were embittered and unwilling to accept what they regarded as humiliation by the Romans, it was good sense to recover Carthaginian power in Spain as a first step. It was an obvious and attractive step, in any case, something that Carthage was almost bound to undertake. Yet anyone who knew Rome's history and understood its normal procedure might have predicted that the recovery of Carthaginian power was bound to arouse Roman suspicion, perhaps its hostility. Whatever the intentions of Hamilcar and his supporters, therefore, the Carthaginian decision to expand in Spain ran the risk of provoking another war with Rome.

In 237 Hamilcar took his young son Hannibal and his son-in-law Hasdrubal and sailed to Spain. Before his death in 229 he succeeded in recovering and expanding the Carthaginian Empire in southern and southeastern Spain. The Romans appear to have taken no notice of his activities until 231, when they sent ambassadors to see what was happening. Hamilcar received them with courtesy and explained that his operations in Spain were intended to make it possible for Carthage to pay the war indemnity to Rome. Faced with such a reply, and since Rome had no interest in Spain, they had no cause of complaint and went home.[44]

If Dio is right that Rome as yet had no interest in Spain, and the absence of any reference to such an interest in the other ancient writers suggests that he is, why did the Romans send an embassy at all? One view is that it was provoked merely by general curiosity, that Hamilcar's smooth reply gave them nothing to complain of, and that their inquiry "does not bear the implication that the Senate would have *done* anything if the *legati* had found anything of which they could disapprove."[45] At the other extreme is the idea that the Romans had been warned by their friends in the West, especially Massilia (modern Marseille). The Romans had been friendly with the Massilians for centuries and may have concluded a formal alliance with them already.[46] Massilia conducted extensive trade with Spanish tribes through its colonies Emporion, Rhode, and Hemeroscopiae, which would be threatened by Carthaginian expansion along the coast. It would have been in the Massilians' interests to warn the Romans about Carthage's growing Spanish empire and the threat it posed to Rome. In this view "the reports of her western friends led the Senate to dispatch a fact-finding mission which would at the same time serve notice on Hamilcar that he was being watched."[47] It implies that Rome was attentive to Spanish concerns already, and engaged in a policy of curbing Carthaginian expansion.

The first approach provides no explanation at all, but the latter goes beyond what the evidence requires. It is likely that the Massilians were alarmed and that they asked Rome to intervene. "If so, Rome could scarcely refuse the token gesture of sending an embassy to Hamilcar,"[48] even if they had no interest in Spain and did not take the warning seriously. Still, it is far from clear that if Hamilcar had given a less satisfactory answer the Romans would have taken no action. His soft answer, however, succeeded in turning away Roman wrath, and the moment passed without conflict. The Romans probably were reassured rather than alarmed.

When Hamilcar died in 229 his troops in Spain elected his son-in-law

Hasdrubal to take his place, and the people back in Carthage confirmed their decision.[49] Hasdrubal swiftly set out on a campaign to punish the tribe that had killed Hamilcar. By a combination of marriage to an Iberian princess, diplomatic skill, and a powerfully increased army, he greatly expanded the Carthaginian Empire in Spain. He founded the city of New Carthage (Cartagena), an excellent port and close to valuable silver mines, and from there he regally governed and extended the boundaries of his province.

In 226 the Romans sent another embassy to Carthaginian Spain. They concluded a treaty with Hasdrubal, whose only reported clause is that he agreed "not to cross the Iber [modern Ebro] in arms."[50] Modern scholars have engaged in fierce arguments about its form, content, significance, and chronological relationship with another Roman agreement in Spain with the city of Saguntum, because the evidence is so slim and because Hannibal's alleged violation of the Ebro treaty was the core of Rome's subsequent claims that Carthage started the Second Punic War.

If Polybius's report is correct, the treaty bound only Carthage and would be another example of the Romans imposing their will on the Carthaginians. The language, however, inescapably implies a Roman concession, for if Hasdrubal agreed not to cross the Ebro, presumably he could go as far as its southern bank. Yet the limit of Carthage's Spanish empire was still a considerable distance short of the Ebro, so the implied concession would have the effect of recognizing that empire and permitting its extension northward to the river. Included in this yielded territory was the Massilian colony of Hemeroscopiae. Why should the Romans voluntarily acquiesce to further Punic expansion and abandon the interests of their ally without prompting from the Carthaginians? Some scholars have tried to explain the geographical problem away by suggesting that the Ebro mentioned by the ancient writers is not the Ebro we know but another river farther south[51]; their arguments rightly have convinced few.

Polybius tells us that Rome acted because it was alarmed by the growing strength of Hasdrubal in Spain: "They discovered, as they thought, that they had allowed their suspicions to be lulled to sleep, and had meanwhile given the Carthaginians the opportunity of consolidating their power." If that was so, why didn't they attack Hasdrubal, or at least impose crippling conditions upon him? Polybius's answer is that they were prevented by troubles closer to hand: "they were in almost daily dread of an attack by the Celts." The Ebro treaty, therefore, was meant "to mollify Hasdrubal by gentle measures, and so to leave themselves free to attack the Celts first . . . for they were convinced that with such enemies on their flank, they would not only be unable to keep their hold over the rest of Italy, but even to reckon on safety in their own city."[52]

That explanation, of course, is consistent with Polybius's theme of a determined Barcid vendetta against Rome and has therefore come under criticism. Why should the Romans feel the need to appease Hasdrubal, who was "neither ruffled nor irritated?"[53] The Romans had no interests of their own in Spain, and there was no danger of the Carthaginians joining with the Celts against them: "For all purposes, theoretical and practical, the Ebro simply was not on Rome's map at the time of the treaty."[54] The answer, once again, is that it was Massilia that brought the matter to the Romans' attention and urged them to stop Hasdrubal before he could lay hold of their colonies and put an end to their lucrative trade in Spain.[55]

Apart from the fact that no ancient writer mentions Massilia in connection with the Ebro treaty, these explanations raise a difficult question already noted: why should the Massilians have asked the Romans to set a limit at the Ebro, thereby abandoning their colony to its south? The objectors to Polybius's interpretation do not confront this obstacle, which seems a greater problem than those posed by the Polybian explanation. His account is coherent and persuasive. For some years the Romans had feared an attack from the Celts to their north. When it came in 225 the vast and ferocious invading army plunged into the heart of Italy and was defeated only with the greatest of difficulty. In their concern not long before the onslaught, the Romans naturally sought to forestall additional problems and dangers. Very likely the Massilians had been calling their attention to the growth of Carthaginian power in Spain with regularity. No doubt, they had tried to frighten the Romans into action by raising the threat of a Carthaginian alliance with the Celts on the Roman side of the Pyrénées.

The Romans would have had to be more obtuse than is reasonable not to know that there was no love for them in the hearts of the ever more powerful Carthaginians and their leader in Spain. The prudent action was to appease him at a dangerous moment and deal with him later, if need be. This was not a typical Roman response, but it was made at a moment of great fear and danger. As they would do again only after their terrible defeat at Cannae in 216, the Romans buried victims alive to ward off a catastrophe predicted by religious authority.[56] In such threatening circumstances they were willing to sacrifice some of the interests of their allies.

The form of the treaty salvaged their pride, since it had the appearance not of a concession but of an order delivered, *de haute en bas*. The Romans could console themselves with the thought that it was only a temporary expedient; nonetheless, as Polybius makes clear, it was an attempt at appeasement in a moment of weakness and fear. Appeasement is a perfectly respectable and often useful instrument of policy. It can be effective when applied from a position of strength, when it is a freely taken action meant to allay a grievance and create good will. It is an unsatisfactory and dangerous device when it is resorted to out of fear and necessity, for then it does not reduce resentment but shows weakness and induces contempt. The Romans' attempt through the Ebro treaty was still a worse kind of appeasement, for even as its content displayed weakness, its form was insulting. Its effect was to neither soothe nor deter but to inflame and encourage the Carthaginians. Even after the Celtic emergency had passed, the Romans took no military measures to guard against the Carthaginians in Spain, nor did they work to conciliate them.

THE ACCESSION OF HANNIBAL

In 221 Hasdrubal was assassinated. As before, the Army elected a new leader, selecting Hannibal, the son of Hamilcar Barca, and the Assembly back at Carthage confirmed him unanimously.[57] Hannibal is judged widely to be one of the great generals in history who learned the lessons of Hellenistic warfare from the career of Alexander the Great, digested and passed on by his father, Hamilcar. He was a master of the tactics of the day, combining infantry with cavalry, and even war elephants, to permit maneuvers that often led to the surrounding and annihilation of the enemy. He was a great natural leader who could command the allegiance even of mercenary troops and allies in the most difficult times. "Above all it is his character . . . that counts and that has given to the Hannibalic war its epic quality and invested his name with an undying glamour."[58] He, too, married an Iberian princess, and then he launched a vigorous military campaign, resuming his father's policy of conquering by the sword. He swiftly occupied central Spain and then began to move along the coast up toward the Ebro. All went well until he came upon the town of Saguntum. "No one," says Polybius, "south of the Ebro rashly ventured to face him except the people of Saguntum."[59] Their boldness rested on their relationship with the Romans, which led Hannibal to regard them warily. Hannibal's attack on Saguntum in 218 was the immediate cause of the Second Punic War, so the nature and timing of that city's connection with the Romans is very important.

Unfortunately, the evidence on both questions is inexact.[60] It seems more likely that the relationship between Saguntum and Rome was not based on a formal treaty. Polybius says merely that the Saguntines "gave themselves over to the *fides* of the Romans."[61] He does not say they made a treaty. Since he carefully looked up and quoted all the relevant treaties that existed, that strongly suggests there was no treaty to be found. It would, moreover, have strengthened the case that Polybius and the Romans wanted to make, i.e., that the Carthaginians were to blame for the war, if Hannibal had attacked a town formally allied to Rome. Finally, if Saguntum were formally an ally when Hannibal attacked there would have been no cause for debate in Rome as to whether to go to its defense, yet such a debate took place. For these reasons it appears that Saguntum was not a formal ally but only a "friend" and client. The significance of that point is that Rome was not legally obliged to come to its aid when Hannibal attacked.

The date of the agreement is also obscure but important. Polybius says that it was made "a good number of years before the time of Hannibal," but it is not clear whether "the time of Hannibal" means when he came to power in 221, or when he became embroiled with Saguntum a year or so later. That is less important than determining the meaning of "a good number of years before,"[62] because we would like to know if Rome became associated with Saguntum before or after the Ebro treaty in 226. If it happened before, it is hard to explain why the Romans did not mention it in the Ebro treaty. Failing to do so could have the implication that Rome was abandoning its client. If, on the other hand, the agreement were made after the Ebro treaty, in 224 or 223, it would mean that the Romans were deliberately challenging Hannibal, in contravention of the Carthaginians' implied right to do as they liked south of the Ebro.

Neither interpretation is excluded, but the former seems preferable, not only because it better suits the language of Polybius (see note 60) but also because it makes reasonable sense of the actions of the participants. Let us assume that the Romans agreed to take the Saguntines into their *fides* in the years before 226. They might have been called upon to settle a quarrel between factions, as they were in 220, or to deter the advance of Hasdrubal and his forces. The Romans would have accepted the request in part to please their Massilian allies and in part to keep an eye on the growing power of Carthage. The client–patron relationship did not oblige them to become involved, but it offered them grounds for doing so if they judged it necessary. It was a typical Roman association, employed many times in the past, and does not imply a Roman interest in Spain per se.

In their anxiety of the year 226 the Romans would have had no hesitation in ignoring this association in making the Ebro treaty. Saguntum simply did not matter in the face of an impending Celtic war. If the Romans thought of the city at all they must have thought it dispensable, just like Massilia's colonies south of the Ebro. To the Carthaginians, on the other hand, it reasonably would have seemed that Rome's abandonment of Saguntum was part of the concession implied in the treaty. They would have regarded the Saguntines as no longer under Roman protection. It was in the interest of the Saguntines, on the other hand, to act as though they were still Rome's friends and clients. These diverse understandings make it easier to comprehend the events of 220–18.

THE CRISIS

In 221 or 220 a quarrel broke out between factions in Saguntum over dealings with a neighboring tribe.[63] One of the factions wanted to call in the Carthaginians to arbitrate, the other, the Romans. It appears that Rome's uncertain policy had given rise to this internal division, as each side gambled on whether Rome would or would not resume its association and protection. The Roman faction won out, and the Romans arrived and executed the leaders of the Punic party. The Romans did not hesitate to act as the patrons of Saguntum, regardless of the Ebro treaty. They might have been willing to abandon the Saguntines by implication when under pressure from the Celts, but freed of that menace, they chose to reassert their patronage. Hannibal, as yet, took no action. Polybius tells us that his father's advice had been to keep clear of Saguntum, "wishing to give the Romans no avowed pretext for war,"[64] and he tried to follow it.

The victorious party at Saguntum had reason to believe that their victory was not permanent and their position precarious so long as Hannibal and his army were in the vicinity and the Romans not committed clearly to Spain, with their armies far away. So "they kept sending ambassadors to Rome, partly because they foresaw what was coming, and trembled for their own existence, and partly that the Romans might be kept fully aware of the growing power of the Carthaginians in Iberia."[65] For some time the Romans paid no attention, but at last, probably in the autumn of 220, they sent ambassadors "to investigate the report."[66]

They found Hannibal at New Carthage, back from a successful season of campaigning. Their instructions were plainly more than merely to make inquiry; they told him "to keep clear of Saguntum, since it was under their *fides,* and not to cross the Ebro, as had been agreed in the time of Hasdrubal."[67] The ancient writers do not say why the Romans chose this moment to heed the Saguntines nor what were Rome's intentions.[68] Some scholars see the embassy as only a small development from Rome's policy of no real interest in Spain.[69] They took notice, after all, only after neglecting many previous warnings, permitting considerable delay. What moved the Romans to action was the Saguntines' assertion that their safety was in question. Then, "the credibility of Roman *fides* was at stake; and it might prove embarrassing elsewhere if Rome's solitary friend in Spain was seen by the world to have fallen seriously foul of Hannibal while the Senate continued to display its customary lack of concern about Spanish affairs and to ignore the moral implications of its *amicitia.* Both practical politics and the Senate's code of conduct coincided to make it necessary to prevent such an occasion from arising." The mission sent by the Senate had an open mind and was prepared to accept Hannibal's assurances. The ambassadors "were polite enough, even if over-endowed with Roman *gravitas.*" They were merely reminding Hannibal that Saguntum still was under Roman protection and that he was bound by Hasdrubal's Ebro treaty. They only were stating the facts and could see no reason why Hannibal should be offended: "the Roman *legati* [ambassador] naturally could not spell out in detail to Hannibal the awkward nature of Rome's moral obligation to Saguntum, that the Senate had no real desire to intervene and that it was, in effect, asking Hannibal to help it out of a difficult situation by letting the world see that Roman *fides* worked."

To be sure, the sending of an embassy was a slight development of Roman involvement. Hannibal might well have misinterpreted Roman intentions when he reviewed the history of Rome's protection of friends and allies in Italy, Sicily, and Sardinia. He might have seen Rome's claim to protect Saguntum as the opening wedge of a campaign to challenge Carthage's empire in Spain as similar claims had led to the expulsion of Carthage from Sicily and Sardinia. The Romans did not have such an intention, but "it was a tragic, if entirely comprehensible, misunderstanding. From this point onwards Hannibal acted as if war was inevitable, indeed as if the *legati* had brought an unacceptable ultimatum."

Some have taken a less indulgent view of Roman motives and seen Rome's action as a step in a policy of active aggression in which Spanish riches were to be the prize. "Rome began to use Saguntum as a tool to undermine Punic power south of the river, and to loosen the hold of Carthage on the enviable wealth of Spain."[70] But, it must be pointed out, there is no direct evidence to support such an assertion. Even the most vigorous critic of Rome as a predatory imperial power concedes that greed of one sort or another can only be part of a full explanation of Rome's behavior. "Hopes of glory, power, and wealth, together with the habits of armed reaction to foreign opponents, mingled with what were seen as the needs of defence."[71]

Neither of the extreme interpretations seems adequate. The Romans were not using the situation at Saguntum as a pretext for engagement against Hannibal and his Spanish empire. They brought no troops and made no military preparations. Subsequent events would show that there was no plan for aggression. On the other hand, the Romans were not compelled to take any action at all in defense of their *fides* in 220. Hannibal neither had attacked Saguntum nor taken any threatening action toward it at that time. Instead he had held his peace even when the Romans became involved and punished the friends of Carthage in the city. They could easily have waited for some hostile gesture before feeling any legitimate concern for their reputation or prestige. It was they who took the initiative in raising difficulties in the land south of the Ebro, if not by their arbitration in Saguntum then surely by sending the embassy to Hannibal. The embassy was not making a polite inquiry but issuing a stern warning. For the benefit of their allies, for their own prestige, and out of concern about Carthage's growing power in Spain, the Romans were ostentatiously asserting their authority and putting the new Carthaginian leader to the test. No doubt, they expected him to respond as Hamilcar had done in 231, to return a soft answer, to give Saguntum a wide berth, and to concede by his demeanor and actions Punic deference to Rome.

But the situation facing Hannibal was different from the one his father had confronted a decade earlier. In 231 the Romans had indeed made an inquiry, received an answer, and gone home. They had made no demands, issued no orders, made no threats, direct or implied. Hamilcar was free to continue with his expansion in Spain. In 220, however, Hannibal was assaulted with demands, orders, and implied threats. If he accepted them quietly the knowledge that he had done so would diminish his personal prestige and the honor of and prestige of Carthage in Spain. That would have material as well as emotional results. Saguntum would be encouraged to trouble tribes allied or subject to the Carthaginians, as they may have been doing already,[72] and others might do the same, in the belief that Rome would protect them. The diminution of Carthage's prestige would have the effect of reducing its power and security, as the Spanish empire began to unravel, undermined by Rome's humiliation of Carthage and its Spanish commander.

Even without believing that the Romans were planning a more complete and active intervention in Spain, therefore, Hannibal had reason for alarm. In addition, if he thought about the history of Roman relations with Carthage, he could well believe that the embassy was only the first step that would lead to the expulsion of his city and its forces from Spain as they had been driven from Sicily. Hannibal did not misunderstand the meaning of the Roman action. If there was any misunderstanding it was on the part of the Romans, who ought to have known how difficult it would be for any Punic leader to accept their insulting message quietly, which, among other things, had the effect of unilaterally annulling the Ebro treaty, as the Carthaginians must have understood it and had a right to understand it. They also misjudged Hannibal, who was less likely than most to accept the insult and its practical implications.[73]

He answered the ambassadors "with all the heat of youth, inflamed by martial ardor, recent successes, and his long-standing hatred of Rome."[74] Harking back to the Romans' arbitration in Saguntum, he charged them with using it as a pretext to put some of the leading citizens to death. Throwing the claims of honor and noblesse oblige back at the alleged defenders of *fides*, he told them that Carthage would not permit so treacherous an action, "for it was the traditional policy of Carthage to protect all persons so wronged."[75] This was not only the bitter response of an angry young man; it also established a new policy and stance toward the Romans.

It amounted to a rejection of subordination and an assertion of equality. Since their defeat in the First Punic War, Carthage and its leaders had been forced to take orders from Rome or to face unacceptable consequences. Hannibal now set out on an independent course, at least in Spain, free of Roman dictation and interference.

For this purpose he needed the support of the government back home, so he sent to Carthage asking for instructions, "since the Saguntines, trusting in their alliance with Rome, were mistreating some of the peoples subject to Carthage."[76] What Hannibal really was asking was whether the Carthaginians were prepared to risk war with Rome to defend their empire in Spain. It was, however, a high risk, because Rome's record did not suggest it would sit by idly while a state it had taken into its *fides* was attacked.

Hannibal must have received solid backing from home, for in the spring of 219, perhaps in April or May, he laid siege to Saguntum. Polybius tells of Hannibal's reasons for launching the attack: the Romans had counted on using Saguntum as their base of operations and had expected to fight the war in Spain; by taking the city Hannibal would deprive them of the base and the prospect of fighting the war so far from Italy; the fear inspired by his boldness would consolidate his empire in Spain. The wealth he would obtain from taking the city would provide funds for his projected campaign against Rome, encourage his troops, who would receive their share, and win support in Carthage when he sent the rest of the booty home.[77]

All of this assumes that Hannibal had decided already on a war against Rome, that his attack on Saguntum was not one of the causes of the war but its first action, and we cannot be certain that Polybius and the Roman apologetic tradition is wrong in making that claim. The odds were that an attack on Saguntum would bring a Roman reprisal and the beginning of war. If war was coming in any case, it would be better to deprive the Romans of Saguntum and to launch an attack into Italy, but here a problem arises. The siege of Saguntum took eight months to complete, and there is no reason why Hannibal should have expected to take the city sooner. He had every reason to fear that news of the attack would bring a Roman army into Spain at once, which would make his strategy of a swift march through Gaul into Italy impossible. He would find himself fighting a war in Spain, with no chance to gain support of the Celts across the Pyrénées, much less to disrupt Rome's Italian confederation. For these reasons it seems much more likely that he did not intend to begin the war by besieging Saguntum. Instead, he was calling Rome's bluff, asserting the validity of the Ebro treaty and Carthage's right to expand up to that river, taking seriously the possibility that Rome might not respond.

For all eight months of the siege, in fact, the Romans took no action. Since they had so recently made it clear that Saguntum was under their protection and warned Hannibal off, why did they fail to defend their client? The simplest answer is that they were occupied elsewhere. In 219 both Consuls were leading armies in Illyria, on the east coast of the Adriatic, where cities under Roman protection were under attack by a certain Demetrius of Pharos. He had been a client of the Romans, but he "had conceived a contempt for its power, when he saw it threatened first by the Gauls and then by Carthage," and he counted on his connections with the mighty kingdom of Macedon to protect him. This was precisely the kind of concern that had turned their attention to Hannibal, but they regarded Demetrius as the closer and more dangerous threat and sent both Consuls against him, "feeling convinced that they would have ample time to correct the errors of the Illyrians and rebuke and chastise Demetrius' ingratitude and temerity."[78] It has been pointed out that, nevertheless, Rome could have raised another army commanded by a proconsul and sent it to Spain on the news of the siege, but "probably her leaders had complacently assumed that her warnings had been enough."[79]

That might explain the initial decision to send both Consuls to Illyria and none to Spain, but not why an additional army was not raised later and sent to relieve Saguntum. The likeliest explanation is that there was division of opinion within the Roman Senate. Raising a third army would have been an unusual step, reserved for what was generally perceived to be an emergency, but why should the Romans think an emergency was at hand? Hannibal had no fleet, yet the First Punic War seemed to prove that naval power was essential to victory. As yet the Romans had no idea of Hannibal's plan, bold to the point of rashness, of marching overland into Italy. The very fact of the siege, as we have seen, tied him to Spain and made it seem that there would be plenty of time to deal with him after the Consuls had completed their campaign against Demetrius. Some Senators, moreover, might have thought that Saguntum was not worth the effort. Even if it fell to Hannibal that would still leave Hannibal south of the Ebro, where the Romans, after all, had permitted him to be. Hannibal might turn out to be no more of a threat than Hamilcar and Hasdrubal had been. There were more important problems closer to home and plenty of time to deal with Hannibal, if need be.

Some time during December 219 or January 218 Saguntum fell. The news cannot have reached Rome later than mid-February, probably earlier, and the Roman Consuls did not go out to take up their commands against Carthage until late August 218.[80] Sometime in between the Romans sent an embassy to Carthage to deliver an ultimatum, but whenever that may have taken place, there was a surprising delay before the Romans took decisive action. Polybius insists with unusual firmness and argumentation that there was no debate in Rome when the news of the fall of Saguntum arrived, but the Senate immediately sent the embassy to Carthage to deliver their ultimatum. On this occasion he must be wrong, for apart from the fact that he does not notice or explain the delay, the debates were reported by both pro-Roman and pro-Carthaginian sources.[81] The Senate, more- over, would need to decide on the language of the ultimatum, the descrip- tion of the grievance, and what the demand for satisfaction should be. All that would require discussion and surely lead to debate. One of the issues must have been whether to confine the Roman response to attacking Hannibal in Spain and then negotiating a peace after his defeat or to aim at the destruction of all Carthaginian power. The ancient writers do not report that discussion, but the latter position must have won out, as the ultimatum makes clear. Then the debate focused on what specific action Rome should take. A distinguished senator made the proposal to declare war immediately and send consular armies to Spain and Carthage, while another more cautiously proposed to send an embassy demanding the disavowal and surrender of Hannibal.[82] Hannibal had political enemies in Carthage, but it was unlikely that the Carthaginians would yield to the Roman demand. Perhaps the idea was the same as that of the Spartans in 432 when they demanded the expulsion of Pericles as a condition for peace.[83] In each case the demand was not expected to be met, but the plan was to discredit its object, make him the issue and the apparent cause of the city's troubles, and thereby create political turmoil and division in the enemy camp.

The latter proposal was adopted, so the Romans sent an embassy to Carthage composed of five distinguished men, including both Consuls of the previous year, to demand the surrender of Hannibal and his staff.[84] The Carthaginians listened to the ultimatum in anger, but they responded with an argument of their case. It rested on their reading of the treaty ending the First Punic War, which never mentioned Spain but promised security to the allies of both powers. Reading the treaty aloud, they pointed out that Saguntum was not a Roman ally at the time and was, therefore, not protected. It was a plausible reading, but not the only one possible. The treaty did not bar either side from taking on new allies, and it could hardly be expected that either side should be free to attack the other's new allies with impunity.[85] Legalities, in fact, were not the issue. The Carthaginians really were insisting on their freedom to do as they liked in Spain. They meant *all* Spain, because they also rejected the legality of the Ebro treaty accepted by Hasdrubal, since they claimed it had not been ratified by the government in Carthage.[86] This was not meant to be the beginning of negotiation but a declaration of defiance.

The Roman ambassadors rejected legal discussions entirely. While Saguntum was still free and unharmed it might be possible to talk about legal points and justifications and settle the matter by discussion, but now that it had been taken by force the Carthaginians had only two choices: to give up the guilty parties as evidence that the deed had not been sanctioned by Carthage, or to face war. The ambassadors would hear no further argument; "the senior member among them pointed to the folds of his toga, saying that it held both war and peace. He would let fall from it and leave with them whichever they chose. The Suffete of the Carthaginians told him to let fall whichever he liked. When the Roman ambassador said it would be war, many of the Carthaginian senators shouted together, "We accept it!"[87] War had been declared.

THE CAUSES OF THE WAR

Hannibal, of course, was counting on the outbreak of war and already had been in touch with Celtic tribes in Gaul and northern Italy. He did not, however, set out at once for Italy. Instead, he left New Carthage in the spring, perhaps April or May, crossed the Ebro and gained control of much of the territory between there and the Pyrénées. He needed to make that first leg of his route secure, but he was probably also trying to conceal his purpose. If so, he succeeded, for the Romans sent their two armies to sea, to Sicily on the way to Carthage with one and toward Spain with the other, only late in August. By September Hannibal was on the Rhône, and the Roman Army on its way to Spain landed at its mouth, too late to stop him. By October he was in Italy, ready to launch the series of victories in the field that almost brought Rome down and would keep the Romans fighting for more than sixteen years.

From antiquity to our own time historians have argued over the responsibility for the war. The Roman apologetic tradition worked hard to fix the blame on Carthage, on the wrath of the Barcids, and on Hannibal's oath. From that perspective it is a war of revenge and was inevitable from the end of the First Punic War in 241. Polybius's revision of that view produces a mixed judgment. He, too, believes in the wrath of the Barcids and Hannibal's oath, but blames Rome's unjust behavior in seizing Sardinia in 238 for inflaming Carthaginian feeling and setting Hamilcar and his successors on the road to vengeance. He, also, saw the war as inevitable, but only after 238.

Modern scholarship, however, has raised questions about these ancient evaluations. The Romans appear to have violated at least the spirit of the Ebro treaty. The Roman apologists invented a clause in it guaranteeing the independence of Saguntum and sometimes spoke as if the Saguntum were north of the Ebro,[88] thereby blaming Hannibal for breaking the treaty when he attacked Saguntum. All this suggests that the Romans felt guilty about their own behavior. There are also doubts about the wrath of the Barcids and Hannibal's oath, which, if not an invention of the Roman apologists, may have been invented by Hannibal to convince King Antiochus of his reliability against Rome.

The rejection of the wrath and the oath leads to a diminution in the responsibility of Carthage. It is possible to see its behavior as entirely reactive and defensive. After the first war the Carthaginians sought only to recover their security and prosperity, expanding their empire in Spain for that purpose alone. The failure of any of the Barcids to build a fleet may suggest that they had no plans for war against Rome. The mild responses of Hamilcar and Hasdrubal to Roman probes suggest the same thing. In this view Hannibal's attack on Saguntum broke no treaty and was justified by any fair understanding of the Ebro treaty. In any case, it was a response to an intolerable Roman provocation.

A case can also be made on the other side. Polybius, who knew Carthaginian as well as Roman sources and was no simple apologist for

Rome, believed in the oath of Hannibal, and so did King Antiochus. The Carthaginians had every reason to hate Rome after its seizure of Sardinia and increase of the war indemnity. The Barcids could easily have felt a special resentment, for Hamilcar had been forced to surrender an un-defeated army when the Carthaginian homeland still was unconquered. They could have felt betrayed by a home government that had made a peace meant to preserve Carthage's dignity but one that left it helpless to prevent its insulting revision by the Romans. The Carthaginians were a proud people with a high sense of their own honor, accustomed for centu-ries to ruling others. The arrogant behavior of the Romans must have made many Carthaginians, not only the fiery Barcids, contemplate re-venge.

The expansion of the Punic Empire in Spain could have had more than one purpose, but it was an essential step toward any war of revenge against Rome. It provided money, soldiers, and a field of combat where good generals could train and harden an army capable of challenging the Romans. The failure to build a fleet does not necessarily demonstrate peaceful intentions, for Hannibal's strategy required none. He planned a swift dash into Italy, gathering allies in Gaul and Italy as he went, using the element of surprise to his advantage, and shattering Rome's confederation by a series of swift, devastating, and decisive battles. Building a fleet would have been a great mistake, for it would have alarmed the Romans and brought an attack before the Carthaginians were ready to fight, in Spain, not in Italy. The mild responses can be seen as tactical maneuvers to put off conflict until Carthage was ready for war. Hannibal knew clearly that Saguntum was under Roman protection when he attacked, and he must have known that the Romans would not tolerate his action. Before he could launch his march to Italy he needed to destroy the base Rome planned to use against him in Spain. That attack was the first act of the war, yet it took the divided and distracted Romans well over a year to take action, giving Hannibal time to take the war into their land.

Although there is some merit on both sides of the argument, it is hard not to place the major responsibility upon the Romans. They cannot be blamed for winning the first war, and the first treaty offered by Lutatius was generous. When the Roman people refused to ratify it, however, and raised the indemnity they sowed the seeds of a new resentment. When they rode roughshod over the helpless Carthaginians in 238 they guaranteed bad feelings for the future. Whenever they accepted Saguntum into their protection, they further provoked Carthaginian suspicion and ill will. Their intervention in that city's affairs was a violation of the very agreement they had imposed on Hasdrubal. Their warning to Hannibal was a threat to the Carthaginian position in Spain and a provocation. Legally and morally the main responsibility for the war was theirs.

From a practical point of view, their policy between the wars is even more blameworthy. We need not sympathize with the Romans or their behavior to see that they wanted peace, for it was a peace they had established, and it was in their interest. Had they wanted to destroy Carthage or do it some lesser harm, there were several opportunities when it easily could have been done. The responsibility for keeping the peace was plainly theirs, for they alone had the power to do so; instead, their confused and shortsighted policy helped bring about a war that almost destroyed them. By imposing a harsher peace than was first proposed in 241 and then by doing the same again and taking Sardinia in 238 the Romans created inevitable resentment and hostility without effectively disarming their defeated opponent. That is the best recipe for provoking a war of revenge at some time in the future. Perhaps the Romans might have appeased and conciliated the Carthaginians by a calculated policy, although after 238 it may already have been too late. In any case the Romans made no attempt to do so. Nor did they take all the steps needed to prevent a war of revenge. They permitted Carthage to recover its strength by establishing a great empire in Spain. Pressed by dangers elsewhere, they tried to appease Carthage out of weakness by means of the Ebro treaty, probably encouraging those who thought of vengeance. The association with Saguntum was a half measure, a compromise between letting Carthage alone and checking the growth of its power. It involved Roman honor and prestige without making the firm commitment that might have made the Carthaginians hesitate. Still less did it take the practical measures that might have deterred war. Instead, the relationship with Saguntum further angered the Carthaginians and put Roman policy, to a considerable degree, into the hands of the Saguntines.

The warning to Hannibal was another error. It put him on notice that the Romans would stand in his way and give him trouble. No doubt, it increased his anger and made him decide that the time had come to launch his attack. It did nothing, however, to prevent him from taking the town, possession of which would have allowed the Romans to hamper a Hannibalic march on Italy. It resembles the error made by the Athenians in the winter of 433–32, when they ordered Potidaea to take down its seaward walls.[89] In each case, if the demand seemed to be necessary, it should have been accompanied by a military force to make it effective. Instead, each demand provoked a strong reaction that proved very costly to those who made it. If the Romans thought they must warn Hannibal to keep away from Saguntum they should have sent a garrison into the town. That might have deterred the attack; failing that, it might have saved the city; if not, the presence of a Roman garrison under siege surely would have brought a Roman army into Spain before Hannibal could launch his surprise attack on Italy. Without a garrison, Rome's failure to send an army as soon as Saguntum was besieged was another error, which allowed Hannibal to take the initiative. Whether their half measures and inaction were caused by hesitation, internal division, distraction, lack of foresight and imagination, arrogant complacency, or all of these, they were serious and costly failures to protect Roman security and keep the peace.

Whatever the reasons, between the wars Rome pursued an ill-conceived, reactive policy that was confused and contradictory and was responsible for bringing on a war under the most unfavorable and dangerous conditions. The Romans wanted to prevent Carthage from becoming too powerful and threatening the status quo that suited Roman interests. At the same time, they did not want to make a military commitment to Spain. Given Carthaginian attitudes the Romans had themselves provoked, it was not possible both to limit Carthaginian power and take no effective action in Spain. The Romans looked away, then they took actions that were inadequate for their purpose.

After 238 some form of conflict was inevitable. Except for the time of the Gallic invasion of Italy the Romans could have crushed the Punic Empire in Spain whenever they chose to make the effort or, at least, put severe limits to its extent and growth. Even as late as 220 a clear military commitment to Saguntum might have deterred war, and would certainly have prevented another invasion of Italy. Another strategy could have left Saguntum to Carthage, but checked Carthaginian power by a policy of containment. That would have required placing a Roman army north of the Ebro and keeping it there as a limit to Punic expansion and a barrier to Punic ambition. That would have been an unpleasant and costly novelty, but it stood a good chance of preventing war and an even better one of confining it to Spain, if it broke out. Instead the Romans pursued a policy that was both too hard and too soft, unclear, self-deceptive, and, therefore, dangerous. Unwilling to commit themselves clearly and firmly to the price of defending the peace they wanted to maintain, they had to pay the price of a long, bloody, costly, devastating, and almost fatal war.

1. All dates are B.C.

2. References are to the *Histories* of Polybius unless otherwise attributed. Numbers for infantry and cavalry come from 3.35.7; elephants from Appian, *Hannibalic War,* 1.4.

3. 3.56.4 and F. W. Walbank, *A Historical Commentary on Polybius,* vol. 1, Oxford, 1957, p. 366.

4. The numbers come from *Livy* (22.49.15), which here are preferable to the larger ones given by Polybius (3.117). See J. F. Lazenby, *Hannibal's War* (Warminster, 1978), pp. 84–85.

5. 22.57.6. The translation is by B. O. Foster in *Livy,* vol. 5 (Cambridge, Mass., and London, 1953), p. 387.

6. 1.1.

7. E. Badian, *Foreign Clientelae (264–70 B.C.),* Oxford, 1958, p. 1.

8. W. V. Harris, *War and Imperialism in Republican Rome, 327–70 B.C.,* Oxford, 1979, p. 41.

9. 6.19. For discussion see A. J. Toynbee, *Hannibal's Legacy: The Hannibalic War's Effects on Roman Life,* vol. 2, (London, 1965), pp. 79–80; P. A. Brunt, *Italian Manpower 225 B.C.–A.D. 14* (Oxford, 1971), pp. 399–402; Harris, *War and Imperialism,* pp. 11–12, 44–46.

10 Harris, *War and Imperialism,* pp. 10, 256–57.

11. Among the most influential have been Theodore Mommsen *(Römische Geschichte,* 12th ed., Berlin, 1920; English translation by W. P. Dickson, London, 1901); Tenney Frank, *Roman Imperialism* (New York, 1914); and Maurice Holleaux, *Rome, la Grèce et les monarchies hellénistiques au IIIme siècle avant J>C> (273–205)* (Paris, 1921).

12. Cicero, *De Republica* 3.35; Augustine, *The City of God* 22.6, cited by Harris, *War and Imperialism,* p. 164.

13. 1.10, translated by E. S. Shuckburgh, *The Histories of Polybius,* Bloomington, 1962.

14. *Livy,* 10.40.13.

15. Badian, *Foreign Clientelae,* pp. 30–31.

16. *De officiis,* 2.26 and *Philippics,* 8.12, cited by Harris, *War and Imperialism,* pp. 165–66.

17. For a thorough critique of the self-defense theory of Roman expansion see Harris, *War and Imperialism, passim.*

18. Ibid., p. 67.

19. 6.15.8.

20. Plutarch, "Aemilius Paullus." In *Lives of the Noble Grecians and Romans.* Translated by John Dryden, revised by A. H. Clough, New York, n.d., pp. 340–41.

21. 6.54.2.

22. Scullard, *A History of the Roman World 753–146 B.C.,* London and New York, 1980, p. 485 and Cambridge Ancient History.

23. 3.22–24 gives the texts of the treaties and comments on them. Philinus, a Sicilian Greek from Agrigentum, reports a third treaty, dated to 306, whereby the Carthaginians promised to stay out of Italy and Rome out of Sicily. He specifically accuses the Romans of breaking that treaty when they crossed into Sicily to fight the First Punic War in 264. Polybius flatly denies the reality of that treaty (3.26), and scholars have differed on the subject. The reality, chronology, and meaning of the reported treaties remain vexing questions. For useful commentary on the treaties before 264 see Walbank, *Commentary,* vol. 1 (Oxford, 1957), pp. 337–55 and H. H. Scullard, *A History of the Roman World 753–146 B.C.* (London and New York, 1980), pp. 482, 486–88.

24. Plutarch, *Pyrrhus,* 23.6.

25. 1.7.

26. 1.10.4.

27. Harris, *War and Imperialism,* p. 189.

28. 1.10.

29. 1.11.2.

30. Walbank, *Commentary,* vol. 1, p. 61.

31. Harris, *War and Imperialism,* p. 190; Polybius, 1.20.1–2.

32. 1.63.

33. 1.62.

34. 1.83.

35. 1.88.10.

36. 3.10.4.

37. 3.9.6–8.

38. 3.11.7–8.

39. See Walbank, *Commentary,* vol. 1, pp. 312–15.

40. H. H. Scullard ("The Carthaginians in Spain," *Cambridge Ancient History,* 2nd ed., vol. 8, p. 22) believes "there is no good ground to reject" the story of Hannibal's oath. Lazenby (*Hannibal's War,* p. 20) says, "the story [of Hannibal's oath] has inevitably been doubted, . . . [but] it is probably true." He also thinks that Polybius may have been right about the causal importance of Hamilcar's anger: "who is to say, for example, how much the personal feelings of Adolf Hitler contributed towards the outbreak of war in 1939?"

41. Lazenby, *Hannibal's War,* p. 19.

42. 2.36.

43. 3.10.6.

44. The incident is reported in a broken fragment of a passage by the historian Dio Cassius (12, fr. 48), who wrote in the third century A.D. Its correct restoration is not disputed, but some scholars reject its authenticity on the grounds that it is absent from the major sources closer to the events and because they believe Rome had no concern with Spain in this period whatever. (See R. M. Errington, "Rome and Spain Before the Punic War," *Latomus* 29[1970]: 32–34.) Most scholars, however, have accepted it, and a thorough argument in its defense is offered by G. V. Sumner, "Roman Policy in Spain Before the Hannibalic War," *Harvard Studies in Classical Philology* 72(1967): 205–46.

45. Errington, "Rome and Spain," p. 33.

46. F. R. Kramer, "Massilian Diplomacy Before the Second Punic War." *American Journal of Philology* 69(1948): 1–2.

47. Sumner, "Roman Policy," p. 215.

48. Scullard, *Cambridge Ancient History,* p. 25.

49. Diodorus of Sicily, 25.12.

50.   2.13.7. For discussion of some of the issues raised by the Ebro treaty see Walbank, *Commentary,* vol. 1, pp. 168–72, and Scullard, *CAH,* vol. 8, pp. 28–31.

51.   J. Carcopino, "Le traité d'Hasdrubal et la responsibilité de la deuxième guerre punique." *Revue des études anciennes* 35(1953), pp. 258–93; Sumner, "Roman Policy," pp. 228–30.

52.   2.13.

53.   Sumner, "Roman Policy," p. 218.

54.   Errington, "Rome and Spain," p. 38.

55.   Sumner, "Roman Policy," p. 218; Errington, "Rome and Spain," pp. 39–41.

56.   Zonaras, 8.19.

57.   3.13.4.

58.   H. H. Scullard, "Hannibal," *The Oxford Classical Dictionary,* 2nd ed., N. G. L. Hammond and H. H. Scullard, eds., Oxford, 1970, p. 487.

59.   3.14.9.

60.   For useful discussions see Badian, *Foreign Clientelae,* pp. 49–52 and Scullard, *CAH,* pp. 25–27.

61.   The Greek word is *pistis,* "faith," a precise translation of the Latin *fides.*

62.   The Greek is *pleiosin etesin édé proteron,* which is not perfectly clear. *Pleión* is the comparative of *polys,* "many," and its simplest meaning is "more." Polybius clearly did not know the exact date of the agreement with Saguntum and was honest enough to avoid a false precision. Among the words obviously available to him were "many" years, *polla,* or "a few" years, *oliga.* Instead he chose *pleión,* which is more than a few and fewer than many. It seems to me that the Romans could not have been making agreements with Spanish towns in the year of the Celtic invasion, 225, so the greatest stretch of time available from 219, when Hannibal attacked Saguntum, is five years back to 224, if the Romans were ready to act even then. If "the time of Hannibal" means his appointment as commander in 221 that leaves a period of only three years. In either case, that seems to qualify as "a few," *oliga.* To be "a good number," *pleión,* I believe, the period would need to go back before the Ebro treaty in 229. Polybius's care to avoid a false precision seems to make this analysis of his language worth the trouble.

63.   Walbank, *Commentary,* vol. 1, p. 322.

64. 3.14.10.

65. 3.15.1.

66. 3.15.2.

67. 3.15.5–6.

68. Scullard (*Cambridge Ancient History*, p. 34), who believes Rome had no interest in Spain and was concerned only to protect Saguntum, rejects the authenticity of the mention of the Ebro treaty on the grounds that since Saguntum was a hundred miles south of the river "it would have been needlessly offensive of the Roman ambassadors to have brought the Ebro into the discussion, . . ." but there is no objective reason to do so.

69. The following is a precis of the argument presented by Errington, "Rome and Spain," pp. 46–49.

70. B. L. Hallward, *CAH*, 1st ed., vol. 8, p. 28.

71 Harris, *War and Imperialism*, p. 204.

72. 3.15.8.

73. Polybius (3.15.12) says that after Hannibal's response the ambassadors, knowing that war could not be avoided, sailed on to Carthage to make their complaints to the home government. He tells us nothing of what happened there. If this mission really took place, it may have been intended to give Hannibal's political opponents an opportunity to undercut and disavow him, but some scholars question its historicity. See Scullard, *CAH*, p. 35, n. 29.

74. 3.15.6.

75. 3.15.7.

76. 3.15.8.

77. 3.17.5–7.

78. 3.16.

79. Lazenby, *Hannibal's War*, p. 26.

80. The chronological problems are difficult, and there has been much debate about them. For helpful discussions see Walbank, *Commentary*, vol. 1, pp. 331–34 and Scullard, *CAH*, pp. 36–39.

81. Scullard, *CAH*, pp. 36–37. Extant accounts of the debate can be found in Dio Cassius, fr. 55.1-9, and Zonaras, 8.22.

82.   Zonaras, 8.22.

83.   See Chapter I, p. 59.

84.   3.20.8. The names of the ambassadors are provided by *Livy*, 21.18.1.

85.   In 3.29.4–10 Polybius persuasively makes the case for the Roman view of this point.

86.   3.21.1–6.

87.   3.33.1–4.

88.   *Livy*, 21.2.7.

89.   See Chapter I, p. 49.

4

THE
SECOND
WORLD
WAR
1939-1945[1]

HE GERMAN INVASION of Poland on September 1, 1939, launched a conflict even more terrible and destructive than the Great War of 1914–18. This second world war was more truly global, for heavy fighting took place in Africa and Asia as well as Europe, and the people of every continent were involved to some degree. The battle casualties were enormous, even greater than the enormous losses of the first, and the assault on civilians was unprecedented. Massive aerial bombardment of cities became common and concluded with the use of the new and terrifying atomic weapons against Japan in 1945. Hitler in Germany brutalized conquered peoples, and he and Stalin in the Soviet Union made war on designated populations within their own countries. The cost of this world war in life and property was even greater than that of the first, and its outcome put an end to Europe's domination of the globe, placing its constituent nations at the mercy of two vast powers that were largely non-European.

Like the Hannibalic War, the Second World War emerged from flaws in the previous peace and the failure of the victors to alter or vigilantly and vigorously to defend the settlement they imposed. The story of its origins, therefore, begins with the way in which the First World War came to an end.

THE END OF THE FIRST WORLD WAR

In March 1918 the new Soviet government of Russia left the war, freeing the Central Powers, at last, from the burdens of a two-front conflict. But the Germans had suffered terrible casualties, and their agricultural and industrial production had been reduced severely. The defection of Russia from the Allied coalition, moreover, was swiftly being balanced by the entry onto its side of the United States of America. The Americans were

281

pouring hundreds of thousands of fresh, well-supplied troops into France, and the enormous economic resources of the North American continent were flowing in vast amounts to bolster the exhausted forces of France and England. The German response was to launch a last, all or nothing attack on the Western front in the same month; it would either bring a swift victory or end Germany's capacity to continue fighting.

The Allies checked the German assault and took the offensive themselves. Before they could break through on the Western front, however, the collapse of the Central Powers' armies in the Balkans forced the Germans to seek peace. General Erich von Ludendorff, the effective commander of the German Army and virtual dictator of Germany, told his government that "the condition of the army demands an immediate armistice in order to avoid a catastrophe." He urged that they approach President Woodrow Wilson of the United States at once to begin peace negotiations on the basis of his Fourteen Points. He also recommended the establishment of a more representative and liberal government, in part because he thought only such a regime could gain an acceptable peace or rally the nation to resist an unacceptable one, in part, also, to lay the blame for Germany's defeat not on the military leadership and their political allies but on the democratic parties that would form the new government. "Let them conclude the peace that now will have to be concluded," he told the approving Kaiser.[2]

On October 3–4 the new government asked for an armistice. The Allies took some time to answer, for they did not all agree on the advisability of a cease-fire or on its terms if adopted. The day before he called for an armistice, when asked if he would grant such a request were he the commander of the Allied forces, Ludendorff responded, "No, certainly not; I would attack even harder."[3] The same view was taken by some Americans. The commander of the American forces, General John Pershing, wanted to march his troops into Berlin. He wrote to Foch, "We should take full advantage of the situation and continue the offensive until we compel [Germany's] unconditional surrender."[4] British Prime Minister Lloyd George told a secret session of his Cabinet that "industrial France had been devastated and Germany had escaped. At the first moment when we were in a position to put the lash on Germany's back she said, 'I give up.' The question arose whether we ought not to continue lashing her as she had lashed France. Mr. [Austen] Chamberlain said that vengeance was too expensive these days. The Prime Minister said it was not vengeance but justice."[5] Foch and the British commander Douglas Haig, however, were more cautious and less aggressive. They sought armistice terms that would prevent the Germans from resuming the war, whatever the outcome of peace negotiations.

Theirs was the view that triumphed, because Wilson sided with them. His Fourteen Points had never been officially accepted by the Allies, and they all quarreled with one or more of them. With victory in sight they were still less eager to tie their hands by a commitment to liberal general principles, but Wilson forced them to comply by threatening to carry on separate peace negotiations. To the Germans he made it clear that the Allies would not offer generous peace terms to the monarchical regime that had brought on the war. He left little doubt that the Germans must abandon the monarchy or submit to unconditional surrender.

Meanwhile, the German Army was being driven back to its own frontiers, and the government in Berlin was in serious trouble. News that peace was being sought struck the German people like a thunderbolt. They had been led to believe that victory was only months away, a claim made plausible by the surrender of Russia and the early success of the offensive in France only months before. Ludendorff's military dictatorship had concealed the Army's reverses as well as possible and done nothing to prepare the people for the truth. The feeling grew that the people had been deceived and that the military government must go. The new government included the liberal Progressives, the Catholic Centrists, and the first Socialist ministers in the history of the German Empire, and its members were prepared to go forward as a democratic, parliamentary, constitutional monarchy, but events overtook them. Wilson's notes and growing popular opinion demanded the departure of the Kaiser. Increasingly the Germans saw the Kaiser as an obstacle, and on November 9, after a popular revolution, he abdicated. In a railway car in the forest of Compiègne, a representative of the new republican government signed an armistice that made it impossible for the Germans to renew the fighting, and at the eleventh hour of the eleventh day of the eleventh month of 1918, the armistice took effect.

The Germans had asked for peace on the basis of the Fourteen Points that President Wilson had declared as the American war aims, including self-determination for nationalities, open diplomacy, freedom of the seas, disarmament, and establishment of a league of nations to keep the peace, "a peace without victors." The German people, for the most part, were

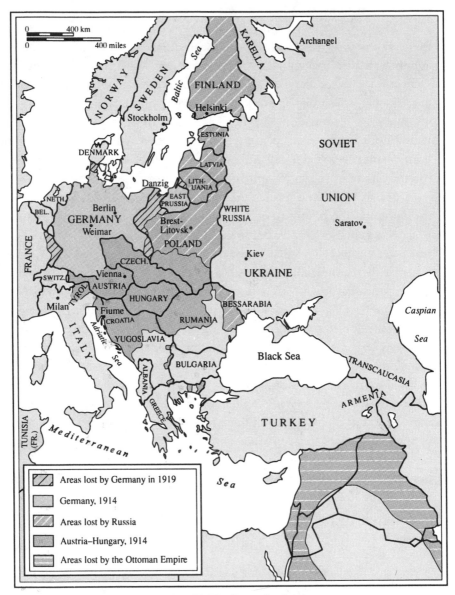

Archangel

KARELIA

NORWAY

SWEDEN

Baltic Sea

FINLAND

Helsinki

SOVIET

Stockholm

ESTONIA

DENMARK

LATVIA

UNION

Danzig

LITH-
UANIA

Saratov

EAST
PRUSSIA

NETH.

Berlin

WHITE
RUSSIA

BEL.

GERMANY

Brest-
Litovsk

Weimar

POLAND

FRANCE

CZECH.

Kiev

Vienna

UKRAINE

SWITZ.

AUSTRIA

TYROL

Milan

HUNGARY

BESSARABIA

Fiume

CROATIA

RUMANIA

Adriatic Sea

YUGOSLAVIA

ITALY

Caspian

Sea

ALBANIA

BULGARIA

Black Sea

TRANSCAUCASIA

GREECE

ARMENIA

TUNISIA
(FR.)

Mediterranean

TURKEY

Sea

	Areas lost by Germany in 1919
	Germany, 1914
	Areas lost by Russia
	Austria–Hungary, 1914
	Areas lost by the Ottoman Empire

First World War Peace Settlement

unaware that their Army had been defeated and was crumbling. No foreign soldier stood on German soil. The Socialist Chancellor of the newly founded Republic greeted returning soldiers with the words "As you return unconquered from the field of battle, I salute you,"[6] and it was generally believed that Germany had voluntarily laid down its arms only when Wilson made a reasonable offer of peace. One German town greeted its returning troops with a banner, reading "Welcome, brave soldiers, your work has been done, God and Wilson will carry it on."[7] The peace the Germans ultimately were required to sign was quite different from their expectations, and many of them came to believe that Germany had not been defeated, but had been tricked by the enemy and betrayed—even stabbed in the back—by pacifists, Jews, republicans, and Socialists at home.

THE PEACE

The representatives of the victorious states gathered at Versailles and other Parisian suburbs in the first half of 1919. Wilson speaking for the United States, David Lloyd George for Britain, Georges Clemenceau for France, and Vittorio Emanuele Orlando for Italy, made up the Big Four. Neither Germany nor the new Bolshevik Russia was present.

Wilson's idealism at once came into conflict with the more practical war aims of the victorious powers. The British and French people had been told that Germany would be made to pay for the war and for the damage done, chiefly to France, as a result of its aggression. France was keenly conscious of its numerical inferiority to Germany and of the low birth rate that would keep it inferior. Naturally, the French wanted a settlement that would weaken Germany permanently and preserve French political and military superiority, and, therefore, its security.

Finally, the peacemakers of 1919 faced a world still in turmoil. The greatest immediate threat appeared to be posed by the spread of bolshevism. The revolution seemed likely to spread as Communist governments were established in Bavaria and Hungary. Berlin also experienced a dangerous Communist uprising led by the "Spartacus group" of Communist extremists. The Allies were worried sufficiently by these developments to allow and support suppression of these Communist movements by right-wing military forces. The fear of the spread of communism played a part in the thinking of the diplomats at Versailles, but it was far from dominant. Fear of Germany remained the chief concern for France; attention to interests that were more traditional and more immediate governed the policies of the other Allies.

Formal sessions began on January 18, 1919, and the last treaty was signed on August 10, 1920. The notion of "a peace without victors" became a mockery when the Germans simply were presented with a treaty and compelled to accept it in a manner that justified their complaint that the treaty had not been negotiated but dictated. The principle of "national self-determination," the leitmotif of the Paris peace conference of 1919, was violated many times, as was unavoidable. The adulation accorded Wilson on his arrival gradually turned into scorn as many of his ideals gave way to the irresistible force of reality, but his rhetoric remained on a lofty plane.

Although a united Germany was less than fifty years old, there was little thought of undoing Bismarck's work and dividing it into its component parts. The French would have liked to detach the Rhineland and set it up as a separate buffer state, but Lloyd George and Wilson would not permit that. Still, they could not ignore France's need for protection against a resurgent Germany. France received Alsace-Lorraine and the right to work the coal mines of the Saar for fifteen years. To compensate for the rejected buffer state, Germany west of the Rhine and fifty kilometers east of it was to be a demilitarized zone permanently, and Allied troops on the west bank could stay there for fifteen years. In addition to this physical barrier to a new German attack, the treaty provided that Britain and the United States would guarantee to aid France if it were attacked by Germany. Such an attack was made more unlikely by the permanent disarmament of Germany. Its army was limited to 100,000 men on long-term service; its fleet was all but eliminated; and it was forbidden to have warplanes, submarines, tanks, heavy artillery, or poison gas. As long as these provisions were observed, France would be safe.

The settlement in the East ratified the collapse of the great defeated empires that had ruled it for centuries. Germany's frontier was moved far to the west, excluding part of Silesia, West Prussia, and Posen.[8] What was left of East Prussia was cut off from the rest of Germany by a corridor carved out to give the revived state of Poland access to the sea. The Austro-Hungarian Empire disappeared entirely. Most of its German-speaking people were gathered into the small republic of Austria, cut off from the Germans of Bohemia and forbidden to unite themselves with Germany.

The Czechs of Bohemia and Moravia joined with the Slovaks and Ruthenians to the east to form Czechoslovakia, and this new state also included several million unhappy Germans. The southern Slavs were united in the kingdom of Serbs, Croats, and Slovenes, or Yugoslavia. Italy gained the Trentino, containing many Germans from the old Habsburg Empire, and Trieste, desired by the Yugoslavs. Rumania was enlarged by receiving Transylvania from Hungary and Bessarabia from Russia. Bulgaria was diminished by the loss of territory to Greece and Yugoslavia. Russia lost vast territories in the West. Finland, Estonia, Latvia, and Lithuania became independent states, and a good part of Poland was carved out of formerly Russian soil.

Wilson was able to accept and rationalize his many unpalatable concessions because of his faith in a new instrument for achieving peace and justice, the League of Nations. Its covenant was an essential part of the peace treaty. The League was not intended as an international government but as a body of sovereign states who agreed to pursue some common practices and to consult in the common interest, especially when war threatened. In that case, the members promised to submit the matter to arbitration or to an international court or to the League Council. Refusal to abide by this agreement would justify League intervention in the form of economic and even military sanctions.

But the League was unlikely to be effective because it had no armed forces at its disposal. Any action required the unanimous consent of its council, envisioned as consisting of Britain, France, Italy, the United States, and Japan, as well as four other states that had temporary seats. The covenant of the League bound its members to "respect and preserve" the territorial integrity of all its members; this was generally seen as a device to ensure the security of the victorious powers. The exclusion from the League Assembly of Germany and the Soviet Union further undermined its claim to evenhandedness. Provisions for general disarmament were doomed to be ineffective. Members of the league remained fully sovereign and continued to pursue their own national interests.

Another provision of the covenant dealt with colonial areas. These were to be placed as mandated territories under the "tutelage" of one of the great powers under League supervision and encouraged to advance toward independence. The old Ottoman Empire disappeared. The new republic of Turkey was limited to little more than Constantinople and Asia Minor. The former Ottoman territories of Palestine and Iraq came under British control and Syria and Lebanon under French control as mandates of the League of Nations. Germany's former colonies in Africa were divided among Britain, France, and South Africa. The German possessions in the Pacific went to Australia, New Zealand, and Japan.

Perhaps the most debated part of the peace settlement dealt with reparations for the damage done by Germany during the war. Before the armistice, the Germans promised to pay compensation "for all damages done to the civilian population of the Allies and their property." The Americans judged that Germany would be able to pay what that would cost. France and Britain, however, worried about repaying their war debts to the United States, and were eager to have Germany pay the full cost of the war, including pensions to survivors and dependents. There was general agreement that Germany could not afford to pay such a sum, whatever it might be, and no total was fixed at the conference. In the meantime Germany was to pay five billion dollars annually until 1921. At that time, a final figure would be set, which Germany would have to pay over thirty years. The French did not regret the outcome. Either Germany would pay and be bled into impotence, or Germany would refuse to pay and invite French intervention.

To justify these huge reparation payments, the Allies inserted the notorious Clause 231 into the treaty:

> The Allied and Associated Governments affirm, and Germany accepts, the responsibility of Germany and her allies for causing all the loss and damage to which the Allied and Associated Governments and their nationals have been subjected as a consequence of the war imposed upon them by aggression of Germany and her allies.

The Germans bitterly resented the charge. They had suffered the loss of vast territories containing millions of Germans and great quantities of badly needed natural resources; they were presented with an apparently unlimited reparations bill. To add insult to injury, they claimed, they were required to admit to a war guilt that they did not feel. Over the years German politicians ranted about the injustice of "unilateral war guilt"[9] but Clause 231 said nothing about "guilt," and its essence was also part of the treaties with Austria and Hungary. There could be no doubt, moreover, that Germany had committed aggression against Belgium, and as we have seen, an excellent case can be made that the Germans were the aggressors against the other Allies. That case, however, was not the one being made at the time or in the next two decades, even in the victorious countries. Finally, to heap insult on insult, they were required to accept the entire treaty as it was written by the victors, without any opportunity for negotiation. The treaty, with its "war guilt clause" and its imposition on a German people not convinced of their military defeat was received as a terrible blow to German honor, and the determination to undo the treaty that was the symbol of that dishonor was a central goal of almost every German statesman thereafter. The Weimar Republic's first chancellor, the Socialist Philipp Scheidemann, spoke of the treaty as the imprisonment of the German people. He accused the Allies of trying to make the Germans "slaves and helots . . . doing forced labour behind barbed wire and prison bars," and asked, "What hand would not wither that binds itself and us in these fetters?"[10] But there was no choice. The Liberals left the Cabinet in protest, but the Social Democrats and the Catholic Center party formed a new government, and their representatives signed the treaty. These were the parties that formed the backbone of the Weimar government that ruled Germany until 1933, and they never overcame the stigma of accepting the Treaty of Versailles. In retrospect Winston Churchill suggested that it might have been wiser to establish a constitutional monarchy with the Kaiser's grandson as monarch: "Instead, a gaping void was opened in the national life of the German people. All the strong elements, military and feudal, which might have rallied to a constitutional monarchy and for its sake respected and sustained the new democratic and parliamentary processes, were for the time being unhinged. The Weimar Republic, with all its liberal trappings and blessings, was regarded as an imposition of the enemy. It could not hold the loyalties or the imagination of the German people."[11] But such a step was entirely at odds with with the liberal ideas that dominated the times, personified most potently by Wilson. The victorious powers' expectations of a lasting peace relied in considerable part on the democratic nature of the new regime, believing that democracies are by nature not warlike. Whatever the merits of that view, the new democratic Republic was unpopular from the first, its patriotism and even its legitimacy deeply in question. Its leaders were compelled to resist enforcement and work for revision or overthrow of the treaty rather than to accept its provisions and move on from there.

Few peace settlements have undergone more severe attacks than the one negotiated in Paris in 1919. The Germans had the greatest complaints. They lost 25,000 square miles of territory containing a population of 6 million people, although many of them were not ethnic Germans. Their loss of valuable raw materials included 65 percent of Germany's iron ore, 45 percent of its coal, 72 percent of its zinc, 57 percent of its lead, 12 to 15 percent of its agricultural products, as well as significant losses of petroleum and potash. In losing its overseas colonies it lost a million square miles of territory with a population of 12 million people and 25 percent of its rubber supply.[12] Germany's new Weimar Republic launched a well-organized, government-financed, and largely covert effort of unprecedented proportions to discredit the Peace of Versailles. Planning began at Versailles during the negotiations, and soon the Foreign Office established a subsection, the *Kriegsschuldreferat,* to direct and finance propaganda to prove that Germany was not responsible for the war and, therefore, that the treaty was unjust.[13] The peace soon came under bitter criticism in the victorious countries as well. Many of the French thought that it failed to provide adequate security for France, because it tied that security to promises of aid from the unreliable Anglo-Saxon countries. In England and the United States, a wave of bitter criticism arose in liberal quarters because the treaty seemed to violate the idealistic and liberal aims and principles that the Western leaders had professed. It was not a peace without victors. It did not put an end to imperialism but attempted to promote the national interests of the winning nations. It violated the principles of national self-determination by leaving significant pockets of minorities outside the borders of their national homelands. Perhaps the most flagrant example was the veto imposed by the victors when the National Assembly of the rump state of Austria voted to join the German Republic.

The most influential critic was John Maynard Keynes, a brilliant British economist who took part in the peace conference. When he saw the direction it was taking, he resigned in disgust and wrote a book called *The Economic Consequences of the Peace,*[14] a scathing attack, especially on reparations and the other economic aspects of the peace. Keynes called the Treaty of Versailles immoral and unworkable, a Carthaginian peace, referring to the utter destruction of Carthage by Rome after the Third Punic War. He argued that such a peace would bring economic ruin and war to Europe unless it were repudiated. Keynes had a great effect on the British, who were already suspicious of France and glad of an excuse to withdraw from Continental affairs.[15] "Meaculpism was born. Doubt flourished; German guilt faded; British guilt spread."[16]

Other criticisms came from those in Britain who had opposed entry into the war on the grounds that there was no need for a quarrel between Britain and Germany, that Germany's goals and policies were acceptable, that Germany was no more responsible for the war than others, perhaps less. Their views became those of the revisionist historians in Britain and America between the wars who so powerfully shaped educated opinion. From their point of view, since Germany bore no special responsibility for the war, the "war guilt" clause was unjustified and with it the justice of the punitive treaty. "Appeasement was born in the minds of those who said that the war need never have come, that it was accidental. . . . It was a determination to prevent by all means a second accidental, 'guiltless' war."[17] The decent and respectable position came to be one that aimed at revision of the treaty in favor of Germany. H. A. L. Fisher, Minister of Education, even as the negotiations were concluded, could defend the treaty only on the grounds that once it was signed "an appeasement, and by degrees readjustments and modifications can be introduced which will give Europe a prospect of stability." Before the failure of Neville Chamberlain's policies in the 1930s "appeasement" carried no stigma in Britain. On the contrary, it was thought to be a decent, even a noble goal, affirmed by most British statesmen. Longings for withdrawal and isolation could be joined with high moral indignation and the call for justice. "By becoming the leading advocate of appeasement, Britain could redress the balance of injustice. The British sense of fair play could operate in Germany's behalf. The British desire for a quiet life, undisturbed by European alarms and cross-channel excursions, could be satisfied. Appeasement was the balm for a guilty conscience."[18]

No less important was Keynes's influence in the United States. It fed the traditional tendency toward isolationism and gave powerful weapons to Wilson's enemies. Wilson's own political mistakes helped prevent U.S. ratification of the treaty. Consequently, the United States was out of the League of Nations and not bound to defend France. Britain, therefore, also was free from its obligation to France. France was left to protect itself without adequate means to do so for long.

Many of the attacks on the Treaty of Versailles are unjustified. If it was a Carthaginian peace then it was like the peace ending the Second, not the Third, Punic War. Germany was neither dismembered nor ruined. Reparations could be and were scaled down and, until the great world depression of the 1930s, the Germans recovered a high level of prosperity. As early as 1921 the establishment of the London schedule of payments which determined the real amount the Germans were required to pay amounted to about 6 percent of their annual national income, an amount "roughly comparable to the burden of some Western economies as a result of the explosion in oil prices during the 1970s,"[19] one that could have been paid without undue sacrifice. The Dawes Plan of 1924 reduced that still further to 3.3 percent of national income and the Young Plan in 1929 to 2.6 percent. Germany never paid even these amounts in full, and the payments were cancelled entirely in 1932. "For the whole period 1919–1931, Germany transferred to the Allies in cash and kind together an average of only 2.0 percent of national income." During this same period Germany enjoyed

> a windfall profit resulting from the devaluation of foreign-owned mark-denominated assets during the 1919–1923 inflation. Then, after 1931, it defaulted on most private foreign investments. These items combined a unilateral transfer equal to a startling 5.3 percent of German national income for 1919–31. On balance, the United States and to a lesser extent the European Allies subsidized Germany during the Weimar era, and not the other way around.[20]

Complaints against the peace should also be measured against the treaty the Germans had imposed on France in 1871, the plans they had made for a European settlement in case of victory and the peace that the victorious Germans had imposed on Russia at Brest-Litovsk. In 1871 Germany had intended to cripple the French economy for a long time and to keep the French in line by means of the occupying army. We have seen the extraordinary character of Germany's plans (see pp. 207–8) and the actual terms imposed on Russia were in the same spirit. One way or another, the Germans gained control of Poland, the Baltic states, and Finland. Before long, the Germans ignored the treaty, occupying the Crimea, where Ludendorff wanted to establish a permanent German colony, and pushing into Transcaucasia. In September 1918, even while their armies were collapsing in the West, the Germans reached the Caspian Sea and occupied Baku.[21] Russia was reduced to a size smaller than it had been at the accession of Peter the Great in the seventeenth century. The intention of the first peace had been to cripple the defeated power, and both Germany's war plans and its treatment of Russia were far more severe than anything enacted at Versailles. There the attempt at achieving self-determination for nationalities was less than perfect, but it was the best solution Europe had ever accomplished in that direction. Viewed from a relevant comparative perspective, the peace imposed on Germany at Versailles was not unduly harsh.

The peace, nevertheless, was unsatisfactory in important ways. At the core of the difficulty was the inherent contradiction between the idealistic, supernational principles and goals enunciated by Wilson and the need of a secure and sustainable balance of the true distribution of power in Europe. Leaving aside such generalities as the desirability of "open covenants openly arrived at" that, in a democratic world dominated by mass media works to make moderate solutions to difficult problems impossible, "freedom of the seas," free trade, disarmament, and a League of Nations to guarantee "the political independence and territorial integrity" of all states, the single principle behind the Fourteen Points effectively acted upon in Paris was that of national self-determination based on ethnic homogeneity.

Philosophically, no reason was given for making it the dominant consideration and, practically, the goal could not possibly be achieved. National minorities necessarily were left encapsulated within foreign states, with greater or lesser degrees of unhappiness. New, conglomerate states of similar nationalities, such as Yugoslavia and Czechoslovakia were created. Their recent disintegration suggests that the experiments were not successful. Focus on ethnic differences as a fundamental basis for social and political arrangements seems to intensify ethnic separatism and mutual hostility. Since ethnic distribution rarely accords perfectly with geographic and economic realities, the chances of achieving ethnically pure states that are viable are slim. A peace strongly guided by the effort to meet the impossible demands of ethnic nationalism was doomed to failure and to charges of hypocrisy. At the same time, the dominance of the principle severely damaged the prospects of creating a peace that confronted reality and had a good chance of success.

The elimination of the Austro-Hungarian Empire, however inevitable that might seem in retrospect, created a number of serious problems. Economically it was disastrous, for it separated raw materials from manufacturing areas and producers from their markets by new boundaries and tariff walls. In hard times, this separation caused friction and hostility that aggravated other quarrels also created by the peace treaties. Poland contained unhappy German minorities. Czechoslovakia held many more Germans no less unhappy, part of a collection of nationalities that did not find it easy to live together as a nation. Even if they could coalesce for mutual defense the newly created states would not be a match for a Germany or a Russia restored to its previous power, but on the contrary, they were full of mutual suspicions and competing desires, more "Balkanized" than ever. Disputes over territories in Eastern Europe promoted further tension. The settlement in Eastern Europe was inherently unstable.

The most critical problem facing postwar Europe was, once again, the future of Germany. Even with the losses imposed by the Treaty of Versailles it remained Europe's largest and most populous nation west of Russia, with a well-educated, disciplined, highly skilled people and a higher birth rate than victorious France. Relatively, it was even more powerful than before the war, since Russia, in the form of the Soviet Union, devastated by military defeat and social revolution, had been driven out of Europe, a pariah among nations, and both the Habsburg and Ottoman Empires were gone. "The immediate problem," one historian has written, "was German weakness":

> [B]ut given a few years of "normal" life, it would again become the problem of German strength. More than this, the old balance of power, which formerly did something to restrain Germany, had broken down. Russia had withdrawn; Austria–Hungary had vanished. Only France and Italy remained, both inferior in man-power and still more in economic resources, both exhausted by the war. If events followed their course in the old "free" way, nothing could prevent the Germans from overshadowing Europe, even if they did not plan to do so.[22]

These facts threatened the future security of the victorious powers and the settlement they were making. Something needed to be done to contain the power that Germany was otherwise certain to recover. One obvious possibility would have been to dismantle Germany and rearrange it in such a way as might prevent its resurgence. Such division of territory in disregard of ethnic considerations was commonplace in Europe from the seventeenth to the early nineteenth century. Even after the cult of nationalism had been born in the French Revolution similar segmentations had taken place. Germany had separated the Danes of northern Schleswig from Denmark in 1864 and then incorporated the people of Alsace-Lorraine, Frenchmen at least since the seventeenth century, without a qualm. Germany had been only a geographical expression until less than a half-century before. Why should it not be dismembered?[23] The French plan for establishing a separate Rhenish republic as a buffer state made considerable sense from the traditional point of view of establishing a durable balance of power and was no more outrageous than the annexation of Alsace-Lorraine had been in 1871. But in the climate of high Wilsonian moralism based on the sanctity of ethnic nationalism that was impossible. The eventual superiority of sixty-five million Germans with greater natural resources over thirty-nine million Frenchmen with a lower birthrate was not checked by the Versailles Treaty.

The peace was inadequate, also, because it rested on a victory whose reality and legitimacy Germany did not admit. Many Germans believed that they had been cheated rather than defeated, and others who knew better chose to believe the same. The Allied decision not to carry the war into Germany made it easier to hold such a view. So did the determination to hold the defeated powers uniquely responsible for the war. Very little of the evidence on which the interpretation offered here rests was available at the time; writers and historians in the *victorious* states immediately went to work to show that the "war guilt" clause was unjustified, some of them awarding chief blame to the Allies. It would take more than fifty years for most of the historical profession to present a different view. The interpretation then dominant made reparations, whose legitimacy depended on the truth of Clause 231, seem completely unfair. The critiques of the German view of reparations cited above are objectively correct, but it is important to note that the realities were unknown or poorly understood at the time. The publicly announced sums were vast and unreasonable; those that were really expected were much smaller, but ignored. The capital inflow that did so much for the German economy was private in nature, whereas reparations were paid out of public funds, i.e., taxes paid by German citizens. The policies of the victorious powers actually made reparations *seem* much worse than they were, increasing the Germans's sense of being mistreated, cheated, and dishonored, and strengthening the power of those political groups who opposed accommodation and the Weimar Republic.

At the same time, the Germans could reject a peace as hypocritical and unjust that proclaimed the principle of ethnic self-determination and then forbade the Germans of Austria to join with the German Republic. Critics of the peace, Germans as well as others, were free to judge the peace's justice not by comparison with others in the relevant history of the world but with some unattainable ideal, a test it could not help but fail. In the United States the traditional desire to remain aloof from continued involvement outside the Western Hemisphere took greater strength from the disappointment with the peace. Britain's traditional preference for maintaining a free hand and avoiding commitments on the Continent was strengthened by the weakness of its economy and still more by the pain of the terrible losses it had suffered in the war. The generation that had experienced the slaughter in the trenches on the Western front was trauma- tized powerfully by it and shrank instinctively from the idea of another such Continental war. Supporting French efforts to enforce the peace meant some form of military engagement on the Continent. Resisting it in the name of fairness, generosity, and justice required no such effort and yet preserved a good conscience.

Finally, the great weakness of the peace was its failure to accept reality. Germany and Russia must ultimately and inevitably play an impor- tant part in European affairs, yet they were excluded from the settlement and from the League of Nations. The League itself represented a flight from reality. A product of the idealistic Kantian tradition of internationalism, it was introduced into a world of nationalistic states, unwilling to abandon any sovereignty. It was undermined badly by the absence of the world's most powerful nation, the United States. At the same time, it provided no certain mechanism for peacefully adjudicating quarrels between states nor for bringing force to bear to maintain peace or prevent aggression. It would work only if the victorious powers were ready to make the commitment and sacrifices necessary to carry out its purposes. In the event, the League made it easier for the Western powers to avoid their responsibilities, for they could always stand aside and invoke it as the proper venue for taking action.

Given the many discontented parties, the peace was not self-enforc- ing. The Germans could defeat some of its critical provisions merely by inaction and subterfuge. If they surreptitiously violated the disarmament provisions of the peace someone must act to enforce them. If they defaulted on reparations payments someone must compel them to deliver, yet no satisfactory machinery for enforcing these clauses was established. It was left to France, with no guarantee of support from Britain and no hope of help from the United States, to defend the new arrangements. Indeed, as we shall see, both Britain and the United States soon came to resist France's efforts at enforcement. Poland, Rumania, Czechoslovakia, and Yugoslavia were created in response to the principle of ethnic nationalism, but also as a threat in the rear to deter German revival as a menace to the peace. These states, however, would have to rely on France in case of danger. France alone was simply not strong enough for the task if Germany were to rearm.

The tragedy of the Treaty of Versailles was that it was neither conciliatory enough to remove the desire for change, even at the cost of war, nor harsh enough to make another war impossible. More than most peaces it required an active commitment on the part of the victors to preserve it. The only hope for a lasting peace required the enforcement of the disarmament of Germany while such clauses of the peace treaty as needed revision and could be changed safely were revised and until the Germans were prepared to accept the new situation. Such a policy required continued attention to the problem, unity among the victors, and farsighted leadership, but none of these was present in adequate supply during the next two decades.

The victors rejoiced, but they also had much to mourn. The casualties on all sides came to about ten million dead and twice as many wounded. The economic and financial resources of the European states were strained badly. The victorious Allies, formerly creditors to the world, became debtors to the new American colossus, itself barely touched by the calamities of war. The old international order, moreover, was dead. Russia was ruled by a Bolshevik dictatorship that preached world revolution and the overthrow of capitalism everywhere. Germany was in turmoil. Austria-Hungary had disintegrated into a swarm of small national states competing for the remains of the ancient empire. These changes stirred the colonial territories ruled by the European powers; overseas empires would never again be as secure as they had seemed before the war. Europe was no longer the center of the world, free to interfere when it wished or to ignore the outer regions if it chose. Its easy confidence in material and moral progress had been shattered by the brutal reality of four years of horrible war. The memory of that war lived on to shake the nerve of the victorious Western powers as they confronted the new conditions of the postwar world.

TESTING THE PEACE, 1919–1933

In a sense, the quality of the Versailles settlement never was tested, for its first article, dealing with its most important issue, was never ratified and so never came into effect. Article 1 of the Versailles Treaty promised immediate assistance to France "in the event of an unprovoked movement of aggression against her being made by Germany." The British version of the treaty, however, made Britain's promise contingent upon "a similar obligation . . . entered into by the United States of America. . . ."[24] When the United States Senate rejected the treaty on November 19, 1919, Britain was absolved of responsibility. France was now protected neither by physical guarantees of her security nor even by the promise of assistance against aggression. By the end of 1919, United States and British defection left the French to fend for themselves. Their policy between the wars would be guided and dominated by fear.

Their attempts to achieve security brought them no sympathy but suspicion, blame, and often opposition from their allies. In the Anglo-Saxon countries the French were depicted increasingly as the villains and the Germans as their victims, a view enshrined in orthodox historiography for half a century. "In terms of national policies, the struggle is usually represented as a conflict between America, moderate and conciliatory, and France, anxious for a crushing 'Carthaginian' peace."[25] Toward the end of the war and at the peace conference, in fact, neither the Americans nor the British were especially conciliatory to Germany, but Lloyd George and Wilson soon changed their tack. From 1919 at least until the onset of the great depression in 1929 Britain and the United States generally worked to prevent France from rigorously enforcing the Versailles Treaty and tried to revise its provisions in an effort to conciliate Germany. Why did they set out to undermine the peace treaty even before it came into force? Wilson and the Americans entertained conflicting and contradictory ideas and desires. They took a characteristically moralistic approach to the war and the peace that should conclude it. The Germans had behaved badly and should be punished for it. France had been the victim of aggression. Understandably, it feared for its security and deserved assistance in its quest for safety, but that was not to be achieved through balance of power politics. A disciple of current British liberal thought, Wilson regarded the balance of power as "part of the old order, inherently unstable, and the source of competitive armaments and international rivalries." He did not want the United States to play any part in such a system nor would he countenance the dismemberment of Germany or the weakening of her economy. In the long run, he believed, France would be safest if Germany were conciliated, not alienated. "The president wanted Germany to pay for her mistakes, but he also wanted to reintegrate Germany into a postwar liberal capitalist order that would be both prosperous and stable. Wilson assumed that, once a participant in such an order, Germany would be peaceful and cooperative, French security would no longer be jeopardized, and American economic interests would be enhanced."[26] It did not occur to him that questions of prosperity and peace might be subordinated to those of national pride and resentment; that the Germans might be driven to restore their honor and the power needed to recover it, by whatever means necessary; nor that an integral Germany restored to its full potential power would dominate the Continent and threaten the safety of its neighbors, east and west.

The apparently contradictory goals of achieving German restoration and French security, Wilson believed, would be attained through the League of Nations, but his notion of U.S. involvement was no less inherently contradictory. Article 10 of the covenant obliged League members to protect each other against aggression, which would appear to commit the United States to the military defense of France if attacked by Germany. Wilson, however, wanted to retain U.S. freedom of action, so he resisted the assignment of practical sanctions to the article, opposed the creation of an international army and planning staff, and repeatedly referred to Article 10 as a moral obligation only, while insisting on its vital importance. The United States retained a veto in the decisive League Council and opposed compulsory arbitration. "These actions reflected Wilson's efforts to balance his desire for French security with his reluctance to compromise independent American decision making in military matters."[27] Small wonder that the French were reluctant to accept U.S. promises as the basis for their safety. When the United States Senate rejected the treaty in November 1919 their doubts were confirmed.

America was protected by its vast distance from Europe and its inherent strength, and its honor was not engaged. To most Americans, free to pursue their nation's interests as they perceived them, those interests seemed to dictate a return to their traditional isolation from foreign entanglements in the political, diplomatic, and military concerns of the old world, to what President Warren G. Harding called "normalcy." This meant support of the rapid return of Germany to full prosperity as a rich market for American industry and commerce, an opportunity for profitable investment, and in a rapidly diminishing degree, as a bulwark against bolshevism. For that to happen all that Americans need do was, in cooperation with Britain, to restrain French efforts at strict enforcement of the peace and to lend money to the Germans to help them rebuild their economy. Meanwhile, they could express moral disapproval at French vindictiveness in trying to squeeze all they could out of Germany in reparation payments, all the while insisting on full repayment by their allies, including France, of their debts to the United States incurred during the war, on the grounds, as President Calvin Coolidge put it, that "they hired the money, didn't they?" To recognize France's true predicament, on the other hand, would have required responsibility, commitment, expense, and action. It was much easier and more pleasant to believe the sensational tracts by revisionist publicists and more sober narratives by respectable revisionist historians showing that Russia, and her allies, not Germany, were responsible for the war or, at least, no less responsible than anyone else; that the "war guilt" clause of the Versailles Treaty, therefore, and the sanctions imposed on Germany based on it, were unjust; that reconciliation with Germany through a favorable revision of the treaty would be both expedient and just; that nothing difficult need be done.

In fact, that reading of American interest was badly out of date. America's intervention in the war responded to the new and as yet badly understood reality that it was involved willy-nilly in a world economy and political system that it was not free to ignore. It had economic ties with the democracies of Western Europe and poorly understood ties of sentiment with them that would prove to be powerful bonds. The new situation imposed new responsibilities for the preservation of peace. The Americans chose to ignore them for the moment, but they proved to be inescapable.

The British reaction was more complicated. One historian has summarized and explained Great Britain's policy as follows: "It never abandoned France entirely, encouraging false hopes here, and it never supported Germany completely, causing bitterness there. But in general, it supported concessions to Germany at the expense of France. This policy, largely instinctive, . . . derived from isolationism and imperial crises, reaction against the cost in blood and money of the First World War, tradition and economic concerns, reluctance to do the job of treaty enforcement, and from fear of France."[28] An economic slump and high unemployment in the early 1920s persuaded the British that only the restoration of prewar levels of trade with Germany would restore strength to its industries and prosperity for England. They believed that significant reparations payments would hamper German recovery and unduly stimulate German exports in competition with British goods.[29] Lloyd George, who had talked of hanging the Kaiser and promised the British electorate that he would squeeze the Germans "until the pips squeaked," now "proposed a new mystique: the economic reconstruction of Europe through German recovery."[30] This meant British opposition to French insistence on full payment of reparations in cash and in kind and on strict enforcement of the treaty in general. French efforts to achieve such enforcement were seen as brutal and selfish bullying, "kicking a man when he is down," and other forms of bad sportsmanship. And they lent credence to the unlikely notion that Britain had more to fear from France than from Germany.

It might seem strange that Britain should fear its recent ally, itself dominated by fear of a resurgent Germany. To be sure, British and French interests clashed at several places around the world, especially the Near East, but these were not serious problems. It was the great *immediate* military predominance of the French Army, the only powerful one left in Europe, that impressed the British, who had raced to disarm immediately. Their sudden, self-imposed military weakness relative to France, and Germany's enforced disarmament, helped lead them to oppose the French and support the Germans in a traditional, if only semiconscious, attempt to establish a balance of power. In a remarkable failure of judgment the British focused their attention on the short-range situation, ignoring long-range realities. "The momentary superiority of the French army and air force, along with France's submarine building program, alarmed Britain's leaders who seriously thought the next war might be against France."[31]

For England to take sides for a defeated Germany against a suddenly more powerful France, moreover, accorded with long-standing habit. Like Sir Edward Grey, Lloyd George and the British leaders who followed him sought to pursue a policy that allowed Britain to maintain a "free hand," to hold the decisive balance between contending powers on the Continent without being committed to any of them. More than ever they wanted to be free of a Continental commitment such as might compel them to fight a land war in Europe. But their error was greater than his. Grey, at least, helped shape and hold together the Triple Entente that might deter an aggressor or defeat him if deterrence failed. British leaders between the wars, on the contrary, steadfastly fought off European commitments until the war was almost upon them. Grey and his colleagues competed in and won the naval race upon which Britain's salvation depended. They carried on military conversations with the French and made at least the minimal preparations that permitted a British expeditionary force to land in time to save France. British leaders between the wars disarmed swiftly and thoroughly and refused to rearm in the face of obvious danger until it was too late to save France and almost too late to save Britain. Europe from 1919 to 1939, moreover, was far less well able to resist the power of a resurgent and dissatisfied Germany than it had been in 1914, and Britain was far weaker, far less able alone to redress the imbalance of power. When the Americans withdrew from their responsibilities it was left for Britain to take on its considerable share of the burden of keeping the peace it so badly needed, but for too long the British preferred to take refuge in illusions.

The burden, therefore, fell on France alone, hampered by the general opposition of their former allies. In 1919 the French were not well equipped for the task in most respects. To maintain their security in the long range they needed to rebuild their industrial capacity and their devastated lands, both shattered by the German invasion; they needed money to stabilize their financial situation and repay their war debt, to acquire the raw materials, sources of energy, and markets without which they could not achieve the economic growth needed to support their military forces and maintain a stable society. Deprived of support from their allies, they were left no choice but to take advantage of their temporary military superiority, to pursue a policy of strict enforcement of the Versailles Treaty to strengthen France and weaken Germany. Then they would need to make alliances with the antirevisionist states of central Europe in a policy meant to contain German power and ambition. For these purposes France needed German disarmament, control of the resources from the Saar and the Ruhr, and the necessary reparations payments. But the Germans resisted all these things with determination. By a variety of devices, including secret collaboration with the Soviet Union, they defied the disarmament clauses.[32] They pressed hard for France's early withdrawal from the Saar and the return of the Ruhr, occupied by the French in 1921, and the Rhineland to full German sovereignty. They failed to make full reparations payments, whether in money or in kind, unless compelled by force, even as they insisted that the amount they owed be reduced. They and their apologists in the West often put forth complicated arguments of economic theory to justify their failure to pay, but whatever the truth about the Germans' ability to pay, it was irrelevant; the central fact was that they chose not to.

Reparations and the Ruhr Crisis of 1923

The Versailles Treaty, chiefly at British insistence, had left the amount Germany must pay in reparations unfixed.[33] On May 5, 1921, the sum finally was set in the London Schedule of Payments. Ostensibly, the figure was placed at 132 billion gold marks, the amount publicly announced and subsequently vehemently denounced. It was a sum far greater than the Germans could pay, as those setting it fully understood. It was set and publicized to deceive public opinion in the countries scheduled to receive payment. The German debt was to be paid for by three series of bonds, A, B, and C, with most of it contained in C. "The C bonds were deliberately designed to be chimerical." Germany's real liability was contained in the A and B bonds and came to a total of 50 billion gold marks, $12.5 billion, "an amount smaller than what Germany had recently offered to pay."[34]

Since the Allies held their Western customhouses, the Germans made their first cash payment in full in the summer of 1921. When the Allied occupation forces withdrew, the Germans failed to make full payments in cash or kind until after the Dawes Plan scaled back its obligations in 1924. By the summer of 1922 it was clear that the Germans were not going to pay. Whenever a reparations payment was due a burst of inflation depreciated the mark. The Germans claimed that reparations were causing the destruction of their currency; their complaints were believed by contemporaries in the West, and by historians since, but German inflation went back to the war, when the government chose to finance their campaigns by loans rather than by taxation. By the end of the war the mark was worth only about half of its 1914 value. Reparations payments, moreover, did not coincide with inflation. In 1921 and 1922 Germany paid very little, yet inflation grew at a great pace. There was practically no inflation in the late 1920s, when payments were supposed to be highest. In the early twenties "British and French experts agreed that Germany was deliberately ruining the mark, partly to avoid budgetary and currency reform, but primarily to escape reparations," and German archives have since revealed that these suspicions were justified.[35]

The British and French did not agree, however, on what to do. The inflation gave a great advantage to German businesses over their competitors in France. They borrowed heavily in Germany, where inflation swiftly reduced their debts, undersold their competition abroad, and used their profits to modernize their plants. The French could match none of these opportunities: "By 1922 the unthinkable was occurring: Germany rebounding with Anglo-American tolerance, while France had achieved neither financial stabilization, nor economic recovery, nor security."[36] During the peace conference Clemenceau had made the argument for a lengthy occupation of German territory as a surety for compliance: "[Germany] will sign the treaty with the intention of not complying with it, she will raise difficulties on one point or another, and if we have no means of imposing our will, everything will slip away bit by bit."[37] To avoid that, the French wanted the Allies to seize a tangible, revenue-yielding German resource as a guarantee of payment, but the British thought otherwise. Compulsion, they claimed would hurt German recovery. Conceding that the Germans had deliberately destroyed their own currency to avoid reparations, they nevertheless recommended a four-year moratorium on all payments to allow Germany time to get its finances in order. The French, naturally, objected to rewarding the Germans for their recalcitrance, believing with justification that a moratorium of that length would mean the end of reparations. There was no agreement.

In December 1922 the Reparation Committee declared Germany in default on its timber deliveries. Although there was no disagreement on the fact or that the Germans were guilty of bad faith, the British dissented, reasoning "that nothing should be asked of Germany because Germany would refuse and then something would have to be done."[38] They knew that the only plausible response was the occupation of the Ruhr, an idea they abhorred. In January 1923 the Germans defaulted on their monthly obligation to deliver a quota of coal for the thirty-fourth time in thirty-six months, and by the same three-to-one vote the commission declared the Germans formally in default, and the Belgians and French chose to occupy the Ruhr, the great industrial area critically important to the German economy. The British denounced the action as illegal and immoral but did not interfere with it.

The French, under Prime Minister Raymond Poincaré, former President of the Republic, were driven to press for this action by the refusal of the British and Americans to help them deal with their serious problems. Poincaré would have liked to avoid the occupation by assuring the delivery of German reparations through British support and American loans. But German industrialists in the Ruhr, the British, and the Americans all insisted that the French first abandon the guarantees they had received in the treaty and counted upon as their last hope of security. Occupation of the Ruhr, therefore, "was to be the guarantee necessary to oblige the Anglo-Saxons to underwrite German payments without obliging France to scrap the Versailles controls."[39]

The German government ordered a campaign of passive resistance. The French reacted by crushing strikes and sending in their own workers, miners, and officials, protected by soldiers. The Germans were deprived of the vast majority of the coal that ran their industry, causing unemployment all over Germany, as well as in the Ruhr. The government was forced to support the great numbers placed in distress from an already overstrained budget. Since the Reichstag refused to impose new taxes, the only alternative was the printing press. The result was a staggering inflation: the mark, which was 4.2 to the dollar in 1914 and 8.9 after the wartime inflation in January 1919, had risen to 17,972 in the month of the occupation of the Ruhr. In July 1923 it was 353,412, in October over 25 *billion,* and in November 1923 it had reached over 4 *trillion* to the dollar.[40]

The effects on most of the German people were serious. Workers suffered from the unemployment, the drop in real wages—which even their strong unions were unable to prevent—and the loss of their savings. Hardest hit were small businessmen, self-employed artisans, and the middling class *(Mittelstand),* in general. They saw their life's savings destroyed and many were forced to accept public relief. They lost not only their money but also their self-respect, their confidence in the government, many their belief in the system itself. It is not surprising that such people were represented disproportionately in the burgeoning Nazi movement of the late twenties and early thirties.

The British revisionists claimed that the occupation profited no one and blamed the political and economic unrest and the people's suffering entirely on France and its vindictive policy. They were wrong in both respects. The occupying powers netted almost nine hundred million gold marks, most of which went to the United States in debt payments. The inflation permitted the German government to pay off its internal debt in a currency debased to the point of worthlessness. Individual German industrialists and speculators made huge profits. Even the British economy benefited from the lapse in German competition. "The astronomic inflation was a result of German policy, not of the occupation itself,"[41] as the rapid restoration of the German currency quickly demonstrated.

As the occupation became longer, nastier and more costly, the French conceived greater goals: control of mines in the Ruhr, permanent Allied control of railroads in the Rhineland, even the creation of an independent Rhenish state, the buffer state they had always sought as a guarantee of their security.[42] Poincaré knew this was France's last chance to use the single advantage it had to prevent the collapse of the Versailles settlement, the resurgence of German preponderance, and the menace to French security it represented.

At last, the Germans gave way. In August 1923 Gustav Stresemann became German Chancellor, committed to compliance with the treaty. Poincaré tried to get support for a plan that would give France control of important German assets in the Ruhr and the Rhineland, depriving the Germans of sovereignty in the area. International agreements would support the new arrangement and provide stability for Europe based on two principles: "economic integration of France with a weakened Germany, and Anglo-American financial support."[43] This, of course, was unacceptable to the British and Americans, who increasingly turned away from France and toward support of Germany. Isolated, threatened by collapse of the franc, pressed by political opponents, Poincaré was forced to yield. Settlement of the problems of reparations, financial stability, the future of the Ruhr and the Rhineland—the de facto revision of the Versailles Treaty, that is—would be determined not by the French in possession of the Ruhr but by international groups in which the French would stand alone.

Such a group produced the Dawes Plan in April 1924. It reorganized Germany's finances, supported by a large international loan and effectively reduced its reparations debt and payment schedule. Payments, in any case, were made easier by considerable American investment in Germany. The Germans enjoyed the opportunity to make almost no payments in the first two years and rightly expected to achieve further reductions when heavier payments became due. Arrangements for the implementation of the new reparations plan and the withdrawal of France from the Ruhr were left to the London Conference in the summer of 1924. By that time Poincaré had been forced out of office and replaced by the pliable and inexperienced Édouard Herriot. France was required to end economic occupation of the Ruhr almost immediately and to withdraw its troops within a year. The Reparations Commission was revised in such a way as to make future punishment of default all but impossible. It was a major defeat for the French, who were deprived of all means to enforce the provisions of the treaty meant to afford them security. The treaty had been revised against their wishes and interests and the process of revision was far from over. The British welcomed the outcome of the Ruhr crisis, but it revealed that Britain and France no longer stood together as a check against German ambitions. The French were too weak to withstand the opposition of their former allies again. "The result was a decisive French moral defeat; never again was France to hold the upper hand which she had enjoyed from 1918 to 1923. . . . Henceforth that military strength with which France could alone offset the potentially overwhelming superiority of German national power, relapsed into a posture of defensiveness and passivity."[44] Britain and the United States, to a much lesser extent, would pay later for undermining French power and confidence in this period.

The Locarno Agreements

After their Ruhr debacle the French sought other ways to defend their security. The first possibility they explored was collective security through the League of Nations. Together with Britain's Socialist Prime Minister, Ramsay MacDonald, Herriot promoted the Geneva Protocol for the Pacific Settlement of Disputes. It provided that all members of the League agree to submit unsolved disputes to binding arbitration rather than resort to war and to give military aid to the victims of aggression.[45] The French government hoped this would provide the protection they needed, but such hopes were excessive. MacDonald was chiefly interested in conciliating Germany, pressing forward with disarmament, especially of France, and avoiding the use of force. In the conditions of 1924 he did not imagine that fighting would be needed. Less even than most British statesmen did he believe that Germany was a menace, even potentially. The promises of military aid to defend France against a German attack looked "black . . . and big on paper," said MacDonald, but were really "a harmless drug to soothe nerves." Problems could be solved by "the strenuous action of good-will."[46] Negotiations produced a document full of loopholes; even so, the British Dominions opposed anything that committed Great Britain to military action, and the Conservative government that succeeded MacDonald rejected the Protocol in March 1925.[47]

The new British Foreign Minister was Austen Chamberlain, the son of Joseph Chamberlain, who had played so large a part in British politics at the turn of the century,[48] and half-brother of the future Prime Minister, Neville Chamberlain. Austen Chamberlain described himself as "the most pro-French member of the government."[49] Convinced that only a specific guarantee would calm justified French fears, he responded positively to a suggestion for a firm British alliance with France. Rumors of such an alliance reached Stresemann. A second menace to his policy of revision without confrontation, the impending final report of the committee investigating German disarmament, moved him to action. The Versailles Treaty provided that the Allies should withdraw their occupation of the Rhineland in three stages. The first was to be the evacuation of Cologne and the surrounding district on January 1, 1925, provided that the Germans had fulfilled their treaty obligations. Although Germany was still effectively disarmed, the commission's preliminary report issued in December 1924 revealed major German failure to meet significant disarmament requirements. (The final report of February 15, 1925, "announced Germany's failure to disarm in 160 pages of damning detail."[50]) On that basis the Allies informed Germany that the withdrawal would not take place until Germany had given clear evidence of compliance.

In January 1925, therefore, Stresemann proposed to the British a plan for the preservation of European peace through international agreement in which France, Germany, and Great Britain, among others, would all take part, the basis for what would become the Locarno agreements. In its final form it consisted of two main elements: the Treaty of Mutual Guarantee, or the Rhineland Pact, a treaty of nonaggression by the states bordering on the Rhine, Germany, France, and Belgium; and a mutual guarantee and promise of assistance in which Britain, France, Germany, Belgium, and Italy agreed to maintain the demilitarization of the Rhineland, "to defend the existing borders between Germany and France and Germany and Belgium and to render military assistance to any signatory who was the victim of a violation of these two promises."[51] The arbitration agreements, the second element, were between Germany and her neighbors, France, Belgium, Poland, and Czechoslovakia.

Chamberlain rightly suspected that the proposal was intended to prevent a Franco-British alliance and to drive a wedge between France and Britain. But he was the only important British official who favored a commitment to France. Members of the Committee of Imperial Defense wanted to give the French no commitment of any kind. Arthur Balfour, former Prime Minister, took the lead. "I am so cross with the French," he said. "I think their obsession [with security] is so intolerably foolish. . . . They are so dreadfully afraid of being swallowed up by the tiger, but they spend all their time poking it."[52] Conservative imperialists such as Balfour, Lord Curzon, Leopold Amery, and Winston Churchill, now returned to the Conservative fold, were opposed entirely to an Anglo-French alliance and against any commitment in Europe "that might restrict Britain's freedom to mediate between the powers."[53] It was only with the greatest difficulty, including a threat of resignation, that Chamberlain got Prime Minister Stanley Baldwin's help in persuading the government to take part in the plan proposed by Stresemann. It was not what Chamberlain had wanted, but it was the best he could get.

The Locarno agreements were greeted with rapture by ordinary people, the press, the diplomats, and for a long time, by historians. Headlines in the *New York Times* announced FRANCE AND GERMANY BAR WAR FOREVER, and the London *Times* proclaimed PEACE AT LAST.[54] Stresemann made much of the voluntary nature of the agreements. Unlike the Versailles treaty, Locarno had been negotiated and accepted by Germany; it was therefore legitimate in the eyes of the Germans and would therefore be effective and lasting. Germany tacitly accepted the loss of Alsace-Lorraine and the permanent demilitarization of the Rhineland, and the Rhineland Pact seemed to bind Britain to give France the assurance it wanted against a German attack. The East, to be sure, was not so protected, but at least Germany had agreed to arbitration treaties with the new states.[55] Beyond all that there was "the spirit of Locarno," a spirit of accommodation and cooperation more important, many said, than the particular provisions. Germany would be conciliated and France reassured, and a true peace would emerge. Chamberlain told the House of Commons that the Locarno agreements were "yet more valuable for the spirit that produced them. . . . We regard Locarno, not as the end of the work of appeasement and reconciliation, but as its beginning."[56]

The realities were very different from these pleasant imaginings. Germany emerged from Locarno with a great victory and the certainty that its position would improve still further. The Locarno agreements left the Germans free to pursue revision of their frontiers in the East. Pressed to negotiate an "eastern Locarno," Stresemann flatly refused. After much discussion, he agreed not to try to change the Eastern settlement by force, but even that he refused to put in writing. Territorial revision in the East was supported by just about every German, and Stresemann called it "the most important task of our policy."[57] The Locarno agreements, in fact, prevented the French from providing effective military help to their eastern allies. If a war should break out over the Polish corridor, for instance, France could not attack Germany without violating the Rhineland Pact. The alliances with Poland and Czechoslovakia lost much of their value to France and, of course, to its eastern allies, because of Locarno. As one perceptive German diplomat put it: "I am a poor German but would not wish to be Polish for there would not pass a night when I would sleep tranquilly."[58] Abandonment of the Poles and Czechs would save the Germans from the threat of another two-front war.

In the west France was out of the Ruhr and in five years would be out of the Rhineland.[59] If the French ever tried to reenter German territory, even to seize customhouses, they would be chastised by the League Council, and Britain and Italy would be bound to come to the aid of Germany. If the Germans refused to meet reparations or disarmament requirements the French had abandoned all means of enforcement. The main point of the Rhineland Pact was to fix the German frontiers with France and Belgium permanently by consent and so remove a major danger of war, but not even that was secure. Days after the conclusion of the Locarno agreements Stresemann asked Belgium to return Eupen and Malmédy, "claiming that he had only promised not to alter the frontier by military means."[60] The French accepted these disadvantages because they seemed to have no choice. Desperate for some kind of protection and unwilling to be isolated, they accepted what they could get: Germany's promise of nonaggression and Britain's conditional promise of military assistance.

The promise of British military assistance was a weak reed on which to support French security, for it was not a firm guarantee against German attack. In case of war between Germany and France the British and Italians would need to decide who was the aggressor and then support the victim. The French and British could not make concerted plans against a German attack, as they had before 1914, because Britain could not prejudge which of the two might be the aggressor. Locarno was not "a guarantee against invasion," only a guarantee to come to the aid of the attacked party after the fact. "Once the Rhineland was evacuated, Locarno guaranteed [only] that British troops would return to the Continent to liberate France from the German Army."[61]

In 1925, moreover, the British had no thought of going to war to defend France. For the moment a German attack was impossible. For the future, the British government hoped and expected that all would be well. Austen Chamberlain believed that the British guarantee of its border would calm the French and remove their fears. Their own safety would also be assured by Germany's conciliation and its return to the Concert of Europe. British friendship and support of France would remove tensions and allow peaceful resolution of outstanding issues.[62]

Winston Churchill, among others, insisted that Britain must not make a commitment that tied its hands, that prevented it from standing between France and Germany as an arbiter. Chamberlain, to be sure, said in 1926 that "the true defence of our country . . . is now no longer the Channel . . . but upon the Rhine,"[63] but not even he expected ever to fight in defense of that line. Still less did the British contemplate defending Germany's eastern neighbors, who were deliberately excluded from Locarno. Of the Polish corridor, which had now become "the danger-spot in Europe,"[64] Chamberlain considered it a place "for which no British Government ever will or ever can risk the bones of a British grenadier."[65] In the ratification debate Chamberlain rightly told Parliament that Britain's obligations could not "be more narrowly circumscribed as they are in the Treaty of Locarno."[66] To a historian writing with the benefit of hindsight: "It seems incongruous that a largely disarmed Britain became the primary instrument for the enforcement of peace."[67] But the British did not feel the incongruity because they did not really feel the obligation.

Had the French or British considered their situation in strategic terms after Locarno they would not have had cause for hopeful rejoicing. Locarno went far toward completing the dismantling of the system France had created to protect itself. Germany was bound to become stronger, especially in the main necessity for modern warfare, a powerful industrial base. By 1929 per capita production was higher than it had been in 1913; between 1924 and 1929 German exports doubled. Germany's improvement in organization and investment in industry swiftly outpaced the other European powers.[68] But in spite of its prosperity and industrial growth and in spite of Locarno, the Germans neither were conciliated nor satisfied. Even such a "good European" as Stresemann worked for the unraveling of Versailles, the restoration of German economic supremacy in Europe, rearmament, revision, as we have seen, of the border with Belgium, and far more grandly, of the entire Eastern settlement. But Stresemann was a moderate in the German political spectrum. When he returned from Locarno he and his agreements were assaulted savagely by more radical nationalists. Hitler's Nazi party urged Stresemann's assassination, and the more respectable German Nationalist Party (DNVP) was angry at the concession of Alsace-

Lorraine and of the rest of the agreements. They withdrew their ministers from the Cabinet and caused a government crisis. Army officials told President Paul von Hindenburg that Stresemann was handing their country over to the Western powers. For the rest of Stresemann's life and after he died criticism continued.

Whatever his own intentions might have been, there were Germans who were entirely unreconciled and ready to use force to restore Germany to dominance whenever the chance should arise. Stresemann's acceptance of the Dawes Plan and the work of the London Conference in 1924 had been denounced in the Reichstag as a "policy of enslavement," and Ludendorff declared: "This is a disgrace to Germany! Ten years ago I won the battle of Tannenberg. Today you have made a Jewish Tannenberg!"[69] Should such people come to power the agreements made at Locarno provided few realistic means for preventing Germany's rearmament and the forcible revision of the situation in Europe. As a practical matter France's security after 1925 relied on her own arms; on her alliances with the Little Entente, i.e., Poland, Czechoslovakia, Rumania, and Yugoslavia, especially on the first two states, which bordered Germany; and on the British military guarantee of its frontier with Germany. Unless France could protect its eastern allies they would be a great liability instead of an asset, but the only effective way to do so was to attack Germany from the west. A sound defensive strategy, therefore, required a strong offensive component that was mobile and swift and always ready to attack. Such a force and such a strategy could have had a strong deterrent effect on Germany and served as a protection for France's allies, and it was something the French could do for themselves. The Ruhr debacle, however, and the rift it had caused with Britain and the United States, had pushed the French totally onto the defensive, psychologically as well as strategically. Their military planners designed only a mass army that could fight only after a long delay, one entirely unsuited for the most important task. "The French system of alliances rested on strategic nonsense."[70]

The British guarantee was even weaker than its inherently equivocal character and the absence of any real expectation ever to honor it might suggest. In November 1918 the British forces consisted of more than 3.5 million men; two years later the figure was 370,000. In August 1919 the British adopted a defense policy based on the Ten Year Rule, according to which "it should be assumed . . . that the British Empire will not be engaged in any great war during the next ten years, and that no Expeditionary Force is required for that purpose." While this made a certain amount of sense in 1919, the rule was kept in force until 1932. In the years 1919–20 and 1920–21 the defense budget was cut from £502 million to one-fifth of that amount, and the sums fixed for annual expenditure in the Ten Year Rule were £60 million for the navy and £75 million for the Army and Air Force combined.[71] "The army was allowed to degenerate in the 1920s to the extent that by 1933 it was incapable of providing in reasonable time even a second-class Expeditionary Force equipped to meet even a second-class opponent outside Europe."[72] The British disarmed so swiftly and fully after the war that they were "wholly incapable of fulfilling the British guarantee, as the Chiefs of Staff pointed out in their annual review for 1926 and on many later occasions."[73]

This rapid and extraordinarily deep cut in defense expenditures was understandable in light of Britain's serious financial problems. Interest payments on the national debt, some 12 percent of the government's spending in 1913, had grown to about 40 percent by the late 1920s.[74] It was natural to try to reduce that figure as much and as quickly as possible. But the cost of so drastic a cut would be enormous, not only in the short run, but more seriously later on. When, at last, the British discovered the need to rearm as quickly as possible in the late 1930s, the neglected war industry found it hard to meet the challenge:

> The long lean years of virtually no construction, the lack of incentive for technological innovation, the unwillingness to invest capital in fields regarded as unprofitable, and in general the steady decay of the country's industrial sinews during the depression, produced their own results. The productive capacity of the country as a whole and those of specialized armaments firms in particular, were too run-down to be reversed without major investment in factories and machine-tools. Thus, even when money for new weaponry was released, it proved impossible to construct, say, as many fighters and bombers as was desired; and until 1939 the Admiralty could do little more than supervise the construction of vessels to bring the navy's strength up to what it should have been in 1930, even under international treaty restrictions.[75]

For the moment, however, the "spirit of Locarno" appeared to work. In September 1926 Germany entered the League of Nations as a permanent member and member of the council, a symbol of the end of its disgrace and isolation. French Foreign Minister Aristide Briand proclaimed the end of Franco-German antagonism and declared: "Away with rifles, machine guns, and cannon! Make way for conciliation, arbitration and peace!"[76] For Germany the new approach brought quick dividends. The Cologne zone of the Rhineland was evacuated on December 1, 1925, and the number of troops in the other zones were reduced in the following year. The committee inspecting German disarmament was deprived of any serious function and withdrew entirely in January 1927, leaving the Germans free to continue their violations of the treaty without fear of complaint, although Germany remained largely disarmed.

After Locarno German foreign policy became "a carefully calibrated series of diplomatic steps calculated to achieve detailed and related goals which in their sum would gradually dismantle the Treaty of Versailles." Germany's ultimate goal was to "reconstruct and even to expand the pre-war Great Power position of the German Reich."[77] Stresemann hoped to achieve all or most of this goal without war, but other Germans expected to use force and some regarded the borders of March 1918, not of 1914, as the appropriate target. Entry into the League of Nations was not merely a symbol of Germany's return to the status of a great power but part of the revisionist plan.[78] One card that strengthened Germany's revisionist hand was its relationship with the Soviet Union. In 1921 the Germans had begun a secret military collaboration with the Russians in whose land they could produce the tanks, airplanes, and poison gases forbidden by Versailles and where they could train both Russians and Germans in their use.[79] In April of the next year they signed the Treaty of Rapallo whereby Germany granted formal recognition to the Soviet Union and encouraged trade by establishing mutual most-favored-nation status. This greatly alarmed the Western powers, who feared the spread of communism and Soviet power. To some extent they had supported German territorial integrity to provide a barrier to Soviet penetration of Europe. The threat of closer German relations with the Soviets helped persuade Western diplomats to support German claims and demands, and Stresemann cleverly took advantage of their fears. At Locarno he had obtained exemption from Article 16 of the League's covenant, which required Germany to permit transit of League troops to apply sanctions to another country and from Germany's participation in the sanctions. This was useful for the goal of revision in more ways than one. Inherently it weakened the League's capacity to pursue collective security through the application of sanctions. In any quarrel between Poland and Russia, moreover, the Poles would be isolated, since no Western troops could cross Germany without consent. "Thus . . . the first step was taken toward weakening the Franco-Polish alliance and the eventual demotion of French continental hegemony."[80] On no account, finally, would Stresemann even give the appearance of helping the West against the Russians, for the fear of Soviet-German collaboration was a useful tool.

To reassure the Soviets, alarmed at Germany's entry into the League, Stresemann signed the treaty of Berlin in April 1926, which essentially confirmed the Treaty of Rapallo. The first Western reaction was shock and anger, which Stresemann used to achieve his ends. In May 1927 Chamberlain told Briand: "We are battling with Soviet Russia for the soul of Germany. . . . [T]he more difficult our relations with Russia became, the more important was it that we should attach Germany solidly to the Western Powers."[81] Disturbing news came out of Germany. An article in the *Manchester Guardian* revealed the secret collaboration between the Soviet and German armies; rumors were rife that the Germans were preparing a future attack on the Polish corridor; the Stahlhelm, a paramilitary organization of extreme nationalists hostile to a settlement with the West and to the Weimar Republic, grew to the point that in 1927–28 its leaders claimed a membership of a million men. A nervous member of the German left warned "that for every French soldier who left the Rhineland ten Stahlhelm troopers would spring up,"[82] yet Stresemann was able to obtain from the Western powers the troop withdrawals and the end to arms inspections already mentioned.

Stresemann continued to press for further revision. There were still occupation forces in the Rhineland, and he abandoned his conciliatory tone and demanded their prompt evacuation, calling the occupation an "iron curtain."[83] The first of heavier reparations payments under the Dawes Plan would come due soon, moreover, and he sought reductions, insisting, however, that the Germans would accept no new payment schedule without an end to the occupation. In August 1929 the powers involved met at the Hague to discuss both problems in what they called "The Conference on the Final Liquidation of the War." Britain was represented by Philip Snowden, Chancellor of the Exchequer in the new Labour government that recently had replaced the Conservatives. He was determined to increase Britain's share of the reparations payments and to eliminate the expense of supporting British troops occupying the Rhineland. With ruth-less arguments in which "he conceded neither a farthing nor a polite word,"[84] he gained a greater share of reparations for Britain in the new Young Plan, which replaced the Dawes Plan and once again scaled down Germany's payments. Briand pressed for continued inspection of German disarmament and for continuation of the Rhineland occupation until the 1935 date, but the British would have none of it, threatening to remove their own troops from the northern zone unilaterally. Under their pressure the French yielded and agreed to evacuation by June 30, 1930.

The Young Plan was proposed to a Germany already suffering serious unemployment and economic decline, which added to its unpopularity. Alfred Hugenberg, leader of the German Nationalist party, formed a com-mittee to direct a campaign against ratification and against Stresemann's policies in general. He was joined by the leader of the Pan-German League, the head of the Stahlhelm, Fritz Thyssen, an important industrial leader, and Adolf Hitler, the heretofore disreputable leader of the Nazis. This group proposed a new law "against the slavery of the German people" for consideration in a national referendum.[85] This so-called Freedom Law demanded repudiation of the war-guilt clause and immediate evacuation of all occupied German territory. It declared the signing of the Young Plan as high treason and insisted that the Chancellor and his ministers be impris-oned for their role in its negotiation. This extraordinary proposal obtained over four million signatures, enough to put it before the Reichstag. There it was defeated soundly, but over five million Germans voted for it in the popular referendum that followed. A historian of Germany has neatly de-scribed its significance: "the fact is that the 5,825,000 Germans who voted for the Feedom Law were apparently willing to repudiate the work of the Republic's greatest statesman, to brand him and his associates as traitors, and to opt for a policy that defied the rest of the world and its notions of public law was surely not insignificant. This and the techniques employed to effect the result were ominous signs of the radicalization of German politics and the beginning of attempts to mobilize the masses against the parliamentary system."[86]

It is a common opinion that Germany came to be a menace to the peace of Europe only after the Great Depression had shattered its prosper-ity, dicredited the Weimar Republic, and opened the way for the dark forces symbolized by Adolf Hitler and his National Socialist party. There is, of course, some truth in a view so widely held, for the Depression and the rise of Hitler were critically important events without which the course of history would have been very different. The Weimar Republic was neither Nazi Germany nor William II's empire. For the most part, it was a democratic republic with many of the checks on militant aggressive foreign policies that modern democracies have. It is possible that, given time, interest in the more adventurous and dangerous of its goals would have faded, as the desire to recover Alsace-Lorraine, even by war, had faded in France. Yet it is important to observe that by the end of the decade of the 1920s, Germany was essentially free of the checks imposed on it by the Versailles Treaty, was rearming with modern weapons and training officers and their men in modern tactics, and was already restored to leadership in industrial power. Almost all Germans were still resentful over the territorial settlement, especially in the east, and its legitimacy and permanence had been undermined by the silence of the Locarno agreements. The nations threatened by Germany's return to independence and power could not resist Germany effectively without the threat of a French attack in the west, yet the chances of such an attack were all but eliminated by the evacuation of the Rhineland and the purely defensive strategy and cast of mind adopted by France. In these circumstances it is not certain that a European war would have been averted, even if Hitler had never come to power. Germany certainly would have pressed an isolated Poland for territorial adjustments that the Poles surely would have resisted. A German attack on Poland carried out by a conservative, nationalist regime would have been less alarming than the one Hitler launched in 1939, but it would have been serious. The German problem was once again at the center of the question of European peace, but there was no one either in Germany or elsewhere who was willing and able to take the steps needed to preserve it.

That situation had been created by a more-or-less conscious policy of neglect and appeasement by the United States and Great Britain. American refusal to provide a guarantee for French security had helped create the situation. American support for the Germans, in the form of pressure against France and the investment of capital in Germany, had put an end to Versailles.[87] Although the British had little capital to invest, they pursued the same policy that, by 1929, had produced a major change in the balance of power and an increasingly unstable international situation.

In 1950 Winston Churchill distinguished in the House of Commons between two kinds of appeasement: "Appeasement in itself may be good or bad according to the circumstances. Appeasement from weakness and fear is alike futile and fatal. Appeasement from strength is magnanimous and noble, and might be the surest and perhaps the only path to world peace."[88] In the years from 1919 to 1935, it has been said, "the principal tenet of [British] appeasement was concession through strength." Its practitioners did not act from fear; they were not "misguided men who mistook weakness for charity." For them "appeasement was a policy of optimism and hope, even at times of strength."[89] The British statesmen of these years were certainly full of optimism and hope, but it is hard to credit the view that they acted from strength. They swiftly dissipated British military strength and established a policy to make sure it could not be restored quickly. Then they worked to restrain and discourage France's military strength, which was their only tangible defense against the possibility of a revived and revanchist Germany. Finally, they powerfully assisted Germany's restoration as the mightiest industrial power in Europe and put an end to serious checks on its clandestine rearmament, even as they hampered France's industrial recovery and deprived it of tangible means of resisting Germany's growing power. Whatever strength Britain may have had after the war, its true weight and effectiveness rapidly diminished and was soon only theoretical. Had the British retained a considerable military establishment; had they made a defensive treaty with France and backed it with concrete military plans and then backed them with the appropriate forces; had they then undertaken such revisions in the Versailles settlement as seemed appropriate and possible and assisted German recovery after French security was guaranteed; such a policy would deserve to be called appeasement from strength. By making a German program of militant defiance obviously suicidal, it also would have strengthened the hand of more moderate politicians such as Stresemann. Leaders like Stresemann were nationalists and sought revision of the treaties, but they were rational, practical men who could be deterred in a way that Hitler could not. True appeasement from strength was a policy worth trying, but that is not the policy the British pursued.

British policy, in fact, *was* weak and misguided: it "did not merely display a characteristic escapism and self-deception but, the realities of power and strategy having been left so far behind, now veered positively into fantasy, like an unsound financier who, devoid of cash resources, deludes himself and his creditors with grandiose paper transactions."[90] It is worth considering why the British acted so. There is no denying that Great Britain faced very serious practical problems that made a significant Continental commitment difficult and unpleasant to contemplate. Victory and the mandate system had increased British imperial responsibilities vastly all over the globe. At the same time the dominions were becoming more independent and less willing to offer military assistance to the British. Nationalism, sometimes in the form of rebellion, was making its way into the colonial empire and imposing heavier burdens on Britain's military resources. In nearby Ireland the troubles were serious enough to require the commitment of between three and four divisions of troops. In July 1920 a General Staff appreciation of the "Military Liabilities of the Empire" reported that "our liabilities are so vast, and at the same time so indeterminate, that to assess them must be largely a matter of conjecture."[91] The same forces that led many British leaders to turn away from the Continent and to concentrate on the Empire before the war worked in the same direction after it, when the challenge was even greater.

At the same time, British finances were far more difficult. The national debt had grown from £650 million to £7,500 million, and taxes had quadrupled.[92] Britain's capacity to compete in the modern industrial world was diminishing in comparison with more up-to-date competitors such as the United States and Germany. Other nations, chiefly the United States, were taking over the responsibilities and profits formerly belonging to Britain as the world's banker and insurer, the "invisible assets" that had contributed so much to British wealth and influence. In October 1922 Bonar Law declared that "we cannot act alone as the policeman of the world . . . the financial and social condition of the country makes that impossible."[93] In the tradition of the nineteenth-century liberal politicians, the parties from Conservative to Labour looked to economic prosperity as the national goal and also as the solution to the problem of war. "The interests of the British Empire in foreign countries," said Stanley Baldwin, "are first of all economic and commercial. When we speak of peace being the greatest British interest, we mean that British trade and commerce, which are essential to the life of our people, flourish best in conditions of peace." Ramsay MacDonald said he repeatedly sought agreements at Geneva in order to attain "international confidence upon which we can base a fabric of peace . . . [because] we want security and stability for the working class and for the economic interest of this country."[94] Such men believed that the restoration of economic well-being would mollify resentments and bring peace. This pointed to assistance for the German economy, to recognizing German economic predominance in *Mitteleuropa,* to providing credit to help Germany obtain raw materials, and to bringing it back into the international trading system. Their actions rested on "a hope, perhaps a belief, that there could be an economic breakthrough which would avoid war. There was a pervasive 'economism' which believed that states did go to war for economic reasons."[95] To a historian writing soon after the outbreak of the Second World War it seemed "amazing that the British, even when dealing with Hitler, so frequently put faith in the ability of some purely economic arrangement or settlement to satisfy nations or to divert their attention from political or territorial aspirations unwelcome to Great Britain."[96]

Missing from all this was an understanding that peoples and nations go to war for deeper and less "rational" motives than economics and a recognition of the need to adopt a sound strategy and to provide the military capacity to carry it out. The Germans were openly resentful about issues of territory and nationality and honor that had little to do with economics. They bridled at what they thought were the injustices of the settlement. Yet if Germany were accorded "justice" by the rectification of her frontiers, would this not once again result in her domination of the Continent, unless her neighbors once more joined forces against her? "And if she did again dominate the Continent, what security could there be for a Britain who now for the first time in her history really *was* vulnerable."[97]

In this sense of vulnerability we arrive, perhaps, at a deeper explanation of British behavior and policy, even in the years before Hitler, less "rational" than economic arguments, less admirable than arguments for "fair play," reconciliation, understanding, even Christian charity. British losses in the war were terrible: over 700,000 dead, some 9 percent of all men under forty-five, and some 1,500,000 seriously wounded.[98] Over 37,000 of the dead were officers, chiefly of what were then spoken of as "the governing classes." Their deaths especially were mourned by poets and other writers who created the powerful metaphor of a "Lost Generation" whose loss deprived the nation of vital leadership and contributed to British decline. In a typical statement made in 1935 Stanley Baldwin said, "We live under the shadow of the last War and its memories still sicken us. . . . Have you thought what it has meant to the world to have had that swathe of death cut through the loveliest and best of our contemporaries, how our public life has suffered because those who would have been ready to take over from our tired and disillusioned generation are not there?"[99]

The sense of vulnerability emerged not only from these bitter memories of loss in the last war but from intensified fears of even greater dangers in the next. The new terror that threatened was aerial bombardment, and it was generally depicted as irresistible and unbearable. As early as 1922 a Sub-Committee of the Committee of Imperial Defence reported its estimate of the probable results of an enemy air attack: "Railway traffic would be disorganized, food supplies would be interrupted, and it is probable that after being subjected for several weeks to the strain of such an attack the population would be so demoralized that they would insist upon an armistice."[100] Although it recommended work on ground defenses, it assumed that they would have only a marginal effect. The dominant theory was that bombers could not be stopped. In 1932 Baldwin told the House of Commons: "I think it well . . . for the man in the street to realise that there is no power on earth that can protect him from being bombed. Whatever people may tell him, the bomber will always get through." The only hope was through deterrence provided by an equal threat: "The only defence is offence, which means that you will have to kill women and children more quickly than the enemy if you want to save yourselves."[101]

As early as 1923 Arthur Balfour, serving on another committee that helped set British policy, had reached the same conclusion: the only ultimate guarantee of peace was "the certainty of every civilized man, woman and child that everybody will be destroyed if there is a war: everybody and everything." Here we see the birth of the policy later adopted by the United States in the nuclear age, Mutually Assured Destruction (MAD), that deliberately eschews serious efforts at defense against attack from the air and relies completely on the terror of retaliation to prevent a future war, leaving no means of defense in case deterrence fails. Had the British kept to it faithfully they would have been devastated and defeated in the Second World War. There can be no doubt that such memories of losses in the war and fears of such future terrors played a powerful part in shaping policy between the wars. "Some time during these celebrations [of victory] there was formulated that simple phrase which the people not only of Great Britain but of the Dominions resolved should be the epitaph of their million-odd war dead: Never Again. Unfortunately, it was to be more than an epitaph; it was to be a policy—and one which would have disastrous results"[102]

British appeasement in the 1920s was not the work of a narrow group of ideologues isolated from the mood of the rest of the country. Prime ministers and Cabinets representing the Liberals, Conservatives, and Labour pursued the same course. Some started on that course even before the peace treaties were complete; most of the governing class quickly joined in. The doughty nationalist and imperialist, the very symbol of Britain's bull-dog tenacity and courage, Winston Churchill, said in 1921: "The aim is to get an appeasement of the fearful hatreds and antagonisms which exist in Europe and to enable the world to settle down. I have no other object in view."[103] Lesser men held doggedly to that policy even after conditions changed and called for a new assessment, but "appeasement was the cor-ner-stone of inter-war foreign policy."[104] The men who shaped and exe-cuted British policy in the 1930s have much to answer for, but it would be a mistake to ignore how bad was the hand dealt them by their predecessors. After 1930 appeasement from strength was no longer an option. The only choice was to continue the well-established policy and continue to yield to German pressure, even as it grew increasingly risky to do so, or to under-take a sharp reversal of course, a policy sure to be unpopular, difficult to bring about, and full of immediate costs and dangers.

The Fall of the Weimar Republic

The year 1929, the midpoint in the two decades between the wars, was an important watershed. In October of that year Gustav Stresemann died and with him the politically careful, if determined, program of the peaceful revision of the Versailles settlement in Germany's favor. In the same month the Wall Street stock market crash gave impetus to a great depression that swept across the industrialized world, causing political shock waves of great significance in Europe, especially Germany. Germany had been suffering from an economic depression well before the crash in the New York stock market, but because of its impact on Germany's creditors, "The Wall Street Crash marked not only the end of the Strese-mann era, but also the beginning of the end of Weimar parliamentarian-ism."[105]

The financial panic led the Americans to set up high tariff walls against foreign imports and to recall their loans. The new barriers to exports and the flight of American capital devastated the Germans. Busi-ness suffered, unemployment grew, and the results were felt in the political arena. The fortunes of the parties who had always supported the Weimar Republic sank, as the extremist, antirepublican, anticapitalist parties, the Communists and Nazis, gained new strength. Each of them, and others as well, fielded paramilitary organizations who fought one another in the streets. The Republic seemed unable to govern, and Germany resembled "Rome in the fifth decade before Christ, when the civil power lost its authority and the soldiers and demagogues took over."[106]

Leaders of the Army were alarmed that the country might disintegrate and fall into civil war, but they were unwilling to take direct responsibility for governing, preferring to work through political intermediaries they hoped to control. It was a delicate task that proved to be beyond their capabilities. In March 1930 the broad government led by a Socialist, Hermann Müller, fell. General Wilhelm Groener, Minister of War, and his associate, General Kurt von Schleicher, head of the ministry's political bureau, took leading roles in shaping the new government. Their aim was to select a Cabinet amenable to their views that was above parties, independent of the Reichstag, and dependent for its authority on President Hindenburg, who could be trusted to pursue the army's policies.[107] They chose as the new chancellor Heinrich Brüning of the Catholic Center party.

Brüning's plan as Chancellor is sometimes interpreted as one seeking to solve domestic problems by achieving success in foreign policy, specifically, to reduce or put an end to the reparations payments and arms limitations imposed by the Versailles Treaty.[108] There is good evidence, however, that foreign policy, in the sense of restoring Germany to political independence and the status of a great power, was his chief concern and that he was prepared to run great risks and cause terrible suffering on the domestic side in order to achieve his goals in the other sphere.

The Chancellor launched a program of the strictest fiscal rigidity with deliberate deflationary consequences, raising taxes and reducing government expenditures, including unemployment insurance, but not reducing the military budget. When this proposal was turned down by the Reichstag, Brüning resorted to the infamous Article 48 of the Weimar constitution, which permitted him to promulgate the law by presidential decree. It was a sharp departure from the principles of republican government, and it would not be the last. Brüning then called for new elections, hoping to achieve a Reichstag more friendly to his policies, but his political judgment was faulty. The elections of September 14, 1930, produced a great victory for the extremist parties: the Communists won seventy-seven seats, but the greatest winners were Hitler's Nazis. In the elections of 1928 they had received 809,000 votes and 12 seats in the Reichstag. In 1930 they polled

6,400,000, "which meant that 107 brown-shirts were going to march into the new Reichstag."[109]

Political leaders in Britain and America thought of Brüning as an exponent of financial responsibility and political moderation, but his memoirs and other evidence suggest that he had something else in mind. He told the Army, the Nationalists, and Hitler that he welcomed their public opposition "so that he could exploit this in diplomacy, . . . by making himself appear as the moderate German to whom concessions had best be made."[110] In October 1930 he explained his plans to the newly influential Adolf Hitler. In the first stage economic policy would be completely in the service of foreign policy. Deflationary measures of every kind would be used to harden Germany "so that she could resist any external pressure and be in a position to exploit the world economic crisis in order to bring pressure to bear on the remaining Powers."[111] Economic hardship would show the Western nations that Germany could not afford to pay reparations. Germany would become as independent of imports as possible; together with fiscal soundness created by domestic austerity, autarchy would allow Germany to shake free of the Young Plan, reparations, and arms limitations. Although Brüning had called for a domestic political truce when he took office, he told Hitler that "sharper opposition on the part of the NSDAP [Nazi Party] to foreign policy" could help bring about the treaty revisions he sought. Success in foreign policy would then allow Brüning to bring about the domestic change nearest to his heart, the restoration of the monarchy.[112]

Meanwhile, the German economy was in terrible decline. Unemployment grew from 3 million in March when Brüning took office to 4.38 million in December 1930, to 5,615,000 a year later, close to 10 percent of the population and a much higher percentage of the workforce.[113] While cutting government expenditures for unemployment benefits, reducing wages and salaries and jobs, however, he refused to make equivalent reductions in the military budget, reflecting the political power of the military in the late Weimar Republic and also Brüning's determination to strengthen Germany's position as a great power. At the same time he continued to provide economic support for the inefficient grain-growing Junkers east of the Elbe. This made the price of bread artificially high at a time when wages and other prices were low and placed a burden on industry, on the poor, and on the small mixed and dairy farmers. All of this increased the flight to the extreme parties on the right and left, especially to the Nazis, but Brüning was prepared to run the risk and also to use it to achieve his goals in foreign policy. The very growth of Nazi power and the threat it posed helped to convince the Western powers to make concessions.

Rather than depart from his policy of tight money and retrenchment meant to "discipline" the Germans and demonstrate Germany's incapacity to continue paying reparations, therefore, Brüning would take no measures to lighten the suffering. He would not consider the compromise of a five-year moratorium on reparations instead of a complete end to them.[114] His own approach was to "stick it out *[Durchhaltepolitik]*" which, as some scholars have pointed out, "constituted nothing less than diplomatic extortion" by presenting creditors the choice "between settlement or the threat of impending collapse of the German economy and utter domestic chaos."[115] The world depression, he told the Reichstag on May 11, 1932, contained hope as well as danger. It would do great harm to many nations but, "if the German people can keep their nerve . . . then the German people will certainly not be among those who . . . succumb. . . . We must not weaken in the last five minutes!" It seems to have been Brüning's plan to have Germany be the first European nation to emerge from the depression.[116] The result would have been to give Germany an economic, and then political, domination over the states of Eastern Europe, which would entirely undermine France's plan for security through Eastern alliances, already badly weakened by the evacuation of the Rhineland.

Brüning's chancellorship was a period of intensified pressure against the Versailles settlement. When France agreed to withdraw from the Rhineland in September 1929 its Foreign Minister, Briand, proposed a new plan for a European federation that somewhat resembled the plan for a united Europe of our own time. He hoped, by involving Germany in a politically and economically integrated Europe, to preserve the states of Eastern and Southeastern Europe and so to defend French security in a new way. The Germans saw it as an attempt to defend Versailles and French domination. Their response was to take a bold and aggressive line. German diplomats pressed for an end to demilitarization in the Rhineland. Brüning went forward with building a second armored cruiser even as he complained of Germany's poverty and its inability to pay reparations.[117]

Most striking of all was Germany's announcement on March 21, 1931, of the intention to form a customs union with Austria. It was done without the prior notice and discussion characteristic of the Stresemann era, but resembled "a forcing manoeuvre in the Wilhelmine manner";[118] it was also a precursor of the unpleasant surprises that Hitler would so often present to the world. This action was intended as a step in the direction of gaining new influence in Eastern Europe and, as the French, Poles, Czechs, and Yugoslavs quickly saw, the first step in the *Anschluss,* the union of Germany and Austria forbidden by the treaties of Versailles and St. Germain. It was also a way of undermining Briand's plan for a federated Europe, although, as the German diplomat Bernhard von Bülow said, "We will dress the matter up with a pan-European cloak."[119] The French responded by using their financial power to break the Creditanstalt bank in Vienna, wreaking economic havoc in Austria, and by bringing the case to the International Court at the Hague, where the union was declared a violation of the treaties.

Germany's behavior aroused suspicions among the other nations and delayed the concessions Brüning sought. Economic effects of the depression and increased public violence between the paramilitary forces of the Nazis and Communists further reduced his political strength. What brought Brüning down, however, was the loss of support from President Hindenburg and from the Army, represented by its most political general, Kurt von Schleicher. Hindenburg was unhappy that the Chancellor could not get the Nazis to support an extension of his term as President without a contest. He blamed this humiliation on Brüning. The military officers were determined to break through the limitations placed on the German Army, and this led them to seek a new and more pliant leader.

Throughout the history of the Weimar Republic the German military leaders worked, often secretly, to build the most effective military force possible with the intention, "under favorable circumstances, to use war as an instrument of policy."[120] Their greatest concern was to achieve a capacity for large-scale mobilization, which required the accumulation of a trained reserve, difficult to achieve so long as conscription was banned. By 1931 Germany's reserves from the last war were becoming too old to fight, and a crisis in reserve manpower loomed. The long-range solution would be to gain freedom from the limiting clauses of the Versailles Treaty, and the Army looked to a new chancellor to achieve that at the forthcoming disarmament conference. Meanwhile, they encouraged and worked with right-wing paramilitary organizations, especially the Nazi SA (Sturmabteilung [Storm Troopers]). The German government, pressed by the Prussian government, which was under Socialist control, banned the

SA, but by 1932 the Army's plans for military expansion contained a role for the SA, so a chancellor must be found who would protect it.

Schleicher used Brüning's efforts to stop the violence of Hitler's paramilitary SA and SS (Schutzstaffel [Defense Squadron]) organizations as the means of bringing him down. He persuaded Hindenburg that Brüning was too responsive to the Socialists and prevailed upon the President to withdraw his support. Since Brüning had been ruling by presidential decree, without the support of Parliament, he was forced to go on May 30, 1932.

Even before the regime of Hitler, however, Brüning's successors had the good fortune to benefit from the work he had done. While he was still in power the Hoover Moratorium suspended reparations payments for a year. At Lausanne in July 1932 the reparations conference revised the Young Plan: Germany would have to make only a token payment in three years, and that would be the end of reparations. Disarmament was also discussed at Lausanne, but the French and British were unwilling to grant the Germans the equality in armaments they insisted upon. At the Geneva Disarmament Conference in September, therefore, the Germans walked out. In response Britain and the United States put pressure not on the Germans but on the French; in December the conference agreed to the principle of equality of rights for Germany in the field of armaments, and the German military leadership already had firm plans for the restoration of their country's military might.[121] Well before Hitler came to power, therefore, Germany had thrown off some of the most crucial restraints imposed by the Versailles Treaty: occupation of the Rhineland, reparations, and disarmament. When rearmament had been achieved it would be far more difficult to prevent the rejection of what remained.

Even before Hitler's ascension to power and Germany's full remilitarization its leading diplomats favored an aggressive foreign policy that foresaw the complete destruction of the settlement in Eastern Europe, including a fourth partition of Poland.[122] These men, such as Foreign Minister Konstantin von Neurath and State Secretary Bernhard von Bülow, remained in their positions quite comfortably for years after Hitler took over. As we shall see, Hitler had some different goals that went far beyond theirs, but for quite a long way their aims were the same. Sharing common ground with most officials in the Foreign Office, conservative politicians, the Army, and the right-wing of the Nazi Party, at least after Hitler came to power, they set forth their views early in March 1933.[123]

They sought to tear up what remained of the Versailles Treaty: the Rhine-land must be remilitarized, the Saar recovered, along with all the lost territories. These should include, apart from the destruction of Poland, Danzig, Memel, parts of Czechoslovakia, some of Schleswig in Denmark, Malmédy in Belgium, the return of Alsace-Lorraine and Germany's lost colonies overseas. Further plans to be pursued later foresaw union with Austria, and the seizure and exploitation of markets and the domination of the economies of the states of Eastern Europe. Bülow's thinking not only encompassed the war aims discussions of 1917–18, which had conceived of a Polish client state subordinate to Prussia, but also embraced territorial expansion to the east as in 1918, when it had been sanctioned by the Treaty of Brest-Litovsk."[124]

These were the goals not of the frightening leader of the Nazis, but of the comforting, traditional diplomats who negotiated with the Western powers in 1932 and who contributed to the impression, widespread in Britain and America,

> that Germany had learned from its defeat in 1918, that the country had a moderate, responsible government, and that in military affairs, the Germans now wanted only the disarmament of others, for the sake of their own security. Germans did not want war, and they had no significant military power; thus there was no need to think of trying to balance German military power. If anything, it was French power that needed to be reduced.

The German people's disinclination toward another war was "the only element of truth in this general impression."[125]

In the last years of the Weimar Republic many of Germany's civilian and military leaders continued to aim at the extreme goals formulated during the last war. If even some of them were achieved the result would be to give Germany the same domination of Europe that the Allies had come into the war to prevent. It was only a matter of time until rearmament would permit a determined leader to act to achieve Germany's unacceptable goals.

Why had the Allies permitted so dangerous a situation to arise? Since the French could not act alone and the Americans were even less inclined to become involved in European affairs because of the economic depression, the real question concerns the British. The terrible memory of the recent war; the weakness of the British economy in the face of an increased demand for social services and increased imperial responsibilities; the ideal-istic rhetoric surrounding the making of peace; the hopes placed in the League of Nations—all have been discussed above. They all strengthened the already powerful forces in British society favoring disarmament, uninvolvement, and appeasement.

There was broad support for the notions that the Great War and the terrible destruction that came from it were caused by the arms race, the alliance system, and the willingness of Britain to commit a land army of significant size to a war on the Continent. British leaders were persuaded easily that the Western Allies had been at least as responsible as the Germans for the war; that the arms race, stirred up by munitions makers and their associates, had been a major cause of bringing it on; that greater under-standing, more generosity, and patience were better ways to avoid war than by military deterrence. There was a general feeling that to think and act on the basis of strategic considerations, to try to preserve a balance of power, to admit to the pursuit of national interest supported by military strength was not only dangerous but immoral. By the end of the twenties such opinions were limited not to radicals or pacifists but influenced the thoughts and actions of both Liberal and Conservative governments and politicians and came to be orthodox, the only ones respectable among educated peo-ple.

Between 1928 and 1930 a number of books about the Great War were published and received with great acclaim and popularity, including such influential volumes as Robert Graves's *Goodbye to All That*, Siegfried Sas-soon's *Memoirs of an Infantry Officer*, and an English translation of Erich Maria Remarque's *All Quiet on the Western Front*. They all delivered the same message: "the futility and dreariness of war, the incompetence of generals and politicians, and the ordinary men on both sides victims of this incompetence."[126] On a more academic and political plane historians on both sides of the Atlantic were publishing revisionist interpretations of the causes of the war with tremendous effect. A. J. P. Taylor has neatly de-scribed the effect of these intellectual efforts:

> Few educated people now believed that the war had been caused by a deliberate German aggression. . . . In the general opinion, wars were started by mistake—the view of Lord Grey; the negotiating machinery of the League would prevent these mistakes

in the future. Or they were caused by great armaments, the view of Lloyd George; the remedy for this was disarmament. Or they were cause by "grievances"; the clear moral here was that these, now predominantly German, should be redressed. Or finally they were caused by "capitalism"; hence Labour's contribution to peace was to bring capitalism to an end. A refinement of this last view was the doctrine . . . that wars were deliberately fostered by the private manufacturers of armaments—a doctrine which produced a royal commission on the "war traffic" in this country in 1935 and a Senate inquiry in the United States.

These explanations were usually mixed together. Whichever were adopted, it led to the same conclusion. Since there was nothing to choose between the governments of each country and since war was always a purposeless evil, the duty of those who wanted peace was to see that their own government behaved peacefully and, in particular, to ensure this by depriving their government of arms.[127]

The decline of the Weimar Republic and its turn toward more aggressive policies after the death of Stresemann coincided with the rule of the second Labour government between 1929 and 1931, a regime, it has been said, that "marked the blooming high summer of moralising internationalism in Britain between the world wars."[128] Labour's election manifesto included among its objectives the establishment of "peace, freedom and justice by removing from among the nations the root causes of international disputes, by conciliation and all-in arbitration, by renouncing war as an instrument of national policy, by disarmament and by political and economic co-operation through the League of Nations."[129] The government put its faith in disarmament and the League and was prepared even to accept a decline in both the absolute and relative strength of the Royal Navy, Britain's ultimate line of defense. At the Washington Naval Conference of 1921–22 a Conservative government already had agreed to parity in battleships with the United States and allowing Japan three ships to their five. To please the Dominions and the Americans they also abandoned the alliance with Japan. To please Japan both Britain and the United States agreed not to develop their naval bases at Hong Kong and the Philippines. "Japan thus received a local supremacy which she later used with results disastrous for the Far East, for British interests, and ultimately for herself."[130]

We can gain some idea of the mood of the day by considering the behavior of Winston Churchill, the indomitable navalist and aggressive imperialist who would be the Cassandra of rapid rearmament against the threat of Nazi Germany in the 1930s. As Chancellor of the Exchequer in the Conservative government of Stanley Baldwin of 1924–29 he pressed for a program of social reform that included expanded old-age insurance, pensions, and cheap housing and repeatedly used the Ten Year Rule to reduce naval appropriations to help pay for it. To the Navy's fears of a war with Japan he replied, "Why should there be a war with Japan? I do not believe there is the slightest chance of it in our lifetime." The admiralty should make plans "on the basis that no naval war against a first class Navy is likely to take place in the next twenty years."[131]

The Washington treaty would have permitted the construction of new battleships in 1931, but at the London Naval Conference of 1930 the Labour Government extended the naval holiday for six more years, and Britain accepted limits on destroyers and submarines at the same five-five-three level. They also allowed the Japanese to have 70 percent as many cruisers as Great Britain and the United States, reducing the British number to fifty, although the Admiralty for years had insisted that seventy was the lowest figure needed to protect British trade. Naval officials regarded the outcome as dangerous, but the government was confident that the new treaty had enhanced British security:

> [T]he advance within the last few years in the development of
> international machinery for the settlement of disputes by pacific
> means had greatly reduced the risk of the outbreak of any war.
> . . . Japan in particular having joined the British Commonwealth
> of Nations and the United States of America in signing the London
> Naval Treaty . . . was unlikely to disturb the peace.[132]

For the same reasons Britain decided to stop work on the base at Singapore for five years.

Disarmament, universal if possible but partial and even one-sided if necessary, was the panacea to men like Arthur Henderson, Foreign Minister of the Labour Government, who was prepared to cut Britain's naval budget in anticipation of the disarmament conference scheduled for 1932.

In this he was much encouraged by the Treasury, which pressed for disarmament and reliance on the League of Nations for financial reasons as the depression strained British resources. In Correlli Barnett's colorful simile: "The British were like a family which, having a large house and rich possessions but a currently reduced income, wished to save money on anti-burglar devices. What cheaper and better way than to persuade all likely burglars that larceny is immoral, and that they should give up their jemmies?"[133]

Prime Minister Ramsay MacDonald, while holding most of the same views as Henderson, was more realistic. Germany's troubles and the rapid growth of Hitler's Nazis alarmed him. In 1931 he thought "the risks of war were greater today than they had been twelve months ago, and a militarist spirit was controlling Europe more to-day than it had been for many years."[134] He was able to stop the naval cuts, and even wanted to revoke the Ten Year Rule, but in the latter effort he was defeated by Henderson, who was convinced that there was no trouble in Europe, and by the majority of the party.[135]

However bad the naval situation, the condition of the Army and the Air Force were still worse. In 1925 a memorandum from the Foreign Office stated that "the true strategic frontier of Britain is on the Rhine. . . . Any policy which permitted Germany first to swallow up France, and then to deal with Great Britain would be fatal strategically." In 1930 the Chiefs of Staff warned that "the country is in a less favorable position to fulfill the Locarno guarantees than it was, without written guarantee, to come to the assistance of France and Belgium in 1914."[136] In 1922 the Cabinet agreed to establish an Air Force of about 250 planes, less than half the size of the French. In quest of parity, a force of 52 squadrons, 394 bombers, and 204 fighters was authorized in 1923 for completion five years later. The "spirit of Locarno" intervened, and completion was postponed until 1936. In 1930 it was put back further to 1938. Expenditures for all the armed services declined from £116 million in 1926–27 to £110 million in 1930–31, to £102.7 million in 1932–33, the year when Hitler took power.[137]

This situation could be accepted by those who put their faith in the League of Nations, but events soon revealed the danger of relying on that institution. In September 1931 Japan invaded Manchuria, the first important challenge to the League of Nations and the whole concept of collective security, and the reaction ought to have made clear the vanity of placing any faith in either.

The two powers best situated to resist Japan militarily were the Soviet Union and the United States, but neither was a member of the League. Like all the other nations, Britain had no intention of taking military action. At British urging the League appointed the Lytton Commission, which examined the situation and completed its report almost a year after the invasion. The report found that Japan had some legitimate grievances, but it condemned the use of force and the occupation and recommended the withdrawal of the Japanese forces. No nation suggested that Japan be branded an aggressor, which would invoke Article XVI of the covenant and call for sanctions, certainly not Britain. Sir John Simon, Foreign Secretary of the new National Government of Britain, insisted at a Cabinet committee meeting in February 1932 that "he had never for one moment favoured the adoption of the League of any kind of sanctions, not even of an economic character." What concerned him was that even a declaration complaining of Japan's behavior might "provoke a situation that precipitated Japan's resentment." His fear was justified, for the British achieved the neat trick of failing to stop the Japanese while gaining their hostility.[138] In February 1933 the League accepted the Lytton Report, and the Japanese resigned in protest. Small or weak nations who feared coercion by stronger states could draw no comfort from the episode.

The Manchurian affair compelled the British armed forces and the government to face a few realities. The British took note of their inability even to defend Singapore and Hong Kong, much less fight the Japanese. In February 1932 Sir Robert Vansittart, permanent undersecretary at the Foreign Office, recognized the danger from Japan, which "may well spread to the Middle East," that Britain alone could do nothing to check it and would be "done for in the Far East" and "must eventually swallow any and every humiliation" there unless the United States were prepared to use force.[139] But during the Manchurian affair the Americans had shown just how little prospect there was of that. Their response was limited to a note issued by Secretary of State Henry Stimson that his government would recognize no agreement between China and Japan that violated American treaty rights or impaired Chinese sovereignty or gained territory by means that violated the Kellogg-Briand Pact.

A few in Britain, like Lord Robert Cecil, along with the Greek scholar Gilbert Murray, the chief enthusiast for the League of Nations, advocated collective security and some kind of useful action, but these were the same people who had insisted on disarmament and resisted the idea that the world faced any dangers. A week before the Japanese invasion of Manchuria Cecil told the League of Nations assembly: "there has scarcely been a period in the world's history when war seems less likely than it does at present."[140] Stanley Baldwin, now Lord President of the Council in the National Government, a coalition that had been formed to deal with the effects of the depression, spelled out the difficulty of acting among the realities that shaped the situation:

> The very people like Bob Cecil who have made us disarm, and quite right, too, are urging us forward to take action. But where will action lead us to? If we withdraw Ambassadors, that is the first step. What is the next? and the next? If you enforce an economic boycott you will have war declared by Japan and she will seize Singapore and Hong Kong and we cannot, as we are placed, stop her. You will get nothing out of Washington but words, big words, but only words.[141]

Events proved him perfectly right. Britain's helplessness led the military leaders to advocate the end of the Ten Year Rule. Neville Chamberlain, Chancellor of the Exchequer, objected on the grounds that the state of the British economy would not permit that. Baldwin maneuvered around him, and on March 23, 1932, it effectively came to an end.[142] That did not mean, however, that the British were ready for serious rearmament.

THE ROAD TO WAR

Hitler in Power

Brüning's fall, it has been said, "was a real turning-point in the collapse of German democracy."[143] It forced the Army to take a more direct role in politics and to deal with the growing problem of Hitler and the Nazis. During the brief chancellorships of Franz von Papen and Kurt von Schleicher there was endless maneuvering to produce a regime that was able to govern and would be acceptable to the Army. The growth of public support for the Nazis made it impossible to omit Hitler, but he refused to participate, except as Chancellor. Papen was President Hindenburg's favorite, and he was convinced he could control Hitler by placing himself in the government and surrounding the Nazi leader with men able to restrain him. He was able to persuade the reluctant President to name Hitler Chancellor and, on January 30, 1933, the sworn enemy of democracy and the Weimar Republic took office with full legality. Papen and his associates were confident that "we'll be boxing Hitler in."[144] In a matter of months, however, Hitler had torn up the constitution, reduced his colleagues to subservience, and made himself dictator of Germany. Before long he would tear up what remained of the Versailles Treaty and the Locarno agreements and start on his march of conquest and extermination.

To Western governments who evaluated Hitler when he came to power he seemed just another German revisionist who would seek to undo what was left of Versailles and "would be content with carefully measured doses of appeasement."[145] The notion that in foreign policy he was just an ordinary German statesman, not very different in his goals from predecessors such as Stresemann, was revived in the 1960s, most influentially by A. J. P. Taylor, who conceded that Hitler's domestic arrangements were novel. "In one sphere alone," however, "he changed nothing. His policy was that of his predecessors, of the professional diplomats at the foreign ministry, and indeed of virtually all Germans. Hitler, too, wanted to free Germany from the restrictions of the peace treaty; to restore a great German army; and then to make Germany the greatest power in Europe from her natural weight."[146] Such goals ought to have troubled the Western powers greatly, even if, as Taylor and others argue, Hitler had no fixed plans but was a mere opportunist who followed the lure of power without guideposts, but the evidence clearly shows the opposite. Hitler was "a fanatic idealogue," and well before he came to power he set out his fundamental goals and policies

> with absolute frankness in *Mein Kampf,* a book he had written . . . to explain the objectives of his movement to his followers and to set down the basic elements of his doctrine in permanent form. . . . *[Mein Kampf]* contains a clear and frighteningly logical exposition of Hitler's political and racial principles, the goals he intended to pursue in both domestic and foreign affairs, and the means he proposed to employ in the realization of those goals. Far more important, Hitler remained true to those principles, which constituted fundamental guidelines for his political conduct from the time he emerged from his prison in Landesberg am Lech in 1924 to his death in the rubble of Berlin.[147]

At the core of Hitler's ideas were his linked concepts of race and of the living space *(Lebensraum)* that would be needed by the German people. He held to a vulgarized version of Social Darwinism that regarded the world as a jungle in which the fittest survived and the unfit would perish. It was popular in Germany, among other countries, for several decades before the war of 1914, where the racial composition of each society was central to its character and future. The Nordic, or Aryan, "race," of whom the Germans were the leading exemplar, were naturally superior and destined to rule the inferior races such as the Slavic and Mediterranean peoples. His special targets were the Jews, a base race without a national home, without roots in the soil, and therefore internationalist and dangerously influential, a people he was determined to destroy. Even after murdering some six million Jews he concluded his testament with the words: "Above all I pledge the leadership of the nation and its followers to the scrupulous observation of the racial laws and to an implacable opposition against the universal poisoner of all peoples, international Jewry."[148]

For Hitler the struggle between the races was basically a contest for control of agricultural land. "In this struggle the stronger won, took the space, proliferated on that space, and then fought for additional space."[149] The only acceptable policy for a superior race was to conquer new space to accommodate its expanding population. The conquered natives of the new lands must not be assimilated, for that would damage the racial purity of the conquerors and dilute their superior qualities. Instead, they should be expelled or exterminated. War, therefore, was not merely a possible result of a dynamic policy but a preferred, inevitable, and essential part of the plan. The space Hitler sought was in the East, chiefly in Russia and the areas it ruled. The point is made plainly and repeatedly both in *Mein Kampf* and in Hitler's *Second Book,* sometimes called his *Secret Book* because, although written in 1928, it was not published in Hitler's lifetime. In *Mein Kampf* he flatly and openly rejects the limited revisionism of a return to the 1914 situation:

> And so we National Socialists consciously draw a line beneath the foreign policy of our pre-War period. We take up where we broke off six hundred years ago. We stop the endless German movement to the south and west, and turn our gaze toward the land in the east. At long last we break off the colonial and commer-

cial policy of the pre-War period and shift to the soil policy of the future.

If we speak of soil in Europe today, we can primarily have in mind only *Russia* and her vassal border states.[150]

In *Secret Book* he spells out his purpose with total clarity: "An additional 500,000 square kilometers in Europe can provide new homesteads for millions of German peasants, and make available millions of soldiers to the power of the German people for the moment of decision. The only area in Europe that could be considered for such a territorial policy therefore was Russia."[151]

The conquest of Russia would be easy, because the Slavs were an inferior race who had been further weakened by the influence of the Jews and Bolsheviks. Weimar revisionists sought friendship with Russia at the expense of Poland. Hitler was little concerned with Poland, trivial as it seemed compared to his plans for the Soviet Union. Its chief importance for him was in its alliance with France, Germany's "grimmest enemy." Since "an eastern policy in the sense of acquiring the necessary soil for our German people" was the core of his plan, "and since France, the mortal enemy of our nation, inexorably strangles us and robs us of our strength, we must take upon ourselves every sacrifice whose consequences are calculated to contribute to the annihilation of French efforts to hegemony in Europe."[152] Germany first must defeat France to clear the road for victory in Russia.

Hitler hoped to carry out his plans in alliance with the British, whom he saw as a nordic, Germanic people whom he admired for their imperial success. To make such an alliance possible Germany would give up, at least in the short run, competition in overseas colonies, world trade, and a great navy. It would avoid the mistakes that had brought on the war of 1914 and acquire what it needed from the conquered territory in the East and the domination of the rest of Continental Europe. As Hannibal and the other Barcids did without a fleet to avoid giving alarm to the Romans, so Hitler was prepared to do with the British. He hoped, also, to work in alliance with Mussolini's Italy, in part because he admired the Fascist dictator, but more because of Italy's value against France. For the Italian alliance he was prepared to sacrifice the Germans who lived in the Italian-ruled South Tyrol (Alto Adige), in spite of his desire to bring all Germans into the Reich. Hitler, then, for all his agreement with most of the goals of the

Weimar revisionists, was something very different. Domestically, he was not merely an enemy of democracy but an advocate of totalitarian tyranny achieved and maintained through the brutal methods of the police state. In foreign affairs he sought, at the least, the domination of the European Continent, including the expropriation, expulsion, and extermination of millions of its inhabitants. In all areas he stood for a crude racialism that aimed at the enslavement or elimination of "inferior" peoples in multiples of millions.

None of this had been kept secret from the German people or the world. On the contrary, Hitler had not only published his ideas and plans in a book but had pounded the message home in countless public speeches. On May 23, 1928, for example, he proclaimed: "I believe that I have enough energy to lead our people whither it must shed its blood, not for an adjustment of its boundaries, but to save it into the most distant future by securing so much land and space that the future receives back many times the blood shed."[153] Hitler benefited from class conflict combined with the fear of bolshevism, and from the economic distress caused by the depression. Although many Germans opposed his rise to power and some continued to resist throughout his career, most found one or more elements in the Nazi program attractive and rallied around their new leader.

In his first few years Hitler needed to concentrate on domestic affairs, establishing and shaping his dictatorial police state, crushing his political opponents, controlling the press and radio, suppressing all political parties but his own, ending all independence of the federal states, and launching a campaign against the Jews. Germany was still weak and isolated, so Hitler worked at reassuring the democratic Western states while he prepared for a major rearmament program and studied their reaction to the new German regime. As we have seen, he kept the leading Weimar officials at the Foreign Office, which produced a comfortable feeling of continuity, and his public statements were gentle and not alarming. In May 1933 he gave a conciliatory speech on disarmament that promised cooperation and moderation meant to encourage the West in its delusions until he was ready to act. The disarmament conference that had begun at Geneva in 1932 presented a challenge, for Hitler feared the proposal of a generous offer that would deprive Germany of a grievance and the freedom to proceed with full rearmament. He therefore insisted that Britain and France disarm to Germany's level at once, a demand they were sure to refuse. That provided him with a pretext for abandoning the disarmament process entirely. In

October he announced Germany's withdrawal from the conference and also from the League of Nations, but he then made speeches promising to hold to agreements on arms control if Germany were treated equally. The Western powers were eager to believe his words and were not turned from their path by his actions any more than they had been deterred from appeasement by the misbehavior of the Weimar regime. In answer to the German withdrawal from the disarmament conference in 1932 the British had produced a new disarmament plan, which they presented on January 30, 1933, exactly the day Hitler became Chancellor. When he, in turn, abandoned the conference, the British, nevertheless, continued to feel "that if they treated Hitler adroitly and did not make the mistake of threatening him, he would return of his own accord to the League and the arms talks."[154]

The Western leaders were not ignorant of the nature of the Nazi government. André François-Poncet, the French ambassador to Germany, warned that Hitler was dangerous and aggressive, seeking vast new goals: "his objective is not, like that of M. Hugenberg, [leader of the German Nationalist Party] to restore, purely and simply, the state of things in 1914."[155] Sir Horace Rumbold, British ambassador to Germany, issued dark reports of the character of the new regime. He told of its rule by terror, its harsh measures against Jews, Communists, Social Democrats, and even nonpolitical critics, its removal of them from their positions and their imprisonment, and he reported that "large concentration camps were being established in various parts of the country."[156] He said there was little hope of "a return to sanity" by the Chancellor and warned that "Germany's neighbors have reason to be vigilant." He also recommended the serious study of *Mein Kampf,* which would demonstrate why Hitler was certain to pursue a course of aggression and war. As early as November 1933 Churchill began the series of warnings against Nazi power and ambitions that would intensify throughout the decade until the war began, insisting that Germany already had begun to rearm and asking the government "to assure us that adequate provision is made for our safety."[157]

The French took the warnings seriously and tried to find a way of containing German power. In 1934 Louis Barthou, French Foreign Minister, tried to organize what amounted to an Eastern Locarno whereby France and the Soviet Union would guarantee the Eastern settlement just as France, Britain, and Italy did the one in the West. It was an attempt to restore a new version of the old Franco-Russian alliance, but Polish hostility to the idea of Russian involvement helped prevent its conclusion. Barthou's successor, Pierre Laval, was able to conclude a Franco-Soviet Pact in May 1935. In it each side promised to consult, to appeal to the League, and finally to take action if a European country threatened or attacked either country, but it lacked any specific miliitary provisions.[158] On the French side its real purpose was to keep Hitler and Stalin apart and prevent the Soviet Union from supplying Hitler in case of war. It never played a serious role in international calculations, though it would provide Hitler with a handy excuse for one of his boldest initiatives.[159]

The British refused to heed the warnings entirely. *Mein Kampf* was not taken seriously but regarded as the ravings of a rabble-rouser that would be discarded once he assumed the responsibilities of power. Typical was the view the weekly magazine *The Spectator* expressed a couple of years later:

> It is true, and it is a pity, that that notorious volume *[Mein Kampf]* is still circulated in unrevised form and regarded as the gospel of the Nazi movement. But even so, if there is some incompatibility between the policies embodied in a volume written in prison by a defeated rebel in 1924 and those proclaimed to the world by the titular head of the German Reich in 1935, it is reasonable to regard the latter as the more authoritative, pending proof to the contrary.[160]

Such proof, of course, was not long in coming, but it was not enough to break through the resistance of the appeasement mentality. An expert on German affairs who would later take the lead in criticism of the Nazis and of their appeasement insisted in March 1933 that "Hitler . . . does not want war. He is susceptible to reason in foreign policy. . . . He may be described as the most moderate member of his party." Only during the question period after his speech did he admit that he had not yet read *Mein Kampf*.[161]

Accepting the warnings of Hitler's evil regime and intentions would have implied taking action against him, but the mood of the country seemed firmly opposed even to the thought of armaments and war, for whatever reason. Only a month after Hitler took power, in February 1933, the Oxford Union held a debate on the motion: "That this House will in no circumstances fight for its King and Country." A noted writer and lecturer, C. E. M. Joad, spoke for the affirmative, asserting that the question was put wrongly. It should have read: "that this House would never commit murder on a large scale whenever the Government decided that it should do so."[162] He described a future war in which bombers would attack Britain within twenty minutes of the outbreak; aerial defenses would be useless since "a single bomb can poison every living thing in an area of three quarters of a square mile." He ridiculed the last war as an exercise in futility and recommended that even if Britain were invaded "only at most a policy of passive resistance should be adopted."[163] The motion passed 275 to 153; when, later on, a motion was proposed to expunge the "King and Country" motion from the record, the proposal was defeated 750 to 138. It has been pointed out that many of those voting were foreigners and that many odd motions are approved by undergraduate debating societies, but when all such considerations have been accounted for the vote must be seen as reflecting widespread resistance among those educated in universities to any idea of pursuing national interests and security or trying to preserve the peace through armaments and deterrence. In 1927 the Cambridge Union had voted for "uncompromising pacifism," and in 1933 in more than twenty universities resolutions like that of the Oxford Union were approved. Whether such actions came to the notice or affected the thinking of Hitler or Mussolini can be debated, but it is hard to believe that they failed to attract the attention of British politicians.

A surer and more potent influence came from a by-election in the London district of East Fulham in 1934. The Labour candidate portrayed his Conservative opponent, who favored maintaining Britain's military strength, as a warmonger. George Lansbury, the Labour Party leader, made a campaign speech in which he promised to "close every recruiting station, disband the Army and disarm the Air Force," and the Labour candidate won, turning a Conservative majority of 14,000 into a Labour victory by 5,000.[164] Studies suggest that domestic issues were more important in what was a general swing to Labour, but the issue of defense versus pacifism surely played a role. In any case "East Fulham frightened the government out of what sense they had."[165] Baldwin's biographer said: "I always felt that the nerve, injured in October 1934, the East Fulham nerve, never quite healed."[166]

There is considerable reason to doubt the accuracy of Baldwin's perception. In the spring of 1935 a survey was conducted in Great Britain, with the blessings of the League of Nations Union, consisting of five questions. The first four were meant to solicit support for the League of

Nations and for disarmament. The fifth, however, asked: "Do you consider that if a nation insists on attacking another, the other nations should combine to compel it to stop by: (a) economic and non-military measures, (b) if necessary, military measures?" Participation was extraordinary: eleven and one half million people, a good majority of all householders, answered. Ten million said yes to all questions except the second half of the last. To that question six and three-quarter million said yes, over two million said no, and two million made no reply. The questionnaire, of course was contradictory, for a yes on question 5(b) was not consistent with support for disarmament in earlier questions, and it was called widely a Peace Ballot and taken as a vote for pacifism, but that was clearly a misinterpretation. "The Peace Ballot had become undesignedly a ringing assertion of support for collective security by all means short of war, and a more hesitant support even for war."[167] The British people appear to have been far more firm and determined to resist aggression than their rulers and betters and would demonstrate their character again before the war came. Churchill was right to say that the response to question five "affirmed a positive and courageous policy which could, at this time, have been followed with an overwhelming measure of national support,"[168] but no politician was prepared to run the risk.

Baldwin's was not the only nerve affected by the belief that the British people as a whole would not support rearmament or military resistance to aggression; there was much better reason to believe that such an effort would encounter powerful opposition from the politicians and the better educated, politically active classes. The Chiefs of Staff warned that "Germany is not only starting to rearm but that she will continue this process until within a few years she will again have to be reckoned with as a formidable military power."[169] The newly formed Defence Requirements Committee (DRC), containing the military chiefs and representatives from the Treasury and Foreign Office, recommended in February 1934 that Japan be replaced by Germany as Britain's first concern and proposed a plan for rearmament to face the challenge. It would increase the home Air Force to defend the British Isles; it would create a very small expeditionary force of six divisions to protect Belgium and Holland; it would start new ship construction for the Navy and complete the fortification of Singapore by 1938. All this would cost some eighty-two million pounds beyond the regular military budget over a five-year period.

These were not excessive goals in light of the dangers facing Britain, but they ran into powerful opposition. Baldwin had by now replaced Mac-Donald as the de facto leader of the National Government, and he was caught between two fires. Clement Attlee, leader of the Labour party, attacked even the trivial increase contained in the 1934 military budget saying, "We on our side are for total disarmament because we are realists," while Churchill assailed the inadequacy of the proposal. Baldwin characteristically tried to appease both sides, telling Attlee that he still had not given up hopes of disarmament and promising Churchill air parity with any country that could reach Britain. "It was, almost verbatim, the same promise Baldwin had made in 1923, when the fifty-two squadron program was first authorized—unfulfilled in the decade that had since elapsed, and destined to remain so for the greater part of another."[170] But the most effective resistance to the DRC plan came from within the government, from the Chancellor of the Exchequer. Neville Chamberlain declared the program financially impossible, cutting the total expenditure to fifty million pounds over the five years. He argued for increasing the share of what remained of the home Air Force, reducing the naval program, postponing work on Singapore, and eliminating the creation of an expeditionary force entirely. The plan finally adopted, though the work on Singapore was restored, was close to Chamberlain's and was therefore quite different from the original DRC proposal. It focused on home defense and entirely abandoned the "continental commitment" dreaded by so many. As its critics pointed out, however, it would signify to Britain's potential allies that it was "abandoning them to their fate," while "the arrival of even small forces which we propose to provide will have an incalculable moral effect out of all proportion to the size of these forces."[171]

Baldwin met violent criticism from the Labour and Liberal members, although he told the House of Commons only about the proposed increase in air power. In his defense he repeated the statement heard first in 1923 and repeated at the time of Locarno: "The old Frontiers are gone. When you think of the defence of England you no longer think of the chalk cliffs of Dover; you think of the Rhine. That is where our frontier lies."[172] Yet no more than before did the government have a plan or the weapons to defend that frontier. "The government, still anxious to maintain economy, virtually decided not to have an army at all. There was to be a 'limited liability' army, fit only for colonial defence. In this odd way, the practical effect of rearmament was actually to increase British isolation: not only the will, but the means, for British intervention on the continent were lacking."[173]

In spite of the decision to rearm, in however a limited fashion, the military budget for 1935 was only slightly higher than the previous years. A group of senior civil servants, worried that the nation was not being informed of the dangers facing it, on their own initiative drew up a white paper that told of German rearmament and the British rearmament required in response. The Cabinet softened its anti-German rhetoric and allowed it to be published in March 1935, but it had little impact. No responsible political leader would take the message of danger from Germany, the consequent requirement of expensive rearmament, and the need to plan for war, at least as a deterrent, to the British people.

The paper appeared as the British and French governments were in the process of presenting to Hitler a new plan for disarmament and European security, in spite of the collapse of the conference. Before he could receive it, using the white paper as an excuse, Hitler announced that, contrary to the Versailles Treaty, Germany had an Air Force. A week later he flatly denounced the remaining military limitations imposed by Versailles and announced the return of military conscription, proclaiming his intention to replace the army of 100,000 long-term volunteers prescribed at Versailles with a force of 36 divisions, about 550,000 short-term conscripts who would provide a deep corps of trained reserves. The new German Army would be larger than the French, and such a force would change fundamentally the European balance of power. In response, Mussolini for Italy and Laval for France met with MacDonald at Stresa, but all that came out of the conference was a common denunciation of Hitler's announcement and a suggestion that they would stand together against future violations of the treaty. It is not cynical to say that "the 'Stresa front' was a front in the sense of a 'bold front' to conceal inner quaverings, . . . as Hitler correctly assumed."[174] It also encouraged Mussolini's plans to conquer Abyssinia as an early step on his establishment of a new Roman Empire. When Mussolini added the words "in Europe" to the official communiqué of the conference no one objected. "The Duce concluded that the path to conquest in Ethiopia [Abyssinia] was open."[175]

The British soon revealed the emptiness of their commitment to defend what was left of the treaty's limitations on German armaments. The chiefs of the Navy were deeply alarmed by the inadequacy of the resources available to meet their responsibilities in the home waters, the Mediterranean, and the Far East. The truculence of Japan and the new threat posed by Germany made the folly of years of retrenchment and neglect of the armed forces, combined with the denial of growing dangers, inescapably clear. The consequences of the errors of the past fifteen years produced a panicky response and serious new errors. Baldwin, who had become Prime Minister in 1935, was pressed by the Admiralty to accept Hitler's offer to negotiate naval limitations, chiefly because of the threat felt from Japan. In the face of a forthcoming election and convinced that the British people opposed rearmament and connected the Conservatives with it, "Baldwin was inclined to accept any agreement that might provide a counter-argument."[176] The result was a naval treaty that granted Germany the right to build a fleet up to 35 percent of the British, a ratio of 45 percent in submarines, which could go to parity when the Germans wished.

The treaty gained nothing for Britain. Even if Britain did not build another ship it would take many years for the Germans, who had a fleet of only 86,000 tons, to reach the 425,000 tons that amounted to the 35 percent of British tonnage, and they would need to do so at the expense of their army. The ratio, moreover, might be comforting so long as the entire British Navy were kept in the North Sea, but if detachments were needed in the Mediterranean or the Far East it would surely be inadequate. Churchill exclaimed in the Commons: "What a windfall this has been to Japan! . . . The British Fleet . . . will be largely anchored in the North Sea [and] when this German fleet is built we shall not be able to keep any appreciable portion of the British Fleet so far from home [as the Far East.]"[177] The diplomatic consequences were no less unfortunate. The Anglo-German agreement was a breach of the Versailles Treaty undertaken without the approval of the other powers. It destroyed the Stresa front and further shook the confidence of the French, which led them to seek help elsewhere, from the USSR, and it widened their rift with Britain. Admiral Erich Raeder, chief of the German Navy, was right to call the naval agreement "a political success for Germany," because Britain, thereby "sanctioned Germany's right thereafter to rearm."[178] Mussolini, whose designs on Abyssinia were well known, took courage when the British said nothing about it at Stresa, and their new appeasement of Hitler and the break the Anglo-German naval agreement had caused with France could only have increased his confidence that Britain would not interfere with his plans.

The Abyssinian Crisis

In 1934 Mussolini was preparing for an attack on the poor and backward African nation of Abyssinia (Europeans called it Ethiopia). In 1896 the Italian Army had been humiliated by a defeat there at the Battle of Adowa, one of the rare defeats suffered by a European power at the hands of a non-European nation. Mussolini was determined to avenge the defeat, begin the restoration of Roman imperial glory, and perhaps to turn the thoughts of Italians from his corrupt and nasty Fascist regime and their economic problems.[179] He began diplomatic preparations in talks with French Prime Minister Pierre Laval in January 1935. They agreed to consult if Germany threatened Austria or continued to rearm in violation of the Versailles Treaty. Laval also made some concessions to Italy in north and northeastern Africa and gave Mussolini a free hand to deal with Abyssinia. The desire for a friendly accommodation led to a misunderstanding on the last point. Mussolini appears to have expected French support, while Laval seems to have been surprised by the Italian desire for a complete conquest.[180]

Alarmed by the Anglo-German naval agreement, the French signed a military agreement with Italy to cooperate against a possible German military action against Austria. The estrangement of Great Britain from France caused by the naval agreement would be a serious problem during the crisis over Abyssinia. Within a few weeks Italian forces and equipment were moving through the Suez Canal to get into position for an attack on Abyssinia, and by June the British could no longer ignore the likelihood of a war. Before the Great War it would have been extremely unlikely that an Italian assault on a weak African nation of no particular value or interest to any of the other European powers would have provoked any meaningful reaction from any of them. The creation of the League of Nations, however, and the accompanying commitments to collective security and to the resistance against aggression changed the situation. In England, especially, popular opinion had seized upon the idea, and any government that openly played by the old rules and neglected the new commitments would be in serious trouble. Faced with the continuing threat of Japan in the Far East, the growing danger presented by Germany, the evidence of French rapprochement with Italy, and the terrible inadequacy of their own military preparations, the Baldwin government found itself in an unhappy position. Trying to avoid the Hobson's choice that awaited them, they sent Anthony

Eden, Minister for League of Nations Affairs, to Rome carrying a proposal that would give Italy part of Abyssinia and, in return, would provide compensation by giving part of British Somaliland to the Abyssinians. Mussolini rejected it, and Eden returned to London just before the results of the "Peace Ballot" were announced.[181]

Within the British government there was little sentiment for a strong stand against Italy, but a considerable feeling that the League could not be abandoned. Yet there was great reluctance to antagonize the Italians and risk driving them to the side of Germany and an unwillingness to resist Mussolini without French support. There was also a keen sense of Britain's military weakness. A new subcommittee called the Defence Policy and Requirements Committee, whose chairman was Baldwin himself, issued a report at the beginning of July 1935, warning that "it is of the utmost importance that this country should not become involved in a war within the next few years. . . . No opportunity should be lost to avoid the risk of war . . . as long as possible." Baldwin personally told Foreign Minister Samuel Hoare, "Keep us out of war, we are not ready for it." Finally, there was the terrible fear engendered by memories of the Great War. King George V pleaded with Hoare, "I have been through one world war. How can I go through another? If I am to go on, you must keep us out of one."[182]

Faced with the need to reconcile these contradictory goals, Hoare pursued what he called "a double policy . . . of negotiation with Italy and respect for our collective obligations under the Covenant, based on Anglo-French cooperation."[183] The difficulty was that Mussolini was not interested in an acceptable deal and France did not wish to oppose him, so that negotiating with Mussolini was inconsistent with collective security and opposing him was at odds with Anglo-French cooperation. As Mussolini demonstrated his intransigence by rejecting all compromises, Baldwin instructed the Navy to take measures necessary should there be war with Italy. The Navy was most unhappy about the prospect. Low levels of support over fifteen years found it in a poor state of preparation. The First Sea Lord, Admiral Ernle Chatfield, asked for delay in imposing sanctions on Italy for as long as possible. The Mediterranean fleet lacked sufficient cruisers and destroyers equipped to fight submarines. The Admiral's second in command told the British ambassador at Cairo "that his ships had enough ammunition to shoot for fifteen minutes!" Hoare took Chatfield's letter to heart: "This country has been so weakened of recent years that we are in no position to take a strong line in the Mediterranean . . . we should be very cautious as to how far and in what manner we force the pace in Paris, with an unstable France and an unready England."[184] Throughout the crisis the British government was discouraged consistently from taking stronger action by similar advice from the Navy.

France's attitude was another deterrent to strong action. The French could not understand Britain's enthusiasm for collective security to defend a backward African nation that still practiced slavery, at the cost of alienating Italy, an ally in the last war and a potential ally against Nazi Germany, when it had been so unwilling to employ it in defense of France's security against German rearmament and revenge. In September at Geneva, Laval, now French Foreign Minister, asked if Britain would be equally willing to apply sanctions in Europe against Germany. Eden could not give a direct and satisfactory answer. Instead he made the case for the League, sanctions, and collective security: to hold the line at Abyssinia would give strength to the League, "and our moral obligation to assist in supporting and enforcing the Covenant correspondingly increased. If, however, the Covenant were now violated with impunity, the authority of the League would be so impaired that its future influence must be negligible in Europe or anywhere else." Laval pointed out that this did not answer the question and, writing years later, Eden conceded, "This may have been true, but the British Government's wariness *and the state of our defences* made it impossible for me to promise unconditional support of the Covenant in the future."[185] (emphasis added) Hoare met with Laval on September 9 and 10 in Geneva, where they agreed that war was too dangerous to risk, so any military action was ruled out lest it provoke Mussolini.

In spite of that, on September 12, Hoare delivered a speech to the Assembly of the League astonishing in the boldness of what it seemed to say. He promised that Britain's government would be "second to none to fulfill, within the measure of their capacity, the obligations which the Covenant lays upon them. . . . The League stands, and my country stands with it, for the collective maintenance of the Covenant in its entirety, and particularly for steady and collective resistance to all acts of unprovoked aggression."[186] This was no sudden burst of enthusiasm by a single minister but had been crafted with the collaboration of Baldwin and Chamberlain. Hoare later described his intentions: it was to be a "revivalist appeal" meant to put "new life" into the League. "At best, it might start a new chapter of League recovery, at worst, it might deter Mussolini by a display of League fervor. If there was any element of bluff in it, it was a moment when bluff was not only legitimate but inescapable."[187]

For internationalists it was "the very speech which they had always hoped to hear from an English foreign minister in such a crisis," but it was empty bombast, as Hoare was quick to communicate to Mussolini. Through his ambassador in Rome he told the Italian dictator that Britain was eager for a settlement, had no wish to humiliate Italy, and neither would employ military sanctions nor close the Suez Canal.[188] Reassured by such communications, Mussolini rejected further proposals for compromise and invaded Abyssinia on October 3, 1935.

The League condemned Italy's action as a violation of the covenant, which called for sanctions of some kind. The ones imposed, and these did not go into effect until November 18, were economic only and did not include an embargo on oil, which, apart from military action, was the only sanction that might have caused Mussolini serious trouble. France continued to hold back; indeed, according to Hoare, Laval secretly was intriguing with Mussolini. The debate in Britain revealed the contradiction and confusion that underlay the government's policies and public opinion. The military chiefs, especially the Navy, continued to advise against any action that might provoke Mussolini, and leading civil servants such as Vansittart in the Foreign Office and Sir Warren Fisher in the Treasury, their eyes focused on the German menace, were strongly of the same opinion.[189] The ministers shared all these misgivings but were unwilling to abandon the League and collective security, especially in light of public opinion. That opinion, however, was ill-informed about the realities and unclear about the strategic issues and their implications. The journalist Kingsley Martin reported the arguments presented at a combined Popular Front meeting he attended in Birmingham:

> The first speaker urged that we must carry out economic sanctions, but in no circumstances must the Labour Party support a war. I followed next and said that, though there was good ground for hoping that economic sanctions would be enough, there was a risk that war would follow, that we should be committed to it if there was war and that we ought to run the risk. The next speaker thanked me for my frankness and said that since sanctions might lead to war, he was altogether opposed to them. The fourth speaker demanded that Britain should at once take drastic steps,

including blocking the Suez Canal, but that there must in no circumstances be a war . . . the meeting ended with an eloquent expression of the Christian pacifist case by Canon Stuart Morris, who was later to be chairman of the Peace Pledge Union.[190]

The same divisions existed within the Labour Party itself. The leadership supported the League and sanctions; Labour's Stafford Cripps denounced the League as "an International Burglars' Union," insisting that "every war entered upon by a capitalist government is and must be an imperialist and capitalist war"; George Lansbury, a radical Labourite, continued to oppose anything but passive resistance. The final vote was overwhelming in support of the leadership, but its meaning remained ambiguous: "Nearly all Labour supporters of collective security continued to say: collective security will stop the aggressor, therefore rearmament is unnecessary."[191]

The government won a huge majority in the elections of October 1935 with a platform containing planks supporting sanctions and the League, but the sanctions did not prevent Italian success in Abyssinia. Voices were raised in favor of an embargo on oil for Italy, but the British Cabinet was reluctant. Hoare and his colleagues were afraid that imposing the petroleum sanction would provoke Mussolini into a "mad dog" act, an attack on the British fleet and a war. The Navy warned again of its unpreparedness, and Hoare complained about the "serious gap in our system of Imperial Defences, which were in a weak state as compared with an Italy mobilised for war."[192] Throughout the crisis he and most other British leaders greatly overestimated Italy's military power and readiness, frightened by the knowledge of Britain's long neglect of its own forces.

By December, however, the Cabinet was on the point of approving an oil embargo, when Hoare went off to Paris and produced the Hoare-Laval agreement meant to provide a peaceful settlement without risking such a provocation. It would have given some sixty thousand square miles of Abyssinia to Italy, and the Italians would have gained a monopoly of economic development in south and southwestern Abyssinia. In return Abyssinia would get a narrow corridor to the sea. The British Cabinet approved it and Mussolini was ready to accept it; if the Emperor of Abyssinia would not, so much the worse for him. News of the deal was greeted in Britain by an outburst of angry disapproval. It was seen widely as a reward for aggression, a blow to the idea of the League and collective security, and an act of cowardice. Hoare was forced to resign and was replaced by Eden, and yet it was not until the end of February that the Cabinet agreed to support oil sanctions that, in fact, were never imposed. By May Haile Selassie fled to London and Addis Ababa fell; the war was over. In July the League ended its sanctions.

In the end, Britain's attempt at a double policy was a disaster that brought about results worse that following either one consistently. Mussolini had achieved his goals, the League and collective security were finished, Britain's prestige was damaged badly, and Italy was alienated, shortly to join forces with Hitler. The democracies seemed weak, indecisive, and cowardly, and their failure and inaction gave courage to their enemies. Lloyd George personified the disgust felt by the British people toward their own government's behavior when he told the House of Commons: "I have never before heard a British Minister . . . come down to the House of Commons and say Britain was beaten . . . and that we must abandon an enterprise we had taken in hand." Pointing to the members of the government on the front bench, he said: "Tonight we have had the cowardly surrender, and *there* are the cowards."[193]

Then and later on critics have blamed the government for not pursuing one of the alternative policies or the other. A few, like Vansittart and Fisher, the Navy chiefs, and some Conservative politicians argued at the time for a prudent, realistic policy that recognized British military weakness and the need to hold Mussolini as an ally against Hitler and so was prepared to sacrifice Abyssinia as Britain almost surely would have done in previous centuries. But this, as Correlli Barnett, points out, "was 1935, not 1835 or 1735. English foreign policy was no longer a matter simply for the foreign secretary or even the Cabinet."[194] Whatever the merits of a policy purely of *Realpolitik* it was all but impossible in the Britain of 1935, as it has remained in Western democratic countries ever since. It is, in fact, a requirement of true realism in the modern world to recognize the inescapable role of what has come to be called ideology but is not very different from what once was called honor. By 1935 the British public would not ignore the commitment to resist aggression, especially on the part of a dictator against a weak country, even without regard to their country's capacity to resist effectively. A government trying to ignore that would be rejected not only as mistaken but, as the reaction of many Conservatives and of Lloyd George made clear, as dishonorable.

What of the alternative, a decision to take strong measures against

Mussolini, e.g., an oil embargo, a naval barrier in front of the Suez Canal, even a war? There is reason to think that an oil embargo might have been effective. In 1938 Mussolini told Hitler at Munich that its imposition might have brought him down.[195] In the mood of the day such actions would have gained public support and acclaim. Why did the British government shy away from them? We have seen that they were, in general, eager to avoid a war of any kind. They were especially reluctant to lose the friendship of Italy, probably to the advantage of Hitler. They knew that France did not support such a policy and were reluctant to carry the full burden of a possible war almost alone. Perhaps the most powerful explanation, however, was their belief that their military and naval forces were inadequate and unready to fight, a belief that was repeatedly and forcefully presented to them by the service chiefs and officials.

In part, the Navy's negative evaluations and recommendations arose from its leaders' distaste for the newfangled foreign policy of the League and collective security and a wish to carry on in the traditional way of pursuing purely national interests. Admiral Chatfield's views were probably typical. He "in common with the other service chiefs, had little use for the League and none for the policy of sanctions." The nation's commitment to them were misguided and dangerous. He could not see why they should create a menace to their communications with the Far East "for a moral motive."[196] At the same time, however, the leaders of the Navy had a legitimate sense of the inadequacy of their resources caused by fifteen years of disarmament.

The result of this combination of attitudes and concerns was an excessive caution, a defensive mentality, an emphasis on risks over opportunities, a willingness to present political opinions in the guise of military estimates, and most seriously, a loss of strategic imagination. To the government the Navy leaders spoke of the threat of Italian air power but did not take it seriously themselves. Admiral of the Fleet Lord Cunningham confirmed many years later essentially what Admiral Chatfield said at the time of the Italian Air Force: "we were not disposed to attach too much weight to its ability to affect the issue. As the war was to prove we were right."[197] They emphasized the dangers of fighting alone against Italy, without French help. At one point the Chiefs of Staff sent a report that Cunningham described as "a very pessimistic, not to say defeatist, view of the Mediterranean Fleet's capacity to deal with the Italians."[198] But neither the attitude of the French nor the fear of Italian air power "seriously affected the supreme confidence of the Admiralty in the ability of its fleet to handle the Italians in the Mediterranean, even in a singlehanded war."[199] What they seemed to fear was that in the course of winning they would suffer such losses as would make them vulnerable and encourage other enemies—Germany, but particularly Japan—to strike and cause Britain to lose the next war. There is no reason to believe that these fears were justified. Germany was in no condition to take any military action, and Japan was occupied fully in Manchuria and China. As for significant losses caused by Italy, it is hard to take such fears seriously in light of the justified contempt the British officers expressed for the Italian Navy, whose performance in the war to come would be far from impressive. Nor did they give adequate thought to the larger strategic consequences of giving way to a breach of the international order. They failed to see the important advantages for keeping the peace of demonstrating Britain's will and capacity and the dangers of inaction and perceived weakness. They thereby were failing in their responsibility to keep the peace and encouraging those who would break it at Britain's expense.

The lessons learned by the Army leaders, however, were different. They breathed a sigh of relief at the demise of the covenant and collective security. Now they would be "freed from the vague, wholesale and largely unpredictable military commitments which we at present incur under the League Covenant."[200] But Britain's situation required international alliances and associations to protect its interests and security, and these inevitably must involve "unpredictable military commitments" to interests that seem marginal to one's own if these associations are to function. The Army leaders sought to pare down the conditions in which Britain might fight to those that could not provide the needed protection, and the politicians accepted their advice without complaint.

But what if the British had taken a bolder course and taken a clear position in opposition to Mussolini's aggression? It seems more than likely that France and other states would have provided assistance. It is a paradoxical truth that for a nation to lead a coalition into risky actions it needs to show its willingness to act alone, while an unwillingness to act without prior agreement encourages hesitation. Even acting alone, moreover, the British had no good reason to fear the outcome. "To us in the Mediterranean Fleet," wrote Admiral Cunningham, it seemed a very simple task to stop [Mussolini]. The mere closing of the Suez Canal to his transports which were then streaming through with troops and stores would effectively have cut off his armies concentrating in Eritrea and elsewhere. It is true that such a drastic measure might have led to war with Italy; but the Mediterranean Fleet was in a state of high morale and efficiency, and had no fear whatever of the result of an encounter with the Italian navy.[201]

Adolf Hitler, it seems, expected Britain to do exactly what Admiral Cunningham described. When the Italians asked him for a loan of ships for their expedition he told the minister carrying the message:

Let the Italians have a hundred ships! We'll go back, undamaged. They will go through the Suez Canal, but they will never go further. The British navy's battleship *Repulse* will be waiting there and signalling: "Which way are you going?" "South," the Italians will reply. "Oh no you're not," the *Repulse* will reply. "You're going north!" and north they will go.

To his personal adjutant he said:

If I had a choice between the Italians and the English, then I would take the English. Mussolini is closer to me, but I know the English from the last war. I know they are hard fellows. If Mussolini thinks he can chase away the English fleet from the Mediterranean with his own, he is very much mistaken.[202]

But the English stood aside of their own accord, and Mussolini took Abyssinia. Eden defended his government's policy in the House of Commons by saying that "you cannot close the Suez Canal with paper boats,"[203] but Hitler and Mussolini knew that the British ships were of steel and fully capable of stopping the Italian fleet. Admiral Cunningham believed that "had we stopped the passage of Italian transports through the Suez Canal, and the import of fuel oil into Italy, the whole subsequent history of the world might have been altered."[204] Instead, in the midst of the crisis in which the British were demonstrating their weakness of will, on March 7, 1936, the Germans marched an army into the demilitarized

Rhineland, violating the Versailles Treaty, which they had been compelled to sign and the Locarno pact to which they had agreed voluntarily.

The Remilitarization of the Rhineland

The remilitarization was a violation of Clauses 42 and 43 of the Versailles Treaty, therefore a "hostile act" meant "to disturb the peace of the world." A "flagrant violation" of Article 4 of the Locarno treaty required its signatories to bring immediate assistance to the state whose claim to assistance was approved by the League. France, therefore, was free to call on Italy, Belgium, and Britain for military aid and to take military steps of its own.[205] The demilitarized Rhineland, besides, was the most important element in the security structure for France created by the Versailles Treaty. It made a German attack on France or the low countries all but impossible, and it opened Germany to an attack from the west that would be difficult to resist. This served as a guarantee for the small countries of Central and Eastern Europe, for any aggression in that direction would open Germany to a French invasion and a two-front war. France's security relied on the credibility of the threat that it could attack Germany successfully, and the demilitarized Rhineland was essential to that credibility.

For Hitler the demilitarization was especially damaging. It interfered with his plans for rearmament and for the expansion to the east to achieve *Lebensraum* for the German people. In addition to the other differences between Hitler and his predecessors there was one of pace. Hitler was in a great hurry. He had huge plans, and he rightly believed that his own participation was necessary for undertaking and achieving them, yet he feared that he might suffer an early death. He must, therefore, force the pace and create opportunities where none seemed to exist. He seems to have spoken about remilitarization as early as the summer of 1935, although as late as February 1936 he appears to have thought that the action might have to wait until 1937.[206] The distractions of the Abyssinian affair, however, the divisions it caused among the Stresa Front powers, and the hesitation and inefficacy of the British and French reaction made him speed up the timetable.

By November 1935 the French and British began to receive warnings from their ambassadors and others that Hitler would soon move troops into the Rhineland. One of those making the prediction was General Maurice

Gamelin, Commander-in-Chief of the French Army, who clearly underscored the danger such a move would present. In January he warned that Germany would take the Rhineland in order to "neutralize the French Army by constructing on its western frontiers a fortified barrier comparable to our own. . . . Hence, free from any fear of an offense from us, Germany would be completely at liberty to settle the fate of the Little Entente powers."[207]

In spite of their clear understanding of the dire consequences that would follow remilitarization, the French "not only lacked a previously prepared plan for a military countermove to remilitarization but did not even begin to prepare one while all . . . intelligence and diplomatic sources were telling them that such a step was impending."[208] Scholars have written of the French military's cast of mind prior to the First World War as being part of a "cult of the offensive,"[209] but after that war, as we have seen, they appear to have formed a "cult of the defensive," symbolized by the Maginot Line, which was to prove far more devastating in the war to come. To be sure, there was an offensive element in French military doctrine that projected offensive operations after a defensive phase. "The defensive phase would wear down enemy strength and permit France and its allies to mobilize their forces. Methodical attacks sustained by massive firepower would then overwhelm hostile positions."[210] In the years between the wars, however, French military leaders became ever more impressed with the increased advantage offered by firepower: "The great destructive power of the new weapons strengthened the defense, and relatively fewer men could establish a virtually impenetrable barrier of fire."[211] As a result, the offensive element continued to shrink as the defense came to the fore and dominated the French military mentality. The logic of France's situation from 1919 on required a not very large mobile force always at the ready to perform just such a task as presented itself in March 1936, but that would have meant thinking offensively on a tactical level as part of a larger defensive strategy. Such thinking was rejected not only by the soldiers but also by their civilian masters: one government after another had held to the position that there was no need for the Army to be prepared for "spontaneous offensive action." The only plan of action called for a general mobilization of all the forces that would take weeks. What was wanted was "a kind of military flyswatter, supple and relatively unmenacing; instead military doctrine prescribed a sledge hammer."[212]

Hitler sent his small force into the Rhineland on March 7, another of his "Saturday surprises" meant to catch the more casual diplomats of the day on weekend, hampered from making a swift response. His formal excuse was that the Franco-Soviet Pact, clearly directed against Germany, was a violation of the Locarno treaty that nullified its demilitarization of the Rhineland. This was a thin pretext later rejected by the League of Nations, but it was accompanied by a burst of promises for future good behavior: Hitler claimed to be ready to negotiate with France and Belgium for new demilitarized zones on either side of their borders; to sign nonaggression pacts with them guaranteed by Britain and Italy; to make such agreements also with the Eastern states; to work out the guarantees against air attacks so eagerly sought by the British; and to return to the League of Nations when it was properly reformed.[213] Speaking in the Reichstag for foreign consumption that same night, he concluded his speech with the pledge that "now, more than ever, we shall strive for an understanding between the European peoples. . . . We have no territorial demands to make in Europe. . . . Germany will never break the peace." The French ambassador in Berlin characterized all this as follows: "Hitler struck his adversary in the face, and as he did so declared: 'I bring you proposals for peace!.' "[214]

Neither the French ministers nor soldiers had any thought of a military response. As far back as February the government had decided that in case of such an action by the Germans France would appeal to the League of Nations, "a course of action which implicitly meant that France considered the violation to be of a nonflagrant character against which unilateral countermeasures would not be justified."[215] On the day after the German action the French formally sent their protest to the League. Thereafter, in spite of arguments within the French government and tough talk from French Foreign Minister Gaston Flandin to the British about sanctions, even military ones, to be taken, there was no chance that France would move. The civilian leaders found it convenient to blame the timidity of the military for their inaction. The military leaders angrily denied the charge, but the documents reveal that in the midst of the crisis, as early as March 9–10, General Gamelin told his fellow officers that "the soldiers had been forced to restrain the politicians."[216] Still, the politicians were not hard to restrain. Apart from their own unwillingness to act, they took note of the attitudes of the French people as reflected in the press. From the royalist Action Française on the right came the cry "We do not march against Hitler with the Soviets!" The left, which had no sympathy for Hitler, nonetheless argued for understanding and inaction. The Socialist *Populaire* said: "It was stupid to believe that a great country of more than sixty million people would put up with, seventeen years after the war, the demilitarization of part of its territory. . . . Hitler has torn up a treaty, he has broken all his promises, but at the same time he speaks of peace and of Geneva. We must take him at his word."[217]

The British, too, had been well warned about the likelihood of a German move in the Rhineland, and the new Foreign Minister, Anthony Eden, was aware of its significance. In February he told his colleagues that the disappearance of the demilitarized zone would "not merely change local military values but is likely to lead to far-reaching political repercussions of a kind which will further weaken France's influence in Eastern and Central Europe."[218] Nonetheless, he was unwilling to fight to protect the zone, preferring to negotiate, using remilitarization as a bargaining chip. In response to the question from Flandin of what Britain would do if Germany broke the Locarno agreement by remilitarizing the Rhineland, Prime Minister Baldwin said that neither country was in a position to take military action against Germany. The plan, then, was to find a way to get Germany back into the Rhineland without violating treaties and to try to get in return an air agreement—all with France's participation. Before there was time for negotiation Hitler moved into the Rhineland. Eden immediately urged the French "not to make the situation more difficult." Over the weekend he wrote a memorandum for the Cabinet arguing against military action or even demands that Germany withdraw its troops. The thing to do was to "conclude with [Germany] as far-reaching and enduring a settlement as is possible whilst Herr Hitler is in the mood to do so."[219]

The government perfectly reflected the feelings of most of the people of Britain. Ardent appeasers like Lord Lothian, Lord Waldorf and Lady Astor and Baldwin's close friend and adviser Tom Jones met at Lothian's country house to formulate a policy for the country. Jones telephoned the results to the Prime Minister, urging him to welcome what had happened, which was trivial in comparison to the accompanying peace proposals, to refuse to be dragged into danger by France, and to "accept Hitler's declaration as made in good faith and put his bona fides to the test by trying it out." The historian Arnold Toynbee was also at the party. He had just come back from a visit with Hitler where he had heard two hours worth of talk delivered "with masterly coherence and lucidity" that convinced him "of the Führer's sincerity in desiring peace in Europe and close friendship with England." The *Times* of London's editorial was called A CHANCE TO REBUILD, and it called Hitler's offers as the best hope of stabilizing Europe. George Bernard Shaw said it was just as if the British had reoccupied Portsmouth.[220]

The politicians in Parliament had a similar reaction. In the Labour party even Hugh Dalton, an advocate of resistance to Germany, said that "the Labour Party would not support the taking of military sanctions or even of economic sanctions against Germany at this time," while his colleague Arthur Greenwood was delighted to find the new situation "pregnant with new and great possibilities for the future of the world."[221] The Conservative member Harold Nicolson did not distinguish between parties when he described the mood in Parliament and looked beneath the surface to explain its source: "The country will not stand for anything that makes for war. On all sides one hears sympathy for Germany. It is all very tragic and sad." In his diary he wrote: "General mood of the House is fear. Anything to keep us out of war."

Ordinary people also took the occupation of the Rhineland calmly. Eden reported the comment of a taxi driver: "I suppose Jerry can do what he likes with his own back garden, can't he?"[222] It was a phrase that has been attributed to Lord Lothian, Lord Halifax, and to Geoffrey Dawson, a leading champion of appeasement who was editor of the *Times,* and it caught on widely. It reflected the understandable ignorance of most people about the strategic significance of what had happened and of the character of the regime that had carried out the coup, as well as eighteen years in which educated opinion had minimized the threat from Germany, sympathized with its grievances, and complained of the aggressive unreasonableness and selfishness of France. They found it especially hard to understand what was wrong with the Germans gaining full sovereignty over a part of their own country, even if that required the violation of international treaties. In the midst of the crisis the British Secretary of State for War told the German ambassador that the British people would not fight on account of the coup in the Rhineland: "The people did not know much about the demilitarization provisions and most of them probably took the view that they did not care 'two hoots' about the Germans reoccupying their own territory."[223] Their leaders had given them no help in understanding these things over the years nor did they in 1936.

British policy was to avoid war at all costs, to seek negotiations with

Hitler, and to speed the pace of rearmament. In their unwillingness to fight, the government was supported strongly by the military leadership. The Chiefs of Staff saw war with Germany as "a disaster for which the Services with their existing commitments in the Mediterranean are totally unprepared."[224] To be sure, their estimates were pessimistic as usual. They were keenly aware of how badly their forces fell short of what might be required of them in all eventualities, but they also grossly overestimated the capacity of the enemy, and in war it is comparative rather than absolute strength that counts. In the Rhineland itself, although General Gamelin claimed that Hitler had placed 265,000 troops there, the actual number was 22,000 men and 14,000 local police.[225] In overall military strength there were seventy-six French Army divisions plus twenty-one Belgians against thirty-two Germans. At sea the Western powers had an overwhelming superiority. In the air the Germans had an advantage in bombers but not in fighters; besides the Luftwaffe was hardly out of its infancy. The German Air Staff reported that in the spring of 1936 its strength would not be enough to fight a war against France and Czechoslovakia "with the slightest chance of success."[226] In addition, the Czechs and Rumanians had offered France their support. On March 9, thinking France would move, Poland offered to activate its military alliance.[227] If France had moved and all the promises were kept, well over a hundred divisions would have moved into Germany from several directions at a time when "German rearmament was only beginning and the first conscripts had only been taken into the army a few months before."[228] A. J. P. Taylor was only exaggerating to a degree when he said that "The actual move on 7 March was a staggering example of Hitler's strong nerve. Germany had literally no forces available for war. The trained men of the old Reichswehr were now dispersed as instructors among the new mass army; and this new army was not yet ready. Hitler assured his protesting generals that he would withdraw his token force at the first sight of French action: but he was unshakably confident."[229] In his testimony at Nuremberg General Alfred Jodl, high in the ranks of the Wehrmacht, said: "Considering the situation we were in, the French covering army could have blown us to pieces." Hitler himself later said that "a retreat on our part would have spelled collapse. . . . The forty-eight hours after the march into the Rhineland were the most nerve-wracking in my life. If the French had then marched into the Rhineland we would have had to withdraw with our tails between our legs, for the military resources at our disposal would have been wholly inadequate for even a moderate resistance."²³⁰

The consequences of the remilitarization of the Rhineland were enormous. Hitler emerged much strengthened internally, and Germany's power and influence were greatly increased. His evident success raised the dictator's popularity with the German people to new heights. The American ambassador to London wrote that " 'an overwhelming majority of Germans' would support any venture which Hitler might undertake."²³¹ Hitler's stature with Germany's diplomats and military leaders, mostly carryovers from the old regime, was much increased, and their willingness to challenge him and his plans undermined. Success also increased his own self-confidence. As he sped home from a triumphant tour of the Rhineland, Hitler "turned to his cronies in the special train and once again expressed his relief at the limpness of the Western powers: 'Am I glad! Good Lord, am I glad it's gone so smoothly. Sure enough, the world belongs to the brave man. He's the one God helps.' "²³² The inaction of the French and British emboldened him to proceed with his aggressive plans. He was now convinced that France would not attack without British support and that Britain would not fight to prevent Germany from taking Austria or Czechoslovakia.²³³

The most important results were strategic. The presence of a German army in the Rhineland, however small and unprepared, confirmed the French Army in its commitment to a purely defensive strategy. The Germans were free to build fortifications on their western front that could be held with relatively few troops. Even more important, they could now use all of Germany's industrial capacity to prepare for war. Eighty percent of Germany's coal lay in the Rhineland and the Ruhr, and while these regions were open to French invasion they could not be developed safely and counted on. "The action of 7 March enabled Hitler to launch his four-year programme, which was designed to mobilize the German economy for a large-scale war by the autumn of 1940."²³⁴ France's inaction, moreover, encouraged Belgium to break off its alliance, made in the 1920s with France, and to move to neutrality, which left a critical gap at the end of the Maginot Line, further increasing France's defensive mentality and putting even the defensive strategy in greater doubt. It helped persuade Mussolini to conclude the "Rome-Berlin Axis" in October 1936, an agreement between the dictators that further complicated France's strategic problems. It also entailed withdrawal of Italian protection from Austria, a prerequisite for Hitler's annexation of Austria. After March 1936 "there could be no doubt that, with the disappearance of the demilitarized Rhineland, Europe had lost her last guarantee against German aggression."[235] That, in turn, meant that the French would not take offensive action in the West if Germany attacked their allies in Eastern and Central Europe. "The Rhineland *coup* sounded the deathknell of the eastern pacts."[236] As Premier Albert Sarraut said in April 1936: "the essential point is that France cannot allow Germany to build fortifications in the formerly demilitarized zone. We would find it impossible to intervene effectively in order to assist our eastern alies."[237] Having permitted the *coup,* however, the French could not prevent the fortification nor defend their allies.

For many years it was common for historians to look upon the remilitarization of the Rhineland as a critical moment. A typical statement by a distinguished scholar reads: "It was one of the great turning points in history, of higher significance than what occurred in Munich two years later."[238] That view was challenged sharply by A. J. P. Taylor:

> It was said at the time, and has often been said since, that 7 March 1936 was "the last chance," the last occasion when Germany could have been stopped without all the sacrifice and suffering of a great war. Technically, on paper, this was true: the French had a great army and the Germans had none. Psychologically it was the reverse of the truth. The Western peoples remained helpless before the question: what could they do? The French army could march into Germany; it could exact promises of good behaviour from the Germans; and then it could go away. The situation would remain the same as before, or, if anything worse—the Germans more resentful and restless than ever.[239]

There is no trouble in answering that challenge. A decisive military action by the French might have humiliated and discredited Hitler, putting an end to his especially dangerous regime. As Hitler himself told the British ambassador, "with dictators, nothing succeeds like success."[240] By the same token, nothing fails like failure. It is also important to ask what might not have happened. Belgium surely would not have sought safety in neutrality. The industrial power of the Rhineland and the Ruhr would not have been safely available to the German military machine. There would have been no effective fortifications of Germany's western frontier to deter a French invasion the threat of which, in turn, could deter a German attack on France's eastern allies. Finally, the Rhineland would not be available "for its traditional purpose of providing the assembly area for great armies intended for the invasion of France and the Low Countries."[241]

A different challenge to the traditional view has more merit. Its advocates point out that the die had been cast well before 1936. To point to the real superiority of the French Army ignores "all those factors of opinion, nerve and determination which made it a foregone conclusion that the superior French power would not be used in the event." The remilitarization was only "the culmination . . . of all that had already passed between Germany on the one hand and France and England on the other in the three years since Hitler had come to power in Germany."[242] It is possible to go further and say that it was the result of almost two decades in which the terrible memories of the last war and the frightening horrors of aerial bombardment projected for the next, disguised and made respectable by revisionist interpretations of the causes of the last war and of the unfairness of the treaties that concluded it, led to a refusal to face unpleasant realities and to think strategically, to maintain a system of defense and the will to use it that would be adequate to deter aggression and preserve the peace.

For all the truth in such a line of thought, however, it is still correct to think of March 1936 as a lost opportunity, a last missed chance to stop Hitler before he became a deadly menace. The great misfortune of the Western powers was that they lacked leaders at this moment of crisis wise enough to understand the situation and strong enough to move against the current. Even had the French chosen to use their "sledgehammer" after a slow and full mobilization, there can be no question of their ability to drive the German troops out of the Rhineland. But no one in their weak interim government had the will, the persuasive ability, or the power to order such an action. British encouragement or even support could have had a powerful effect, but the members of the Baldwin government, although they had proclaimed that Britain's frontier was on the Rhine, although the stationing of German forces in the Rhineland and even more, a German conquest of France, would assist immensely those air attacks on Britain that so terrified them, were not willing to take the step. Baldwin and his Cabinet had the power to act, and no one can be certain that an effort to make the danger clearly understood combined with bold leadership, especially if it brought success, would not have found support. As a careful student of the crisis has put it: there is no "way of knowing what might have been the effect if public opinion had been given a strong lead by the government, both during and after the crisis."[243] But Baldwin and his colleagues were men of their time and place, averting their eyes from unpleasant realities, paralyzed into inaction and hoping for the best.

From the Rhineland to Vienna

At the very beginning of *Mein Kampf* Adolf Hitler, born in the town of Braunau am Inn in Austria, wrote that the reunion of Germany and Austria was

> a task to be furthered with every means our lives long. German-Austria must return to the great German motherland, and not because of economic considerations of any sort. No, no: even if from an economic point of view this union were unimportant, indeed, if it were harmful, it ought nevertheless to be brought about. *Common blood belongs in a common Reich.*[244] [Emphasis in original]

Because of its intrinsic importance and because it was essential for his future plans, Hitler's next major goal was *Anschluss,* the union of Germany and Austria. On the diplomatic front Hitler hoped to win over to his side both Britain and Italy, isolating France. In *Mein Kampf,* once again, he designated Britain as potentially the most valuable of allies, but his attempts to draw closer failed. For all their internal confusion and weakness, the British never completely lost sight of the fact that their security was intertwined with the security of France.

The relationship with Italy went better. Hitler had expressed his admiration for Mussolini in *Mein Kampf* as early as 1923, but the latter's resistance to Germany's machinations in Austria in 1934 had led to tension between the dictators. Hitler's friendly neutrality during the Abyssinian war, however, helped bring them together. The occupation of the Rhineland, moreover, helped divert the Western powers from employing the oil sanction, allowing Mussolini to win his war. Hitler then recognized the conquest of Abyssinia, which France and Britain refused to do, bringing Fascist Italy and Nazi Germany still closer together. Finally, the outbreak of the Spanish Civil War in July 1936 provided a further opportunity for rapprochement.

Both Germany and Italy aided the rebel dictator Francisco Franco against the Popular Front loyalist forces of the Spanish Republic, ostensibly as part of their fight against Marxism. For Mussolini it was an opportunity to flex his military muscles and to assert his claim as the leading Mediterranean power. For these purposes he sent comparatively large forces to Spain. Hitler's goals were more complex. He hoped to get economic advantages in return for his aid to Franco. The Spanish War also usefully diverted Mussolini's attention away from the defense of Austria, further alienated him from the Popular Front government in France, and strained relations between Britain and France. For these reasons, as well as from the desire to limit Germany's risk, Hitler made only a small, if important, contribution to Franco's campaign. His goal was to keep the war going as long as possible since, for Germany, "a hundred percent victory for Franco [was] not desirable."[245] In November 1936 the two dictators agreed on a declaration of common interests in foreign policy that came to be known as the "Rome-Berlin Axis." At the same time Germany signed an Anti-Comintern Pact with Japan, and a year later Italy joined it as well, loosely uniting the three revisionist powers that had abandoned the League of Nations. The Axis Powers came into being, ending Germany's diplomatic isolation and putting further strain on the resolve of Britain and France.

The Spanish War weakened France by intensifying its internal political disunity, distracting its attention from Central and Eastern Europe, and placing it further under the dominance of Britain. The French Left thought that fascism must be fought in Spain, not in Central Europe, and supported Soviet involvement on the side of the Republic and closer relations between France and the Soviet Union. The Right was friendly to Franco, denounced Soviet involvement as an attempt to start a European war, and bitterly opposed any thought of a Franco-Soviet alliance. The Popular Front government under Léon Blum annoyed both sides by its policy of ineffective friendship with the Spanish Republic and its half-hearted cooperation with the British policy of nonintervention.

To strengthen their position against Germany the French attempted to establish firmer agreements with Poland and the Little Entente, the association formed by Czechoslovakia, Yugoslavia, and Rumania in 1920 and 1921, but they were brushed aside or flatly rejected. The Yugoslavs preferred to make a nonaggression pact with Italy, and President Edvard

Beneš of Czechoslovakia considered a similar agreement with Germany. The remilitarization of the Rhineland had changed the balance of power fundamentally, and the attitudes of the small states changed with it. The French began conversations with the Soviet Union but got nowhere. Military leaders did not want a true military alliance with the Soviets, in part because of their hostility to communism, in part because they feared that an alliance would enrage Hitler, and in part because they doubted its military value. When the Blum government fell in June 1937 discussions of such an alliance stopped until shortly before the outbreak of war. These failures and the dangers to which France was exposed pushed the French even further to take their lead from Britain. "By 1936 Great Britain was the leading rider in the Anglo-French tandem."[246]

British Rearmament

One consequence of the events of 1935–36, both in France and in Britain, was to launch a serious effort at rearmament. Abyssinia and Spain clearly demonstrated the incompetence of the League of Nations and the inefficacy of collective security. The Rhineland coup underscored the boldness and strength of the new Germany. Reluctantly, the Western democracies were driven to the conclusion that armed force must play some role in deterring aggression and keeping the peace, and that the dictatorships were challenging their military superiority. In Britain the general election of 1935 had given the Baldwin government a mandate for rearmament. In July 1937 even the Labour party decided thereafter to abstain on armaments expenditure instead of continuing to vote against them, but the vote within the party was close "and was provided mainly by inarticulate trade unionists. The leaders were still mostly on the other side."[247] Torn between the contradictory positions that Germany had legitimate grievances and that Nazism had to be resisted, between a commitment to collective security and an opposition to the use of force, Labour still seemed to oppose rearmament. Attacked by Churchill in the Commons for his slowness in getting started, Baldwin defended his actions:

> Supposing I had gone to the country [in 1933], and said that Germany was re-arming, and that we must re-arm, does anybody think that this pacific democracy would have rallied to that cry at

that moment? I cannot think of anything that would have made the loss of the election from my point of view more certain.[248]

But it was not public opinion that shaped British policy in those years. The government leaders themselves were opposed to rearmament for all the reasons already described; it was only the alarm caused by recent events, chiefly the growing menace of Germany that changed their policy. The arms budget for 1936, increased to £159 million, was still only half of Germany's annual expenditure, and Baldwin created the office of Minister of Public Defence, although he placed in it the unprepossessing Sir Thomas Inskip[249] instead of the fire-eating Churchill. He had little power or influence, and the post "became little more than a fresh treasury brake on the demands of the services."[250]

The questions shaping British rearmament can be divided into two fundamental categories: economic and strategic. How much did Britain need to spend, and how much could it afford? How should the expenditure be distributed among the forces, and how should those forces be used? In reality, of course, these questions could not be separated clearly, and different decision makers approached them from different perspectives. From 1933 on the Chiefs of Staff recognized Germany as a serious potential threat to British interests and security, so they saw the resulting need for an expeditionary force that could be swiftly and effectively landed on the Continent to defend the Low Countries in collaboration with France. Even as it deplored the state of Britain's small professional army, the Field Force as it was called, to avoid memories of the Expeditionary Force of 1914, the annual review for 1935 of the Chiefs of Staff reaffirmed that "the integrity of the Low Countries is, with the advent of air power, of greater importance than ever in our history, and the Army must be prepared in conjunction with the French, to attempt to deny those countries to German invasion."[251] In spite of strong differences of opinion between the services they continued to present a united front on this point, but powerful forces worked against its implementation. The public and, even more, their leaders, were haunted by terrible memories of the trench warfare in the last war and the frightful casualties that came with it. They were persuaded by the revisionist views that the British had been dragged into a war not vital to them by commitments to the Continent and by secret talks between French and British military staffs, all of these views reinforced by antiwar books and films. These opinions were further supported by a pervasive dislike and suspicion of the French, the notion that they were grasping and ambitious, had a powerful army, and could well take care of themselves, alternating with its opposite, that they were corrupt, weak, and degenerate, bound by treaties to a lot of eastern countries of no importance to Britain that were certain to bring them into a disastrous war against Germany, dragging the British along with them. Basil Liddell Hart, the influential military writer, wrote persuasively and often about the need to return to "an allegedly historic 'British Way in Warfare' founded upon sea power and the instrument of blockade, associated with a policy of 'limited liability' towards any military commitment to the Continent."[252]

Another proposed escape from the Continental commitment was the magical force imputed by some to air power. By concentrating expenditures on the Navy and the Air Force, it was said, Britain might deter a future war or even substitute for the Army in winning one. General John Burnett-Stuart was an outspoken advocate of the policy of "limited liability." He scorned the idea of training the Army for another "Battle of the Marne." The Royal Air Force (RAF) should take over the job of the Expeditionary Force, which would be conducted "without risk and without the entanglements which developed as soon as we landed troops on the continent." Aware that the plan of sending an army to the Continent was still part of the plan, he was certain that "to send the British Army to a Continental War in its then condition would be to condemn it to disaster." Such a sacrifice would do no good either for France or for Britain. The idea, in his view, shattered "when faced with the fact that we had no Expeditionary Force fit to send." He remained "obsessed by the iniquity of a policy which accepted for the army a most exacting and hazardous commitment, and at the same time denied it the means of making itself fit to meet it."[253] He was certainly right about the miserable condition of the Army, which was tiny in size, poorly equipped, badly trained, backward in military doctrine and weapons, uncoordinated with its likely allies, and without a clear strategic mission. The natural response of the Army might be expected to include demands for an increase in money and men, even the conscription that would surely be required to recruit the numbers needed, but Army requests remained polite and modest.

In part this reflected the realities of public and ministerial opposition to great expenditures for military purposes, to sending British armies to fight on the Continent, and to conscription, but there was also another element. British officers remembered not only the bitter experience of casualties expended in ground offensives that produced little or no military gain, but also the terrible criticism of the generals like Haig and French who had ordered them. "Flanders" and "Passchendaele" had the same paralyzing effect on British generals as "Vietnam" and "the Tet Offensive" have had on American generals since 1975. They had their own "Never Again." They "were worried that the ill-prepared Expeditionary Force would be dispatched in an emergency and that they would be unjustly held responsible for the resulting massacre."[254] Never again would they expose their armies to conditions in which they could not be certain of having a decisive advantage and a prospect of victory without heavy casualties and of being immune themselves to charges of stupidity, incompetence, or callous bloody-mindedness.

Between the wars, therefore, "there was no equivalent of Sir Henry Wilson . . . pressing single-mindedly and almost fanatically for a military undertaking to support France." Any such attempt would have played into the hands of critics like Liddell Hart, "who believed that the army was led by Colonel Blimps eager to repeat the blood-letting of the Somme and Passchendaele."[255] The Chiefs, therefore, pressed the diplomats and ministers to delay war at all costs, strongly supported attempts to appease potential enemies, and vigorously opposed staff conversations with potential allies. When British inaction at the Rhineland coup helped persuade the Belgians to withdraw into neutrality, the Belgians, nevertheless, sought staff talks with the British Army. The Chiefs of Staff "remained adamantly opposed to staff talks with either France or Belgium on the grounds that news of them would be leaked and Britain would be committed. It would be a repetition of 1914 all over again."[256]

In November 1935, nonetheless, as we have seen, the Defence Requirements Committee produced a report recommending a broad program of rearmament: the Navy should be built up to a Two-Power Standard that would allow it to defend Britain's interests in the Far East against Japan and the home waters against Germany; the Air Force was to be expanded vastly; in case of war with Germany the five regular divisions of the field force should be backed up by twelve divisions of the territorial army, trained and equipped for modern warfare, the regulars to be on the Continent within two weeks, the territorials within four to eight months. The proposals were passed on to the Defence Policy Requirements Committee, headed by the Prime Minister, who added William Douglas Weir, a Scottish lord and manufacturer with considerable experience in military production. Weir riddled the Army proposal, asserting that it would be less effective than air power and objecting to its cost: "there appears to be no more difficult or costly method of making our contribution to our Allies in Europe than through increased British Army strength." A devoted adherent to the idea of strategic bombing, he proposed instead shifting expenditures toward the offensive element of the Air Force so that it would "represent the most effective possible deterrent to any European enemy."[257] The Chiefs pointed out that an earlier study had demonstrated that, given the limited range of the bombers of that day, Britain must defend the Low Countries to protect the home islands from German air attacks. They might also have pointed out that British bombing attacks on Germany would also be far easier and more likely to be effective if launched from bases on the Continent closer to their targets.

Without meeting such arguments, Weir trumped them by overwhelming the military men with economic and industrial difficulties. Accepting all the committee's suggestions would be too costly, requiring excessive interference with normal business activities. Besides, it would be impossible to move forward with the entire program because of the industrial bottlenecks that would result, caused chiefly by the shortage of skilled labor. This was and remains a telling point and presents an important example of how the policies of the 1920s helped determine the limits within which the men of the 1930s could work. By disarming all but totally, the British not only left themselves incapable of meeting current challenges but also mortgaged the future. When key industries are reduced to a skeleton force or abolished entirely they also destroy the pool of trained workers without which future expansion in the face of new necessities is badly, sometimes fatally, delayed. One important lesson to learn from a study of this period is:

> As long as a nation maintains its military forces and industries so that they can withstand the strain of rapid expansion and contraction, there need again be no agonizing four-year lag, such as the British endured, during which the British foreign office was obliged to weigh virtually every diplomatic move on the basis of whether it would gain or lose time for rearmament.[258]

Neville Chamberlain, Chancellor of the Exchequer, firmly supported Weir on all points. One of his most powerful arguments over the years was that finance was the fourth branch of the armed services. Economic stability was an essential part of the defense program; economic stability and strength would serve as a deterrent to possible enemies. By maintaining the strength of its currency and international credit Britain could buy what military equipment it needed until its own industry could take on the load. In a long war economic power would be decisive, so it was necessary to limit the pace of rearmament. But if Hitler meant Britain harm, could not be appeased, and was not stopped, the war might be short and disastrous. Chamberlain refused to be moved by such a possibility. He feared that rearmament at the most rapid pace would weaken the pound, encourage inflation, hurt British trade, and destabilize both the economy and the society. "The aim of keeping armament expenditure constantly below the inflationary threshold by means of the twofold strategy of détente and moderate rearmament, thus forced the British to fix defensive priorities in armament expenditure and military strategy."[259]

From his powerful position in the Treasury Chamberlain insisted that the economy could not bear the strain and that public opinion would not support the effort. The appeal to public opinion was frequent, but it was selective, and Chamberlain did not hesitate to circumvent it when convenient.[260] In March 1936 the Cabinet was very sensitive about the great increase in expenditures recommended in the "Defence White Paper" they put forth. Chamberlain suggested that it would be better "to avoid figures which could be added up to a larger amount than public opinion was anticipating."[261] The published document did not give a total amount, and concealed a great many vital and expensive details.

Against a Continental Army Chamberlain argued that if Germany attacked the Eastern countries there would be no need of a British Expeditionary Force in the West. If, on the other hand, the attack came in the West, a British force might arrive too late to help. "By this marvelous logic," says Telford Taylor, "the need for a field force appeared to be entirely eliminated."[262] Chamberlain also urged the shift of resources from the Army to the Air Force, and he won the argument. At first Baldwin was pressured into a compromise in which the regular forces would be made ready, but the preparation of the territorials put it off for three years. When Chamberlain became Prime Minister in May 1937, however, it was decided not to prepare the regulars for Continental service either. By December Minister for the Coordination of Defence Sir Thomas Inskip's list of defense priorities put cooperation "in defence of the territories of any allies we may have in war" in last place, to be provided only "after the other objectives have been met."[263] The new Secretary for War, Leslie Hore-Belisha, whom Chamberlain had appointed in place of Sir Alfred Duff Cooper, a vigorous advocate for a Continental Army, agreed and saw a bright side to the decision: "he thought that when the French realized that we could not commit ourselves to send an expedition they would be the more inclined to accelerate the extension of the Maginot Line to the sea."[264] By February 1938 Great Britain had cut the field force down to three divisions for use "in an Eastern theatre," to be used on the Continent only after a review by the General Staff of "the whole field of possible action open to the enemy." In the same month Chamberlain persuaded the government to tell the French "that they must not *count* upon any force whatsoever, and that the maximum we could send would be two divisions."[265] In the words of Michael Howard, "a policy of 'limited liability' in continental warfare had now shrunk to one of no liability at all."[266]

From 1936 to 1938 Britain's military leaders had argued that a Continental commitment was needed to protect the Low Countries, from which an enemy might launch deadly air raids and even an invasion. Their defense demanded the cooperation of France, and French morale required the preparation and commitment of an adequate British Expeditionary Force, as well as staff talks to facilitate their military preparations. Throughout 1936 and 1938, however, they took their cue from the powerful new Prime Minister who was determined to avoid a repetition of the war of 1914. "The last thing they now wanted was any kind of involvement on the Continent which would, they feared, saddle them with obligations they could not possibly fulfill."[267] They shied away from the suggestion of staff talks with the French, saying that "the very term 'staff conversations' has a sinister purport and gives an impression . . . of mutually assumed military collaboration." If news of them leaked the result would be "the very situation we wish to avoid, namely the irreconcilable suspicion and hostility of Germany." Such statements led Eden to believe that the Chiefs of Staff wanted "to clamber on the bandwagon with the dictators, even though that process meant parting company with France and estranging our relations with the United States."[268] That view was too strong, but the Chiefs did want the politicians and diplomats to pursue a policy of appeasement that would "reduce the number of our potential enemies and to gain the support of potential allies." They wanted the government to do what it had done in the first decade of the century, to use diplomacy to improve the odds.

> But the world had changed since 1904. Britain's potential adversaries did not include a France willing to purchase European security at the price of colonial expansion, or a Russian Empire torn by internal revolution and external defeat [or a less powerful and aggressive Japan]. They consisted of predatory powers who regarded appeasement as a surrender and came back for more.[269]

But neither the soldiers nor the politicians and diplomats were prepared to believe that. Chamberlain's policy of appeasement was meant to avoid war altogether and so make it unnecessary to send an army to the Continent. The soldiers, many of whom saw war as unavoidable, only wanted time for further rearmament. Few of them considered that the Germans might make better use of the delay than the British and become still more formidable. "They consistently gave 'worst case' appreciations over the possibility of supporting Czechoslovakia, in the process ignoring evidence that the latter would put up a formidable defence."[270] It was only after Munich, when the strategical balance had shifted so obviously in Germany's favor, and especially after the German occupation of Bohemia in March 1939, when appeasement obviously had failed, that they returned to a plan for putting an army on the Continent, now with the full support of the government. The cost of the previous policy, however, was great. "Belgium and France had lost confidence in Britain's support on land, while conversely Hitler was strengthened in his belief that she would remain aloof if he launched a quick, decisive attack in the West."[271] When war came France and the Low Countries quickly fell, providing bases close enough to permit the heavy aerial bombardment of the British Isles that almost drove Britain from the war.

Paradoxically, it was the growth of air power that persuaded Chamberlain and many others that the British Army need not be sent to the Continent. It was the fear of a "knockout blow" from the air and an obsession with the promise and danger presented by the airplane that helped rationalize the rejection of the traditional importance of the Army: "to the British Government rearmament came to seem almost a question of air power alone. Cabinet discussions tacitly assumed that the next war, if it came, would take the form of a direct, almost a private duel between the

British and German Air Forces."[272] At the heart of such thinking was the paralyzing fear of the effects of aerial bombardment. In 1937 the experts expected that in case of war the Germans would launch an attack that would last for sixty days, producing casualties of 600,000 dead and 1.2 million injured. Other estimates added millions suffering from psychological disorders. Accepting these estimates, health officials later calculated that 1 to 3 million beds would be needed as soon as war broke out.[273]

These appraisals were grossly exaggerated. Although the Luftwaffe had given serious thought to strategic bombing, German efforts and expenditures for air power went chiefly to support for ground forces in the *Blitzkrieg* to come. Such bombers as they had and were building lacked the range to be effective against Britain from German bases and were vulnerable to attacks from fighters. The fighter escorts that might have protected them had even shorter ranges. Even after the fall of France and the Low Countries gave the Germans bases close to Britain, British defenses imposed fearful losses. In the six years of the war civilian casualties from air attack in Great Britain, including the dreaded V-1 and V-2 unmanned rockets toward the end of the war, were about 295,000, of whom 60,000 were killed.[274] But few put any stock in defense against aerial attack in the mid 1930s. The dominant theory was that of strategic bombing formulated most influentially by the Italian Giulio Douhet and embraced enthusiastically by Sir Hugh Trenchard as marshal of the RAF. Right up to the beginning of the war the RAF put its hopes in the deterrent effect of the threat of massive bombardment from the air and minimized the prospects of a defensive strategy. It is astonishing, therefore, that in the 1930s, after two decades in which these notions ruled British air strategy, the RAF had only foggy notions of just how they would use their bomber force and whether it was capable of achieving its task. By 1938 it clearly was not and would not be before 1941 at the earliest.

The civilian ministers, however, had been pressing for the reverse strategy, a heavier reliance on fighters and defense at the expense of bombers and offense. This was not because of their superior strategic or technical cleverness. They were "right but for the wrong reasons, which were that fighters were cheaper and less disturbing to the financial 'ration,' and quicker to build so that front-line strength could be more quickly increased toward the politically magic 'parity.' "[275] Early in 1935, moreover, a British scientist, Robert Watson Watt, supported by a government committee established by Baldwin, successfully demonstrated the principle of a system that could detect approaching airplanes by reflected radio waves that came to be called radar, and within two years a chain of coastal radar stations was begun. Within another year, swift, fast-climbing fighter planes, the Hurricane and the Spitfire, armed with eight guns, lethal to slower, unescorted bombers, had been tested successfully. The foundations for the effective air defense that would win the battle of Britain were in place. Churchill respectfully called this competition in applied science and technology the "wizard war," just as a later generation would sardonically call a similar effort to defend against attacks by missiles "Star Wars," but his contemporaries were not much impressed. When the RAF was granted additional funds as late as 1939 and permitted to spend them as they chose they spent them on bombers, even though until shortly before the war few of them could reach Berlin. "Two sevenths of them could reach the Ruhr from British airfields. Three sevenths of them would have to use French or Belgian bases, though expenditure on aeroplanes had made it impossible to provide an army with which to protect these bases."[276] Except for the almost fortuitous developments in aerial defense, therefore, British rearmament was both too little and too late to serve as a deterrent, and it left Britain in poor shape to fight the war when it came. The material, psychological, and moral disarmament carried out in the 1920s made the task of those governing Britain in the next decade very hard. The men of the 1930s, however, largely shared the outlook and attitudes of their predecessors. They were reluctant to revise or abandon them in the face of new circumstances and the increasing evidences of danger. Only slowly and reluctantly did they begin to rearm materially; their psychological and moral recovery came even later.

Chamberlain replaced Baldwin as Prime Minister in May 1937, with important consequences for Britain's rearmament, strategy, and foreign policy. Like so many of his contemporaries Neville Chamberlain was moved by the horror of war, the fear of its reappearance, and the belief that an attitude of conciliation and generosity toward the beaten foe, never mind at what cost to its potential victims, would somehow keep the peace. The chief lesson he learned from his complete focus on the one most recent analogy was to avoid the "mistakes" he believed had caused the previous war. A recent, not unsympathetic examination of Chamberlain's performance makes this very clear:

At the public level, Chamberlain was like most of his contemporaries, profoundly affected by the First World War, and he later entered politics with the conviction that, above all else, the mistakes of the past must not be repeated. So powerful were these historical memories that in 1938 at Munich, and in the months that followed, it was almost as if Chamberlain saw not Hitler and his unique threat to the peace of Europe, but rather the kaiser of 1914 repeating the same disastrous mistakes which had led to the "Great War."

Chamberlain believed that the alternative to coming to terms with Hitler would be another world war, infinitely more devastating than the last, and that therefore almost any act of political accommodation was fully justified, not only justified, but indeed the only conceivable course of moral action. It was these considerations rather than a belief that the Treaty of Versailles ought to be revised, or an appreciation of British weakness, or the need for domestic political unity, which were in the end decisive. As a result, Britain backed resolutely into war with Germany with her eyes focused doggedly on the past.[277]

Such attitudes were at least understandable while Germany ostensibly was disarmed and led by the divided, weak, and relatively unpopular governments of the Weimar Republic, but the advent of Adolf Hitler and his powerfully centralized, militaristic Nazi regime, openly dedicated to the destruction of the treaties ending the previous war and the balance of power they had created, produced no change of course. Chamberlain put little faith in the League of Nations or collective security. Britain must accept the responsibility of creating and maintaining a peaceful world. He was not a pacifist. Before the Great War he had been an aggressive proponent of a strong national policy. In 1908 during the Bosnian crisis he made a speech in which he said that "treaties are not to be depended on for keeping the peace . . . we have got to make ourselves too strong to be attacked."[278] In the next year he was one of those demanding eight new battleships instead of the four proposed by the government to win the naval race against Germany, and in 1910 he spoke in favor of conscription.[279] But the experience of the war changed him profoundly. Beyond the horror of the general slaughter he was shaken profoundly by the deaths of two cousins on the Western Front. "Thereafter he was inspired by a profound detestation of force as a means of solving disputes between nations."[280] He had always felt the need to equal or surpass his father, who had earned his reputation as a champion of empire, and his half-brother Austen, who had negotiated the Treaty of Locarno. "Neville believed his place in history would be secured as the prime minister who achieved the appeasement of Europe."[281]

He was a strong, active leader, convinced that only he had the understanding and talents to bring Britain through those trying times; he had a secure majority in the House of Commons; he was the unchallenged leader of his party; and he had a clear plan of action to preserve the peace. It was a dual program of rearmament to achieve a position of strength and respect that would permit an active and aggressive policy of appeasing the complaints of the discontented powers. Although in many respects it seemed to continue the policies pursued by Baldwin, there were important differences between the quiet drift of Baldwin's approach and Chamberlain's active appeasement: "The main ingredients of Chamberlain's diplomacy—sense of urgency and mission, determination to be his own foreign secretary, dislike of the foreign office, faith in personal diplomacy, willingness to make unreciprocated concessions, contempt for France and the League—taken together formed a distinctive approach."[282]

Even before becoming Prime Minister he had favored increased spending for armaments. As Chancellor of the Exchequer he took bold steps to pay for the cost of rearmament, at some political risk to himself, introducing deficit spending, a rise in the income tax, and a tax on business profits called the National Defence Contribution. All he was prepared to support, however, was a "quick fix," a single investment in 1936 and 1937 that would raise the low level of British military power to a point that would permit the kind of diplomacy he had in mind. Thereafter he resisted calls for increased expenditure on armaments even as Germany's power grew and her policy became more menacing.

His plan was to achieve stability and peace by the active attempt to discover Hitler's demands and to allow and even help him to achieve them without war. He regarded Hitler and Mussolini as rational men like himself with limited goals who could be dealt with by flexibility and reasoned discussion, and he was eager to get on with it. He did not permit himself to consider the possibility that their demands might be unacceptable or even unlimited. Nor did he let strategic considerations affect his willingness to accept actions and demands, such as Germany's annexation of Austria and of the Sudeten area of Czechoslovakia, that threatened the security of Poland and the rest of Eastern Europe, and therefore of France and Britain. To think of strategy was to consider the possibility of war, to plan for it, and to prepare for it, and that was a course of action that was unthinkable.

For that reason he accepted the decline of French influence in Central Europe and the inevitability that Germany would become the dominant power in that area and in the Balkans. After all, that had been Britain's view since the 1920s, ratified by the Locarno agreements negotiated by his brother Austen.[283] He also understood that Germany was bound to fill the vacuum and regarded that as acceptable, so long as the changes were brought about peacefully. He did not concern himself with the worry expressed on some occasions by Eden and a few others that with France so weakened and power so unbalanced, a Germany so strengthened might turn against the West and achieve the Continental domination that would alarm even Chamberlain. He was not without doubts about the Germans, sometimes expressing the opinion that *they* were the source of danger in Europe and that force was the only language they understood, but he refused to be driven off course by such thoughts. After reading a book that accurately laid out the true nature of the Nazi system, he wrote in 1937: "If I accepted the author's conclusion, I should despair, but I don't and won't."[284] (emphasis added)

In less than a year Chamberlain rid the crucial positions in his government of those men who held the wrong views. Duff Cooper was removed from control of the Army, where he had insisted on arguing for a Continental commitment, and sent to the Admiralty, where he was kept under tight rein. Neville Henderson, a man who became notorious for putting the German case in London better than he put the British case in Berlin, was appointed ambassador to Germany. He was instructed personally by Chamberlain and faithfully carried out his program of appeasement because he fully agreed with it. Sir Robert Vansittart, permanent undersecretary in the Foreign Office, increasingly outspoken in his criticism of Nazi Germany, was kicked upstairs to a position without power and replaced by Sir Alexander Cadogan, who presented no such problem. Chamberlain's industrial adviser, Sir Horace Wilson, actually became his principal adviser and representative in foreign affairs. His greatest experience was in industrial relations. He "shared the illusion that the same arts of round-table negotiation which served with English employers and trade unionists would also serve with Adolf Hitler."[285] Wilson, likewise, shared Chamberlain's views and faithfully served his master. In February 1938 Eden resigned as Foreign Minister. He was by no means an enemy to the policy of appeasement, as few British politicians and officials were at the time, but he was not enthusiastic for it and had and expressed moral scruples about it that caused discomfort among others. Both in policy and personality he was too independent, and he was replaced by Lord Halifax, a novice to foreign affairs who was Chamberlain's man. Surrounded by men who agreed with him, or were his creatures, or lacked knowledge, experience, and independent standing, Chamberlain was free to conduct his policy toward Germany without interference.

Even before he became Prime Minister, in April 1937, he set forth his ideas to the Cabinet Committee on Foreign Policy. He argued that it was time to end the policy of drift and discuss with Germany the political guarantees Britain wanted as part of a general settlement: a new agreement for the security of Europe to replace the shattered Locarno agreements; Germany's return to the League; an arms limitation agreement; a set of treaties in which Germany promised to respect the integrity of European states, including one with Czechoslovakia. How would Germany be persuaded to agree to these things? Chamberlain's suggestion was that Britain could offer "financial help in restoring her economic system." In light of Germany's currently booming economy and Britain's financial troubles, this suggestion was "not a little amazing."[286] Until the outbreak of the war Chamberlain would continue to try to win German good will and good behavior by offering economic incentives, a program that has been called "economic appeasement." A student of that program offers the following evaluation:

> Economic appeasement, like appeasement as a whole, was based in the final analysis on a total misinterpretation of the National Socialist regime and its objectives. In return for every agreement, Berlin demanded prior unconditional recognition of its political hegemony on the Continent. Britain could not grant these concessions without sacrificing her own security and risking another continental blockade. Again and again she laid her hopes on the "moderates" among German politicians and businessmen, but they never really stood a chance against the party extremists led by Hitler. According to the aggressive ideology of *Lebensraum* the German economy had the sole function of preparing for autarky

and war. Such a policy, which from 1938 manoeuvred constantly on the brink of war, was incompatible with a concept based on "economic reason" for which the preservation of peace was the basis for combatting national difficulties.[287]

Chamberlain, of course, made different assumptions and eagerly sought a chance of starting discussions with Germany.

The opportunity came when Halifax, not yet Foreign Minister but in his capacity as master of the Middleton hounds, was invited to the International Hunting Exhibition in Berlin. Chamberlain seized upon the event as an opportunity to begin the dialogue with Hitler, and Halifax went on from Berlin to meet with the Führer at Berchtesgaden. Halifax began the new policy at once:

> I said there were no doubt other questions arising out of the Versailles settlement which seemed to us capable of causing trouble if they were unwisely handled, e.g., Danzig, Austria, Czechoslovakia. On all these matters we were not necessarily concerned to stand up for the *status quo* as to-day, but we were concerned to avoid such treatment of them as would be likely to cause trouble. If reasonable settlements could be reached with the free assent and goodwill of those primarily concerned, we certainly had no desire to block.

This was an invitation for Hitler to press forward with the revision of those remaining aspects of Versailles that displeased him, with advance notice that Britain had no intention of getting in the way if only he behaved with some small degree of decorum. Chamberlain regarded the visit as a "great success, because it achieved its object, that of creating an atmosphere in which it is possible to discuss with Germany the practical questions involved in a European settlement."[288]

The next step was to come to an understanding with the French, for the great danger to Britain's policy of appeasement was that France might honor its commitments to it allies in Central and Eastern Europe, especially to Czechoslovakia, with whose people the French were very popular and with which France was particularly close. If Hitler should attack the Czechs, France come to their aid, and Germany attack France, Britain would find it hard to stay out of the war. On November 29 and 30, 1937, therefore, Camille Chautemps and Yvon Delbos, Prime Minister and Foreign Minister since late June, came to London to seek closer relations with the new British government. Chautemps was conscious of French weakness externally and internally. He lacked Chamberlain's determination and direction. He described his own policy as one of "wait and see," and Delbos's idea of a policy was one of "making concessions to Germany piecemeal in order to stave off war." Édouard Herriot, President of the Chamber of Deputies, gave words to a general feeling that the limited manpower and resources of France made it impossible for it to act like a great power and support its Eastern allies. Édouard Daladier, Minister of War, whose nickname was "the bull of the Vaucluse," said that France could not afford "the Napoleonic luxury" of fighting any but a completely defensive war, and the General Staff report of February 8, 1939, placed any offensive action against Germany to help the Central European allies last among the Army's priorities, to be undertaken only "if possible" and "at a convenient time."[289] The Germans got the same impression about France's intentions as Halifax had given to Hitler at Berchtesgaden: the French would not raise an objection "to an evolutionary extension of German influence either in Austria . . . or in Czechoslovakia."[290]

It is conceivable that the French might have taken a stronger stance had they been confident of British support, but nothing had changed in that respect. It is interesting to speculate what would have happened had France firmly stated an intention to go to the aid of Czechoslovakia or Poland if they were attacked, forcing the British to face the realities of a German war with France, but Chautemps and Delbos were not the men to take such a position, if any French statesman could have been. They went to London only to seek, if they could, what increasingly seemed France's only hope for security: closer cooperation, perhaps even an alliance, with Great Britain. During their November visit to London, Chamberlain "took over the reins of the Franco-British team and guided it until the outbreak of war."[291] The French appeared to be asking British support for a stand in defense of Czechoslovakia, but hard questioning from Chamberlain made it clear that they were not serious and had written the Czechs off already. What they wanted was an excuse for not acting, which Chamberlain readily supplied, making it clear that Britain would not join in a war for Czechoslovakia. In the face of such a declaration Chautemps "saw reason." "The abandonment of a weak nation," he said, "aroused feelings of indignation. But it was not necessary to see the matter in such a direct and crude way. . . . The important thing was to maintain peace," and there was no point in anticipating events. "Frightened by what they glimpsed, the French ministers closed their eyes to the Czech problem." Chamberlain set forth what had been agreed as follows: "It seemed desirable to try to achieve some agreement with Germany's aims, even if she wished to absorb some of her neighbors." On his forthcoming trip to Prague Delbos would ask Beneš "how far he is able to go in making concessions to the Sudeten Germans."[292]

Hitler's Plans

While the Western powers were thinking how they might give Hitler what he wanted he was planning how he might take it. On November 5, 1937, he called together his Foreign Minister, Konstantin von Neurath, and his military chiefs, Werner von Blomberg and Fritsch for the Army, Erich Raeder for the Navy, and Hermann Göring for the Air Force, and Hitler's own adjutant, Colonel Friedrich Hossbach, whose memorandum is the source of our knowledge of what took place.[293] Hitler told those assembled that the subject was so important that it could not be discussed in a wider circle; that his views were the result of long and careful thought and experience; that they represented his basic ideas about Germany's international position; and that, in case of his death, they were to be considered his last will and testament. In almost every respect these ideas were the same as those expressed in *Mein Kampf,* the one important exception being that he no longer expected a British alliance. His views now were expressed with regard to the opportunities then available to Germany and the consideration of a number of plans of action contingent on the course of events. He emphasized Germany's need for living space to be acquired in the East, but now he counted on the opposition of "the two hateful antagonists England and France,"[294] which would have to be removed before the Eastern expansion could take place. This must be accomplished before 1943–45 because by then Germany's military efficiency would have begun to decline and economic problems would cause further difficulty. Before France and Britain could be attacked, however, Austria and Czechoslovakia must be removed as a danger "to our flank in any possible operation against the West."[295] The best moment for the removal of that menace would be if France were paralyzed by internal strife or by war with another major power (presumably Italy). In any event, a favorable opportunity must be seized as soon as possible because the military strength of the two Central European states was growing, and the advantages of gaining control of them would be great:

> The annexation of Czechoslovakia and Austria would mean an acquisition of foodstuffs for five to six million people. . . . The incorporation of those two states with Germany meant . . . a substantial advantage because it would mean shorter and better frontiers, the freeing of forces for other purposes, and the possibility of creating new units up to a level of about twelve divisions.[296]

Although Germany must be ready to strike with the speed of lightning, Hitler was not sure that fighting would be needed, for he believed that France and Britain already had given up the idea of any military assistance to Austria or Czechoslovakia.

Such were Hitler's plans as revealed to his Foreign Minister and military chiefs. The conference reveals a man with fixed aims from which he never departed who was also entirely opportunistic as to when and how they should be achieved. Until then there had been little disagreement between the Führer and the conservative leaders who had stayed on since the end of the Republic. Some of them were very nervous during the Rhineland reoccupation, but so was Hitler, and there was no real rift. At the November conference, however, his auditors were shaken badly by the grandeur of his ambitions and the risks they presented. Blomberg, Fritsch, and Neurath openly expressed doubts and reservations. Fritsch was especially alarmed because he had a memorandum from his Chief of Staff, Ludwig Beck, painting a frightening picture of Germany's unreadiness for war. In case of war, said Beck, "our position would be inconceivable."[297] Even Göring, not a man from the old order but as close as anyone to Hitler, expressed concern about Hitler's plans. Fritsch and Blomberg warned against risking war with Britain and France and, even without help from the West, regarded Czechoslovakia as a serious obstacle. To clear the way for action Hitler soon purged Fritsch, Blomberg, and Neurath, eliminating the doubters, and replacing them with men who were entirely his creatures, prepared to carry out his program with enthusiasm.

There can be little doubt that Hitler had speeded up his timetable because of the behavior of the new Western leaders. The Halifax interview had made that clear at Berchtesgaden, and Delbos made a similar statement soon after: "France . . . had no essential objection to a further assimilation of certain of Austria's domestic institutions with Germany's."[298] Together with the removal from power in Britain of Eden and Vansittart, these were clear signs that German expansion in Central Europe would not meet serious resistance from the West. The one remaining potential obstacle was Italy. Mussolini always had resisted German unification with Austria. In 1934, when an attempted coup by the Austrian Nazi party threatened to bring that about, Mussolini sent an army to the Austrian border to prevent German intervention. It was the low point of German-Italian relations, but the events of 1935–36 changed their direction. Western policy helped drive the two dictators together. In the Abyssinia affair the Western powers had alienated Mussolini without frightening him, while Hitler behaved with benevolence. The remilitarization of the Rhineland showed the democracies' weakness and lack of resolve and greatly strengthened Germany. The civil war in Spain found the dictators fighting on the same side and drew them closer together. Finally, in November 1937, Mussolini told Joachim von Ribbentrop, Germany's new Foreign Minister, that "France knows that if a crisis should arise in Austria, Italy would do nothing. . . . We cannot impose independence upon Austria."[299]

The Anschluss

All that was left was to bring Austria into the Reich, which Hitler seemed to expect could be done without war. He called the Austrian Chancellor, Kurt von Schuschnigg, to Berchtesgaden and bullied him into legalizing the Austrian Nazi party, as well as bringing pro-German Austrians into key positions in his government. It seemed only a matter of time until Austria and Germany would be joined fully, when Schuschnigg surprised everybody with a call for a plebiscite to determine whether or not the Austrian people wished to retain their independence. The question was posed in such a way as to guarantee a positive vote and the frustration of Hitler's plans. This forced Hitler's hand, and he prepared for military action, but at the last moment he worried about Mussolini's reaction and sent Prince Philip of Hesse to the Duce to get reassurance. The night before the scheduled invasion, which Hitler insisted upon even though the Austrians had by then yielded on all points, the Führer anxiously awaited the call from Rome. Here is the record of the call:

HESSE: I have just come back from the Palazzo Venezia. The Duce accepted the whole thing in a very friendly manner. He sends you his regards. . . .

HITLER: Then please tell Mussolini that I will never forget him for this.

HESSE: Yes.

HITLER: Never, never, never, whatever happens. . . . As soon as the Austrian affair is settled, I shall be ready to go with him, through thick and thin, no matter what happens.

HESSE: Yes, my Führer.

HITLER: Listen. I shall make any agreement—I am no longer in fear of the terrible position which would have existed militarily in case we got into a conflict. You may tell him that I thank him ever so much; never, never shall I forget.

HESSE: Yes, my Führer.

HITLER: I will never forget, whatever may happen. If he should ever need any help or be in danger, he can be convinced that I shall stick to him, whatever may happen, even if the whole world were against him.

HESSE: Yes, my Führer.[300]

The fervor of Hitler's gratitude may have been justified, for when his untested new army moved into Austria on March 12, 1938, many tanks and other vehicles broke down and littered the sides of the road, but they were not needed. A jubilant population also lined the roads, cheering and throwing flowers. There were many who had no reason for cheers. In the next few weeks the Nazis made seventy-six thousand arrests in Austria and also instigated and assisted mobs engaged in anti-Semitic riots. On March 13 Austria was annexed officially to the German Reich. France and Britain made formal protests, but their hearts were not in it. The French had never intended to fight, and such suggestions as they made to Britain for resistance of any kind were strictly for internal political purposes.[301] In spite of their complacency in advance of the event, the British were somewhat shocked when it took place. Henderson and Chamberlain blamed

Schuschnigg's foolishness for bringing it about, and Chamberlain also put the blame on Eden for having stood in the way of a rapprochement with Mussolini that might have prevented it. Cadogan, Vansittart's successor as permanent undersecretary at the Foreign Office, blamed his predecessor for making a great fuss about Austria "when we can't do anything about it."[302] But their deepest feeling appears to have been relief. A month before Hitler marched into Austria Cadogan said: "Personally, I almost wish that Hitler would swallow Austria and get it over." A month after the *Anschluss* he wrote Henderson: "Thank goodness Austria's out of the way. . . . After all, it wasn't our business: We had no particular feeling for the Austrians: We only forbade the *Anschluss* to spite Germany."[303]

The fall of Austria was a blow to Chamberlain's plan for active appeasement, not because it had put Austria under German control, but because of the manner in which that had happened. The military invasion and the immediate annexation were not lawful and nonviolent, and they violated international decorum, but Chamberlain refused to be discouraged. He told an emergency meeting of the Cabinet on the day of the invasion that Germany's action was "most distressing and shocking to the world," making "international appeasement much more difficult."

> In spite of all, however, [Chamberlain] felt that this thing had to come. Nothing short of an overwhelming display of force would have stopped it. Herr Hitler had been planning to take this action for some time and Dr. Schuschnigg's blunder had given him the chance. . . . So he believed that what had happened was inevitable unless the Powers had been able to say "If you make war on Austria you will have to deal with us."

Such a statement, of course, was out of the question, and Chamberlain, too, seemed to be greatly relieved, concluding by saying, "At any rate the question was now out of the way."[304]

Not everyone took the matter so calmly. Winston Churchill pointed out to the House of Commons that since Vienna was the center of communications of what had been the Habsburg Empire its control gave Germany "military and economic control of the whole communications of Southeastern Europe, by road, by river, and by rail."[305] Such statements showed Chamberlain that the *Anschluss* had strengthened greatly the hands of those "who urged that we should cease to have any dealings of any kind

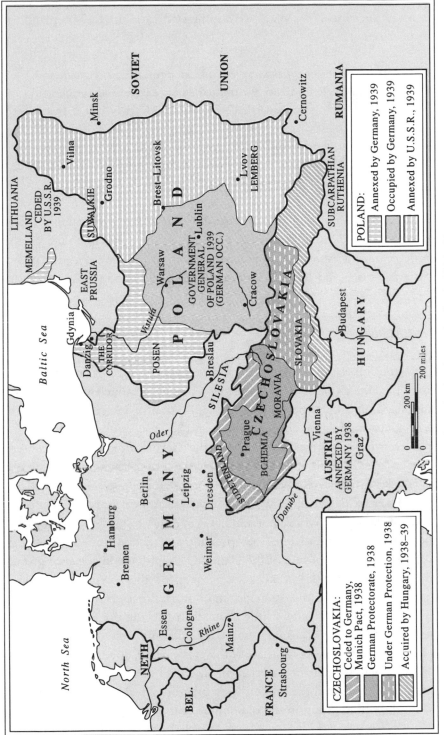

POLAND:

Annexed by Germany, 1939

Occupied by Germany, 1939

Annexed by U.S.S.R., 1939

CZECHOSLOVAKIA:

Ceded to Germany,
Munich Pact, 1938

German Protectorate, 1938

Under German Protection, 1938

Acquired by Hungary, 1938–39

SOVIET

UNION

RUMANIA

LITHUANIA

MEMELLAND
CEDED
BY U.S.S.R.
1939

EAST
PRUSSIA

Minsk

Vilna

Grodno

Brest-Litovsk

Lvov
LEMBERG

Cernowitz

SUWALKIE

P O L A N D

GOVERNMENT
GENERAL
OF POLAND 1939
(GERMAN OCC.)

Lublin

Warsaw

Cracow

POSEN

Vistula

Gdynia

Danzig

THE
CORRIDOR

Baltic Sea

Breslau

SILESIA

SUBCARPATHIAN
RUTHENIA

SLOVAKIA

C Z E C H O S L O V A K I A

MORAVIA

BOHEMIA

Prague

SUDETENLAND

Budapest

HUNGARY

Vienna

AUSTRIA
ANNEXED BY
GERMANY 1938

Graz

Danube

Berlin

Leipzig

Dresden

Weimar

Hamburg

Bremen

North Sea

Oder

G E R M A N Y

Essen

Cologne

Rhine

Mainz

NETH.

BEL.

FRANCE

Strasbourg

200 km

200 miles

0

0

Partitions of Czechoslovakia and Poland, 1938–39

with the Dictators."[306] Many were impressed by Churchill's demand for stronger action:

> If a number of states were assembled around Great Britain and France in a solemn treaty for mutual defence against aggression; if they had their forces marshalled in what you may call a grand alliance . . . if that were sustained, as it would be, by the moral sense of the world; and if it were done in the year 1938—and, believe me, it may be the last chance there will be for doing it— then I say you might even now arrest this approaching war.[307]

But Chamberlain remained firm: "He did not think that anything that had happened should cause the Government to alter their present policy, on the contrary, recent events had confirmed him in his opinion that that policy was a right one and he only regretted that it had not been adopted earlier."[308]

Munich

The annexation of Austria was a strategic advance of critical importance for Hitler's plans. It put Germany directly in touch with Hungary, Yugoslavia, and Italy, permitting the application of increased pressure on them and reducing the chance they would act in defense of Czechoslovakia. Even more important, it enabled the Germans to surround western Czechoslovakia on three sides. The *Anschluss* set the stage immediately for an attack on Czechoslovakia itself.

The state of Czechoslovakia was invented at the peace conference that concluded the First World War and illustrated the impossibility of applying the Wilsonian notion of self-determination of nationalities to European realities. With the collapse of the Habsburg Empire the idea was to give its northern Slavic peoples an independent nation of their own, but to make it viable from an economic, strategic, and historical perspective. The Czechs themselves made up only a little more than half the population, and together with the Slovaks came to some ten million people. Because the new state followed the old boundaries of the provinces of Bohemia and Moravia and also included part of Austrian Silesia it had defensible frontiers, but it also had more than three million Germans. They had been accustomed to being the ruling group in the old empire and deeply resented their inclusion as a minority in a Slavic republic. There were also about a million Poles, Magyars, and Ruthenians, and the regions in which they lived were coveted by Poland and Hungary. Finally, the Czechs and Slovaks, though similar in many ways, were not in their own minds a single people, as the voluntary dissolution of Czechoslovakia in 1992 later confirmed.

The greatest problem came from the Germans, not merely because of their numbers but also of their location. They were settled on and about the western frontier, adjacent to Germany and Austria. To grant independence or autonomy to the Germans would not only damage the country's economic viability and chief railroad arteries but also remove its natural barrier against attack and make it strategically untenable. Concessions to the Germans, moreover, would invite similar demands from the other minorities and lead to the dissolution of the state. These problems existed from the first, but the hard times brought by the Great Depression of the 1930s made them worse. The advent of Hitler's ardently nationalist and racialist regime in Germany made matters still worse, and the *Anschluss* with Austria meant that a crisis was imminent. Political parties in Czechoslovakia were organized along nationalistic lines, and by 1938 almost all the Germans were attached to the Sudeten German party (the land occupied by the Germans was called the Sudetenland) under the leadership of Konrad Henlein. By the time of the crisis he was entirely a tool of Hitler's, accepting his subsidies and taking orders from him.

Hitler always had intended the destruction of Czechoslovakia. In accordance with his racial theories he regarded the Slavic Czechs as subhuman and thought it was intolerable that they should rule over Germans. Czechoslovakia stood in the way of Germany's expansion to the east and was allied to France. It was less than an hour by air from Berlin, and Hitler called Czechoslovakia "a French aircraft-carrier in the middle of Europe."[309] At the meeting with his military leaders and Foreign Minister on November 5, 1937, he had expressed his determination to remove the danger at the first opportunity. When the military situation was favorable Germany would launch "an offensive war against Czechoslovakia, so that the solution of the German problem of living space can be carried to a victorious end even if one or other [sic] of the great powers intervene against us." He might not, in fact, wait that long if "a situation arises which, owing to Britain's aversion to a general European war, through her lack of interest in the Central European problem" or where France and Italy came into conflict, "creates the probability that Germany will face no other opponent than Russia on Czechoslovakia's side."[310] A month later the military leadership produced a plan for an attack on Czechoslovakia called "Operation Green." Hitler counted on a victory that would shorten his frontiers, free troops for other uses and increase his strength further to enlarge his army by enlisting the Sudeten Germans and others, and use the considerable economic and industrial resources of Czechoslovakia to bolster his own power. He hoped that he could isolate Czechoslovakia and fight an entirely local war, keeping the Western powers out of it.

To this end he worked with Henlein to undermine the Czech state. Hitler understood very well Britain's fascination with the idea of national self-determination and the rights of national minorities. It was, therefore, important to claim that Germany sought not the conquest of Czechoslovakia but the protection and vindication of the rights of the Sudeten Germans against their Czech oppressors. The Sudetens were not without some legitimate grievances for understandable reasons, and the Czechs had not moved with the greatest alacrity to remove them, but Hitler did not want them removed. When Henlein came to Berlin for instructions at the end of March 1938 Hitler told him that the Czech questions would be solved very soon and gave him instructions, which Henlein repeated to be sure he had them right: "we must always demand so much that we cannot be satisfied."[311] Throughout the ensuing crisis the British chose to accept at face value the claims of Hitler to be concerned only with the legitimate complaints of the Sudeten Germans, refusing to recognize the mounting evidence to the contrary.

It was the French who had a treaty committing them to defend Czechoslovakia in case of attack, but they were unwilling to undertake war against Germany without British support. The Soviet Union also had a treaty with the Czechs, but it only came into force if the French kept their promise first, so everything ultimately depended on the British. On March 21 the Chiefs of Staff carried out Chamberlain's instructions to report on "The Military Implications of German Aggression against Czechoslovakia."[312] It was a deeply pessimistic document that painted a gloomy picture of Britain's general situation and of its prospects if it fought alongside France and Czechoslovakia in a war against Germany. It found the allies inferior in every relevant respect and it saw Britain threatened by a "knockout blow" from the Luftwaffe. The chiefs considered it possible that a public announcement of Britain's intention to fight for Czechoslovakia might deter Germany unless the Germans realized that "public opinion in Great

Britain was not unanimously behind the Government" and believed that they had, "in the present inadequate state of our defences, of which [they] must be fully aware, a good chance of dealing a knock-out blow on Great Britain, in which case our undertaking would lose almost all its deterrent value." Their conclusion was that "we are not yet ready for war."[313] The report vastly overestimated German strength and underestimated that of Britain and its allies. In the jargon of our time, it matched a best-case analysis of the German situation with a worst-case analysis of Britain's. As we shall see, many of their key facts were wrong, and their estimates deeply flawed. Here it is enough to point out that just two months later General Beck, Commander-in-Chief of the German Army, wrote two memoranda in which he emphasized the weakness of Germany's forces and their un-readiness for war, "describing the superior potential strength of the allies, which must spell Germany's ultimate defeat."[314]

It would be wrong to conclude that these inaccurate British military reports that argued against action had a decisive influence on the course of events. Days before this report by the Chiefs of Staff was received, Chamberlain and his supporters in the inner circle of the Cabinet had decided not to defend Czechoslovakia but to proceed vigorously with a policy of active appeasement aimed at achieving a solution at the expense of Czechoslovakia but without a war.[315] The importance of such military reports lay in the assistance they gave Chamberlain in persuading the rest of the Cabinet to go along. On the same day the report was submitted, a meeting of the Cabinet Foreign Policy Committee considered the proposal by one of its members, Oliver Stanley, to give France a guarantee for the support of Czechoslovakia. Halifax, the Foreign Minister, responded that he and Chamberlain himself had both inclined in such a direction, but the report of the Chiefs, "an extremely melancholy document," had dissuaded them. Instead they proposed to try to "induce the Government of Czecho-slovakia to apply themselves to producing a settlement with the Sudeten Deutsch" and to "persuade the French to use their influence to obtain such a settlement." He called it a "disagreeable business which had to be done as pleasantly as possible." Chamberlain made a similar case, saying that it was hard to believe that "the French would not be glad to find some method to relieve them of their engagement."[316] The Cabinet fell into line and agreed that Britain and France should work to prevent a military outbreak by pressing the Czechs to treat the Sudeten Germans fairly and address their grievances. That policy assumed that they had legitimate grievances that were limited and could be granted without the destruction of Czechoslovakia and that attention to those grievances was Hitler's concern. That is what Chamberlain told the Cabinet. He had sometimes considered other possibilities, writing on one occasion that "force is the only argument Germany understands,"[317] but if he thought of them in the spring of 1938 he brushed them aside. The course he followed was by now habitual for Britain: "The liberal-minded intelligentsia, spurred by their fear of war, were quick to see and sympathize with the Sudeten-German point of view, and, adopting like the Government, a posture of high-minded concern for 'fairness,' were at pains to persuade the nation of the justice of the Sudeten-German case."[318]

The French had acquired a new government led by Édouard Daladier on April 10. He and his Foreign Minister, Georges Bonnet, came to London at the end of the month, ostensibly to ask for a firm promise of support for Czechoslovakia. Daladier painted a dark picture of Hitler's intentions: "the ambitions of Napoleon were far inferior to the present aims of the German Reich. . . . If and when Germany had secured the petrol and wheat resources of Roumania, she would then turn against the Western Powers. . . . War could only be avoided if Great Britain and France made their determination quite clear to maintain the peace of Europe."[319] Chamberlain rejected such thinking, expressing his strong doubts that Hitler "really desired to destroy" Czechoslovakia, and Daladier backed down. This was to be the pattern until the outbreak of war. Daladier would take a strong stand and then allow himself to be talked out of it. In part, Daladier was concerned "to preserve French honour," but he may also have been bluffing to convince Britain that France would fight for Czechoslovakia in order to get greater commitments from Britain and to force Britain to take the lead in negotiations. "British support, it was reasoned, might yet deter Germany from attacking Czechoslovakia and, if the worst happened, Britain would be committed to France."[320] Just as in 1937, the French turned diplomatic leadership over to Chamberlain and counted on him to get them out of their obligations. "Chamberlain was now free to play a diplomatic role of such pre-eminence as . . . even Palmerston and Castlereagh had never enjoyed. For the destiny of Europe lay between him and one other man."[321]

As Henlein orchestrated a chorus of protests, demonstrations, and riots in the Sudetenland, and Hitler unleashed a torrent of propaganda and threats against the Czech government, the French and British were putting pressure on the Czechs to make concessions. Rumors of troop movements on their borders led the Czechs to mobilize their forces on the weekend of May 19–22 to meet what seemed to be the threat of a German attack. In fact, these appear to have been routine movements of German troops that, in the heated atmosphere of the day, were misconstrued.[322]

Britain issued a warning of support for France in case of a war with Germany over Czechoslovakia, as the French had persuaded the British to do at the April meeting, but neither side was serious. Bonnet scolded the Czechs for mobilizing without consulting their ally and maneuvered to get the British to make clear their reluctance to fight as a way of excusing France from its obligation. After sending the warning to Germany, the British sent a warning in the opposite sense to France. The French "should not be under any illusion" that because of the warning Britain "would at once take joint military action" to defend Czechoslovakia.[323]

The chief effect on the French was to increase their determination to avoid war over Czechoslovakia at any cost. Bonnet said that if the Czechs proved too "unreasonable" France could well declare that she "considered herself released from her bond,"[324] and the British felt that way even more strongly. Halifax stressed to his ambassador in Paris "the importance of putting the greatest possible pressure upon Dr. Beneš without delay"; Cadogan was more forceful, reporting the decision "to use the big stick on Beneš."[325] The impact of the May crisis was powerful. The Western press had treated it as if Hitler had been planning some action and had been thwarted and forced to retreat by Western resolve. This infuriated him, and he acted swiftly, changing the introduction to his plan of attack to read: "It is my unalterable decision to destroy Czechoslovakia by military action in the foreseeable future," and setting October 1 as the date for the attack.[326] He then set to work urging the Poles and Hungarians to make demands for territory at Prague, sent agents to Slovakia to stir up separatist activity, and ordered the formation of a Sudeten vigilante unit to plan violent disruptions in the Sudeten towns of Eger and Asch.[327]

Hitler continued to express confidence that the Western powers would not fight to save Czechoslovakia, and their behavior seemed to confirm his view. As negotiations between the Czech government and Henlein got nowhere the French and British put ever more pressure on the Czechs to yield. In July they forced upon Beneš the acceptance of an "independent mediator," Lord Runciman, to assist in negotiations between the government and the rebellious minority. The tension, however, increased over the summer, and military action by Germany seemed increasingly likely, so, on August 30, the British Cabinet met to discuss a course of action. The suggestion was considered to repeat the warning made on May 21, but Halifax and Chamberlain produced the usual arguments of opposition by public opinion and the Empire, and this time Chamberlain added a new one: because of Britain's military weakness a threat to fight could only be a bluff, and "no democratic state ought to make a threat of war unless it was both ready to carry it out and prepared to do so."[328] Here is the first instance in which Chamberlain used Britain's military inadequacy as a justification for his policy of appeasement. Yet it was he who had adamantly and persistently opposed any additional expenditures on rearmament beyond what had been voted originally, in spite of the growing menace. It was he, more than anyone else, who had brought about the decision not to prepare an army for use on the Continent. He had presented these military measures as being in the best interests of British security, yet now he used the condition of Britain's armed forces as an excuse for a weaker foreign policy than others demanded. "Clearly, Chamberlain was using military weakness as an ex post facto justification for conclusions which he had already reached by other means."[329] The Cabinet decided to issue no warning, but decided, in Halifax's words: "to keep the Germans guessing."

On September 4, 1938, President Beneš agreed to all the demands of the Sudeten Germans. Henlein escaped embarrassment when, three days later, a violent confrontation in a Sudeten town between Czechs and Germans gave him an excuse to break off negotiations. Rioting continued in the Sudetenland, and war seemed imminent. At a Cabinet meeting on September 12 Halifax speculated that Hitler might be mad and for that reason argued against issuing an ultimatum because of the risk of "driving Hitler over the edge." It was the last time that there was serious discussion of protecting Czechoslovakia by the threat of a general war, and it raises the question as to whether Hitler could have been stopped or deterred. There is no doubt that some leaders of the German Army were powerfully opposed to an attack on Czechoslovakia at that time because they believed it would lead to a general war for which Germany was not prepared and which it was bound to lose. When they confronted Hitler he assured them that Britain and France would not fight, but they were not convinced. On August 27 General Beck resigned after a last attempt to hold Hitler back, and other generals plotted to overthrow the Führer if he should attack

Czechoslovakia.[330] Other Germans were in touch with the British, assuring them that a coup to overthrow Hitler would follow a British ultimatum. Although it seems unlikely that there would have been such a coup, it has been suggested that "the combined moral pressure of his own generals' opposition and of an English declaration to stand by Czechoslovakia might therefore have dissuaded Hitler from issuing the order to march."[331] Hitler's firm support for Henlein's most outrageous demands, and the harshness of the assault he made on Beneš and the Czechs in his speech at Nuremberg on September 12, however, make it seem more probable that his mind was set for war, regardless of British action.[332] By then it was too late for deterrence; neither Hitler nor Germany could any longer be stopped except by superior force.

In that speech at the Nazi party rally Hitler proclaimed that "through forebearance one will never reconcile so irreconcilable an enemy as the Czechs. . . . The Germans in Czechoslovakia are neither defenceless nor are they deserted." The Czechs put down an armed uprising, and Henlein and his colleagues fled to Germany and announced their newly proclaimed goal that had nothing to do with civil rights, equal treatment, or autonomy: "We wish to live as free Germans. We want peace and work again in our homeland. We want to return to the Reich."[333]

In these circumstances war seemed hard to avoid. On the thirteenth the French Cabinet met to consider whether to mobilize. The previous day Daladier had asked Gamelin what the French forces could do to help the Czechs. Practically nothing, was the reply. An attack on Germany's Westwall, in the view of the General Staff, would be a "modernized battle of the Somme"[334] with no chance of a breakthrough and horrendous casualties. Small wonder that the French lost their nerve, as Daladier sent a message to Chamberlain saying, "Entry of German troops into Czechoslovakia must at all cost be prevented."[335] This cleared the way for Chamberlain to carry out a plan he had been contemplating for two weeks. The timing probably was influenced by several considerations: the crisis itself and the French collapse under its pressure; a hardening of public opinion in Britain that might reduce the room for maneuver; a fear that Hitler might take some unexpected action beforehand; and a need not to miss the dramatic moment when things looked most hopeless and the intervention was most unexpected.[336] On the day before he left, the Cabinet received a new report of the military situation not calculated to stiffen the British back. One of its observations was: "It is our opinion that no pressure that Great

Britain and France can bring to bear, either by sea, on land, or in the air, could prevent Germany from overrunning Bohemia and from inflicting a decisive defeat on Czechoslovakia." It did not speak to the question of what would be the consequence of the Czechs abandoning their defensible borders by yielding the Sudetenland, or what the effect would be on the balance of power and British security of the German conquest of Czechoslovakia, or whether it would be better for the Western powers to fight Germany then or later, for they had not been asked those questions.[337] They were not the sort of questions that Chamberlain wished to consider. Without consulting the French or his full Cabinet he sent a wire to Hitler proposing to fly to Germany for a discussion that might lead to a peaceful outcome of the crisis. Hitler agreed, and on September 15 Chamberlain undertook at the age of sixty-nine the first air voyage of his life to meet the German leader at his lair at Berchtesgaden in Bavaria.

In one respect the British Prime Minister looked to the future, not merely to the escape from a particular crisis but to the beginning of a general understanding between Britain and Germany that would appease Hitler's allegedly legitimate demands once and for all and bring a lasting peace to Europe. At the same time he looked to the past, as so often to his understanding of the First World War, telling the Führer that "after 1914, it was said that if we had told Germany that we would have come in, there would have been no war, and I thought that they should understand beforehand what were the necessary implications."[338] But Chamberlain was not there to warn Hitler off his intended course by threat of war. It was Hitler, instead, who demanded the annexation of the Sudetenland, making it clear that "he would face any war, even the risk of a world war, for this."[339] The Prime Minister had been authorized by the Cabinet to discuss only a plebiscite in the Sudetenland. The difference between that and the Führer's demand was not great, in a practical sense, for the Sudeten Deutsch were certain to vote for a union with Germany, but it lay at the core of the policy of appeasement. The essential quality of that program was that it should settle problems peacefully, without the threat or actuality of force. To be sure, a plebiscite in those circumstances would have occurred only because of the threat of German force, but the truth would have remained covered by a veil, however transparent. Chamberlain, ever the practical man of business, therefore, went beyond his mandate and never mentioned a plebiscite. He chose to view Hitler's demand as a request for "self-determination" to which he personally did not object, but he would need to seek the approval of his government and the French. Nothing was said about the approval of the Czechs. Chamberlain agreed to the annexation by Germany of all regions in Czechoslovakia where Germans were a simple majority and was returning to London only to gain the needed approval from others. Hitler graciously promised, in return, not to take military action while Chamberlain was engaged in the effort, not a difficult concession since we know his invasion plans were set for October 1.

On his return Chamberlain reported to the Cabinet on his mission. His goal was to get from his colleagues, and then the French and the Czechs, support for a plebiscite to decide the fate of the Sudetenland. He had found Hitler somewhat excitable but not insane. The situation was more serious than he had thought, and he believed that only his intervention had prevented an immediate attack. He was convinced that Hitler's goals were strictly limited, that the Sudetenland was the end of his demands, not the beginning, that Hitler "meant what he said" and was telling the truth.[340] The Prime Minister met considerable opposition. Several members of the Cabinet spoke of the dangers of the proposed policy, and Duff Cooper put their position most fully and forcefully. He argued for the importance of the balance of power and against the view that Britain's military weakness prevented action. He pierced the fog of the argument for delay on military grounds: "As regards the condition that we should not intervene unless we had overruling force, we had not got it now and were unlikely to attain it." He did not trust Hitler and thought that acquiescence to a plebiscite "might lead to complete surrender." Nor did he believe this was the last of Hitler's demands. So long as the Nazis ruled Germany there was no chance of peace. Another member was indiscreet enough to mention the Czechs and raise the question of honor: the required concessions were "unfair to the Czechs and dishonourable to ourselves." Still another objected to yielding to Hitler's bullying, comparing the present crisis with 1914, when the Germans invaded Belgium: "There was a hard fibre in the British people which did not like to be told that, unless they acquiesced in certain things, it was all up with them." Oliver Stanley, President of the Board of Trade, impressed by the strategic issues, said: "If the choice for the Government in the next few days was between surrender or fighting, we ought to fight. . . . The present was a better rather than a worse time to fight."

Halifax and Chamberlain defended their policy against this onslaught.

The Foreign Minister conceded that there was an element of blackmail in Germany's actions, but this must be overlooked in order to revise, at long last, the defects of the 1919 peace treaties. As for war, it could not be justified by arguments over geography but only over great moral questions. "There was no greater urge to fight for Czechoslovakia than to fight for [sic] Japan because of the bombing of civilians in Canton." It was strategic innocence of this kind that had provoked Stanley's remarks, and those of still other ministers who asserted that it was better to fight than surrender. To them Chamberlain replied that those were not the only alternatives: "Acceptance of the principle of self-determination was not an abject surrender." Reversing his claim that military weakness prevented Britain from resisting by war, he now asserted that Britain's rearmament program had made it "a formidable power" and that "it had never entered his head to go to Germany and say to Herr Hitler that he could have self-determination on any terms he wanted." One historian has called Chamberlain's response "a shifty performance for an honourable man,"[341] but there is some question about the aptness of the adjective. Chamberlain had spoken to his colleagues only about accepting the principle of self-determination and had said nothing about the cession of territory. Chamberlain's answer, therefore, "was a piece of deliberate deception since at Berchtesgaden Hitler had demanded and Chamberlain had acquiesced to the principle of cession."[342] The Prime Minister's control of the Cabinet, however, was still firm, and he came away with a hand free to continue negotiations.

On September 18 Daladier and Bonnet came to London again and heard Chamberlain assert that the only alternative to war was to discuss with the Germans means of achieving self-determination in Czechoslovakia. Daladier cut through the illusions that veiled Chamberlain's policy. He believed that Hitler aimed at nothing less than the destruction of Czechoslovakia as a step toward further conquests in the East that would soon lead to a turn against the West in much worse circumstances. He argued against a plebiscite, because it would quickly lead to the dissolution of the state by the minorities. Chamberlain brushed these arguments aside and brutally stated his case: "Negotiations could not be resumed except on the basis of considering ways and means to put the principle of self-determination [for the Sudetens] into effect. If we would not accept this basis it meant war. Let there be no mistake about that."[343] The French gave way and agreed to press Czechoslovakia to cede the Sudetenland without a plebiscite, but in return they got Chamberlain to give a British guarantee for the integrity of the Czech state that remained. In these discussions Chamberlain was accompanied only by Halifax, Hoare, and Simon, three reliable supporters of his policy. Without consulting the full Cabinet he had committed Britain to the dismemberment of Czechoslovakia and a Continental commitment, not to France but to a small Central European country whose defenses he was about to give away. "In this strange way," A. J. P. Taylor points out, "the British government guaranteed a weak, defenceless Czechoslovakia, where they had previously declared it impossible to assist a heavily armed one."[344] But the reality was that neither France nor Britain expected to keep its commitment, and British newspapers understood that well. The press, Cadogan wrote in his diary for September 21, engaged in a campaign "against betrayal of Czechoslovakia," but he was not easily shaken. The contemplated action was "inevitable, and must be faced. . . . *How* much courage is needed to be a coward!"[345]

To gain Czech approval the French and British ambassadors presented an ultimatum on September 21 to President Beneš, "the brutal clarity of language of which would have been admirable if addressed to the aggressor rather than the victim":

> *One*   That which has been proposed by England and France is the only hope of averting war and the invasion of Czechoslovakia.
>
> *Two*   Should the Czechoslovak Republic reply in the negative, she would bear the responsibility for war.
>
> *Three*   This would destroy Franco-English solidarity, since England would not march.
>
> *Four*   If under these circumstances the war starts, France will not take part; i.e. she will not fulfill her treaty obligations.[346]

On the next day, carrying Beneš's unconditional acceptance, Chamberlain flew to Bad Godesberg in the Rhineland to report his success to Hitler, but the Führer greeted him by saying, he was "very sorry" but that "after the developments of the last days that solution [would not] work."[347] These "developments" were riots caused by the Sudeten vigilantes under his instructions, and his new demands were that German troops should occupy designated parts of Czechoslovakia immediately. He also spoke of the rights of the Poles and Hungarians, talking of a plebiscite to be held later to deal with all the claims of minorities, which would surely have resulted in the dissolution of Czechoslovakia. Hitler probably expected the Czechs to refuse and the allies to stand back while he took what he wanted, which would have given him control of the strategically vital areas before the Czechs could take action to defend them. His chief fear seems to have been that the Czechs might accept his demands.[348]

Instead of declaring Britain's determination to stand by the Czechs and the French in the face of this unexpected ultimatum, Chamberlain continued to negotiate, desperately trying to find a way to get Hitler to withhold military action and accept what would be given him without it. It seems clear that Chamberlain himself would have been prepared to accept Hitler's action, but he had come to realize that it would not be possible to do so. During the meeting at Godesberg the Czechs ordered mobilization, indicating their unwillingness to yield. Hitler's ultimatum was also too much for Daladier, who refused to agree to what he called "the strangulation of a people."[349] There was also significant opposition in Britain. Chamberlain had heard boos at the airport as he left for Godesberg; a poll published on the day of his departure showed only 22 percent in favor of his policy and 40 percent opposed. Of the newspapers only the staunchly proappeasement *Times* stood firmly behind him. The Labour party had come around to a position that flatly opposed further appeasement. On September 8, their National Council published a manifesto that asserted that BRITAIN SHOULD LEAD AGAINST AGGRESSION . . . The British Government must leave no doubt in the mind of the German Government that they will unite with the French and Soviet Governments to resist an attack on Czechoslovakia."[350] On the eve of Chamberlain's flight to Godesberg the leaders of the party protested that "this dishonour will not bring us peace. Hitler's ambitions do not stop at Czechoslovakia." The Liberal party now proclaimed vigorously similar views. Within the Conservative party itself Eden and Churchill kept making speeches critical of Chamberlain's policies and were beginning to ally themselves with the opposition. Moved by news of outrages by the German Sudeten forces, a meeting of the Inner Cabinet on the same day of Chamberlain's departure sent a message to him at Godesberg saying that "the great mass of public opinion seems to be hardening in sense of feeling that we have gone to the limit of concession and that it is up to the Chancellor to make some contribution."[351] Chamberlain continued to argue and plead for some concession that would allow him to deal with public opinion, but the Führer was obdurate.

The Prime Minister, nonetheless, was determined to pursue the course he had set. He reported to the Cabinet his belief that "he had now established an influence over Herr Hitler, and that the latter trusted him and was willing to work with him. If this was so, it was a wonderful opportunity to put an end to the horrible nightmare of the present armaments race. That seemed to him to be the big thing in the present issue."[352] He asked whether the difference between the Berchtesgaden and Godesberg proposals was great enough to justify a war, and he pulled out all the stops, playing once again on the terrible fear of aerial bombardment:

> That morning he had flown up the river over London. He had imagined a German bomber flying the same course. He had asked himself what degree of protection we could afford to the thousands of homes which he had seen stretched out before him, and he had felt that we were in no position to justify waging a war to-day in order to prevent a war hereafter.[353]

A heated discussion followed in which even Halifax and Hoare opposed accepting Hitler's latest demands and the Cabinet as a whole was "deeply and evenly divided," and it was agreed to put off a decision until the conversations with the French scheduled for that evening.

In France, too, Hitler's Godesberg demands had changed the climate of opinion and stiffened the French spine. Once again, Daladier made the argument for defending Czechoslovakia and, in spite of Chamberlain's efforts to browbeat him with questions about France's willingness and ability to fight, the best the British Prime Minister could do was win agreement for one more effort to avoid war. It was agreed to send Horace Wilson to see Hitler with "one last appeal" for negotiations. In exchange, however, Chamberlain was forced to make the guarantee to France that British governments had always refused. In case Hitler refused, Wilson was told to say that if the Czechs rejected Hitler's ultimatum and France chose to fight against Germany, "we shall feel obliged to support them."[354]

Wilson arrived in Germany on the evening of September 26 and gave Hitler Chamberlain's letter urging discussions "about the way in which the [Sudeten] territory is to be handed over," but the negative reaction was so strong that he did not deliver the authorized warning at the first meeting. The same night Hitler delivered a speech at the Berlin Sportpalast in which he violently denounced the Czechs. Chamberlain heard the speech, issued a press statement expressing his determination to continue his efforts for peace, and sent instructions to Wilson to deliver the warning to Hitler "more in sorrow than in anger." Hitler, however, continued to insist on his Godesberg terms. Even now, although the political situation would not allow him to press the Czechs to accept Hitler's terms, Chamberlain sent them a message expressing the view that "Bohemia would be overthrown and nothing that any other Power can do will prevent this fate for your country and people."[355]

Halifax had made the British warning to Hitler public, the French were mobilizing troops, and the British their Navy, air raid trenches were dug in London parks, gas masks were distributed, hospitals emptied in anticipation of vast casualties from air raids, and children were evacuated to the country. In that atmosphere Chamberlain addressed the British people in a radio broadcast that same night of September 27, 1938:

> How horrible, fantastic, incredible it is that we should be digging trenches and trying on gas masks here because of a quarrel in a far-away country between people of whom we know nothing. It still seems impossible that a quarrel which has already been settled in principle should be the subject of war. . . .
>
> However much we may sympathize with a small nation confronted by a big and powerful neighbor, we cannot in all circumstances undertake to involve the whole British Empire in war simply on her account. If we have to fight it must be on larger issues than that. I am myself a man of peace to the depths of my soul. Armed conflict between nations is a nightmare to me; but if I were convinced that any nation had made up its mind to dominate the world by fear of its force, I should feel that it must be resisted.
>
> Under such a domination life for people who believe in liberty would not be worth living; but war is a fearful thing, and we must be very clear, before we embark on it, that it is really the great issues that are at stake, and that the call to risk everything in their defence, when all the consequences are weighed, is irresistible.

Chamberlain clearly was not so convinced, and it has been pointed out that his speech "was nothing less than a repudiation of the pledge privately given to France."[356]

After the broadcast Wilson reported to the Cabinet, suggesting further pressure on Czechoslovakia, but the Cabinet would not have it. Duff Cooper threatened to resign, and the wavering Halifax also opposed the plan. It was agreed that in his speech in the House of Commons the next day Chamberlain would make public the guarantee to France. Then, in the depths of depression, the Prime Minister received a conciliatory letter from Hitler that said: "I regret the idea of any attack on Czechoslovak territory. . . . I am even ready to give a formal guarantee of the remainder of Czechoslovakia."[357] It may be that this was only some sort of ruse, but there is considerable evidence that the hard line taken by the allies, and the possibility that war was imminent compelled Hitler to back down. The reception of the British warning and its publication by the Foreign Minister, news of French and British mobilization, demonstrations of the reluctance of the German people for another war, appear to have converted Göring and Goebbels, heretofore aggressive optimists, to the pessimistic views of the generals, and these things appear "to have given Hitler pause."[358] A revived Chamberlain, without consulting anyone, immediately wrote a letter to Hitler to suggest a four-power conference and another inviting Mussolini to take part.

The letters were sent the next morning, the German ultimatum was set to expire at 2 P.M., and when Chamberlain addressed the House of Commons, which convened at 2:45 in the afternoon, he had not yet received a reply. At least one observer was reminded of the occasion when Sir Edward Grey had spoken on the eve of the Great War on August 4, 1914, and Chamberlain himself made the connection, saying, "Today we are faced with a situation which has no parallel since 1914." After going through the course of events for an hour he was handed a note which he read aloud: "I have now been informed by Herr Hitler that he invites me to meet him at Munich tomorrow morning. Signor Mussolini has accepted and I have no doubt M. Daladier will also accept. I need not say what my answer will be." A member shouted, "Thank God for the Prime Minister!" and the House went wild with enthusiasm.[359] In the House and outside there was widespread support for one more attempt to save the peace.

The next day the conference gathered at Munich. Chamberlain had asked for a meeting at which the Czechs would be represented. Hitler had accepted one that excluded them, and there was no complaint. It was agreed easily that Germany would occupy the Sudetenland, not all at once, but in stages from October 1–10. An international commission of the four powers and a Czech representative would determine the conditions of evacuation and the final boundaries. France and England would guarantee the remainder of Czechoslovakia and, after the Polish and Hungarian claims were settled, Italy and Germany would join the guarantee of what was still left. The only change from Godesberg was that the occupation would be spread over ten days instead of taking place at one stroke, a technical impossibility, in any case.[360] The Czechs then were informed of the agreement and instructed to accept it unconditionally and immediately.

For many years the dominant interpretation of Munich, the crowning moment of the policy of appeasement, was that it was the work of Chamberlain himself or at least of the "guilty men," which included the Prime Minister and his colleagues in government. Later scholarship rightly has pointed out that the general policy was one widely approved by the country at large for quite a long time, that appeasement was a policy of long standing in British history, and that the military and financial weakness of Britain in the 1930s made any other policy difficult and unlikely. We should go still further and emphasize that the disastrous policies of disarmament and appeasement in the 1920s made it still less likely that statesmen would be found willing and able to reverse those policies in more dangerous times.

It is possible, however, to agree with these latter-day judgments and yet conclude that Chamberlain played a decisive role in the course of events, even to say that without his determined, single-minded effort to preserve peace at almost any cost there would have been war over Czechoslovakia in 1938, not over Poland in 1939. The *Times* was quite right, on Chamberlain's return from Munich, to say that "had the government of the United Kingdom been in less resolute hands, it is as certain as it can be that war . . . would have broken out."[361] Hitler not only wanted the dissolution of Czechoslovakia but preferred to achieve it by force of arms in a war from which he expected the Western powers to stand clear. It is also obvious that opinion in Britain and France, both within the governments and without, would not have permitted a peaceful outcome unless Chamberlain, with his unique determination and power, took matters into his own hands, ignored his colleagues and public opinion, and forced the concessions that Hitler demanded. The irony is that, even so, he probably would have failed had not the defiance of almost everyone else convinced Hitler to give way.

But Chamberlain had not come to Munich merely to settle the

Czech crisis. He clung fast to the hope that this would be the beginning of a general settlement that would bring a lasting peace. The next morning he presented Hitler with a statement for his signature: "We regard the agreement signed last night and the Anglo-German Naval Agreement as symbolic of the desire of our two peoples never to go to war with one another again. We are resolved that the method of consultation shall be the method adopted to deal with any other question that may concern our two countries." Hitler signed with pleasure and that, not the four-power agreement on Czechoslovakia, was the piece of paper that Chamberlain waved at the crowd when he returned to the England, proudly saying, "I've got it." That night, from his residence at Downing Street, he told an excited crowd: "This is the second time that there has come back from Germany to Downing Street peace with honour. I believe it is peace for our time."[362] Chamberlain referred to the return of Disraeli from the Congress of Berlin in 1878, but the analogy hardly could have been less appropriate. At Berlin a great power had been forced to disgorge part of the gains it had won by military aggression because of the firm resistance of the concerted powers of Europe and the dispatch of the British Navy to the Dardanelles. At Munich the aggressor was handed what he wanted without the need to move a soldier, in return for the promise of polite conversation in the future.

Contemporaries in Britain and around the world hailed Chamberlain's achievement, and a month later tributes and presents were still pouring in. A quarter century later a distinguished historian could write, apparently without irony, that the settlement at Munich "was a triumph for all that was best and most enlightened in British life; a triumph for those who had preached equal justice between peoples; a triumph for those who had courageously denounced the harshness and shortsightedness of Versailles."[363] If the motives alleged were the only ones at work we should nonetheless need to point out that Munich was also the triumph of an unrealistic muddle-headedness that based its idea of justice on a gross misreading of history and its notion of safety on the promises of a demonic and ruthless leader of a brutal totalitarian regime whose writings, speeches, and actions over a decade and a half showed that he had no intention of keeping them. It is also hard to find nobility in a policy that sought to achieve peace at the expense of a small and weak nation that had put its trust in the nations who threw it to very ferocious wolves to preserve, so they thought, their own safety. Whatever nobility can be found in such a policy, however, is marred by the fact that the agreement to the dismemberment of Czechoslovakia at Munich, whatever its other bases, rested not on questions of right and wrong but largely on fear.

Events soon made that clear. Hitler's cruel treatment of the Czechs made a mockery of all talk of justice. He boasted of Munich as a victory for German power, not for the spirit of peaceful conciliation. Not everyone applauded the Munich settlement. In the British Cabinet Duff Cooper resigned in protest of what he took to be a surrender to brute force. The opposition in Parliament introduced a motion to reject the Munich agreement, and thirty Conservatives abstained from supporting their leader. In the debate in Commons Clement Attlee, head of the Labour party, called the agreement "one of the greatest diplomatic defeats this country and France have ever sustained."[364] Churchill, speaking for the dissident Conservatives, agreed with Attlee's assessment and made one of the most memorable speeches of his life:

> [W]e have sustained a total and unmitigated defeat, and . . . France has suffered even more than we have. . . .
>
> We really must not waste time after all this Debate upon the differences between the positions reached at Berchtesgaden, at Godesberg and at Munich. They can be very easily epitomized if the House will permit me to vary the metaphor. One pound was demanded at the pistol's point. When it was given, £2 were demanded at the pistol's point. Finally, the dictator consented to take £1 17s. 6d and the rest in promises of good will for the future. . . .
>
> All is over. Silent, mournful, abandoned, broken Czechoslovakia recedes into the darkness. She has suffered in every respect by her association with the Western democracies and with the League of Nations, of which she has always been an obedient servant. . . .
>
> I venture to think that in the future the Czechoslovak State cannot be maintained as an independent entity. I think you will find that in a period of time which may be measured by years but may be measured only by months Czechoslovakia will be engulfed in the Nazi regime. . . . We have been reduced [in the last five years] from a position of safety and power—power to do good, power to be generous to a beaten foe, power to make terms with Germany, power to give her proper redress for her grievances,

power to stop her arming if we chose, power to take any step in
strength or mercy or justice which we thought right—reduced in
five years from a position safe and unchallenged to where we stand
now. . . .

The responsibility must rest with those who have had the undis-
puted control of our political affairs. They exploited and discredited the vast institution of the League of Nations and they neglected to make alliances and combinations which might have
repaired previous errors, and thus they left us in the hour of trial
without national defense or effective international security. . . .

We are in the presence of a disaster of the first magnitude which
has befallen Great Britain and France.[365]

Both Attlee and Churchill saw and expressed the true meaning of Munich,
as almost all their contemporaries did not, but it is only fair to point out
that each had made a contribution to bringing the debacle about, Churchill
when he ruthlessly slashed British defenses as a minister in the 1920s, Attlee
when he and his party continually pressed for disarmament and then op
posed rearmament in the 1920s and 1930s.

A hardheaded historian, appalled by the failure of Britain's leaders to
think strategically, has pointed out that the opposition Labour and Liberal
parties made their case "not on strategic grounds, but on the score of
morality and ideology. A robber power, and, what was worse, a Fascist
power—had been positively helped by the British Government to enlarge
itself at the expense of a small country, and, what was worse, a democratic
country."[366] There is good reason to regret the absence of strategic
thought in the making of national decisions, then and now, but it is a
mistake to underestimate the importance of these other concerns. In states
where there is direct or representative democracy it is not possible to
exclude issues of morality and ideology from consideration, for that is how
the ordinary citizen thinks about affairs, both foreign and domestic, and the
politicians cannot afford to ignore their feelings. In fact, the politicians,
with few exceptions, think the same way. Arguments about morality and
ideology involve what Thucydides called honor, and nations from antiquity
to our own world cannot ignore it. To exclude such considerations is to
engage in the opposite of "realism." It is likely that the swing in British
opinion away from appeasement to resistance was moved far more by the
proddings of honor than of interest.

Chamberlain was forced to defend his policy against those who did not believe it rested on high principle; in so doing he conceded at least part of their case. "He himself 'didn't care two hoots' about the Sudeten Germans one way or the other. He was more at home arguing that he had saved the Czechs, the French, or finally the British people themselves from the horrors of war; and . . . that the state of British armaments made war impossible."[367]

One defense of the policy that led to the Munich agreement, often used by historians later on,[368] was that there was value in delay, that Britain was better able to fight in 1939 than it would have been in 1938 when radar, air defenses, Hurricanes, and Spitfires were available to resist German air attacks. As we have seen, that was not the argument Chamberlain emphasized at the time. He thought and said that the purpose and, after Munich, the result of his policy was not to improve Britain's military situation for a stand later, but to achieve peace through diplomacy. The fact is that he continued to oppose any substantial increase in expenditures for rearmament after Munich. The improvement in Britain's defenses that were achieved by September 1939 resulted from the carrying out of programs that had been put in place as a result of the white paper of 1935, before Chamberlain became Prime Minister.

As a defense of Chamberlain's policy the argument has no merit, but it remains an interesting and important question.[369] In 1938 Britain's greatest fear, the terror of aerial attack, was not well founded. The Luftwaffe lacked bombers, and the fighters needed to protect them, with sufficient range to do important damage to Britain from the German bases they would have been confined to in 1938. The powerful attacks launched during the Battle of Britain in 1940 depended on the bases acquired after the defeat of France and the Low Countries, which had not yet taken place. The Luftwaffe's limited resources were devoted chiefly to providing support for the ground forces' *Blitzkrieg*. Britain's radar, Hurricanes, and Spitfires were barely enough to save the country in 1940; the British would have faced no such menace even without them in 1938, and the Germans most closely involved knew it. As the commander of Germany's Second Air Force put it, "given the means at his disposal, a war of destruction against England seemed to be excluded."[370]

The British and French also vastly overestimated the size and quality of the German Army and undervalued the quality of the Czechs, who were well equipped, had good morale, and had strong fortifications in the West.

Still, it seems likely that fighting alone against the Germans they would have been defeated in a month or two. In such a war, however, the considerable stocks of war matériel and the excellent Czech armaments factories would have been exhausted and destroyed, which, without a war, "would prove of great use to the German war machine when they fell, undamaged into German hands in March, 1939."[371] It is possible, furthermore, that the Czechs might not have fought alone. "The Poles were in a position to intervene with perhaps decisive impact," and such intervention was far from inconceivable. "A Czech politician quite correctly categorized Polish policy during the crisis as planning to move against Czechoslovakia if France and England remained neutral, to maintain neutrality and wait upon events if only France intervened, but to join the war against Germany if Britain came in."[372] In mid September 1938 the Poles informed the British government "that their actions in the crisis would depend on what Great Britain did."[373] Critics of Chamberlain's policy have written of his unwillingness to seek the "Grand Alliance" advocated by Churchill that would have included the Soviet Union. For a variety of reasons it is unlikely that the Soviets would have become involved or been able to provide significant help if they had, but it would have been far better for the Western democracies to have the Soviets neutral, as they were in 1938, than allied to the Germans, as in 1939, supplying Hitler with vast quantities of essential raw materials, as they did right down to the German invasion of Russia in June 1941.

The Germans' main fear in 1938 was the danger from the West. They had only five regular divisions with which to protect the porous defenses of the whole frontier with France and Belgium. French forces alone on that front were vastly greater and could have broken through easily had they attacked. In spite of a superiority of fifty-six divisions to a total of eight German ones, however, it is no more likely that Gamelin and the French would have attacked if the war had broken out in Czechoslovakia than they did when it broke out in Poland a year later.

Germany's greatest problem would have been an economic crisis caused chiefly by a shortage of raw materials. Having used great stocks of weapons and munitions in defeating the Czechs, without the acquisition of the undamaged weapons and factories from them, without the resources they acquired from the Soviet Union and Eastern Europe in the interim, the Germans would have been hardpressed. The economy probably would not have collapsed but would have suffered a "slow steady disintegration.

. . . The *Wehrmacht*'s fighting capacity would have suffered a corresponding decline."[374] Here is the considered conclusion of a careful student of the question:

> In terms of numbers of divisions, economic resources, industrial capacity, and naval forces, Germany would have faced overwhelming Allied superiority in 1938 whether she faced only Britain and France, or an enlarged coalition that included Russia and perhaps Poland. Even so, the war against Germany would not have been easy, nor would it have been quickly won. But the results would have been inevitable and would have led to the eventual collapse of the Nazi regime at considerably less cost than the war that broke out the following September.[375]

Less than six months after Munich Hitler shattered whatever hopes of conciliation remained by marching into Czechoslovakia and occupying the entire country. This action destroyed the pretext on which the appeasers rested so many of their hopes: that Hitler only wanted to restore regions inhabited mainly by Germans to the Reich, a limited aim in accord with the principle of national self-determination and no threat to the general stability of Europe. It also made a mockery of his promise that he had no more European territorial demands and, more important, of his formal guarantee of Czechoslovakia's territorial integrity. His apologists could no longer claim that he had only legitimate and limited goals or, as Chamberlain had claimed, that he was a man of his word. For most Britons Hitler's occupation of Prague was a turning point, the end of their hope for and belief in appeasement. Chamberlain himself was shaken. In the days after the occupation of Prague, still dominated by the analogy of 1914, he invoked the name of Lord Grey over and over again, this time, however, musing that Grey had not been wrong about Germany, after all.[376] But he and his supporters clung to their hopes. In the Munich agreement Britain, no less than Germany, had guaranteed the independence of Czechoslovakia. To honor its word Britain would need to take up arms at once in defense of the victims of German aggression. Hitler, however, had arranged things so that it might appear to those who desperately wanted to believe it that Czechoslovakia had suffered a collapse that was largely internal and that Germany was only picking up the pieces. This was the view seized on by Chamberlain, who told Parliament that Britain could not be bound to guarantee a state that no longer existed. He went on to say that he meant to stay with his policy of substituting "the method of discussion for the method of force in the settlement of differences."[377]

Such an approach, however, was no longer possible. A free country with a free press and any pride and sense of honor, one that permits some degree of independence within the governing party and criticism by the opposition, will not easily bear the kind of humiliation caused by the Nazi occupation of Prague. Many Englishmen came to agree with Churchill's assessment of Munich: "The government had to choose between shame and war. They have chosen shame and they will get war." In the summer of 1939 a Gallup poll found that three quarters of the British public believed it was worth a war to stop Hitler. An angry rumbling in the country, and especially within his own Conservative party, forced Chamberlain to take a very different line in public. Only two days after his refusal to act in defense of Czechoslovakia he made a speech in which he declared that "any attempt to dominate the world by force was one which the Democracies must resist." Such talk was greeted with enthusiasm, and it soon became clear that the British people would no longer put up with appeasement and weakness but demanded a new policy of resistance and strength. The tenor of the criticism strongly suggests that the new resolve came from a sense of shame and anger over honor betrayed more than from a need to protect British interests. In this atmosphere, fearing the charge of inaction, Chamberlain gave way to overreaction. Rumors of a German plan to attack Rumania, almost certainly false but in any case unproven, as well as ill-founded fears that Hitler was about to attack Poland, led the British to guarantee Poland against aggression and then extend the same guarantee to Rumania and Greece. It is still valuable to read Churchill's judgment on this belated change of course:

> There was sense in fighting for Czechoslovakia in 1938 when the German Army could scarcely put half a dozen trained divisions on the Western Front, when the French with nearly sixty or seventy divisions could most certainly have rolled forward across the Rhine or into the Ruhr. But this had been judged unreasonable, rash, below the level of modern intellectual thought and morality. Yet now at last the two Western Democracies declared themselves ready to stake their lives upon the territorial integrity of Poland. History, which we are told is mainly the record of the crimes and

follies and miseries of mankind, may be scoured and ransacked to find a parallel to this sudden and complete reversal of five or six years' policy of easy-going placatory appeasement, and its transformation almost overnight into a readiness to accept an obviously imminent war on far worse conditions and on the greatest scale[378]

The British, in fact, lacked the military resources needed to defend the guaranteed states or any plan for doing so. They sent neither money nor arms to the Poles, nor, of course, did they even consider the possibility of attacking Germany from the west should Hitler move east. In spite of Britain's very real economic and financial difficulties, the British government at last vastly increased their planned expenditures for rearmament. In spite of their powerful aversion to compulsory service and a Continental commitment, they instituted conscription in peacetime. Chamberlain did not take these steps because he expected war, which he still hoped to avoid by diplomacy. Events had made a policy of full and open appeasement impossible; now he hoped to bring Hitler to his senses by the threat of confrontation backed by the commitments in Eastern Europe, the rearmament program, and conscription. Then he could negotiate a peaceful settlement. As steps to deter war these came far too late, for their results would not be felt for years. Perhaps the most important reason for the failure of this belated attempt at deterrence was that it lacked credibility. Whatever its military capabilities, would Britain have the will to use them? Whatever their commitments, would the British have the courage to honor them? Even after Prague and the shift to a policy of deterrence in the political and military spheres Chamberlain continued to employ appeasement by offering economic and colonial concessions. Small wonder that Hitler never seems to have taken his opponents' warnings seriously. As he laid plans for the attack on Poland he discounted the danger from the leaders of Britain and France. "I saw them at Munich," he said. "They are little worms."

The exposure of the self-deception, weakness, and fear that lay behind the appeasement policy created an enormous political pressure that forced the government to reverse itself sharply and dramatically; in its embarrassment and in its eagerness to be rid of the charge of weakness and dishonor, the Chamberlain government was driven to actions that were both vain and foolish. Chamberlain never really gave up all hope of finding a way to conciliate Hitler. Even when Hitler invaded Poland the British Prime Minister delayed keeping his commitment until the fury of his

Conservative colleagues forced his hand. Finally, however, Hitler's attack on Poland forced Britain to enter a war for which it was still ill prepared, for which it had no realistic strategic plan, and one, we should not forget, that it came within a hair's breadth of losing.

THE CAUSES OF THE WAR

The Second World War, like the Second Punic War, was the product of the failure of the victors to use the opportunity to construct a solid basis for peace after it ended and work consistently at the difficult task of preserving a peace that was not without flaws. Even more than the struggle between the Romans and Carthaginians it deserves the title applied to it by Churchill, "the unnecessary war." The victorious nations in the First World War brought it to an end using language of idealistic generosity in which they did not really believe, creating utopian expectations whose inevitable collapse produced bitterness and cynicism, permitting complaints used to excuse irresponsible behavior of more than one kind. They vaguely put their hopes for peace in international organizations such as the League of Nations, though no nation abandoned any sovereignty and the League had no armed forces. When the United States failed to ratify the treaty, join the League, and give a guarantee for French security, the entire basis for preserving the peace in the face of a large, bitter, and largely intact Germany was undermined. The task of preserving the peace fell to France and Britain and, given France's many weaknesses, that meant chiefly Britain.

British leaders in the years between the wars were powerfully impressed by what they took to be the lessons of the First World War. For them the Great War and the terrible destruction that came from it were caused not by German ambition abetted by British hesitation but by the arms race, the alliance system, and the willingness of Britain to commit a land army of significant size to a war on the Continent. British leaders easily were persuaded by the liberal and radical intellectuals of the day who rejected traditional ideas of power balances and military strength as the devices for keeping the peace. They were the products of the Enlightenment's belief in not merely technological but social progress, and whether or not they were Marxists, they gave great weight to economics as the most important element in international relations. They also shared the confidence of the Enlightenment and of nineteenth-century social science that problems of human society were thoroughly susceptible to rational analysis and amendment. They thought they had a new vision, different from and superior to all previous ones, and often these views were oddly combined with a self-righteous religiosity that believed that sin and evil could be overcome successfully by the example of unilateral virtue, trust, and good will. Not for them the darker picture painted by a Thucydides of a human nature that remained largely the same over the centuries or of a human race that escaped chaos and barbarism by preserving with difficulty a thin layer of civilization by means of moderation and prudence based on a careful study of experience.

Britain's governing class came to believe that the Western allies had been at least as responsible as the Germans for the war, that greater under-standing, more generosity, and patience were better ways to avoid war than by military deterrence. They failed to react to the menace created by German ambitions between the wars even to the extent they had before 1914. Few took the League of Nations seriously. It served chiefly as a form of self-delusion or an excuse for inaction. Whenever tested it proved the emptiness of the concept of "collective security" when not led by one or more responsible states with the will and the means to resist aggression.

In Britain pacifism, isolationism, and other forms of wishful thinking were widespread and contributed to the mood favoring disarmament and concessions. The idea of maintaining peace through strength was not in fashion. The main damage to international security and the prospect of peace was done in the 1920s when Britain rapidly disarmed and abandoned Continental responsibilities, deliberately disregarding and denying the threat that Germany would inevitably pose. They were driven by the traditional desire for remaining aloof from Continental involvements and maintaining "the free hand," by an unwillingness to spend money for arms rather than for increased social spending and lower taxes, but most of all by the horrible memories of the last war and the deadly fear of a new one.

The French, much less influenced by the intellectual currents so powerful in Britain and America, were psychologically crippled by the memory of the slaughters of 1914–18, when excessive reliance on the offensive had led to disaster. French military and political leaders were dominated by that one historical analogy only. They built the Maginot Line and tried to hide behind it, though it was incomplete and provided an inadequate defense. Their war plans, such as they were, contained no thought of taking the offensive, even against so puny a force as the Germans placed in the Rhineland in 1936.

Had the French and the British between the wars examined their political and strategic situation objectively and realistically they would have seen that an offensive element was essential to their very defensive goals of maintaining peace and the security of the new Europe. There was no point in feeling guilty about what they had done to Germany at the peace conference. If the peace was unjust they should change its terms willingly, without compulsion, but what changes would satisfy Germany? Only those made at the expense of the new nations of Eastern Europe established on the high principle of national self-determination and the lower one of security for France against a revived and far more powerful Germany. Even a reasonable German nationalist such as Stresemann sought changes unacceptable to the successor states. Hitler had repeated many times in speech and writing that he wanted the new nations obliterated. Changes such as the Germans wanted were not possible without abandoning both principles. The Western democracies, therefore, had no choice but to defend the status quo against all but minor revisions unless they were prepared to abandon all principle and all security. Once they faced that hard fact they would have seen that the easiest, cheapest, and safest way to accomplish that end was to keep the Germans effectively disarmed for the foreseeable future. Failing that, they must keep the Rhineland demilitarized and be prepared to launch an attack through it if the Germans attacked the Eastern states. Whatever its faults, such a program would have been operationally easy and inexpensive, it would have protected the security of Britain, France, and the successor states, and it would have avoided a major war.

Such a program was not undertaken because the Western leaders, and many of their people, did not examine their situation objectively and realistically but emotionally and hopefully. They were moved by the horror of war, the fear of its reappearance, and the blind hope that a refusal to contemplate war and prepare for it, combined with an attitude of conciliation and generosity toward the beaten foe, never mind at what cost to its potential victims, would somehow keep the peace.

Such attitudes were at least understandable while Germany was largely disarmed and led by the divided, weak, and relatively unpopular governments of the Weimar Republic, but the advent of Adolf Hitler and his powerfully centralized, militaristic Nazi regime, openly dedicated to a revision of the treaties ending the previous war and the balance of power they had created, produced no change of course. Chamberlain, the most determined, powerful, and effective executor of the policy of apppeasement, did not permit himself to consider the possibility that Hitler's demands might be unacceptable or even unlimited. Nor did he let strategic considerations affect his willingness to accept actions and demands, such as Germany's annexation of Austria and of the Sudeten area of Czechoslovakia, that threatened the security of Poland and the rest of Eastern Europe, and therefore of France and Britain. Rearmament, moreover, would be terribly costly; it would get in the way of important social programs and even threaten the solvency of Great Britain.

There is no doubt that the cost of rearmament put a great strain on the British economy, already weakened by the First World War and the Great Depression. The British seemed to face the dilemma of whether to rearm as quickly and fully as possible and endanger the economy or to accept what appeared to be necessary restraints without achieving security. In fact, both the economy and national defense had been damaged already by the government's unwillingness to pay for reasonable armaments in the 1920s and early 1930s. As one distinguished scholar has put it: "for a modest increase in defence expenditure not only would the services have had fewer deficiencies when the war came but unemployment would have been cut and unused resources exploited."[379] Keeping defense industries alive at a reasonable level, moreover, would have made it much easier to achieve faster rearmament later when the Nazi menace arose. As it turned out, the need for a sudden and great acceleration in rearmament put a terrible strain on an unprepared arms industry and a weak economy.

But this entire line of argument, which tries to justify the policy of Baldwin and Chamberlain because of the need to preserve the economy, examines only one side of the problem. The question is, after all, was there a real and serious threat to Britain's security? If there was, then a failure to meet the challenge at any cost might mean that there would be no independent economy to preserve. The economic costs of all-out rearmament, in other words, must be measured against the economic as well as other costs of the alternative. In the event, Britain lost access to the European Continent, was compelled to fight a war at high cost for more than five years, suffered heavy military and civilian casualties and terrible damage to London and other cities, and within a few years, almost all of its empire. Yet had the British been prepared materially and psychologically to resist at any time up to 1936, all of this could have been averted. Had they been ready even by 1938 the costs of the war would have been far smaller in every respect.

When important segments of British opinion began to swing in the direction of resistance to Hitler, Chamberlain was able to use the very military weakness he had helped create as a reason to avoid confrontation and to continue to seek accommodation. He had created what proved to be a vicious circle: commitment to appeasement prevented adequate rearmament, and the resulting military weakness supported the case for more appeasement. In his efforts he received much help from the military chiefs, no less traumatized than their Prime Minister by the horrors of the previous war. In democratic societies especially, military leaders, though influenced by the codes and ideas of the profession, are not immune to the same forces, intellectual and political, as the rest of society. The British "Cassandras in gold braid"[380] consistently assessed Britain's strategic situation using the darkest of worst-case analyses at the same time as they wildly overestimated the economic, diplomatic, and military power of the enemy. Down to 1939 their testimony repeatedly made it easy for Chamberlain to persuade his colleagues that military action was unthinkable and appeasement the only course.

It may never have been possible to deter the fanatical Hitler from war but *Germany* could have been prevented from launching any serious adventure down to the occupation of the Rhineland. Had the democracies not disarmed both materially and psychologically but remained responsible and alert, his plans of conquest would have been ludicrous. Neither he nor any other German leader could have posed a danger so long as France and Britain chose to prevent it. The means for preserving the peace were not lacking, only the understanding and the will.

1. The Asian aspect of the war can be thought to have begun earlier, with the Japanese attack on Manchuria in 1931, or later, with the attack on Pearl Harbor in 1941. Although the wars in Asia and Europe had important connections, and many of the combatants were the same in both regions, the stories and explanations of the origins of war in the two areas were fundamentally different. The concern here is with the coming of the war in Europe.

2. Hajo Holborn, *A History of Germany 1840–1945,* New York, 1969, p. 502.

3. *Ibid.,* p. 505.

4. Richard M. Watt, *The Kings Depart,* New York, 1968, p. 171.

5. Minutes of October 26, 1918, cited by Marc Trachtenberg, "Reparations at the Paris Peace Conference." *Journal of Modern History* 51(1979): 32.

6. Sally Marks, "1918 and After: The Postwar Era." In *The Origins of the Second World War Reconsidered,* Gordon Martel, ed., Boston, 1986, p. 24.

7. Holborn, *Germany,* p. 561.

8. Other losses included part of Schleswig to Denmark and Eupen-Malmédy to Belgium.

9. Sally Marks, "The Myth of Reparations," *Central European History* 11(1978): 232.

10. Craig, *Germany,* p. 425; Holborn, *Germany,* p. 572.

11. Winston S. Churchill, *The Gathering Storm,* Boston, 1948, p. 11.

12. Holborn, *Germany,* p. 567.

13. Immanuel Geiss, "The Outbreak of the First World War and German War Aims." In *1914, The Coming of the First World War,* Walter Laqueur and George L. Mosse, eds., New York, 1966, pp. 71–74.

14. New York, 1920.

15. Sally Marks ("1918 and After," n. 49, p. 43), with references to memoirs by Keynes, concludes that his positions "were shaped by his passion for Carl Melchior, the German financier and reparations expert whom he met during negotiations at Spa shortly after the armistice." In a review of a collection of Keynes's writings Stephen A. Schuker (*Journal of Economic Literature* 18[1980]: 126) quotes his posthumously published confession that "in a sort of way I was in love with him [Melchior]." Schuker points out that at a critical stage of the Ruhr occupation in 1923 Keynes "journeyed secretly to Berlin and, with Melchior, rewrote a key German diplomatic note. Back in England, he lauded the note for its fairness. Then, as the Ruhr crisis intensified, he kept up a steady drumfire of support for German objectives in the *Nation,* denounced the French as the 'new Goths,' and promoted Melchior's access to senior officials in Whitehall. Meanwhile, he used his privileged access to financial information to speculate on the forward exchanges. If he ever wondered whether he was involved in a conflict of interest, he gave no sign of it."

16. Martin Gilbert, *The Roots of Appeasement,* London, 1966, p. 62.

17. *Ibid.,* p. 9.

18. *Ibid.,* p. 52.

19. Stephen A. Schuker, "The End of Versailles." In *Origins Reconsidered,* Martel, p. 55.

20. *Ibid.,* p. 56. The subject of reparations remains controversial, although Schuker's view is characteristic of that of a number of scholars whose work, based on the opening of new archives and the fuller exploitation of evidence previously available, has appeared in the last fifteen years or so. For help in understanding the issues see the debate in *The Journal of Modern History* 55(1979): 4–85, which includes articles by Walter A. McDougall, Marc Trachtenberg, and Charles S. Maier, comments by Klaus Schwabe and Gordon Wright, and replies by the authors, and *"Review Essay,* Is There a New International History of the 1920s?" by Jon Jacobson in *The American Historical Review* 88(1983): 617–45.

21. Holborn, *Germany,* pp. 488–89.

22. A. J. P. Taylor, *The Origins of the Second World War,* New York, 1985, p. 24.

23. For an interesting discussion of the question see Gerhard L. Weinberg, "The Defeat of Germany in 1918 and the European Balance of Power," *Central European History* 2(1969): 248–60.

24. Arnold Wolfers, *Britain and France Between Two Wars,* New York, 1940, p. 14, n. 7.

25. Marc Trachtenberg, "Reparations," p. 24.

26. *Ibid.*

27. *Ibid.,* p. 5.

28. Marks, "1918 and After," p. 29.

29.   Marks, "Myth of Reparations," p. 236.

30.   Maurice Baumont, *The Origins of the Second World War*. Translated by Simone de Couvreur Ferguson, New Haven and London, 1978, p. 16.

31.   Marks, "1918 and After," pp. 27–28.

32.   Hans Gatzke, "Russo-German military collaboration during the Weimar Republic." In *European Diplomacy between Two Wars,* Hans Gatzke, ed., Chicago, 1972.

33.   Trachtenberg, "Reparations," p. 39: "It was British policy, especially British intransigence on figures, that was ultimately responsible for the failure of the treaty to include a fixed sum."

34.   Marks, "Myth of Reparations," p. 237. My discussion of the reparations issue prior to the Dawes Plan of 1924 is indebted most to this article.

35.   *Ibid.,* pp. 238–39. For references see note 31.

36.   Walter A. McDougall, "Political Economy versus National Sovereignty: French Structures for German Economic Integration after Versailles." *Journal of Modern History* 51(1979): 13.

37.   Marc Trachtenberg, "Reply." *Journal of Modern History* 51(1979): 84.

38.   Marks, *Illusion of Peace,* p. 48.

39.   McDougall, "Political Economy versus National Sovereignty," p. 18. For a similar argument see Jacques Bariéty, *Les Relations franco-allemandes après la première guerrre mondiale,* Paris, 1977, pp. 109–20.

40.   See table in Craig, *Germany,* p. 450.

41.   Marks, "Myths of Reparations," p. 245.

42.   McDougall, "Political Economy," pp. 18–19.

43.   *Ibid.,* p. 19.

44.   Correlli Barnett, *The Collapse of British Power,* New York, 1972, p. 327.

45.   The arbitration clause is reminiscent of the Thirty Years' Peace that concluded the First Peloponnesian War in 445, and the Geneva Protocol also provided for multinational force against an aggressor who refused arbitration. Even had it been ratified its success, like the earlier arbitration clause, would have depended on political and military realities at the time of crisis.

46. Taylor, *Origins,* p. 52. Taylor's account of MacDonald's thinking deserves quotation: "The important thing was to launch negotiations. If the French could be lured into negotiating only by promises of security, then the promises should be given, much as a small child is lured into the sea by assurances that the water is warm. The child discovers that the assurances are false; but he gets used to the cold, and soon learns to swim. So it would be in international affairs. Once the French began to conciliate Germany, they would find the process less alarming than they imagined. British policy should urge the French to concede much, and the Germans to ask little. As MacDonald put it some years later: 'Let them especially put their demands in such a way that Great Britain could say that she supported both sides.' "

47. Marks, *Illusion,* p. 61.

48. See Chapter II, pp. 142–43.

49. Jon Jacobson, *Locarno Diplomacy, Germany and the West 1925–1929,* Princeton, 1972, p. 16.

50. Marks, *Illusion,* p. 63.

51. Jacobson, *Locarno,* p. 3.

52. *Ibid.,* p. 15.

53. *Ibid.,* p. 19.

54. *Ibid.,* p. 3.

55. Even these arbitration agreements were nonbinding, therefore not enforceable, which understandably worried the Czechs and Poles.

56. Gilbert, *The Roots of Appeasement,* p. 115.

57. Piotr S. Wandycz, *The Twilight of French Eastern Alliances, 1926–1936,* Princeton, 1988, p. 20.

58. Marks, *Illusion,* p. 71.

59. At the time of Locarno, however, evacuation of the Rhineland was not scheduled until 1935.

60. *Ibid.,* p. 70.

61. Jacobson, *Locarno,* p. 38

62. *Ibid.,* p. 24–25.

63. Barnett, *Collapse,* p. 332.

64.   *Ibid.*, p. 333. The comment was made by Lord d'Abernon, British ambassador to Berlin, perhaps "the true father" of Locarno (Marks, *Illusion,* p. 65).

65.   Taylor, *Origins,* p. 54.

66.   Jacobson, *Locarno,* p. 36.

67.   Marks, *Illusion,* p. 72.

68.   *Ibid.,* p. 334.

69.   Craig, *Germany,* p. 514.

70.   Barnett, *Collapse,* p. 328.

71.   Brian Bond, *British Military Policy between the Two World Wars,* Oxford, 1980, pp. 8, 21.

72.   *Ibid.,* p. 24.

73.   *Ibid.,* p. 332.

74.   Paul M. Kennedy, *The Realities Behind Diplomacy,* London, 1985, p. 228.

75.   *Ibid.,* p. 230.

76.   Marks, *Illusion,* p. 80.

77.   Marshall M. Lee and Wolfgang Michalka, *German Foreign Policy 1917–1933, Continuity or Break?,* Leamington Spa, Hamburg, and New York, 1987, p. 98.

78.   *Ibid.,* p. 86.

79.   Holborn, *Germany,* pp. 604–6; Marks, *Illusion,* pp. 44–45; Hans W. Gatzke, *Stresemann and the Rearmament of Germany,* New York, 1969.

80.   Lee and Michalka, *German Foreign Policy,* pp. 86–87.

81.   Jacobson, *Locarno,* p. 123.

82.   Craig, *Germany,* p. 522.

83.   Marks, *Illusion,* p. 99.

84.   *Ibid.,* p. 104.

85.   Holborn, *Germany,* p. 643,

86.   Craig, *Germany,* p. 528.

87.   W. Link, "Die Beziehungen zwischen der Weimarer Republik und den USA." In *Die USA und Deutschland, 1918–1975. Deutsch-amerikanische Bziehungen*

zwischen Rivalität und Partnerschaft, M. Knapp, et al., Munich, 1978, pp. 82 and 102ff., cited by Lee and Michalka, *German Foreign Policy,* p. 108.

88.   Gilbert, *Roots,* p. ix.

89.   *Ibid.,* pp. 11–12.

90.   Barnett, *Collapse,* p. 332.

91.   Michael Howard, The *Continental Commitment,* London, 1989, p. 78.

92.   *Ibid.,* p. 76.

93.   Keith Robbins, *Appeasement,* Oxford, 1988, p. 30.

94.   Wolfers, *Britain and France,* p. 209. Baldwin spoke in 1923, MacDonald in 1934.

95.   Robbins, *Appeasement,* p. 34.

96.   Wolfers, *Britain and France,* p. 209.

97.   Howard, *Continental Commitment,* p. 80.

98.   Bond, *British Military Policy,* p. 10.

99.   Barnett, *Collapse,* p. 425.

100.   Howard, *Continental Commitment,* p. 82.

101.   Barnett, *Collapse,* p. 436.

102.   Howard, *Continental Commitment,* p. 74

103.   *Ibid.,* p. ix.

104.   Gilbert, *Roots,* p. 54.

105.   Lee and Michalka, *German Foreign Policy,* p. 110.

106.   Craig, *Germany,* p. 535.

107.   Gordon A. Craig, *The Politics of the Prussian Army, 1640–1945,* Oxford, 1955, pp. 436–37.

108.   Craig, *Germany,* p. 554.

109.   Craig, *Germany,* p. 542.

110.   E. W. Bennett, *German Rearmament and the West,* Princeton, 1979, p. 49.

111. Heinrich Brüning, *Memoiren, 1918–1934,* Munich, 1972, p. 203, cited by Lee and Michalka, *German Foreign Policy,* p. 115.

112. Brüning, *Memoiren,* p. 204. It is difficult to know how much of Brüning's talk with Hitler was aimed at gaining his support, but there is reason to believe that what is cited here was sincere. Since Hitler was opposed entirely to a restoration of the monarchy, there is no reason for Brüning to have said what he did unless he meant it. As for his foreign policy goals, as Lee and Michalka point out (p. 16), his statements accord well with his actions. Important questions have been raised about the reliability of Brüning's memoirs. It has been suggested that he exaggerated his right-wing sympathies to meet criticisms from that quarter. It is possible, therefore, that his talk about a restoration of the monarchy is insincere.

113. Craig, *Germany,* p. 553.

114. A. J. Nichols, *Weimar and the Rise of Hitler,* 3rd ed., Basingstoke and London, 1991, p. 156.

115. Lee and Michalka, *German Foreign Policy,* p. 121.

116. *Ibid.,* pp. 121–22.

117. Craig, *Germany,* p. 555.

118. *Ibid.,* p. 556.

119. Marks, *Illusion,* p. 116.

120. E. W. Bennett, *German Rearmament,* p. 507.

121. Bennett, *German Rearmament,* pp. 209–72.

122. Lee and Michalka, *German Foreign Policy,* p. 136.

123. Their memorandum is published by G. Wollstein, *"Eine Denkschrift des Staatssekretärs Bernhard von Bülow von März 1933. Wilhelminische Konzeption der Aussenpolitik zu Beginn der nationalsozialistischen Herrschaft." Militärgeschichtliche Mitteilungen* 1(1973): 77ff. It is the chief source for the discussion in Lee and Michalka, *German Foreign Policy,* pp. 144–48.

124. Lee and Michalka, *German Foreign Policy,* p. 145.

125. Bennett, *German Rearmament,* p. 506.

126. A. J. P. Taylor, *English History 1914–1945,* Oxford, 1965, p. 361.

127. *Ibid.,* pp. 361–62.

128.   Barnett, *Collapse,* p. 282. The following discussion owes much to Barnett's analysis.

129.   *Ibid.,* pp. 282–83.

130.   A. J. P. Taylor, *English History,* p. 151.

131.   Telford Taylor, *Munich, the Price of Peace,* New York, 1979, p. 203.

132.   Barnett, *Collapse,* p. 291.

133.   *Ibid.,* p. 295.

134.   *Ibid.,* p. 296.

135.   *Ibid.*

136.   T. Taylor, *Munich,* p. 205; Barnett, *Collapse,* p. 337.

137.   T. Taylor, *Munich,* p. 206.

138.   Barnett, *Collapse,* pp. 302, 305.

139.   T. Taylor, *Munich,* p. 208.

140.   A. J. P. Taylor, *English History,* pp. 298–99.

141.   Barnett, *Collapse,* p. 301.

142.   T. Taylor, *Munich,* p. 209.

143.   Nichols, *Weimar,* p. 133.

144.   Joachim C. Fest, *Hitler.* Translated by Richard and Clara Winston, New York, 1975, p. 362.

145.   Craig, *Germany,* p. 673.

146.   A. J. P. Taylor, *The Origins of the Second World War,* 2nd ed., New York, 1985, p. 68. The first edition was published in 1961. The second edition is unchanged except for the addition of a preface for the American reader and a new introduction called "Second Thoughts."

147.   N. Rich, *Hitler's War Aims,* New York, 1973, p. xiii. In addition to Rich's work, I rely chiefly for an understanding of Hitler's goals and policy on E. Jäckel, *Hitler's* Weltanschauung, translated by Herbert Arnold, New York, 1972, and G. L. Weinberg, *The Foreign Policy of Hitler's Germany, Diplomatic Revolution in Europe 1933–1936,* Chicago, 1970.

148.   Jäckel, *Hitler's* Weltanschauung, p. 66.

149. Weinberg, *Foreign Policy,* p. 6.

150. A. Hitler, *Mein Kampf.* Translated by Ralph Manheim, Boston, 1943, p. 654

151. *Hitler's Secret Book.* Translated by Salvator Attanasio, New York, 1961, p. 74.

152. *Mein Kampf,* p. 666.

153. Weinberg, *Foreign Policy,* p. 22.

154. Craig, *Germany,* pp. 679–80. Craig goes on to say that "this belief was remarkably stubborn, particularly in England; as late as the spring of 1939 Neville Chamberlain professed to believe it and told reporters that he thought there was a good chance of reopening disarmament talks, with German participation, before the end of the year."

155. *Ibid.,* p. 674.

156. Martin Gilbert and Richard Gott, *The Appeasers,* Boston, 1963, p. 10.

157. T. Taylor, *Munich,* p. 211.

158. See N. Rostow, *Anglo-French Relations 1934–36,* London, 1984, p. 154.

159. See p. 357.

160. B. Morris, *The Roots of Appeasement, The British Weekly Press and Nazi Germany during the 1930s,* London, 1991, p. 6.

161. Gilbert and Gott, *The Appeasers,* p. 13. It is worth mentioning that no English translation was available until 1939.

162. This account of the debate and surrounding events is based on that of Telford Taylor *(Munich,* pp. 197–99).

163. *Ibid.,* p. 198.

164. *Ibid.,* p. 204.

165. A. J. P. Taylor, *English History,* p. 367.

166. G. M. Young, *Stanley Baldwin,* p. 210, cited in *ibid.,* p. 367.

167. A. J. P. Taylor, *English History,* p. 379.

168. Winston S. Churchill, *The Gathering Storm,* Boston, 1949, p. 170.

169. T. Taylor, *Munich,* p. 212.

170. *Ibid.,* p. 213.

171. Ibid., p. 214.

172. Ibid.

173. A. J. P. Taylor, *English History*, p. 375.

174. Ibid., p. 377.

175. T. Taylor, *Munich*, p. 225.

176. Craig, *Germany*, p. 687.

177. T. Taylor, *Munich*, p. 224.

178. Ibid., p. 222.

179. On the origins of Mussolini's policy, see G. W. Baer, *The Coming of the Italian-Ethiopian War*, Cambridge, Mass., 1967.

180. For the French side, see Franklin D. Laurens, *France and the Ethiopian Crisis, 1935–1936*, The Hague, 1967.

181. Barnett, *Collapse*, p. 359.

182. T. Taylor, *Munich*, p. 227.

183. Ibid., p. 228.

184. A. Marder, "The Royal Navy and the Ethiopian Crisis of 1935–36." *American Historical Review* 75(1970): 1328, n. 4; 1329.

185. Barnett, *Collapse*, p. 364.

186. T. Taylor, *Munich*, p. 229.

187. Ibid.

188. Barnett, *Collapse*, p. 366.

189. T. Taylor, *Munich*, p. 227.

190. Barnett, *Collapse*, p. 370.

191. A. J. P. Taylor, *English History*, p. 382.

192. Barnett, *Collapse*, p. 372.

193. T. Taylor, *Munich*, p. 233.

194. *Collapse*, p. 375.

195. P. O. Schmidt, *Hitler's Interpreter*, London, 1951, p. 112.

196.   Marder, *Royal Navy,* p. 1342.

197.   Ibid., p. 1344.

198.   Ibid., p. 1339.

199.   Ibid., p. 1338.

200.   Ibid., p. 1356.

201.   Ibid., p. 1340.

202.   L. Mosley, *On Borrowed Time, How World War II Began,* London, 1969, p. 7. For the sources of the quotations see p. 477.

203.   J. T. Emmerson, *The Rhineleand Crisis,* London, 1977, p. 246.

204.   Marder, *Royal Navy,* p. 1341.

205.   P. S. Wandycz, *The Twilight of French Eastern Alliances,* Princeton, 1988, p. 431.

206.   Weinberg, *Foreign Policy,* p. 241; Craig, *Germany,* p. 688.

207.   R. J. Young, *In Command of France, French Foreign Policy and Military Planning 1933–1940,* Cambridge, Mass., and London, 1978, p. 119.

208.   Weinberg, *Foreign Policy,* p. 243.

209.   S. Van Evera, "The Cult of the Offensive and the Origins of the First World War." In *Military Strategy and the Origins of the First World War,* S. E. Miller, ed., Princeton, 1985, pp. 58–107.

210.   Steven Ross, "French Net Assessment" in *Calculations, Net Assessment and the Coming of World War II,* W. Murray and A. R. Millett, eds., New York, 1992, p. 152.

211.   Robert A. Doughty, *The Seeds of Disaster: The Development of French Army Doctrine 1919–1939,* Hamden, 1985, p. 3.

212.   Young, *Command,* p. 120.

213.   Craig, *Germany,* p. 690.

214.   W. L. Shirer, *The Collapse of the Third Republic,* New York, 1969, pp. 261–62.

215.   Ibid., p. 121. For an explanation of the legalities, see note 62 on pp. 282–83.

216.   Ibid., p. 122.

217. Shirer, *Collapse*, p. 265.

218. T. Taylor, *Munich*, p. 241.

219. *Ibid.*, p. 243.

220. The quotations from Jones and Toynbee are from T. Taylor, *Munich*, pp. 243–44; the remark by Shaw is in Barnett, *Collapse*, p. 384.

221. A. J. P. Taylor, *English History*, p. 386.

222. T. Taylor, *Munich*, p. 244.

223. Weinberg, *Foreign Policy*, p. 259.

224. T. Taylor, *Munich*, p. 245.

225. Craig, *Germany*, p. 691.

226. T. Taylor, *Munich*, p. 248.

227. For a good discussion of Czech and Polish relations with France during the Rhineland crisis see Wandycz, *Twilight*, pp. 431–47.

228. A. Bullock, *Hitler, A Study in Tyranny*, New York, 1962, pp. 342–43.

229. *Origins*, p. 97. Weinberg, *Foreign Policy*, p. 252, believes that the Germans were to stage "a fighting withdrawal," which implies the willingness to risk a war, but Hitler "clearly did not think the contingency very likely." He also reports that Hitler had a "last minute attack of nerves" (p. 253) before issuing the final orders.

230. P. Schmidt, *Hitler's Interpreter*, London, 1951, p. 320.

231. Emmerson, *Rhineland*, p. 237.

232. J. Fest, *Hitler*, p. 499. Craig (*Germany*, p. 691) translates part of the passage: "The world belongs to the man with guts! God helps him."

233. Emmerson, *Rhineland*, p. 238.

234. *Ibid.*, p. 239.

235. *Ibid.*, p. 248.

236. A. Adamthwaite, *France and the Coming of the Second World War 1936–1939*, London, 1977, p. 41.

237. *Ibid.*

238. Holborn, *Germany*, pp. 769–70.

239. *Origins,* p. 101.

240. Emmerson, *Rhineland,* p. 237.

241. Barnett, *Collapse,* p. 385.

242. *Ibid.,* pp. 385–86.

243. Emmerson, *Rhineland,* p. 245. For a different view see S. A. Shuker, "France and the Remilitarization of the Rhineland, 1936," *French Historical Studies* 14(1986): 299–338.

244. *Mein Kampf,* p. 3

245. Craig, *Germany,* p. 695.

246. Adamthwaite, *France,* p. 51,

247. A. J. P. Taylor, *English History,* p. 414.

248. Barnett, *Collapse,* p. 438.

249. The appointment became the butt of jokes and was called the most extraordinary since the Emperor Caligula had appointed his horse Consul.

250. A. J. P. Taylor, *English History,* p. 390.

251. B. Bond, *British Military Policy Between the Two World Wars,* Oxford, 1980, p. 215. See also Bond's article, "The Continental Commitment in British Strategy in the 1930s," in *The Fascist Challenge and the Policy of Appeasement,* W. J. Mommsen and L. Kettenacker, eds. (London, 1983), pp. 197–206, and Michael Howard, *The Continental Commitment,* London, 1972.

252. Bond, *British Military Policy,* p. 215.

253. *Ibid.,* p. 216–17.

254. Bond, "Continental Commitment," p. 202.

255. *Ibid.,* p. 200.

256. Bond, *British Military Policy,* p. 212.

257. T. Taylor, *Munich,* p. 236.

258. Emmerson, *Rhineland,* p. 246.

259. B-J. Wendt, " 'Economic Appeasement'—A Crisis Strategy." In Mommsen and Kettenacker, eds., *The Fascist Challenge,* p. 161.

260. His biographer writes: "Chamberlain often attributed to the public views with which he sympathized though he had no real evidence to support such a claim. He had no objective evidence as to what public opinion would or would not support in a situation like 1914, but he knew very well that he himself could not support a repetition of the Great War." (L. W. Fuchser, *Neville Chamberlain and Appeasement,* New York and London, 1982, p. 66.)

261. T. Taylor, *Munich,* p. 238.

262. *Munich,* p. 237.

263. Howard, *Continental Commitment,* p. 116.

264. *Ibid.*

265. Fuchser, *Chamberlain,* p. 89.

266. *Ibid.,* pp. 116–17.

267. *Ibid.,* p. 117.

268. *Ibid.,* p. 118.

269. *Ibid.,* pp. 119–20.

270. Bond, "Continental Commitment," p. 203.

271. *Ibid.,* p. 205.

272. Barnett, *Collapse,* p. 4.

273. A. J. P. Taylor, *English History,* p. 411.

274. *Ibid.*

275. T. Taylor, *Munich,* p. 648.

276. A. J. P. Taylor, *English History,* p. 391.

277. L. W. Fuchser, *Neville Chamberlain and Appeasement,* New York, 1982, p. xi. It is worth noting that the author is by no means hostile to his protagonist. He describes his work as a "not unsympathetic reexamination" of the "popular image of Chamberlain as a weak and ineffectual old man feebly waving his umbrella, promising 'peace in our time' while the Wehrmacht marched into the Rhineland, Austria, and Czechoslovakia." (p. x)

278. K. Feiling, *The Life of Neville Chamberlain,* London, 1946, p. 48.

279. Barnett, *Collapse,* p. 458.

280. *Ibid.*

281. Fuchser, *Chamberlain*, p. 73. In a speech he gave in 1938 he declared his object to be "the appeasement of the whole world." (Feiling, *Chamberlain*, p. 335)

282. A. Adamthwaite, "War Origins Again," *Journal of Modern History* (1984): 101.

283. A. J. P. Taylor, *English History*, p. 415.

284. Barnett, *Collapse*, p. 460.

285. *Ibid.* A similar idea had great currency in American universities in the 1960s and 1970s, when "peace studies" programs sprung up like wildflowers, and it still has its devotees today.

286. *Ibid.*, p. 462.

287. Wendt, " 'Economic Appeasement,' " pp. 170–71.

288. Barnett, pp. 467–68.

289. Adamthwaite, *France*, p. 62.

290. *Ibid.*, pp. 59, 62.

291. *Ibid.*, p. 67. The words are those of the French diplomat Robert Coulondre, who applied them to the period just after the *Anschluss* in March 1938, but I think Adamthwaite is correct to place the moment even earlier, at the end of November 1937.

292. Both quotations come from *Ibid.*, p. 69.

293. The reliability and significance of the "Hossbach Memorandum" have been challenged, most notably by A. J. P. Taylor in his *Origins* (pp. 131–35). For a brief but convincing defense on both counts see Rich, *Hitler's War Aims* (pp. 287–88). Few scholars any longer doubt that the memorandum is a substantially accurate account of the meeting or that Hitler's message was intended seriously.

294. Craig, *Germany*, p. 698.

295. Rich, *Hitler's War Aims*, p. 97.

296. *Ibid.*

297. Craig, *Germany*, p. 699.

298. Rich, *Hitler's War Aims*, p. 98.

299. *Ibid.*, p. 97.

300. Bullock, *Hitler,* pp. 431–32.

301. Adamthwaite, *France,* p. 80.

302. T. Taylor, *Munich,* p. 576.

303. Ibid., p. 617.

304. Fuchser, *Chamberlain,* p. 112.

305. Rich, *Hitler's War Aims,* p. 101.

306. Barnett, *Collapse,* p. 473.

307. T. Taylor, *Munich,* p. 619.

308. Fuchser, *Chamberlain,* pp. 113–14.

309. Craig, *Germany,* p. 702

310. Rich, *Hitler's War Aims,* p. 104.

311. Weinberg, *German Foreign Policy,* p. 334.

312 Barnett, *Collapse,* p. 505.

313. Ibid., p. 509.

314. Ibid., p. 511.

315. Fuchser, *Chamberlain,* pp. 116–17; Barnett, *Collapse,* p. 509.

316. Fuchser, *Chamberlain,* p. 117.

317. Feiling, *Chamberlain,* p. 342.

318. Barnett, *Collapse,* p. 514.

319. Adamthwaite, *France,* p. 180.

320. Ibid., pp. 180–81.

321. Barnett, *Collapse,* p. 515.

322. There have been many suggestions of chicanery on the part of one state or another, but, as Weinberg *(Foreign Policy,* p. 367) says: "When the times are appropriate for them, many omens or flying saucers will be seen."

323. Adamthwaite, *France,* p. 190.

324. Ibid.

325. Fuchser, *Chamberlain,* pp. 128–29; Adamthwaite, *France,* p. 191.

326. Weinberg, *Foreign Policy,* pp. 369–71.

327. Craig, *Germany,* p. 705.

328. Fuchser, *Chamberlain,* p. 136.

329. *Ibid.,* p. 137.

330. Barnett, *Collapse,* p. 522.

331. *Ibid.*

332. Weinberg, *Foreign Policy,* p. 431.

333. Barnett, *Collapse,* p. 523.

334. Weinberg, *Foreign Policy,* p. 400.

335. A. J. P. Taylor, *English History,* p. 210.

336. Fuchser, *Chamberlain,* pp. 139–40; Weinberg, *Foreign Policy,* pp. 424–31.

337. Barnett, *Collapse,* pp. 526–27.

338. Fuchser, *Chamberlain,* p. 142.

339. Rich, *Hitler's War Aims,* p. 107

340. Barnett, *Collapse,* 427–28; Weinberg, *Foreign Policy,* pp. 437–38; Fuchser, *Chamberlain,* pp. 133–34.

341. Barnett, *Collapse,* p. 531. The account of the Cabinet meeting, including quotations, comes from pp. 527–31.

342. Fuchser, *Chamberlain,* p. 145.

343. Barnett, *Collapse,* p. 532.

344. *English History,* p. 427

345. T. Taylor, *Munich,* p. 794.

346. Barnett, *Collapse,* p. 533.

347. Craig, *Germany,* p. 705.

348. Weinberg, *Foreign Policy,* p. 447.

349. Craig, *Germany,* p. 706.

350. Barnett, *Collapse,* p. 536.

351. Fuchser, *Chamberlain,* p. 150.

352. Barnett, *Collapse*, p. 538.

353. Fuchser, *Chamberlain*, p. 151.

354. Adamthwaite, *France*, p. 218.

355. Fuchser, *Chamberlain*, pp. 154–56.

356. *Ibid.*, pp. 156–57.

357. *Ibid.*, p. 158.

358. Weinberg, *Foreign Policy*, p. 452.

359. Fuchser, *Chamberlain*, pp. 159–60.

360. A. J. P. Taylor, *English History*, p. 429.

361. K. Robbins, *Munich 1938*, London, 1968, p. 327.

362. *Ibid.*, pp. 429–30.

363. A. J. P. Taylor, *Origins*, p. 189.

364. Craig, *Germany*, p. 707.

365. W. S. Churchill, *Blood, Sweat, and Tears*, pp. 55–65.

366. Barnett, *Collapse*, p. 549.

367. A. J. P. Taylor, *English History 1914–1945*, New York and Oxford, 1965, pp. 430–31.

368. For a list of some of these see Williamson Murray, "Munich 1938: "The Military Confrontation." *Journal of Strategic Studies* 2(1979): 297, n. 2.

369. The following discussion rests on the work of Williamson Murray, which is the most thorough and professional evaluation of the military realities I have seen. It is set forth in "German Air Power and the Munich Crisis," *War and Society*, II, Brian Bond and Ian Roy, eds. (London, 1977), and in the article cited in the previous note. A fuller discussion that places the question in the context of the broader European issues can be found in Murray's *The Change in the European Balance of Power, 1938–1939*, Princeton, 1984.

370. W. Murray, *Luftwaffe*, Baltimore, 1985, p. 20.

371. Murray, "Munich," p. 286.

372. This is Murray's paraphrase (p. 286) of the account by Hubert Ripka, *Munich, Before and After* (London, 1939), p. 83.

373. A. M. Cienciala, *Poland and the Western Powers, 1938–1939,* Toronto, 1968, p. 54.

374. Murray, "Munich," p. 294.

375. Murray, *The Change in the European Balance of Power, 1938–1939,* Princeton, 1984, pp. 262–63.

376. Fuchser, *Neville Chamberlain,* p. 175, n. 6.

377. *Ibid.,* p. 175.

378. Churchill, *The Gathering Storm,* Boston, 1948, p. 347.

379. Paul M. Kennedy, *The Rise and Fall of British Naval Mastery,* London, 1983, p. 298.

380. Barnett, *Collapse,* p. 439.

5

THE
CUBAN
MISSILE
CRISIS

N THE NIGHT of October 22, 1962, President John F. Kennedy addressed the American people and the world, announcing that the Soviet Union was in the process of constructing "offensive missile sites" on the island of Cuba, ninety miles from the American mainland, for the purpose of achieving a "nuclear strike capability against the Western Hemisphere."[1] Complaining against the "sudden and clandestine" nature of the action, he called it a "deliberately provocative and unjustified change in the status quo which cannot be accepted by this country," and announced a "quarantine," that is, a blockade, of Cuba as the first step in bringing about the removal of the missiles and their launching sites. He reported his directive to America's armed forces "to prepare for any eventualities" and announced that any missile launched from Cuba against any nation in the hemisphere would bring "a full retaliatory response upon the Soviet Union." He called upon the leader of the Soviet Union, Nikita S. Khrushchev, to "halt and eliminate this clandestine, reckless, and provocative threat to world peace." The Cuban missile crisis, as it has always been known in the West,[2] became public. The world's two nuclear superpowers appeared to be on a collision course and, for the first time, many people believed that a nuclear war was not only possible but imminent.

THE COLD WAR

The missile crisis was an episode in the Cold War, the rivalry between the Soviet Union and the United States that developed in the years following their victory as allies over the Axis powers in the Second World War. The alliance between the Soviet Union, on the one side, and Great Britain and the United States on the other, was strictly a marriage of convenience. The Western states were representative democracies with free-enterprise economies, while the Soviet Union under Stalin was a totalitarian dictatorship with a state-controlled socialist command economy. Communist ideology aimed at the destruction of such "bourgeois capitalist" systems as those of its wartime allies, and the Western states had been hostile to the Bolshevik revolution of 1917 and to the Communist empire it had produced. Only their mutual enemies kept them together, and even that unity was achieved only with great difficulty. As victory drew closer, cracks in the alliance became clearer, and the war ended with important issues unresolved.

Unlike the First World War, the second ended without a comprehensive set of formal peace treaties. Treaties were signed with the smaller defeated powers in 1947. The United States concluded a peace agreement with Japan in 1951 and the USSR a separate one five years later, but there was no treaty with Germany, for the victorious powers could not agree. In the tradition of Woodrow Wilson, whom he had served as undersecretary of the Navy, U.S. President Franklin D. Roosevelt laid great stress on a new international organization, this time the United Nations Organization: "Through the United Nations, he hoped to achieve a self-enforcing peace settlement that would not require American troops, as well as an open world without spheres of influence in which American enterprise could work freely."[3]

It was not long, however, before differences of opinion and mutual distrust arose between the United States and the Soviet Union. Some scholars place responsibility for the growing rift on the Soviet Union, seeing its cause in the revolutionary imperialism of Stalin and the Soviet leaders who followed him. Others place the blame for the Cold War on the United States, whether because of its insensitivity to the needs and feelings of the Soviet Union, because of some irrational hatred of communism, or because of the inherent expansive, even imperialistic character they attribute to capitalism. In part, the new coldness among the Allies arose from the mutual feeling that each had violated previous agreements. The Soviets plainly were asserting permanent control of Poland and Rumania under puppet Communist governments. The United States, on the other hand, was taking a harder line on the extent of German reparations to the Soviet Union. In retrospect, however, it appears unlikely that friendlier styles on either side could have avoided a split that rested on basic differences of ideology and interest. The USSR's history is a story of constant pressure against its neighbors and, when possible, expansion of its sphere of control over them. After the Second World War the Communist regime was eager to defend the Western approaches to their country and to set up secure buffers in the states of Eastern Europe so that they would never again have to fight a war in the USSR. Another goal has been to gain hegemony over the Balkans. When the combative and apocalyptic Communist ideology is added to Russia's historical tradition the result is not likely to be a peaceful accommodation unless other nations are willing to yield the entire Eurasian land mass to Soviet domination in one form or another.

The Americans had hopes of reaching a friendly settlement with Stalin, working out remaining disagreements through the United Nations Organization, withdrawing and demobilizing their forces, and turning their attention to other things. They could not do so. The war had started over the invasion of Poland. The Allies could hardly abandon that hapless nation to Stalin without protest, but any truly independent Poland would seem an intolerable threat to the Soviet Union. Promises about Polish independence and democracy made during the war were sure to be broken, and their breach surely would be taken as signs of Soviet bad faith and unacceptable ambition. Conflict was inevitable, too, over Germany for similar reasons and over Western Europe, where Communist parties under the influence or control of Stalin disrupted attempts to return to normal conditions. No American government was likely to stand aside.

In 1945 American military forces were the greatest in their history, American industrial power was unmatched in the world, and atomic weapons were an American monopoly, but the Americans made no attempt to roll back Soviet power where it existed. In less than a year from the war's end, American forces in Europe were reduced from 3.5 million to half a million. The speed of the withdrawal was the result of pressure to "get the boys home" but was fully in accord with American plans and peacetime goals.

These goals were the traditional ones of support for self-determination, autonomy, and democracy in the political area, free trade, freedom of the seas, no barriers to investment, and the "open door" in the economic sphere. They agreed with American principles, and they also served American interests well. As the strongest, richest nation in the world, the one with the greatest industrial plant and the strongest currency, the United States would benefit handsomely if such an international order were established.

From the Soviet perspective the extension of its frontiers and the domination of formerly independent states in Eastern Europe were necessary for the security of the USSR. They were seen as a proper compensation for the fearful losses that they had suffered in the war. American resistance to the new state of things could be seen as a threat to the Soviets' security and legitimate aims. American objections over Poland and other states could be seen as attempts to undermine regimes friendly to Russia and to encircle the Soviet Union with hostile neighbors. Such behavior might seem to justify Russian attempts to overthrow regimes friendly to the United States in Western Europe and elsewhere.

The growth in France and Italy of large Communist parties plainly taking orders from Moscow led the Americans to believe that Stalin was engaged in a great worldwide plot to destroy capitalism and democracy by subversion. Even today, in the absence of reliable evidence about Stalin's intentions, certainty is not possible, but most people in the West thought the suspicions plausible. Rivalry between the Soviet Union and the United States dominated international relations for almost half a century. In the flawed world of reality it is hard to see how things could have been otherwise. The important question was whether the conflict would take a diplomatic or a military form.

Evidence of the new mood of hostility among the former allies was not long in coming. In February 1946 both Stalin and his Foreign Minister, Vyacheslav Molotov, gave public speeches in which they spoke of the Western democracies as enemies. A month later Churchill gave a speech in Fulton, Missouri, in which he viewed Russian actions in Eastern Europe with alarm. He spoke of an Iron Curtain that had descended on Europe, dividing a free and democratic West from an East under totalitarian rule. He warned against Communist subversion and urged Western unity and strength as a response to the new menace.

Franklin Roosevelt had been convinced that America's withdrawal from world affairs after the First World War and its failure to participate in collective security through the League of Nations had contributed to the coming of the second. The formation of the United Nations Organization, therefore, was one of his major goals toward the end of the war. He hoped that the United Nations could be an organization that would permit international military intervention against aggression as well as a site for negotiation and consultation. The U.S. commitment to such an international organization indicated that it would accept the responsibilities of a world power this time and not retreat from that responsibility. To demonstrate that commitment the new organization would be located in the United States.

By the late 1940s hopes that the United Nations would resolve the world's major conflicts had been disappointed. Like the League of Nations, it was (and is) dependent on voluntary contributions of money and troops. The UN Charter, moreover, forbids interference in the internal affairs of nations, and many of the problems of the late 1940s were internal in nature. In the UN the rivals were members of the Security Council, where the Americans could count on a majority. During the late 1940s and throughout the 1950s, therefore, the Soviet Union repeatedly used its veto in the Security Council and in this way frustrated the capacity of the United Nations to resolve existing problems.

One important new element in the world of international relations was the advent of atomic energy. The Americans ended the Asian portion of the war by exploding atomic bombs on Japan. The new weapon and its far more powerful successor, the thermonuclear or hydrogen bomb, appeared to change the nature of warfare, threatening its victims with swift annihilation, so the question of how such weapons would fit into the international order immediately presented itself. In 1945 the United States had a monopoly on atomic weapons and their secrets, but it was only a matter of time until others acquired them. As the Cold War developed there were suggestions, the best known by the philosopher Bertrand Russell, that the bomb should be used to coerce cooperation and good behavior from the Soviet Union.[4] Instead, the Americans put forward a plan to place the manufacture and control of atomic weapons under international control. The Russians balked at the proposed requirements of on-site inspection and for limits on the veto power in the United Nations. The plan fell through. The United States continued to develop its own atomic weapons in secrecy, and the Russians did the same. By 1949, with the help of information obtained by Soviet spies in Britain and the United States, the Soviet Union exploded its own atomic bomb, and the race for nuclear weapons was on.

In the years immediately following the war "there existed genuine confusion in Washington as to both Soviet intentions and appropriate methods for dealing with them."[5] But Western resistance to what the West increasingly perceived as Soviet intransigence and Communist plans for subversion and expansion took clearer form in 1947. Since 1944 civil war had been raging in Greece between the royalist government restored by Britain and insurgents supported by the Communist countries, chiefly Yugoslavia. In 1947 Britain informed the United States that it was financially no longer able to support the Greeks. On March 12 President Truman asked Congress for legislation to support Greece and also Turkey, which was under Soviet pressure to yield control of the Dardanelles. Congress voted funds to aid Greece and Turkey, but the Truman Doctrine, as enunciated in a speech of March 12, had a broader significance. The President advocated a policy of supporting "free people who are resisting attempted subjugation by armed minorities or by outside pressures," by implication anywhere in the world.

American aid to Greece and Turkey took the form of military equipment and advisers, but the threat in Western Europe was the growth of Communist parties encouraged by postwar poverty and hunger. To deal with this menace, the Americans devised the European Recovery Program, named the Marshall Plan after George C. Marshall, the Secretary of State who introduced it. This was a plan for broad economic aid to European states on the condition only that they work together for their mutual benefit. The invitation included the Soviet Union and its satellites. Finland and Czechoslovakia were willing to participate, and Poland and Hungary showed interest. The Soviets, fearing that American economic aid would attract many satellites out of their orbits, forbade them to take part.

The Marshall Plan was a great success in restoring prosperity to Western Europe and in setting the stage for Europe's unprecedented postwar economic growth. It also led to the waning of Communist strength in the West and to the establishment of solid democratic regimes. From the Western viewpoint this policy of "containment" was a new and successful response to the Soviet and Communist challenge. To Stalin it may have seemed a renewal of the old Western attempt to isolate and encircle the USSR. His answer was to put an end to all multiparty governments behind the Iron Curtain and to replace them with thoroughly Communist regimes completely under his control. He also called a meeting of all Communist parties around the world at Warsaw in the autumn of 1947. There they organized the Communist Information Bureau (Cominform) dedicated to spreading revolutionary communism throughout the world. The era of the popular front was officially over. Communist leaders in the West who favored friendship, collaboration, and reform were replaced by hard-liners who attempted to sabotage the new structures.

In February 1948 a more dramatic and brutal display of Stalin's new policy took place in Prague. The Communists expelled the democratic members of what had been a coalition government and murdered Jan

Masaryk, the Foreign Minister and son of the founder of Czechoslovakia, Thomas Masaryk. President Edvard Beneš was forced to resign also, and Czechoslovakia was brought fully under Soviet rule.

These Soviet actions, especially those in Czechoslovakia, increased America's determination to go ahead with its own arrangements in Germany. The wartime Allies never had agreed on the details of a German settlement and kept putting off decisions. At first they all agreed on the dismemberment of Germany but not on the form it should take. By the time of Yalta, Churchill had come to fear Russian control of Eastern and Central Europe and began to oppose dismemberment.

There were differences in economic policy, too. The Russians proceeded swiftly to dismantle German industry in the Eastern zone to improve their own economy, but the Americans acted differently. They concluded that such a policy would require the United States to support Germany for the foreseeable future. It would also cause political chaos and open the way for communism. They preferred, therefore, to try to make Germany self-sufficient, and this meant restoring rather than destroying its industrial capacity. To the Soviets the restoration of a powerful industrial Germany, even in the western zones only, was frightening and unacceptable. The same difference of approach hampered agreement on reparations. The Soviets claimed the right to the industrial equipment in all the zones, and the Americans resisted their demands.

Disagreement over Germany produced the most heated of postwar debates. When the Western powers agreed to go forward with a separate constitution for the western sectors of Germany in February 1948, the Soviets walked out of the joint Allied Control Commission. In the summer of that year the Western powers issued a new currency in their zone. Berlin, though well within the Soviet zone, was governed by all four powers. The Soviets feared the new currency that was circulating in Berlin at better rates than their own. They chose to seal the city off by closing all railroads and highways to West Germany. Their purpose was to drive the Western powers out of Berlin. To many it seemed that war threatened, but the Western allies responded to the Berlin Blockade with an airlift of supplies to the city that lasted almost a year. In May 1949 the Russians were forced to back down and to open access to Berlin.

The Berlin blockade, however, greatly increased tensions and suspicions between the opponents, and it hastened the separation of Germany into two states. West Germany formally became the German Federated

Republic in September 1949, and the eastern region became the German Democratic Republic a month later. Ironically, Germany had been dismembered in a way no one had planned or expected.

Meanwhile the nations of Western Europe had been coming closer together. The Marshall Plan encouraged international cooperation. Consequently, in March 1948 Belgium, the Netherlands, Luxembourg, France, and Britain signed the Treaty of Brussels, providing for cooperation in economic and military matters. In April 1949 these nations joined with Italy, Denmark, Norway, Portugal, and Iceland to sign a treaty with Canada and the United States that formed the North Atlantic Treaty Organization (NATO). NATO committed its members to mutual assistance in case any of them was attacked. For the first time in history the United States was committed to defend allies outside the Western Hemisphere. The NATO treaty formed the West into a bloc. A few years later West Germany, Greece, and Turkey joined the alliance.

Soviet relations with the states of Eastern Europe were governed by a series of bilateral treaties providing for close ties and mutual assistance in case of attack. In 1949 the Council of Mutual Economic Assistance (COMECON) was formed to integrate the economies of these states. Unlike the NATO states, the Eastern alliance system was under direct Soviet domination through local Communist parties controlled from Moscow and overawed by the presence of the Red Army. The Warsaw Pact of May 1955, which included Albania, Bulgaria, Czechoslovakia, East Germany, Hungary, Poland, Rumania, and the Soviet Union, merely gave formal recognition to a system that already existed. Europe was divided into two unfriendly blocs. The Cold War had taken firm shape in Europe.

In fundamental ways the new situation resembled the structure of international relations in the Hellenic world after the Peloponnesian War, a similarity often remarked upon during the Cold War. The world was "bipolar," divided into discrete blocs led by powers of very different kinds, rivals for the leading position, fearful and suspicious of one another. It was common in the West to identify the open, individualistic, democratic society of Athens with the similar one of the United States and the closed, communal, statist society of Sparta with Russia but, as we have seen, although the analogy between the internal character of the societies is reasonable, it breaks down when applied to external affairs. In ancient Greece, Sparta led a coalition of states, many of whom were quite independent, that resembled NATO more than the Warsaw Pact, and its policy was essentially static, intended to maintain the status quo that preserved its primacy and security. It was democratic Athens that was the dynamic, disruptive state, whose expansion and power the Spartans found threatening. The Delian League, which really had become an Athenian Empire, more closely resembled the Warsaw Pact, which badly disguised a Soviet Empire. In the twentieth century it was the Soviet Union, like Athens after the Persian Wars, that had used its victory swiftly to expand its territory and power, which challenged and alarmed the United States, a state, like Sparta, generally satisfied with the status quo and eager to preserve its advantages.

As late as 1950 America's policy of "containment" of the Soviet Union went hand in hand with a rapid disarmament and reduction in military expenditures. American armed forces dropped from a high of over 12 million to only 660,000 by 1949. In the last war year of 1945 American expenditures for defense amounted to 85.7 percent of the annual budget and 38.5 percent of the gross national product. By 1950 those figures had dropped to 30.4 percent and 4.6 percent respectively.[6] The original containment strategy aimed at strengthening key points in the world chiefly through economic assistance and thereby restoring the confidence needed to resist the pressures exerted by the Soviet Union and international communism. The West's monopoly of atomic weapons was a further reason for allowing conventional forces to decline so swiftly and precipitously.

Events in 1949 undermined this minimal approach to containment. Mao Tse-tung's Communist forces gained control of China and allied themselves with the Soviet Union, appearing to offer a vast and growing threat to the rest of the world. The announcement in September of that year that the Soviets had exploded an atomic bomb was yet another shock. Suddenly the West's enormously inferior conventional forces seemed terribly inadequate to contain the tremendous populations under Communist rule, disposing of great armies and armed with the most potent weapons of destruction. To meet the new challenge President Truman early in 1950 appointed a committee of American officials under the leadership of Paul H. Nitze to assess the situation and recommend a course of action. The result was NSC-68, a report that shaped American policy in the next phase of the Cold War.

Recognizing that the confidence needed to hold out against the great new threat required a military as well as an economic element, the report recommended a great expansion of American military forces to help defend a perimeter of lands. A century of history shaped an outlook quite different from the one that dominated the West after the First World War. It accepted the need for the United States, as the world's most powerful nation, to assume the responsibility for leading the defense of the nations threatened by Soviet power and maintaining the peace through strength. It looked with approval at the system based on a balance of power that had served Europe before that war when "it had proved impossible for any one nation to gain such preponderant strength that a coalition of other nations could not in time face it with greater strength."[7] The report's drafters were also powerfully influenced by the events leading to the Second World War. Hitler's ability to intimidate his opponents even without using military force by threats, by the mere display of military might, by creating the sense of a power that was growing while his opponents were inactive, fearful, decadent, and declining clearly had made a powerful impression. Their report asserted that the Soviets wanted "to demonstrate to the free world that force and the will to use it are on the side of the Kremlin [and] that those who lack it are decadent and doomed."[8] Western security required vigorous resistance. The goal of the policy was to contain Communist power where it existed around the world, to deter adventures and aggression and thereby, ultimately, to bring about peaceful diplomatic settlements and normal relations; in the report's words: "by developing the moral and material strength of the free world [so] that the Soviet regime will become convinced of the falsity of its assumptions and that the preconditions for workable agreements can be created,"[9] that is, essentially, what has happened in the last few years. All these long-range goals required the construction of powerful military forces at once and their maintenance for the foreseeable future.

It is not clear, however, that the American Congress would have been willing to undertake the great expense of such a program had not the North Koreans launched an attack on the South in June of 1950. The Americans appear to have had no thought of involvement on the Continent of East Asia. They had observed unhappily the victory of the Chinese Communists but had taken no action, and Secretary of State Dean Acheson had omitted mentioning Korea when describing the perimeter that the United States was prepared to defend. The Korean invasion, however, clearly approved if not instigated by Stalin, touched a nerve. It was an unprovoked aggression that "resembled nothing so much as the Japanese invasion of Manchuria in 1931,"[10] the first step in the collapse of collective security and the safety of the European system. It challenged the authority of the United Nations and it seemed to be an example of the kind of pressure, the "salami tactics" that NSC-68 warned against, and Truman gained United Nations support for a "police action" to resist the North Korean aggression.[11] In response to the Korean War American defense expenditure tripled in three years and remained at levels about twice that of 1950 through 1962. Russia's explosion of a hydrogen bomb in 1953, its continued alliance with China, and continuing disagreement about the future of Germany seemed to justify the new American course.

KHRUSHCHEV COMES TO POWER

The death of Stalin in March of 1953 brought hopes of a new relationship. These hopes were strengthened by the Twentieth Communist Party Congress in 1956. There was a "thaw" in Soviet intellectual life, talk of "peaceful coexistence" in place of inescapable conflict between the capitalist and Communist worlds, a summit conference at Geneva in 1955 and, at the Twentieth Congress, a speech by Nikita Khrushchev, the new Soviet leader, revealing and denouncing the evils of Stalin and his brutal system of repression. None of that, however, brought an end to the Cold War, merely changed its character in various ways. To an unprecedented degree the conflict spread around the world, as insurgent forces turned the rivalry between the great powers to their own advantage. Rebellions against European colonial powers or against conservative native regimes gained support from the Soviet Union and Communist China, while their opponents sought help from the United States and its allies. Civil wars broke out in Asia, the Middle East, and Latin America, and their course demonstrated the continuing persuasiveness of Thucydides's analysis:

> Later on [after the outbreak of civil war at Corcyra in 427 B.C.], one may say, the whole Hellenic world was convulsed, struggles being everywhere made by the popular chiefs to bring in the Athenians, and by the oligarchs to introduce the Lacedaemonians. In peace there would have been neither the pretext nor the wish to make such an invitation; but in war, with an alliance always at the command of either faction for the hurt of their adversaries and their own corresponding advantage, opportunities for bringing in the foreigner were never wanting to revolutionary parties.[12]

In this respect the Cold War was more like war than like peace, as the competition for power and influence spread to "the third world." The competition for strategic sites and allies throughout the world took on great significance, not only for their intrinsic importance, but as signs of momentum in the Cold War. The alignment of some third world state with one side could be seen as adding to its power in a practical sense, but also psychologically as evidence of its prospects for victory. Each side came to see a gain for its rival as a loss for itself, a blow to its prestige and honor, and thereby a weakening of its power.

The competition also intensified in the area of weaponry. In 1955 the Soviet Union exploded a hydrogen bomb dropped from an airplane before the United States was capable of such a feat. In 1957 the Soviets put into orbit Sputnik, the first artificial earth satellite propelled by rockets of a power not yet achieved by the Americans. It was now theoretically possible for the Soviets to place a nuclear warhead on a rocket-driven missile powerful enough to reach the United States and against which there was no defense. This was the outcome of a major strategic and doctrinal revolution in the Soviet Union begun in 1953, placing primacy on nuclear weapons delivered by rocket-launched missiles. It produced what Soviet military writers called "a revolution in military affairs," which dominated the thinking of Khrushchev and the Soviet military establishment. The same term had been used by Friedrich Engels to describe the invention of gunpowder, which "caused a complete revolution in military affairs and ushered in a new era in the development of the military art and in the organization of the armed forces."[13] The new development was seen as equally revolutionary. According to *Military Strategy,* the definitive statement of Soviet military doctrine: "the nuclear-armed missile . . . is now the decisive factor. The quantity and quality of divisions no longer matter."[14] The Soviet Armed Forces were augmented by a fifth service, the Strategic Rocket Forces, which quickly replaced the ground forces as the main service and became the prime focus of military thought and effort.

In January 1960 Khrushchev laid out the new military doctrine in a speech to the Supreme Soviet. A future war would not begin with the invasion of the frontiers, as in the past, but with a strike deep into the interior: "not a single capital, no large industrial or administrative center, and no strategic area will remain unattacked in the very first minutes, let alone days, of the war. A surprise strike is possible but could not by itself win a war. Rockets will be duplicated in such a way that those surviving the initial strike would be able to rebuff the aggressor effectively."[15] He made it clear that the Soviet Union was prepared to fight a nuclear war, to survive the inevitable heavy casualties, and win. The West, on the other hand, would not survive; for them nuclear war would mean the end of capitalism. This was not mere bravado but the beginning of a new military era. In the same speech he announced a plan to reduce Soviet troops by 1.2 million men, and in 1961 Defense Minister Rodian Malinovsky told the Twenty-second Party Congress that Khrushchev's speech was now the basis of Soviet military doctrine. Malinovsky made it clear that since nuclear missiles were now central to Soviet doctrine all other services had to be shaped to prepare for nuclear war.

But in the late 1950s the Russians did not yet have a guidance system that would make the missiles effective weapons, nor could they bear the great expense of producing and deploying enough nuclear missiles for a safe and effective first strike in the face of vast American superiority in long-range bombers armed with atomic bombs. As late as 1960 the Soviets could deploy only a few operational ICBMs. At a time before there were high-level reconaissance planes or satellites to photograph the entire Soviet Union and reveal what forces it actually disposed of, Khrushchev under-took an aggressive policy of bluff, talking and acting as though the Soviets had nuclear and military dominance. Even before Sputnik he threatened Britain and France with attacks by nuclear missiles during the Suez Crisis in November 1956[16] and crushed the Hungarian revolution without fearing a Western response. Afterward Khrushchev and other Soviet spokesmen threatened often and boldly to use nuclear missiles in support of their goals. This policy of "strategic deception"[17] was very effective in alarming the West. There was increasing belief in a "missile gap" that was thought to be in the Soviets' favor and was believed to have erased the American military advantage. The Eisenhower administration had based its strategy on a threat of "massive retaliation" by atomic and later hydrogen bombs in response to any Soviet aggression, allowing America's conventional forces to fall far behind. Now that strategy appeared to have been defeated by the leap in Soviet missile technology, undermining the credibility of America's deter-rent power and permitting the Soviets to take more forceful action.

The most important target of Khrushchev's new strategy was Ger-many, and especially Berlin. The Potsdam agreements of July 1945 pro-vided for a de facto, presumably temporary, division of Germany into an Eastern part, governed by the Soviet Union, and a Western part, overseen by Britain, France, and the United States, and Berlin was divided the same way. This proved to be annoying and embarrassing for the Soviets and their Communist puppets ruling East Germany, for the freedom and economic recovery of West Germany and West Berlin presented a stark contrast to the bleak and brutal Eastern zones. The solidification of the division of Germany and the growing economic miracle in West Germany made the Soviets more eager still to drive the Western powers out of Berlin.

To these continuing concerns two others were added by 1958. The Soviet alliance with China was coming apart as each side realized the other was trying to use it for its own purposes alone. Khrushchev may have wanted to demonstrate his toughness and resolve by having his way in Berlin, thereby responding to Chinese criticisms of his alleged weakness. He may also have wanted to act while he could still make the Western powers believe that the two great Communist states were united.[18] A second new pressure came from the tactical and intermediate-range nuclear weapons the United States had recently introduced into the NATO forces in West Germany as a response to the perceived "missile gap." Khrushchev feared that control of these might be turned over to the West Germans, something he dearly wanted to prevent. "By threatening Berlin," it has been suggested, "the Russians would exact a German peace treaty which would make it impossible for West Germany to possess or produce atomic weapons."[19]

In November 1958, therefore, Khrushchev tried to use his putative advantage in nuclear missiles to force a solution. Unlike previous demands and threats, this one took the form of an ultimatum, promising to turn over control of the routes of access to Berlin, including those in the air, to the East German government, who would certainly close them to the Western powers if they did not conclude a satisfactory treaty within six months. To emphasize the point Soviet Foreign Minister Andrei Gromyko rattled the Soviet missiles, warning that in an outbreak of war over Berlin "modern military technology" guaranteed that the horrors of war "would inevitably spread to the continent of America."[20]

During what remained of the Eisenhower administration the bluff did not work. The general who was President of the United States was confident of American nuclear superiority and counted on its deterrent power. Looking back on the Berlin crisis of 1958–59 Eisenhower said: "If resort to arms should become necessary, our troops in Berlin would be quickly overrun, and the conflict would almost inevitably be global war. For this type of war our nuclear forces were more than adequate."[21] Soon the character of Khrushchev's bluff became more generally obvious. By this time the Americans had made great and visible progress in the power and quality of their own rockets and missiles. The results of secret reconaissance flights over the Soviet Union by the new high-flying U-2 planes revealed how limited was the deployment of Soviet missiles. Insiders in the American government, at least, knew there was no "missile gap" in the Soviets' favor, so it could not be exploited.

Even before these developments Soviet military planners worried about the danger of a nuclear first strike by the United States and how to prevent or deal with it. The growing nuclear imbalance *in favor* of the United States, however, raised this fear to a high place in the Soviet consciousness. In his 1961 speech Malinovsky declared: "It must be expected that the most probable method of umleashing war by the imperialists against the Soviet Union, if they risk going into it, will be a surprise attack with the wide use of nuclear weapons. Under these conditions the main task of [Soviet] Armed Forces will be to repulse the attack of the enemy and instantly deliver a retaliatory crushing strike on him."[22] Any war, no matter how small or local, if it involved the nuclear powers, would become a nuclear and world war. It was essential, therefore, to prepare for the critical danger of a first strike.

Soviet theory regarded most wars as the consequence of capitalist imperialism and, therefore, unjust. Early in 1961, shortly before the inauguration of Kennedy as President, Khrushchev spoke of the kinds of wars that might be fought. World war and local war were characteristically imperialist wars and therefore unjust, but he spoke of a third kind of war, the wars of national liberation. These, such as those waged in Algeria and Vietnam, "are liberation wars, wars of independence waged by the people . . . sacred wars. We have helped and shall continue to help people fighting for their freedom."[23] This idea was embodied in the Third Party Program adopted in 1961. The party program to party members was the equivalent of official military doctrine to the armed forces. They were supposed to study and know its content and to act accordingly. The program made clear that it was the Communists' duty "to support the sacred struggle of the oppressed peoples and their just anti-imperialist wars of liberation."[24] By that time a revolution had taken place in far-off Cuba, and its struggle against the United States might qualify as a candidate for such support.

CASTRO AND CUBA

Cuba had been a colony of Spain until the Spanish-American War of 1898. Thereafter, it achieved independence within a sphere of U.S. influence, which took the form of economic domination and occasional military intervention. The fluctuating governments of the island had been both ineffective and corrupt. During the 1950s, Fulgencio Batista, a dictator supported by the U.S. government, ruled Cuba. In the years since independence, usually under unpopular governments, Cuba had experienced much political unrest. During the 1940s, as often in the past, university student groups led antigovernment agitation. In one of them was Fidel Castro Ruz, the son of a wealthy landowner. On July 26, 1953, he and others unsuccessfully attacked a government Army barracks. The revolutionary movement that he came to lead in exile took its name from that date: the Twenty-sixth of July Movement. In 1956, Castro and a handful of followers set sail on a yacht from Mexico and landed in Cuba. From the Sierra Maestra Mountains they organized guerrilla attacks on Batista's government and supporters. By late 1958, Castro's forces were in a position to topple Batista, who fled Cuba on New Year's Day in 1959.

There has been considerable dispute as to whether Castro was already a Communist when he took power and was planning to ally Cuba with the Soviet Union from the first. It is difficult to be certain, for he has made many different statements on the subject to different people at different times in different circumstances, some of them about the need to conceal one's intentions if the revolution is to succeed.

Among the men closest to Fidel Castro, his brother Raul and Che Guevara appear to have been devoted Marxists, and they had considerable influence upon him. There can be little doubt that Castro, at least, was a Cuban nationalist revolutionary with some socialist leanings, eager to transform Cuban society and free it from domination and influence by the United States and American business interests.[25] At any earlier time developments in Cuba, no matter how unwelcome, would have posed little threat to American interests or security, but the situation in 1959 was different. "The most extraordinary chronological coincidence affecting the Cuban Revolution was the fact that Fidel Castro came to power at almost the precise moment when the Soviet Union acquired both the capability and willingness to underwrite the survival of a revolution 6,000 miles from its border and 90 miles from the United States.''[26]

The first significant step made by the Soviet Union to bring Cuba into its orbit came in February 1960 when Anastas Mikoyan, the Soviet First Deputy Prime Minister, came to Havana to open a trade exhibit. There he negotiated an agreement, beginning the process of ending Cuban economic dependence on the United States. The next month the Cubans signed trade agreements with Yugoslavia and Poland and announced a large sale of sugar to China, "thereby in effect inaugurating trade relations with Peking."[27] At the beginning of July the Cuban government seized the Texaco, Esso, and Shell oil refineries after they had refused an order to refine Russian crude oil. The United States retaliated by suspending the sugar quota, some 80 percent of Cuban exports to the United States. The very next day the Soviets agreed to buy the sugar that would have been sold to the Americans. In October the Cubans used the suspension of the sugar quota as a pretext for nationalizing almost a billion dollars in private American investments.

By then the United States had imposed an embargo on trade with Cuba.[28] Of the many ways in which Cuba had been tied to the American economy before the revolution by far the most important was the dependence on the guaranteed American market for sugar and the almost complete reliance on American oil for fuel and power. Within less than a year of Castro's victory the confiscation of American property, the end of the sugar quota and its replacement by the markets of the Soviet Union and other Communist states, and the replacement of American oil by shipments from the Soviet Union, freed the Cubans from economic subservience to the United States. Time would show that economically they had only traded one subordination for another.

Soviet support for Castro went far beyond economics. In May 1960 the Soviets established formal diplomatic relations. In July Khrushchev delivered a speech in Moscow in which he promised to support the threatened socialist brothers against the menace of the United States. Figuratively speaking, in case of need, Soviet

> artillerymen can support the Cuban people with their rocket fire if the aggressive forces in the Pentagon dare to launch an intervention against Cuba. And let them not forget in the Pentagon that, as the latest tests have shown, we have rockets capable of landing directly

in a precalculated square at a distance of 13,000 kilometers. This, if you will, is a warning to those who would like to settle international issues by force and not by reason.[29]

President Eisenhower responded by invoking the Monroe Doctrine and asserting that the United States would not "permit the establishment of a regime dominated by international communism in the Western Hemisphere." To which Khrushchev scornfully replied: "We consider that the Monroe Doctrine has outlived its time, has outlived itself, has died, so to say, a natural death. Now the remains of this doctrine should best be buried as every dead body is so that it should not poison the air by its decay."[30] The Soviet leader was now rattling rockets and using his strategy of "strategic deception" not on behalf of Berlin but of a small island with which the Soviet Union had had no previous connection and could in no way be considered a part of the USSR's important interests. He also had taken the opportunity to reject America's traditional claim to hegemony in the hemisphere. An equivalent American action might have been the promise to use nuclear weapons to defend the Hungarian revolution of 1956 and to challenge Soviet hegemony in Poland, Rumania, and the rest of Eastern Europe.

By September arms shipments from the Soviet bloc were arriving in Cuba, and technicians from the Soviet Union and Czechoslovakia were instructing Cuban troops and setting up equipment and weapons. In December Cuba and the Soviet Union issued a joint communiqué in which the Cubans declared their alignment and solidarity with the Soviet-Chinese bloc.[31] The Cold War had come to the Americas with a vengeance.

There has been little discussion of why Khrushchev chose to assist the Cuban revolution so strongly beginning in February 1960. Perhaps that is because some motives seem so obvious. Khrushchev, as we have seen, was an adventurous leader who had chosen to seek and expand Soviet power all over the world when opportunity presented itself. As Castro's revolution became more radical, more Marxist, and more anti-American during 1959, the opportunity to spread Soviet influence to an island just off the American coast must have been very tempting. The Americans had allies, bases, platforms for propaganda and surveillance at many points close to the Soviet Union; here was a chance to gain a first foothold in the Western Hemisphere to begin to achieve some parity in these areas, perhaps to put the Americans off balance by helping Castro sponsor subversion and

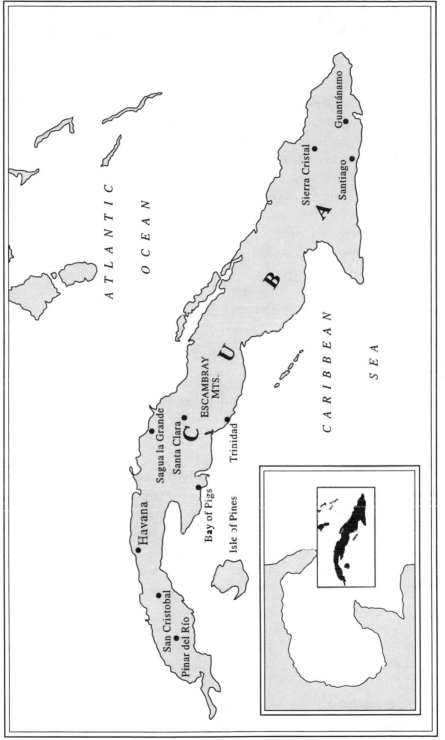

Cuba

revolution in the Americas more effectively than he was already doing. Khrushchev gave a different explanation. In a speech to the Supreme Soviet in December 1962 he set forth the reasons for Soviet support of Cuba:

> The freedom-loving Cuban people, after raising the banner of the people's antiimperialist revolution, rallied around their leader, Fidel Castro, and his comrades-in-arms and by 1959 had cleared their soil of North American plunderers and their accomplices. This was a truly heroic struggle, deserving of admiration. . . . In a brief time a radical agrarian reform was carried out, industrial enterprises, firms and banks were nationalized, and a cultural revolution was carried through. The republic of Cuba became a democratic state laying the foundations of socialism. . . .
>
> This notable victory gladdened everyone to whom the cause of freedom and socialism is dear. And the socialist countries, and above all the Soviet Union, naturally came to Cuba's aid when the people of Cuba, having won independence, were subjected to economic and then military pressure from their imperialist neighbor.[32]

It is easy but mistaken to dismiss such an explanation as hypocritical rhetoric. There is evidence that Khrushchev, a man of the lower classes who had made his way to the top through the Communist system, had fought to victory in World War II, which the Russians call the Great Patriotic War, and who had taken great risks to undermine the Stalinist system for the purposes of creating a more effective state better able to compete with the capitalist world, was a true believer. To him Castro was a difficult, hard to control, but uniquely admirable man who had made a socialist revolution on the doorstep of the leader of the "capitalist-imperialist" camp. As the Soviet leaders themselves said, the Cuban revolution "made them feel young again."[33]

KHRUSHCHEV VERSUS KENNEDY

The Bay of Pigs

On the Eisenhower administration it had the opposite effect. Developments in Cuba led the American government to support plans aimed at

overthrowing the Castro regime. In March 1960 Eisenhower accepted a
CIA recommendation to arm and train Cuban exiles for the purpose. At
first the idea was to support Cuban guerrillas only, but by November 1961
problems in security had led the CIA to decide on an invasion of the island,
with American planes flown by Cuban pilots providing air cover. The men
training Cuban guerrillas in Guatemala were replaced by those preparing
for a "conventional attack, with tanks, artillery and air support."[34] Since
the Republicans lost the election and never carried out the plan they were
never compelled to explain their motives. President Kennedy, who did
undertake a version of it and sustained an embarrassing defeat, had that
responsibility, and in a speech in November 1963, he said that the Americans objected to subversion, dictatorship, to a Soviet satellite in the Caribbean. Many years later Kennedy's Secretary of Defense, Robert S. McNamara, explained the administration's thinking more fully, giving reasons
that could not have been very different from the thoughts of the men who
had originally conceived and approved the plan:

> Our principal concern was Cuba's military relationship with the
> Soviet Union. . . . Our second concern was Cuba's support for
> armed groups whose goal was to overthrow many, if not all, of the
> governments in Latin America and the Caribbean.
> Our third concern was the constant, hostile rhetoric directed at
> the government of the United States and other governments in the
> hemisphere. . . .
> Our fourth concern was that the Cuban government betrayed
> its promises of a free election and began to establish a dictatorship
> that violated the civil and political liberties of the Cuban people.[35]

For such reasons the United States was planning to launch and support an invasion of Cuba by exiles from that island, recruited, trained, and
supplied by Americans, when Kennedy took office, although the decision
to attack had not yet been made. This was only one of several difficult
problems awaiting the new President, whose experience in the intricacies
of foreign affairs was limited and whose political position at home was
unusually tenuous. At forty-three he was the youngest man elected President in American history, and he had won in the closest race since 1888.
With 118,000 more votes than his Republican opponent, Richard Nixon,
out of a total of about 68 million, some two tenths of 1 percent, he did not

have quite a majority of the popular votes. In spite of his victory the Democrats lost two seats in the Senate and twenty-two in the House, a rare result in a victorious presidential race. It was not an overwhelming mandate, and it provided little leverage to use in Congress, where every legislator had won election by a higher percentage than the president. The Democrats, as usual, were divided between liberals and conservatives, the latter, chiefly from the South, entrenched by seniority in powerful positions. They were likely on many issues to side with the Republicans, leaving the President without a majority.

Apart from these open and practical challenges the new President, the first Catholic to hold that office, confronted unusual personal ones. After the patriarchal Eisenhower, the general who had guided the victory in the war, Kennedy seemed young and callow. Insiders knew that his political victories had been won, in considerable part, with the vast sums of money spent by his father, Joseph P. Kennedy, that in his years in the Senate he had been a dilettante who had few achievements, little weight, and not much respect. In conducting the nation's affairs he would have little leeway or margin for error.

Like many candidates without practical experience in foreign policy and with no record to defend, Kennedy during the campaign was free to challenge the incumbent from both sides. He criticized the Eisenhower administration for not achieving a nuclear test ban and for a national defense policy too weak in conventional forces. In one of his few memorable senatorial speeches he had called for an end to French colonialism, "but he condoned American involvement in place of the French in Southeast Asia."[36] He blamed the administration for risking war, perhaps even nuclear war, to defend two tiny islands off the Chinese coast from the Communists, but he hammered away at the administration's weakness in resisting the Soviet Union, charging that Soviet economic growth was outpacing the Americans'. Even more vigorously and repeatedly, he charged Eisenhower with permitting a "missile gap," a great advantage in long-range missiles, to emerge in favor of the Soviet Union. During the campaign he made a speech that implicitly rejected the attitude and rhetoric that suggested that the struggle against communism was a holy war from which the United States must emerge as the sole victor: "We must face the fact that the United States is neither omnipotent—that we are only six percent of the world's population—that we cannot impose our will upon the other ninety-four percent of mankind—that we cannot right every wrong or reverse every adversity—and that therefore there cannot be an American solution to every world problem."[37]

But in another speech he said:

The enemy is the Communist system itself—implacable, insatiable, unceasing in its drive for world domination. . . . This is not a struggle for supremacy in arms alone. It is also a struggle for supremacy between two conflicting ideologies: freedom under God versus ruthless, godless tyranny.[38]

His inaugural address followed this latter path:

Let the word go forth . . . to friend and foe alike, that the torch has been passed to a new generation of Americans, born in this century, tempered by war, disciplined by a hard and bitter peace, proud of our ancient heritage. . . . We shall pay any price, bear any burden, meet any hardship, support any friend, oppose any foe to assure the survival and success of liberty.[39]

As President, Kennedy was divided between the sense of caution and restraint implied by the first statement and the boldness of the second. During the campaign he strongly emphasized the tougher, more aggressive stance, criticizing Eisenhower's defense and foreign policy chiefly from the right.

On no subject was this clearer than on the administration's treatment of Cuba. Kennedy accused the Republicans of creating "Communism's first Caribbean base" there. He blamed them for allowing "a Communist menace" to arise "only eight jet minutes from Florida. . . . We must make clear," he said, "our intention not to let the Soviet Union turn Cuba into its base in the Caribbean—and our intention to enforce the Monroe Doctrine . . . and that we will not be content till democracy is restored to Cuba. The forces fighting for freedom in exile and in the mountains of Cuba should be sustained."[40]

Soon after the election Kennedy was told about the planned invasion of Cuba, a scheme remarkably well suited to what he had been urging in the campaign. He was impressed, and told the head of the CIA, Allen Dulles, to continue with the planning, although, according to Arthur Schlesinger, Jr., he also had grave doubts about it from then on. "Thus

Kennedy, Hamlet-like, encouraged what he in fact mistrusted, perhaps already caught up by the dilemma between the policy which he had advocated in the campaign and what he thought wise—a dilemma that was to haunt him all the time he was in office."[41]

Soon after his inauguration Kennedy was pressed to make a decision about a Cuban invasion. On the one hand, Soviet military supplies and Soviet-bloc advisers were arriving every day and strengthening Cuba's capacity to resist, as well as Communist control of the island. The Cubans were supporting revolutionaries in the Caribbean and Central America, and the CIA warned that some of the affected nations might "go like Castro" in a few months. With remarkable foresight Dulles warned Kennedy that "Cuba might become a Sino-Soviet bloc missile base in this hemisphere, right close to our own coastline." On the other hand the presence of Cuban exiles training in Guatemala was a secret hard to keep. "A group of such Cubans now training in Guatemala . . . can not remain indefinitely where they are."[42]

Kennedy received conflicting advice and appears to have hesitated in making up his mind. There is no doubt that he wanted to get rid of Castro; in the course of his brief presidency he seems, in fact, to have developed a fixation on the subject. He took the threat of Soviet operations from Cuba seriously and wanted to eliminate the possibility. Apart from that, it would have been personally and politically embarrassing to take no action after his aggressive rhetoric during the electoral campaign. Even more embarrassing was the prospect of what Dulles called "the disposal problem," what to do with the Cubans training in Guatemala if there were no invasion. They and their supporters were sure to return to Miami full of recriminations against a new President who had talked tough during the campaign but who cancelled an effort to overthrow the Cuban dictator planned by his predecessor, whom he had criticized for weakness.

Against these considerations he feared the hostility open American involvement in the attack would provoke in Latin America, where he was planning the "Alliance for Progress," and elsewhere around the world, where he was hoping to present the United States in a new, freedom-loving guise, as the first home of democratic revolutions, aligned with the emerging nations. More serious than that was his fear that an American military operation in Cuba would move the Soviets to launch a retaliatory action against Berlin, compelling the Americans to resist and risk a war or lose its credibility and risk the collapse of NATO.

The original CIA plan aimed at forming small groups who would find their way into Cuba, establish effective bases, be armed and supplied by air, increase their operations, and gain more adherents, as Castro had done against Batista, until they could challenge and overthrow the regime. No American forces would take part in any fighting.[43] By the time of the 1960 election that plan had been abandoned and replaced by a scheme for a landing by a Cuban exile force on the coast of Cuba. It resembled the plan that had successfully overthrown the Arbenz government in Guatemala in 1954. American B-26 bombers would gain control of the air and disrupt Cuban communication and the transportation needed to oppose the landing. Opponents of Castro would arise in their tens of thousands, and the dictator would be forced to flee. By the time Kennedy took office that plan was seen as impractical and was replaced by another. A considerable amphibious force, supported by paratroopers dropped behind the town, would land at the town of Trinidad, which was far from Castro's main army and near the Escambray Mountains, to which the Cuban exiles could escape for safety if the landing failed. This would be supported by air strikes in American planes that would protect the beachhead. Once it was safe, a provisional government would arrive by air, and in a week or two be recognized as the Cuban government. Then they could ask the United States for aid, presumably in the form of arms and supplies, not fighting forces. The plan was modeled on the Anzio landing in Italy in 1944 and provided for a gradual increase in forces and expansion of territory over a period of time. "If by any chance the attack failed, Trinidad was near enough to Escambray for the invaders to disappear into the hills."[44]

Kennedy did not like the plan because it was "too spectacular" and would "put us in so openly, in view of the world situation." Later on he would tell his confidante Theodore Sorensen that he had been reluctant to use American force in Cuba because he feared that Khrushchev might use American involvement as a pretext to move against Berlin.[45] To meet his objections the CIA framed a compromise plan. The landing would be at the Bay of Pigs, west of Trinidad, and in the words of presidential adviser McGeorge Bundy, "unspectacular and quiet and plausibly Cuban in its essentials."[46] At Kennedy's further request the "noise level" was reduced by a decision to make the landing at night, and the President reserved the right to call off the invasion as late as twenty-four hours beforehand. Kennedy was comforted further by the thought that if the mission failed the invaders could still "melt into the mountains." It seems that somewhere in the discussions there was a failure of communication that concealed the fact that the new landing site was too far from the mountains to permit such an escape. If the invasion failed and American armed forces did not intervene, the invaders would be slaughtered on the beach.

In retrospect it seems extraordinary that anyone should have thought that such an attack could have been launched without revealing very plain American fingerprints. American recruitment and training of Cuban exiles was an open secret. Prisoners certainly would testify that the whole affair had been organized by the CIA. If the Soviets wanted an excuse to act against Berlin the curtailed plan would serve just as well as the bolder one, but without military support, at least in the air, it was far more likely to fail. The plan ran into considerable opposition within the administration on grounds ranging from the ideological to the practical. The Joint Chiefs, the CIA, and the Secretary of Defense, however, were keenly in favor. On his return from a visit to his father in Florida, so too was the President. Bundy says that by April 4 Kennedy "really wanted to do this. . . . He had made up his mind and *told* us. He didn't *ask* us," and Sorensen reports that he had lost patience with doubters.[47] At the same time, he was determined not to use American military forces, and at a press conference on April 12 he announced that "there will not be, under any conditions, any intervention in Cuba by United States armed forces."[48] On the fourteenth he gave final permission for the plan to proceed.

The first step was to be an air strike against Cuban airfields flown by Cuban exiles flying American B-26 bombers. These relics from World War II were "slow, unwieldy, unsuited to air cover, and constantly developing engine trouble."[49] As part of the plot to conceal American involvement, they took off from relatively distant bases in Nicaragua, which made the flights longer, more dangerous, and more exhausting, requiring the replacement of Cuban fliers by Americans, some of whom died in the fighting. In addition, Kennedy at the last moment reduced the number of bombers below the sixteen originally intended, saying, "I want it minimal." Only six planes flew.[50] The air strikes did not complete their mission, but a second strike was scheduled for the next day.

The United States continued to deny involvement, and Adlai Stevenson, American Ambassador to the United Nations, was not told the truth until after a public denial before the General Assembly. He threatened to resign, and along with other foreign policy advisers, argued against further American involvement. Kennedy cancelled further air strikes "that could have decimated the remainder of Castro's air force: the strikes were not to be flown until after the exiles had secured a Cuban beachhead. Then the new attacks could be plausibly portrayed as launched from Cuban soil."[51] On April 17 about fourteen hundred Cuban exiles landed at the Bay of Pigs. Without air cover they were easy targets for Castro's Air Force and were pinned to the beach. When news of the developing disaster reached Washington on Monday, orders were given for a second air strike, but a combination of cloud cover and the lateness of the decision "made this postponement fatal. The last opportunity to neutralize the air over the beach by destroying [the Cuban planes] was gone."[52]

On Tuesday April 18 Khrushchev broadcast a message on Radio Moscow. He dismissed the notion that the United States was not involved: "the armed bands which invaded that country [Cuba] have been trained, equipped and armed in the United States of America." He accused the Americans of aggression and warned them against the spread of "the flames of war" beyond Cuba. "Any so-called 'small war' can produce a chain reaction in all parts of the world As for the Soviet Union, there should be no misunderstanding of our position: We shall render the Cuban people and their government all necessary assistance in beating back the armed attack on Cuba."[53] Kennedy believed this to be a clear threat to move against Berlin if the Americans became openly involved in the fighting in Cuba. In December 1962 he told survivors of the disaster flatly that "the Soviet government had threatened to attack West Berlin if the United States continued to launch raids on Cuba and backed the invasion." He described his choice as either to "support the Bay of Pigs operation and risk a Soviet confrontation in Berlin which could touch off a large-scale war, or maintain world peace and risk the defeat of fourteen hundred men in Cuba."[54]

After the failure at the Bay of Pigs former president Eisenhower asked why Kennedy had failed to provide air cover, and the President responded that he had been worried that the Soviets would make trouble in Berlin. Eisenhower asserted that "that is exactly the *opposite* of what would really happen. The Soviets follow their own plans, and if they see us show any weakness, then is when they press us the hardest. . . . The failure of the Bay of Pigs will embolden the Soviets to do something that they would otherwise not do."[55] There was considerable evidence that the old general, who had been dealing with the Soviets since the Second World War, including eight years as President, from the time of Stalin through the transition following his death and into the time of Khrushchev, was right. Throughout his time at the Soviet helm Khrushchev counted on a policy of bluff, drawing back when the bluff was called. Years later his son described his father's methods:

> At one point [Nikita] Khrushchev said that we built missiles like sausages. I said then, "How can you say that, since we have only two or three?" He said, "the important thing is to make the Americans believe that. And that way we prevent an attack." And on these grounds our entire policy was based. We threatened with missiles we didn't have. That happened in the Suez crisis, and the Iraqi crisis.[56]

Just before midnight of Tuesday, April 18, Kennedy met with his civilian and military advisers at the White House to decide how to cope with what was turning out to be a catastrophe at the Bay of Pigs. The Navy asked to be allowed to send jet planes from an aircraft carrier to protect the men on the beach and the planes bringing them supplies. Admiral Arleigh Burke of the Joint Chiefs of Staff said, "Let me take two jets and shoot down the enemy aircraft." Kennedy refused, repeating that he was determined not to use American forces in combat. Burke then suggested bringing in a destroyer. Later he said that "one destroyer opening fire could have knocked hell out of Castro's tanks. It might have changed the whole course of the battle." The President refused; "Burke," he said, "I don't want the United States involved in this." The admiral replied in a loud voice, "Hell, Mr. President, but we *are* involved." Under pressure Kennedy compromised: he agreed to send six unmarked planes from the carrier. They were instructed "not to attack planes or ground targets. They could defend the [Cuban exile] Brigade bombers if they were attacked. When Secretary of State Dean Rusk objected against committing American forces, after all, the President raised his hand just below his nose and said, "We're already in it up to here."[57] But the American action did not accord with that statement. If they were in so deep they might be expected to have taken actions that could produce success or, at least, protect the men on the beach.

Schlesinger thought "the instructions given were 'somewhat tricky.' " So they were, no less tricky than the instructions given the Athenian admirals at Corcyra in 433 B.C., but the outcome was very different. The limited, at first hesitant, but finally serious Athenian intervention helped save Corcyra; the American simulacrum of an effort was useless. The carrier jets arrived at the beaches the next morning too early to do any good. The supply planes were shot down or driven away. By Wednesday afternoon it was all over. Of all the men engaged in the landing about one hundred were killed in the fighting, and the rest were captured.

The day after the debacle Kennedy delivered a speech that sounded the bold note of his inaugural address:

> We face a relentless struggle in every corner of the globe. . . . We dare not fail to grasp the new concepts, the new tools, the new sense of urgency we will need to meet it, whether in Cuba or South Vietnam. . . . History will record the fact that this bitter struggle reached its climax in the late 1950s and the early 1960s. Let me then make clear as the President of the United States that I am determined upon our system's survival and success, regardless of the cost and regardless of the peril![58]

One of Kennedy's aides warned that the speech seemed to contain a threat of a future invasion of Cuba, but the President replied that "I didn't want us to sound like a paper tiger. We should scare people a little, and I did it to make us appear as tough as possible."[59] In the view of one administration official some evidence of American toughness after the Bay of Pigs might be needed. Abram Chayes, Kennedy's legal adviser in the State Department, estimated the effect of the Bay of Pigs misadventure on the Russians as follows: "I think the Russians could not possibly understand why, having undertaken this and gone and done what we did, we didn't finish it off. That, I think, raised at least the possibility in the minds of many Russian leaders that there was some failure of nerve here to be played."[60]

To the man who had sent tanks into Hungary to assert Soviet control, the behavior of the United States toward Cuba must have seemed all but incredible. In his memoirs Khrushchev observed that Cuba was "only a few miles from the American shore and it is stretched out like a sausage, a shape that makes it easy for attackers and incredibly difficult for the island's defenders."[61] When he heard of the invasion, according to his son Sergei, he "honestly didn't think that Cuba could put up serious resistance against the landing troops."[62] We can only imagine his reaction when he heard that the Americans had allowed the assault to fail, with the loss of all the invaders, and taken no military action of their own, although Khrushchev's generals had told him that an invasion of the island by American forces would take no more than three or four days to complete.[63] Arkady Shevchenko, of the Soviet Foreign Ministry, later reported that the Bay of Pigs "gave Khrushchev and the other leaders the impression that Kennedy was indecisive."[64] To the Soviet leader the fiasco of the Bay of Pigs may have suggested that his American counterpart lacked resolve; that he was, as some American critics asserted in a play on the title of a book published by the President, all profile and no courage.

The Summit Meeting at Vienna

From the beginning of his presidency Kennedy wanted a summit meeting with Khrushchev, and as early as February 22, 1961, he suggested one in a letter to the Soviet leader, chiefly, as he told the press, "so that he and Khrushchev could understand each other's purposes and interests."[65] The reason the President gave to his aide Kenneth O'Donnell, however, reveals his concern lest he appear weak: "I have to show [Khrushchev] we can be just as tough as he is. I'll have to sit down with him and let him see who he's dealing with."[66] Kennedy had admitted privately to Richard Nixon in April that the Bay of Pigs disaster might have led Khrushchev to believe that he could "keep pushing us all over the world," and he told O'Donnell that "it was one thing to become involved in a fight between Communists in Laos or Cuba, but this is the time to let [Khrushchev] know that a showdown between the United States and Russia would be entirely something else again."[67]

Khrushchev made no reply for nine weeks, perhaps waiting for a favorable moment. In May, at last, he sent word that he wished to proceed with the summit meeting at Vienna early in June. George Ball, high in the State Department, thought the timing unpropitious, "just after the 'series of defeats we have suffered' in space, Cuba, and Laos." There were questions also as to whether Kennedy was up to the task.[68] Perhaps the desire to dispel such assessments helped Kennedy decide to go to Vienna. Perhaps, also, the wish to demonstrate his toughness led him to give an unprecedented second State of the Union Address on May 25 in which he asked Congress for increased funds for defense, including a tripling of expenditure for fallout shelters, as well as for a large sum for the space program to enable the United States to place a man on the moon by 1970.

Kennedy gave yet another reason for seeking a meeting with Khrushchev in his talk to the press. He was going, he said to "avoid the 'serious miscalculations' which had produced the earlier wars of the century."[69] This was one of Kennedy's pet ideas. He had taken a course in the origins of the First World War at Harvard just before the Second World War, when the revisionist views of Harvard's Sydney Fay were dominant, as they were in colleges across the country. This had impressed him with the ease with which "one nation's misinterpretation of another's intention could set them sliding into war." He had, moreover, been much impressed by Barbara Tuchman's *The Guns of August,* which he thought supported that view, recommended it to his staff, and lectured them "on the fatal miscalculation known to experts as 'accidental war.' "[70] His meeting with Khrushchev had as its goal, too, to lecture Khrushchev on the same point and thereby help avoid war by miscalculation.

It is, as usual, more difficult to know why the Soviet leader at last decided to press for a meeting. Fyodor Burlatsky, one of Khrushchev's assistants, suggests that the Soviet leader

> thought he would be able to exert greater influence and pressure on Kennedy than on [Eisenhower], the experienced "political wolf." . . .
>
> Khrushchev went to Vienna with quite different feelings from those with which he went to Camp David. Not only had he gained confidence, he had even become somewhat self-opinionated. If before his meeting with Eisenhower he had been concerned not to lose face, before meeting Kennedy he was more preoccupied with how to put the young president "in his place" and secure the concessions he wanted from him.[71]

For Kennedy dealing with the Russians, as for Lord Grey dealing with the Germans before the First World War, the goal was to settle particular issues of concern to his nation in the hope that this might lead to a general entente, step by step. Kennedy, therefore, hoped to resolve the problems that pressed on him—arms control, Southeast Asia, Soviet incursions into the third world. The hottest spot was Berlin, but since there the status quo was the best the Americans could hope for, any change could only be for the worse and would surely produce a serious confrontation. Kennedy, therefore, hoped to avoid the subject of Berlin, get Khrushchev to freeze the current situation there, and allow progress on particular issues on which it was easier to agree. Khrushchev, on the contrary, like Kaiser William II, wanted a general realignment of power that would permit his nation to gain ground, to win recognition at least equal to that of his opponent's, to proceed with dynamic growth, and perhaps to gain ultimate domination. Khrushchev challenged Kennedy's conventional idea of the status quo. For him, as Arthur Schlesinger has put it, "it was in essence the communist revolution in progress (as he hoped) across the world. From this perspective Kennedy's conception of a global standstill was an attempt not to support but to alter the status quo; it was an attack on the revolutionary process itself."[72] In the same way, the Kaiser had seen Britain's attempt to stop the building of a German fleet and Germany's attempts to force its way into other people's colonies. Reminiscing about the meeting in Vienna, Khrushchev later told Senator William Benton that " 'we in the USSR feel that the revolutionary process should have the right to exist. The question of the right to rebel, and the Soviet right to help combat reactionary governments . . . is the question of questions. . . . This question is at the heart of our relations with you. . . . Kennedy could not understand this.' " This, as Schlesinger points out, was Khrushchev's notion of coexistence: "the democracies had no right to intervene in the Communist world, while the communists had every right to intervene in the democratic world."[73] Khrushchev appears to have come to Vienna seeking a general political breakthrough,[74] and the weakness already displayed by the young American President encouraged him to believe that in a face-to-face meeting he might bully Kennedy into giving way.

The first meeting took place on the morning of June 3.[75] Kennedy argued that the struggle of ideas should be carried out "in a way which would not involve the two countries directly and would not affect their national interest or prestige."[76] That amounted to a plea for the maintenance of the political status quo, and Kennedy supported it with the understanding of history he had learned in college and was eager to share with Khrushchev. "My ambition is to secure peace. If we fail in that effort, both our countries will lose. . . . Our two countries possess modern weapons. . . . If our two countries should miscalculate, they would lose for a long time to come." The Soviet leader did not want to follow this path that suggested mutual danger and mutual accommodation. He wanted to increase the pressure, not to cool the atmosphere. As Kennedy described it to an aide soon after the meeting, "Khrushchev went berserk":

He started yelling, "Miscalculations! Miscalculations! Miscalculations! All I ever hear from your people and your news correspondents and your friends in Europe and everyplace else is that damned word 'miscalculation'! You ought to take that word and bury it in cold storage and never use it again! I'm sick of it." It was a vague Western concept and just another "clever way of making threats."[77]

Did America want the Soviet Union "to sit like a schoolboy with hands on top of the desk"? The Soviets believed in its ideas and would not guarantee that they would stop at its borders. "The Soviet Union was going to defend its vital interests, whether or not the United States regarded such acts as miscalculations; it did not want war but it would not be intimidated either."[78] To calm the atmosphere Kennedy explained that he was talking only about the difficulty of predicting what any country might do next. He conceded that the United States had made "certain misjudgments," for instance, in failing to foresee Chinese intervention in the Korean War. The purpose of this meeting, he said, "is to introduce precision in judgments of the two sides and to obtain a clearer understanding of where we are going."[79] That was not, of course, Khrushchev's purpose, but as the time for lunch was approaching, he left the matter there.

After lunch Kennedy took Khrushchev for a stroll in the garden, for he had learned that the Chairman became easier when he walked in the woods of Camp David with Eisenhower in 1959. It did not seem to help, for Kennedy's aide, watching from a distance, reported Khrushchev "shaking his finger" and "snapping like a terrier" at the President. Kennedy's report is that he returned to the theme that both leaders were responsible for peace: "I propose to tell you what I can do and what I can't do, what my problems and possibilities are, and then you can do the same." Khrushchev's version is that Kennedy "described the narrowness of his 1960 victory and his weakness in Congress and asked him not to demand too many concessions because he could be turned out of the Presidency."[80] In any case, that was not the conversation Khrushchev had in mind, and he launched into a harangue on Berlin before they returned for the afternoon session.

The former Harvard history major doggedly returned to the instruction of the less well-educated Soviet leader, arriving at his favorite subject of miscalculation. "Hoping to win Khrushchev over with a self-deprecating remark, he said that he himself had miscalculated at the Bay of Pigs. By his own account, 'It was more than a mistake. It was a failure.' " In return Khrushchev was happy to point out that "in the speech before the Twentieth Party Congress I admitted Stalin's mistakes."

He complained of the Americans' tendency to blame all revolutions on Communist instigation. It was American support of reactionaries like Batista in Cuba and the Shah in Iran that caused revolutions. How could the Americans claim to fear Castro in tiny Cuba? How should the Soviet Union feel about Turkey and Iran, "followers of the United States," who "march in its wake, and they have U.S. bases and rockets"? It was the Americans who were the first to intervene in the internal affairs of other countries. "He warned that, 'to use the President's term,' this situation might generate some miscalculation, too."[81] In the face of this assault Kennedy retreated, disclaiming any brief for Batista and conceding that if the Shah did not improve the condition of his people, his country also would have to change. When this remark was leaked to the Shah it made him worry that the Americans might be thinking of removing him from power.[82]

Khrushchev used the discussion of Laos once again to repeat the same themes: "If the United States supports old, moribund, reactionary regimes, then a precedent of intervention in internal affairs will be set, which might cause a clash between our two countries." After this scarcely veiled threat Kennedy made a truly remarkable statement: "We regard . . . Sino-Soviet forces and the forces of the United States and Western Europe as being more or less in balance." Even had it been true it would have been a gratuitous admission that could undermine American deterrence of Soviet adventures, but it was not true. The Soviet Union and China, far from being partners in a unified bloc, were at each other's throats, so their forces should not have been lumped together. In 1961, moreover, the Americans had an overwhelming advantage in nuclear missiles and knew they did. So, of course, did Khrushchev. What could he have made of an American President who admitted to military parity while enjoying enormous superiority? As Michael Beschloss points out:

> The President's declaration sent Khrushchev into near ecstasy. For the rest of his life he boasted that at this summit the leader of the United States had finally acknowledged that there was rough parity between the two great powers. Dictating his memoirs in the late

1960s, he praised Kennedy for understanding that the Soviet bloc had amassed such economic and military might "that the United States and its allies could no longer seriously consider going to war against us."

In Washington, when the Joint Chiefs learned of Kennedy's comment, they were furious.[83]

Before the meeting in Vienna the President had been told by a Soviet intermediary that Khrushchev would be prepared to make concessions on nuclear testing and Laos if Kennedy were willing to come to the summit.[84] He therefore returned the conversation to Laos. Here again Kennedy conceded that American policy had not always been "wise," but the concession brought no profit.

Kennedy took up the theme of "wars of national liberation," which Khrushchev had endorsed in a speech in January. The President did not argue the rightness of the American case or make any threats, explicit or implicit, but once again, Kennedy's restraint did not soften the Chairman's response. Wars of national liberation were sacred wars. Additions to the Communist side, in Africa, for example, "would be examples of the popular will. If there were to be interference, there would be a chain reaction and ultimately war between the two countries." As Dean Rusk said much later, "In diplomacy you almost never use the word war."[85] The Chairman's threatening tone had moved beyond the bounds of normal diplomatic discourse. Again Kennedy turned the other cheek, saying that he had no trouble with different social systems, such as those of Yugoslavia, Burma, and India, so long as they were not closely tied to the Soviet Union, in which case they might pose "strategic problems" for the United States. To clarify this veiled reference to Cuba, Kennedy asserted that Khrushchev would be troubled if the Poles joined the West. "Khrushchev angrily replied that what happened in Poland was none of the President's business. . . . If the premise of American policy was to preserve the balance of power, the United States must not really want peaceful coexistence. Maybe it was seeking a pretext for war."[86]

The two men met again the next day at the Soviet Embassy, and at once Khrushchev resumed the attack. "What business did the United States have claiming special rights in Laos? . . . [It] is so rich and powerful that it believes it has special rights and can afford not to recognize the rights of others." The Soviet Union insisted on its right to help other peoples gain their independence.

Khrushchev then made use again of Kennedy's extraordinary statement of the day before: "As the President has stated, the forces of the two sides are now in balance. . . . A great deal of restraint is required because the factors of prestige and national interests are involved here." Kennedy again undercut his own position by saying that "frankly speaking," the American commitments in Laos antedated his assumption of office. He wanted to reduce those commitments and sought only a way to have a cease-fire. Instead of permitting that retreat, Khrushchev questioned the President's veracity, another extraordinary procedure in normal diplomacy. "Hadn't the President ordered U.S. military advisers in Laos to wear American uniforms? Hadn't he ordered and then canceled a Marine landing in Laos?"[87] The President truthfully denied that he had ordered in the Marines, but Khrushchev said that was not what he read in the American newspapers and delivered yet another warning: "if the United States were to send Marines, other countries might respond with Marines or some other forces. Another Korea or an even worse situation might result." Kennedy said he was eager to remove U.S. forces from Laos and had not wanted even to consider using the Marines, recognizing that that would bring a "counteraction, and thus peace in that area might be endangered."[88] Khrushchev at last agreed to work for a cease-fire in Laos. "The two men thus completed the one piece of business transacted at Vienna."[89] On a nuclear test ban, however, there was no agreement. Once again the Chairman rejected adequate inspection within the Soviet Union as an excuse for espionage.[90]

At last they turned to the subject of greatest importance to them both —Berlin. Khrushchev asserted that the situation in Germany was intolerable. There was still no peace settlement long after the end of the war; West Germany was rearmed and the leading European power in NATO. "This meant the threat of a third world war." If the West did not agree to a treaty the Soviet Union would sign one with East Germany alone. Such a treaty, by ending the state of war, would cancel all occupation rights, administrative structures, and rights of access, which would have to be negotiated with the East German government.[91] It was implicit that such negotiations with the subservient Soviet satellite would not be successful.

Kennedy responded firmly: this was not a question of legal technicalities, nor was the argument about Laos. This was a matter of great importance to the United States. The Americans were not in Berlin by anyone's permission; they had fought their way in:

> This is an area where every President of the United States since World War II . . . has reaffirmed his faithfulness to his obliga- tions. If we were expelled from that area and if we accepted the loss of our rights, no one would have any confidence in U.S. commit- ments and pledges. . . . If we were to accept the Soviet proposal, U.S. commitments would be regarded as a scrap of paper. Western Europe is vital to our national security, and we have supported it in two wars. If we were to leave West Berlin, Europe would be aban- doned as well.

He conceded that the situation in Berlin was "not satisfactory," but conditions all over the world were unsatisfactory. The Soviet Union would not accept a change in the balance against its interests; no more could the U.S.

Beschloss is critical of Kennedy for his unbending position on Berlin and for asking for "a standstill in the Cold War." At Camp David, Eisen- hower had talked vaguely about some interim agreement that would "not involve the prestige of our two countries";[92] Kennedy, on the other hand, was asking Khrushchev "to renounce the ideal of dynamic world commu- nism that he privately cherished and publicly championed. . . . Simply to drop the Berlin demands that he had been making since 1958, whatever the political humiliation."[93] But Eisenhower, in fact, had imposed political humiliation on the Chairman in 1958 by ignoring his Berlin ultimatum, and the world had not come to an end. What compromise was possible, after all? The United States could not abandon West Berlin without hand- ing the Soviets a major victory and suffering the consequences Kennedy correctly described to Khrushchev. What choice, moreover, did an Ameri- can leader have but either to try to stop the march of "world communism" or succumb to it if the Soviet Union insisted on pressing forward? Any errors Kennedy made at Vienna were not the result of stubborn intransi- gence.

Further debate did not improve the atmosphere. Khrushchev threat- ened to sign a treaty with East Germany in six months. "If the U.S. wants to start a war over Germany, let it be so. Perhaps the USSR should sign a peace treaty right away and get it over with."[94] According to Schlesinger this "was not quite a tirade; it was too controlled and hard and therefore more menacing." He reports that

> Kennedy replied that the United States did not wish to precipitate a crisis. The Soviet Union was doing so by threatening unilateral changes in the existing situation. Was this the way to achieve peace? If the United States surrendered to the Soviet demand, it would not be regarded as a serious country any longer.
>
> Khrushchev became even harsher. The Soviet Union, he said, would never under any conditions accept American rights in West Berlin after the treaty. . . . [R]esponsibilty for subsequent violations of East German sovereignty would be heavy.

Kennedy replied that the United States did not wish to deprive the Soviet Union of its ties in Eastern Europe and would not submit to the loss of its own ties in Western Europe. He had not assumed office to accept arrangements totally inimical to American interests.[95]

It was time for lunch, but Kennedy was most dissatisfied with the course and outcome of the talks. He told his aides that he must see Khrushchev again to pin down the Soviet position on Berlin and leave the Chairman with no doubts about his firmness: "I can't leave here without giving it one more try."[96] After lunch they met again. Once again, Kennedy hinted at the dangers of miscalculation. He hoped that Khrushchev would not bring about a situation "so deeply involving our national interest, [because] no one can predict what course it would take." After a further exchange Khrushchev slammed his open hand on the table. *"I want peace. But if you want war, that is your problem."* Kennedy replied, *"It is you, and not I, who wants to force a change."* Like the Roman legates at Carthage in 218 B.C. Khrushchev answered, "It is up to the U.S. to decide whether there will be war or peace." His decision to sign the peace treaty was "firm and irrevocable. . . . The Soviet Union will sign it in December if the U.S. refuses an interim agreement." Kennedy answered, "If that is true, it's going to be a cold winter."[97]

The meeting had not gone as Kennedy had hoped. The mood had not been conciliatory, as he had been led to believe it would be. All he had gained was a promise to ease the pressure in Laos; he had not even achieved the expected agreement on a test-ban treaty. What he had learned about Khrushchev was neither comforting nor helpful. His attempts to impress his counterpart with the dangers of miscalculation had fallen flat. Worst of all, his plan to show Khrushchev his toughness had miscarried entirely. In the face of Khrushchev's undiplomatic language; his questioning of Kennedy's veracity; his insistence on the Soviet Union's right and intention to intervene in behalf of "sacred" "wars of national liberation"; his announcement of an inflexible determination to change the status of Berlin, regardless of Western protests; his repeated threats of war; the President appeared weaker than before. He had conceded a military parity that did not exist; he had spoken of his domestic political weakness; he had distanced himself from positions taken by his predecessors, which implied a willingness to make concessions in those areas at the expense of allies. He had admitted to errors in his own policies in the hope of achieving reciprocal admissions, to no avail. He had been bullied.

Kennedy loyalists have tried to put the best face on this catastrophic encounter. Schlesinger says: "Each man came away from Vienna with greater respect for the mind and nerve of his adversary."[98] Sorensen asserts that it was "neither a victory nor a defeat for either side."[99] More than three decades later he still insisted that "as the transcript shows, Kennedy gave as well as he got throughout."[100] That was not how the President saw it. Rusk, who rode back with him after the meeting, later said that "Kennedy was very upset. . . . He wasn't prepared for the brutality of Khrushchev's presentation. . . . Khrushchev was trying to act like a bully to the young President of the United States."[101] When he reached the American residence in Vienna Kennedy was interviewed by James Reston of the *New York Times,* who asked, "Pretty rough?" The President replied, "Roughest thing in my life."

> I think he did it because of the Day of Pigs. I think he thought that anyone who was so young and inexperienced as to get into that mess could be taken. And anyone who got into it and didn't see it through had no guts. So he just beat hell out of me. . . . I've got a terrible problem. If he thinks I'm inexperienced and have no guts, until we remove those ideas we won't get anywhere with him. So we have to act.

Kennedy's fears about Khrushchev's perceptions seem to have been justified. The Chairman had been amazed "when Kennedy undercut his own arguments by saying he had inherited many of his policies and had no choice but to defend them. To a leader of Khrushchev's belief this absence of emotional conviction hinted at weakness; if Kennedy was motivated only by abstract geopolitical gamesmanship, he might fold under pressure."[102] Burlatsky, who was present at Khrushchev's debriefing after the summit, thought that Kennedy seemed to Khrushchev more like "an adviser, not a political decision-maker or President. Maybe in a crisis he would be an adviser, but not even the most influential." He thought that Khrushchev looked down on Kennedy as a self-made man regards a rich man to whom all has been handed: "This guy was here as a result of his own activities. And he understood the feelings of simple people. John Kennedy had no such feelings. Maybe his relations with workers and peasants were like a political game."[103] At a conference in 1988 he said the two leaders "left Vienna without understanding or sympathy. . . . Khrushchev thought Kennedy too young, intellectual, not prepared well for decision making in crisis situations." Another participant asked, "Too weak, or too ineffective?" "Too intelligent and too weak," was the answer.[104] That was the same impression of Khrushchev's evaluation received by some of the men close to Kennedy. George Ball, looking back in 1987, said, "We all thought that Khrushchev saw him as young and weak," and Kennedy's military adviser, General Maxwell Taylor, recalled that "the meeting of Khrushchev with President Kennedy in Vienna had so impressed him with the unreadiness of this young man to head a great country like the United States, plus the experience that he had seen in the Bay of Pigs, [led him to believe that] he could shove this young man around any place he wants."[105] In his speech reporting to the American people Kennedy must have confirmed Khrushchev's estimate. The "most somber" exchange, the President said, concerned Germany and Berlin. He told the American people: "We and our allies cannot abandon our obligations to the people of West Berlin." He did not tell them of the ultimatum Khrushchev had delivered; in fact he told them a lie, saying that there had been "no threats or ultimatums by either side."[106] Khrushchev, of course, knew otherwise and could draw his own conclusions as to why Kennedy had chosen to suppress the truth.

The Berlin Wall

Khrushchev's threats about Berlin made a powerful impression on Kennedy. After Vienna, even more than before, the problem of Berlin became an obsession with him. Secretary of the Interior Stewart Udall complained, "He's imprisoned by Berlin." Kennedy knew that defense of the city and access to it was an inescapable test of America's will and of its commitment to NATO and Western Europe as well. At the same time, its geographical position well within Soviet-controlled East Germany, where the West was at a hopeless military disadvantage, made it difficult to stand firm in a crisis without risking a nuclear confrontation. Khrushchev's threats created a nightmare that explains why Kennedy "tracked incoming cables and cleared many messages before they went to the Secretary of State for signature . . . [and] read transcripts of every conference."[107] He deeply resented the situation he had inherited and had little love for the people he was obliged to defend. "We're stuck in a ridiculous situation," he told his aide. "It seems silly for us to be facing an atomic war over a treaty preserving Berlin as the future capital of a reunited Germany when all of us know that Germany will probably never be reunited. . . . [I]t seems particularly stupid to risk killing millions of Americans over access rights on an Autobahn. Before I back Khrushchev against the wall and put him to the final test, the freedom of all Western Europe will have to be at stake." Access from the East to the West through Berlin was a terrible drain of manpower from East Germany. "You can't blame Khrushchev for being sore about that."[108]

It sometimes seemed as if Kennedy were more annoyed with his German allies than with the Soviets, but it was Khrushchev who was determined to press the issue and force a crisis. Apart from his other troubles at home and abroad, the Soviet leader could not ignore Berlin easily. For a long time Walter Ulbricht, the Communist dictator of East Germany, had been pressing Khrushchev to take action that would stop the flight of East Germans to the West. Since the end of the war some 4 million had left; in 1960 the figure was 200,000, and the rate of flight in the early months of 1961 indicated the total might be greater in that year. The refugees were disproportionately young, well-educated, skilled professionals. The East German population rapidly was becoming an aging society ever more difficult to support as the ablest younger people fled to the West.[109] The threat all this posed to the stability of East Germany, combined with the Soviets' continued fears that West Germany would soon acquire nuclear weapons, pushed Khrushchev toward action in Berlin.

The first sign perceived by the Americans was the appearance in *Pravda* on June 10 of the complete text of Khrushchev's aide-mémoire revealing his six-months' ultimatum on Berlin. Rusk had told Kennedy that if Khrushchev kept the ultimatum secret that would be evidence that he did not want a crisis on Berlin.[110] Its publication pointed clearly in the opposite direction. Only a few days later the influential Democratic senator from Montana, Mike Mansfield, came out in favor of making Berlin a "free city," as Khrushchev was proposing. Kennedy could no longer remain silent, so at a press conference on June 28 he separated himself from Mansfield's suggestion and warned that "the Soviets would make a grave mistake if they supposed that Allied unity and determination can be undermined by threats or fresh aggressive acts."[111]

As early as March Kennedy had called on Dean Acheson, Truman's Secretary of State, well known for his hardline views on the Cold War, to give advice on Berlin and the German problem. Acheson presented his views at a meeting of the National Security Council on June 29. He argued that the pressure on Berlin was only part of a general move to gain a broad range of goals in Germany and, beyond that, to test the will of the United States. There could be no negotiation and no concession. The United States must hold fast to the "three essentials" laid out by the Eisenhower administration for West Berlin: "(1) the preservation of Allied garrisons; (2) freedom of air and surface access; (3) the city's freedom and viability."[112] This had the effect of abandoning Western interests in East Berlin, which appalled West German leaders when they later learned of it, but not Eisenhower, nor Acheson, nor, in the event, Kennedy, thought it worth fighting for.

Acheson's proposal called for a major increase in American nuclear forces, in conventional forces in West Germany, in reserves in America ready for swift movement to Germany, and for the declaration of a national emergency. Word of this contingency planning leaked into the press; it may have been sprung deliberately by the White House "to send a stiff alarm to Khrushchev."[113] On July 8 Khrushchev reversed his plan to cut the size of the Red Army in light of the new importance of missile forces. Instead he would increase the Soviet military budget by a third, turning away from his cherished plan to divert as much military spending as possible toward improving the economy. This was pressed on him by military leaders, but there is no reason to doubt the effect of some of the reasons he gave publicly: "Adenauer was 'shouting himself hoarse for nuclear weapons,' [and] Kennedy has increased military spending."[114]

After considerable debate within the administration, President Kennedy decided to reject the call for a national emergency and the refusal to negotiate. His intention was to establish his and America's determination, after which he would seek to reopen discussions with the Soviets. In other respects he followed Acheson's advice, setting forth the American policy in a speech delivered on July 25. He revealed the increase in American forces in Germany, the call-up of reserves, and the use of new funds for fallout shelters. Although he spoke of removing "irritants" in Berlin and hinted at negotiation, his speech was tough, speaking publicly of war, as Khrushchev had spoken privately of it at Vienna:

> We have given our word that an attack upon that city will be regarded as an attack upon us all. . . . Any dangerous spot is tenable if men—brave men—make it so. We do not want to fight, but we have fought before. . . . The lives of those families which are not hit in a nuclear blast and fire can still be saved—*if* they can be warned to take shelter, and *if* that shelter is *available*. . . . We cannot negotiate with those who say, "What's mine is mine, and what's yours is negotiable." . . . The source of the world trouble and tension is Moscow, not Berlin. And if war begins, it will have begun in Moscow and not Berlin. . . . To sum it all up, we seek peace, but we shall not surrender.[115]

On the other hand, Kennedy made no reference to the guarantee of free access between East and West that was part of the Potsdam agreement; he spoke of the boundary between the two sectors as a "frontier of peace," and of the defense of "West Berlin," not of "Berlin." It was easy for a careful reader to see the speech as including an invitation to shut East Berlin off from the West.

The next day Khrushchev told his visitor, John McCloy, Kennedy's disarmament adviser, that the United States had declared "preliminary war," insisted that the Soviets would sign a German treaty "no matter what," and rattled his rockets: "If you attempt to force your way through, we will oppose you by force. War is bound to be thermonuclear." McCloy reported that the Chairman was "really mad . . . after digesting the President's speech."[116]

On July 30 J. William Fulbright, chairman of the Senate Foreign Relations Committee, suggested on national television that it might be a good thing if the Soviets closed the border in Berlin: "the Russians have the power to close it in any case. . . . If they chose to close their borders, they could without violating any treaty. I don't understand why the East Germans don't close their border because I think they have a right to close it."[117] The remarks caused outrage in West Berlin, but the East German newspapers greeted it as a splendid formula that could resolve the crisis. Fulbright's comment brought to mind the remarks of Senator Mansfield, and some thought that both Democratic senators had been inspired to suggest a compromise favored by Kennedy, who did not dare to make the proposal himself.[118]

There is no direct evidence that the President had anything to do with the senatorial statements, and it should be remembered that he publicly disagreed with Mansfield's statement. On the other hand, he never commented on Fulbright's remarks, and there is reason to believe that he agreed with them. Not long after Fulbright's television appearance Kennedy told foreign policy adviser Walt Rostow that Khrushchev "will have to do something to stop the flow of refugees. Perhaps a wall. And we won't be able to prevent it. I can hold the Alliance together to defend West Berlin, but I cannot act to keep East Berlin open."[119]

At least since March Ulbricht had been pressing Khrushchev to stop the flow of refugees, urging him to take control of the air lanes to the West and even to seize West Berlin.[120] When these ideas had been rejected he suggested putting up a barbed-wire barrier along the sector frontier, but there was considerable opposition, and he was allowed only to prepare for such an action at some future time. The suggestion of building a wall was not taken up until the Warsaw Pact leadership meeting in Berlin at the beginning of August. This time Ulbricht asserted that if the flight from the East was not stopped the East German economy would no longer be able to meet the demands of the Soviets and the other Eastern allies and asserted that there was danger of a workers' uprising like that of 1953. He also assured his listeners that the Americans would not act to prevent a border closing, citing Senator Fulbright's belief that East Germany had the right to do it. On August 5, therefore, Khrushchev agreed to the construction of a barrier at the sector border the following weekend, at midnight of the night of August 12–13. First they would erect a barbed-wire fence. If, as they expected, the West did not use force against it, they would replace it with a solid wall. Khrushchev gave his permission, along with the firm warning, "not one millimeter farther." The East Germans were not to step into the Western Zone, and Soviet officers would be there to see that they did not.

Apparently Khrushchev had read the signals from the West and concluded that the Americans would resist any interference with West Berlin but that it was safe to close the border from the East. On August 9 he told his generals that "we'll just put up the serpentine barbed wire, and the West will stand there like dumb sheep. And while they're standing there, we'll finish the wall,"[121] which is exactly what happened. In the next few days, however, he delivered messages meant to intimidate Kennedy and the Allies. Through intermediaries Kennedy received a message from Italy's Prime Minister, Amintore Fanfani. In a series of meetings with Khrushchev the Soviet leader had been terribly belligerent, threatening "a dozen times, no less," that a conflict over Berlin would mean nuclear war. Referring several times to the statements by Mansfield and Fulbright, he said he was willing to negotiate, but Kennedy must "not wait too long."[122] A few days later at a gathering in the Kremlin he threatened the Western allies with crushing not only "the orange groves of Italy but also the people who created them," as well as the olive orchards and the Acropolis in Greece. "In cutting off the head, nobody worries about the hair."[123]

Kennedy's reaction was like "the curious behaviour of the dog in the night" in the Sherlock Holmes story. The curious behavior was that he did nothing. The bullying of Fanfani was a probe meant to get back to Kennedy, who might then have used the occasion to send a warning back in direct or indirect fashion, privately or publicly. On August 10, at a news conference, the President had a splendid opportunity to send a public message, when a reporter asked him if the United States had any policy in regard to the flight of refugees from East Germany to the West. Here was the chance to reject the comments made by Fulbright and to deliver a warning. Kennedy responded that "the United States does not attempt to encourage or discourage the movements of refugees." Khrushchev had every reason to take that answer as a signal that the United States would not challenge the closing of the Berlin frontier.[124]

On the same day Marshal Ivan S. Konev, one of the most important Soviet generals in the Second World War, the conqueror of Prague and Dresden, appeared in Berlin as Commander-in-Chief of the Soviet forces there. It was an act sure to suggest some major undertaking; it was "as if the Americans had decided to call Eisenhower out of retirement."[125] In fact, the appointment was a bluff meant to impress the West with the seriousness of Soviet intentions. As Khrushchev later revealed, "The fact that Konev spent most of his time in Moscow proves that we weren't expecting the confrontation to escalate into a full-scale military conflict."[126] Asked by one of the Western generals about significant military movements in the vicinity, Konev announced, "Whatever may occur in the foreseeable future, your rights will remain untouched and nothing will be directed against West Berlin." This assurance convinced many West Germans that the West had made a deal with the Soviets approving the construction of the wall, another "stab in the back." Kennedy, speaking of the characteristic mistrust the Germans felt toward his administration, compared them to the wife who continually asked her husband if he loved her. "When he keeps saying that he does, she demands, 'But do you *really* love me?'—and then has him trailed by detectives."[127] German politicians were, indeed, often unduly suspicious, but in this case, their suspicions seem to have been justified. To be sure, there was no formal deal, but Kennedy had given repeated public indications that he did not include access to East Berlin as one of his requirements and, as we have seen, had privately made it plain that he would accept the closure of the frontier. The Soviets acted with the justly confident expectation that they would not be resisted.

At midnight on August 12 the barbed-wire fences separating West from East Berlin began to go up. The Western military commanders in Berlin took no action, in spite of the urging of West Berlin's mayor, Willy Brandt, who told them, "You let Ulbricht kick you in the rear last night!" The only response from Washington was a statement that "the violations of existing agreements will be the subject of vigorous protest through appropriate channels," a clear indication that the Americans would not take military action.[128] It was very much like the response the French made to Hitler's reoccupation of the Rhineland in 1936, an analogy that came to the mind of Wolfgang Leonhard, a former Communist who had been in Moscow during the war and was a charter member of the East German government under Ulbricht after the fall of Berlin. He urged that Western military forces move right up to the frontier at once. He was confident that Khrushchev would retreat, just as Hitler would have done had he been confronted by military force.[129] Brandt also had wanted a show of force, at least to reassure the West Berliners that they were not in danger. A Social Democrat who had been vehemently pro-American and a great admirer of Kennedy, he felt badly let down. "*Kennedy* is making mincemeat of us," he said, and those who knew him best say that the failure of American reaction to the wall caused his subsequent turn away from the United States toward accommodation with the Communist East and the advocacy of antinuclear and disarmament, goals that opposed American policies in the years to come. Later his close associate Egon Bahr said, "On August thirteenth we became adults." He reported Brandt as believing that by closing the border "the Soviet Union had defied the major power in the world and effectively humiliated it. . . . The curtain went up and the stage was empty."[130] Brandt wrote a letter to Kennedy complaining of American inaction that made the President very angry. When he showed it to the reporter Marguerite Higgins, however, she said, "Mr. President, I must tell you frankly: the suspicion is growing in Berlin that you're going to sell out the West Berliners." That her perception was right was proved by 300,000 Berliners who crowded into the square in front of Berlin City Hall carrying homemade signs that read: BETRAYED BY THE WEST. WHERE ARE THE PROTEC-TIVE [Western] POWERS? and THE WEST IS DOING A SECOND MUNICH.

Privately, the American position was that nothing need be done. The immediate reaction of America's ambassador to the Soviet Union, Foy Kohler, was that "the East Germans have done us a favor. That refugee flow was becoming embarrassing."[131] The President looked upon the building of the wall as a way out of the Berlin dilemma. He told a trusted aide: "This is [Khrushchev's] way out of his predicament. It's not a very nice solution, but a wall is a hell of a lot better than a war."[132] The private attitude of the American leaders was remarkably similar to that of the British at the news of Hitler's occupation of Austria, when Sir Alexander Cadogan, permanent undersecretary at the Foreign Office, said, "Thank goodness Austria's out of the way. . . . After all, it wasn't our business: We had no particular feeling for the Austrians: We only forbade the *Anschluss* to spite Germany."[133] But such statements could not be made publicly, for they would surely be seen as evidence of America's lack of commitment and would be denounced as appeasement. American officials in Germany and members of his own administration in Washington warned Kennedy of sagging morale in Berlin and of the dangers of inaction. General Lucius Clay, the hero of the first Berlin crisis of 1948–49 and the airlift, thought back to those days, convinced that if he had been allowed to send an armored column into Berlin then "the Korean War never would have taken place. If he were President now, he'd tear the Wall down."[134] Kennedy, of course, would do no such thing, but he felt the pressure to take some action to reassure those who doubted his courage and

America's determination. On August 17 he decided to send a battle group of fifteen hundred men overland from West Germany into Berlin to demonstrate American commitment to keep open access to Berlin. With them went Vice President Lyndon Johnson to represent the President and General Clay, a symbol of American steadfastness.

The mission had considerable success; the Berliners and even Brandt were reassured that at least the Americans intended to protect West Berlin. Not all Americans and their friends, however, were satisfied. On his return from Berlin Johnson told reporters off the record that the Berlin crisis was the result of the American performance in Laos and at the Bay of Pigs. Khrushchev, he said, "has tasted blood in Cuba and Laos and now Berlin, and he's out for more. He thinks he can push a young President around and a new administration and is probing to see how far he can go."[135] Eisenhower privately was appalled by Kennedy's failure to defend the Potsdam agreement. Dean Acheson and Lucius Clay thought that if the Americans had acted vigorously and swiftly they could have prevented the erection of the wall without danger. Couve de Murville, the French Foreign Minister and De Gaulle himself believed that "it might have been better to have an immediate reaction against the Wall . . . and maybe the Russians would have withdrawn."[136] In retrospect it does not seem likely that an assault on the wall, however early, even when the barrier was only barbed wire, would have been useful. Had the wall been ruptured, the Communist forces always could have drawn further back and built another, and the Western forces could hardly penetrate the border at any great depth to keep knocking down barriers. Nor was it reasonable to risk a war over the issue, but there were considerable risks, too, in the manner in which the President had allowed the wall to be built and the complaisance with which he seemed to accept it.

He had refused conspicuous opportunities to warn the Soviets away from their unilateral violation of the Potsdam agreement, appearing to invite such an action as a way of buying a relaxation of the tension over Berlin. Years later Bundy admitted that Kennedy's speech of July 25 may have encouraged Khrushchev to close the frontier. "It might have been wise at least to be less clear about it—to leave Khrushchev with greater uncertainty—to leave room in his mind for the possibility that a wall might mean a war." Such a speech might have been "more broadly deterrent to Khrushchev."[137] But that was the opposite of Kennedy's approach. He sought "definition and clarity," always fearing that war would come by

miscalculation. He did not appear to consider that when some clear defini-
tions might signal weakness and retreat they could lead to the miscalculation that such a retreat might continue indefinitely. After the building of
the wall, moreover, an action that could be characterized fairly as "secret,
swift and extraordinary," a "sudden, clandestine decision," a "deliberately
provocative and unjustified change in the status quo" (these are the words
he would later use to describe the introduction of nuclear missiles into
Cuba),[138] he made no public statement for over a week and barely mentioned the matter for the rest of his life. It was open to both friend and foe
to interpret his behavior as part of a policy of appeasement under duress. It
might be thought, especially by the man who had treated him so harshly at
Vienna, that the American President was a man who was tough in his
public speeches and military gestures but soft and accommodating in his
thoughts and policies; whose political weakness did not permit him to
make concessions publicly in open negotiations, but who was willing to
permit a fait accompli and to accept it without retaliation; who could be
pushed to abandon positions taken by tougher predecessors in his search for
peaceful accommodation.

Khrushchev was very different, a man both calculating and reckless.
Fyodor Burlatsky, one of his aides, called him an "adventurer," a "risky
man" who liked to probe and test his opponent. "We tested this," he said,
in Berlin: "if we press the United States, what happens?" For Kennedy the
Berlin crisis was a terribly dangerous situation that might lead to nuclear
war, which therefore called for restraint and concessions. But Khrushchev
and his assistants saw things differently: "We had no . . . feelings that it
was a dramatic story with Berlin. It was one more step in the Cold War, but
we did not think it was that dangerous. We pressed you, you pressed us, but
it was not that dangerous. Only games—political games. That is all." Sergo
Mikoyan, the son of Khrushchev's close associate and his father's secretary
during the crises of 1961 and 1962, does not always see eye-to-eye with
Burlatsky, but on this matter they are agreed: "I remember one phrase
Khrushchev used at home; he said Berlin is the tail of imperialism, and we
can yank it when they do something wrong to us. I think this was his idea,
but I do not believe it was important for us."[139] For Kennedy, however,
there was no game, only a deadly and frightening pressure that occupied his
mind throughout the crisis to come.

Rattling Missiles

Even before the construction of the wall Kennedy had pressed Rusk to find a way to begin negotiations over Berlin with Khrushchev. He was prepared to ignore or overcome the resistance of his allies and begin talks with the Soviets as soon as possible. To prepare for them he suggested the formation of a small working group excluding such hardliners as Acheson and Kohler. He proposed instead Charles Bohlen, Bundy, and Sorensen, "three men whom critics might deem insufficiently tough on Berlin," telling Rusk that the group "should be as nearly invisible as possible," for its members were to seek fresh, new proposals, not "warmed-over stuff from 1959."[140]

It is not certain what new proposals he had in mind, but it is clear that in 1961 and 1962 "the shift in U.S. policy was dramatic."[141] In that period the Kennedy administration, de facto, accepted the Oder-Neisse line and with it the division of Germany and considered moving toward separate treaties and a nonaggression pact between the two Germanies. Kennedy was prepared not to insist on occupation rights in West Berlin "if other strong guarantees can be designed." He was ready to discuss "a zone of limited armaments" in Central Europe, and the United States moved away from the idea of sharing nuclear weapons with Germany. And, of course, he had accepted the construction of the wall, an open breach of the Potsdam agreement.

> The world at the end of 1962 was very different from the world of November 1958. In the 1950s, the German question was still an open issue. In the 1960s, the division of Germany was accepted as a fact of life. In the late 1950s, it seemed Germany was well on its way to acquiring nuclear weapons. By the early 1960s it had become clear that the Federal Republic was not going to control nuclear forces of its own.[142]

These changes were major achievements for Khrushchev and his policy of aggressive bluffing. As one scholar has put it, "It is in fact striking how far the Soviets were able to go with what amounted to a crude strategy of just keeping the pot boiling and giving it a stir from time to time—and this during a period when the Americans clearly had the upper hand in terms of the strategic nuclear balance."[143]

Kennedy's note urging Rusk to press ahead with negotiations was written on August 21. Just one week later the President learned that the Soviet Union was undertaking a new series of nuclear tests. This was a direct violation of Khrushchev's assurance at Vienna, repeated in July, that he would not be the first to resume testing. "Fucked again," was the President's response to an action that Sorensen believes was the deepest disappointment Kennedy suffered at the hands of the Soviets during his presidency.[144] Kennedy understood the action to be some form of intimidation, but he still could not understand the decision. Throughout his presidency neither Kennedy nor his colleagues seem to have understood consistently Khrushchev's methods nor his belief that the American President could be bullied. The Chairman had told Soviet nuclear scientists on July 10 of his plans to resume testing. Andrei Sakharov passed him a note warning of the dangerous consequences of resumption. Khrushchev's response reveals his view of Kennedy.

> Look, we helped elect Kennedy last year. Then we met with him in Vienna, a meeting that could have been a turning point. But what does he say? "Don't ask for too much. Don't put me in a bind. If I make too many concessions, I'll be turned out of office." Quite a guy! He comes to a meeting but can't perform. What the hell do we need a guy like that for? Why waste time talking to him?[145]

The first Soviet test took place on September 1. Kennedy was reluctant to resume American testing, so he and British Prime Minister Macmillan the next day proposed an atmospheric test ban *without inspection,* a vital concession that no Western leader had been willing to make previously. The only answer was the explosion on September 3 of another Soviet nuclear bomb, followed the next day by a third nuclear test. The President felt he no longer had a choice, explaining: "I had waited two days for an answer to the message Macmillan and I sent to Khrushchev. That was plenty of time. All they did was shoot off two more bombs," so he ordered a resumption of nuclear testing, but not in the atmosphere. He appears to have understood Khrushchev's intentions, but only in part. To Rusk he explained that it was too soon to expect a response from the Russians to

American invitations to negotiate on Berlin. "They are bent on scaring the world to death before they begin negotiating, and they haven't quite brought the pot to a boil. Not enough people are frightened." To Adlai Stevenson's complaints he responded: "They had spit in our eye three times. We couldn't possibly sit back and do nothing at all. . . . All this makes Khrushchev look pretty tough. He has had a succession of apparent victories—space, Cuba, the Wall. He wants to give out the feeling that he has us on the run." To his friend Ben Bradlee of the *Washington Post,* however, he revealed his belief "that the foul winds of war are blowing," that "Khrushchev is moving inevitably toward the brink."[146] He clearly did not understand Khrushchev's reliance on bluff, his delight in games-manship, but took his threatening words and actions with full seriousness, in spite of America's overwhelming strategic advantage.

He continued to try to find a road to accommodation, using an interview with James Reston of the *New York Times* to send the message of his eagerness to negotiate. Khrushchev responded through the same me-dium, using an interview with C. L. Sulzberger to communicate his views. He insisted again on the conclusion of a German peace treaty and on making West Berlin a "free city." Such was his confidence that he made public for the first time a sanitized version of his picture of the American President. He was "too young. He lacks the authority and the prestige to settle this issue. . . . If Kennedy appealed to the people, if he voiced his real inner thoughts and stated that there is no use fighting over Berlin . . . the situation would be settled quickly." Eisenhower could have said these things, and "no one could have accused him of being young, inexperi-enced, or afraid." If, however, Kennedy said them, "the opposition will raise its voice and accuse him of youth, cowardice, and a lack of statesman-ship. He is afraid of that." At the same time, privately and secretly through Sulzberger, he offered to undertake discussions, but only "on the basis of a peace treaty and a free Berlin."[147] The remarks in the *Times* amounted to a public insult, challenging Kennedy to prove his maturity and courage by yielding to Khrushchev's demands. The secret message presumed the Presi-dent would not take umbrage and refuse further discussions in his eagerness for a settlement, a correct assumption.

In the second half of September Rusk carried out the President's instructions to talk to Gromyko and see if negotiations over Berlin were possible. Rusk told Gromyko that "if the atmosphere can be improved, we are quite ready for businesslike and constructive discussion." He said the

United States would fight to defend its rights in Berlin, and Gromyko responded that war over Berlin would be foolish, "unthinkable and unnecessary." Bohlen, one of the three men Kennedy had chosen to plan for negotiations on Berlin, took this to mean that "there may be some real give in the Soviet position."[148] The Soviets had reason to believe that there was considerably more "give" on the other side, whose government had come seeking negotiations immediately after Khrushchev had broken an important promise in a most public and violent way and capped that with a public insult to the American President.

Khrushchev continued to play the cat-and-mouse game, alternating harsh threats and insults with friendly gestures, sometimes combining the two. He sent a messenger to communicate with Kennedy through his press secretary, Pierre Salinger. The envoy reported that "the storm in Berlin is over." The Chairman was willing to meet with Kennedy at a time when the President's political troubles permitted, to talk about American ideas about Berlin, but he urged haste, because the dangers of a major military confrontation in Berlin were great. Kennedy took the message to mean that Khrushchev would not sign a treaty with East Germany that year.[149] Soon afterward Gromyko confirmed that to Rusk. When Gromyko then came to the White House for a conversation in which "he had nothing new to offer," Kennedy concluded, "It looks like a thaw."[150]

Khrushchev's envoy advised the President not to let his forthcoming speech at the UN be warlike, like the one on July 25, but Kennedy made no change in his text. He reaffirmed the Western position on West Berlin and once again raised the spector of nuclear war: "We in this hall will be remembered either as part of the generation that turned this planet into a flaming funeral pyre or as the generation that met its vow 'to save succeeding generations from the scourge of war.' The decision is ours. For together we shall save our planet—or together we shall perish in its flames." He painted a picture of *Götterdämmerung,* where all would perish alike. That is not, of course, the way that Khrushchev rattled his rockets, always giving the impression that it was his enemies who would be destroyed while the Soviet Union survived, precisely the official Soviet military doctrine. "To ensure that no one mistook this rhetoric for weakness," as Beschloss points out, Robert Kennedy had appeared on the television news program *Meet the Press* the previous day to say, "I would hope that in the last few weeks [Khrushchev] would have come to the realization that the President will use nuclear weapons."[151]

There was reason to doubt whether not only Khrushchev but Kennedy's fellow Americans had come to that realization. In his interview with Sulzberger the President recalled that Republican Senator Margaret Chase Smith had been one of several people to doubt that he had the will to use nuclear weapons. He assured his interlocutor that "I think we have convinced Khrushchev on that," but he had not convinced all Americans of his nerve. On October 27, with Soviet tanks confronting an equal number of American tanks at the frontier in Berlin, the President spoke to General Clay on the telephone. The general expressed his opinion that the Soviets were not going to do anything. Kennedy responded: "I'm glad of that. I know you people over there haven't lost your nerve." Clay answered: "Mr. President, we're not worried about our nerves, we're worrying about those of you people in Washington."[152] At a luncheon in the White House a hawkish Texas publisher told the President, "We can annihilate Russia and should make that clear to the Soviet government. . . . You and your Administration are weak sisters." The situation called for "a man on horseback. . . . Many people in Texas and the Southwest think that you are riding Caroline's tricycle." His newspaper received over two thousand responses to the story, 84 percent of them in support of the accusation.[153]

For domestic political reasons and also to influence Khrushchev's behavior Kennedy needed to take some action to increase confidence in America's strength. As early as February, just a few months after Kennedy had won election claiming the Republicans had permitted a "missile gap" in favor of the Soviets, McNamara had let slip the news that "there is no missile gap." He said that each side had about the same number of missiles in place, not volunteering that the United States had about six thousand nuclear warheads to some three hundred for the Soviets. His information came chiefly from imperfect satellite photographs that were hard to read. In June, using information supplied by the secret agent Oleg Penkovsky, the CIA judged that the Soviets had fifty to a hundred working intercontinental ballistic missiles (ICBMs). Using a fuller collection of much improved photographs taken by the Discoverer satellite, their estimate on September 6 was of fewer than thirty-five. A week later that figure was amended to ten to twenty-five ICBMs that were in unhardened silos, slow and difficult to launch.[154] Such missiles were of no value for a second strike; pinpointed on American photographs they were of little more use for a first strike, which, in any case, would be suicide against a vastly superior American arsenal of missiles that could be launched from airplanes, submarines, and land-based missile launchers. "The whole Soviet ICBM system was suddenly obsolescent."[155]

The temptation to reveal this information to the Soviets was enormous. If they knew that the Americans had overwhelming nuclear superiority, that the Americans were aware of it, and that they had clear aerial photographs of each and every Soviet missile installation, that would deter bullying and nuclear blackmail. Some thought that it was important that such a revelation should be private, so that Khrushchev was not embarrassed publicly and forced to speed up his own production of missiles and warheads or to undertake some dangerous maneuver to recoup his position. But Kennedy had a compelling reason for making the announcement public. As we have seen, domestic critics doubted American military capacity to meet the Soviet threat, as well as Kennedy's resolve to use the forces available. With midterm elections coming up the President wanted to dispel any suggestion of unpreparedness and of his own weakness. He might hope that a public announcement of American nuclear superiority would meet both problems.

The announcement was made on October 21, 1962, by Roswell Gilpatric, undersecretary of defense. He listed specific types and numbers of America's nuclear weapons, summing them up by saying: "The total number of our delivery vehicles . . . is in the tens of thousands, and, of course, we have more than one warhead for each vehicle." The core of his message was:

> The destructive power which the United States could bring to bear even after a Soviet surprise attack upon our forces would be as great as, perhaps even greater than, the total undamaged force which the enemy can threaten to launch against the United States in a first strike. In short, we have a second-strike capability which is at least as extensive as what the Soviets can deliver by striking first.[156]

The immediate response from Khrushchev was to order another nuclear blast two days after Gilpatric's speech. Soviet Defense Minister Malinovsky also made a speech in which he breathed defiance, denied American nuclear superiority, and warned of the destruction that would befall Western Europe in case of war.[157] At the end of March 1962 the President gave an interview to Stewart Alsop in which he said that "Khrushchev must *not* be certain that, where its vital interests are threatened, the United States will never strike first. . . . In some circumstances we might have to take the initiative." The intention, once again, must have been to demonstrate Kennedy's toughness and resolve; if so, the ploy did not work any better than Gilpatrick's speech. To Khrushchev the interview must have seemed an attempt to intimidate the Soviets and use the newly proclaimed nuclear superiority as a political weapon. When Salinger visited him in May the Chairman said, "Your President has made a bad mistake, a very bad mistake, for which he will have to pay. . . . He has said you will be the first to use the Bomb. . . . Not even Eisenhower or Dulles would have made the statement your President has made. He now forces us to reappraise our own position."[158] The Soviet reaction and subsequent behavior does not suggest fear that the Americans would make use of their nuclear superiority, now publicly proclaimed. Neither these statements nor other Western actions appear to have affected the pace of Soviet missile production, which had been moving as fast as possible since the late 1950s.[159] Khrushchev's decision to place missiles secretly in Cuba, with the expectation that the American President would take no military action when their presence was revealed, makes no sense if the Soviet leader thought that Kennedy was capable of a nuclear "bolt from the blue." The best explanation of the Chairman's behavior is that he believed that the President would not launch his nuclear weapons even under threat and provocation, so that Khrushchev could right the strategic and political balance without serious danger.

In retrospect, from the standpoint of policy and strategy, the decision to make a public statement revealing America's superiority appears to have been amateurish and a mistake. The public revelation that Khrushchev had been bluffing about Soviet leadership in nuclear weapons, that the opposite was emphatically true, was embarrassing. It would make trouble for him in the struggle against China within the Communist bloc and strengthen the hand of his critics at home. The main effect, very likely, was to make it even more difficult to contemplate an American attack on Cuba to remove Castro, although there was already reason enough for Khrushchev to want to avoid that further embarrassment. It has been common for students of the Cuban missile crisis to praise Kennedy for leaving Khrushchev a way out, a means of retreat without resort to war. Whatever the validity of that judgment as to the October crisis, his decision on this occasion led in the opposite direction. Out of his political and diplomatic weakness the President had pushed his opponent further into a corner, putting greater pressure on him to take a counteraction. Gilpatric's speech and the Alsop interview were errors because they embarrassed Khrushchev with an attempt to use America's nuclear advantage as a weapon of public diplomacy without removing his doubts that the American President had the will to use them as weapons of war.

Missiles to Cuba

Developments in Cuba provided Khrushchev with a new challenge and with an opportunity to resolve many of his continuing problems. Since the Bay of Pigs, Castro had become ever clearer in his adherence to the Soviet bloc and his defiance of the United States. He openly announced a Marxist-Leninist course for Cuba, received economic aid and military supplies from the Soviet Union, and secretly sent some of the latter, along with other forms of support, to revolutionary forces in several places in Latin America. Publicly, he vehemently announced his hostility to the United States and his contempt for its prospects of removing him from power. In reality, he believed that the Americans were sure to make another attack on Cuba, and he was deeply concerned about it.

The Kennedy administration was obsessed with Castro, regarding him as a menace to the stability of the Western Hemisphere. To the President "Castro was a symbol of Khrushchev's claim that communism was on the march, a beachhead for Soviet influence in Latin America, a lingering sign of his own failure at the Bay of Pigs. Dean Rusk was surprised that 'this man with ice water in his veins' was so 'emotional' about Castro. McNamara recalled that they were all 'hysterical.' "[160] To deal with him the administration used diplomatic and economic sanctions, covert action aimed at his overthrow, even attempts at assassination. None of these tactics nor all of them together worked or gave serious promise of success. The one sure way to succeed, although it might be costly in casualties and in alienating opinion in Latin America and the world, was by invasion, but Kennedy was unwilling to pay that price. The United States made plans for a possible invasion and even rehearsed some of them, but the evidence indicates he had no intention of carrying them out. He did not want Cuba to become "another Hungary"; even more importantly, Kennedy remained fixed by the fear that Khrushchev would use such an event as an excuse to act against West Berlin, which would raise the specter of nuclear war. Yet Kennedy never publicly denied an intention to attack Cuba, in considerable part because of the political cost of seeming soft on Castro when American public opinion was very hostile to him. Speaking almost three decades after the crisis, McNamara stated "categorically, without qualification, and with the certainty that I am speaking . . . of the mind of President Kennedy . . . that we had *absolutely no intention* of invading Cuba." McNamara's memory of the missile crisis does not always square with his views in 1962 as revealed by records that have since been made public, but nothing in them seems to contradict this statement. More important, however, is his admission that "if I had been a Cuban leader at that time, I might well have concluded that there was a great risk of U.S. invasion. . . . If I had been a Soviet leader at that time, I might have come to the same conclusion."[161]

An American invasion of Cuba that would remove Castro was not something Khrushchev could contemplate with equanimity. He was under attack for softness against the West from Mao's China. He had retreated twice from ultimatums about Berlin, and the NATO countries continued to station their troops in the free, capitalistic Western sector. Gilpatric's speech had revealed his policy of bluff and the Soviet Union's gross inferiority in nuclear weapons. The removal of Castro, the first reversal of a revolution by an avowed Marxist-Leninist, would be a terrible additional blow to Soviet credibility and prestige, and therefore to its power. The lesson easily drawn would be that America had used its nuclear advantage to roll back the tide of communism, and that Khrushchev lacked the means and the courage to prevent it. What further concessions might the United States demand, and what could the Soviet leader do to counter its superior power?

Khrushchev first revealed the idea of placing missiles in Cuba late in April to Mikoyan. While vacationing in the Crimea, he said, he looked across the Black Sea and expressed resentment at the bases there from which the Americans "could in a short time destroy all our southern cities. . . . They have surrounded us with bases on all sides, and we have no possibility and right to do the same!" This was an old complaint of Khrushchev's that he had made to several Americans about their bases in such places as Turkey, Britain, and Greece, and he had not been satisfied with the response, given, for instance by Adlai Stevenson, that they were not aggressive but defensive.[162]

On his return to Moscow he told Mikoyan of his plan: he would place the missiles in Cuba, "very speedily in September and October, but not . . . reveal it before the American elections in November." Khrushchev planned to announce the action in a letter to be delivered by Dobrynin to the President, and "he expected it would be received in the United States as the Turkish missiles were received in the Soviet Union."[163]

Khrushchev's motives have been the subject of great debate. Among the reasons that have been suggested are: the desire to defend Cuba; an attempt to close the missile gap; as a bargaining chip to trade for the missiles in Turkey and, perhaps, elsewhere; to create an opportunity for bringing about a favorable settlement in Berlin; as a way of gaining ground against China within the socialist bloc; to achieve a general victory in the Cold War that would allow gains on many fronts; to gain a victory in Soviet domestic politics.[164] Although arguments have been brought against some of them, there is no reason why all could not have played some part in Khrushchev's thinking, for a successful implantation of the missiles might have helped achieve each of the objectives. The two reasons offered by Khrushchev himself, however, can reasonably be seen as the most pressing for him: the defense of Cuba and the closing of the missile gap.

> [O]ne thought kept hammering away at my brain; what will happen if we lose Cuba? I knew it would have been a terrible blow against Marxism-Leninism. It would gravely diminish our stature around the world, but especially in Latin America. If Cuba fell, other Latin American countries would reject us, claiming that for all our might the Soviet Union hadn't been able to do anything for Cuba except to make empty protests to the United Nations. We had to think up some way of confronting America with more than words. We had to establish a tangible and effective deterrent to American interference in the Caribbean. But what exactly? The logical answer was missiles. . . . In addition to protecting Cuba, our missiles would have equalized what the West likes to call "the balance of power." The Americans had surrounded our country with military bases and threatened us with nuclear weapons, and now they would learn just what it feels like to have enemy missiles pointed at you; we'd be doing nothing more than giving them a little of their own medicine.[165]

Mikoyan gave essentially the same account privately in 1962 to a member of the Hungarian mission in Washington: "the missile deployment in the Caribbean . . . was aimed on the one hand to defend Castro and on the other to achieve a definite change in the power relation between the socialist and capitalist worlds."[166]

On hearing of Khrushchev's plan, Mikoyan expressed doubts about the possibility of maintaining secrecy while the missiles were going in and about Castro's willingness to risk accepting them, and he argued that the Americans would not accept them.[167] Khrushchev, however, appears not to have questioned Kennedy's willingness to accept the situation once the missiles were in place, yet this would seem to be one of the riskiest features of the adventure. What would happen if the Americans discovered the missiles before they were operational? In that case, the American President, having overwhelming superiority in conventional forces in the region, might attack the island and take out the bases, attacking the Soviet troops in the process. Any Soviet threat to launch a counterattack elsewhere or to launch a nuclear strike would face the same unsatisfactory odds that had provoked the adventure in the first place. Even if the missiles were operational, any threat to use them faced the same reality of a vast American advantage in nuclear weapons. A nuclear attack launched from Cuba would cause terrible damage in the United States, but the response from the United States sure to follow would totally destroy Soviet power at an unimaginable cost in casualties.

It is hard to believe that such risks were justified by the goal of achieving a temporary adjustment in the balance of power, while Soviet missile construction caught up with the Americans, yet Khrushchev took the chance. Why? Burlatsky says, "I am not sure Khrushchev's analysis went far enough—[to the point of asking] 'What will be the U.S. answer?' Many people thought this was an adventure, but he was willing to try anyway. As I understand, it was the first step to strategic parity, and he tested what would be." Sergo Mikoyan agrees "that Khrushchev did not think through the American reaction."[168] Both men portray Khrushchev as believing that the placement of missiles in Cuba would not bring a hostile reaction from Kennedy, but the opposite. Sergo Mikoyan, as we have seen, says he expected an improvement in Soviet-American relations to ensue. Burlatsky says, "I also believe Khrushchev's aim was to begin détente with the U.S.—this was his general aim. But it is very difficult to imagine how placing rockets in Caba can support this."[169] His puzzlement is natural, but a suggestion is available that would explain not only this surprising expectation but Khrushchev's willingness to undertake the entire risky adventure: he expected Kennedy to accept the new situation without resistance. Thereafter, the balance of power having been restored, the United States would be more accepting of the Soviet point of view, cease to interfere with its activities, and accept "peaceful coexistence" in the Soviet sense. Khrushchev's decision was not simply impulsive and unconsidered. Before making his decision, toward the end of May, Khrushchev discussed his idea with a small group of his closest advisers, consisting of Frol Kozlov, secretary of the Central Committee, Sergei Biryuzov, commander of the Strategic Rocket Forces, Foreign Minister Andrei Gromyko, Defense Minister Malinovsky, and Sharaf Rashidov, an alternate member of the Presidium (Politburo).[170] As we have seen, he first consulted Mikoyan, who warned him of a negative American response. He also spoke to Gromyko, who told him that "putting missiles into Cuba would cause a political explosion in the United States. I am absolutely certain of that, and this should be taken into account."[171] Khrushchev assured Gromyko that "we don't need a nuclear war and we have no intention of fighting." Forewarned and challenged, he held to his original view. Clearly, he did not fail to think his actions through but, instead, based his analysis on his understanding of Kennedy's likely reaction—that he would accept peacefully the change in the power balance.

For this Khrushchev appears to have had considerable grounds.[172] Kennedy's failure to support the Bay of Pigs invasion suggested a lack of will and determination, a fear of Soviet action elsewhere, an unwillingness to risk a war against a weak opponent in his own neighborhood, even at the cost of personal and national humiliation. At Vienna the President had backed away from American commitments, undercut the positions taken by allies, and put up with unprecedented bullying. His acceptance of the Berlin Wall was further evidence of timidity. "If the President had not used his nuclear superiority to dictate terms on Berlin, where the United States had treaty commitments, why should he use it over Cuba?"[173]

Kennedy, moreover, had displayed a willingness to swallow unwelcome Soviet actions without protest and even to conceal what had happened from the public to avoid political embarrassment. He had denied publicly that Khrushchev had delivered an ultimatum on Berlin at Vienna, only to be embarrassed when Khrushchev revealed the truth. Khrushchev's messenger, Bolshakov, had led Kennedy to expect a test-ban treaty as a reward for the summit meeting in Vienna. When none was forthcoming, Kennedy made no protest about the deception. At the same meeting Khrushchev promised not to be the first to resume testing and then broke his promise without warning. Again, Kennedy did not complain. "The Chairman may have presumed that Kennedy accepted such trickery as a staple of international politics."[174]

There were other signals that tended to confirm Khrushchev's estimate. After the Bay of Pigs Khrushchev wrote to Kennedy, pointing out that while the Soviet Union did not plan to establish a missile base on Cuba, the United States used the territory of other countries to threaten Soviet security. This provoked no answer from Kennedy. During the summer of 1961 Kennedy had indicated carefully which American rights in Berlin the Americans would defend, but he laid down no similar line in regard to Cuba. "The Chairman could be excused for presuming that Kennedy's failure to warn against nuclear missiles in Cuba was not accidental."[175] In a news conference in March Kennedy said that there was no difference between a missile fired from close range or from five thousand miles off, a further suggestion that the President might not take the placement of missiles in Cuba as cause for undue alarm. Then in June Senator Fulbright made another contribution to international communication. In the Senate he said, "I suppose we would all be less comfortable if the Soviets did install missile bases in Cuba, but I am not sure that our national existence would be in substantially greater danger than is the case today."[176] Once again, Kennedy did not contradict the senator, any more than he had rejected Fulbright's invitation to the Communists to seal the border in Berlin a year earlier. Khrushchev could be forgiven for believing that the chairman of the Senate Foreign Relations Committee was speaking for the President once again.

Combined with the evidence of Kennedy's willingness to go to great lengths to avoid confrontation and the risks of fighting, these signals provided considerable support for a belief that the President would accept missiles in Cuba without great risk to the Soviets. He might respond to the "sudden and secret" installation of missiles in Cuba just as he had responded to the "sudden and secret" installation of the Berlin Wall: "he would claim surprise, send Moscow a formal protest, and then tell the American people that this was not an issue on which the West was prepared to go to war."[177]

Khrushchev's meeting with his advisers late in May resulted in a decision to send a delegation to Cuba to see whether Castro would cooperate and if it would be possible to install and deploy the missiles in secrecy. Sharaf Rashidov was chairman, and he was joined by Sergei Biryuzov and Alexander Alexeyev, the newly appointed ambassador to Cuba. The Soviet mission, using the cover story that they were to advise on irrigation, arrived in Havana on May 29. The Cubans accepted the proposal with alacrity. Then and ever since, Castro and his colleagues have claimed that they did so "not so much to defend Cuba as to change the correlation of forces between capitalism and socialism," explaining that "to defend Cuba other measures could be taken without resorting to installing missiles."[178] Khrushchev had instructed the mission to make both arguments and, in fact, was offering the Cubans a package. He would send a military force, a significant number of troops, to the island, where they would serve as a trip wire, like the Western troops in Berlin, meant to deter an American invasion that would lead to fighting with Soviet troops, which might then bring on a larger war. In the event, Khrushchev *did* place forty-two thousand troops on the island, a number considerably larger than was needed to patrol the missile sites. The missiles, of course, were valuable for the same purpose also. Once they were operational they would assist powerfully in the goal Mikoyan's son Sergo continues to insist was primary: to "deter an invasion *beforehand.*"[179] But, of course, they would also "change the correlation of forces." The Cubans hardly could accept one offer and refuse the other. As Castro later put it, "It was impossible not to share the risks which the Soviet Union was taking to save us."[180] Expressing revolutionary zeal and courage and solidarity, they agreed to cooperate. To the second question the mission had been sent to answer Biryuzov reported that the missiles could be hidden in the mountains where they would not be found;[181] speedy installation and camouflage would take care of the rest.

Early in July a Cuban military delegation led by Raul Castro arrived in Moscow, where its members met with Khrushchev and other officials to plan for the installation of the missiles. They made a formal agreement, renewable every five years, whereby the missiles would be fully under the control of the Soviet military command.[182] The operation was given the code name "Anadyr," the name of a river in a cold area far to the north, to help conceal its tropical target. Great pains were taken to preserve secrecy. Eighty-five ships were scattered among seven ports, needing 185 trips to complete the movement of the Soviet forces to Cuba. A new command structure was created, with General I. A. Pliyev, a hero of the Second

World War, at its head. He led a group of officers from every branch of the services to select appropriate sites for deploying their forces. General Gramov, sent to Cuba as a representative of Malinovsky to check on how the operation was going, received orders from his chief to convey the instructions from both the Defense Minister and Khrushchev himself to Pliyev: in case of an invasion tactical nuclear weapons could be used in case of "a direct invasion by the aggressor," but "in case of extreme need only." The use of tactical nuclear weapons when necessary was a regular part of Soviet military doctrine, but the rest of the message was: " 'The missile forces will fire only if authorized by Nikita Sergeievich Khrushchev'—it was repeated—'only if instructed by the Supreme-Commander-in-Chief himself.' "[183] Control of the nuclear weapons that could reach the United States was always to be solely in the hands of Khrushchev himself.

Soviet ships had been bringing arms to Cuba since the summer of 1960, but the pace slowed early in 1962. During the first half of that year an average of fifteen dry-cargo ships arrived each month. Late in July the pace quickened sharply. Thirty-seven ships arrived in August, twenty of them carrying arms.[184] During that time U.S. intelligence received reports of Soviet missiles in Cuba. Investigation showed these to be describing surface-to-air (SAM) or cruise missiles, or to be mistaken. Late in August sightings of Soviet warplanes, MIG-21s, and IL-28 bombers were reported. A CIA memorandum dated August 22, recently declassified, describes the arrival in Cuba of unusual numbers of ships carrying military equipment and personnel. It says, "The speed and magnitude of this influx of bloc personnel and equipment into a non-bloc country is unprecedented in Soviet military aid activities; clearly something new and different is taking place."[185] As early as August 10 John McCone, director of the CIA, came to the conclusion that the Soviets were sending medium-range ballistic missiles (MRBMs) to Cuba. Over the objection of his subordinates, who thought he lacked hard evidence for his belief, he wrote a memo to the President setting forth his suspicions. A week later additional information led him to claim again at a high-level meeting that the Soviets were installing offensive missiles in Cuba.[186] McCone was a Republican and well known for his strong anti-Communist opinions. Kennedy, Rusk, and McNamara dismissed the first warning on those grounds and responded to the second by insisting that any missiles being constructed in Cuba were defensive; that is, they would not be surface-to-surface weapons capable of reaching the United States.

On August 23, nonetheless, the President called a meeting of the National Security Council (NSC) to consider McCone's assertions. Once again, Rusk and McNamara rejected his claims, but Kennedy asked for a contingency plan in case the CIA chief was right. Studies were to consider the advantages and disadvantages "of a statement warning against the deployment of any nuclear weapons in Cuba; the psychological, political, and military effect of such a deployment; and the military options that might be exercised by the United States to eliminate such a threat." He also asked the Defense Department to see what could be done about removing U.S. Jupiter missiles from Turkey. On August 29 a high-altitude flight by a U-2 plane reported firm evidence of SAM missile sites at eight different places in Cuba, and soon after new evidence showed the installation of coastal defense cruise missiles as well. This information reached the President on August 31, two days too late for a press conference in which he said that he had seen no evidence of Soviet troops or air defense missiles on the island.[187] It was also on August 31 that Senator Kenneth Keating of New York rose in the Senate to say that he had evidence that the Soviets were installing medium- and intermediate-range ballistic missiles (IRBMs) in Cuba, which the administration was covering up. He urged the President to act, suggesting that the Organization of American States (OAS) send a team to Cuba to investigate. Kennedy and the CIA dismissed these claims as coming from Cuban exiles and other unreliable sources, but a group of prominent Republicans, including Richard Nixon, demanded a blockade of Cuba to stop further Soviet arms deliveries. At a time when midterm congressional elections of great importance to his presidency were approaching, Kennedy found himself under assault for his failure to respond to what Nixon called "a clear and present danger" to the United States. Cuban refugees demanded that he "enforce the Monroe Doctrine." The *New Republic* questioned his courage, accusing the Kennedy administration of following the example of the Broadway musical *The King and I:*

> Whenever I'm afraid,
> I hold my head erect
> And whistle a happy tune
> So no one will suspect
> I'm afraid.[188]

Even in the face of such sharp criticism, Kennedy still did not take any meaningful action. Khrushchev had every reason to believe that Kennedy knew much of what was happening in Cuba, since the Chairman knew that the claims of Keating and others were true. If a mere Senator knew of the missiles, how could the President be ignorant? If he was in doubt, why did he not press the Soviets for assurances, insist on inspection, put on some kind of pressure to halt the clearly visible deliveries of military personnel and equipment? Why did he make a public denial of SAM installations that were real? Khrushchev had good reason to believe that his calculations were right, that Kennedy knew what was happening and preferred to conceal it from the American people. That must surely mean that he would accept their presence once it was officially revealed.

During the first week in September troops from four elite armored brigades began arriving in Cuba and kept coming until the middle of October, but American intelligence learned of their presence only on October 25.[189] Increased evidence of SAM sites and a possible submarine base led the President to send his brother to see Soviet Ambassador Anatoly Dobrynin on September 4. The ambassador delivered Khrushchev's assurance that no surface-to-surface missiles or other offensive weapons would be installed in Cuba, "that this military build-up was not of any significance and that Khrushchev would do nothing to disrupt the relationship of our two countries during the period prior to the election."[190] On the day before, Walt Rostow had submitted his evaluation of the situation in Cuba. He judged that the Soviet deliveries did not present "a substantial threat to U.S. security," but suggested that the Soviet Union was "in a mood to double its bets rather than cut its losses." They were, however, a challenge to the United States and a cause of unrest in the United States. He recommended that the President publicly draw the line "at the installation in Cuba or in Cuban waters of nuclear weapons or delivery vehicles, sea or land based."[191]

Robert Kennedy suggested a course of action like the one proposed by Rostow: the President should make a statement that the United States will not tolerate offensive weapons in Cuba. He did so, but in the context of rejecting the reports that the Soviets were currently engaged in emplacing them:

> There is no evidence of any organized combat force in Cuba
> from any Soviet bloc country; of military bases provided to Russia;

of any violation of the 1934 treaty relating to Guantanamo; of the presence of offensive ground-to-ground missiles; or of other significant offensive capability either in Cuban hands or under Soviet direction and guidance. Were it to be otherwise, the gravest issue would arise.[192]

Kennedy did not make even this statement with the intention of changing Soviet behavior, but as a way of responding to his critics at home. Years after these events Bundy explained: "We did it because of the requirements of domestic politics, not because we seriously believed that the Soviets would do anything as crazy from our standpoint as placement of Soviet nuclear weapons in Cuba." It had never occurred to them to issue a warning before. Sorensen, who appears to have had a closer rapport with the President and a better understanding of his thinking than any of the others except his brother Robert, provides an explanation of the President's intentions. By expressing his willingness to accept the vast amount of military capability of all kinds that was pouring into Cuba except offensive missiles, "the President drew the line precisely where he thought the Soviets would not be. . . . If we had known that the Soviets were putting forty missiles into Cuba, we might under this hypothesis have drawn the line at one hundred, and said with great fanfare that we would absolutely not tolerate the presence of more than one hundred missiles in Cuba. I say that [as] one believing very strongly that that would have been an act of *prudence,* not weakness."[193] Here is the conclusion one student of the crisis draws:

> Kennedy therefore issued a warning that was too late to stop Khrushchev's Cuba operation and so precise that it caused him to forfeit the option of responding to the discovery of missiles in Cuba with anything less than a full-fledged confrontation with the Soviet Union. Had the President issued such a warning five months earlier or not painted himself into a corner now, history might have been different.[194]

Combined, these remarkable statements suggest that Kennedy was willing to accept Soviet offensive missiles in Cuba without complaint; that only political pressure forced him to warn the Soviets against them; that it was only the mistake of refusing to believe that Khrushchev would really put offensive weapons into Cuba that compelled Kennedy to take serious measures to remove them after they were discovered. If that is correct, then Khrushchev was entirely right in his understanding of Kennedy, and the risk he took in installing the missiles was much smaller than has been thought. Khrushchev's only mistake, then, would have been to underestimate the political pressure that would be applied to the President of a free country who appeared unwilling to protect his country's safety and interests. It was precisely the mistake Hitler made in expecting Chamberlain to accept the invasion of Poland as he had accepted the dismemberment of Czechoslovakia, in spite of the public guarantee the British leader had given. There is considerable evidence that Chamberlain, too, regretted that he had "painted himself into a corner" in 1939, but when the invasion took place, political pressure from inside and outside his government forced his hand. Had he failed to respond he would have been forced from office. Hitler had not misread his man but only failed to understand the workings of free countries.

If Kennedy truly thought as his colleagues say he did, one can only marvel at his own lack of understanding of the military and political realities. If he had been right and the Soviets had not emplanted offensive missiles but only placed on the island more than forty-five thousand Soviet troops, equipped, as they could be expected to be, with tactical cruise missiles with nuclear warheads, with SAM emplacements to prevent aerial surveillance, and with all other modern equipment, this would not have violated the conditions he publicly proclaimed as acceptable, though it would have turned Cuba into a Soviet aircraft carrier from which it could threaten and help subvert the governments of the Western Hemisphere. The political cost of that alone was sure to be more than Kennedy could bear. Even if he were not impeached, as he later said he would have been for not ensuring the removal of the missiles after they were discovered, he would surely have been defeated for a second term. The greater likelihood is that he would have been forced into a confrontation even without the issue of offensive missiles. It is extraordinary that he could view what he took to be a Soviet conventional military buildup with such complacency. It called for deep concern and resistance, even at the cost of a confrontation. Such a confrontation, however, would have been far less dangerous than the one that actually took place after some offensive nuclear missiles were already in place. Had Kennedy not painted himself into a corner history would surely have been very different, but it is hard to see how a confrontation could have been avoided once he had acquiesced in the unprecedented Soviet adventure.

In the following weeks, by public and private messages Khrushchev assured Kennedy that he did not plan to put offensive weapons into Cuba and promised again to make no trouble before the elections. In one meeting with Sorensen, Dobrynin assured him repeatedly that "all the steps were defensive in nature and did not represent any threat to the security of the United States."[195] It may be true that in communicating this message Khrushchev was not only trying to deceive the President but also encouraging him "if the missiles were found before November, to explain them away to his own generals as purely defensive and conceal them from the public until the balloting was done."[196]

The game continued as the Soviets issued a statement condemning American bases overseas, insisting that the weapons being sent to Cuba were entirely defensive, and denying that any offensive weapons would go to Cuba, since the Soviet missiles at home were so powerful that there was no need to bring them to Cuba. Kennedy responded in a press conference that if Cuba should attempt to export aggression or become an "offensive military base of significant capacity for the Soviet Union," the United States would do "whatever must be done to protect its security and that of its allies." But he also repeated that the Soviet personnel streaming onto the island did not constitute a serious threat, so that "unilateral military intervention on the part of the United States cannot currently be either required or justified."[197] If it was a warning to the Soviets, it was no less a response to the administration's domestic critics. A few days later Khrushchev spoke to the visiting Austrian vice chancellor, certain that his message would be passed on to Kennedy. As a respected student of the Kremlin at that time reports, he said that the Soviet Union "would fight any blockade of the island. He proclaimed to all and sundry that the Americans had lost their fighting spirit. . . . In short, he seemed confident at the time that all he had to do was raise his voice a little. Khrushchev's heightened self-assurance of those days was that of a gambler who had made his move."[198]

By the middle of September that move was traveling toward completion. United States intelligence sources reported what seemed to be MRBMs unloading at the Cuban port of Mariel from the fifteenth to the seventeenth and seeing at least eight of them on a convoy going to San Cristobal, where the first missile site was built.[199] On the nineteenth the United States Intelligence Board approved a report on the military buildup on Cuba. It spoke of reports of continuing deployment of nuclear missiles, reports of sightings of these missiles and of the boast of Castro's private pilot that the Cubans might win in a confrontation with the Americans "because we have everything, including atomic weapons." It also mentioned the construction of an "elaborate SA-2 air defense system." It also observed that the Soviets "could derive considerable military advantage" from the establishment of missiles in Cuba, but regarded such an installation as "incompatible with Soviet Policy as we presently estimate it. . . . [They] would almost certainly estimate that this could not be done without provoking a dangerous U.S. reaction."[200] McCone challenged this conclusion because it ignored the increase in Soviet bargaining power Khrushchev would gain by the emplacement of strategic missiles, but he lost the argument.[201]

Late in September crates appropriate for Soviet Il-28 bombers, technically capable of carrying nuclear payloads, though not previously used for the purpose, were spotted on the decks of ships bound for Cuba. At an intelligence briefing on October 1 evidence of the possible installation of IRBMs was presented to McNamara and the Joint Chiefs. The Defense Department went forward with contingency planning for a blockade of Cuba, for air attacks, and for amphibious landings on the island.[202] Meanwhile, a Soviet program of disinformation combining attempts at deception and deterrence was in full swing; Gromyko told the UN General Assembly that the United States was planning to invade Cuba, denied that the Cuban buildup was a threat to the United States, and warned that an attack on Cuba or on a ship going to Cuba could mean war. The last statement was clearly intended to discourage discovery of the missiles, most of which had not yet arrived in Cuba. At the same time, Khrushchev continued his secret correspondence with Kennedy, talking about the possibility of a test ban even as the missiles were on their way to the island. Later on, the President compared this to the deception practiced by the Japanese in carrying on negotiations in Washington even as the bombers were on their way to Pearl Harbor. Khrushchev also sent a private message by Bolshakov, his back channel to the President, to soothe and deceive him, insisting that all he was sending to Cuba were "defensive weapons."[203]

On October 13 Chester Bowles, ambassador-at-large in the State Department, told Soviet Ambassador Dobrynin that the Americans "had some evidence" that the Soviets were bringing offensive nuclear missiles into Cuba. Dobrynin, it appears, had not been told and denied that the

Soviets had any such plans.[204] The conversation, of course, would have been reported to the Kremlin. Khrushchev may have taken this as evidence that Kennedy had discovered some missiles; in any case, work on the missiles was accelerated, even before the SAMs needed to protect them for surveillance were ready.[205]

On October 14 the administration's official position was stated on a national television show by McGeorge Bundy: "there was 'no present evidence,' nor was there any likelihood that the Soviets and Cubans would try to install a 'major offensive capability.' . . . So far, everything that has been delivered in Cuba falls within the categories of aid which the Soviet Union has provided, for example, to neutral states like Egypt and Indonesia, and I should not be surprised to see additional military assistance of that sort."[206] The statement did not accord entirely with all the facts. Combined with the report of Dobrynin's conversation with Bowles it provided Khrushchev with further evidence that his hopes and expectations might be true: that Kennedy knew what was happening and was concealing it from the American people.[207] Why did the President and his administration fail to take seriously the plausible conclusions drawn by McCone from the same evidence available to them? Abram Chayes later explained his own thinking: "I for one didn't believe the reports of offensive missiles because I didn't *want* to believe them. I didn't want to be lying to senators when I reported on the Cuba situation, and I certainly wasn't inclined to take Keating and McCone at face value, because I didn't think they were reliable anyway. I don't want to accuse anyone else of this, but it was very easy for me to disregard Keating and the other hotheads who were screaming about missiles in Cuba."[208] It is unlikely that he was alone in this attitude. The same day as Bundy's denial a U-2 flight over western Cuba took photographs that revealed the first hard evidence of MRBM sites in Cuba.[209] By the morning of the sixteenth they had been studied and analyzed, and the news was revealed to the President.

The Crisis

To help him in the crisis he now faced, the President appointed an advisory board officially called the Executive Committee of the National Security Council that came to be known as the "ExCom." Its members were his brother, Attorney General Robert Kennedy, Secretary of State Dean Rusk, Secretary of Defense Robert McNamara, Secretary of the

Treasury Douglas Dillon, National Security Advisor McGeorge Bundy, Chairman of the Joint Chiefs of Staff Maxwell Taylor, the President's Special Council, Theodore Sorensen, Under Secretary of State George Ball, Director of the CIA John McCone, and the Soviet specialist in the State Department, Llewellyn Thompson. In addition, Kennedy consulted Dean Acheson, John McCloy, and Robert Lovett, who were not members of his administration. Without the participants' knowledge, the group's meetings were tape-recorded by the President. Transcripts of the meetings are now available, serving as the primary evidence with which it is possible to correct and supplement recollections and published accounts of what took place.

The ExCom's first meeting was held at midday on Tuesday, October 16, 1962, and its second that same evening. The group never devoted serious discussion to allowing the missiles to remain. Most of the talk centered on what military course of action would be best: (1) a "surgical" air strike aimed at the missile installations alone; (2) a general wave of air strikes at a broader range of targets; or (3) an invasion of Cuba. Still another option mentioned was a blockade of Cuba. The President concluded the first session by saying: "Maybe we just have to just take *them out,* and continue our other preparations . . . because that's what we're going to do *anyway.* We're certainly going to do number one; we're going to take out these, uh, missiles."[210] In the evening session McNamara presented three courses of action to get the missiles out: a political route involving communications with Castro and Khrushchev; one that would be partly political and partly military, which would include full and open surveillance and a blockade of weapons; and a third that would involve some kind of military action.[211] No decision was reached.

Although, and perhaps because, there was consensus on the need to remove the missiles, there was little discussion of why. General Taylor and others thought that the Cuban missiles would have substantial strategic importance, while others, McNamara foremost among them, thought they had none. The President agreed with McNamara. In his "Summary of Agreed Facts and Premises, Possible Courses of Action and Unanswered Questions," written the next day, Sorensen says, "It is generally agreed that these missiles, even when fully operational, do not significantly alter the balance of power—i.e., they do not significantly increase the potential megatonnage capable of being unleashed on American soil."[212] Wherever he may have discovered this consensus, it does not emerge from the transcript of the meetings. McNamara asserts it, the President appears to accept it, and it is Sorensen's own view. Taylor asserted a different view, but he did not defend it in detail, and he did not challenge McNamara's claim, so perhaps silence from him and the others implies consent. But there was little reason for those who did not agree to speak, since no one argued against removing the missiles, whatever their importance.

There is reason, however, to question this "consensus." At a conference in 1987 some of the members of the ExCom expressed other opinions. Douglas Dillon said he thought that the Cuban missiles made a great difference in the strategic balance: "Before the Soviets put missiles in Cuba, it was doubtful whether they could deliver any warheads from Soviet territory at all. . . . My impression at the time was that they radically altered the number of *deliverable* warheads, and in that sense, they significantly increased Soviet capability." Nitze thought the deployment in Cuba "militarily . . . would be a major step toward nuclear parity—effective nuclear parity, not in numbers but in military effectiveness—because their capability in an initial strike from those sites would be tremendous. After all, these could cover almost all targets in the United States. Between the MRBMs and the IRBMs there was hardly any part of the United States that wasn't vulnerable to these missiles. And if they really got off a first strike they could raise havoc."[213] One of the scholars at the meeting made a more specific point on the threat Soviet missiles in Cuba would pose to America's strategic bombing force. There were only forty-six SAC bases in the United States at the time, almost all of them within range of the IRBMs. It "looked like a significant threat to our bomber force, and this is what the Joint Chiefs worried about."[214]

Some Soviet officials express similar views. Georgi Shaknazarov, aide to Mikhail Gorbachev in 1988, fully agreed with Dillon and Nitze: "It is the ability to deliver a missile that is important for parity, not the quantity of missiles. We had no missiles near the United States. The United States had bases encircling the Soviet Union. It was an attempt by Khrushchev to get parity without spending resources we did not have."[215] Most telling of all, at a conference in Moscow in 1989, General Dimitri Volkogonov, a member of the Soviet Ministry of Defense and a historian with full access to Soviet records, reported that at the time of the crisis the Soviets had only twenty ICBMs. The forty missiles shipped to Cuba would be twice as many and, although each warhead was smaller than on an ICBM, "those missiles which we were putting in Cuba could support nearly the same payload."[216] The installation of the Cuban missiles almost doubled Soviet nuclear missile power at a stroke and increased the capacity to hit American targets by considerably more.

General Volkogonov used biblical language to express the same idea: "Saint John the Divine said that God has seven cups of anger which he could pour onto the earth. So, applying this analogy to us, we should say that the Soviet side had at that time only half-a-cup. The Americans had seven cups. Therefore if we placed our missiles in Cuba, then we had a full cup." One purpose of the plan was "to raise our position as a nuclear power,"[217] and the Cuban missiles, even one "full cup," would have done that. The installation of the missiles would have brought the Soviets from having no credible threat to having a relatively small one, but one that was very significant against an opponent that could be paralyzed by a minimal nuclear deterrent. At the 1987 conference Arthur Schlesinger expressed the point clearly. The missiles

> had a considerable effect on the world *political* balance. The emplacement of nuclear missiles in Cuba would prove the Soviet ability to act with impunity in the very heart of the American zone of vital interest—a victory of great significance for the Kremlin, which saw the world in terms of spheres of influence and inflexibly guarded its own. . . . It was a bold move into the American political sphere which, had it worked, would have dealt a severe blow to the American position worldwide.[218]

Yet McNamara and those who agreed with him did not see the military point of the Cuban missiles. A puzzled President Kennedy asked, "If the, uh, it doesn't increase very much their strategic, uh, strength, why is it, uh, can any Russian expert tell us why they—[did it]?"

No one in the ExCom provided a satisfactory explanation, nor has anyone since. That is because there can be none based on the assumption that the missiles did not alter the strategic balance. Khrushchev, after all, decided to put the missiles in Cuba at great expense and at great risk to himself and his country. He could have avoided such risks if all he wanted was to defend Cuba, as the Cubans continue to point out. There was no need to run the greater risk unless he believed it would produce a change in the strategic balance that could then be used to good advantage for a multitude of purposes. The reason for the puzzlement of McNamara and

Kennedy is that they believed, explicitly or implicitly, in the doctrine of "minimal deterrence." If one side had any capacity whatever to deliver even a few nuclear warheads on the cities of its opponent, that opponent would be deterred from using nuclear weapons against it. In 1962 the United States had a master nuclear-war plan called the Single Integrated Operational Plan (SIOP). Although he was bound by it and appears not to have challenged it at that time, in 1987 McNamara said: "SIOP 1(a) was totally unreasonable *before* Cuba, and it was totally unreal *after* Cuba. . . . Does anyone believe that a President or a Secretary of Defense would be willing to permit thirty warheads to fall on the United States? No way! And for that reason neither we nor the Soviets would have acted any differently before or after the nuclear deployment."[219] But, without an Anti-Ballistic Missile Defense system, the doctrine of Mutually Assured Destruction (MAD) that McNamara always championed requires that these American officials be willing to do just that and to retaliate (or get the enemy to believe they will) if they are to protect American interests and security from nuclear blackmail. Since Kennedy and McNamara had no intention of using nuclear weapons themselves, and since they believed Khrushchev thought as they did, there seemed to be no point to his moving missiles to Cuba. They assumed that he "was much too sensible to challenge us in the way that nuclear weapons in Cuba so obviously would." As Bundy later put it, "We did not suppose that nuclear superiority conferred on us the opportunity for political coercion that Khrushchev took for granted."[220] The trouble was that Khrushchev did not think as they did and did not believe in minimal deterrence. He believed that nuclear war was possible, that it could be won, and therefore that nuclear superiority mattered very much.

But how would the achievement of greater parity by installing missiles in Cuba help the Soviets? They were still overwhelmingly behind in nuclear power. If they launched a first strike they would not destroy the United States or its capacity to destroy the Soviet Union. Khrushchev did not want to launch a first strike or any nuclear strike at all. What he wanted was a credible nuclear force that would paralyze the Americans and prevent them from using their nuclear threat to prevent Soviet advances around the world. Its purpose was like the minimal one of the Kaiser's "risk fleet": to prevent the British from using their fleet to contain German power and to block German expansion. It was based on Khrushchev's conviction that the Americans would not use nuclear weapons if, as McNamara later enthusiastically affirmed, there was any chance of *some* nuclear weapons falling on the United States. Before the Cuban missiles the Soviets had only twenty inaccurate ICBMs, an insufficiently credible force. The additional forty missiles fired from as near as Cuba would surely and obviously do great harm. Faced with that prospect, the Americans would have to be more circumspect and stay out of the Soviet path.

Confronted inescapably with the proof of their misunderstanding of his views, McNamara and those who agreed with him were forced to cope. There is some reason to think they would have preferred to accept the missiles rather than force a confrontation. At the first meeting of the Ex-Com McNamara said: "I'll be quite frank. I don't think there is a military problem here. . . . This is a domestic political problem."[221] Kennedy always had inclined to McNamara's position: "you may say [as the President also had said in March] that it doesn't make any difference if you get blown up by an ICBM flying from the Soviet Union or one that was ninety miles away. Geography doesn't mean that much. . . . Last month I should have said . . . that we don't care." What had changed the situation since "last month" was Kennedy's public statement forbidding the installation of offensive weapons into Cuba. "But when we said we're not going to and then they go ahead and do it, and then we do nothing, then . . . I would think that our risks increase. Uh, I agree. What difference does it make? They've got enough to blow us up anyway. I think it's just a question of—after all, this is a political struggle as much as military."[222] The domestic political price of accepting the missiles was clear. Bundy later said, "The basic problem for us was that we had repeatedly taken the public position that the presence of offensive missiles in Cuba was unacceptable. . . . Soviet nuclear missiles in Cuba posed a particularly difficult problem, because our public simply would not tolerate them so close to us."[223] The President told his brother that if he hadn't acted against the missiles, "I would have been impeached."[224] If only, the implication emerges, he had not misjudged the Soviets and drawn the line where he did! As one sympathetic writer puts it, "How different these Cabinet Room conversations might have been had Kennedy phrased his September pledge more vaguely or not at all. Instead of discussing how to take the missiles out, he and his advisers would now be able to consider the option of explaining to the Americans that they had little to fear from the missiles in Cuba."[225]

The presumption is that the American people would not be alarmed unless the President told them there was cause for alarm, but the American people's predicted anger was sure to arise from the fact that they had much to fear from missiles in Cuba. Once the missiles were installed and accepted Khrushchev would have believed himself free from the deterrent effect of American nuclear power, in spite of its superiority. The President himself lamented his failure to carry through at the Bay of Pigs; a success there would have avoided the current crisis. "That's why it shows that the Bay of Pigs was really right," he said, but it was Robert Kennedy who saw the strategic problem in its immediate and concrete aspect. "The other problem is in Latin America a year from now. And the fact that you got *these* things in the hands of Cubans here and then you—say, your—some problem arises in Venezuela. You've got Castro saying, 'You move troops down into that part of Venezuela, we're going to fire those missiles.' "[226] The missiles, no doubt, would not be in Cuban but Soviet hands, but there was nothing to stop Khrushchev from saying something similar, secure in the belief that the Americans would not call his bluff. It would be even more likely for him to insist on the changes in Berlin he sought, where he had the overwhelming advantage in conventional forces, secure in the expectation that the United States would not resort to nuclear weapons while the Cuban missiles were pointed at its heart. If the Americans would accept the emplacement of missiles, why wouldn't they accept expulsion from Berlin rather than risk a nuclear attack made possible by those missiles? The place for them to have made a stand, if they were to make a stand at all, ought to have been at the emplacement of the missiles, or earlier, at the construction of the Berlin wall.

For the President, McNamara, Bundy, and Sorensen, however, the problem was one of "domestic politics," and this greatly affected their view of how to proceed. General Taylor later described the American options for removing the missiles: (1) talk 'em out, i.e., achieve the goal by negotiation; (2) shoot 'em out, by military action; (3) squeeze 'em out by various kinds of pressure; (4) buy 'em out by some kind of trade.[227] The U.S. ambassador to the United Nations, Adlai Stevenson, repeatedly urged negotiations in which the United States should be willing to discuss the abandonment of the American base at Guantanamo in Cuba as well as the removal of the Jupiter missiles from Turkey and Italy in exchange for the removal of the Cuban missiles: "I feel you should have made it clear that the existence of nuclear missiles anywhere is negotiable before we start anything."[228] Kennedy, for the time being, rejected these suggestions. They would imply that "we had been frightened into abandoning our position," and asserted that there would be "no bargains over our bases in Turkey and Italy." After the meeting Robert Kennedy told the President that Stevenson was not strong enough to represent the United States and should be replaced. The President agreed that Stevenson may have gone too far in suggesting concessions, but had shown courage in risking the charge that he was an appeaser. That same evening Stevenson told a presidential aide in language like that used by Sir Alexander Cadogan in 1938: "I know that most of those fellows [in the ExCom] will probably consider me a coward for the rest of my life for what I said today, but perhaps we need a coward in the room when we are talking about nuclear war."[229] Cadogan had said, *"How* much courage is needed to be a coward!"

The President and some of the others, as we have seen, seemed at first to lean toward the "shoot 'em out" school, the idea of taking out the missiles with air strikes, which might have had to be followed by an invasion of the island, but they soon backed away from that approach. It needed to compete with a second approach that quickly gained favor, a variety of the "squeeze 'em out" method. The plan, proposed and strongly urged by McNamara, was to put pressure on the Soviets by imposing a naval blockade on Cuba.

The arguments for an assault were obvious. The missiles were not yet operational, but every passing day brought the moment closer when the Soviets would be in a position to use them, or threaten their use, against the United States. For most this was a powerful reason to launch an aerial attack to destroy the missiles and their site, and McNamara expressed the need for speedy action.

> The question is one of readiness of the, to fire and—and this is highly critical in forming our plans—that the time between today and the time when the readiness to fire capability develops is a very important thing. . . . If we are to conduct an airstrike against the installations, or against any part of Cuba, we must agree now that we will schedule that prior to the time these missile sites become operational. I'm not prepared to say when that will be, but I think it is extremely important that our talk and our discussion be founded on this premise: that any airstrike will be planned to take place prior to the time they become operational. Because, if they

become operational before the airstrike, I do not believe we can state we can knock them out before they can be launched; and if they're launched there is almost certain to be, uh, chaos in part of the east coast or the area, uh, in a radius of six hundred to a thousand miles from Cuba.[230]

Years later McNamara vehemently denied that he was concerned with the pressure of time: "I don't think we put great weight on the date on which they might become operational. At least I didn't. I know the later writing on the subject makes it sound like an important issue, but it had no effect on my decision."[231] Since McNamara soon showed himself hostile to an air strike and in favor of a blockade, there is reason for him retrospectively to reject the importance of time, but the transcript of his remarks at the first ExCom meeting reveals that he did not do so in October 1962.[232]

For the others the pressure of time clearly argued for a swift attack to remove the missiles, and General Taylor and Dean Acheson argued strongly in its favor. The air strike, however, was less attractive to some because it was an irrevocable military action. It would kill Soviet troops and seemed more likely to lead to war. A second objection to the air strike was that the Air Force insisted on a much larger aerial attack than the "surgical" one limited to the missile sites, where damage and casualties would be relatively small. They argued for a thorough attack, requiring hundreds of sorties and causing many casualties among civilians, as well as among Cuban and Soviet military personnel. Even then, they could guarantee the destruction of only 90 percent of the missiles.[233] General Taylor did not think the remaining 10 percent were significant. His view has been characterized as follows: "the crisis contained little, if any, risk of nuclear war. . . . American military superiority both locally and at the strategic nuclear level gave the United States a virtually free hand in dealing with the Soviet missiles in Cuba. . . . The event was only a crisis because of the unwarranted level of anxiety among the President's principal civilian advisors."[234] Nitze held the same view: "the decisive factor was our undoubted strategic superiority. McNamara didn't believe in that, but I believed in its significance. And I therefore didn't think that the risk of the Russians responding in a way that would bring into action our undoubted strategic superiority was very great."[235]

But such views lost ground. At the ExCom meeting on the morning of Thursday the eighteenth Robert Kennedy responded to the Joint

Chiefs' recommendation of an air strike by raising a moral question: wouldn't a sneak attack be a violation of American tradition and undermine "our moral position at home and around the globe"? It was a question, he reported, that occupied more time in the discussions than any other in the first five days.[236] The "moral" argument, and its championship by the President's brother, the attractions of a blockade that could be thought of as only the first step that would not preclude stronger measures later, and the fear of the undestroyed missiles carried the day. McNamara continued to argue forcefully for a "quarantine" and, after much discussion, a straw poll showed six members favoring an aerial attack and eleven for a blockade.

The President, no longer participating in the ExCom meetings, did not express his opinion openly. Years later General Taylor said that the report of Air Force General Walter C. Sweeney on October 21, that "you can't expect me to get 'em all; some of the missiles would get away," "certainly tilted the President, if he needed any real tilting, to the quarantine option."[237] Kennedy, however, did not need "any real tilting" to prefer the blockade, or "quarantine," which was the euphemism that had been chosen to apply to it. On the twenty-first he had already given final approval to the blockade plan before the meeting at which Sweeney spoke.[238]

Over the night of October 18–19, however, some important opinions changed. As the President prepared to leave on a campaign trip, Rusk, Bundy, and the Joint Chiefs told him they now favored an air strike. Kennedy's reaction reveals his own inclinations. He asked his brother and Sorensen to convene another meeting of the ExCom, offering to call off his trip if it should be necessary. "Sorensen found him impatient and 'a bit disgusted' that people were still changing their minds."[239] He and his brother were especially annoyed at Bundy, who had changed his mind more than once and, as Robert Kennedy later put it, "finally, he led the group which was in favor of a strike—and a strike without prior notification, along the lines of Pearl Harbor." Sorensen's recollection was that it was not a good week for Bundy, and the President "didn't like it." It seems a fair conjecture that "Kennedy may have expected Bundy to realize that he was leaning heavily toward quarantine and [wanted him to] help him get the Joint Chiefs on board."[240]

Any lingering doubts must be erased by what took place at the ExCom meeting on the nineteenth. An unidentified speaker ventured the opinion that the discussion with the President the night before had led to a tentative decision in favor of a blockade and he "thought the President had been satisfied at the consensus."[241] General Taylor quickly stated that he and the Joint Chiefs were not part of that consensus. Bundy then made it clear that he was opposed, neatly making the case against the blockade. It "would not remove the missiles. Its effect was uncertain and in any event would be slow to be felt. Something more would be made more difficult by the prior publicity of a blockade and the consequent pressures from the United Nations for a negotiated settlement. An air strike would be quick and would take out the bases in a clean surgical operation. He favored decisive action with its advantages of surprise and confronting the world with a fait accompli."[242] General Taylor argued that a decision for a blockade would have the effect of preventing the air strike he favored. In a few days the missiles would be operational. "Thus it was now or never for an air strike." This was an important point, for it required the participants to choose between the two options, destroying the more comfortable view that favored the blockade: that if it failed, a military solution was still available. Dillon and McCone supported the air strike. McNamara announced for the blockade, and George Ball said he was undecided.

At that point the President's brother made a decisive intervention. To be effective, it was argued, an air strike on the missiles had to be swift and secret. During the very first meeting of the ExCom Robert had passed a note to his brother that read, "I now know how Tojo felt when he was planning Pearl Harbor." At the meeting of the nineteenth he expanded on that analogy. He had spoken with the President very recently that morning, and

> he thought it would be very difficult indeed for the President if the decision were to be for an air strike, with all the memory of Pearl Harbor and with all the implications this would have for us in whatever world there would be afterward. For 175 years we had not been that kind of country. A sneak attack was not in our traditions. Thousands of Cubans would be killed without warning, and a lot of Russians too. He favored *action,* to make known unmistakably the seriousness of United States determination to get the missiles out of Cuba, but he thought the action should allow the Soviets more room for maneuver to pull back from their overextended position in Cuba.[243]

The analogy, repeated once again, is entirely specious. In 1941 the Japanese attacked without specific provocation while their ambassadors were engaged in negotiations ostensibly aimed at settling differences peaceably. An American attack would come only after the United States had warned the Soviet Union specifically against doing what it was doing. The analogy, in fact, seems better to fit the Soviet act of implanting the missiles secretly while repeatedly denying they were doing so. Robert Kennedy's moralism, moreover, fits badly with his earlier suggestion that the United States invent a pretext for taking action against Cuba: "one other thing is whether, uh, we should also think of, uh, uh, whether there is some other way we can get involved in this through Guantanamo Bay, or something, er, or whether there's some ship that, you know, sink the *Maine* again or something."[244] His intervention, nonetheless, had a crucial effect on the course of the discussion. Dillon, as we have seen, was very much in favor of a swift "surgical" air strike, a view to which he returned many years later, but Robert Kennedy's statement changed his mind. "I finally agreed with Bobby Kennedy that a surprise attack on Cuba at that time was unacceptable because it was too much like the Japanese attack on Pearl Harbor. If we attacked like that, we would be forsaking the ideals for which I believed we had fought World War II."[245] We should not doubt that Dillon and others were moved sincerely by the Attorney General's argument, but it would be naive to ignore the fact that he also had removed the veil, revealing the President's own preference and asking the group not to recommend an action that would make things "very, very difficult indeed for the President." As one ExCom member said later, "We all knew Little Brother was watching and keeping a little list of where everyone stood."[246]

The ExCom then divided into two working groups, each to produce the case for one of the choices. When they came together again there was further discussion about the options. Taylor's claim that they could not eat their cake and have it, too, that they must choose between the air strike and the blockade, clearly presented a problem to those who favored the blockade. McNamara, therefore, announced that an air strike could be made some time after Sunday if the blockade did not work. This gave Robert Kennedy the opportunity he needed: "The Attorney General took particular note of this shift, and toward the end of the day made clear that he firmly favored a blockade as the first step; other steps subsequently were not precluded and could be considered; he thought it was pretty clear what the decision should be."[247] There was no response to Taylor's fear that the missiles would become operational before an aerial attack could now be launched. Waverers were encouraged to believe that both options were still available. The decision for a blockade effectively had been taken, although it would not become formal until the twenty-first.

Robert Kennedy's "moral" argument against an air strike rested on the premise that it must be a "sneak attack," but that is by no means clear. Sorensen, in fact, tried to compose a letter the President could send to Khrushchev prior to the air strike. To avoid giving Khrushchev a chance to stall, hide the missiles, make propaganda, and take other unwelcome steps, it was to be "an airtight letter" delivered by a high-level personal envoy. It would say that "only if he agreed in his conference with that courier (and such others as he called in) to order the missiles dismantled would U.S. military action be withheld while our surveillance oversaw their removal." The idea appealed to "many of those originally attracted to the air-strike course . . . in the hope that a warning would suffice."[248] Besides the warning, Sorensen's draft included an invitation by the President to meet with Khrushchev, should he come to New York, to discuss, among other things, "the NATO bases in Turkey and Italy."[249] Years later Burlatsky wondered why the President had begun with a public announcement of the blockade and not with a private communication to Khrushchev.[250] Sorensen's explanation is that "no matter how many references I put in to a summit, to peaceful intentions and to previous warnings and pledges, the letter still constituted the kind of ultimatum which no great power could accept, and a justification for either a pre-emptive strike against this country or our indictment in the court of history."[251] While Sorensen was working on the letter that was never sent the President was meeting with the Soviet Foreign Minister. Gromyko complained about American actions toward Cuba and delivered a message from Khrushchev firmly assuring Kennedy that the assistance the Soviets were giving Cuba were not offensive in nature. The President read from his previous warnings against the installation of offensive weapons, to which Gromyko did not reply. The President did not ask any direct questions about the missiles or reveal their discovery.[252]

Kennedy regretted not mentioning the missiles to Gromyko as soon as he left, but he did not say why. Burlatsky, many years later, saw this as a lost opportunity: "I am convinced that if John Kennedy said when he met Gromyko, 'We know everything about rockets in Cuba,' maybe there would be no crisis; because Khrushchev must understand he was discovered and that he would need now to negotiate about a new situation. But Kennedy did not say anything to Gromyko."²⁵³ We will never know whether an earlier revelation that the missiles had been found, together with a stiff note demanding their removal, might have averted the crisis that followed before any missiles were operational. What is clear is that Kennedy preferred the risks of delay and inaction to the risks of action.

On Friday, October 20, Kennedy held another meeting. Although the final decision had not been taken, he made it clear that the blockade was the way he would go, calling it "the only course compatible with American principles." Adlai Stevenson suggested that even as the blockade was announced the United States should propose an offer for a settlement removing the American missiles from Turkey and the American base at Guantanamo. This suggestion earned much criticism, including some from the President, but his difference from Stevenson was only tactical. At the ExCom meeting of the day before, McNamara, whose thinking through-out the crisis seems to have been close to Kennedy's, had expressed the view "that the U.S. would have to pay a price to get the Soviet missiles out of Cuba. He thought we would at least have to give up our missile bases in Italy and Turkey and would probably have to pay more besides."²⁵⁴ Now, on the twenty-first, Kennedy "agreed that at an appropriate time we would have to acknowledge that we were willing to take strategic missiles out of Turkey and Italy if this issue was raised by the Russians. . . . But he was firm in saying we should only make such a proposal in the future."²⁵⁵ That future would come only a few days later.

On Monday, October 22, envoys informed America's major allies of the installation of the missiles on Cuba and of the plan to blockade the island. That same afternoon, only two hours before his speech to the nation, the President informed seventeen congressional leaders from both parties. Richard Russell, the influential senator from Georgia, had asked to be briefed before the meeting, so he was the only congressman present who was prepared for what they were about to hear. As he listened to the President he wrote a note for himself, "Khrushchev believes what he says —we are afraid." In response to the President he denounced the quarantine as a halfway measure. He urged an attack that would remove the missiles and also rid Cuba of Castro and his government. To the President's shock he was joined by Fulbright, who also favored an invasion, saying "it would be less provocative and less inclined to precipitate a war with Russia." Others then joined in the criticism, saying the blockade was too slow and not an adequate response to the danger. They would support the President in the crisis, but the Republican leaders of the House and Senate insisted that they be recorded as informed, not consulted.[256] They clearly regarded Kennedy's plans as too weak. He had little further room to retreat. He understood American politics even if Khrushchev did not. His understanding of what was politically possible may already have led him to be firmer than he might have liked. If he did not get the missiles out the political price would be enormous.

That night Kennedy delivered his speech to the nation. He announced that "it shall be the policy of this nation to regard any nuclear missile launched from Cuba against any nation in the Western Hemisphere as an attack by the Soviet Union on the United States, requiring a full retaliatory response upon the Soviet Union."[257] United States military forces were placed on DEFCON 3, and the nuclear forces on DEFCON 2, the highest alert level short of war. SAC planes were in the air, Polaris nuclear submarines left port for their stations at sea, and ICBM crews were placed on full alert. Never before or since has the world been brought so close to nuclear war.

Just how close that catastrophe really was we shall never know. Khrushchev responded angrily to Kennedy's speech. There is a report that his first reaction was to order an acceleration of the emplacement of the missiles and to instruct the captains of the ships approaching Cuba to ignore the blockade and sail on through. The story claims that it was only the intervention of Mikoyan that stopped the ships.[258] It is not unlikely that Khrushchev's first instincts were bellicose. Kennedy had reacted in a similar way, angrily saying, "He can't do this to *me*," on first hearing of the missiles[259] and having no doubt at first that an air strike was the smallest possible response. Khrushchev, like Kennedy, had time for second thoughts. If Mikoyan ordered the captains to halt he could not have done so without the Chairman's approval. The construction of the Cuban missiles, moreover, continued at an accelerated pace. Khrushchev's actions thereafter, in any case, were cautious, far more so than Kennedy and his advisers expected. They seriously anticipated trouble in Berlin and even considered the possibility of a Soviet attack on the Turkish missiles, but Khrushchev undertook no provocative action whatever.

The day after the speech Khrushchev sent a letter to Kennedy that denounced the blockade but assured the President that the missiles were in Cuba for purely defensive purposes; he avoided the harsh language and threats he had used on previous occasions but instead asked the United States "to display wisdom" and avoid taking actions that might lead to war. Ambassador Kohler noted that both the statement and the letter "avoided specific threats and are relatively restrained in tone."[260] The messages can, in fact, be interpreted as an appeal to the President not to launch an attack. The Soviet military forces did not match the American alert, canceling leaves and discharges, but making no redeployments and not placing its units on a wartime alert. Khrushchev also issued a public statement for Soviet consumption that spoke of an American blockade of Cuba but said nothing of the Soviet missiles. It depicted the issue as one between the United States and Cuba. "Perhaps the Russians felt that if they had to back down later, it would be far less embarrassing to do so under the fiction of resolving a conflict between the United States and a third country . . . than to appear to be retreating from a naked confrontation between the superpowers."[261] That is the way the State Department saw it, reporting that "the Soviet reaction thus far suggests a high degree of circumspection and implies that the Soviet Union may be carefully leaving the back door open for a retreat from the danger of a general war over Cuba."[262]

The Resolution

That estimate turned out to be correct. The rest of the crisis was really a matter of tense bargaining over the terms under which the Soviets would withdraw the missiles, in spite of the understandable alarm of American officials, who could not be sure of Soviet intentions. They prepared for a blockade of Berlin and agreed to attack SAM sites if American surveillance planes were shot down.[263] Their most immediate fear was that Soviet submarines or merchant ships would challenge the blockade and start the shooting. Kennedy consistently chose the least provocative action and was ready to make concessions, some of which he could not admit publicly, in order to avoid confrontation and to end the crisis. He considered offering to meet Khrushchev at a summit, but rejected another talk as valueless "until Khrushchev first accepted, as a result of our deeds as well as our statements, the U.S. determination in this matter."[264] That was an acknowledgment of how little Khrushchev had been impressed by Kennedy's previous warnings. As the ships kept their course toward Cuba, over passionate protests by the Navy, Kennedy pulled back the quarantine line from eight hundred miles, originally set to keep American ships out of range of Soviet MIGs on Cuba, to five hundred miles. The next morning, Wednesday, October 24, the blockade formally went into effect, but the ships kept coming. The President appeared to feel that even the imposition of a blockade may have been too provocative a step. He said to his brother, "It looks really mean, doesn't it. But then, really, there was no other choice. If they get this mean on this one in our part of the world, what will they do on the next?" Robert Kennedy comforted him by reminding him of the domestic political considerations that had made total inaction impossible: "If you hadn't acted you would have been impeached." It was then that the President responded, "That's what I think—I would have been impeached."[265]

As the tension mounted word came that the ships had stopped at the limit or turned around to head back before they got there. That was the moment when Rusk made his famous remark to Bundy: "We're eyeball to eyeball and I think the other fellow just blinked."[266] Rusk was wrong in two ways: more ships were coming and would challenge the blockade line the next day; the "blink," moreover, had taken place the previous night, when the *Poltava*, carrying twenty nuclear warheads, turned back, along with several other ships capable of carrying large missiles.[267] Khrushchev seems to have decided to pull back ships carrying the incriminating missiles and warheads so they could not be seized by the American Navy, but the others kept going. He may have thought that his opponent might yet fail the test of action.

Kennedy, in fact, continued to exercise restraint. His response to Khrushchev's letter, sent to Moscow in the early hours of October 25, was moderate and unthreatening, concluding: "I repeat my regret that these events should cause a deterioration in our relations. I hope that your Government will take the necessary actions to permit a restoration of the earlier situation."[268] His actions were in the same vein. Oil tankers were not on the quarantine list, but when the *Bucharest* approached the line some members of the ExCom wanted it stopped so that Khrushchev would "make no mistake of our will and intent,"[269] but Kennedy wanted to avoid any confrontation, so he ordered the tanker to be let through. It was greeted in Havana with a celebration.[270] Later he also allowed the East German passenger ship *Voelker Freundschaft* to pass the line without inspection. The first ship to be stopped was the *Marucla*, a freighter of Panamanian ownership and Lebanese registration, bound from Riga to Cuba under Soviet charter. Robert Kennedy says that "the *Marucla* had been carefully and personally selected by President Kennedy to be the first ship stopped and boarded. He was demonstrating to Khrushchev that we were going to enforce the quarantine, and yet, because it was not a Soviet-owned vessel, it did not represent a direct affront to the Soviets, requiring a response from them." To make sure that there would be no misunderstandings, the American destroyer assigned to stop it radioed the *Marucla* the night of the twenty-fifth to let its captain know it would be boarded the next morning.

Not everyone in the ExCom was sure that such sensitive treatment was the best policy. At the meeting on the morning of the twenty-sixth, Undersecretary of State George Ball called for extending the embargo to include petroleum, such as the *Bucharest* had carried into Havana. Secretary Dillon was not happy about the policy of stopping Soviet ships. In that way "a confrontation with the Russians would not be over missiles, but over Soviet ships. He believed we should go for the missiles rather than force a confrontation with the USSR at sea."[271] Since the only way to "go for the missiles" was by aerial attack and/or invasion, it appears that Dillon was calling for an air strike. Secretary Rusk read a cable whose content is censored in the released account of the meeting, but it produced the comment from Nitze that it was important to get the "Soviet missiles out urgently." McCone was dissatisfied with the limited goal of obtaining the removal of the missiles. "Even if the Soviet missiles are removed, Castro, if he is left in control, will be in an excellent position to undertake the Communization of Latin America." Both Rusk and Bundy rejected any goal but removing the missiles, and the President agreed with them.

Rusk put serious hopes in UN Secretary-General U Thant's efforts to bring about a negotiated solution and wanted nothing to interfere with his efforts. He asked for a delay in adding oil to the embargo list. When McNamara pointed out that construction on the missile sites was continuing and asked for night reconnaissance flights with flares, Rusk "asked that the night mission not be flown because of the unfortunate effect which it might have on the U Thant negotiations in New York." He contemplated the substitution of a UN quarantine for the American one, to which McCone objected. He insisted on an American quarantine "until the Russians accepted all our conditions." Rusk wanted it to be clear to U Thant that the quarantine was only against the missiles and not other Soviet military shipments to Cuba.

Stevenson reported on the discussions under way with U Thant and the talks with the Russians that would follow if the Russians agreed. Of the immediate talks he "acknowledged" that "it would be impossible to obtain an agreement to make the weapons inoperable." If the Russians were willing to agree to stop further construction he wanted to know "whether in return we would be prepared to suspend the quarantine." He predicted that in talks with the Soviets "the Russians would ask us for a new guarantee of the territorial integrity of Cuba and the dismantlement [sic] of U.S. strategic missiles in Turkey." Reaction was sharply negative. Bundy insisted that negotiations for a standstill were not good enough; there must also be guarantees of the inspection of Cuba. Dillon said, "We could not negotiate for two weeks under the missile threat which now exists in Cuba." McCone objected to any comparison between the Cuban and Turkish missiles. It is in the context of this conversation that we must understand Kennedy's reaction. He could not go so far in the direction of conciliation as Stevenson suggested, if he wanted to, without running into stiff resistance within his administration. His other decisions took the most cautious path possible. Following Rusk's advice, he declined to add oil to the embargo list or to order night reconnaissance flights. He made only one significant intervention of his own: "The President said we will get the Soviet strategic missiles out of Cuba only by invading Cuba or by trading. He doubted that the quarantine alone would produce a withdrawal of the weapons. He said our objective should be to prevent further military shipments, further construction at missile sites, and to get some means of inspection."272

Although the President was very cautious in these discussions, not willing to show any more of his hand than necessary, his statement sheds considerable light on his views. It rejects McCone's desire to include the removal of Castro in the list of American goals. He would have liked to achieve the removal of the missiles, but that could not, he said, be done by the quarantine. How then? The reference to an invasion cannot be taken seriously. Not even the most aggressive military leaders advocated an invasion as the next step. The policy of choice for those who wanted military action was an air strike. When the President asked what could be done if negotiations and the quarantine failed to remove the missiles, Bundy replied, "Then our choice would be to expand the blockade or remove the missiles by air attack," but the President never even mentioned an air strike as a possibility. By referring to the invasion, instead, he signaled that he did not plan any military action at all. The serious part of his comment was the reference to a trade. Even before Stevenson's comments Kennedy had asked whether the United States could commit itself not to invade Cuba, and Rusk said that it was already so committed by the UN Charter and the Rio Treaty. To this guarantee Stevenson added the Turkish missiles as a necessary part of any trade, thereby foreshadowing the deal that was made eventually.

As we have seen, the idea of a trade for the Turkish and Italian missiles already had been floated by Stevenson. The same suggestion had come from a source closer to Kennedy and much more influential with him. "More than once" at the morning meeting of the nineteenth Secretary McNamara voiced the opinion that the United States would have to pay a price to get the Soviet missiles out of Cuba. He thought we would at least have to give up our missile bases in Italy and Turkey and probably would have to pay more besides."[273] Robert Kennedy was present, but the record does not show that either he or anyone else objected. There is good reason to believe that the President was ready to make such a trade even before the Soviets proposed it.

Events later in the day, however, suggested that it might not be necessary. Aleksander Fomin, officially public affairs counselor to the Soviet embassy but really the Washington station chief for the KGB, invited John Scali, State Department correspondent for ABC News, to lunch. He proposed a settlement of the crisis on the following terms: "[Soviet] bases would be dismantled under United Nations supervision and Castro would pledge not to accept offensive weapons of any kind, ever, in return for a U.S. pledge not to invade Cuba."[274] Then, at 6 P.M. of the same day the State Department began receiving a private letter from Khrushchev to the President. It arrived in four parts from the American embassy in Moscow, the last section coming at 9 P.M., about twelve hours after it had been delivered in Moscow. From its language and style it generally has been thought to have been written by Khrushchev himself. It is long, tortuous, and in places emotional, asking Kennedy to cease the blockade and not to force the issue to war. Its best known passage reads:

> If you have not lost command of yourself and realize clearly what this could lead to, then, Mr. President, you and I should not now pull on the end of the rope in which you have tied a knot of war, because the harder you and I pull, the tighter the knot will become. And a time may come when this knot is tied so tight that the person who tied it is no longer capable of untying it, and then the

knot will have to be cut. What that would mean I need not explain to you, because you yourself understand perfectly what dread forces our two countries possess. . . . Let us not only relax the forces straining on the ends of the rope, let us take measures for untying this knot.

The most important passages, however, contain a proposal suggesting a solution of the crisis:

> If the President and Government of the United States would give their assurances that the United States would itself not take part in an attack upon Cuba and would restrain others from such action; if you recall your Navy—this would immediately change everything. . . . Then the question of armaments would also be obviated, because when there is no threat, armaments are only a burden for any people. This would also change the approach to the question of destroying not only the armaments which you call offensive, but of every other kind of armament. . . .
>
> I propose: we, for our part, will declare that our ships bound for Cuba are not carrying any armaments. You will declare the United States will not invade Cuba with its troops and will not support any other forces which might tend to invade Cuba. Then the necessity for the presence of our military specialists in Cuba will be obviated.[275]

Even as the message was coming in Scali reported his meeting with Fomin to Roger Hilsman. The State Department believed that the letter must have been drafted about the same time as the instructions to Fomin: "the two communications were clearly related: the cable indicated a willingness to negotiate, and the unofficial approach through Scali suggested a formula for the negotiations."[276] Rusk sent Scali back to tell Fomin that the United States was willing to pursue his suggestion, but that time was of the essence. Recently, a Soviet official has claimed that Fomin had no orders from Moscow but was working on his own.[277] If that is true it would be a most remarkable coincidence, because at just about the same time that Fomin was talking to Scali, U Thant was making virtually the same proposal to Adlai Stevenson in New York. Years later Thant told Rusk that the proposal came from a Soviet official who Rusk knew to be a

KGB agent. Thant also said that Gromyko was aware of what was happening.[278] The Americans, in any case, had every reason to believe at the time that a proposal from a highly placed KGB agent in the midst of a great crisis came from the Kremlin and, without further evidence, so should we.

The Americans assumed the offer was authorized and genuine. Using what appears to have been a favorite metaphor, Rusk told Scali: "Remember when you report this—that, eyeball to eyeball, they blinked first."[279] It appears that this time he was right. Why had Khrushchev abandoned the refusal to make any concessions of his first communication for the new message that clearly sought a peaceful outcome that included concessions by the Soviets? It has been suggested that Khrushchev was unpleasantly surprised that the United States had won the support of the Organization of American States and many other nations and that the blockade was really in effect and functioning; that he realized that his nuclear inferiority made a diversionary blockade on Berlin too dangerous; and that the conventional superiority of the United States in the Western Hemisphere would make it impossible to defeat an army invading Cuba.[280] It is hard to believe, however, that public opinion could determine the actions of a man who had invaded Hungary in spite of the almost unanimous denunciations of the nations of the world. As for the blockade, it had not prevented the installation of some nuclear missiles in Cuba that must by now be presumed to be operational.[281] If even ten or so were ready they could serve much the same purpose of minimal deterrence as the forty originally planned. As for the military superiority of the United States, both nuclear and conventional, that had been no less true when the adventure had been conceived and on October 23, when Khrushchev had sent his first note offering no concessions. Perhaps Khrushchev was feeling pressure at home, either to withdraw or to take risks he was unwilling to consider; we have no reliable evidence. Kennedy, moreover, had not shown himself to be so bellicose as to cause alarm. On the contrary, as we have seen, all his actions were cautious and pacific. On learning of the missiles and the deception Khrushchev had practiced on him he had not launched air strikes and an invasion, as were urged by many of his advisers and as might have been expected. Even after ordering a blockade, he had allowed ships to pass through without inspection and carefully had selected a non-Soviet vessel to stop. Throughout these events he had avoided threatening language. Such evidence might have encouraged the Soviet leader to believe that patience and toughness might yet yield the outcome he wanted: the American acceptance of the Cuban missiles and the advantages they would give the Soviet Union.

On the other hand, there was also some evidence that might have caused alarm. American military forces around the world had been put on high alert. Two other actions, moreover, both taken without the permission or knowledge of the President, might have caused still more concern. On October 22, the very day Kennedy revealed the discovery of the Cuban missiles, the first U.S. Jupiter missile site was formally turned over to the Turkish Air Force. The decision makers in Washington seem not to have known of what must have been a long-planned and routine action.[282] In Turkey, however, it received publicity and was probably reported to the Kremlin within a couple of days. Then, on the twenty-fourth General Thomas Powers, commander-in-chief of SAC, decided that it was now "important for [the Soviets] to know of SAC's readiness." On his own authority he informed SAC commanders by uncoded messages that the alert was going smoothly and that SAC plans were well prepared.[283] It seems at least plausible that Khrushchev might have read these actions, unknown to Kennedy and in no way planned by him, as dangerous and threatening warnings of American willingness and preparedness for a fight and that his offer of a solution might, ironically, have resulted from these unintended messages that were so much at odds with the President's own approach.

The delivery of Khrushchev's message was completed too late for the Americans to respond on Friday, October 26, when it was received. By the next morning everything had changed. A CIA memo reported at six in the morning that "three of the four IRBM sites at San Cristobal and the two sites at Sagua La Grande appear to be fully operational."[284] At 9 A.M. Radio Moscow began broadcasting a new message from Khrushchev. It added to the requirements for the withdrawal of the Cuban missiles the withdrawal by the Americans of their missiles from Turkey. None of this was to be done quietly, moreover, but in the full glare of the world's attention. The mutual pledges would take place in the United Nations. The Soviets would promise to remove their missiles from Cuba; the Americans would promise to remove their missiles from Turkey; the Soviets would promise not to attack or disturb Turkey; the Americans would promise the same to Cuba. These were equations that the American President could not accept publicly, whatever he might think privately. At the very least, it would seem to be a sellout of a NATO ally under pressure from the Soviets, an act of weakness and fear. Kennedy's political opponents were sure to ask why he had accepted such terms instead of acting strongly and decisively.

What had caused the change in the Kremlin? Why had Khrushchev, so eager to end the confrontation in his previous message, added the Turkish missiles to his requirements, thereby increasing tension and giving the Americans more time to decide on a military action that he presumably feared? Khrushchev presents himself as being under great pressure from the military,[285] but there is no question that he was always in charge during the crisis and able to take his own decisions. There is no reason to believe that he felt free to send the first letter but then felt constrained by hardliners to send the second letter almost immediately. Apart from such a suggestion, scholars have had a difficult time explaining Khrushchev's *volte face*. Here is a distinguished example: "It may be that Khrushchev simply had not thought through the implications of the proposal; 'irrational reasons' may have been at work here as well as in his decision to deploy missiles in Cuba in the first place. But whatever the explanation, he committed a serious gaffe at the climax of the confrontation."[286] Before assuming irrationality, however, it might be better to seek an answer elsewhere. As we have seen, American leaders, Kennedy very much among them, had considered the possibility of a trade early on. On October 25 Walter Lippmann suggested a trade of the Turkish for the Cuban missiles as a way out of the crisis. Kennedy had been known to complain of Khrushchev's belief that Lippmann's columns spoke the President's opinions. There is no evidence that the column had been inspired by the White House, but Kennedy's failure to respond to it has provoked an interesting speculation:

> Once Lippmann made his Thursday proposal, Kennedy may have thought it useful to call Khrushchev's attention to one route by which he could negotiate an end to the crisis. Had he wished to warn the Chairman away from such a route of bargaining, he could have easily asked Salinger to issue a statement to the effect that the United States could not accept the suggestion of a Turkey-for-Cuba trade that had appeared in public prints. Knowing Khrushchev might assume that Lippmann was proposing a trade on his behalf, the President let the column stand.[287]

It is possible, therefore, that Lippmann's suggestion and the President's silence may have persuaded Khrushchev to raise the ante. However that may be, an even stronger signal was sent to the Soviets on the night of the twenty-sixth when Robert Kennedy came to Anatoly Dobrynin for a visit known only to the President, unreported by Robert Kennedy in his memoir of the crisis, and unknown to historians until just recently. According to Dobrynin it was Robert Kennedy who suggested making the Turkish missiles part of a settlement. The Attorney General asked: " 'You are interested in the missiles in Turkey?' He thought pensively and said: 'One minute, I will go and talk to the President.' He went out of the room. I do not know what he did, I assume he spoke with the President, and when he appeared he said: 'The President said that we are ready to consider the question about Turkey—to examine favorably the question of Turkey.' "[288] There was time for Dobrynin to get the message to the Kremlin in time for Khrushchev to have composed his message demanding the trade of Cuba for Turkey. Thus, it has been suggested "that Khrushchev's public demand for a Turkey-Cuba missile trade—made on the morning of the 27th—may have been based on Robert Kennedy's remarks, relayed through Dobrynin."[289] In fact, it seems highly likely that Khrushchev reversed himself because Kennedy made him an offer of the Turkish missiles without being asked. His reversal, therefore, was neither "irrational" nor a "gaffe," but the hardheaded bargaining of a veteran player taking advantage of the weakness of an inexperienced and nervous opponent.[290]

As Khrushchev's latest message came in on the twenty-seventh the ExCom met to consider a reply, unaware that the President already was committed to a trade involving the Turkish missiles. He had made the offer in the context of Khrushchev's gentler letter of the twenty-sixth when, presumably, the trade could be made quietly, without public fanfare, some time after the Cuban missiles had been removed. As the new, harsher letter came in, demanding a very public trade, Kennedy found himself in a most difficult position. At an earlier meeting of the ExCom he had insisted that "there would be no bargains over our bases in Turkey and Italy."[291] Some members of the ExCom, unaware of the President's commitment made the night before, were bound to take a hard line and make a trade seem a retreat under threat rather than a voluntary diplomatic ploy, and the President could not afford to seem weak and yielding. No less serious was the difficulty of getting Turkey and NATO to accept the trade under the glare of Khrushchev's demand. The President's behavior at the ExCom meetings throughout the day takes on new meaning when these problems are understood.

Kennedy's first question was "where are we with our conversations with the Turks about the withdrawal of these [missiles]?"[292] The answer was not encouraging. On the twenty-fourth a cable had been sent to U.S. Ambassador to Turkey Raymond Hare and to U.S. Ambassador to NATO Thomas Finletter to tell them that a trade for the Turkish missiles was under consideration. On the twenty-fifth Finletter responded that the Turks saw the missiles as "a symbol of the alliance's determination to use atomic weapons" in defense of Turkey. The Turks would reject any deal that did not replace the missiles with some form of nuclear weapon.[293] In answer to the President's question at the meeting Nitze pointed out the difficulties: "Hare says this is absolutely anathema, and is a matter of prestige and politics." Ball, reporting on Finletter's reaction, said the Turks were a problem. They might give up the missiles if they were replaced by Polaris submarines off the coast, "and even that might not be enough." The decision to install the missiles in Turkey, moreover, had been taken not by the United States but by NATO, so removing them implied consultation and permission. It might not be easy for the President to fulfill the promise Robert Kennedy had made on his behalf the night before.

Bundy was not eager to make the trade. He made the suggestion that has come down in the literature of the missile crisis as the "Trollope Ploy," a reference to the habit of maidens in Anthony Trollope's Victorian novels of taking the innocent remarks of a suitor to be a marriage proposal and accepting it. "I would answer back [to Khrushchev's more recent message] saying I would prefer to deal with your interesting proposals of last night."[294] Kennedy was uncomfortable with the suggestion: "in the first place, we last year tried to get the missiles out of there because they're not militarily useful, number one. Number two, it's going to—to any man at the United Nations or any other rational man it will look like a very fair trade." Nitze objected that a trade would shake allied confidence: "everybody else is worried that they'll be included in this great big trade, and it goes beyond Cuba." Kennedy asked how much negotiating had gone on with the Turks and was told by George Ball that he had the opinions of Hare and Finletter, but there had been no direct talks with the Turks: "if we talked to the Turks, I mean this would be an extremely unsettling business." The President was not impressed. "Well *this* is unsettling *now*, George, because he's got us in a pretty good spot here, because most people will regard this as not an unreasonable proposal." Bundy interjected, "But what most people, Mr. President?" To which he answered: "I think you're going to find it very difficult to explain why we are going to take hostile military action in Cuba, against these sites—what we've been thinking about—the thing that he's saying is, if you'll get yours out of Turkey, we'll get ours out of Cuba. I think we've got a very tough one here." Bundy returned to the idea of ignoring the second message with the demand for the Turkish missiles and responding to the first, omitting any consideration of the trade, but the President continued to insist that the second message was the real one; it superseded the first and must be dealt with. "There are disadvantages also," he said, "in the private one [i.e., the first message], which is a guarantee of Cuba. But in any case this is now his official [sic] and we can release his other one, and it's different, but this is the one that the Soviet government obviously is going on."

Robert Kennedy came to the President's support, arguing that Bundy's plan would cause confusion, giving Khrushchev the initiative and causing delay. He recommended a response to Khrushchev offering the trade. Given that momentum the President once again raised the problem that had been troubling him from the beginning of the discussion, the Turks.

> "The first thing we ought to do is not let the Turks issue some statement that's wholly unacceptable . . . not have the Turks making statements, so that this thing—Khrushchev puts it out and the next thing the Turks say they won't accept it. I think we ought to have a talk with the Turks because I think they've got to understand the peril that they're going to move in the next week. When we take action in Cuba, the chances are that he'll take some action in Turkey, and they ought to understand that. . . . So I think the Turks ought to think a little. We ought to try to get them not to respond to this till we've had a chance to consider what action we'll take. Now how long will it take to get in touch with the Turks?

The President's interest in putting pressure on the Turks was ignored in an outburst of concern by others about the danger such an action would present to the integrity of NATO. "Most of the group argue[d] that an open trade could fragment the NATO alliance."[295] Bundy was the clearest spokesman for this view: "I think that if we sound as if we wanted to make this trade, to our NATO people and to all the people who are tied to us by alliance, we are in real trouble. . . . We'll all join in doing that if it's the decision, but . . . that's the assessment of everyone in the government that's connected with these alliance problems. . . . If we appear to be trading our—the defense of Turkey for the threat to Cuba we . . . just have to face a radical decline in the—" The President interrupted to say: "as the situation is moving, Mac, if we don't for the next twenty-four or forty-eight hours, this trade has appeal. Now if we reject it out of hand and then have to take military action against Cuba, then we also face a decline." The situation would simply have to be explained to NATO. By now, at least, McNamara appears to have realized that the President was determined to remove the Turkish missiles, so he presented an ingenious plan meant at the same time to permit their withdrawal without asking NATO's permission; to tie it to the idea of military action, thereby removing the stigma of weakness; to pour cold water on the Joint Chiefs' proposal for an air strike, even as he presented a scenario so frightening that it tacitly argued for making the trade:

> Mr. President, I wonder if we should not take certain actions with respect to the Jupiters in Turkey and Italy *before* we act in Cuba. . . . Then we could *tell* NATO that at the time we talked to them about this proposal from Khrushchev and our response to it. If we act in Cuba, the only way we can act now is with a full attack . . . we would not dare to go in with the kind of limited attack that we've been thinking about the last twenty-four hours without taking out their SAM sites. The moment we take out the SAM sites and the MiG airfields we're up to the [excised] sortie program. If we send [excised] sorties against Cuba, we must be prepared to follow up with an invasion in about [excised] days. If we start out on that kind of program, it seems to me the Soviets are very likely to feel forced to reply with military action someplace, particularly if these missiles—Jupiter missiles—are still in Turkey. We might be able to either shift the area in which they would apply their military force or give them no excuse to apply military force by taking out the Turkish Jupiters and the Italian Jupiters before we attack Cuba.[296]

The President's attention, however, remained fixed on NATO and the Turks: "They don't realize that in two or three days we may have a military strike which could bring perhaps the seizure of Berlin or a strike on Turkey and they'll say, By God we should have taken it." McNamara was worried about the imminence of an American air strike against Cuba and pressed for a delay until there could be a NATO meeting, but the President again focused on the Turks: "I think that . . . the real problem is what we do with the Turks first . . . what we're going to do is say to the Turks—which they're bound to think is . . . under Soviet pressure, we want to get your missiles out of there." McNamara was ready with a message for the Turks:

> What I'd say to the Turks [is]: "Look here, we're going to have to invade Cuba. You're in mortal danger. We want to reduce your danger while at the same time maintaining your defense. We propose that you defuse those missiles tonight. We're putting Polaris submarines along your coast. We'll cover the same targets that your Jupiter missiles did, and we'll announce this to the world before we invade Cuba and thereby would reduce the pressure on the Soviet Union to attack you, Turkey, as a response to our invasion of Cuba."[297]

The Turks, of course, might think that the removal of the missiles, installed in the first place to serve as a deterrent against Soviet attack, was evidence of American weakness and lack of resolve, and they might prefer to put their faith in the missiles instead of American promises. Robert Kennedy saw the flaw in McNamara's argument: "Now, then they say . . . what if the Soviet Union attacks us anyway. Will you use the missiles on the nuclear submarines?" McNamara responded: "Then, I think, before we attack Cuba . . . we've got to decide how we'll respond to Soviet military pressure, and I'm not prepared to answer that question."

The record does not show that he ever was so prepared. It seems likely, in fact, that neither McNamara nor the President expected to take any military action at all. To be sure, there was pressure from the Joint Chiefs, whose opinion was presented by General Taylor, to launch air strikes on the missile sites as soon as possible, probably Monday, October 29, and at the conference in 1987, Dillon said that "by Saturday the 27th, there was a clear majority in the ExCom in favor of taking military action,"[298] but he conceded that the President had not made such a decision, and that the decision on what action to take would be made by an "inner group" consisting of the President, Robert Kennedy, Rusk, and McNamara. None of these men favored military action. McNamara's memory, as we have seen, can be imperfect, but in 1987 he was repeatedly adamant in saying that neither he nor the President planned any military action. "What would have happened if Khrushchev hadn't accepted President Kennedy's terms? . . . I believe we could have done a lot more with the blockade. We could have continued to turn the screw for quite some time, and I believe that's what we would have done." He conceded that there was *tremendous* pressure for military action, "but that didn't mean that we were going to do it right away. We had lots of time left to turn the screw on the blockade, and a lot of pressure to take that route, too." He was entirely confident, moreover, that there would be no military action soon: "If President Kennedy were going to strike on Monday or Tuesday, then he would have told me about it so we could make the necessary preparations. He hadn't told me, so I don't think he was going to strike." He was definite in rejecting the idea that the United States would use nuclear weapons under any conditions. "I *knew* what I was going to do with SIOP. *None* of the options was going to be used at all. I had procedures in place for withholding, which, of course, would have given the military a fit; but before the Cuban missile crisis, I had recommended to President Kennedy that he never make use of SIOP in any circumstances." When asked how he would respond to a Soviet action somewhere in the world, he responded: "Turn the screw on the blockade and avoid the air attack and invasion," and Bundy confirmed his opinion that "the 'turn of the screw' option would have won out."[299] If all this is true, McNamara's talk of attack, invasion, and further escalation was only for effect, a tactic meant to prepare the ground for the trade of missiles.

Llewellyn Thompson, however, was not willing to accept the trade. The President continued to argue for it, ostensibly on the grounds that the "Trollope Ploy" would not work, that the last message represented the Soviets' true position. But Thompson argued otherwise: "The important thing for Khrushchev, it seems to me, is to be able to say, I saved Cuba, I stopped an invasion." Kennedy remained skeptical, but Bundy supported the idea. At that point General Taylor presented the recommendation of the Joint Chiefs—a big air strike no later than Monday to be followed by an invasion days later. Robert Kennedy sardonically responded, "That was a surprise."

Further discussion was interrupted by the news that an American U-2 had been shot down by a missile from a SAM site. The decision to fire had been made by a local commander without the knowledge of or permission from the Kremlin. He was reprimanded by Malinovsky, who said: "You hastily shot down the U.S. plane; an agreement for a peaceful way to deter an invasion of Cuba was already taking shape."[300] It was assumed, however, in ExCom that this was a deliberate escalation by the Soviets that called for retaliation, since the ExCom had decided on Tuesday the twenty-third that if such a thing happened the Americans would take out a SAM site. Kennedy, however, decided not to retaliate against any SAM sites but to wait to see if any other American surveillance planes were attacked before making a military response. The "order to call off the planned reprisal [was] reportedly received with disbelief in the Pentagon."[301] But Kennedy still was worried about Turkey and NATO. In the midst of the discussion about attacking SAMs Kennedy told Gilpatrick, "Ros, why don't you write this out, . . . and then we'll get back to what we're going to do about the Turks." As the discussion of the SAMs continued he once again raised the question of a NATO meeting: "I'm just afraid of what's going to happen in NATO, to Europe, when we get into this thing more and more."

McNamara was quick to agree and to start a discussion on what to tell the NATO allies. The President left the room for a time, and the Secretary of Defense went back to painting frightening scenarios of military escalation, concluding with his idea of removing the Turkish missiles *before* any attack on Cuba. Ball pointed out the flaw in the proposal: withdrawing the Turkish missiles might only open the door to a Soviet reprisal elsewhere. When McNamara was forced to concede the point Ball demolished the proposal by saying, "I think you're in a position where you've gotten rid of your missiles for *nothing.*"

McNamara lost the argument with Ball, but the focus on escalation and his more extreme suggestion of removing the missiles without a trade won converts to the plan for a trade as a more moderate approach. Vice President Lyndon Johnson and George Ball spoke in favor, Ball saying, "Well, I would far rather if we're going to get the damned missiles out of Turkey *anyway,* say, We'll trade you the missiles." Even McCone accepted the idea of a trade as part of a tough message to Khrushchev demanding "that he stop this business and stop it right away, or we're going to take out those SAM sites *immediately* . . . and I'd trade these Turkish things out right now. I wouldn't even talk about it." McNamara embraced the suggestion, interpreting it as an attempt "to try to negotiate a deal," which was not the way McCone intended it. "I wouldn't try to negotiate a deal," he said, "I'd send him a threatening letter." Thompson joined in the argument favoring a tough stand: "These boys are beginning to give way. Let's push harder. I think they'll change their minds when we take continuing forceful action, stopping their ship or—or taking out a SAM site." Lyndon Johnson said that it was a forceful action, the downing of a U-2, not Khrushchev's letter, that had made the greatest impression on the ExCom.

At that point President Kennedy returned and changed the course of the discussion decisively, derailing all talk of immediate military action of any kind. Bundy told him that there were substantial differences of opinion, but Kennedy again focused on getting messages to the Turks and NATO. Then he made his position clear: "We can't very well invade Cuba with all its toil, and long as it's going to be, when we could have gotten them out by making a deal on the same missiles in Turkey. If that's part of the record I don't see how we'll have a very good war."

Kennedy's statements during the rest of the meeting strongly suggest that he was determined to close a deal with the Soviets before the next day, Sunday, October 28, was over, if at all possible. This is when he revealed his decision not to keep the commitment to take out a SAM site in retaliation for the downing of a U-2. "I think we ought to wait until tomorrow afternoon, to see if we get any answer. . . . I think we ought to keep tomorrow clean, do the best we can with the surveillance. If they still fire, and we haven't got a satisfactory answer back from the Russians, then I think we ought to put a statement out tomorrow that we were fired upon, and we are therefore considering Cuba as an open territory and then take out all the SAM sites." Thereafter he was ready to support proposals for attacks on the SAM sites, tightening of the blockade, stopping Soviet ships, so long as nothing was done *until Monday.*

McNamara quickly got into the spirit of the President's suggestion, proposing a call-up of more air reserve squadrons and the preparation of troop carrier transports that would be needed for an invasion. These would be a form of pressure. It would be an indication of seriousness and toughness in place of immediate military action. The President agreed at once. McNamara asked if it would be better to take the Turkish Jupiters out right away. He thought the decision should be made before any discussion with NATO. The President answered, "Can't we wait? Isn't it possible to get through tomorrow at three or four o'clock without even getting into NATO with the Turkey business? . . . Why don't we just wait another eighteen hours, see if that's been eased at all. We're hard and tough on this.

We called up the planes tonight, and we wait." The best explanation for Kennedy's action is that he did not want to raise the question with NATO of removing the Turkish missiles because he feared they would get in the way of the trade. Robert Kennedy expressed the fear that half would be in favor and half opposed. Pressed to inform Hare, the ambassador to Turkey, the President laid out the decision he was prepared to communicate. It was the Trollope Ploy, a way to satisfy, for the moment, those who did not want to trade, but one that gained time for the trade's completion:

> Let's give him an explanation of what we're trying to do. We're trying to get it back on the original proposition of last night, and— because we don't want to get into this trade. If we're unsuccessful, then we—it's possible that we may have to get back on the Jupiter thing. If we do, then we would of course want it to come from the Turks themselves and NATO, rather than just the United States. We're hopeful, however, that that won't come. . . . We'll be in touch with him in twenty-four hours when we find out if we're successful in putting the Russians back on the original track.[302]

With the decision made, Sorensen and Robert Kennedy prepared a draft of a letter responding to Khrushchev; after some revision the President approved it. It provided that the Soviets would remove "all weapons systems in Cuba capable of offensive use." In return, the United States would end the quarantine and "give assurances against an invasion of Cuba."[303] The original draft by Sorensen and Robert Kennedy included a passage saying, "As I was preparing this letter, I learned of your public message attempting to connect NATO bases and Cuba. I must tell you frankly that this is not a way to go forward with a settlement of the immediate crisis."[304] The President removed that passage, and the final letter said that an agreement on the terms proposed "would enable us to work toward a more general arrangement regarding 'other armaments,' as proposed in your second letter which you made public." This was an unmistakable hint that a deal on the Turkish missiles could be negotiated privately after the current crisis was over.

The letter was sent off at 8:05 P.M., but before that the President met with his inner circle in the Oval Office. They decided to strengthen the message by sending Robert Kennedy to deliver it orally to Dobrynin. He was told to say that if the missiles are not removed there will be military action against Cuba, but if they were the United States would pledge not to invade. In addition, while there could be no public deal, the Turkish missiles would be removed after the crisis was over. Sorensen later said at a conference in 1989 that Kennedy recognized that Khrushchev's request "had some basis" and that "it would undoubtedly be helpful to him [in removing the Cuban missiles] if he could say at the same time to his colleagues in the Presidium, 'And we have been assured that the missiles will be coming out of Turkey.' "[305] None of this was revealed to the other members of ExCom.[306]

Robert Kennedy's memoir reports that he met with Dobrynin at the Justice Department at 7:45 P.M. It has the President's brother saying, "We had to have a commitment by tomorrow that those bases would be removed. I was not giving them an ultimatum but a statement of fact. . . . If they did not remove those bases, we would remove them." When Dobrynin raised the question of the Turkish missiles, the published memoir reports, Kennedy replied: "that there can be no quid pro quo or any arrangement made under this kind of threat or pressure."[307] In 1989, however, Sorensen revealed he had been the editor of the published book. He admitted that the "diary was very explicit that this was part of the deal, but at the time it was still a secret even on the American side, except for the six of us [in President Kennedy's inner circle] who had been present at the meeting. So I took it upon myself to edit it out of his diaries."[308] It hardly matters, for even in the published version Robert Kennedy is represented as saying that "President Kennedy had been anxious to remove those missiles from Turkey and Italy for a long period of time. He had ordered their removal some time ago, and it was our judgment that, within a short time, those missiles would be gone."[309] It should not have taken much imagination to understand that the missiles were part of the deal even in the sanitized version, but after the fact the Kennedy team felt it important to project the idea that they had ended the crisis through calm toughness, not by making concessions at the expense of allies without consultation.

In 1989 Dobrynin told of his memory of the meeting. Robert Kennedy said "that he confirmed the agreement of the president to remove the missiles from Turkey. The president again said that he has it in his mind, and that I may convey this to my government. But it cannot be made a part of the package and publicized."[310] Kennedy told Dobrynin that the military was pressing the President to launch an air strike and urged a speedy reply. His parting words were: "time will not wait. We must not let it slip away." The President's brother "did not put forth an ultimatum. . . . But he persistently asked, it is true, to convey the President's request that if possible he wanted to receive an answer on Sunday." In 1971 Gromyko's son Anatoly published a book in which he reports that Robert Kennedy told Dobrynin that "the Pentagon was exerting strong pressure on his brother. . . . He did not exclude the possibility that the situation could get out of control and lead to irreparable consequences."[311] In his own memoirs Khrushchev recounts an undated meeting between Dobrynin and Robert Kennedy whose general contours fit the meeting of October 27. Here is his version of Dobrynin's report:

> The President is in a grave situation and he does not know how to get out of it. We are under very severe stress. In fact we are under pressure from our military to use force against Cuba. Probably at this very moment the President is sitting down to write a message to Chairman Khrushchev. . . . President Kennedy implores Chairman Khrushchev to accept the peculiarities of the American system. Even though the President himself is very much against starting a war over Cuba, an irreversible chain of events could occur against his will. That is why the President is appealing directly to Chairman Khrushchev for his help in liquidating this conflict. If the situation continues much longer, the President is not sure that the military will not overthrow him and seize power. The American army could get out of control.[312]

These memoirs are an imperfect source. Khrushchev wrote them chiefly from memory, years after the events, without access to all his papers. He also had reason to exaggerate the desperation of the American President and to present him as a suppliant rather than a negotiating partner. When the drama and exaggeration are removed, however, the basic picture does not vary greatly from what the facts require. Kennedy *was* under pressure from the military, and civilians as well, to take immediate military action, and the President *was* reluctant to do so. Years later Sorensen said:

> I do not believe that John Kennedy wanted war at the time, and I don't think he wanted war with Cuba in particular. He was mindful of that when he ruled against the idea of an air strike—even the so-called "surgical" air strike. . . . As reinforcement of Bob

McNamara's point that new military escalation on our part was not imminent, I point out that when the U-2 plane was shot down, a man ready for military action would have responded immediately by an air attack on one of the SAM missile sites. President Kennedy held off authorization for any such action, and I agree with Bob that he would have found other ways to tighten the screws, so to speak, tighten the blockade, but not given the green light for either an air strike or an invasion. . . . So I do not believe that air strike or invasion was imminent; but I have to remind you that John Kennedy was not a dictator, and . . . that the pressures on him from the military, and from others, were rising, and one man alone is not able to hold out against that rising tide indefinitely.[313]

Nor is there doubt that he needed and urged a speedy response. If a solution did not come soon, the pressure would increase and the President's position become more difficult. We need not believe in the likelihood of a military coup to understand that there were *some* limits to the freedom Kennedy had before he must launch a military action. We have seen that Robert Kennedy's account of a tough and laconic communication is not perfectly accurate. Dobrynin's is brief and incomplete, but it agrees more closely with Khrushchev's than with Kennedy's. The reader must decide which best reproduces the mood and tone of the communication but, properly read, they all present much the same picture: confirmation of the missile trade and pressure for a swift response to end the crisis before the President might be forced to take military action.

Even then the President was not satisfied. He must have been concerned that Khrushchev would not accept the request that the trade be concluded secretly but would insist on a public announcement, so he prepared for that contingency as well. Unknown to any other member of the ExCom Kennedy asked Rusk to call his friend Andrew Cordier, dean of Columbia University's Schools of International Relations and a former UN official, "and dictate to him a statement which would be made by U Thant . . . proposing the removal of both the Jupiters and the missiles in Cuba. Mr. Cordier was to put the statement in the hands of U Thant only after further signal from us."[314] Should the signal be given, of course, the United States would accept the proposal. This secret plan was revealed only a quarter of a century later, when Rusk and others emphasized that it was only a contingency plan that was never put into effect. The crisis came to an end before that assertion was put to the test, but it is clear at least that President Kennedy was seriously considering even a public trade rather than a military response. At least one distinguished scholar of the missile crisis thinks that that was the course the President might have taken: "I don't know whether the McNamara/Bundy view that the next step would have been another turn of the screw rather than an air strike is a revision of history, but I suppose there is a chance that POL [petroleum, etc.] would have been added to the embargo list and even that it might have done the trick. I wonder, though, whether the President would even have opted for this, given the preparations being made for a public deal on the Turkish missiles. He may have gone for the quick exit."[315]

That judgment, along with all others, must remain a speculation, because at 9 A.M. on Sunday, October 28, a new message came over the airwaves from Radio Moscow. Khrushchev announced the issuance of "a new order on the dismantling of the weapons which you describe as 'offensive,' and their crating and return to the Soviet Union."[316] Even before receiving the official text Kennedy responded with a letter in which he said, "I consider my letter to you of October twenty-seventh and your reply of today as firm undertakings on the part of both governments which should be promptly carried out."[317] For all practical purposes, the crisis was over. In 1987 Abram Chayes, a member of the Kennedy administration, looked back to the solution of the crisis: "Max Taylor said that there were three options. . . . There was a fourth: buy 'em out. This one gets talked about much less than the others because of the power of the Munich stigma and because it sounds a lot less courageous. But in fact we did, in part, buy 'em out, and the President seems to have been willing to go even further than he did in this direction if need be. He was willing to pay an enormous price in world opinion and in his domestic standing, but the other options had prices, too, and who's to say that this one was the highest."[318] If Chayes is right, there is no obvious limit to what concessions Kennedy might have made had Khrushchev stuck to his guns.

Why, then, did Khrushchev agree to end the confrontation? To be sure, Kennedy had agreed to the essence of his terms, a promise not to invade Cuba and another to remove the Turkish missiles. But that does not account for the swiftness of his announcement. Kennedy, moreover, had not agreed to the public announcement of the missile trade. Khrushchev might have delayed and continued the pressure, insisting on the public announcement of the American retreat to compensate for the political price the Soviet leader would need to pay for his own withdrawal of the missiles and apparent abandonment under pressure of an ally. Castro, in fact, when he learned of the trade and was told he must not shoot at any more American planes, went berserk. He kicked the wall, shattered a mirror, and denounced Khrushchev as a "son of a bitch . . . a bastard . . . an asshole, a man with no *cojones,* a *maricon* [homosexual]."[319] The affair, in fact, was a major reason why Khrushchev was driven from power the following year. There was every reason for him to squeeze everything he could out of Kennedy before closing the deal, perhaps the Italian Jupiters, as well as the Turkish, all announced publicly in the UN to help shake the faith of the NATO allies in the strength, nerve, and reliability of the Americans.

That he did not, but settled as quickly as possible, suggests that he had reason to fear delay. From his point of view the situation may well have seemed to be getting out of hand. A Soviet commander had ordered the shooting down of a U-2 without permission. There might be similar unordered and unwanted provocations. The Cubans, moreover, were pressing for more dangerous actions. On Friday the twenty-sixth Castro had written a letter to Khrushchev predicting an air strike or invasion within the next one to three days. He asked the Soviet leader to prevent such actions and, if such an invasion took place, "that would be the moment to eliminate such danger forever through an act of clear legitimate defense, however harsh and terrible the solution would be."[320] Khrushchev assumed that Castro wanted him "to preempt the invasion and inflict a nuclear strike on the U.S." The next day Castro ordered Cuban antiaircraft forces to fire on all U.S. aircraft and refused the Soviet ambassador's request to rescind the order.[321] There seemed to be danger that events might get out of the Kremlin's control.

Then, on Saturday the twenty-seventh, an American U-2 lost its way and wandered over Soviet territory in Siberia. It called for help, and an American fighter plane scrambled to help at the same time that a Soviet MIG took off to intercept the U-2, which managed to get away without shooting.[322] Khrushchev might at first have thought that it was a reconnaissance mission prior to an American attack, although the location of the incursion made that unlikely. At the very least, it might have made him aware of the danger that an unintended military encounter might flare up into serious fighting and that, if that happened, Kennedy might not be able to control his military leaders and prevent them from launching an attack that the Soviet Union could not answer without committing suicide.

Ironically, such a conclusion might result from the very assessment of Kennedy's character that had led Khrushchev to launch the Cuban adventure. A man as weak as the Chairman thought Kennedy to be could not for long prevent stronger action by stronger men. During the previous summer Khrushchev had told Llewellyn Thompson that he suspected the military of planning to gain control of the American government. As one scholar has pointed out, "He lived in a political culture where such things actually happened. When Dobrynin cabled Moscow of Robert Kennedy's comment that the Pentagon was pressuring his brother for an air strike, Khrushchev evidently read it to mean that the President was in danger of being overthrown."[323] Perhaps that interpretation is overdrawn, but there is good reason to believe, at least, that Robert Kennedy's words pointed to the loss of full presidential control. With the prospect of the collapse of control on all sides, Khrushchev called off the crisis before disaster could befall.

The Americans were triumphant. The President called congressional leaders to the White House. "We've won a great victory," he told them. "We have resolved one of the great crises of mankind." In the ExCom Rusk said that all members deserved credit for the "highly advantageous resolution" of the missile crisis. Bundy, one of the hawks, generously said that everyone knew who the hawks and doves were and that this was the day of the doves. The President warned them to be careful in their statements to the press. "Khrushchev has eaten crow. Let's not rub it in." Rusk said much the same to reporters who, amazingly to those who know the press of today, largely did what they were told.[324] It was self-serving advice. In the euphoria of the moment, later turned into the standard version by the publications of books by Robert Kennedy, Schlesinger, and Sorensen, the end of the crisis had come about as a result of the calm and measured toughness of the brave young President, who had refused to yield under pressure, who had made no concessions except the promise not to invade Cuba, which he had no intention of doing anyway. Boastful statements from Washington might cause Khrushchev to break his vow of silence and to reveal the fact that the President had made a bargain under pressure at the expense of a NATO ally, a trade of Cuban for Turkish missiles, without consulting either Turkey or NATO, a bargain so embarrassing that he concealed it from the American people and made secrecy about it a condition for an agreement. As late as January 30, 1963, McNamara "lied outright to Congress on the issue of whether Kennedy had secretly traded Jupiter missiles in Turkey for removal of the Cuban missiles, assuring the House Armed Services Committee that there was 'absolutely no connection' between the 'forced removal' of Soviet missiles in Cuba and the removal of the missiles 'in Turkey or Italy.' "[325]

Nor was everyone on the American side satisfied with the outcome. Worried about domestic criticism, Kennedy called the Joint Chiefs to the White House, where he expressed his admiration and gratitude for their advice and efforts during the crisis. The Navy's chief, Admiral Anderson, shouted, "We have been had!" Air Force chief Curtis Le May called it "the greatest defeat in our history."[326] These reactions may be excessive, but a more sober judgment might conclude that Kennedy had let Khrushchev off cheaply. In light of the vast military advantage enjoyed by the United States, it might have been possible to insist on an end to Soviet aid to Cuba, which would soon have rendered Castro unable to assist the Communist insurgents in El Salvador, Nicaragua, and other parts of Latin America that were to cause the United States so much trouble over the next quarter century. Still, with the benefit of hindsight, Kennedy's very great caution may well seem justified. It was America's great military strength that brought safety in the crisis and it was its vast military, political, and economic power that permitted it to win the Cold War without the need of a hot war against the Soviets, although those overwhelming advantages were not so clear in 1962. Nations that wish to preserve the peace frequently can afford a degree of forbearance when their superiority in power is sufficient.

THE CAUSES OF THE CRISIS

It is not the management of the Cuban missile crisis, however, that is at issue here, but its origins. How did it happen that the two great powers ever got to the point where careful crisis management seemed to be necessary to avoid a conflict that might grow to nuclear proportions? Geoffrey Blainey in his interesting book on the causes of war believes that wars occur when competing states disagree about their relative power.[327] The missile crisis arose, however, in spite of the fact that both the Soviet and American leaders *agreed* on America's superiority. Khrushchev undertook his adventure because he had become convinced that Kennedy lacked the will to use American military superiority when challenged and hoped to use his opponent's weakness of character to change the balance of power. Kennedy's behavior at the Bay of Pigs, in Vienna, in response to the Berlin Wall, and in response to the flow of Soviet armaments to Cuba consistently pointed to the conclusion that he could be intimidated into acquiescence. Khrushchev's plan was not irrational, although it was risky and wrong on two major points. He made a mistake in thinking the missiles would be implanted in secrecy. If they had been, it seems entirely possible, in light of his performance when they *were* discovered, that Kennedy would have been willing to accept the fait accompli. Khrushchev's second mistake was to misunderstand the nature of the American government and political system, putting too much importance on the role of the President. His assessment of Kennedy's likely response does not seem to have been far from the mark, judging from the President's behavior in the crisis and from the statements of some of his closest associates. But, as Sorensen has pointed out, an American President is not a dictator, no more than is a British Prime Minister. Had Khrushchev delayed in bringing the episode to a close, Kennedy, in spite of his pacific inclinations, might have been compelled to take military action, just as Chamberlain was forced to turn to a policy he disliked when his Cabinet and public opinion turned against him. When Khrushchev realized that such a danger existed in 1962 he understood the mistake he had made and agreed to the best deal he could get in the circumstances.

President Kennedy was impressed deeply by the idea that wars come about chiefly through miscalculation. This led, as it often does, to the assumption that his opponent was playing by the same rules and that his goal was much the same as Kennedy's own. The differences in the position of each side and, therefore, in their intentions, was slighted. Like the revisionists of the post–World War I era, the President was concerned chiefly with positive actions that might lead an opponent to miscalculate his own pacific intentions and make war as a result. He ignored or discounted the possibility that his opponent might be bluffing, trying to use Kennedy's reluctance to fight to gain advantages out of proportion to the Soviet Union's power. It did not occur to him that inaction that could be interpreted as weakness and timidity might cause a different kind of miscalculation equally, and perhaps more, dangerous than the other, the kind made by Tirpitz and Kaiser Wilhelm that the British lacked the will to match Germany's naval building program and to resist its expansion before 1914 or that Hitler had made when he thought the men he called "little worms" were free not to keep their promise to defend Poland in 1939. The analysis offered here leads to the suggestion that it was this latter form of miscalculation that brought on the missile crisis. A stronger line, as Kennedy himself sometimes perceived, might have avoided it altogether. In the difficult world of international competition there is no greater guarantee of safety in cautious passivity than in bold activity, perhaps less. In each case the particularities must determine which course of action or which combination is best.

The Cuban missile crisis demonstrated that it is not enough for the state that wishes to maintain peace and the status quo to have superior power. The crisis came because the more powerful state also had a leader who failed to convince his opponent of his will to use its power for that purpose.

1. The quotations from President Kennedy's speech are from D. L. Larson, *The "Cuban Crisis" of 1962, Selected Documents, Chronology and Bibliography,* 2nd ed., Lanham, Maryland, 1986, pp. 59–64.

2. B. J. Allyn, J. G. Blight, and D. A. Welch, *Back to the Brink,* Cambridge, Mass., 1992, pp. xvii–xxii. The Soviets refer to "the Caribbean Crisis" and the Cubans to the "October Crisis."

3. R. O. Paxton, *Europe in the Twentieth Century,* New York, 1975, p. 487.

4. A. B. Ulam, *The Rivals, America and Russia Since World War II,* New York, 1971, p. 104.

5. J. L. Gaddis, *Russia, the Soviet Union, and the United States: An Interpretive History,* New York, 1978, p. 181.

6. The figures come from a chart compiled by J. L. Gaddis in *Strategies of Containment* (New York, 1982), p. 359. His sources are the U.S. Bureau of the Census and the U.S. Office of Management and Budget.

7. Gaddis, *Strategies,* p. 91.

8. *Ibid.,* p. 92.

9. Gaddis, *Russia,* p. 198.

10. *Ibid.,* p. 201.

11. The United States benefited from the accident that the Soviet Union was boycotting the Security Council at the time, a mistake it did not repeat.

12. Thucydides, *The Peloponnesian War,* 3.82.1, translated by Richard Crawley.

13. V. D. Sokolovskiy, ed. *Voyennaya Strategiya* (Military Strategy), 1st, 2nd, and 3rd eds. Moscow, 1962, 1963, 1968, p. 226. Cited by H. F. Scott and W. F. Scott, *Soviet Military Doctrine,* Boulder and London, 1988, p. 22.

14. Scott, *Soviet,* p. 22.

15. *Ibid.,* p. 30.

16. A. L. Horelick and M. Rush, *Strategic Power and Soviet Foreign Policy,* Chicago, 1966, p. 31.

17. Gaddis, *Russia,* p. 226.

18. Ulam, *The Rivals,* pp. 294–95.

19. Ibid., p. 295.

20. Horelick and Rush, *Strategic Power,* pp. 119–20.

21. D. D. Eisenhower, *The White House Years: Waging Peace, 1956–1961,* Garden City, New York, 1965, p. 336 note.

22. Scott, *Soviet,* pp. 30–31.

23. Ibid., p. 31.

24. Ibid., p. 34.

25. The following discussion of developments in Castro's Cuba depend chiefly on Hugh Thomas, *The Cuban Revolution* (New York, 1971); Theodore Draper, *Castro's Revolution* (New York, 1962); and Maurice Halperin, *The Rise and Decline of Fidel Castro* (Berkeley, Los Angeles, and London, 1972).

26. Halperin, *Rise,* p. 43.

27. Ibid., p. 77.

28. L. Chang and P. Kornbluh, eds., *The Cuban Missile Crisis, 1962: A National Security Documents Reader,* New York, 1992, pp. 347–48;

29. Cited by N. T. Carbonell, *And the Russians Stayed, the Sovietization of Cuba,* New York, 1989, p. 100.

30. Ibid., pp. 100–1.

31. Chang and Kornbluh, *Cuban,* p. 348.

32. R. R. Pope, *Soviet Views on the Cuban Missile Crisis,* Washington, D.C., 1982, pp. 78–79.

33. Herbert R. Dinerstein, "The Soviet Union and the Communist World," *Survey.* (Spring 1973); 147.

34. Thomas, *Cuban Revolution,* p. 524.

35. J. G. Blight, B. J. Allyn, and D. A. Welch, *Cuba on the Brink,* New York, 1993, pp. 45–46. I am grateful to the book's editor, Linda Healey of Pantheon, for allowing me to see the bound galleys before publication.

36. J. M. Blum, *Years of Discord, American Politics and Society, 1961–1974,* New York, 1991, p. 18.

37. S. E. Morison, H. S. Commager, W. E. Leuchtenburg, *The Growth of the American Republic,* vol. 2, 7th ed., New York and Oxford, 1980, p. 749.

38. M. Beschloss, *The Crisis Years, Kennedy and Khrushchev 1960–1963*, New York, 1991, p. 25.

39. Blum, *Years*, p. 26.

40. Beschloss, *Crisis*, p. 28; Thomas, *Cuban*, pp. 518–19.

41. Thomas, *Cuban*, p. 525.

42. Beschloss, *Cuban*, p. 104.

43. A. M. Schlesinger, Jr., *A Thousand Days*, Boston, 1965, p. 228.

44. *Ibid.*, p. 238.

45. Beschloss, *Crisis*, pp. 106, 128.

46. *Ibid.*, p. 106.

47. *Ibid.*, pp. 107–8.

48. T. C. Sorensen, *Kennedy*, New York, 1965, p. 298.

49. *Ibid.*, p. 300.

50. P. Wyden, *Bay of Pigs*, New York, 1979, p. 170.

51. *Ibid.*, p. 116.

52. Sorensen, *Kennedy*, p. 301. Sorensen tries to minimize the importance of cancelling the air strikes but also to place the blame for the decision on the military officials for not communicating their importance to the President. Beschloss, *(Crisis*, p. 116) on the basis of the diary of Le Moyne Billings, a school friend of Kennedy's, writes: "Later, after rerunning that fateful Sunday night endlessly in his mind, the President reproached himself about barring the second air strike. He thought his decision an error, although not a decisive one. Still, he told Lem Billings that if he 'hadn't stayed all weekend in Glen Ora [his estate in Virginia] and had gone back Sunday night,' he 'might have learned more about the situation' in Cuba that might have changed the course of events."

53. T. Higgins, *The Perfect Failure, Kennedy, Eisenhower, and the CIA at the Bay of Pigs*, New York, 1987, p. 145; Beschloss, *Crisis*, p. 120.

54. Carbonell, *And the Russians Stayed*, p. 190. Kennedy gave the same explanation to Eisenhower after the Bay of Pigs disaster (Beschloss, *Crisis*, p. 144).

55. *Ibid.*, p. 145.

56. J. G. Blight, et al., *Cuba on the Brink*, pp. 130–31.

57. Wyden, *Bay of Pigs,* p. 270–71.

58. Beschloss, *Crisis,* pp. 128–29.

59. *Ibid.,* p. 129.

60. P. Wyden, *Wall, The Inside Story of Divided Berlin,* New York, 1989, p. 54. (H. Catudal, *Kennedy and the Berlin Wall Crisis,* Berlin, 1980, pp. 66–67)

61. N. S. Khrushchev, *Khrushchev Remembers,* translated and edited by Strobe Talbott, Boston, 1970, p. 492.

62. Beschloss, *Crisis,* p. 118.

63. Blight and Welch, *On the Brink,* p. 241.

64. A. N. Shevchenko, *Breaking with Moscow,* New York, 1985, p. 110.

65. Schlesinger, *A Thousand Days,* p. 356.

66. K. P. O'Donnell and D. Powers with J. McCarthy, *"Johnny, We Hardly Knew Ye,"* Boston, 1972, p. 286.

67. Beschloss, *Crisis,* p. 158.

68. *Ibid.,* p. 164.

69. Schlesinger, *A Thousand Days,* p. 356.

70. P. Wyden, *Wall, The Inside Story of Divided Berlin,* New York, 1989, p. 49.

71. F. Burlatsky, *Khrushchev and the First Russian Spring,* translated by D. Skillen, New York, 1988, p. 162. Schlesinger (*A Thousand Days,* p. 367) made a similar judgment: "Khrushchev came to Vienna ready to collaborate on Laos and on nothing else; for the rest, he hoped to unnerve Kennedy and force him into concessions."

72. Schlesinger, *A Thousand Days,* p. 366.

73. *Ibid.*

74. Ulam, *Rivals,* p. 326.

75. The account of the Vienna conversations between Kennedy and Khrushchev depends on the reports given by Schlesinger (*A Thousand Days,* pp. 358–74) and Beschloss, who had the benefit of interviews with informed sources and, best of all, of seeing the official memoranda of conversations drafted by Kennedy's interpreter at the meetings.

76. Beschloss, p. 196.

77. O'Donnell, *"Johnny,"* pp. 341–42.

78. Schlesinger, p. 361.

79. Beschloss, p. 197.

80. *Ibid.*, pp. 198–99.

81. *Ibid.*, pp. 200–1.

82. *Ibid.*, p. 201, note.

83. *Ibid.*, p. 202.

84. *Ibid.*, pp. 155, 203.

85. *Ibid.*, pp. 203–4, 224.

86. *Ibid.*, p. 205.

87. *Ibid.*, p. 212.

88. *Ibid.*, pp. 212–13.

89. Schlesinger, *A Thousand Days*, p. 368.

90. Beschloss, *Crisis*, p. 215.

91. Schlesinger, *A Thousand Days*, 370–71.

92. Beschloss, *Crisis*, p. 219.

93. *Ibid.*, p. 217.

94. *Ibid.*, p. 219.

95. Schlesinger, *A Thousand Days*, p. 372.

96. O'Donnell, *"Johnny,"* p. 297.

97. Beschloss, *Crisis*, pp. 223–24.

98. Schlesinger, *A Thousand Days*, p. 378.

99. Sorensen, *Kennedy*, p. 543.

100. Blight and Welch, *On the Brink*, p. 35.

101. Beschloss, *Crisis*, p. 224. Robert Kennedy later said that this meeting was "the first time his brother had really come across somebody with whom he couldn't exchange ideas in a meaningful way." The President said that dealing with Khrushchev was "like dealing with Dad. All give and no take." (p. 234)

102. Ibid., p. 228.

103. Ibid.

104. Blight, *On the Brink,* p. 236.

105. Ibid., pp. 236, 281.

106. Beschloss, *Crisis,* p. 231.

107. Wyden, *Wall,* p. 55.

108. O'Donnell, *"Johnny,"* pp. 292, 299–300.

109. Wyden, *Wall,* pp. 45–47.

110. Beschloss, *Crisis,* p. 235.

111. Ibid., p. 239.

112. Wyden, *Wall,* p. 72.

113. Beschloss, *Crisis,* p. 244.

114. Ibid., p. 245.

115. Sorensen, *Kennedy,* pp. 590–91.

116. H. Catudal, *Kennedy and the Berlin Wall Crisis,* Berlin, 1980, pp. 113–14.

117. Wyden, *Wall,* pp. 80–81.

118. Ibid., p. 82; Beschloss, *Crisis,* p. 264.

119. W. W. Rostow, *The Diffusion of Power,* New York, 1972, p. 231.

120. The source for the discussions among the Communist leaders is a Czech military official who took part in them, Colonel Jan Sejna, who defected to the West in 1968. He was interviewed by Peter Wyden, and the results are reported in *Wall* (pp. 85–90).

121. Beschloss, *Crisis,* p. 268.

122. Catudal, *John Kennedy,* pp. 226–27.

123. Beschloss, *Crisis,* p. 270.

124. Catudal, *John Kennedy,* p. 203.

125. Wyden, *Wall,* p. 127.

126. Khrushchev, *Khrushchev Remembers,* p. 459.

127. Wyden, *Wall,* p. 127, note.

128. Beschloss, *Crisis,* p. 273.

129. Wyden, *Wall,* p. 165.

130. Beschloss, *Crisis,* p. 274.

131. Ibid., p. 273.

132. O'Donnell, *"Johnny,"* p. 303.

133. See above, p. 386.

134. Wyden, *Wall,* pp. 227–28.

135. Beschloss, *Crisis,* p. 286.

136. Ibid., 281–82.

137. M. Bundy, *Danger and Survival: Choices About the Bomb in the First Fifty Years,* New York, 1988, pp. 367–70.

138. D. L. Larson, *The "Cuban Crisis" of 1962, Selected Documents, Chronology and Bibliography,* 2nd ed., Lanham, Md., 1963, p. 61.

139. Blight and Welch, *On the Brink,* pp. 235, 288–89.

140. Beschloss, *Crisis,* p. 287–88. The characterization of the three men is by Beschloss.

141. M. Trachtenberg, "The Berlin Crisis." In Trachtenberg, ed., *History and Strategy,* Princeton, 1991, p. 226.

142. Ibid., p. 231.

143. Ibid., p. 233.

144. Beschloss, *Crisis,* p. 291; Sorensen, *Kennedy,* p. 619.

145. A. Sakharov, *Memoirs,* translated by R. Lourie, New York, 1990, p. 217.

146. Beschloss, *Crisis,* pp. 307–8.

147. Ibid., pp. 308–9.

148. Ibid., pp. 311 12.

149. P. Salinger, *With Kennedy,* New York, 1966, pp. 191–94.

150. O'Donnell, *"Johnny,"* pp. 304–5.

151. Beschloss, *Crisis,* p. 315–16.

152. Wyden, *Wall,* p. 263.

153. Beschloss, *Crisis,* pp. 327–28.

154. *Ibid.,* pp. 65, 328.

155. R. Hilsman, *To Move a Nation,* New York, 1967, p. 164.

156. Beschloss, *Crisis,* p. 330.

157. *Ibid.,* p. 332.

158. *Ibid.,* pp. 371, 373.

159. As the Scotts put it *(Soviet Military Doctrine,* p. 36), "Many Western analysts believe that the Soviet emphasis on nuclear weapons was the result of U.S. actions during the Cuban Missile Crisis in October 1962. But Khrushchev's speech in 1960 and Malinovsky's address to the Party Congress in 1961 testify that the Soviet Union had made the doctrinal decision to concentrate on nuclear-missile forces years before the crisis. After years of research and development, production lines for missiles were started in the 1950s." Khrushchev's decision to cut conventional forces, later reversed under pressure, is further evidence that the Soviets were putting major emphasis on nuclear missile production.

160. *Ibid.,* p. 375.

161. Allyn, et al., *Back to the Brink,* p. 9.

162. Beschloss, *Crisis,* p. 381–82. The American Jupiter missiles in Turkey, in fact, became operational that same month (Chang and Kornbluh, *Cuban,* p. 351). The story in Khrushchev's *Memoirs* is on pp. 493–95.

163. Blight and Welch, *On the Brink,* p. 238.

164. This, essentially, is the list given by Blight and Welch in *On the Brink* (pp. 116–17). So far as I know, it exhausts the published suggestions.

165. Khrushchev, *Memoirs,* pp. 493–94.

166. Pope, *Soviet Views,* p. 125.

167. Blight and Welch, *On the Brink,* p. 238; Beschloss, *Crisis,* p. 385.

168. *Ibid.,* pp. 234, 239.

169. *Ibid.,* p. 235.

170. R. L. Garthoff, *Reflections on the Cuban Missile Crisis,* 2nd ed., Washington, D.C., 1989, p. 13.

171. Beschloss, *Crisis,* p. 387.

172. The following discussion owes much to the views presented by Beschloss (*Crisis,* pp. 382–93), who seems to me to have a good grasp of the situation and of Khrushchev's thinking. I have learned much from him. My interpretation differs from his chiefly in one particular. He appears to see Kennedy's behavior as presenting Khrushchev with a combination of reasons for fear and confidence. He sometimes seems to believe that Kennedy's statements and actions alarmed Khrushchev into such actions as placing missiles in Cuba, which he was willing to do because other of the President's statements and actions suggested he lacked the will and determination to take military action. But if he were really afraid that Kennedy would use his power for any purpose at all, why should he take the great risk of installing the missiles, when the pressures on the President to act would be greatest? My own view is that Khrushchev did not fear military action by Kennedy by the time of his decision to install the missiles. He felt a long-range danger to his policies and objectives from the Soviet nuclear inferiority that could be expected to last beyond Kennedy's term of office; in the short run, however, he felt that Kennedy did not represent a danger.

173. Beschloss, *Crisis,* p. 383.

174. *Ibid.,* p. 384.

175. *Ibid.,* p. 393.

176. *Ibid.,* p. 392.

177. *Ibid.*

178. Allyn, et al., *Back to the Brink,* p. 51.

179. Blight and Welch, *On the Brink,* p. 241.

180. Beschloss, *Crisis,* p. 391; Szulc, T., *Fidel: A Critical Portrait,* New York, 1986, pp. 576–81.

181. Blight and Welch, *On the Brink,* p. 239.

182. An account of the agreement and of the details of the Soviet military operations is given by General Anatoly Gramov, then head of a bureau of the Main Operations Directorate of the Soviet General Staff in Blight, et al., *Cuba on the Brink,* p. 58.

183. *Ibid.,* pp. 61–62.

184. These figures come from American sources collated and analyzed by G. T. Allison in *Essence of Decision: Explaining the Cuban Missile Crisis,* Boston, 1971, p. 103.

185. Chang and Kornbluh, *Cuban,* Document 11, p. 57.

186. Ibid., p. 353.

187. Ibid., p. 354.

188. Cited by Beschloss, *Crisis,* pp. 414–15.

189. Chang and Kornbluh, *Cuban,* p. 355.

190. R. F. Kennedy, *Thirteen Days,* New York, 1969, pp. 25–26.

191. Chang and Kornbluh, *Cuban,* Document 14, p. 68.

192. Larson, *The "Cuban Crisis" of 1962,* Document 1, p. 17.

193. Allyn, et al., *On the Brink,* p. 43.

194. Beschloss, *Crisis,* p. 420.

195. Sorensen, *Kennedy,* p. 668.

196. Ibid., p. 421.

197. Chang and Kornbluh, *Cuban,* p. 356.

198. Tatu, *Power,* p. 241.

199. Chang and Kornbluh, *Cuban,* p. 356.

200. Ibid., Document 13, pp. 63–65.

201. Beschloss, *Crisis,* p. 424.

202. Chang and Kornbluh, *Cuban,* p. 357.

203. The story is told by Robert Kennedy in an oral history interview (Beschloss, *Crisis,* p. 425). As we shall see, he seems to have been obsessed with the Pearl Harbor analogy.

204. Chang and Kornbluh, *Cuban,* p. 358.

205. Beschloss, *Crisis,* p. 429.

206. Ibid.

207. Graham Allison has observed that Bundy's statement, in full awareness of the shipping of Il-28s, makes it "not inconceivable that a decisionmaker in Moscow could believe that the United States would be willing to accept offensive missiles in Cuba as long as they were put there quietly." (Blight and Welch, *On the Brink,* p. 41)

208. Ibid.

209. Bundy, *Danger and Survival,* p. 301.

210. Chang and Kornbluh, *Cuban,* Document 15, p. 96.

211. Ibid., Document 16, pp. 97–113.

212. Ibid., Document 17, p. 114.

213. Allyn, et al., *Cuban,* p. 141.

214. Scott Sagan in *Ibid.,* p. 32.

215. Ibid., p. 248.

216. Allyn, et al., *Back to the Brink,* p. 53.

217. Ibid.

218. Blight and Welch, *On the Brink,* p. 28.

219. Ibid., *On the Brink,* p. 33.

220. Bundy, *Danger and Survival,* pp. 218–19.

221. Chang and Kornbluh, *Cuban,* pp. 110–11.

222. Ibid., p. 103.

223. Blight and Welch, *On the Brink,* p. 244.

224. Beschloss, *Crisis,* p. 448.

225. Ibid.

226. Ibid., p. 443.

227. The list comes from two accounts, each giving slightly different lists of three. See Abram Chayes's version in Allyn, et al., *On the Brink* (p. 102) and that of Raymond Garthoff in *Reflections* (pp. 44–45). Taylor's own list in an interview given in 1987 did not include the "buy 'em out" option. (p. 77)

228. Chang and Kornbluh, *Cuban,* Document 19, pp. 119 20; Beschloss, *Crisis,* p. 468.

229. Beschloss, *Crisis,* pp. 468–69.

230. Chang and Kornbluh, *Cuban,* Document 15, pp. 87 and 90.

231. Blight and Welch, *On the Brink,* p. 54.

232. The evidence of the transcript is confirmed in a "Memorandum for the Record" written the day after the meeting by Lt. General Marshall S. Carter, Deputy Director of the Central Intelligence Agency, who briefed the group on the significance of the U-2 photographs. He wrote that "Mr. McNamara pointed out that if we are going to take overt military action, it must at all costs be done on a 100% basis and before any of the missiles become operational." (Published by Brassey's [no editor], in *The Secret Cuban Missile Crisis Documents, Central Intelligence Agency,* Washington, New York, London, 1994, p. 146.) McNamara's repeated denial of what he said at the time is caused, presumably, by its contradiction of positions he then held and later came to hold. If it did not matter whether a missile came from Russia or from Cuba, then whether the Cuban missiles were operational or not should not make a difference. The blockade that he soon came to advocate in place of an air strike, moreover, would allow the missiles to become operational. That action, therefore, would contradict the strong emphasis on the need to remove the missiles quickly in the passages quoted above. To sustain the correctness of his view that the Cuban missiles were unimportant except for domestic politics, and that there was never a need to attack them, he needs to suppress what he said at the time.

233. *Ibid.,* Document 25, pp. 144–45.

234. Blight and Welch, *On the Brink,* p. 137.

235. *Ibid.,* p. 147.

236. R. F. Kennedy, *Thirteen Days,* pp. 38–39.

237. *Ibid.,* pp. 79–80.

238. Chang and Kornbluh, *Cuban,* p. 364.

239. *Ibid.,* p. 459.

240. *Ibid.*

241. Chang and Kornbluh, *Cuban,* Document 21, p. 124. The notes of this meeting were taken by the State Department's legal adviser, Leonard Meeker.

242. *Ibid.*

243. *Ibid.,* p. 125.

244. Chang and Kornbluh, *Cuban,* Document 16, p. 107.

245. Blight and Welch, *On the Brink,* p. 152.

246. Beschloss, *Crisis,* p. 432.

247. Chang and Kornbluh, *Cuban,* Document 21, p. 127.

248. Sorensen, *Kennedy,* p. 685.

249. Beschloss, *Crisis,* p. 454. The reference to the NATO bases comes from Sorensen's notes in the John F. Kennedy Library. There is no mention of the offer to talk about them in Sorensen's *Kennedy,* published in 1965, where the tough part of the message is revealed.

250. Blight and Welch, *On the Brink,* p. 244.

251. Sorensen, *Kennedy,* p. 685.

252. Beschloss, *Crisis,* pp. 455–57.

253. Blight and Welch, *On the Brink,* p. 246.

254. Chang and Kornbluh, *Cuban,* Document 21, p. 126.

255. *Ibid.,* p. 363.

256. Beschloss, *Crisis,* p. 480.

257. Larson, *"Cuban" Crisis,* pp. 61–62.

258. The source is Roy Medvedev, *All Stalin's Men,* translated by Harold Shukman, New York, 1985, p. 52. The story was affirmed orally by Mikoyan's son, who said he heard it from his father (Blight and Welch, *On the Brink,* p. 367).

259. *Ibid.* Kennedy's response is reported by Richard E. Neustadt.

260. Chang and Kornbluh, *Cuban,* p. 367.

261. Beschloss, *Crisis,* p. 488.

262. *Ibid.*

263. Chang and Kornbluh, *Cuban,* p. 368.

264. R. F. Kennedy, *Thirteen Days,* pp. 66–67.

265. *Ibid.,* p. 67.

266. Chang and Kornbluh, *Cuban,* p. 370.

267. Beschloss, *Crisis,* p. 497.

268. Chang and Kornbluh, *Cuban,* Document 39, p. 173.

269. Beschloss, *Crisis,* p. 504.

270. Chang and Kornbluh, *Cuban,* Document 42, p. 177.

271. Bromley Smith's "Summary Record of NSC Executive Committee Meeting, October 26, 1962, 10:00 A.M.," Document 42 in Chang and Kornbluh, *Cuban,* p. 178.

272. *Ibid.,* pp. 177–83.

273. *Ibid.,* Document 21, p. 126.

274. *Ibid.,* Document 43, p. 184.

275. *Ibid.,* Document 44, p. 188.

276. Hilsman, *To Move a Nation,* p. 219.

277. Beschloss, *Crisis,* p. 515.

278. *Ibid.*

279. Hilsman, *To Move a Nation,* p. 219. It appears to have been important to Rusk and others in the administration not to appear to have yielded or made concessions.

280. These suggestions are made by Beschloss, *Crisis,* p. 522.

281. At the ExCom meeting on the evening of October 25, McCone reported that some of the missiles were already operational (Chang and Kornbluh, *Cuban,* p. 372).

282. *Ibid.,* p. 367.

283. *Ibid.,* p. 371.

284. *Ibid.,* Document 47, p. 195.

285. Beschloss, *Crisis,* p. 523.

286. Blight and Welch, *On the Brink,* pp. 309–10.

287. Beschloss, *Crisis,* p. 530.

288. Allyn, et al., *Back to the Brink,* p. 143.

289. Chang and Kornbluh, *Cuban,* p. 83.

290. This account accepts Dobrynin's report of his private, unrecorded meeting with Robert Kennedy on October 26. Mark Kramer *(Bulletin* of the Cold War International History Project, Woodrow Wilson International Center for Scholars,

Washington, D.C., 3 [Fall 1993]: 40), however, reports that "Dobrynin's claim was not accurate, as the ex-ambassador himself later acknowledged with considerable embarrassment." This observation is based on the following evidence: a letter dated May 15, 1992, from Ashok Prasad of the BBC reporting a conversation with Dobrynin; the fact that Dobrynin omitted any mention of the October 26 meeting in his article "Karibskii krizis: Svidetel'stvo uchastnika," *Mezhdunarodnaya zhizn'* (Moscow) 7 (July 1992): 54–68; Kramer's own conversation with Dobrynin. It is clear that Dobrynin was untruthful either when he told the story or when he denied it, but it is far from certain which version is correct. Logically, and in the absence of other evidence as to motive or other relevant factors, there is no better reason to believe one instead of the other. Compelled to choose, I find it more likely that the story, not the denial, is true. The story is specific and detailed. I do not see it as self-serving or aggrandizing, for it shows Dobrynin only in the role of a messenger, nor does it make any contribution to Soviet *amour propre*. At the conference where it was told members of the ExCom who were present expressed no surprise and did not question its accuracy. On the contrary, Robert McNamara suggested that future dangers could be reduced "by assuring effective communication, as thank God we had to a considerable degree during the crisis through Robert Kennedy and Ambassador Dobrynin." (Allyn, et al., *Back to the Brink*, p 168) And McGeorge Bundy made a similar point, praising "the way in which the existing personal trust between Robert Kennedy and Ambassador Dobrynin led them to exchange information which was, in the end, helpful to their respective leaders." *(Back to the Brink, p. 190)*

As indicated below, moreover, President Kennedy's agreement to a trade for the Turkish missiles on the night of October 26 makes excellent sense of his obsession, otherwise difficult to understand, with Turkish and NATO reaction to the withdrawal of the missiles from Turkey, at the ExCom meeting of the twenty seventh. For most of the discussants the question was whether or not to attack the missiles in *Cuba,* yet the President kept bringing the discussion back to the missiles in *Turkey.* The most plausible explanation would be that he and few others at the meeting, perhaps only Robert Kennedy, knew that the deal for the Turkish missiles had been made already. The others, therefore, regarded the trade as impossible, since the President had ruled it out earlier, and were thinking of other ways to react to Khrushchev's insistence on it. Kennedy, on the other hand, knowing that the deal was on, concentrated on what might immediately cause trouble: the possible resistance of Turkey and NATO.

If, however, the deal struck on the twenty-sixth is a product of Dobrynin's imagination, Kennedy's performance on the twenty-seventh would suggest that, without having yet made a deal, he had decided to accept Khrushchev's new demand but was worried, in the same way—about Turkish and NATO objections.

In either case, he was unwilling to reveal either what he had done or was planning to do until the ExCom could be brought round to support the trade.

291. Beschloss, *Crisis,* p. 468.

292. The following account of the ExCom meetings of October 27 are from Chang and Kornbluh, *Cuban,* Document 49, p. 200–20.

293. *Ibid.,* p. 373.

294. In later years Robert Kennedy, publicly supported by McNamara, took credit for inventing this approach, but the record shows that it came from Bundy first. See Beschloss, *Crisis,* p. 528, note.

295. Chang and Kornbluh, *Cuban,* p. 377.

296. *Ibid.,* p. 206.

297. *Ibid.,* p. 207.

298. Blight and Welch, *On the Brink,* p. 72.

299. *Ibid.,* pp. 52, 65–67; 69–72; 88–89.

300. Malinovsky's reprimand is reported by General Volkogonov in Allyn, et al., *Back to the Brink,* p. 32.

301. Allison, *Essence,* p. 225.

302. Chang and Kornbluh, *Cuban,* p. 219.

303. The letter is reproduced in Chang and Kornbluh, *Cuban,* Document 51, pp. 223–25.

304. Beschloss, *Crisis,* p. 534, note.

305. Allyn, et al., *Back to the Brink,* pp. 92–93.

306. Chang and Kornbluh, *Cuban,* p. 377.

307. R. F. Kennedy, *Thirteen Days,* p. 108.

308. Allyn, et al., *Back to the Brink,* p. 93.

309. R. F. Kennedy, *Thirteen Days,* pp. 108–9.

310. Allyn, et al., *Back to the Brink,* p. 144.

311. Beschloss, *Crisis,* p. 536, note.

312. N. S. Khrushchev, *Khrushchev Remembers,* pp. 497–98.

313. Allyn, et al., *Back to the Brink,* p. 105.

314. Blight and Welch, *On the Brink,* pp. 83–84.

315. *Ibid.,* p. 110.

316. Chang and Kornbluh, *Cuban,* Document 52, p. 226.

317. *Ibid.,* Document 53, pp. 230–31.

318. Blight and Welch, *On the Brink,* p. 102.

319. Beschloss, *Crisis,* p. 543.

320. Chang and Kornbluh, *Cuban,* Document 45, p. 189.

321. *Ibid.,* p. 375.

322. *Ibid.,* p. 376.

323. Beschloss, *Crisis,* p. 539.

324. *Ibid.,* pp. 542–45.

325. Cited by P. Glynn, *Opening Pandora's Box,* New York, 1992, p. 200.

326. *Ibid.,* p. 544.

327. G. Blainey, *The Causes of War,* London, 1973, p. 122.

CONCLUSIONS

THE STUDY OF war and its causes is both sobering and challenging. No one can examine the grim history of the human race, repeatedly ravaged by the pain and horror of war, without feeling a great sadness at its ubiquity and perpetuity. Yet anyone who analyzes the origins of particular wars must also be struck by a sense that many of them were unnecessary. In spite of the weaknesses and conflicts inherent in human beings and the societies they create, a student of their wars must feel that it is necessary, but also possible, to do better. It is not toward the elimination of war that we must aim, for that is an implausible expectation. Nor would most people, even in the modern world, agree that war must always be avoided. In our time wars of national liberation or for religious or political freedom are thought widely to be justified and preferable to a peace under the old conditions. Few Americans, in retrospect, would condemn the American Revolution or the Civil War for breaking the peace to achieve national independence and the end of slavery. Yet it would also be wrong to despair of reducing the danger and frequency of wars. If war in general cannot be avoided, we may still hope to be able to reduce the danger of war for long stretches of time, to avoid particular wars, to pursue policies that make a satisfactory peace more likely and more lasting.

The end of the Cold War concludes a half century when many people regarded a major war between the NATO countries and the Soviet Union as inevitable or highly likely, yet the crisis has passed. We need to remember that even major conflicts sometimes are resolved without war and that the world has sometimes experienced relatively peaceful eras. If the goal is to preserve peace, the worst mistake we can make is to take inadequate measures to that end because we do not comprehend the nature of the problem.

For these purposes we need to understand more about how they come about, and that requires that we step beyond the opinions and prejudices of our time and place to examine the origins of wars in different ages and kinds of society. The five cases studied here differ from one another in many ways. The states in each international system range from tiny Greek towns to a vast polyglot state stretching across the Eurasian land mass, from city-states to great nations, from a system confined to the Aegean basin to a worldwide empire. The types of government involved include a direct democracy, aristocratic republics, representative democracies, limited monarchies, absolute autocracies, and totalitarian dictatorships. They involve international systems that are bipolar and multipolar and span two and one half millennia of human experience. They are meant to serve as a modest beginning for a base of information and interpretation that may provide illumination across time and culture.

A persistent and repeated error through the ages has been the failure to understand that the preservation of peace requires active effort, planning, the expenditure of resources, and sacrifice, just as war does. In the modern world especially the sense that peace is natural and war an aberration has led to a failure in peacetime to consider the possibility of another war, which, in turn, has prevented the efforts needed to preserve the peace. Perceiving the source of a new war in a time of peace is, to be sure, a difficult task. The hardheaded men who sat at the Congress of Vienna in 1815, for instance, a rare group who thought carefully about the problem and established a system meant to preserve the general peace, did very well but did not succeed fully. They relied neither on idealistic hopes nor on the terror of new weapons to preserve the peace they urgently wanted after so many years of deadly war. They depended instead on the Concert of Europe, a prudent attempt to recognize the realities of power as they existed at the time and to build a stable system of international relations based upon it. The general peace was not shattered fundamentally until 1914. Their achievement was impressive, bringing "a period of peace lasting almost a hundred years," but Henry Kissinger suggests that the international stability was "so pervasive that it might have contributed to disaster. For in the long interval of peace the sense of the tragic was lost; it was forgotten that states could die, that upheavals could be irretrievable, that fear could become the means of social cohesion."[1]

If their successors forgot these things the practical men of affairs who managed Europe's international system in the years after 1815 did not. They knew that peace does not keep itself, that one or more states in any international system must take the responsibility and bear the burdens needed to keep the peace, so they established an international order meant to last, and they were prepared to defend it. Even they, however, could not foresee the changes in society and politics that ultimately undermined the Concert and the peace of Europe. The searing power of nationalism based on linguistic and ethnic ties that would be so important in destroying peace was not yet well understood. "It would have occurred to no one in the eighteenth century that the legitimacy of a state depended on linguistic unity. It was inconceivable to the makers of the Versailles settlement that there might be any other basis for legitimate rule."[2]

Nor could the leaders of the great European powers, Austria, Britain, France, and Russia, imagine that Prussia, a second-rate state in 1815, would one day be the spearhead of a united Germany whose creation would upset entirely the balance of power and pose a problem for a lasting European peace that has not yet been solved. As late as the middle of the nineteenth century Tsar Nicholas I regarded the notion that Germany would be unified, perhaps under Prussian leadership, as "utopian nonsense."[3] Domestically, the Prussian monarchy was shaken badly by the revolution of 1848, and internationally, Prussia was humiliated by Austria at Olmütz in 1850. "Prussia in the first half of the nineteenth century was the least of the Great Powers, disadvantaged by geography, overshadowed by powerful neighbors, distracted by internal and inner-German problems, and quite incapable of playing a larger role in international affairs."[4] So as late as 1863 no one could have forecast the immense power that Prussia would soon achieve as the heart of a unified Germany, but in less than a decade swift victories over Denmark, Austria, and France made Prusso-Germany the most powerful nation in Europe and, after a few more decades, a deadly menace to its peace.

Yet to anyone familiar with history none of this should have been surprising. Unexpected changes and shifts in power are the warp and woof of international history. In the fifth century B.C. the father of history already underscored the inevitable and unforeseeable shifts in the power of states: "I shall go forward with my history describing equally the greater and lesser cities. For the cities which were formerly great, have most of them become insignificant; and such as are at present powerful, were weak in the olden time."[5] Paul Kennedy writes in the same vein about our own world that "wealth and power, or economic strength and military strength, are always relative, and since all societies are subject to the inexorable tendency to change, then the international balances can *never* be still, and it is a folly of statesmanship to assume that they ever could be."[6]

The current condition of the world, therefore, where war among major powers is hard to conceive because one of them has overwhelming military superiority and no wish to expand, will not last. A reunified Germany, with its colossal economic resources, will sooner or later acquire comparable military power, and the same is true for Japan. The power of China is growing with its economic success, and it is unlikely for long to maintain a secondary role on the international scene. Nor should Russia's current difficulties blind us to its inherent strength and the certainty that it will, sooner or later, emerge on the world scene as a great power with desires and goals of its own, not necessarily compatible with those of other nations or with the status quo. It would be foolhardy, moreover, to assume that the return of Germany, Japan, and Russia to full status as great powers will be the only changes in the world system and that we can foresee what others may come. In the past such unforeseen changes often have threatened the peace, and we have no reason to doubt that they will do so again.

Our study of the episodes examined here suggests some general observations about the origins of wars and the preservation of peace. The first is that in a world of sovereign states a contest among them over the distribution of power is the normal condition and that such contests often lead to war. Another observation is that the reasons for seeking more power are often not merely the search for security or material advantage. Among them are demands for greater prestige, respect, deference, in short, honor. Since such demands involve judgments even more subjective than those about material advantage, they are still harder to satisfy. Other reasons emerge from fear, often unclear and intangible, not always of immediate threats but also of more distant ones, against which reassurance may not be possible. The persistence of such thinking in a wide variety of states and systems over the space of millennia suggests the unwelcome conclusion that war is probably part of the human condition and likely to be with us for some time yet.

Most thinking and writing about the subject, however, has assumed tacitly that peace is the natural state of relations among states, that war is an aberration that can be escaped by improving the character of the decision makers, by the evolution of society away from bellicose traditions and institutions, and by avoiding entangling or provocative actions. The suggested solutions since the eighteenth century chiefly have been the education of peoples and their leaders to produce an understanding that war is not only terrible but also wicked, irrational, and unprofitable. Assuming that people go to war chiefly for some rational purpose, usually to gain some material advantage, this approach counts on education to produce a more correct rational understanding of the interests of those involved. To that extent alone is it active. Apart from education the chief course advised to maintain peace is restraint: the avoidance of actions that will destroy the peace that is in the natural order of things.

The evidence provided by the experience of human beings living in organized societies for more than five millennia suggests otherwise. Statistically, war has been more common than peace, and extended periods of peace have been rare in a world divided into multiple states. The cases we have examined indicate that good will, unilateral disarmament, the avoidance of alliances, teaching and preaching of the evils of war by those states who, generally satisfied with the state of the world, seek to preserve peace, are of no avail.

What seems to work best, even though imperfectly, is the possession by those states who wish to preserve the peace of the preponderant power and of the will to accept the burdens and responsibilities required to achieve that purpose. They must understand that no international situation is permanent, that part of their responsibility is to accept and sometimes even assist changes, some of which they will not like, guiding their achievement through peaceful channels, but always prepared to resist, with force if necessary, changes made by threats or violence that threaten the general peace. But this condition is not easy to achieve. In the first place, the natural distribution of power does not necessarily coincide with the needs of peacekeeping. Sometimes the balance is so close as to prevent effective deterrence and to make it tempting to risk war to gain or prevent a preponderance of power. Such appears to have been the case before the Peloponnesian War. Sometimes the power and will are present but the responsible states are arrogant and careless. Such seems to have been true of the Roman Republic before the Hannibalic War.

Such episodes might occur at any time. They seem to illustrate the truth of Thucydides's belief in the general consistency of human nature in the realms of politics, international relations, and war, of the value of his history as "a possession for all time" to such people as "wish to see clearly both the events that have taken place and, in accordance with human nature, will happen again in the future in the same or a similar way."[7] The study of history, however, must concern itself not only with those things that remain the same but also with those that vary from place to place and those that change in the course of time. The states in the modern world and the people in them are different from those in the ancient world in significant ways.

To understand the ancient Greeks and Romans we must be alert to the great gap that separates their views, and those of most people throughout history, from the opinions of our own time. They knew nothing of ideas such as would later be spoken in the Sermon on the Mount, and they would have regarded them as absurd if they had. They viewed the world as a place of intense competition in which victory and domination, which brought fame and glory, were the highest goals, while defeat and subordination brought ignominy and shame. In the world of city-states the sphere of competition was elevated from contests between individuals, households, and clans to contests and wars between *poleis*. The Greek states, moreover, the Athenian democracy no less than any other, were warrior communities that accepted without question the naturalness of war and the absolute obligation of each able-bodied man to do military service and risk his life for his community. He also regarded these actions as among the highest attributes of a man, proof of his freedom and dignity and a source of honor and glory, themselves the highest values for human beings.

The Romans had even fewer hesitations about the desirability of power and the naturalness of war than the Greeks. Theirs was a culture that venerated the military virtues, a world of farmers, accustomed to hard work, deprivation, and subordination to authority. It was a society that valued power, glory, and the responsibilities of leadership, even domination, without embarrassment. The effort needed to preserve these things could be taken for granted; it was in the nature of things and part of the human condition.

Modern states, especially those who have triumphed in the Cold War and have the greatest interest in preserving peace, and most particularly the United States, on whom the main burden of keeping the peace must fall, now and in the foreseeable future, are quite different. The martial values and the respect for power have not entirely disappeared, but they have been overlayed by other ideas and values, some of them unknown to the classical republics. The most important of these is the Judaeo-Christian tradition, and especially the pacifist strain of Christianity that emphasizes the Sermon on the Mount rather than the more militant strain that played so large a role over the centuries. Even as the power and influence of formal, organized religion have waned in the last century, the influence among important segments of the population in the United States and other Western countries of the rejection of power, the evil of pursuing self-interest, the wickedness of war, whatever its cause or goal, have grown. There are now barriers of conscience in the way of acquiring and maintaining power and using it to preserve the peace that would have been incomprehensible to the Greeks and Romans.

At the same time, most of these countries are liberal republics of a democratic character, devoted to and increasingly shaped by an ethical system that is commercial, individualistic, libertarian, and hedonistic, at the other end of the spectrum from the agricultural republics of antiquity, with their respect for the power and glory of their states and the sacrifices these require. Like Great Britain in its heyday, the United States has enjoyed the advantages of insularity, protected from serious dangers by oceans that for many years permitted it to ignore the rest of the world in secure isolation. This has enabled Americans, unlike the peoples of the ancient world, and more than most people in history, to have a long tradition, deriving from the British experience, of distrust of things military and to reject compulsory military service except for brief periods in extraordinary circumstances. Even with professional volunteer armed forces it has demonstrated a powerful aversion to the casualties that are sometimes inevitable in the preservation of peace and civility.

In the nineteenth and twentieth centuries, moreover, the Western countries have made a commitment to the material and physical welfare of their citizens that has produced expensive and growing social programs. In a democratic country subject to the power of public opinion and organized groups that benefit from its largess, governments face increasing pressure to satisfy domestic demands at the expense of the requirements of defense. Expenditures for weapons and armies in peacetime meant chiefly to deter wars are especially difficult to justify. By their nature they will never be used if they are successful, so critics always can claim they are unnecessary. Since such a conclusion will justify ease, inaction, and a turn away from external responsibilities, it will always have a ready audience. For all these reasons, even when modern democratic countries have the material resources to do what is needed to keep the peace they find it hard to rally the spiritual resources that are at least as necessary.

In spite of their victories in the Cold War and, more recently, in the Gulf War, the United States and its allies, the states with the greatest interest in peace and the greatest power to preserve it, appear to be faltering in their willingness to pay the price in money and the risk of lives. Nothing could be more natural in a liberal republic, yet nothing could be more threatening to the peace they have achieved recently. Although the world today is very different in many important ways, a haunting analogy with the victorious powers after the First World War suggests itself. The nature of American society and of its allies and their traditional understanding of the causes of wars and the basis for peace give reason to fear that the United States and the other satisfied states will revert to type. Such countries are always in danger of slipping from the realistic, expensive, and painful policy that they, with some lapses, pursued after the Second World War. It is increasingly difficult even to count on the realistic if not entirely adequate response to danger by Britain that confronted the Kaiser instead of the self-deluding inaction with which Britain tried to appease the Germans in the years between the wars. The character and traditions of such societies, their lack of expansive ambitions, make them long for the closest approximation to their preferred policies of isolation that conditions will permit and sometimes beyond. In a country whose thinking and behavior are shaped by this combination of influences, proposals for the assumption of a continuing commitment to the active preservation of peace, not by resorting to disarmament, withdrawal, and disengagement, but by maintaining a strong military power and the willingness to use it when necessary, are certain to encounter strong opposition.

Our studies suggest that such reactions and longings are futile, and the policies they suggest are dangerous. Whatever the preferences and intentions of such societies and their leaders, their power and their desire for international stability unavoidably place them in the path of dissatisfied states that want to revise the correlation of forces and power in their own favor. They are not free to stand clear. They may insist TO HELL WITH SERBIA, as a London newspaper headline proclaimed in the spring of 1914; they may ask WHERE IS PRAGUE? as did a different London newspaper in 1938, and answer, "If the 'collective-security' madmen get their way you might find yourself in a trench one day. If the policy of isolation triumphs, you will . . . not fight anybody unless they come here looking for trouble." But to no avail. The free and spirited people of a still-powerful nation will not allow the world order to be torn up to its disadvantage and their security endangered, and they will reject any leadership prepared to do so. The only choices available to leaders of such a country is whether to seek to avoid the crisis by working to preserve the peace, to act realistically while there is time, or to avoid the responsibility until there is no choice but war.

ENDNOTES

1. Henry A. Kissinger, *A World Restored,* New York, 1964, p. 6.

2. *Ibid.,* p. 145.

3. Paul Kennedy, *The Rise and Fall of the Great Powers,* New York, 1987, p. 161.

4. Kennedy, *Rise and Fall,* p. 162.

5. Herodotus, 1.5.

6. Kennedy, *Rise and Fall,* p. 536.

7. 1.22.4.

GENERAL

Blainey, Geoffrey. *The Causes of War*. London, 1973.

Ferrill, Arther. *The Origins of War*. London, 1985.

Fukuyama, Francis. "The End of History?" *The National Interest* 16(1989): 3–18.

Glynn, P. *Closing Pandora's Box*. New York, 1992.

Howard, Michael. *War and the Liberal Conscience*. London, 1978.

———. *The Causes of Wars and Other Essays*. Cambridge, Mass., 1983.

———. *The Continental Commitment*. London, 1989.

———. "Men Against Fire: The Doctrine of the Offensive in 1914." In Howard, ed., *The Lessons of History*, New Haven, 1991.

Jones, E. L. *The European Miracle: Environments, Economies and Geopolitics in the History of Europe and Asia*. Cambridge, 1981.

Kagan, Donald. "World War I, World War II, World War III." *Commentary* (March 1987): 21–40.

Kissinger, Henry. *A World Restored: Europe After Napoleon*. Boston, 1973.

Langer, W. L. "A Critique of Imperialism." *Foreign Affairs*, 14(1935–36): 102–19.

Lebow, Richard N. and Barry S. Strauss, eds. *Hegemonic Rivalry from Thucydides to the Nuclear Age*. Boulder, 1991.

Mill, J. S. *Principles of Political Economy*. London, 1848.

Paine, Thomas. *Collected Writings*. London, 1894.

Paxton, R. O. *Europe in the Twentieth Century*. New York, 1975.

Rotberg, R. I., and T. K. Rabb, eds. *The Origin and Prevention of Major Wars*. Cambridge, England, 1989.

Seabury, Paul, and Angelo Codevilla. *War, Ends and Means*. New York, 1989.

Sun Tzu Wu. *The Art of War*. Translated by Lionel Giles. Harrisburg, 1944.

Trevelyan, G. M. *John Bright*. London, 1913.

Waltz, Kenneth N. "The Origins of War in Neorealist Theory." In *Origin and Prevention*, edited by Rotberg and Rabb.

⋆ *A full bibliography of this subject would require a book at least as long as this one. The list given here includes the works cited as well as a few other books, chiefly in English, that are especially interesting and helpful to the general reader.*

The Peloponnesian War

Andrewes, A. "The Government of Classical Sparta." In *Ancient Society and Institutions. Studies presented to Victor Ehrenberg on his 75th Birthday,* edited by E. Badian. Oxford, 1966.

Badian, E. "Thucydides and the Outbreak of the Peloponnesian War." In *Conflict, Antithesis, and the Ancient Historian,* edited by June Allison. Columbus, 1990.

Beloch, Karl Julius. *Die Attische Politik seit Perikles.* Leipzig, 1884.

——. *Griechische Geschichte,* 2nd ed., Strassburg, Berlin, and Leipzig, 1912–27.

Busolt, Georg. *Griechische Geschichte,* vol. 3, pt. 2. Gotha, 1904.

Busolt, Georg, and Heinrich Swoboda. *Griechische Staatskunde,* 2 vols. Munich, 1920–26.

Cartledge, Paul. *Sparta and Lakonia.* London, 1979.

Delbrück, Hans. *Geschichte der Kriegskunst I, Das Altertum.* Berlin, 1910; reprinted 1964.

de Ste. Croix, G. E. M. *The Origins of the Peloponnesian War.* London and Ithaca, 1972.

Forrest, W. G. *A History of Sparta 950–192 B.C.* New York, 1968.

Greenidge, A. H. J. *A Handbook of Greek Constitutional History.* London, 1902.

Hanson, Victor D. *The Western Way of War.* New York, 1989.

Kagan, Donald. *The Outbreak of the Peloponnesian War.* Ithaca, 1969.

——. *The Archidamian War.* Ithaca, 1974.

——. "The Speeches in Thucydides and the Mytilene Debate." *Yale Classical Studies* 24(1975): 71–94.

Meiggs, Russell. *The Athenian Empire.* Oxford, 1972.

Meyer, E. *Geschichte des Altertums,* vol. 4, pt. 1, 2nd ed. Stuttgart and Berlin, 1915.

Thucydides. *The Peloponnesian War.* Translated by Richard Crawley. New York, n.d.

The First World War

Albertini, Luigi. *The Origins of the War of 1914,* 3 vols. Oxford, 1952–57.

Andrew, Christopher M. *Théophile Delcassé and the Making of the Entente Cordiale.* London, 1968.

Bade, K. J. "Imperial Germany and West Africa: Colonial Movement, Business Interests, and Bismarck's 'Colonial Policies.' " In *Bismarck,* edited by Foerster, et al., pp. 121–47.

Balfour, M. L. *The Kaiser and His Times.* New York, 1972.

Barraclough, Geoffrey. *From Agadir to Armageddon.* London, 1982.

Becker, Jean-Jacques. *1914: Comment les français sont entrés dans la guerre.* Paris, 1977.

Benns, F. Lee. *European History Since 1870.* 3rd ed. New York, 1950.

Berghahn, Volker R. *Der Tirpitz-Plan.* Düsseldorf, 1971.

———. *Germany and the Approach of War in 1914.* New York, 1973.

Bestuzhev, I. V. *Borba v Rossii po voprosam vneshnei politiki 1906–1910.* Moscow, 1961.

Bismarck, Prince Otto von. *Reflections and Reminiscences,* 2 vols. Translated by A. J. Butler. New York, 1899.

Bosworth, Richard. *Italy and the Approach of the First World War.* London, 1983.

Brandenburg, Erich. *From Bismarck to the World War.* Oxford, 1933.

Bridge, F. R. *From Sadowa to Sarajevo: The Foreign Policy of Austria-Hungary, 1866–1914.* London and Boston, 1972.

———. *Great Britain and Austria-Hungary 1906–1914.* London, 1972.

———. "Izvolsky, Aerenthal, and the End of the Austro-Russian Entente, 1906–8," *Mitteilungen des Österreichischen Staatsarchivs* 29(1976).

Brock, Michael. "Britain Enters the War." In *Coming,* edited by Evans and Pogge von Strandmann.

Calleo, David. *The German Problem Reconsidered.* Cambridge, Mass., 1978.

Cecil, Lamar. *Wilhelm II Prince and Emperor 1859–1900.* Chapel Hill and London, 1989.

Churchill, Winston S. *The World Crisis 1911–1918,* 2 vols. London, 1938 edition.

Craig, Gordon A. *Europe Since 1815.* New York, 1961.

———. *Germany 1866–1945.* New York, 1978.

Dedijer, Vladimir. *The Road to Sarajevo.* New York, 1966.

Ekstein, Michael G., and Zara Steiner. "The Sarajevo Crisis." In *British Foreign Policy Under Sir Edward Grey,* edited by F. H. Hinsley.

Eley, Geoff. "*Sammlungspolitik,* Social Imperialism and the Navy Law of 1898." *Militärgeschichtliche Mitteilungen* 1(1974): 29–63.

Evans, R. J. W. "The Habsburg Monarchy and the Coming of the War." In *The Coming of the World War.*

Evans, R. J. W., and H. Pogge von Strandmann, eds. *The Coming of the World War.* Oxford, 1988.

Fay, S. B. *The Origins of the World War,* 2 vols., 2nd ed. New York, 1966.

Fischer, Fritz. *Germany's Aims in the First World War.* New York, 1967.

———. *War of Illusions.* Translated by Marian Jackson. New York, 1975.

———. "The Foreign Policy of Imperial Germany and the Outbreak of the First World War." In *Escape,* edited by Schöllgen.

Fischer, Wolfram. *Germany and the World Economy during the Nineteenth Century.* London, 1984.

Foerster, S., W. J. Mommsen, and R. Robinson, eds. *Bismarck, Europe, and Africa.* London, 1988.

French, David. *British Economic and Strategic Planning 1905–1915.* London, 1982.

Gall, Lothar. *Bismarck, Der weisse revolutionaer.* Frankfurt, 1980.

Geiss, Immanuel. *Julikrise und Kriegsausbruch 1914,* 2 vols. Hanover, 1964.

———. "The Outbreak of the First World War and German War Aims." In *1914, The Coming of the First World War,* edited by Laqueur and Mosse. New York, 1966.

———, ed. *July 1914, The Outbreak of the First World War, Selected Documents.* New York, 1974.

———. *German Foreign Policy, 1871–1914.* London, 1976.

Gifford, P., and W. R. Lewis, eds. *Britain and Germany in Africa: Imperial Rivalry and Colonial Rule.* New Haven, 1967.

Gilbert, Felix. *The End of the European Era 1890 to the Present.* New York, 1970.

Gooch, G. P., and Harold Temperley, eds. *British Documents on the Origins of the War, 1898–1914,* 11 vols. London, 1926–1938.

Gordon, M. R. "Domestic Conflict and the Origins of the First World War: The British and German Cases." *Journal of Modern History* 46(1974): 191–226.

Grey, Sir Edward (Viscount Grey of Fallodon). *Twenty-Five Years 1892–1916,* 2 vols. New York, 1925.

————. *Speeches on Foreign Affairs 1904–1914.* London, 1931.

Herrmann, David G. *Armies and the Balance of Military Power in Europe, 1904–1914.* Yale University Dissertation, 1992.

Hildebrand, Klaus. *German Foreign Policy From Bismarck to Adenauer, The Limits of Statecraft.* Translated by Louise Willmot. London, 1989.

————. "Opportunities and Limits of German Foreign Policy in the Bismarckian Era, 1871–1890: 'A System of Stopgaps'?" In *Escape,* Schöllgen.

Hinsley, F. H., ed. *British Foreign Policy Under Sir Edward Grey.* Cambridge, 1977.

Holborn, Hajo. *A History of Modern Germany,* vol. 3, 1840–1945. New York, 1969.

Jarausch, Konrad. *The Enigmatic Chancellor.* New Haven, 1973.

Joll, James. *The Origins of the First World War.* London and New York, 1984.

Kahler, Miles. "Rumors of War: The 1914 Analogy." *Foreign Affairs* 2(1979–80): 374–96.

Kehr, Eckart. *Schlachtflottenbau und Parteipolitik 1894–1901.* Berlin, 1930.

————. *Der Primat der Innenpolitik.* Edited by Hans-Ulrich Wehler. Berlin, 1965.

Keiger, John F. V. *France and the Origins of the First World War.* New York, 1983.

Kennedy, Paul M. "Tirpitz, England and the Second Naval Law of 1900: A Strategical Critique," *Militärgeschichtliche Mitteilungen* 2(1970): 34–54.

————. "German Colonial Expansion: Has the 'Manipulated Social Imperialism' Been Ante-Dated?" *Past and Present* 54(1972): 134–41.

————. *The Rise of the Anglo-German Antagonism 1860–1914.* London, 1980.

————. *The Rise and Fall of British Naval Mastery.* London, 1983.

————. *Strategy and Diplomacy.* London, 1984.

————, ed. *The War Plans of the Great Powers 1880–1914.* Boston, 1985.

————. *The Rise and Fall of the Great Powers.* New York, 1987.

Koch, H. W., ed. *The Origins of the First World War: Great Power Rivalry and War Aims.* London, 1972.

Krumeich, Gerd. *Armaments and Politics in France on the Eve of the First World War.* Translated by Stephen Conn. Leamington Spa, 1984.

Lafore, Laurence. *The Long Fuse.* New York, 1971.

Langer, W. L. *The Franco-Russian Alliance 1890–1894.* Cambridge, Mass., 1929.

————. *The Diplomacy of Imperialism 1890–1902,* 2nd ed. New York, 1951.

————. *European Alliances and Alignments 1871–1890,* 2nd ed. New York, 1966.

Laqueur, Walter, and George L. Mosse, eds. *1914, The Coming of the First World War.* New York, 1966.

Lepsius, J., A. Mendelssohn-Bartholdy, and F. Thimme, eds. *Die Grosse Politik der Europäischen Kabinette 1871–1914,* 39 vols. Berlin, 1922–1927.

Lieven, D. C. *Russia and the Origins of the First World War.* London, 1983.

Marder, A. J. *From Dreadnought to Scapa Flow,* 2 vols. Oxford, 1961.

Miller, Steven E., ed. *Military Strategy and the Origins of the First World War.* Princeton, 1985.

Mommsen, W. J. "Domestic Factors in German Foreign Policy before 1914." *Central European History* 6(1973): 3–43.

————. "Bismarck, the Concert of Europe, and the Future of West Africa, 1883–1885." In *Bismarck,* Foerster.

Monger, George. *The End of Isolation, British Foreign Policy 1900–1907.* London, 1963.

Montgelas, Max, and Walter Schücking, eds. *Outbreak of the World War: German Documents Collected by Karl Kautsky,* supp. IV, no. 2. Translated by Carnegie Endowment for International Peace. (1924): 616–18.

Nichols, J. A. *Germany After Bismarck, The Caprivi Era 1890–1894.* Cambridge, Mass., 1958.

Pogge von Strandmann, H. "Consequences of the Foundation of the German Empire: Colonial Expansion and the Process of Political-Economic Rationalization." In *Bismarck,* Foerster.

Porch, Douglas. *The March to the Marne: The French Army 1871–1914.* Cambridge, 1981.

Remak, Joachim. "The Healthy Invalid: How Doomed the Habsburg Empire?" *Journal of Modern History* 41(1969): 127–43.

Rich, Norman. *Friedrich von Holstein, Politics and Diplomacy in the Era of Bismarck and Wilhelm II,* 2 vols. Cambridge, 1965.

Rich, N., and M. H. Fisher, eds. *The Holstein Papers.* Cambridge, 1957.

Ritter, Gerhard A. *The Schlieffen Plan: Critique of a Myth.* London, 1958.

Röhl, J. C. G. *Germany Without Bismarck: The Crisis of Government in the Second Reich, 1800–1900.* London, 1967.

————. "Admiral von Müller and the Approach of War, 1911–1914." *Historical Journal* 4(1969): 651–73.

————. *1914: Delusion or Design.* London, 1973.

Rupp, G. H. *A Wavering Friendship: Russia and Austria 1876–1878*. Cambridge, Mass., 1941.

Schöllgen, Gregor, ed. *Escape Into War? The Foreign Policy of Imperial Germany*. Oxford, New York, Munich, 1990.

Schroeder, Paul W. "World War I as Galloping Gertie: A Reply to Joachim Remak." *Journal of Modern History* 44(1972): 319–45.

Spring, D. W. "Russia and the Coming of War." In *Coming*, Evans and Pogge von Strandmann.

Steinberg, Jonathan. *Yesterday's Deterrent*. London, 1965.

———. "The Copenhagen Complex," *Journal of Contemporary History*, vol. 1, no. 3 (1966): 23–46.

Steiner, Zara S. *The Foreign Office and Foreign Policy*. New York, 1969.

———. *Britain and the Origins of the First World War*. New York, 1977.

Stone, Norman. *The Eastern Front 1914–1917*. London, 1975.

Stürmer, Michael. "A Nation State Against History and Geography: The German Dilemma." In *Escape*, Schöllgen.

Taylor, A. J. P. *The Struggle for Mastery in Europe 1848–1918*. Oxford, 1957.

Turner, Jr., Henry A. "Bismarck's Imperial Venture: Anti-British in Origin?" In *Britain and Germany in Africa: Imperial Rivalry and Colonial Rule*, edited by P. Gifford and W. R. Lewis. New Haven, 1967.

Turner, L. C. F. "The Significance of the Schlieffen Plan." In *The War Plans of the Great Powers 1880–1914*, Kennedy.

———. *Origins of the First World War*. New York, 1967.

———. "The Russian Mobilization in 1914," *Journal of Contemporary History* 3(1968): 65–88.

Van Evera, S. "The Cult of the Offensive and the Origins of the First World War." In *Military Strategy and the Origins of the First World War*, Miller.

Wehler, Hans-Ulrich. *Bismarck und der Imperialismus*. Berlin, 1969.

———. *The German Empire, 1871–1918*. Translated by Kim Traynor. New York and Oxford, 1985.

William II, Emperor of Germany. *The Kaiser's Memoirs*. Translated by Thomas R. Ybarra. New York, 1922.

Williamson, Jr., S. R. *The Politics of Grand Strategy, Britain and France Prepare for War, 1904–1914*. Cambridge, Mass., 1969.

———. *Austria-Hungary and the Origins of the First World War*. New York, 1991.

Wilson, Keith M. *The Policy of the Entente*. Cambridge, 1985.

Woodward, E. L. *Great Britain and the German Navy*. Oxford, 1935.

THE SECOND PUNIC WAR

Badian, E. *Foreign Clientelae (264–70 B.C.)*. Oxford, 1958.

Brunt, P. A. *Italian Manpower 225 B.C.–A.D. 14*. Oxford, 1971.

Carcopino, J. "Le traité d'Hasdrubal et la responsibilité de la deuxième guerre punique." *Revue des études anciennes*. 35(1953): 258–93.

Errington, R. M. "Rome and Spain Before the Punic War." *Latomus* 29 (1970): 25–57.

Frank, Tenney. *Roman Imperialism*. New York, 1914.

Hallward, B. L. *Cambridge Ancient History*, 1st ed., vol. 8. Cambridge, 1934.

Harris, W. V. *War and Imperialism in Republican Rome, 327–70 B.C.* Oxford, 1979.

Holleaux, Maurice. *Rome, la Grèce et les monarchies hellenistiques au IIIème siècle avant J>C> (273–205)*. Paris, 1921.

Kramer, F. R. "Massilian Diplomacy Before the Second Punic War." *American Journal of Philology* 69(1948): 1–26.

Lazenby, J. F. *Hannibal's War*. Warminster, 1978.

Livy (Titus Livius), Loeb Classical Library edition, vol. 5. Translated by B. O. Foster. Cambridge, Mass., and London, 1953.

Mommsen, T. *Römische Geschichte*, 12th ed. Berlin, 1920. Translation by W. P. Dickson. London, 1901.

Plutarch. *Lives of the Noble Grecians and Romans*. Translated by John Dryden, revised by A. H. Clough. New York, n.d.

Polybius. *Histories*. Translated by E. S. Shuckburgh. Bloomington, 1962.

Scullard, H. H. "The Carthaginians in Spain." *Cambridge Ancient History*, 2nd ed., vol. 8. Cambridge, 1989.

———. "Hannibal." In *The Oxford Classical Dictionary*, 2nd ed., edited by N. G. L. Hammond and H. H. Scullard. Oxford, 1970.

———. *A History of the Roman World 753–146 B.C.* London and New York, 1980.

Sumner, G. V. "Roman Policy in Spain Before the Hannibalic War." *Harvard Studies in Classical Philology* 72(1967): 206–46.

Toynbee, A. J. *Hannibal's Legacy: The Hannibalic War's Effects on Roman Life*, vol. 2. London, 1965.

Walbank, F. W. *A Historical Commentary on Polybius*, vol. 1. Oxford, 1957.

The Second World War

Adamthwaite, A. P. *France and the Coming of the Second World War 1936–1939.* London, 1977.

———. *The Making of the Second World War.* London, 1980.

———. "War Origins Again." *Journal of Modern History* (1984): 100–15.

Aster, Sidney. *The Making of the Second World War.* London, 1973.

Baer, G. W. *The Coming of the Italian-Ethiopian War.* Cambridge, Mass., 1967.

Bariéty, Jacques. *Les Relations franco-allemandes après la première guerre mondiale.* Paris, 1977.

Barnett, Correlli. *The Collapse of British Power.* New York, 1972.

Baumont, Maurice. *The Origins of the Second World War.* Translated by Simone de Couvreur Ferguson. New Haven and London, 1978.

Bell, P. M. H. *The Origins of the Second World War.* London, 1986.

Bennett, E. W. *German Rearmament and the West.* Princeton, 1979.

Bond, Brian. *British Military Policy between the Two World Wars.* Oxford, 1980.

———. "The Continental Commitment in British Strategy in the 1930s." In *The Fascist Challenge and the Policy of Appeasement,* Mommsen and Kettenacker, eds.

Bond, Brian, and Ian Roy, eds. *War and Society,* vol. 2. London, 1977.

Brüning, Heinrich. *Memoiren, 1918–1934.* Munich, 1972.

Bullock, A. *Hitler, A Study in Tyranny.* New York, 1962.

Churchill, Winston S. *The Gathering Storm.* Boston, 1948.

Cienciala, A. M. *Poland and the Western Powers, 1938–1939.* Toronto, 1968.

Craig, Gordon A. *The Politics of the Prussian Army, 1640–1945.* Oxford, 1955.

Dallek, Robert A. *Franklin D. Roosevelt and American Foreign Policy, 1932–1945.* Oxford, 1979.

Deist, Wilhelm. *The Wehrmacht and German Disarmament.* London, 1981.

Doughty, Robert A. *The Seeds of Disaster, the Development of French Army Doctrine 1919–1939.* Hamden, 1985.

Emmerson, J. T. *The Rhineland Crisis.* London, 1977.

Erdmann, K. D., "Zur Echtheit der Tagebücher Kurt Riezlers. Ein Antikritik," *Historische Zeitschrift* 236(1983) pp. 371–402.

Feiling, K. *The Life of Neville Chamberlain.* London, 1946.

Fest, Joachim C. *Hitler*. Translated by Richard and Clara Winston. New York, 1974.

Fuchser, L. W. *Neville Chamberlain and Appeasement*. New York and London, 1982.

Gatzke, Hans W. *Stresemann and the Rearmament of Germany*. New York, 1969.

————, ed. *European Diplomacy between Two Wars*. Chicago, 1972.

————. "Russo-German military collaboration during the Weimar Republic." In *European Diplomacy between Two Wars,* Gatzke.

Gilbert, Martin. *The Roots of Appeasement*. London, 1966.

Gilbert, Martin, and Richard Gott. *The Appeasers*. Boston, 1963.

Hitler, Adolf. *Mein Kampf*. Translated by Ralph Manheim. Boston, 1943.

————. *Hitler's Secret Book*. Translated by Salvator Attanasio. New York, 1961.

Holborn, Hajo. *A History of Germany 1840–1945*. New York, 1969.

Jäckel, E. *Hitler's Weltanschauung*. Translated by Herbert Arnold. New York, 1972.

Jacobson, Jon. *Locarno Diplomacy, Germany and the West 1925–1929*. Princeton, 1972.

————. "Review Essay, Is There a New International History of the 1920s?" *American Historical Review* 88(1983): 617–45.

Kaiser, D. E. *Economic Diplomacy and the Origins of the Second World War*. Princeton, 1980.

Kennedy, Paul M. *The Rise and Fall of British Naval Mastery*. London, 1983.

————. *The Realities Behind Diplomacy*. London, 1985.

Knox, MacGregor. *Mussolini Unleashed, 1939–1941. Politics and Strategy in Fascist Italy's Last War*. Cambridge, 1982.

Langer, W. L., and S. E. Gleason. *The Challenge to Isolation*. New York, 1952.

Laurens, Franklin D. *France and the Ethiopian Crisis, 1935–1936*. The Hague, 1967.

Lee, Marshall M., and Wolfgang Michalka. *German Foreign Policy 1917–1933. Continuity or Break?* Leamington Spa, Hamburg, and New York, 1987.

Lewis, W. R., ed. *The Origins of the Second World War. A. J. P. Taylor and His Critics*. New York, 1970.

MacDonald, C. A. *The United States, Britain, and Appeasement, 1936–1939*. London, 1981.

Marder, A. "The Royal Navy and the Ethiopian Crisis of 1935–36." *American Historical Review* 75(1970): 1327–56.

Marks, Sally. "1918 and After: The Postwar Era." In *The Origins of the Second World War Reconsidered,* Martel.

———. *Illusion of Peace.* New York, 1976.

———. "The Myth of Reparations." *Central European History* 11(1978): 231–55.

Martel, Gordon, ed. *The Origins of the Second World War Reconsidered.* Boston, 1986.

McDougall, Walter A. "Political Economy versus National Sovereignty: French Structures for German Economic Integration after Versailles." *Journal of Modern History* 51(1979): 4–23; 78–80.

Middlemas, Keith. *Diplomacy of Illusion. The British Government and Germany, 1937–1939.* London, 1972.

Mommsen, W. J., and L. Kettenacker, eds. *The Fascist Challenge and the Policy of Appeasement.* London, 1983.

Morris, B. *The Roots of Appeasement, The British Weekly Press and Nazi Germany during the 1930s.* London, 1991.

Mosely, Leonard. *On Borrowed Time, How World War II Began.* London, 1969.

Murray, Williamson. "German Air Power and the Munich Crisis." In *War and Society,* Bond and Roy.

———. "Munich 1938: The Military Confrontation." *Journal of Strategic Studies* 2(1979): 283–302.

———. *The Change in the European Balance of Power, 1938–1939.* Princeton, 1984.

———. *Luftwaffe.* Baltimore, 1985.

Murray, W., and A. R. Millett, eds. *Calculations, Net Assessment and the Coming of World War II.* New York, 1992.

Nichols, A. J. *Weimar and the Rise of Hitler,* 3rd ed. Basingstoke and London, 1991.

Rich, N. *Hitler's War Aims,* vol. 1. New York, 1973.

Ripka, Hubert. *Munich, Before and After.* London, 1939.

Robbins, K. *Munich 1938.* London, 1968.

Robertson, E. M., ed. *The Origins of the Second World War.* London, 1971.

Ross, Steven. "French Net Assessment." In *Calculations,* Murray and Millett.

Rostow, N. *Anglo-French Relations 1934–36.* London, 1984.

Schmidt, P. O. *Hitler's Interpreter.* London, 1951.

Schuker, Stephen A. "The End of Versailles." In *Origins Reconsidered,* Martel.

―――. "France and the Remilitarization of the Rhineland, 1936." *French Historical Studies* 14(1986): 299–338.

Shirer, W. L. *The Collapse of the Third Republic.* New York, 1969.

Smith, Dennis Mack. *Mussolini's Roman Empire.* Harmondsworth, 1979.

―――. *Mussolini.* London, 1981.

Sösemann, H. "Die Tagebücher Kurt Riezlers. Untersuchungen zur ihrer Echtheit und Edition," *Historische Zeitschrift* 236(1983) pp. 328–69.

Taylor, A. J. P. *English History 1914–1945.* Oxford, 1965.

―――. *The Origins of the Second World War,* 2nd ed. New York, 1985.

Taylor, Telford. *Munich, the Price of Peace.* New York, 1979.

Thorne, Christopher. *The Approach of War, 1938–1939.* London, 1967.

Trachtenberg, Marc. "Reparations at the Paris Peace Conference." *Journal of Modern History* 51(1979): 24–55.

―――. "Reply." *Journal of Modern History* 51(1979): 81–85.

Ulam, Adam B. *Stalin.* London, 1974.

Wandycz, Piotr S. *France and Her Eastern Allies.* Princeton, 1962.

―――. *The Twilight of French Eastern Alliances, 1926–1936.* Princeton, 1988.

Watt, D. C. *Too Serious a Business. European Armed Forces and the Approach of the Second World War.* London, 1975.

―――. *How War Came. The Immediate Origins of the Second World War 1938–1939.* New York, 1989.

Watt, Richard M. *The Kings Depart.* New York, 1968.

Weinberg, Gerhard L. "The Defeat of Germany in 1918 and the European Balance of Power." *Central European History* 2(1969): 248–60.

―――. *The Foreign Policy of Hitler's Germany, Diplomatic Revolution in Europe 1933–1936.* Chicago, 1970.

―――. *The Foreign Policy of Hitler's Germany: Starting World War II, 1937–1939.* Chicago, 1980.

Wendt, B-J. " 'Economic Appeasement'—A Crisis Strategy." In *The Fascist Challenge,* Mommsen and Kettenacker, eds.

Wolfers, Arnold. *Britain and France Between Two Wars.* New York, 1940.

Wollstein, G. *"Eine Denkschrift des Staatssekretärs Bernhard von Bülow von März 1933. Wilhelminische Konzeption der Aussenpolitik zu Beginn der nationalsozialistischen Herrschaft."* *Militärgeschichtliche Mitteilungen* 1(1973): 247–72.

Young, G. M. *Stanley Baldwin*. London, 1952.

Young, R. J. *In Command of France, French Foreign Policy and Military Planning 1933–1940*. Cambridge, Mass., and London, 1978.

The Cuban Missile Crisis

Allison, G. T. *Essence of Decision: Explaining the Cuban Missile Crisis*. Boston, 1971.

Allyn, B. J., J. G. Blight, and D. A. Welch. *Back to the Brink*. Cambridge, Mass., 1992.

Beschloss, M. *The Crisis Years, Kennedy and Khrushchev 1960–1963*. New York, 1991.

Blight, J. G., and D. A. Welch. *On the Brink*. New York, 1989.

Blight, J. G., B. J. Allyn, and D. A. Welch. *Cuba On the Brink*. New York, 1993.

Blum, J. M. *Years of Discord, American Politics and Society, 1961–1974*. New York, 1991.

Bundy, M. *Danger and Survival: Choices About the Bomb in the First Fifty Years*. New York, 1988.

Burlatsky, F. *Khrushchev and the First Russian Spring*. Translated by D. Skillen. New York, 1988.

Carbonell, N. T. *And the Russians Stayed, the Sovietization of Cuba*. New York, 1989.

Catudal, H. *Kennedy and the Berlin Wall Crisis*. Berlin, 1980.

Chang, L., and P. Kornbluh, eds. *The Cuban Missile Crisis, 1962: A National Security Documents Reader*. New York, 1992.

Dinerstein, Herbert R. "The Soviet Union and the Communist World," *Survey* (Spring 1973): 240–50.

Dobrynin, Anatoly. *"Karibskii krizis: Svidetel'stvo uchastnika."* *Mezhdunarodnaya zhizn'* (Moscow) 7(July 1992): 54–68.

Draper, Theodore. *Castro's Revolution*. New York, 1962.

Eisenhower, D. D. *The White House Years: Waging Peace, 1956–1961*. Garden City, New York, 1965.

Gaddis, J. L. *Russia, the Soviet Union, and the United States: An Interpretive History*. New York, 1978.

———. *Strategies of Containment*. New York, 1982.

Garthoff, R. L. *Reflections on the Cuban Missile Crisis*, 2nd ed. Washington, D.C., 1989.

Halperin, Maurice. *The Rise and Decline of Fidel Castro.* Berkeley, Los Angeles, and London, 1972.

Higgins, T. *The Perfect Failure, Kennedy, Eisenhower, and the CIA at the Bay of Pigs.* New York, 1987.

Hilsman, R. *To Move a Nation.* New York, 1967.

Horelick, A. L., and M. Rush. *Strategic Power and Soviet Foreign Policy.* Chicago, 1966.

Kennedy, Robert F. *Thirteen Days.* New York, 1969.

Khrushchev, N. S. *Khrushchev Remembers.* Translated and edited by Strobe Talbott. Boston, 1970.

Kramer, Mark. "Tactical Nuclear Weapons, Soviet Command Authority, and the Cuban Missile Crisis." *Bulletin of the Cold War International History Project.* Woodrow Wilson International Center for Scholars, Washington, D.C. 3(Fall, 1993): 40–46.

Larson, D. L. *The "Cuban Crisis" of 1962, Selected Documents, Chronology and Bibliography,* 2nd ed. Lanham, Maryland, 1986.

Medvedev, Roy. *All Stalin's Men.* Translated by Harold Shukman. New York, 1985.

Morison, S. E., H. S. Commager, W. E. Leuchtenburg. *The Growth of the American Republic,* vol. 2, 7th ed. New York and Oxford, 1980.

O'Donnell, K. P., and D. Powers with J. McCarthy. *"Johnny, We Hardly Knew Ye."* Boston, 1972.

Pope, R. R. *Soviet Views on the Cuban Missile Crisis.* Washington, D.C., 1982.

Rostow, W. W. *The Diffusion of Power.* New York, 1972.

Sakharov, A. *Memoirs.* Translated by R. Lourie. New York, 1990.

Salinger, P. *With Kennedy.* New York, 1966.

Schlesinger, Jr., A. M. *A Thousand Days.* Boston, 1965.

Scott, H. F., and W. F. Scott. *Soviet Military Doctrine.* Boulder and London, 1988.

Shevchenko, A. N. *Breaking With Moscow.* New York, 1985.

Sokolovskiy, V. D., ed. *Voyennaya Strategiya (Military Strategy),* 1st, 2nd, and 3rd eds. Moscow, 1962, 1963, 1968.

Sorensen, T. C. *Kennedy.* New York, 1965.

Szulc, Tad. *Fidel: A Critical Portrait.* New York, 1986.

Thomas, Hugh. *The Cuban Revolution.* New York, 1971.

Ulam, Adam B. *Expansion and Co-existence. The History of Soviet Foreign Policy, 1918–67.* London, 1968.

————. *The Rivals, America and Russia Since World War II.* New York, 1971.

United States Arms Control and Disarmament Agency. *Documents on Disarmament.* Washington, D.C., 1959.

Wyden, P. *Bay of Pigs.* New York, 1979.

————. *Wall, The Inside Story of Divided Berlin.* New York, 1989.